MW00653742

DON SHULA

A Biography of the Winningest Coach in NFL History

Carlo DeVito

Sports Publishing books may be purchased in bulk at special discounts for sales promotion, corporate gifts, fund-raising, or educational purposes. Special editions can also be created to specifications. For details, contact the Special Sales Department, Sports Publishing, 307 West 36th Street, 11th Floor, New York, NY 10018 or sportspubbooks@skyhorsepublishing.com.

Sports Publishing® is a registered trademark of Skyhorse Publishing, Inc.®, a Delaware corporation.

Visit our website at www.sportspubbooks.com.

10 9 8 7 6 5 4 3 2 1

Library of Congress Cataloging-in-Publication Data is available on file.

Cover design by Tom Lau
Cover photo credit Associated Press

ISBN: 978-1-68358-233-5
Ebook ISBN: 978-1-68358-235-9

Printed in the United States of America

CONTENTS

INTRODUCTION VII

CHAPTER 1: THE FISHERMAN'S SON 1

CHAPTER 2: PLAYING DAYS 15

CHAPTER 3: COLLEGE DAYS REDUX 40

CHAPTER 4: DETROIT 47

CHAPTER 5: BALTIMORE 56

CHAPTER 6: MIAMI 92

CHAPTER 7: UNDEFEATED 134

CHAPTER 8: WOODSTROCK AND THE KILLER BEES 168

CHAPTER 9: MARINO 215

CHAPTER 10: PURSUING HALAS 241

CHAPTER 11: RETIREMENT 306

CHAPTER 12: LIFE AFTER FOOTBALL 319

ENDNOTES 360

SELECTED BIBLIOGRAPHY 405

ACKNOWLEDGMENTS 411

Dedicated to the one true coach in our family, Thomas DeVito

"He moved from single-bar face mask to Darth Vader visors on players who evolved from crew cuts to curls to shaved heads. He won with Hall of Famers, and he won with a quarterback who taped the plays to his wrist. He won smashing mouths and won airing it out. Always, he won by being a man on fire."

—Dave Kindred in *The Sporting News*

Introduction

There were two things that were important to Don Shula: family and football. It was not surprising that eventually they would intertwine.

He was first and foremost an Ohio boy, raised in a small community with a large and wide network of hardworking laborers. His family was never poor, always had clothes, a roof, and enough to eat. This was accompanied by discipline, love, and religion. Like his mother, Mary, Don was a devout Catholic all his life, yet not proselytizing.

His career as a coach was legendary. He was a head coach in professional football for 33 years. That's a remarkable feat in and of itself. The only man who rivaled that was George Halas, 40 seasons as head coach, but he also owned his team. Shula coached 20 more games than Halas but finished with 23 more wins (including postseason). Halas had a winning percentage of .671, Shula finished with .665. Shula went to six Super Bowls and won two. He helmed the only undefeated championship team in NFL history. He was 6–1 in AFC championship games. He was voted Coach of the Year four times and was was enshired in the Pro Football Hall of Fame.

His career had several other benchmarks. Some of these events alone would be enough to make a notable career for some men. He coached in two of the longest and most memorable playoff games in the history of the league, against the Kansas City Chiefs in December 1971 and the San Diego Chargers in January 1982. During his playing career, he was part of the game that had the most penalties in the history of the NFL. He was involved in one of the largest trades in NFL history. He presided over the famed Snowplow Game and Dan Marino's fake spike and Tom Matte's two playoff games at quarterback. He graduated 13 players to the Pro Football Hall of Fame. But perhaps the most impressive fact was he only had two losing campaigns in 33 seasons.

Perhaps more important, he also helped orchestrate the massive changes that took place in the NFL. He played wearing a leather helmet (and no face mask) and later helped lead the league to the development of the modern passing game that is the hallmark of the game today. Not only was he a coach and a player, but he was cochairman (along with close friend George Young) of the all-powerful competition committee. In an era when he was winning with a smashmouth running attack, he helped forge the new game geared toward passing and offense. The new rule changes that he helped usher in eventually made some of his own teams obsolete. Yet for the better good of the game and the league, he saw its popularity and success would be tied to the new passing attacks of Don Coryell and Bill Walsh.

If we compare him to others, what do we see? Only seven men have ever won 200 or more games in the history of the NFL. In his career, he outlasted such names as Paul Brown, Tom Landry, Chuck Noll, and John Madden.

He was not without his faults. He had a volcanic and titanic anger. And he was known to not only lose his temper, but to let loose with strings of abusive language that he directed at players, coaches, owners, and officials. He would spew venom and anger like a cannon but be perfectly serene minutes later. As he often said, finesse was not his forte.

He was in some ways a hypocrite. As a player, he hung around in the most roguish of circles and performed his own legendary hijinks. As a coach, his favorites often tended to be the bad boys, but on the field, he expected perfection in all other ways, including a devotion to the game that coincided with his own obsessive drive.

His greatest attribute was also his greatest flaw. To quote former Oilers and Saints coach Bum Phillips, "He can take his'n and beat your'n and take your'n and beat his'n." His ability to win with the talent that he had at hand was an amazing attribute. He could win with a smashmouth offense, he could win with the passing offense, he could bludgeon you with a brutal defense. He once won a playoff game with a fourth-string quarterback (a halfback turned quarterback) who only knew a dozen plays, which were taped to his forearm.

Yet this unique ability also betrayed him. He often was able to elevate teams through the regular season and the playoffs masking his own club's flaws, only to be exposed in championship games by teams who were better balanced or more talented. It is still inconceivable that he was able to bring "Woodstrock" to a Super Bowl, or the Marino team that had no real running attack or stout defense.

He also handled some of the greatest players in the history of the game. His up-and-down relationship with the great Johnny Unitas was legendary. He also enjoyed father-son relationships with Larry Csonka, Bob Griese, Dan Marino, and Nick Buoniconti.

Cleveland, Baltimore, and Miami were three of the most important places in his life. The Greater Cleveland area would always be home in his heart and was the seed of his character. Wherever he went and whatever he became was forged there. In his early years, he returned to his family and childhood friends. In later years, he quipped, he returned for weddings and funerals, but that was not entirely true. He helped raise money for local schools and charities, most notably his alma mater, John Carroll University.

Baltimore was the equivalent of his first love. The city would be the backdrop to both his greatest triumph (the 1968 NFL championship) and most memorable losses (the 1964 championship loss to Cleveland; the inexplicable upset in Super Bowl III). And like many first loves, that affair did not end well. But he would always have a warm place in his heart and misty look in his eyes for the city by the Chesapeake.

And then there was Miami. It was the town that he made famous and that made him famous . . . and wealthy. Outrageous triumph, in defiance of all odds, was topped only by more notable losses, and spectacular events.

And through it all lay family. Fealty, pride, and a fierce love made him cherished, despite his professional zeal that sometimes set him apart, made him seem unreachable, or seemingly distant, even to those close to him. He established one of only two three-generation family coaching trees in NFL history. His two sons both became NFL coaches, and now a grandson, as well. Even in retirement, he forged, with the help of others, especially his son David, a top-five largest high-end steakhouse chain in the country, competing with Ruth's Chris, the Palm, and Morton's, among others.

Others may someday win more games. But no one will challenge Shula for his contributions to the sport, for the change he helped engender both on and off the field for the betterment of the league and its popularity. Simply put, over his 40 seasons in the league, he changed the way the game was coached, played, and ruled. It was men like him, George Young, Wellington Mara, Tex Schramm, Pete Rozelle, and Art Modell who helped shape modern football into the national phenomenon it has become.

Always, he won by being a man on fire.

CHAPTER 1

The Fisherman's Son

Grand River, Ohio, is still a small town on the shores of Lake Erie. Dotted with compact homes of many types, the downtown is also petite. The main draw of the area has always been the outdoor sporting life, great for those who like boating, kayaking, or canoeing, with abundant recreational fishing and hunting. Despite a plethora of recreational boats on the water in summer, this is not a wealthy town. It remains hardworking and middle-class.

As of the 2000 census, there were 345 people living in Grand River, made up of 122 households and 96 families residing in the village. If you were born in the town of Grand River, you probably went and did most of your shopping in Painesville, though you might go to Mentor, as well. Even as late as 2000, the makeup of the population remained largely unchanged from the ethnic backgrounds of those of the 1930s. According to consensus information, 26.1 percent were of German, 13.7 percent English, 12.4 percent American, 8.5 percent Irish, 8.2 percent Italian, 6.5 percent Hungarian, and 6.5 percent Polish ancestry.

"Painesville and the surrounding area embody the melting-pot theory. Hungarians, Finns, Poles, Italians, Irish, and blacks make up this blue-collar town. The Painesville phone book begs for a pronunciation guide. Learning to get along wasn't a plea but a way of life," jibed one Florida sportswriter.

Daniel Sule (the family's original name) was born in Hungary on August 1, 1900. He arrived in the United States with his parents when he was six years old. Dan's parents eventually returned to the old country. "[Dan]changed his name to 'Shula' when the first-grade teacher couldn't properly pronounce the old-world 'Sule,' and quit school in sixth grade," wrote *Sun Sentinel* sports scribe Dave Hyde.

"We never knew them," said Irene Battista, Shula's older sister.

"Dan met Mary Miller when they were teen-agers *[sic]* and married in 1921. Dan worked at a rose nursery, earning $9 a week, and the family saved enough to buy the modest home at 615 River St. It was next door to the home of Mary's parents, Anna and Joseph, who ran the main business—grocery store-restaurant—in Grand River," reported the *Sun Sentinel*. Mary Miller was born on December 7, 1902, and was two years her husband's junior.

"Dan converted to Catholicism, Mary's religion. Dan and Mary had twins, Josephine and Joe, in 1922. Irene was born in 1926 and Don in 1930. Josephine died at 5 in an accident. But the siblings doubled in number in 1936 with the birth of triplets—Jane, Jeannette, and Jim. They were the first famous Shulas, the local newspaper chronicling their lives." As Don himself said, when he was growing up, the most famous three people in the house were the triplets.

Years later, Jeannette Shula Moroz, one of his younger sisters, remembered it a little differently. "He just scrawled out his name, Don Shula, and turned it back and said that 'This is the signature that's going to be famous,'" she said with a chuckle.

The Shula family was growing. Dan switched jobs and began working at one of the fish houses down at the end of River Street for fifteen dollars a week. It was more money, but it was also more dangerous.

In every sense—economically, commercially, educationally, recreationally—Cleveland's massive midwestern shadow loomed large over this small region to the northeast. Many in the small region read the *Cleveland Plain Dealer*, and they rooted for either the Cleveland Indians or the Cleveland Browns (Negro League) baseball teams. There was no professional football at that time in Cleveland.

Fishing on Lake Erie dated all the way back to 1796. "Each morning, Dan Shula woke in the night to drop his nets in Lake Erie. The boat he worked held two tons of fish. His younger son often helped fillet the Erie blue pike into 25-pound cans, earning six cents a pound for his work," wrote Dave Hyde.

"My first job," son Don recalled many years later.

According to Hyde, "[Don] didn't like the fishing life, and his dreams took him far from Erie blue pike. But the moral of the generational story is what the son learned from the father in the same way he passed it to his younger son, Mike, and his four other children."

"A work ethic," Shula said. "That's what I remember about my dad. And, for me, all I knew when faced with a problem is how to roll up my sleeves and get to work."

"You're going back to the way I was brought up," Shula remembered. "Everything was planned, orderly, clean. Religion was involved—the way my mom and dad brought me up."

Shula's father would leave the house at 3:00 a.m. and return home twelve hours later, which made a huge impression on the young Donald.

"There were some commercial fishhouses *[sic]* and fishing boats that would go out and lift the nets in Lake Erie and take the fish out and come back with two tons of fish in the bottom of the boat. My dad was a commercial fisherman. One of the early summer jobs I had was going out with him on the boat and learning how to fillet fish and pack them and ship them out in ice and do all the things you had to do." But Shula never warmed to his father's profession. "I never got used to the rough seas. I'd get seasick a lot when I'd go out on Lake Erie. When I got to Miami, everybody wanted to take me deep sea fishing. I said, 'No thanks. I've had enough of seasickness.'

"Dad said, 'You'll get over it.' Every time we went out he said that, 'You'll get over it.' I never got over it.

"My father was one of those guys who just worked all his life. He was a nurseryman, that was the kind of work he loved, but after I was born there were triplets, and he couldn't make it on 16 or 18 dollars a week. He took a job as a commercial fisherman on Lake Erie, and after that we moved to Painesville, where he went to work as a tinner in a factory.

"My dad was never an athlete. He had good coordination, but there was never any time. He worked all his life, and one of the things that makes me happiest now is that before he died I got to take them back over to the old country," Shula recalled. "We went to Budapest, and then we drove about a hundred miles and found the little town he was from and looked up all the relatives. And then we went to Rome and while we were there the pope came out. That was everything he wanted."

"He has always maintained that his mother was the family's disciplinarian. Some years ago, he was on television and was angered at something going on in a game. The microphone picked up some of his language," wrote Gerald Eskanazi in the *New York Times*.

"I hope my mother didn't hear that," he said. Shula later received a phone call from his mother. She did indeed hear it and called to complain.

"It's a unique place with very independent-minded people," said Bill Stanton, who was the counselor to the president of the World Bank, a former congressman, one of Shula's former employers, and a Painesville native. "Down deep, the guy never left that town," Stanton told Jason Cole of the *Sun Sentinel*.

"I still have relatives in the Mentor and Painesville area," Shula once said. "I get back for weddings and funerals."

Cole wrote, "The Mar-Val Bowling Alley, where Shula met first wife Dorothy Bartish, opened in 1932. Gartman's Model Bakery, two blocks away, opened in 1898. Hellriegel's Inn and Restaurant, where Dorothy and Don had their wedding reception, started as a small house in 1841."

Back then, the mercantile trade was dominated by the Gail G. Grant department store. Other notable spots included Toyland (a favorite among youngsters) and the Lockie Lee Dairy Store (a local creamery). Jerry and Bart's Restaurant was the fashionable eatery of the day. Other memorable stores included Kresge's and Newberry's five-and-dime stores, and Fisher Food. Few from the area could forget the Greyhound Bus Station. Main Street in those days was packed with cars and awnings and signs and people. Packards, Hudsons, Studebakers, DeSotos, and Nashes drove the streets with their big, bulbous headlights and whitewall tires.

"Our father may not have been as outward with his emotions, but he had to be tough to go out to work every day, day after day, even when he was sick," said Jeannette Shula Moroz. "When he worked at the rayon plant in Painesville, he used to ride to work with another man. He could have asked that man to come pick him up when it was cold, but he never did. He always made the walk over there."

Many locals said Dan was a quiet man, and that his wife Mary was the disciplinarian and vocal leader of the family. "She was a strict Hungarian mom. She laid down the law," said Lou Gurbach, a pleasant woman and distant relative of the Shulas. According to friends, Mary was disciplined, dedicated to detail, and competitive.

"Every morning she would wake up and start cooking for everyone, but never in a housecoat," said Jane, who along with Jeannette and Irene lived in the Painesville area for many years. "She always had to get dressed first. She had a routine that she followed, and she never broke from it." Mary attended church every day after dropping off her children at school. Don would follow her example.

Once, Shula's high school friend, Jim Mulqueeny, was stopped for speeding in nearby Ashtabula. A few days later, Mulqueeny showed up at the Shula household to fetch Don for a baseball game. Don's mother, Mary, was waiting on the porch. "She didn't say anything, she just gave me that look. I knew what she was telling me, 'Take it easy,'" Mulqueeny recalled many years later.

As she got older, Mary became obsessed with church bingo. "Oh, she hated to lose," Jane said. There was no question where Don got his passion.

"He hated to lose even when he was in elementary school," his mother, Mary, said years later. "When he was eight years old, he would play cards with his grandmother. If he lost, he would tear up the cards and run and hide under the porch. You couldn't pry him out for supper."

Don attended elementary school at St. Mary's Catholic School in Painesville. "His team lost and he went under the stands at the field and cried his head out. That's when he played for the St. Mary's Parish of Painesville team before he went on to Harvey High, John Carroll University, and pro football. He still says that to this day he hates to lose."

Shula marveled that his mother wouldn't allow anyone in the family's living room except for special occasions. Otherwise, no one was allowed in. "It was strictly taboo," Shula remembered years later. "It was nothing more than a showplace with everything in its proper place all neat and clean. I could never understand it."

With a playground directly across the street from their house, Shula was never far from home and was required to come home as soon as the streetlamps went on.

"When I grew up my parents lived next to my grandparents. And they talked Hungarian to each other. And they communicated that way. So I'm one, and two, and three years old, and the first language I learned was Hungarian. So I was going around the neighborhood, and they would point to me and say, 'This kid doesn't speak English.' I think I speak a little better English now," he said years later.

He played almost every day in that park. He played games and got into fights. He considered himself a pretty good scrapper, having won more than he lost. He remembered years later that at one time he'd gotten pretty full of himself and picked a fight with a quiet child. He pressed the issue, and the fight was on. The boy knocked him down. He shook it off and rose up again, and the other boy put him down again, to the point where he saw stars. "That's the first beating I ever took. It really put me in my place a little and made me realize I couldn't go out and lick the world.

"As a kid, I was the one who organized the games," he has said of the sandlot football he played in the lots around Painesville. "In grade school I chose the lineups. In high school I knew what everyone was supposed to do and I corrected their mistakes. That's my background."

"Things were really tough sometimes, but Don was always strong, always truth and justice," said young brother Jim. "He was the one stopping fights. He was the realist."

At Thomas W. Harvey High School in Painesville, Shula played football, baseball, basketball, and was on the track team. He eventually lettered eleven times in high school alone. His real love was for football, where he excelled. He starred playing halfback in a single-wing offense. He began playing football while still quite young and at the tender age of eleven was forbidden by his parents to play the game anymore after sustaining a bad facial cut during a neighborhood scrimmage. But Shula was not to be so easily dissuaded.

In 1942, "I forged my mother's signature so I could play high school football," he later admitted. Ironically, he was sidelined by a case of pneumonia just before the season began. Encouraged by an assistant coach to return to the game as soon as possible, a healthy Shula later rejoined the team but kept his football participation a secret from his parents until he was named a starter. "I guess I got away with one," Shula once said.

"Don was also the one who would carry a football while running a mile down Richmond Street on the way home from football practice, stiff-arming the trees. He was the one who would draw pictures of football players and hang them in the room he shared with Jim in their small, two-story frame house," wrote Bill Plaschke in the *Los Angeles Times*.

Shula's need to excel exhibited itself even back then. "That's been a part of my makeup," he once said. "I enjoy a laugh on the field, as much as the next fellow, but not at the expense of success. As a young boy, I'd get upset if the others didn't work and study."

"It was a habit he would never break," wrote John Underwood in *Sports Illustrated*.

"The coaches didn't always like it," Shula remembered.

Once, when Shula got out of hand for the second time, scuffling with one of the other players, the head coach, the usually mild-mannered Clarence Mackey, slapped Don. Shula's face got red, flaring with anger and embarrassment. After the practice, Shula waited for everyone to leave before going into the coaches' office. The coaches thought he would quit. Instead, Shula apologized.

"There were other guys who were more talented, but Don was tough, fearless," said Tony Cimaglio, who played with Shula and eventually became the equipment manager for the Harvey High football team. "Don was always the aggressor."

Shula's leadership skills were apparent even back then.

"Don performed capably as a varsity guard in basketball and was an outstanding sprinter and quarter-miler. I became very close to him and admired his kind of determination," Assistant football and track coach Don Martin said years later. Martin remembered Shula as a fine sprinter who was a driven member of the mile relay team. Martin began the relay race with two slower runners. He then staged Shula and Eugene "Jeep" Mucciaroni to finish.

"Our last two meets, we fell behind by 15 to 20 yards after the first two runners," Martin said. "Don turned to Jeep and said, 'I'll get half.' It wasn't just that he was going to do his job, he was inspiring Jeep to do better. He had the mind of a coach right then."

"I don't remember him saying it, but I know he got his half," Mucciaroni said. "The funniest thing is that he was so excited he almost made us lose. In the mile relay, the starting line is about 10 yards in front of the finish line. So as I'm coming around the last turn, I see Don standing at the starting line, jumping up and down, waiting for me to come in with the win. I had to dodge him to get to the finish line."

Roy Kropac, who attended school with Shula from third grade through John Carroll, said Shula "was captain of everybody" in high school.

"Charlie Schupska was the quarterback and would bring the play in, but Shula would just tell guys where to run, call all the plays right there himself," Kropac said. Did the coaches mind? "No, because it usually worked."

In Shula's senior season of football, the team posted its best record ever, 7–3, but was denied a league title by neighboring Willoughby. Shula cried after the loss.

Against Ashtabula, Harvey was leading, 12–6, and attempted to put the game out of reach with a trick play. At the snap of the ball, Shula took the ball right, and Kropac faded left, awaiting a pass from Shula. Shula then threw to Kropac. But Ashtabula was ready for it. They read the play perfectly, intercepted Shula's pass, and the defensive back ran toward the goal line with a convoy of blockers.

From the other end of the field, Shula chased down the Ashtabula runner, sliding between the blockers, and tackled the back, saving the touchdown and the game. Afterward, Ashtabula Coach George Guarnieri congratulated Shula.

"[Guarnieri] said it was the finest football play he had ever seen," Martin said.

"As soon as I saw Don make that play, I knew he was going to be somebody," Cimaglio said.

"And he was the one who would carry the ball two dozen times for his high school team on Friday, then report to work as a welder in a nearby mill at 7 a.m.

Saturday," wrote Plaschke. Shula was named All-Ohio quarterback as a senior and graduated in 1947.

"When I got out of high school, the veterans were coming home from World War II, and they were getting all the scholarships," Shula recalled. "I had a good senior year at Harvey, but I wasn't getting any scholarship offers, so that summer I decided I would work a year and then go to college."

"I pulled into a gas station one day, and Howard Bauchman, who had been the coach at Painesville and then went on to Cleveland Heights, saw me and asked me what I was going to do. I told him and he said, 'Don't do that. I have this friend, Herb Eisele, who just got the head coaching job at John Carroll. I'll set up an interview for you and see what he could do to help you financially.'

"He set up the interview, and Herb said he could give me a scholarship for tuition only the first year. If I did OK, it would include room, board, and books plus tuition the following years. I had a good freshman year, and I got a full scholarship after that first year.

"I think about needing gas that day a lot. It's amazing how events shape the direction your life takes."

Despite being at a small Jesuit university, Herb Eisele was no ordinary college coach. Eisele was among the most famous football players and coaches in Ohio history up to that time. He was a local legend as a high school star in the 1920s and later a Walter Camp All-American honorable mention at the University of Dayton. As a high school coach for many years in Cleveland, he amassed 130 victories and only 33 losses, as well as nine city championships and three state titles at Cathedral Latin, his alma mater. From October 17, 1943, to October 10, 1946, his teams went 36 straight games without a loss.

"Eisele was an exceptional coach. He only had two assistants, but they were as fine a small college staff that you could find anywhere. Eisele completely adopted the Cleveland Browns' style of football both offensively and defensively. He and his staff would watch the Browns' practices, see their games, study their style, and emulate it," remembered Shula. Eisele emphasized fundamentals and technique, and they were lessons Shula carried with him right through college and eventually into the pros.

"At Carroll, Don played both ways at halfback," Eisele said. "He was always inquisitive. I only had two assistant coaches, Bill Belanich and Dan Mormile, and there was only so much time we had on the field. During practice, when we worked on defense, Don always wanted to know what everybody else was supposed to do.

I used to say, 'Don, just do what you're supposed to do,' but that was never enough for him.

"He wanted to know where everybody was supposed to be and also what everybody else would do on each play. You could see then that his football mind was developing," said Eisele. "He said that it gave him a good feeling to know all the assignments on a play.

"I remember one day, when I was instructing the team, Shula kept interrupting me with questions," said Eisele, laughing. "I finally said, 'You run the holes, son, and I'll do the coaching.'"

"On the practice field, he always wanted to know why—the reasons for a certain play," said fellow teammate Sil Cornachione. "The significance of this was that he did not accept anything on the surface. He continually reached down for the reasons for things. At Carroll he asked a lot of question, and often offered suggestions, but never asked them to be smart, he just wanted to find out the 'why.'

"Don came from a small town and from a league you did not hear much about. We used to kid him about coming out of a cornfield. Don came to John Carroll with the idea of catching up," said Cornachione. "He made a good effort to learn as much and find out as much as the next person."

"At Carroll we had a play called the '44-off tackle.' If the four hole was closed, Shula used to veer or go outside. He used to do this so well that rather than correct him and make him bulldoze into the line, the coaches put in a play called '44-veer,'" chuckled Cornachione.

Shula played well in his first year. Under the headline "Carroll Is Tuning Up New Battery" in the *Cleveland Plain Dealer,* the newspaper gushed, "Another promising halfback is Don Shula, from Painesville Harvey High School. The rangy Shula runs with high knee action and has been a good target for [Rudy] Schaffer's aerials."

At Carroll, Shula was not the main back; his roommate, Carl Taseff, was. Taseff was born in Parma, Ohio, on September 28, 1928. He attended East High School in Cleveland, Ohio. At 5-foot-11 and between 195 and 200 pounds, he was strong, sturdy, reliable, and versatile, filling in at fullback and halfback, with lots of power and speed. He and Shula played both defense and offense. Taseff was something special. Taseff and Shula would go on to become lifelong friends.

In October 1948, a headline blared across the *Plain Dealer*'s sports page: "Shula, Carroll's Sophomore Backfield Find, Starts Against B.W. Saturday." The accompanying story, written by Charles Heaton, read, "Jim Moran, veteran defensive ace and sparkplug of the John Carroll football squad, probably will be on the sidelines when the Blue Streaks tangle with Baldwin-Wallace Saturday night at Berea, but strangely enough, his absence is causing little consternation in University Heights. The reason for the unusual state of affairs is a 175-pound rookie halfback—Don Shula. . . . A week ago Shula was just another substitute on the Blue Streak squad but on the strength of his brilliant performance against Youngstown College, the sophomore has been shifted to left halfback."

"I think he's going to rate with one of the best we've ever had," said backfield coach Danny Mormile. A photo of Shula, in the famous huckabuck style, with his legs going forward and torso twisted backward, posed for his photo in white football pants and black jersey sans helmet.

In the subsequent game, Schaffer found Shula in the back of the end zone for a touchdown, to take a halftime lead of 12–6 over Baldwin-Wallace. Taseff was his usual stalwart self, but the game ended in a 19–19 tie. Heaton reported that Shula "filled in so capably in the two games, again will get the call at left halfback" for the following week's game against Niagara when Shula caught a few passes and ground out a few more yards on the ground, while Taseff carried the load for a victory.

It even came to the point, when Shula missed a game, it became headline material in the *Plain Dealer.* As the Blue Streaks prepared for their first bowl game, the Knights of Columbus Great Lakes Bowl, Heaton wrote of the injury-plagued squad on November 29, 1948, "The most important backfield addition for the well-rested University Heights club is Don Shula. . . . Shula, when in top shape, rates as one of the best backs on the squad." Yet is was Taseff who pushed over the line in the waning minutes of the game to give Carroll its bowl game victory, 14–13, over Canisius on December 5, 1948.

Before their junior season began, Taseff and Shula were among many to be called up for National Guardsmen training at Camp Atterbury, Indiana. They saw action on the playing field on October 1, 1949, when Shula scored a touchdown and Taseff crossed the plane twice, as Carroll defeated Toledo, 28–14. A week later, an interception by Shula counted for naught, as the Blue Streaks lost in a passing duel to Youngstown. In a subsequent game against Xavier, Shula's costly fumble was the turning point of the game, and, what might have been the tying score instead turned out to be the third score for Xavier, in a stunning 21–7 loss. The Blue Streaks bounced back the next week against Marshall with a 26–7 victory and then defeated Bowling Green, 38–24, scoring five times through the air. Shula made several catches for first downs and hauled in a touchdown pass as well, as they won, 38–24.

The aerial show continued the next week, as Schaffer threw often, with Shula snagging two more important first downs and Taseff running for 87 yards and a touchdown as they cruised to a 27–0 win over Case Tech. The next game was a crowning achievement for Taseff, who bulldozed for 242 yards, and "Shula, who also ran in excellent form from the left half back spot, crashed over for Carroll's third score," wrote Heaton, as they beat Canisius, 26–12, for their fourth win in a row. In their next game, Taseff roared for 99 yards and three touchdowns and Shula scored an extra point as they beat Baldwin-Wallace, 28–7. Don had found extraordinary faith in the Catholic religion at a young age. "Don has faith in himself and faith in God, and everything somehow always seems to work out for him," brother Jim Shula said.

"I was interviewed with him for a network documentary in which he says at one point he wanted to be a seminarian, although that was not included in the final documentary," said Father Juan Sosa, pastor of St. Joseph Parish on Miami Beach, where Shula has been a longtime parishioner following an equally long affiliation at Our Lady of the Lakes Parish in Miami Lakes.

"A great many of the ideas and thoughts that I have, as far as my relationship with God, stem from those early years and the lessons I learned around the house about being God-fearing and doing things the right way," Shula said years later. "We never missed mass. From second grade on . . ."

Shula was known to attend 7 a.m. mass most of his adult life, saying the rosary while waiting for the mass to begin. "I once seriously considered the priesthood myself. But then I decided I couldn't be a priest and a coach too," he chuckled.

There were great expectations for Eisele's John Carroll squad in 1950, but the Blue Streaks lost their first two games of the season. Over the next few weeks, Carroll's fortunes changed. On October 11, 1950, the *Plain Dealer* ran a big headline, "Carroll Offense Clicks as 'Infantry' Advances Under Moderate Air Cover: Shula Is Leader In Ground Attack." Charles Heaton led off the article writing, "Back to the good earth is the football trend at John Carroll and halfback Don Shula has played an important role in this switch in offensive strategy." In their first two games, Carroll had thrown 43 percent of the time and lost both times. In wins against Toldeo and Kent State, that number dropped to 18 percent as the duo of Taseff and Shula rumbled like a pair of Sherman tanks over the opposition. The Blue Streaks threw fewer passes in that same period. And the ones they did throw were higher-percentage completion passes. "Shula did considerable football toting in those victories," wrote Heaton. They beat Toledo, 41–0. Then, Shula had 11 rushing attempts for 113 yards against Kent State in a 48–7 romp. And by that time, Heaton pointed out, Shula had 122 yards receiving on six catches for the season up to that point, which led the team. All of it was positioned near a large photo of Shula himself.

"Don plays offense and defense. He went the distance in all nine games last season . . .," gushed Heaton. "Shula is a football perfectionist and he and Shaffer often can be found on the field after practice working on pass timing."

"I can't praise the boy enough," Eisele said of Shula. "We pile work on him, but there's never any complaining."

"Don is hoping for a crack at professional football after he finishes Carroll in June, but his final aim is a career in coaching and teaching," continued Heaton.

On October 21, 1950, the Blue Streaks routed Case Tech, 51–14. Taseff and Shula again led the way, with quarterback Shaffer and right halfback Burrell Shields also making big contributions. On November 4, Shula ran for 165 yards and a touchdown as Carroll beat Dayton, 24–12.

Then came the big game the following week, when the mighty Syracuse Orangemen came to play little Carroll, the Ohio Jesuit school. The Blue Streaks brought a six-game winning streak into Cleveland Stadium to face a Syracuse team on the rise. Syracuse was coming off a 34–0 dismantling of Lafayette. They'd previously beaten Rutgers, Penn State, Holy Cross, and Boston University. In the lead-up to the big game, Heaton wrote in the *Plain Dealer* that Shula was "turning in his finest season at left halfback."

"When the football game between John Carroll University and Syracuse University was first announced in April of 1950, there were more than a few in Syracuse, N.Y., who wanted to know 'Who is John Carroll?'" wrote Ohio sports historian Timothy L. Hudak. "When the final seconds had ticked off the game clock on Friday evening, November 10, of that year those same people were probably wishing that they had never heard of 'him.'"

Hudak noted about Taseff that Carl had played varsity all four years for the Blue Streaks and was the team's best back. Not only was Taseff the team's star, going into the game, Taseff had 848 yards rushing, which made him the third-best back in the nation up to that point. Taseff had also scored 17 touchdowns, number one in the nation! "Carl was also a very able pass catcher when the ball was thrown to him and he was the Blue Streaks punter. . . .[Shula] had already rushed for 666 yards on the season. JCU backfield coach Dan Mormile considered Shula to be the best collegiate back in Ohio, in part because, unlike Taseff, Shula also played defense."

Midway through the second quarter, the score was tied, 7–7, when Syracuse blocked a punt for a safety and extended their lead to 16–7 by halftime. The third quarter was a stalemate. But in the fourth quarter, Carroll finally scored twice and led the game, 21–16.

Syracuse put together one last drive. Quarterback Avatus Stone, unable to find an open receiver, and flushed from the pocket, scrambled to the Carroll 4-yard line where he was knocked out of bounds.

"Time had expired during the play. The ecstatic Blue Streaks fans were storming the field and some of the stadium lights were even being turned off. But wait, the game was not over. John Carroll had been flagged for holding on that last play," reported Hudak. "The gridiron was cleared of fans and the lights put back on. With no time on the clock the penalty was stepped off from the original line of scrimmage, the ball being placed at the JCU 16. As reporter Lawrence J. Skiddy of the *Syracuse Herald American* put it, 'It wasn't as good as the four-yard line. But you couldn't decline the penalty. That would have meant the game was over.'" With their last snap, Syracuse ran another pass play that seemed to take forever but fell well shy of its intended receiver. This time the game was over for real, and Carroll had prevailed.

"Don Shula, who turned in another fine offensive performance, paced the ground attack with 124 yards in 23 carries. Carl Taseff was right behind with 115 yards in 25 attempts," reported Heaton. Little John Carroll had walloped Syracuse. David had killed Goliath. And Don Shula was the hero, despite having been groggy for a few plays halfway through the game after having his bell rung.

The last game of the season, versus rival Baldwin-Wallace, saw Taseff and Shula continue to dominate. Carroll took a 20–6 lead into halftime. But the third quarter saw Baldwin-Wallace score 19 unanswered points to take a 25–20 lead into the fourth quarter. Carroll scored at the top of the fourth quarter, then intercepted a Baldwin-Wallace pass and drove for the winning score. Taseff and Shula alternated blasting away at the B-W defense, until finally, from four yards out, Shula blasted through the middle and scored the winning touchdown as the Blue Streak prevailed, 33–25. Taseff had scored four times and Shula once to account for all of Carroll's scoring that day.

Shula graduated in 1951 with a sociology degree. He had earned a reputation as a solid, smart, dependable ballplayer. Taseff was one of the leading rushers in college football that year and led the nation with 23 touchdowns. Both players were drafted by the Cleveland Browns, Shula in the ninth round and Taseff thirteen rounds later. Don then sat by the phone waiting for Paul Brown to call to no avail.

"So I called the Browns. 'Aren't you going to sign me?' I asked. I drove to Cleveland, and they gave me a contract—the minimum, $5,000. I was afraid they'd pull it back before I could get my signature on it," Shula recounted with a chuckle. Both Taseff and Shula signed their contracts the same day and looked for a bar where they could celebrate their good fortune.

"Do you think they'll recognize us as being new members of the Cleveland Browns?" Shula asked Taseff. The two shiny newly minted football professionals ordered their first martinis and reveled in their newfound glory.

"We toasted each other. I took a big gulp and almost threw up. It's the last martini I ever drank," Shula recalled years later.

Shula did not know at the time (but he did find out later in life) that he had been drafted at the urging of the then-little known offensive line coach of the Browns—one Weeb Ewbank. The irony would be that the two men's lives would be inextricably linked in some odd way, shape, or form for the next two decades. Each would have a jarring impact on the other. Both men would help forge the modern game and be intertwined in some of pro football's greatest moments.

CHAPTER 2

Playing Days

The middle of July 1951 found Shula and Taseff together at Camp McCoy, Wisconsin, with the 37th Infantry Regiment, which had to defend a hill against the 147th Infantry Regiment in the hot summer heat. Harry Truman was president of the United States. "Tennessee Waltz" by Patti Page was the No. 1 single on both the *Billboard* and *Cashbox* charts. Julius and Ethel Rosenberg were convicted of conspiracy to commit espionage. Truman relieved General Douglas MacArthur of his Far Eastern commands. *All About Eve* won the Academy Award for Best Picture. And *Your Show of Shows* starring Sid Caesar and Imogene Coca was among the favorite shows on television that year.

"Most other members of the platoon were Clevelanders. Among them were Sgt. Carl Taseff, 22, an all-Ohio and Little All-American halfback on the football team of John Carroll University until his graduation in June. Another was Pvt. Don Shula, 21, another halfback on the same team. Both players will go from this summer encampment to train at Cleveland Browns camp at Bowling Green," reported the *Plain Dealer.*

"This is a good deal," Taseff remarked. "We are keeping in shape, running up and down hills, and throwing a ball around the barracks area. Don dug two holes today!" Being a pair of local boys made good, the *Plain Dealer* followed their movements throughout the summer.

"As the safety man, [Stan] Heath will be getting competition from Cliff Lewis, the 160-pound Lakewood boy who is starting his sixth season with the Browns, and Don Shula of John Carroll," wrote *Plain Dealer* sportswriter Harold Sauerbrei in late July. By the second week in September, the newspapers were already writing the duo off. "Shula and Taseff may be making their farewell appearances, for the time being at least . . . when it was announced Ohio's 37th Division of the National Guard would be called to duty in January," Sauerbrei revealed a few days before a matchup against the Rams. In that game, Shula played incredibly well and made an impression on coach Brown.

"I've always been a big Browns fan," Shula said. "Paul Brown meant an awful lot to me and my career."

"The first time I met Paul Brown I stood there shaking," Shula later remembered, standing in Brown's office that first summer. He was "completely in awe of the man. He was practically a legend and I had tremendous respect for him. I watched the Browns play whenever I could." Even in college, Shula pretended to be a high school player, so he could pay the 25-cents fee to get in to watch the team play. He had a hard time scraping together the money to attend games. Shula said it was the best quarter he ever spent.

"I was too excited to talk and just listened to everything that Brown was saying," Shula remembered.

Shula was right to be in utter awe of Brown. If Eisele was a legend in Ohio high school football, Brown was a god. The rest of the league was in awe of him, as well. Paul Eugene Brown had been born on September 7, 1908. The son of a railroad dispatcher, Brown was a football star right from the start. Despite a diminutive size, he took over as quarterback in his junior year at Massillon High School, and posted a record of 15 wins and only three losses in his final two years of school. Brown enrolled at Ohio State University in 1926 but never made it past the tryouts and later transferred to Miami University in Oxford, Ohio. Weeb Ewbank was the school's star quarterback. Brown took over the reigns after Ewbank left and achieved 14 wins against three losses over his junior and senior seasons.

The next year, he became the head coach at Massillon, the archrival of neighboring Canton, Ohio. Brown made massive changes. He emphasized speed and quickness over brute force, using schemes he'd acquired from Duke's Jimmy DeHart and Purdue's Noble Kizer. His teams would be smart. His record at the school from 1932 to 1940 was 80–8–2. That included a 35-game winning streak. Over his last six seasons there, his teams won six state championships and four High School Football National Championships. His teams outscored their opponents 2,393 points to 168 over that span. He was nicknmed the "Miracle Man of Massillon." In 1941, he was named the head coach of Ohio State and went 8–1, losing only to Northwestern and the great Otto Graham. In 1946, he cofounded the Cleveland Browns, a new team whose ownership had courted him, and named the team after him. There, Brown won four AAFC championships before that league merged with the NFL in 1950. That didn't stop Brown. His team won three NFL championships—in 1950, 1954, and 1955.

It was during this time that Brown began to perfect the systems he would use the rest of his life and that would be adopted by the entire league and are still in use today. Brown invented the playbook. He tested his players on their knowledge of it. He also originated the practice of sending in plays to his quarterback from the sideline using hand signals. He created the 40-yard dash, because that was the maximum average distance used to cover a punt. He was the first coach to use game film to scout opponents and to hire a full-time staff of assistants and invented the modern face mask, the taxi squad, and the draw play.

He also helped smash the color barrier a year before Jackie Robinson integrated baseball. In 1946, Brown fielded a team with two African American players—Bill Willis, a hard-nosed lineman, and Marion Motley, a fullback. "It's interesting, in a way, because he did it before they did it in baseball," said Mike Brown, Paul's son, years later. "I'm not sure why professional football is not given more credit for breaking the color line. It's always intrigued me that that was the case, though keep in mind that back in the '40s, baseball was the principal sport in the country. It definitely was the bigger sport. Maybe that was part of it, but it's almost forgotten."

Brown had a strict, systematic approach to coaching and had a keen eye when it came to recruiting players.

"When he coached at Massillon High School, he had many black players on his teams," Mike Brown recalled. "When he coached at Ohio State, he had many black players on his team. When he coached in the service, the same thing was true. When he got to the Cleveland Browns, he looked around and he knew where he had better football players than he had with the Browns. Guys who formerly played for him."

"Paul was a top businessperson who was driven to setting up an organization that would be the best in the world, utilizing the best personnel, developing the best devices to win," Jim Brown, his great running back, said. "Color never came into his philosophy—neither positive nor negative. The way he carried his organization was that everybody was afraid of him, so you didn't have any dissension."

"Check the record. Then you tell me who's the greatest coach of all time," former NFL player Cris Collinsworth, now a prominent sportscaster, once said. "At the time, Paul Brown was Bill Gates. He transformed the game from a physical exercise to an intellectual exercise."

Brown was known for such quotes as "Football is a game of errors. The team that makes the fewest errors in a game usually wins" and "Leave as little to chance as possible. Preparation is the key to success." Brown also espoused the philosophy of "When you win, say nothing. When you lose, say less." The stoic Shula surely took heed of the philosophy that "The key to winning is poise under stress."

Still, Brown had his detractors. He was criticized for being a control freak. "He wanted to control every single detail on the field. He wanted to know exactly what every player was going to do and for them to know exactly what was expected of them on every play," said Mark Bechtel of *Sports Illustrated*.

He was obsessed with finding men who were as absorbed in football as he was. "If they were boozers, or chasers, or things of this nature, he wouldn't have them," Jim Brown said. He loathed agents, was a tough negotiator of contracts, and could be didactic to the point of distraction. Still, his success was undeniable. By the end of his tenure with the Browns, his teams won seven professional titles and played in 11 league championship games. Brown had several disciples he directly coached and mentored, among them Weeb Ewbank, Don Shula, Bill Walsh, Blanton Collier, and Lou Saban.

"The biggest influence on my coaching life has been Paul Brown. Paul believed in the businesslike approach. He emphasized classroom techniques in which he could expound on the five theories, as he called it," said Shula years later. "He said that you learn by seeing, hearing, writing, practicing, and reviewing."

Shula recalled Brown handed out blank playbooks and forced the players to diagram each play themselves, so they would better understand the plays. Shula recalled his first training camp, spent with long late-night sessions with Brown and the coaching staff, diagraming plays, talking strategy. Brown made the players write down certain things he said—word for word. Shula called it "tedious." But it made a big impression on him. "As I looked around the room and saw players like Otto Graham, Mac Speedie, and Marion Motley doing the same thing . . . I realized the importance that Paul put in this method." Shula also saw that Brown was "standoffish and aloof" with his players. In Shula's eye, it was very much a teacher-pupil relationship that Brown cultivated.

The team was loaded with stars. Otto Graham was the charismatic and incredibly gifted Browns quarterback. Not only had Graham won five football championships, he'd also played for a professional basketball championship team in 1946. There was also fullback/linebacker Marion Motley (later to be a Hall of Famer), and receivers Dante Lavelli (known as "Gluefingers," who also made the Hall of

Fame) and Mac Speedie (who led the league in receptions three times, was selected to two Pro Bowls, and named All-Pro three times).

"We were as close as we could be," Shula said of Taseff and himself. "Some of the other rookies were pretty much on their own and it could get lonely at times." It was brutally competitive, and the veterans didn't really start friendships with rookies. Taseff and Shula again got lucky. Two veterans, Lou Rymkus and Lou Groza, befriended the pair and brought them to a bar. "Later we found out why," Shula laughed. "We'd end up in a saloon where the bartender would pass out cigars to the Browns players. Rymkus was a heavy cigar smoker. The owner would come over and give us all cigars." Then Rymkus would insist they sit down in a booth, where Rymkus would relieve the rookies of their cigars, and he and Groza would leave.

"Taseff and I were left on our own."

Shula recalled that much like many years later, veterans did not make friends with rookies unless they made the team, but it was a big deal that Rymkus and Groza took Shula and Taseff to that local bar.

Louis Joseph "the Battler" Rymkus was all All-Pro tackle, playing offensive and defensive lineman. Rymkus quickly established himself as an anchor of the team's lines. Another was Louis Roy "The Toe" Groza. Groza had joined the Army in 1943, as a surgical assistant. Groza saw the wounded hauled behind the lines back to mobile hospital units where he assisted doctors in all manners of procedure. "I saw a lot of men wounded with severe injuries," he said years later. "Lose legs, guts hanging out, stuff like that. It's a tough thing, but you get hardened to it, and you accept it as part of your being there." Groza was one of the people who formed the hub of the Cleveland offense. He gained fame as the team's placekicker in his first few years but later moved to offensive tackle (while he continued to kick). His success rate in 1950 was 68.4 percent in an era when most teams averaged less than 50 percent.

"Anywhere from 40 to 50 yards, he was a weapon," said Groza's holder, Tommy James.

"I never thought I would miss," Lou admitted years later.

"Lou never got all the credit he deserved for his tackle play, probably because his great kicking skills got him more notoriety," said Andy Robustelli, a Hall of Fame defensive end for the Rams and Giants, who played against Groza.

Still starstruck years later, Shula marveled in his autobiography, "I remember the thrill I got lining up one day, when Otto Graham asked me to catch a few balls.

It was during the early weeks of camp. I was a guy from a small college who had the opportunity to catch passes from a star of Graham's magnitude."

"Otto Graham was my idol," Shula said in his later years. "I was just dazed by the whole deal. Otto was the catalyst to help us win all those games . . . he had great athletic ability." Shula pointed out that Graham had been a running back at Northwestern, but Brown had made him into a quarterback. "Otto has to be one of the best of all time. All you gotta do is look at his accomplishments."

Shula's shining moment came one day early on, when he was asked to play middle safety in a scrimmage. The ball was snapped, and in a second, the offensive line had created a hole, wiped out the linebackers, and emerging through the hole was the massive and fast Marion Motley. Shula screwed his courage to the sticking point, collided with Motley, and made a perfect tackle, much to his own surprise.

"Nice tackle, Taseff!" shouted the onlooking head coach.

The rookie bounded up. "The name is Shula. Shula," he repeated, "S-H-U-L-A!"

Brown, amused, responded, "I'll try to remember."

Shula seemed to be acquitting himself well. "The Browns seemed pleased with me. I made a good impression on Blanton Collier, who was the backfield coach." Collier went on to become one of the most successful football coaches in the game's history. He spent many years with Brown through Cleveland's successes and won an NFL title with Cleveland himself in 1964.

Collier had become famous for calling plays for the Browns from the press box, relaying them to Brown down by the bench, when he then instructed his infamous "messenger guards" to call the play in the huddle. Collier also became known as the "ol' professor," for his affable ways and incredible football knowledge. His most famous quote was "You can accomplish anything you want as long as you do not care who gets the credit."

All-Pro tackle Dick Schafrath once said about Collier, "You instilled more attitude, togetherness, motivation, and confidence into the Browns than anyone can imagine by being TOTALLY INVOLVED with us. We hungered for you to teach us more football each day. None of us ever suspected selfishness or greed on your part. The Blanton Collier era I will recall as the best years of my entire football life."

There was the threat at the time that the Army Reserve would call on Shula, which caused the Browns some consternation about taking up a roster spot for him. Shula had played sparingly in the first four preseason games. Mid-September was approaching; the final roster cuts and announcements would need to be made. Shula and Taseff were nervous.

"I later found out that one of the veterans, Tony Adamle, who was captain of the team, recommended to Brown that I be given the final opportunity to make the team. Brown respected the opinions of his veteran players," Shula later remembered.

Brown told Shula he would be given one last shot, starting him in the last preseason game against the Los Angeles Rams. Brown told Shula if he played well, it would enhance his chances of making the team.

"Everything was riding on that one game for me," Shula recalled years later for the September 14 contest. This was no easy task. A field goal by Groza with 20 seconds left in the NFL Championship Game had beaten the Rams to win the league crown the previous season. It was expected that the Rams would play with real tenacity.

Specifically, Shula would be under fire. The Rams featured two dynamic quaterbacks, the wily and accomplished veteran Bob Waterfield and wunderkind Norm Van Brocklin. Shula would be matched up against Tom Fears. In 1950, Fears had lead the NFL in both receptions and receiving yards. His 84 catches that season set a record that lasted for ten years. He would eventually become a Hall of Famer. Shula would be tested.

"Fears caught his first pass on me. I came up and made the tackle and rolled over with him. He felt I was twisting his leg, and he reached down and kicked me in the mouth and uttered profanities," Shula recalled. Despite wanting to retaliate, Shula kept his cool, knowing he could not afford to. Starting a fight, and getting thrown out of a game of this magnitude, would surely spell the early end of his pro football career, and he knew it.

"It took all I had to hold back and not take a swing at Fears," Shula recounted. Shula thought he played well enough, making some open-field tackles. Still, he didn't know what to think.

Harold Sauerbrei in the *Plain Dealer* put an end to any questions with the subheadline, "Shula Stands Out." In a thriller, where Brown paced the sidelines, "the John Carroll boy . . . went the route with the defensive team at safety and right half. He was successful all the way and three times turned in plays that made him conspicuous." Shula intercepted a pass that would have been a sure touchdown, recovered a fumble to halt another drive, and made a "jarring tackle" covering a punt on special teams. The Browns pulled out a 7–6 victory on Graham's 5-yard touchdown pass to Horace Gillom and Groza's extra point with 42 seconds remaining in the contest.

The next day, Shula received an envelope with a note inside: "Congratulations. You have made the Cleveland Browns football team. Report to the Stadium on Wednesday morning for a meeting and a practice at 9:30." Shula was the only rookie to make the club that year. Taseff was not so lucky. He had not made the final roster but had been placed on the taxi squad.

Shula began his first campaign as a special teams player and backup defensive back. Tommy James, a respected defensive player, then went down with pulled a muscle during a practice. Suddenly, Shula was the starting defensive back for the World Champion Cleveland Browns.

In the practice before his first game, Brown and Collier made sure every pass was thrown in Shula's direction. For his part, the rookie and fledgling defensive back was paired against Hall of Famer Mac Speedie and Gillom, the extraordinary back who also served as the Browns' punter.

"Each time I failed to cover . . . I would look back at Brown," Shula recalled of the test. Brown would be shaking his head. Shula would turn to Collier hoping for a different result, only to see the same negative nod. Steeled in such a crucible, Shula responded come game time. Shula also discovered that Brown and Collier had decided to make sure he had plenty of help from his defensive backfield mates and made sure the defensive line put plenty of pressure on the opposing quarterback.

"As a player, he was interested in more than just his position. He wanted to know what other people were doing and why they were supposed to be carrying out other assignments," Collier remembered fondly. "Don was a good player but probably lacked the speed needed for cornerback where we had him with the Browns. He was a vicious tackler and a leader. . . . He always has been highly competitive and with a violent temper." But there was no mistaking that Collier had real affection for his charge, and respect.

Shula performed admirably in his first appearance against the Washington Redskins in Week Three, which the Browns won, 45–0. A week later, they beat the Steelers, 17–0. By October 27, Carl Taseff had been activated to replace the injured Pro Bowler Dub Jones on punts and kickoffs. The two rookies were reunited. From there on in, Shula's entire family would come to see almost all his home games while he was playing for the Browns.

Shula again received good notices in his game against the Philadelphia Eagles on November 11. Harry Jones noted in the *Plain Dealer*, "Don Shula, John Carroll alumnus, played the entire game at defensive right halfback . . . and turned in a distinguished performance."

Harold Sauerbrei wrote, "The absence of James is not nearly as serious now as it was a week ago, for Shula was a more than adequate substitute at defensive right halfback in the Eagles game. Shula tackled well, and displayed such aggressiveness in trailing the receiver on the Eagles pass patterns that he left a deep impression on Brown."

Shula received high praise from Brown, when the coach told reporters, "All last week I wondered if I had made a mistake in keeping Don and sending Ace Loomis to Green Bay. Now I know the right decision was made."

Shula would remember the November 25 game against Chicago Bears in Cleveland for two reasons. First, the two teams combined for a record 37 penalties in one game! It is still an NFL record, as is the 374 yards of penalties.

The lead on the story under the headline in the *Plain Dealer* said it all. "Don Shula intercepted a Chicago Bears pass, headed down the sidelines and went 94 yards for what most of the fans thought was a touchdown. But Shula himself wasn't sure," wrote Harry Jones.

"Soon as I reached the end zone I turned around to see if they were calling it back," Shula told the press.

"Sure enough, they were," wrote Jones.

"This was one of the roughest games I ever saw," an unidentified official told the press. "We had to call 'em—there was nothing else we could do. Why, there would have been a regular riot out there."

"This was the first league game between the Browns and the Bears," said Don Kindt, defensive leader of the Bears. "We really wanted to win it badly, for we were still the 'Monsters of the Midway.' It was the reputation of the older league against the champs of the All-America Football Conference. George Halas really tried to get us up that week. I don't think I ever saw him want to win a game more." The game was supposed to feature the Bears' power against the Browns' finesse.

Both teams were guilty of piling on. Years later, the Bears players admitted they needed help bringing down the behemoth Marion Motley. As play became more and more chippy, with the Clevelanders retaliating, the game soon got out of hand.

"It seemed the harder we tried," said Chicago defensive end Ed Sprinkle years later, "the worse we got and the madder we became."

Most surprising was that Dub Jones scored a record-tying six touchdowns that day as the Browns rolled to a 42–21 win. "I knew Dub needed one more TD to tie the record," said Otto Graham, "so when Paul Brown sent in a running play

I ignored it and called for a pass. Dub cut down and then in and I hit him for the sixth TD."

By the second week in December, Shula had gained notoriety as part of "Browns' Midgets," so dubbed because the Browns started the smallest defensive backfield in the National Football League. Shula had played in nine games and intercepted six passes. But by the time these accolades were coming in, James had fully recovered, and Brown benched Shula in favor of James for the last game of the year against the Eagles and the upcoming NFL title game rematch with Los Angeles. Brown gave Shula the bad news after the Steelers game on December 9.

"I was back on the bench. Although I didn't agree with Brown's decision, I kept my mouth shut. But it hurt. Oh, how it hurt. I felt as if my world had collapsed," remembered a heartbroken Shula. Taseff later said that Shula had plenty to say about that, "but he didn't say it to Brown." On December 23, the Los Angeles Rams avenged their 1950 loss, beating the Browns, 24–17, to win the NFL championship.

Shula and Taseff did not have long to reflect on their first season as professional football players. After the season was over, at the beginning of the New Year, with the Korean War raging on, their National Guard unit was activated, and they reported to the National Guard and were eventually stationed at Fort Bragg, North Carolina. There, they were appointed to run the physical training school for the base. As Shula later pointed out, it taught them both a great deal about leadership. Because of their position, neither Shula nor Taseff was popular. Soldiers were required to finish their day with physical training after the day's work had been accomplished. In late spring and summer, both men were placed on the camp's baseball team and moved to the "special services" branch of the fort. "It was a gas," recalled Shula.

While on the baseball team, Shula and Taseff met Heisman Trophy winner Vic Janowicz of Ohio State, who was also on the team. Janowicz was given a pass to play in the College All-Star Game against the NFL champion Los Angeles Rams in Chicago. The two went AWOL, with the knowledge of a sympathetic sergeant, and they surprised Janowicz at the game. On August 15 at Soldier Field, in the pouring rain, they watched Janowicz score the first touchdown of the game. The Rams won the game with a fourth-quarter touchdown and field goal, 10–7. They all made it back to the Carolinas without incident.

They coached football in the fall of 1952 at Camp Polk, Louisiana, around the time the army was beginning to draw down on its reserves for Korea. It was apparent that their unit would soon be deactivated. A company commander helped secure their early release. Shula recived the news on a Friday and called Brown.

"I could be back in Cleveland for Sunday's game," Shula told Brown.

Brown insisted Shula make it back fast. James had been injured again. They needed Shula. Brown asked if Shula was in shape, and Shula confirmed he was.

"You remember the defenses from last season?"

"How could I forget them?" responded Shula.

Shula flew north and made it to Cleveland the next day. Shula went to practice, and the coaches schooled him hard, trying to get him back to game readiness. Shula was there in time for the November 16 meeting against the Pittsburgh Steelers and was back in the starting lineup a week later.

"It didn't take long for the Philadelphia Eagles to test me," Shula ruefully remembered of his first game back.

Al Pollard, a famed rough-and-tumble running back from Loyola Marymount and West Point, who had been coached by Vince Lombardi, was one of the Eagles' stars. Early in the game, Shula brought Pollard down. But during the play, Pollard kicked Shula in the mouth. Shula bled profusely from his cut lip. He had lost a tooth and had another loosened. He was removed from the game. His lip required multiple stiches, and the team dentist replaced the lost tooth. It was after this incident that Shula began wearing the newfangled helmets with face masks. Shula played in five games after returning to the team and failed to intercept a pass.

The Browns proved human in 1952 and went 8–5 but still made it to the NFL Championship Game, where they lost to the Detroit Lions, 17–7. Although Shula did not know it, his career with the Browns was over.

In late March 1953, Don Shula was finishing his Master's Degree in Physical Education at Case Western Reserve University in Physical Education, which he'd been working on all during his years with the Browns. At the same time, he was selling cars and working construction in the offseason.

"J. William Stanton was a prominent businessman in his native Painesville, Ohio, and a county commissioner. In federal office, he represented a northeastern quadrant of Ohio that included the eastern suburbs of Cleveland and an area near Akron and Youngstown," according to the *Washington Post.* A former Georgetown University foreign service school student, who earned a Bronze Star and the Purple Heart during World War II, Stanton graduated Georgetown in 1949.

He opened his own Lincoln-Mercury dealership in Painesville not too long after. One of his salespeople was Don Shula. Stanton grew the business into one of Ford Motor Company's largest and most successful franchises. Stanton later became a moderate Ohio Republican who served in the US House of Representatives from 1965 to 1983 and then was counselor to the president of the World Bank.

During the 1956 offseason (he was playing in Baltimore at the time), Shula was working for Stanton at the Painesville Lincoln-Mercury dealership. Stanton used to brag that Shula made more money working as a salesman for him ($7,000) than playing for the Colts ($6,800). That summer, Shula requested all his commissions be held until the end of the summer season. Before he returned to training camp, he took his bankrolled commissions and bought a new car for his mother.

"You should have seen her face when she saw that car," Stanton said. Shula once quipped that he stopped selling cars when he ran out of relatives to sell them to.

After one of his classes, he stopped in a local coffee shop. "I bought a newspaper and ordered a cup of coffee. I turned to the sports page and did a double take. I slammed my coffee down and almost spilled half of it," he remembered.

He had been traded to the Colts in the largest multiplayer deal in NFL history. Fifteen players were traded between the two clubs. The ten that were shipped by the Browns off to Baltimore included Shula, Taseff, two of Cleveland's 1952 first-round draft picks, quarterback Harry Agganis, safety Bert Rechichar, linemen Ed Sharkey and Elmer Wilhoite, ends Art Spinney and Gern Nagler, and tackles Stu Sheets and Dick Batten. In return, Brown received center Tom Catlin, veteran defensive tackle Don Colo, offensive tackle Mike McCormack, halfback John Petitbon, and guard Herschel Forester. Of the major trade, Shula said, "That's the first time I knew about, reading it in the newspaper!" And just like that, Shula was going to Baltimore.

At the time, Baltimore was not an impressive place to be. The city was a stalwart of the eastern seaboard, but there was no proud football tradition yet in Baltimore in those days.

The Colts were a Frankenstein of a sports club, made up of parts from other dead sports franchises. Officially, the team was established in 1947 as the Miami Seahawks in the AAFC. They were disbanded after a disastrous 3–11 season. Owner Robert Rodenberg transferred his franchise to Baltimore. Once in Baltimore, they were rechristened the Colts.

According to unofficial Colts historian Mike Devitt, "Baltimore mayor Thomas D'Alesandro Jr. formed a citizen's syndicate that kept the team from going out of business. In 1948, the club tied for the AAFC Eastern title with a 7–7 record before losing in the playoffs to Buffalo. When the AAFC and NFL merged following the 1949 season, the Colts joined the Browns and 49ers as the three AAFC teams that were admitted to the NFL. After losing 11 games in 1950 and considerable money at the box office, Colts owner Abraham Warner gave his franchise back to the NFL on January 18, 1951."

In 1952, the old New York Yankees football franchise was relocated to Texas and renamed the Dallas Texans. Attendance at home games was so lackluster that halfway through the season, their remaining games were rescheduled as away games. The league was forced to operate the team for the remainder of the season. According to the Pro Football Hall of Fame, "The last three games were against the Detroit Lions, Philadelphia Eagles, and the Chicago Bears. It was decided that the Lions and Eagles would serve as hosts to the Texans, while the Bears would meet the vagabond team in Akron, Ohio. The Akron game was actually the second half of a football Thanksgiving doubleheader, with a high school morning game outdrawing the pros. There were so few fans in the stands that in his pregame remarks, Texans coach Jimmy Phelan suggested that rather than introducing the players on the field, they should 'go into the stands and shake hands with each fan.'"

Phelan quipped after the debacle of a season, "We got all the breaks and they were all bad."

According to football historian Barry Shuck, "[NFL commissioner Bert] Bell announced that Baltimore would inherit the franchise provided they could sell 15,000 season tickets. The city went wild with excitement, holding numerous forms of fund-raising drives. Soon, Baltimore had sold 15,753 season tickets sold and raised over $300,000."

Bell then sought an owner for his newly situated franchise. Enter Carol Rosenbloom, called "C.R." by friends and associates. Bell and Rosenbloom had become friends while summering near each other on the Jersey shore. Rosenbloom bought in his share of the Colts for $13,000.

Robert H. Boyle once wrote in *Sports Illustrated*, "Carroll Rosenbloom is a mysterious millionaire who would rather lose a corporation than a ball game. But he seldom has to worry about either—he has a Midas touch."

Even as Rosenbloom would become one of the NFL's most conspicuous owners, he was still a man of mystery. Boyle wrote, "Few people know exactly what he does for a living. . . . He is shirts, stocks, movies and toys and perhaps even snips and snails and puppy-dog tails as well, for his money is spattered across the board. Even when Rosenbloom's interest in a single company is pinned down, his position is still confusing."

Boyle pointed out that Rosenbloom owned several holding companies that loosely owned numerous businesses, few being related. Rosenbloom was "the largest single shareholder (naturally) in Seven Arts Productions Limited, a company that backed *Funny Girl*, the Broadway musical starring Barbra Streisand, and such films as *What Ever Happened to Baby Jane?*, *Lolita*, and *The Night of the Iguana*."

He was as charismatic and flamboyant as he was well known. Born on March 5, 1907, he was one of nine children and grew up on Hollins Street, in Baltimore, the son of Solomon Rosenbloom, a Russian immigrant, and his wife, Anna, who owned a denim manufacturing company. Rosenbloom attended Baltimore City College and then attended and played football at the University of Pennsylvania under a young assistant coach named Bert Bell, who would eventually become commissioner of the NFL.

By 1950, according to Dan Moldea, author of *Interference*, the silver-haired and rugged-faced Rosenbloom was "America's overalls king" and presided over a far-flung empire of more than 7,000 employees. He owned three of the nation's largest overalls manufacturers. "He amassed a fortune manufacturing work clothes, including fatigue uniforms for the military in World War II," wrote Dave Brady in the *Washington Post*. "He got his start in business with help of his father after attending the Wharton School of Business at the University of Pennsylvania."

"I was associated with my father for 30 days," Rosenbloom once quipped, "then I went down to Roanoke, Va., and started a little business." Rosenbloom had been dispatched by his father to liquidate the Blue Ridge Overalls Company, which he had bought. Instead of closing it down, Carroll instead decided he wanted to turn it around. Carroll secured several government contracts for overalls and ensured the success of the company. He later gained distribution through Sears-Roebuck and J. C. Penney, as well.

"There was never a dull moment," said his son, Steve Rosenbloom, who worked for his father in pro football and now lives in Louisiana. "If things ever got too quiet, he would throw a couple of paper clips into the machinery just to watch people scramble."

Art Modell worked with Rosenbloom as a fellow National Football League owner from the early '60s until the late '70s. "Carroll was a very unique character," he said. "He acted on his own a lot, certainly had his own way of doing things. He wasn't universally loved, but he was well liked by the people who knew him best, including myself."

Bert Bell Jr., who worked for Rosenbloom in the 1960s as the Colts' business manager, said succinctly, "You knew he was robbing you, but you liked him anyway."

Bell described his first meeting with Rosenbloom in 1960. Carroll was playing a game of dice for money with a man he identified only as "Colonel Gottlieb." As he's winning, he's watching the Democratic National Convention. The young Bell, the former commissioner's son, was confused, as he was there for a job interview. There were small piles of cash all over, as the two men continued to watch television and play dice, while Rosenbloom alternately discussed the intricacies of the convention (he was a close friend of Joseph Kennedy, the father of nominee John Fitzgerald Kennedy), and the opportunities for the young Bell.

"There's Carroll, rolling dice, dissecting a presidential race, giving Colonel Gottlieb the needle, and talking to me about a job for the summer," Bell recalled years later. Rosenbloom wavered on sending the young man to work at the Atlantic City Race Track or training camp for the Baltimore Colts. Suddenly, in the middle of it all, Rosenbloom abruptly said, "Forget the race track. Go down to training camp." Carroll then counted his winnings and threw half ($200) at the young Bell. "That was Carroll. If Carroll liked you, he took care of you."

That said, Rosenbloom, who eventually owned two NFL franchises in his lifetime, was among the winningest owners in the history of professional sports, with a winning percentage of .660. He was competitive and ruthless.

Shula was surprised when he arrived for training camp at Western Maryland College (now known as McDaniel College) in Westminster, Maryland, in the summer of 1953. Shula assumed he was competing for a job, but he found out there were other reasons for his being there. "The coach, Russ Murphy, wanted to do everything the way it was done in Cleveland. Only, he wasn't familiar with the Browns' system. He asked me to help," Shula remembered. Shula helped with the game plan and making corrections while out on the field.

One of Shula's housemates in Baltimore was Arthur J. Donovan Jr., otherwise known as Art Donovan or infamously as Fatso. Donovan was a loud, brash Irishman from the Bronx. He was outspoken and brusque, but this belied a smart man who was much shrewder than most people realized. Like Yogi Berra, while people laughed at his rough exterior, Donovan laughed all the way to the bank.

"I guess telling stories is an art. I never looked at it that way. I just started talking, and everyone started laughing. So I kept talking, and they kept laughing," Donovan quipped in his autobiography, *Fatso*, years later.

Donovan was the son of famed boxing referee Arthur Donovan Sr., the son of Professor Mike Donovan, the world middleweight boxing champion in the late Victorian era. Art's father had refereed numerous championship bouts in his lifetime. Art himself was a big guy, both athletic and smart, having survived a Jesuit education. He graduated Mount Saint Michael Academy in the Bronx in 1942 and received a scholarship to Notre Dame. But he quit after just one semester, enlisting in the United States Marine Corps in April 1943. Donovan was a highly decorated soldier. Serving in the Pacific during World War II, he participated in some of the fiercest battles of the war including the Battle of Luzon and the Battle of Iwo Jima. He also served on the aircraft carrier USS San Jacinto. Upon his honorable discharge, Donovan completed his degree at Boston College.

"I came to my first Colts training camp in July of 1950, and it was murder, absolute murder. We had a coach named Clem Crow who must have been nuts. You got to remember that I'd been a Marine, had gone through basic training and spent 26 months in the Pacific during WWII, but the Marine drill instructors had nothing on Clem," Donovan remembered.

A colorful character, he was nicknamed "Fatso" because of his heavy physique. He played his entire career at a lusty 270 pounds. "I'm a light eater. As soon as it's light, I start to eat," he once said. "The only weight I ever lifted weighed 24 ounces. It was a Schlitz. I always replaced my fluids." He celebrated his exaggerated diet of bologna, salami, and lots of beer.

Donovan told stories of Shula during his playing days with the Colts. Donovan recalled that once, while away at an exhibition game in Milwaukee, the team went to a local bar for a few drinks. Most of their teammates had left around midnight; even the hard-drinking Donovan had returned to the team hotel. But Shula and Taseff had decided to hang much later. Both were very drunk. Linebacker Bill Pellington was also with them. A while later, the Milwaukee police arrived at the hotel, insisting on interviewing the players.

"We know one of you Colts stole the taxi cab. Who is it?" they interrogated the players.

Apparently, two drunk players had got in a taxi, while the driver was nowhere to be found. They honked the horn several times, to no avail.

"Shula put Taseff, who was stewed to the gills, in the back of the cab, put the cabbie's hat on, and drove back to the hotel," recalled Donovan. "They would never have gotten caught, except Taseff was slow getting out of the cab. He wanted to pay Shula the fare."

Shula demurred, saying that it was Pellington who drove. "We really didn't steal it. We just borrowed it. In the early years, there wasn't anything we didn't do. We did it all," admitted Shula in his later years.

Donovan recalled that "Shula doesn't like to see me coming, especially when his players are around, because I have stories that will knock that hard-guy image right on its keester."

"I played with Don Shula. I lived with Don Shula. When I think back to when we were single guys playing and living together, who the hell would ever believe that Shula would be the great coach he is today?" said Donovan.

Shula was a starter the whole season in the secondary. The Colts started the 1953 season with a victory over the Chicago Bears, 13–9, at Memorial Stadium in Baltimore. It was an optimistic beginning. On October 25, they beat the Washington Redskin, 27–17, to improve their record to 3–2.

The defensive backfield soon earned the nickname of the Radar Corps, as they had recorded an astonishing 17 interceptions in the first five games, many of which were big plays. They lost their next two contests, first to Green Bay at home and then to the Lions at Briggs Stadium. Both were hard-fought games. Then they faced the Eagles at Philadelphia. "The Radar Corps cracked. They took us apart and beat us pretty badly," said Shula of the 45–14 drubbing. The Colts lost their last seven games that season, giving up 35 or more points in five of them.

Despite finishing 3–9 for the season, the Colts led the league with 56 defensive takeaways. Shula only had three interceptions that year, with a 35-yard return on one of them. He had also recovered one fumble. After the season, Shula returned home to Painesville.

Margaret Fitzgerald had married an Englishman named George Hammond. Despite having married him, Margaret never seemed to give up the mores and customs of her native Ireland. George was a motorman on the Cleveland, Painesville & Eastern (CP&E) rail line that linked Painesville, Ohio, to the greater metropolis. Margaret and George gave birth to a daughter, Dorothy Hammond, in 1909 while living in Painesville. A graduate of St. Mary's Parochial School and Harvey High School, she graduated with the class of 1927. Sometime in the late 1920s or early 1930s, Dorothy met John Bartish, who was Hungarian by birth and who also worked in the railroad yards. Margaret disapproved of their match. She preferred that her daughter marry someone of Irish descent. The couple decided to elope. It took some time for Mrs. Hammond to accept the union. On August 8, 1933, Mrs. Dorothy Hammon Bartish gave birth to a beautiful, healthy baby girl. Unfortunately, there were complications. Dorothy died the following morning at Lake

County Memorial Hospital, and her body was later interred at the Evergreen Cemetery.

"When her daughter died in childbirth, the split between [the grandmother and the newborn's father] widened," recounted Shula years later. The little girl was named Dorothy in honor of her deceased mother. "The grandmother raised Dorothy and naturally exerted a great amount of influence over her."

Shula met Dorothy Bartish at a bowling alley in 1954. As Shula remembered it, the bowling alley was a hangout because it featured two things: bowling and a bar. While bowling with friends one night, another group (of three young women) rented the lane next to theirs. The two groups exchanged banter and then introductions. Shula remembered inviting their fellow bowlers to the bar for a drink.

Dorothy was from Painesville and was four years behind Don in school. He had heard her name mentioned many times, as far back as grade school, but still, even in the small town, they had never met. Her family was not well off, but her working-class father had saved enough money for her to attend college after high school. "I remember hearing how much John Bartish had sacrificed for his daughter, and yet this was our first meeting," remembered Shula. He soon learned she had earned a degree in music education from Ursuline College in Cleveland. Before they parted, Shula asked her out on a date, and she accepted.

The first meeting almost was thrown off track. When Shula arrived at Dorothy's door, her unforgiving grandmother coldly greeted him. Luckily, Dorothy came down, saved the moment and the two were off. In the car, Shula asked why her grandmother was so brusque. "She didn't approve of another Hungarian coming around and now dating Dorothy," Shula recalled.

After another exchange, Shula asked Dorothy if she would like to go to the movies. When she balked, it was decided that they would go dancing. While Shula agreed to the idea, secretly he was worried. He was shy with women and lacked confidence in his dancing abilities. They ordered drinks, and then the music began. She taught Don to dance on thatr first date. She made him feel "more confident and better-looking," as he put it. She opened up his personality, and Shula realized there was something about Dorothy that struck true for him.

Dorothy was going to be a teacher, and Don was in the middle of his playing career. The two saw other people, but it was obvious to Shula that they were happiest when they were with each other. Still, it was agreed that they wouldn't rush into anything.

When Shula arrived back at Western Maryland College that summer, for training camp, there was a new head coach. Rosenbloom had pursued Blanton Collier to no avail and then decided on a little-known coach named Weeb Ewbank.

Wilbur Charles "Weeb" Ewbank was born on May 6, 1907, in Richmond, Indiana. One of Ewbank's younger brothers could not pronounce the name Wilbur correctly, calling him "Weeb" instead. The name stuck with him the rest of his life. Ewbank was an excellent athlete. He attended Miami University in Oxford, Ohio, in 1924, where he played quarterback for the football team as well as playing basketball and baseball. The football team finished 8–1 in 1927 and won the Ohio Athletic Conference championship.

From 1928 to 1930, Ewbank coached high school football, baseball, and basketball at Van Wert High School. He then moved to McGuffey High School in Oxford as their football and basketball coach. In 1932, Ewbank took a break from coaching to earn a master's degree at Columbia University in New York City. He returned to McGuffey and recorded three undefeated seasons between 1936 and 1939. In 1943, he enlisted in the US Navy and was assigned to the Naval Station Great Lakes near Chicago. There he met Paul Brown, a former classmate who succeeded him as Miami's starting quarterback. While stationed there, Ewbank served as an assistant to Brown on the football team, and the two began a long friendship and professional association. Ewbank coached for a few more years at Brown University and Washington University (St. Louis).

In 1949, he accepted a position under Paul Brown in Cleveland. Ewbank thought he would oversee the quarterbacks, but Brown insisted that he oversee the offensive line. "He knew I'd have to work very hard at this job and bring a fresh approach," Ewbank recalled many years later. Ewbank also oversaw personnel and had influence on the draft.

Carroll Rosenbloom approached him to become the coach of the Colts in 1954. Brown advised him to pass on the offer, believing it would be difficult to turn around a three-time loser of a franchise. When Ewbank accepted the position, Brown accused Ewbank of passing along to Rosenbloom and his staff the names of players he had targeted while still with the Browns. NFL commissioner Bell concurred, and Ewbank agreed to stay through the draft. However, Brown was not wrong about his suspicions. Ewbank had given a list of players to the Colts through Baltimore sportswriter John Steadman. The most famous of these draftees was future Hall of Fame end Raymond Berry, whom the Colts drafted, and who became a major target later for Johnny Unitas.

Donovan had heard that Ewbank had a reputation around the league as a "tremendous coaching talent and a rat bastard." Ewbank confirmed the description when he told Donovan he had to lose thirty pounds before training camp, or Ewbank would cut him.

"Ewbank began by doing things exactly the way the Browns did them," wrote football historian Michael MacCambridge. "Ewbank was no rube, and possessed a quiet confidence in his own coaching skills."

"Many changes and adjustments had to be made," Ewbank remembered. "I took two defensive ends and made offensive guards out of them. Then Gino Marchetti, who was an offensive tackle, was shifted to defensive end. . . . We kept experimenting with our personnel, and it took time for all the pieces to fall into the right places."

According to Shula, there were "Some rough guys there, but you know, you could learn a lot from some of those old players. Gino Marchetti revolutionized defensive-end play. Most of them were bull rushers in those days, but Gino was a grabber and thrower, a guy with moves who'd blow by the tackle so fast sometimes that he'd never touch him. There were guys who'd play against Gino and say, '[Don] Joyce is much tougher. Look, my uniform isn't even dirty.' But Gino got a lot of quarterbacks and running backs dirty."

"Ewbank is a very meticulous person who put in a great deal of time planning and actually was the coach the Colts needed at the time," said Shula years later.

"When Ewbank came over as the Colts' head coach three years later, he knew he was inheriting a heady player. Ewbank, who recalled that Shula was always talking strategy with veteran players, reportedly had so much confidence in Shula that he allowed Shula to call the defensive signals on the field," wrote sportswriter Brad Snyder.

"Ewbank had entrusted me with the responsibility of calling defensive signals. I had to come into the defensive huddle from my right cornerback spot and hustle back into position," Shula explained.

Known as a strong-willed individual, Shula was often referred to by his teammates as "Captain Red Neck" because of his burning determination and hard competitive instincts. For the next season, Shula thought he deserved a raise and mailed back his 1954 contract unsigned.

"I'd heard that was the way the veterans did it," he said. After a while he got a letter from the front office. "We assume you have decided to retire," it said and asked for his playbook. "I got on the phone right away. Paid for the call myself. 'Listen,' I said, 'you've made a terrible mistake. I'm not retiring.'"

The team opened the 1954 season at home against the Los Angeles Rams. "On the first play of the game they pulled the old sucker pass play. That's when you put ten guys in the huddle and leave one just a few inches in bounds on the sideline to streak downfield when the ball is snapped," recalled Donovan. Rams end Skeets Quinlin was idling over by the sidelines.

"Weeb saw it and began yelling at Shula at the top of his lungs," recalled Art.

"He blended in with them real good. So good, in fact, that I did not see him," said Shula. "When the ball was snapped, Van Brocklin dropped back to pass. He threw a ball that must have traveled sixty yards in the air. I said to myself, 'Where is that dummy throwing the ball?'" Quinlin breezed by Shula for an 80-yard touchdown, and the rout was on. "I looked around embarrassed," Shula admitted. The Rams beat the Colts, 48–0, that day.

Shula, Donovan, Pellington, and Marchetti shared a townhouse in the Campus Hills section of Baltimore. The house was nicely appointed with furniture, fine china, and crystal. The young men would wrestle constantly in the living room and dining room, and Shula remembered the sound of the china and crystal clinking in the cabinets whenever they would jostle one another.

"Donovan would get into his stance, and Pellington and I would try to knock him off his feet," recalled Shula. "Nobody could move him. He was just so strong down in here and up in there. We'd be holding on and that furniture would be rattling." Eventually, Donovan would begin to laugh, and then give way from the laughter, and the three would topple to the living room floor, sending rumbles throughout the house.

Donovan also recalled that Ewbank had assembled a special squad to cart injured players off the field. "In those days, there were no medics. Players came out and carted you off the field. There were three guys in particular Weeb liked to use—Don Shula, Carl Taseff, and Bert Rechichar—because they were defensive backs and they were fast." Donovan said they would drag you off the field quickly, no matter your condition.

Shula had five interceptions for the Colts in 1954, but the team floundered, posting another 3–9 record. The 1955 team showed marked improvement. They finished in the middle of the Western Conference pack with a record of 5–6–1. Shula played nine games and again snagged five interceptions. On November 5, triplets Jeanette, Jane, and James Shula made a road trip to see Don play. Since the Colts did not play the Browns that year, they drove from Bowling Green University, in Bowling Green, Ohio, where they were going to college to see their brother play in Detroit against the Lions (a 24–14 loss).

The Shula triplets had graduated from Riverdale High School in 1954. Janette and Jane had started at Bowling Green the fall following their graduation from high school, but James had put in a year at the Industrial Rayon Corporation in Painesville, where his father now worked, before starting college.

All three lived in the newest living facilities at the school at that time. The girls resided at one end of the campus, and James lived at the other end. They all saw one another regularly. By then, Jane was working summers at her brother Joseph's grocery store back home. Jeanette worked for the local parks and recreation in summers as a playground supervisor.

During the 1955 season, the Colts developed what became a popular prank—dousing a teammate with a bucket of cold water. By midseason, the practice had grown tiresome, and Ewbank was forced to deal with the most notorious of water hoisters by levying a fine of $1,000 for the next man caught in the act. This was no small fine, representing anywhere from 5 to 20 percent of the players' salaries.

Despite the possible harsh penalty, Gino Marchetti convinced Carl Taseff to pull off the prank one more time. Taseff was hidden, unseen in a corner of the locker room with the pail of cold water. Marchetti told Taseff, when he walked in and gave the signal, to douse rookie running back Alan Ameche. But this was all a ruse. The joke was on Taseff. Marchetti waited in a hallway for coach Ewbank, who was dressed in a sports coat and tie, to walk by, leading him into the locker room. When he walked in, Marchetti gave the mischievous and unknowing Taseff the signal. Taseff jumped out and pitched the icy water at the unsuspecting head coach.

Taseff's eyes widened before the water left the pail, and Ewbank froze! Ewbank stood there, in shock, absolutely soaked, while Taseff fumbled all over him apologizing again and again. Weeb was absolutely steaming.

"I'm so sorry, coach! I'm so sorry," repeated Taseff.

"You're sorry, all right. You're a sorry, dirty, no-good son of a bitch!" thundered Ewbank. Marchetti and his cohorts were in stitches. Luckily for Taseff, once Ewbank cooled off and realized Taseff had been duped, he waved off the fine.

Shula's season ended prematurely after an altercation with Tom Fears in a 17–17 tie against the Los Angeles Rams on November 20. According to Donovan, Shula was a "mean sonofabitch, and a wild man to boot. He was a defensive back who would throw an elbow into a receiver's eye as soon as look at him." Shula was constantly holding, hooking, and grabbing the former All-Pro end to the point of distraction. The two had played against each other for half a decade. As the players walked back to their respective huddles, the frustrated Fears screamed at Shula, "Shoes, goddammit, keep your mitts off me. Don't hold me anymore."

"Finally Fears had enough, and toward the end of the game he coldcocked Shula with an elbow that put his lights out. Smashed Shula's jaw," remembered Donovan.

Donovan and Pellington, both fellow housemates with Shula, visited him in the hospital. Shula was in the hospital a few days, and the two players returned to bring him home. They asked what they could do for him, make him something to eat, and he asked for something soft, so they cooked him some eggs.

"So the choosy prick didn't like the way we cooked them. He told Pellington they were too hard," recalled Donovan.

"Screw you, cook your own eggs," yelled Pellington and threw the plate of eggs at Shula, who missed the final three games of the season.

The 1956 season was a breakout year for Ewbank, the Colts, and a new quarterback named Johnny Unitas. "Shula was one of the first players to notice—truly notice—John," wrote Unitas biographer Tom Callahan.

John Unitas was born on May 7, 1933, in Pittsburgh, Pennsylvania. His father died when John was five, and his mother worked two jobs to support the family. He played college ball for the University of Louisville, in Kentucky. At 6-foot-1 and 145 pounds, Unitas appeared slightly built, and wherever he went, there was the worry that he would get hurt. Unitas threw for 3,139 yards and 27 touchdowns in his years at Louisville. He was drafted in the ninth round by the Pittsburgh Steelers, but his performance in camp was lackluster, and he never made the final roster. He played semipro ball on the weekends for the Bloomfield Rams. He played quarterback, safety, and punter for six dollars per game.

Unitas eventually found his way to Baltimore. "It all started when we received a letter about John from one of our fans in Pennsylvania. I always accuse John of having written it himself. In any event, the letter impressed me enough to check with his college coach, Frank Camp," recalled Weeb years later. "We decided to give Unitas a tryout, along with a large group of other candidates. It took a 75-cent telephone call to contact John."

His early appearances were inauspicious, but he started seven games, and the team started to pick up. There was optimism in Baltimore.

"It's an exaggeration to say Shula and Unitas were the same guy, but only a slight one," Callahan wrote. "Shula and Unitas had the same attitude about work, the same competitive spirit, the same tunnel vision, the same stubbornness, the same bluntness. Shula was louder. He was that screamer John had always detested."

But there was also another understanding for Shula. Going up against the likes of receivers such as Lenny Moore and Raymond Berry in practice, Shula understood he was losing a step. "John was just starting to time up with these guys, and I wasn't good enough when Unitas had the ball."

"My future wasn't good. I was really just an average player who knew what I was supposed to do out on the field. I enjoyed the contact and the challenge of learning my assignments but knew I didn't have that good a year in 1956. Most of the time I played with a badly sprained ankle that required injections before each game, and this hampered my performance," Shula recalled. "I could see that the coaches weren't that high on my performance."

Ewbank and the Colts' coaching staff were constantly trying out younger players. During training camp, in 1957, Shula was beaten out by a rookie and an untested veteran. He was the fourth player on the depth chart at his own position.

Ewbank eventually released his starting right cornerback: "He wasn't quite fast enough," Ewbank said many years later. "He was smart enough."

"All of a sudden I had the cold realization that I was no longer a part of the Baltimore Colts organization, and this was a tremendous disappointment," Shula later admitted.

On September 29, 1957, Don Shula found himself in the cheap seats at Memorial Stadium to watch his old teammates defeat the Detroit Lions, 34–14. After the game, the dejected Shula made his way down to the locker room to congratulate his old teammates. To his surprise, they presented him with the game ball.

"It meant a great deal to me," Shula recalled later. "I was walking away with their respect. It meant more than anything else." Shula recalled that it certainly helped to lighten his dejected mood.

Shula was picked up a few days later by the Washington Redskins in time for the second game of the season. On November 10, the Colts played the Redskins at Washington's Griffith Stadium. The Redskins gave up 230 passing yards, and according to Shula, "Raymond Berry had an exceptional day against me, catching nine or ten passes. He set a record of thirteen [actually, twelve] receptions in the game." In fact, Berry's 224 receiving yards still stand as the Colts single-game record.

Despite his employment by the Redskins, Shula spent every free hour in Baltimore, hanging out with his friends and keeping up his relationships. He had no aspirations outside of football and had spent an inordinate amount of time with these guys. And the Colts were winning, which was more than you could say for the Redskins. Despite a 7–5 record, it was becoming clear that the Colts were just starting to take off.

Johnny Unitas to Raymond Berry (and to Jim Mutscheller) was starting to make things happen, as well as the impressive backfield of Alan Ameche and Lenny Moore. Unitas, Ameche, and Mutscheller all earned Pro Bowl honors that season, as well as Donovan and Gino Marchetti on defense. And, of course, his childhood friend, Carl Taseff, was still with the club, albeit in a backup role.

The season ended without fanfare. Winning their last three, after a troublesome start, the Redskins went 5–6–1. Shula had three interceptions for 48 yards (his longest return was 30 yards). Shula went back to selling cars in Painesville and assumed he would play in 1958. He discovered a different fate, though, in an unanticipated way. He had been driving through Washington and decided to stop in at the team offices and chat with the coaches before training camp began. The coaches invited Shula into their meeting room, and there, in front of him, was the big personnel board for the 1958 season. His name was listed below a rookie's. Once again, he had been deemed expendable.

"It was a strange feeling. I suddenly felt cold all over," remembered Shula. He was only twenty-seven years old. He didn't think he could possibly be finished. Maybe he would be traded? Would it be worthwhile to fight for the job? Of course, they would run another rookie against him the next year. In his words, "I had to face the realization that maybe I didn't have it anymore as a player."

When Shula left the Redskins offices, he decided he would not play again. He would retire. All the late-night bull sessions with his fellow players, all the beers and bars and dates and life on the road, and wrestling in the house, and all the football talk and camaraderie was gone. He had played seven seasons of professional ball, played in 73 games, intercepted 21 passes, and recovered four fumbles. And just like that, his playing days were over.

CHAPTER 3

College Days Redux

After Shula had learned of his fate, and decided he would retire, he went back to Painesville and began making phone calls. He was letting people he knew that he was retired and interested in coaching. Shula then decided to drive to Philadelphia, where the 1958 National Collegiate Coaching Convention was being held. "I felt like if I talked to some of the people at the meetings and around the lobby, letting them know that I was looking for a coaching job, then my chances for getting a position would be better," Shula reasoned. "It was just a stepping stone. I don't think he really cared whether he played pro football for any length of time. He was always looking ahead to where he could run a team rather than just playing on it," said Painesville friend and John Carroll classmate Roy Kropac years later.

During his time there, he ran into an old friend, Frank Lauterbur. At the time, Lauterbur was an assistant at Army but had been an assistant coach at Baltimore when Shula was a player. Earl Henry "Red" Blaik was the head coach at Army from 1941 to 1958, and in that time won three national championships.

A week after Shula had run into him, Lauterbur called him, telling Shula he had heavily recommended Shula to the newly appointed coach. A day later, sight unseen, Dick Voris called and, on Lauterburg's recommendation, offered Shula a job on his staff, where he was assigned to coaching the backfield.

Richard J. "Dick" Voris was a formidable character, and a well-seasoned football veteran successful at many different levels. "Coach" (as he was affectionately known) attended Salinas Junior College and enlisted in the Marines for a four-year tour of duty in the Pacific during World War II. He coached two years of college football, and then a year with the Rams. In February 1955, Red Blaik had hired him to coach the offensive line. In 1958, Army finished third in the AP Poll, crushing many of its opponents during the season. At the end of the season, Voris was offered the job as head coach of the football team at the University of Virginia.

"It was an odd beginning," Shula remembered. Shula knew nothing about the University of Virginia and accepted a $6,500 salary (well below his last Redskins salary, but he reasoned with himself that at least he had a job in football). Shula was headed to Charlottesville. Arthur Geupe had lead the program from 1946 to 1952. Geupe compiled a 47–17–2 (.727) record while with the Cavaliers. His '51 team finished 8–1 and was ranked 13th in the nation. He left to coach Vanderbilt University for another ten years.

For Shula, a former professional, the University of Virginia was a wake-up call. The school was a prestigious one, well known for its high standard of academic excellence. Geupe had left Virginia just in time. In 1951, professor Robert Gooch (a former Cavaliers quarterback himself) published the findings of a committee called the "Gooch Report," a treatise on why the school should abolish the football program. The paper had two purposes. The country had seen a rash of suspensions and fines from the NCAA for rules violations where football was concerned. There had been rumblings that an investigation might hit Virginia, and the faculty wanted to avoid the tarnishing of the school's reputation. The other part was to abolish scholarships (to use the money for academics) and to make sure the athletes were students first, football players second. The faculty overwhelmingly supported the Gooch paper. Bending to pressure, University President Darden reduced the number of athletic scholarships given by 80 percent.

Years later, Geupe quipped, "There is no way you can be Harvard Monday through Friday and try to be Alabama on Saturday." With the writing on the wall, Vanderbilt lured Geupe away, and Virginia hired Voris.

"My first year coaching was not a pleasant one," mused Shula. "When I reached Virginia, I discovered that the scholastic standards were so high that it was not only tough to get a player into school, but also once you did, it was tough keeping him in."

Shula thought Voris well organized and was impressed with his fellow coaches. It was a small staff, and Shula remembered them putting together the first playbook. He enjoyed that part of it. More than when he was a player, Shula, in contributing to this new set of schemes, realized how important the playbook truly was.

"We worked hard on fundamentals in spring practice," Shula remembered. But he was shocked about the difference of the athletes they were coaching as opposed to the players they would be competing against.

Meanwhile, Shula began to contemplate life after football. He recalled the time that he was sharing an apartment with a fellow coach, and while alone one night, staring at the ceiling, Shula was trying to understand what direction his life was going in. He realized that he was now in his life's work. He would, for better or worse, be a coach.

"Then I began to think of Dorothy," said Shula. Dorothy was teaching for a year in Hawaii. He began to wonder if maybe she had changed since she had begun her job there. Had she met someone there? "When she left me—you know that saying 'Absence makes the heart grow fonder'? That's when I realized that she was the one."

Shula wrote Dorothy a letter. In it he proposed to her. He suggested she leave when the semester was over and come home and get married. "I just liked everything about her."

"I was playing it cool," said Dorothy. "I didn't think he was ready to give up all those girls I imagined he had." Don wrote her a letter, to which she mused, "'It's the beginning of Lent,' he said. 'Let's pray we do the right thing.' I'd met a pilot and I was thinking about getting married. Don was coaching at Virginia."

"You're making a terrible mistake," Don told her.

"I got three letters talking marriage. The last one said, 'Will you?' Don made all the wedding arrangements," said Dorothy. Dorothy accepted via mail in return. And via handwritten posts, they corresponded about their wedding date, and what life would be life going forward. Years later, Shula joked that the two corresponded like pen pals.

Don and Dorothy were married on July 19, 1958. "Dorothy has always been the most important person in my life. Whenever the big decisions had to be made, we would sit down and discuss all aspects of the situation, and time after time she would always be there with the right answer. It was never, 'How can I leave my friends or the house?' but 'If you think it's the thing to do, let's do it.'" Shula said.

Meanwhile, the season at Virginia was a trying one. They lost their first game, 20–15, at Clemson but came back and upset heavily favored Duke, 15–12. During their third game, a 26–14 loss to North Carolina State, they lost their starting quarterback, Fred Russell, and their season was essentially lost. The team finished 1–9. According to Shula, their home games were played in mostly half-empty stadiums, and the student apathy was evident. Shula wanted out. Unknown to him, so did Voris.

In February of 1959, Shula again attended the coaches' convention and ran into Blanton Collier, whom he'd known from his years with the Browns. He had left the Browns and was now the head coach at his alma mater, the University of Kentucky. After a brief conversation, Collier offered Shula a job. Shula accepted. He drove to Kentucky and met the rest of the staff. Shula liked Collier. "Blanton is probably the best teacher of technical football in the game and a superb organizer."

The offer included a $1,000 raise and free on-campus housing. Kentucky was a much more competitive school athletically speaking. According to Shula, Collier expected a lot from his coaches. He worked them hard. Everything was planned, nothing was left to chance. They spent their daytime in the offices at the school, and nights in Blanton's basement, reviewing film.

Collier had taken over the program in 1954, a year after Paul "Bear" Bryant had left for Texas A&M. What few remember about Collier's years at Kentucky was that the school had been placed on probation for violations that occurred under Bryant. More important, however, Collier had accumulated some of the greatest coaching names in the country when they were still unknowns. Among the staff were (not including Collier and Shula) Howard Schnellenberger, Ermal Allen, John North, Bob Cummings, and Bill Arnsparger. It was one of the greatest brain trusts ever assembled in college football.

Howard Schnellenberger eventually became the offensive coordinator for Bryant at Alabama, helping to win three national championships (1961, 1964, 1965), was the offensive coordinator in 1972 for Shula (winning a professional championship), and was the head coach of Miami University when they won the 1983 national championship. He was 6–0 lifetime in bowl games.

Bill Arnsparger went on to become one of the greatest defensive gurus of the next generation, creating such successful units of the Miami Dolphins as the "No-Name Defense" and the "Killer Bees." He was head coach of the New York Giants and Louisiana State University (including two Sugar Bowl berths). In 1994, he was the defensive coordinator for the Super Bowl–bound San Diego Chargers.

John North had played for the Baltimore Colts from 1948 to 1950 and later coached the New Orleans Saints for three seasons. Ermal Allen went on to become one of the integral people for the Dallas Cowboys in charge of scouting opposing teams. Bob Cummings became an assistant coach for the New Orleans Saints and later became a legendary secondary school coach in Louisiana.

"Years later, when my second son was ready to graduate high school, he was a guard on a strong football team. . . . Philip chose to enroll there, a decision I had agreed with, as I knew that Blanton Collier was the kind of man I wanted my son to play for," recalled Don Martin, Shula's old high school football coach. "And I knew Don would help him make the adjustment to college. . . . I recall Blanton pointing to Shula saying, 'That young man knows as much football as anyone in the country. He's going to make a fine head coach.'"

The Wildcats lost five out of their first six games in 1959 and finished the season with at 4–6. They lost badly to Auburn (33–0), but other than that, never gave up more than 16 points a game, falling victim to their lack of talent compared to the other teams that were stacked with athletic ability in the Southeastern Conference. In his one season with the Wildcats, Shula found information, knowledge, experience, men and relationships that would serve him for decades to come. For Shula this had been a watershed year, possibly the most important in his early career. He would carry much from these years with him forward into his professional life. He pointed out later, "From the standpoint of background, this was the most influential year that I had in coaching."

In the meantime, Shula started hearing about opportunities in the pro game, which was much more to his liking. He enjoyed coaching college players, but he wanted to be in an environment where football was everything. He wanted to be with professional coaches and professional athletes. He heard first from a Canadian team. But Shula was not interested in going north. He then got calls from the Chicago Cardinals and the Detroit Lions.

Shula visited Chicago first. The Cardinals had once been a successful team, but in the 1950s, they had suffered a dismal run, winning only 33 games during the entire decade. They'd only had one winning season in that span. While Shula was interviewing with them, their owners, the Bidwells, were also engineering a move to St. Louis to get out of the shadow of the more popular Bears. The Cardinals were notoriously undercapitalized, and it was well known that several possible suitors were spurned, as the Bidwells did not want to give up control of their franchise.

The head coach of the Cardinals was Frank "Pop" Ivy, possibly one of the most popular coaches in football. Ivy was the only person to be a head coach in the National Football League, American Football League, and Canadian Football League. He had played at Oklahoma University and then played for the Pittsburgh Steelers and then the Chicago Cardinals. After retiring as a player, he served as an assistant at Oklahoma before taking the head coaching job with the Edmonton Eskimos from 1954 to 1957. He then was the head coach for the Cardinals from 1958 to 1961.

Shula then visited with George Wilson of the Detroit Lions. Wilson was an impressive man. As a player, Wilson was part of Northwestern's 1936 Big Ten Conference championship team. By the end of the 1937, he was playing for the Bears. He was on the roster for six NFL Championship Games with them. He retired in 1946.

In 1947, Wilson stayed with the Bears but moved over to the coaching side. He served as an assistant under George Halas for two seasons. In 1949, he took an assistant position with the Detroit Lions. He remained an assistant with the Lions for another eight years. Just prior to the 1957 season, head coach Buddy Parker, who had been with the team since 1951, was introduced at the "Meet the Lions" banquet as the "best coach in the league." Parker rose and told the fans in attendance, "I've got a situation here I can't handle anymore. These ballplayers have gotten too big for me, or something. I'm getting out of Detroit football. I'm getting out tonight. So long." Wilson was named to replace him.

The Lions were the Gashouse Gang of the National Football League, led by their prolific drinker and passer, Bobby Layne.

"Actually, Bobby doesn't live it up any more than most players," a veteran observer of the club once said. "He just doesn't bother sneaking around. He goes in the front door at nightclubs and he comes out the front door. He doesn't spare himself the next day, either. He runs as hard and works as hard as any player on the team."

They were among the most colorful teams in the league. They were famous for fighting with local citizens in bars while on the road as well as among themselves. Famous fights, like the one the night before a 1953 contest in San Francisco (they cleared the bar and won the game the next day), as well as at 18,000 feet (defensive back Tulsa Bob Smith came to fisticuffs with assistant coach Buster Ramsey—he lost the fight and his job while on a team flight).

"I joke around a lot," Wilson said, after he became the Lions' head coach, "but there's only one way to play football and that is to beat down the other guy."

"After Parker's precipitous departure in mid-August, his chief assistant, George Wilson, was made head coach. Wilson cracked down on the Lions; he instituted an 11 p.m. curfew for the athletes and made it stick by fines of $50 per hour for violators. He personally made bed checks at training camp to make sure the team was getting its sleep, and he ran the players unmercifully in practice," reported *Sports Illustrated*'s Tex Maule.

That year, 1957, was the last year the Lions won an NFL championship, beating the 49ers in the playoffs and the Cleveland Browns, 59–14, for the title. In 1958 and 1959, their record started to slide.

"I talked over the opportunities with Dorothy. I decided to accept the job with the Lions as the defensive backfield coach. The pay was good too, $11,000," said Shula. It was the most money he'd ever made in professional football.

When he broke the news to Blanton Collier back in Kentucky, Collier asked him what his long-term plans were. Shula was firm—he wanted to be a head coach. Shula insisted it had been his dream all along.

"Well, if that is your ultimate goal, then there is no doubt that you have to take the job with Detroit," Collier told him.

"Technique-wise, Blanton Collier was head and shoulders above everyone else," says Shula now, referring to Collier's insistence on drilling his team in the classroom and on the field. "I've tried to learn from everyone I've been exposed to, but I've also been very conscious about doing things within the framework of my own personality. I don't want anyone to ever think I'm trying to act like somebody else, but I'd be pretty stupid not to learn things from men I've played under or coached against."

Shula was back in professional football.

CHAPTER 4

Detroit

"Welcome to the Lions," George Wilson said.

The glory days of the Lions were behind them, or so it seemed. Their charismatic and spiritual leader, quarterback Bobby Layne, had been traded to the Pittsburgh Steelers. However, they still had the core of their great and brutal defense. "The Lion team was still reflecting its fame in the past as a tough, roughneck outfit; that is not to say it was undisciplined, but that it was a player's team, molded by . . . "rounders"—which was the old football term for the hell-raisers," recalled literary icon George Plimpton.

"He was a wide-shouldered, dark-haired, deeply tanned man with a voice of resonance—which the players said reminded them of someone speaking through a long pipe," recalled Plimpton of Wilson. "He and the other coaches had been playing golf. All of them wore golfing hats with crossed club-sticks insignia on the front."

Alex Karras, the incredibly ferocious and charismatic All-Pro defensive tackle, recalled meeting Wilson for the first time, saying, "It was the beginning of a beautiful friendship. . . . He never demanded much; only that I should give my full attention to the game while it was being played. The same thing with practice." What a player did off the field, Wilson seemed less concerned about. "Wilson felt that if a player wanted to smoke, drink, or carouse, that was fine. As for curfews, he kept everybody loose."

"I guess you fellows know how to take care of your bodies, or you wouldn't be here," Wilson told his Detroit charges. "And I figure you're all over twenty-one and know the difference between right and wrong. So have a good time and be ready to work when the time comes." Karras recalled later that among his players, Wilson was "a man who had the kind of respect few coaches enjoy."

"It was easy to spot George Wilson. He was usually in the middle of the field, almost always alone, wearing slick-pressed purple knee-length shorts, and socks drawn halfway up his calves," recalled Plimpton. "He would walk with his head down, seeming to inspect the ground before he moved a shoe onto it, and then after the deliberation a foot would move forward, and he would plod slowly in an aimless turn among his players as if unaware of their presence.

"He had been with most of his associates since his Chicago Bears days, and it was apparent that he rarely interfered with them: each knew what he was supposed to do," Plimpton wrote.

Shula was the young man on the staff. "I was happy to be back in pro ball," Shula recalled. When Shula first arrived, Wilson handed him the previous year's defensive playbook and instructed Shula to set it up the way he wanted to teach it.

"He was a tough, hard-nosed player with the Chicago Bears and he dealt with his team like one player to another. George wanted to treat the players the way he wanted to be treated as a coach," said Shula. "I could see a lot of values in the type of relationship Wilson had with his players."

The Lions' coaching staff would pick a bar, and everyone had to be sure to bring a dollar bill to participate in a round of Liar's Poker. "After everyone had studied his dollar, the bidding would start. George Wilson would take a sip of his fancy drink, squint at his dollar bill, and would say, 'No fooling around, I bid six threes,'" remembered Plimpton.

"At Detroit the bed checks were rare. The coaches treated the men as professionals, unlike some of the other training camps where there was a more procrustean attitude. . . . Tom Landry, [the Dallas Cowboys'] head coach, pulled a main switch himself at 10:30 to darken the training camp dormitory corridors," reported Plimpton.

The Lions were loaded with talent. Alex Karras was paired with Roger Brown, staking the inside of the defensive line, with Darris McCord and Bill Glass both playing ends. The team was anchored by the legendary middle linebacker Joe Schmidt, a Hall of Famer, flanked on either side by Wayne Walker and Carl Brettschneider. And the defensive backfield featured the talented corner Dick "Night Train" Lane, paired with their other corner, the amazing Dick LeBeau. Yale Lary and Gary Lowe were the safeties.

This defense was laden with absolute firepower. Schmidt had won two NFL championships with the Lions and went to 10 consecutive Pro Bowls. Karras was the outsize, outspoken four-time Pro Bowler. LeBeau, Lane, and Lary were all Hall of Fame defensive backs.

"George Wilson knew he had the ingredients of a championship team when training camp opened in 1960," Alex Karras remembered. If there was any problem coaching this elite unit, it was that these competitors were each a crazy character in his own right. Alex Karras, known to his teammates as "the Hog," "became the unofficial hazing master," according to Plimpton. He was prone to theatrics in which most team members indulged him. Karras stated repeatedly that he took a pay cut when he graduated from Iowa in 1958 and signed with the Detroit Lions. As he himself said, "I never graduated from Iowa, but I was only there for two terms—Truman's and Eisenhower's."

Lane had earned his nickname as a rookie playing for the Los Angeles Rams.

"[Tom] Fears liked to play records, and his favorite was 'Night Train,'" Lane once recalled. "Every day I'd be going to his room and he'd be playing it. He roomed with a guy named Ben Sheets, and whenever I'd walk into the room, Sheets would say, 'Here comes Night Train.' He started calling me that, and it stuck."

He had 14 interceptions in 1952, his first season in the NFL. He was ferocious on the field, known for his interceptions and his lethal hitting. "Lane was a lifelong jazz devotee. When he was nearing the end of his football career, he married Dinah Washington, known as the Queen of the Blues," Richard Goldstein wrote in the *New York Times*. "His mother was a prostitute, his father a pimp, and he was abandoned when he was three months old. A widow with two children of her own, Ella Lane heard cries coming from a trash bin near her Austin home and found him, covered by newspapers. She raised him."

"I played with him, and against him, and he's the best I've ever seen," former NFL player and broadcaster Pat Summerall once said of Lane. Herb Adderley, the Hall of Fame Green Bay Packers cornerback, called Lane "the best defensive back ever to play the game."

The soul of the defense, despite such outsize characters, was Joe Schmidt. Known by teammates as "the Old Man," Schmidt was the true team leader. At the time, Schmidt was considered as important to his team as Jim Brown or Johnny Unitas were to theirs. While Karras was loud, Schmidt was quiet. "But the same competitiveness glowed in him," wrote Plimpton. "The quality that makes Schmidt a leader," Bob Scholtz, a Lion's offensive lineman once said, "is his absolute honesty. Everybody knows that."

The team was filled with pranksters. Karras was usually the brunt of practical jokes. Teammates planted frogs under ashtrays and anything to startle him. His reactions, almost always over the top, were the favorite payoff of the team. It never seemed to get old, and Karras seemed ever ready for the laugh. Dick LeBeau was the other favorite target. Players would wait until late at night, when LeBeau would be reading in his room. Invariably, the players would take turns sneaking into his room and, wearing grotesque rubber Halloween masks, would scream out at the unsuspecting LeBeau.

Despite his knack for massive amounts of information and preparation, nothing prepared Shula for what happened in his first play as a defensive coordinator in a preseason game against the Cleveland Browns. Shula sat in the press box for the first half of the game, watching the action and making notes. He would come down at halftime to make adjustments and corrections during those 15 minutes. Shula remained on the field for the second half, meeting with the defensive backs and linebackers.

Shula noticed that there was confusion among the defensive backfield players. Milt Plum, the Browns quarterback, took the snap and found a wide-open Ray Renfro, who caught a long, lazy pass and scored an easy 60-yard touchdown. "I almost fell out of the press box."

They lost their first three regular-season games to Green Bay, San Francisco, and Philadelphia before they finally scored their first win against the Baltimore Colts, a bittersweet victory for Shula against his old club.

On December 4, the Lions played the Colts for the second time that season. Could they defeat Unitas and company a second time in the same season? The game was a memorable one. The Colts needed the win to keep their hopes of a third straight NFL championship alive, and the Lions were trying to stay in contention, as well. As Wilson himself said, it was "a 'must-win' game for us. . . . Although we had beaten the Colts earlier in the season, we expected a rough afternoon in Baltimore."

"On any given Sunday during the Colt season," Karras reflected, "the fans can become extremely vicious."

"We spent much of that week with our defensive players, knowing that if they came through with the type of game they were capable of playing, we could beat the Colts," recalled Wilson. "I was proud of our defensive unit and felt it was one of the best in the game."

Wilson was worried by two things—all the parties going on in the team's hotel, and which quarterback he would start the next day. He had his choice of Jim

Ninowski and Earl Morrall. "Jim had the much stronger arm and was a better runner than Earl. However, Earl, in his fourth year as a pro, was a dedicated student of the game."

Luckily, the partying stayed under control and Wilson decided on Ninowski. The bus ride from the hotel was silent. Remembered Wilson, "It was the type of tension that I have always found prevalent before a big game."

It soon became apparent that the game would be a defensive struggle, the first quarter ending with a 3–2 score, with Baltimore forcing a safety and and the Lions kicking a field goal. Wilson called it a "hockey score." Then in the second quarter, Lenny Moore broke free on a pass from Unitas and scored an 80-yard touchdown. Lane blocked the point-after attempt, leaving the score at 8–3.

After the Lions marched the ball down to the Colts' red zone, Bobby Boyd picked off a Ninowski pass and returned it to the Lions' 12-yard line. On the Colts' first play, defensive tackle Roger Brown forced a fumble that the Lions recovered. In the fourth quarter, Wilson put in Morrall, who responded with a 40-yard touchdown pass to Howard Cassady to put the Lions up, 10–8. They added a field goal, increasing their lead to 13–8.

Then Unitas hit Lenny Moore, who stretched out for a long pass against Lane and dived for a touchdown. Karras said Lane was so upset, "I thought he had a heart attack."

The fans went crazy. "One whole section of Memorial Stadium emptied," Karras recalled. A mob stormed the field. An announcement was made over the loudspeakers, asking fan to return to their seats so the game could be finished.

As the crowd dispersed, two inebriated fans lingered around the Lions bench. One of them struck Karras on the helmet. "I took my helmet off and clobbered him," recalled Karras. The beaten man fell to his knees. Just then, the other malingerer pulled out a knife and chased Karras around the bench, with Karras alternately swinging his helmet at the assailant.

All this time, Wilson was screaming to his team, "We can still win!" Finally, a group of police came to the Lions' aid, and the miscreants were removed. With six seconds remaining, Morrall passed to wide receiver Jim Gibbons, who weaved his way downfield for a miraculous 65-yard touchdown with time running out.

Madness ensued. Wilson himself did not actually see the touchdown until the next day on the film. Karras and others sitting on the bench dejectedly never saw the play, either.

"I don't know how we got into the locker room. We had to fight off Baltimore fans, who clawed at our uniforms, spit, cursed, and carried on like uncaged lunatics," Karras recalled, further stating that some of the angry mob included the policemen who were supposed to be protecting them. Wilson recalled that his tie clasp was stolen in the melee, and his suit was torn, as fans grabbed and scratched him, too.

The Lions had derailed the Colts. "Baltimore never did recover," Wilson proudly stated. The 1960 club ended up going 7–5 and beat the Cleveland Browns in the Playoff Bowl (for third place), 17–16.

"There was some feeling of accomplishment by playing the Runner-Up Bowl, but it wasn't the feeling I wanted," remembered Shula years later. He wanted to win a championship. The 1961 Detroit club finished 8–5 and again played in the runner-up game, beating the Philadelphia Eagles, 38–10.

By 1961, Shula started gaining more recognition. "The Lions quarterback situation was in flux, and that side of the team performance appeared sluggish. Their defensive unit played about 70% of the time. But it was a potent offensive force through its interception of passes and its talent for provoking and recovering fumbles," Gordon Cobbledick wrote in the *Plain Dealer.*

Cobbledick did not mention what the linebacker Schmidt would say to quarterback Milt Plum as the two passed each other on the field during exchanges between defense and offense: "Pass, Milt, three times, then punt."

Cobbledick acknowledged the talent difference between the two units. "Much of the credit for the uniformly fine performance of the defense is given by the Detroit staff to Don Shula," he wrote. "When Buster Ramsey quit the Lions to go to the New American League, many of the team's followers predicted the collapse of the defensive backfield. But under Shula's coaching, far from collapsing, it has improved." Cobbledick noted that among Lions fans and NFL followers, Shula was considered "definitely head coach material."

There was obvious improvement on the club, but the 1962 team exceeding all expectations. The most unforgettable game of the season was also one of the most famous Thanksgiving Day games in club history. Fifty years later, Detroit sportswriter Richard Bak anointed the game "the most famous football game ever played in the history of the Detroit Lions: the Turkey Day massacre of the haughty, undefeated Green Bay Packers at Tiger Stadium on November 22, 1962."

The game pitted the 8–2 Lions versus the 10–0 Green Bay Packers led by Vince Lombardi. "Their offense seemed unstoppable," remembered Shula. Earlier in the season, the Packers had beaten the Lions, 9–7. The Lions had clung to a 7–6 lead for most of the game. With two minutes left in the game, the Lions were in Green Bay territory, grinding out yards and eating up the clock, when Milt Plum threw an ill-advised pass that Herb Adderley intercepted and returned to the Lions' 18. The Lions were speechless at first, then angry. Waiting for the rest of the Packers offensive unit, Karras turned to legendary guard Jerry Kramer and said, "C'mon, C'mon . . . I'm gonna bust your face!" Karras made two tackles behind the line, but Green Bay's Paul Hornung kicked a 26-yard field goal with time running out to give Green Bay the victory.

"It still ticks me off," Joe Schmidt said thirty years later. "We never should have thrown the ball. We should have run Nick Pietrosante. Yale Lary could have punted the ball all the way to Milwaukee. Green Bay had only one time-out left. At least we should have made them earn it."

The Lions wanted revenge. "On the Packers' first play from scrimmage, quarterback Bart Starr was swarmed under by several blitzing Lions for a 15-yard loss. It set the tone for the day. Before 57,598 wildly screaming fans and 32 million disbelieving television viewers, the revenge-minded Lions practically chased the Packers out of Tiger Stadium and back to Wisconsin," wrote Bak. "By the time it was over, Starr had been sacked 11 times and lost 110 yards attempting to pass. Jimmy Taylor, the league's leading ground-gainer, was held to a mere 47 yards."

Lions linebacker Wayne Walker explained, "Everything we did that day was just perfect. If we blitzed, they didn't pick it up. If we looped linemen, they didn't pick it up. If we didn't blitz and played a zone, Bart Starr couldn't read it."

The Lions jumped out to a 23–0 halftime lead, with the last nine points the result of two sacks of Starr, the first leading to a fumble that was returned for a touchdown by Sam Williams, followed by trapping Starr in his own end zone for a safety. "We knocked the bejabbers out of them," crowed Karras.

"We demolished them," said Shula proudly. "Practically every time that Starr set up to pass, he was swamped. . . . It was probably one of the greatest defensive performances of all time."

Shula was getting more attention for the Lions' defensive play. "Bill Glass says the Detroit Lions' excellent defense isn't all physical. The Browns' end rates Don Shula . . . as one of the best defensive coaches in the league," wrote Gordon Cobbledick in the *Plain Dealer* after the Green Bay game.

The Lions finished 11–3 and won their third straight Playoff Bowl, 17–10 over the Pittsburgh Steelers. And the humbled Packers went on to defeat the New York Giants for the 1962 NFL championship.

Shula was now seen as a defensive genius. A year later, when George Plimpton was granted unprecedented access, he recalled looking at the Lions playbooks for both the offense and the defense. Shula's handiwork was self-evident: "The defensive book was more interesting." Besides the usual admonitions about such things as penalties, stressing third-down situations, and playing hard the last two minutes of each half, the book "included page after page of statistics, graphs, and charts, and a long section showing assignments for individual players against specific offensive plays." Plimpton effused that the defensive book was incredibly complicated and complete. "Furthermore, it seemed to be written with a zest missing in the offensive book."

Meanwhile, the once-proud Baltimore Colts were looking for a new head coach. Weeb Ewbank had built the team from the ground up and had achieved incredible things, including their famous win over the New York Giants in "The Greatest Game Ever Played" in 1958, the first overtime NFL Championship Game ever. They repeated in 1959, but 1960, 1961, and 1962 had brought mediocre finishes.

"Gino [Marchetti]was the one who got me the job," Shula said. "Carroll Rosenbloom loved Gino."

"We got hammered by the Chicago Bears," Marchetti recalled years later of the 52–0 thrashing at the hands of the Bears in late November 1962. "On Monday, I got a call to meet our owner, Carroll Rosenbloom. I thought maybe he was going to trade me. I felt so bad after the beating the Bears gave us. When I walked in the room, Carroll asked me why I was depressed. I told him because we lost."

"Don't worry; now I got my chance to fire Weeb Ewbank," said the smiling Rosenbloom.

"He asked me to recommend a coach. I told him Shula, who had played with us and was then a coaching assistant for the Detroit Lions. We were playing them the next week. A meeting was set up on the Saturday before the game between Rosenbloom and Shula.

"It was supposed to be secret. No one was to know. But Shula said he was working for George Wilson, and, as the Lions' head coach, he wanted to tell him or he wouldn't go through with the idea. He informed Wilson."

The charismatic owner and the young defensive genius met on December 1 in Detroit. The Colts were in town to play the Lions. The two met the night before the game between the two clubs. One of the first questions Rosenbloom asked of Shula was "Are you ready to be a head coach?" Shula assured Rosenbloom that he was.

"Don Shula should have been the [Lions] head coach," Joe Schmidt said years later. "He knew what the hell he was doing. I told [management], 'Don't let this guy get away. He's going to be a good coach.' He took off. I don't blame him."

Shula and Rosenbloom talked on and off again over the next several weeks. They met again at the Golden Strand Hotel, in Hollywood, Florida. Shula knew that Rosenbloom's hiring of him was a gamble. Marchetti and Colts general manager Don Kellett were both staunch supporters of Shula's hiring. Kellett and Shula had kept in touch from Shula's days as a player with the Colts through his five years of coaching.

On January 8, 1963, the Baltimore Colts introduced Shula as their new head coach. Shula received a two-year, $30,000-a-year contract. At thirty-three, he became the youngest coach in the NFL.

"Letting Ewbank go was one of the toughest things I've ever had to do, and I mean this with regret. I've always had admiration for Weeb," Rosenbloom told the press. Rosenbloom offered Ewbank another job in the organization but was confident other teams would make moves toward his former coach. Ironically, the same newspapers that had called for Ewbank's head during several preceding mediocre campaigns now portrayed the scorned Ewbank as an unappreciated victim.

Shula realized that Rosenbloom was a serious, competitive owner who expected a championship team. Ewbank was an accomplished, winning coach. If Rosenbloom was willing to fire Weeb, it was clear to Shula that nothing short of a championship would suffice.

CHAPTER 5

Baltimore

If Shula didn't know what he was getting himself into, he soon found out.

"On a day when the Baltimore Colts play in the National Football League, Carroll Rosenbloom, their owner, is in torment. His palms are wet with sweat, and his superstitions run wild. In the locker room before the game he always pats the head of Johnny Unitas, the quarterback, and accepts a piece of adhesive tape from Lenny Lyles, a defensive back," wrote sports scribe Robert H. Boyle. "Even when Baltimore is comfortably ahead with only two minutes to go, he worries that the other team will score and try an onside kick. After the gun sounds he slumps in his seat, exhausted but all smiles—until he remembers next week's game."

"I don't want any yachts, and I don't want any castles," Rosenbloom told the writer. "I would just like to have about 30 more championships, and then I'd be all set."

Rosenbloom would spend the entirety of the game chain-smoking and sweating. "Carroll smokes three packs of cigarettes," said Rosenbloom's friend Sig Hyman (president of Pension Planners of Baltimore, Inc.). "One for offense, one for defense, and one for the half."

Gene Klein, owner of the San Diego Chargers, once said about Carroll, "He always gave you the feeling that, if you crossed him, he was capable of slitting your throat, then donating your blood to the Red Cross blood drive."

Expectations were high. And now Shula would have his chance to become a head coach. He would now have a chance to put into effect all that he had learned. He would be somewhat the autocrat that Brown had been, he would be as highly organized as Collier, and hoped to have the same compassion and freedom for his players as Wilson and Ewbank. But if the old guard of the Colts, the men he had played with and who had won several championships without him, thought he was their friend, they had no idea of the fire he held within him. "I try to have mutual respect with all my players. You can't worry about friendship, or whether you're liked or disliked. You can be the most popular guy in the world and not win on Sunday," Shula explained about his style. Ewbank's trait of being too nice would not be Shula's undoing.

"The Colts had gotten old in certain areas," Shula recalled of his first campaign in 1963. "I decided to go with the younger players who demonstrated talent."

Changes were made along the offensive and defensive lines. Key stars such as Raymond Berry, Jim Orr, and Lenny Moore, as well as Gino Marchetti, were retained. There was also a new fullback, J. W. Lockett, who was acquired from the Cowboys.

"I think the players were very much in agreement with the choice. He had left there with a real great reputation and there were still a lot of players who had played with him and knew him. And I think he was a great football coach," said Raymond Berry years later.

"The first guy I had to tell he didn't fit into my plans was Joe Perry," Shula once related of that first season. I'm thirty-three years old and I'm sitting opposite *Joe Perry,* who was a great player and a great guy, and I'm telling him, 'Joe, we're going in a different direction.' I just felt humbled when I did it, but it had to be done."

Shula knew he had a credibility gap. "I had been an average player here, and now all of a sudden I'm back, coaching guys who were great players . . . who had just won a championship," Shula explained later. "I know I had the proving to do all over again. . . . The guys who helped me most were Gino and Pellington. They were player-coaches for me that year. Gino was the team captain, and everybody looked up to him."

Shula hired two men who would become lifelong associates. Shula retained Ewbank's offensive line coach, John Sandusky. Sandusky would go on to become one of Shula's most trusted and long-lasting confidants and professional relationships. John Thomas "Sandy" Sandusky Jr. had grown up in Philadelphia and played tackle for Villanova University, where he was an All-American. He played offensive and defensive tackle for the Cleveland Browns (for six years), winning NFL championships in 1950, 1954, and 1955, and then retired after spending the 1956 season with the Packers. He and Shula had been teammates while Shula was with the Browns.

Shula also retained Charley Winner. Winner had played college ball but had never played in the pros. As a twenty-year-old B-17 "Flying Fortress" radio operator and gunner during World War II, he flew 17 missions over Germany near the war's end. On his final mission, in the early spring of '45, he was shot down.

"We were at about 19,000 feet when we got hit," Winner explained. "We were bombing Hamburg. Pattern bombing. We were the first group over the target. Flak from the ground was way below, but antiaircraft fire was right up where we were and we took a direct hit. Our pilot, who had just turned 19, was killed. We tried to nurse the plane along but lost all our electrical power. So we jumped. Parachuted. On the way down I could see our airplane making a slow big circle, head to ground, and I could see it hit and explode."

Winner had played for Weeb back when Ewbank had been the head coach at Washington University in St. Louis. Winner eventually married Weeb's daughter Nancy. Their first date was at an ice cream parlor. "We've been eating ice cream ever since!" Winner said sixty-six years later. Charley would call on Nancy at the coach's house. However, he knew what the clear signal was, from the coach, when it was time to leave. "Weeb taking his socks off was his way of telling me to go home," he recalled, chuckling.

Sandusky and Winner would form, along with Carl Taseff and one or two other men, the core of Shula's inner circle for most of the rest of his life.

Possibly most important at the time, however, was Don McCafferty, who coached the offensive backfield and who would become instrumental in the relationship between him and veteran star quarterback Johnny Unitas.

Unitas was a gambler. According to biographer Lou Sahadi, "Much of Unitas' success was the result of his daring and improvisation, and he needed the freedom to continue. Unitas wasn't about to change."

The problems had begun during the last year of Ewbank's tenure. Ewbank was complaining that Unitas never followed any of the game plan set up by the coaches. Unitas had a lot of respect for Ewbank and in his silent, classic way never confronted the coach, though he grumbled slightly about him years later.

"As a quarterback, I have to take orders and do what the hell he wants," said Unitas. "I guess you get a little touchy because the man says you don't do what the hell he tells you."

In 1962, Rosenbloom became fed up with the whole situation, especially Ewbank. He went to Unitas behind the coach's back. "Look, you're the boss," Rosenbloom told Unitas. "Call the plays any way you want to. You're in complete charge on the field once the game starts."

Shula had even said to Unitas, privately, "How well I do depends on you."

But there was friction from the beginning. "Early on, it was fourth down and a half yard to go and Shula sent in the field-goal team," Gino Marchetti said. "John waved it off and got the first down. After the game, Shula summoned Unitas to the coaches' room." Marchetti was a player-coach that year, and so he was there. It was just Marchetti, Shula, and Unitas.

"If you're going to show me up like that, I can't be the coach of this team," Shula said in an even tone. No screaming.

"He was very calm," said Marchetti.

"From now on, when I send the field-goal or punting team in, you come off. It has to be my decision whether we kick or not," said Shula.

"John, he's right," Marchetti interjected. However, the relationship never improved.

Shula was philosophical about his experience with Unitas. "It was John's personality. It was my personality. It was his confidence in his own ability. It was my belief in how things should be done. I'm not a guy who finesses things, and John was never a finesse guy, either. You always knew where John stood, just like you always knew what I was thinking. It's not like we didn't listen to him making up the game plans. You're not going to ignore that kind of experience." Shula insisted that they inserted plays Unitas liked, asked for, and felt comfortable playing. Their game plan was tailor-made for him.

There were times the coaches, especially Shula, might call a play, seeing something in the defense that maybe the unit on the field wasn't seeing. One time, Shula sent in such a play, and Unitas refused to use it, instead calling a different play. "Don't let me down," Unitas ordered his teammates.

Shula admitted that during a game against the Packers, they were reading a signal for a blitz. When Shula got the sign from one of the coaches that the Packers were going to blitz, Shula would signal the offensive tackle and tell Unitas, who would then, in turn, change the play for a maximum protect. One time, Shula signaled in the blitz call, but it never came, and the Colts had lost an opportunity for a one-on-one coverage with one of their most dangerous receivers.

"After the play, John glared at me on the sideline and kicked the dirt as he came off the field. I got upset," said Shula.

"Listen," Shula said to Unitas. "It wasn't my fault. They crossed us up, and I blew it by sending in the wrong sign."

"Unless you're sure of what you're doing, don't interrupt my play calling!" Unitas snapped back.

"He came in as a young head coach. He knew the game and was a tough disciplinarian. He was a hollering, screaming-type coach. He prepared you well for the game," Unitas said. "What he did in his first year, which was very smart of him, was not to come in with a new system and force everybody to change. [Shula] made the adjustment to the offense we had."

In one famous story, Unitas had become so enraged with Shula's screaming and shouting that he stopped the practice, walked to Shula, and tossed him the ball, saying, "Here, you be the quarterback."

Shula said he had tremendous respect for Unitas, and that they had their share of good and bad times. But he had nothing but respect for the old gunslinger.

"John had a real toughness about him. He would wait until the last instant to release the football and paid the price. He put his neck on the line all the time, knowing he was going to take the big hit by waiting so long, but he gave Raymond Berry or Jimmy Orr an extra step to get open. He'd pick himself up bleeding off the ground and play the next play. He was one of the toughest guys I've ever coached," recalled Shula years later. "Another thing about John was the two-minute drill. He was the best at that I've ever seen. He just had a clock in his head, and I think I and a lot of other coaches learned a lot about the two-minute drill from watching Unitas operate it."

Petulant as ever, when he was unhappy, Unitas would say to reporters, "Don't ask me, ask Shula. It's his team."

Unitas held a grudge against Shula for the rest of his life. Friends lamented in later years that Unitas would never give up his loathing for Shula. Raymond Berry pointed out that each perceived a lack of respect from the other and held that grudge for a long time. Unitas once told defensive tackle Fred Miller, as long as twenty years later, "If that son of a bitch was across the street, and his guts were on fire, I wouldn't walk over and piss in his mouth."

The Colts got off to a slow start in 1963. They lost their home opener to the Giants, beat the 49ers in San Francisco, and then dropped two in a row to Green Bay and the Bears, both on the road. They sandwiched a pair of two-game winning streaks around a two-game losing streak to reach .500.

On Friday, November 22, President John F. Kennedy was assassinated, throwing the nation into an emotional roller coaster. The Baltimore Colts were already en route to Los Angeles that day. They had a game against the Rams that Sunday.

"We always left for West Coast trips on Friday and then had Saturday to adjust time-wise," said Shula. "Planes were slower and everything was slower. I can't remember whether we were in the air or not, but if the games were going to be canceled, it would have been on Saturday and we would have already been out there. Everything hit so quick I don't think any of us had time to think."

Comissioner Pete Rozelle called his friend and mentor Tex Schramm, who was the Dallas Cowboys' general manager. "He asked me what I thought he should do, and I told him I personally thought he should play," said Schramm. "When you have something very sad like that happen, the faster people can get their minds off it for at least a short period, the better."

Rozelle also called Kennedy's press secretary Pierre Salinger, who told him, "Jack would have said, 'Play.'" Decades later, Rozelle revealed that he thought it was the worst decision of his career but admitted that the call had to be made in haste, and the machinery of the league was also difficult to reverse. Some fans vowed to stay away from the games and were critical of Rozelle's decision.

The slate of seven games went on unencumbered. Many recalled the games being somewhat surreal. There were no marching bands or halftime shows. "Taps" was played at some stadiums. Many of the players, especially Mike Ditka of the Bears, recalled playing in a daze, still stunned by the news. Then during the halftime of several of the games, the players found out that the accused assassin, Lee Harvey Oswald himself, had been murdered by a local nightclub owner.

"I remember sitting in the press box when we got the word about [Jack] Ruby killing Oswald," Schramm said. "That threw everything into a total spin. When we got back to the dressing rooms, it was, 'What happened?'"

Years later, the league remained divided. "That was the only game I ever played on any level that I didn't care about at all. There was no desire, no determination. I kept thinking, 'This is America?' America was a safe haven. Then, all of a sudden, it wasn't. It lives with me to this day," New York Giants Hall of Fame linebacker Sam Huff later recalled. "Worst mistake Rozelle ever made."

"Absolutely, it was the right decision," said Salinger thirty years later. "I've never questioned it. This country needed some normalcy, and football, which is a very important game in our society, helped provide it."

The Kennedy family had agreed with the decision. Robert Kennedy even went so far as to attend an Eagles preseason game in 1964 and spoke with the players. "He came into our locker room," said Eagles backup quarterback King Hill, "and went around shaking our hands. He said he appreciated us playing the games that weekend."

The Colts and Rams and 48,555 fans observed a minute of silence out of respect for the slain President. The Colts took a 16–14 lead in the third quarter when Danny Villanueva kicked the decisive 13-yard field goal for the Rams. The Colts attempted a go-ahead field goal in the fourth quarter from the Rams' 17-yard line but missed.

"What stands out in my mind is the eeriness of the whole thing," Villanueva recalled years later. "We played the game in silence. I think people who wanted to cheer didn't because it wasn't politically correct."

The loss dropped the Colts under .500, but they reeled off three consecutive strong wins to finish with a winning record at 8–6, good for third place in the West Division.

According to Unitas biographer Tom Callahan, "Like a lot of disciplinarians, Lombardi included, Shula was a sucker for the bad boys."

One time, Shula was trying to make a point to wide receiver Jimmy Orr. "Orr was not a very physical player," Shula explained. Shula thought he looked less like a ballplayer than any he had had in his career. One day, in a film study with the team, Shula thought he would embarrass Orr to be more physical and inspire the mercurial 1958 NFL Rookie of the Year. In front of the whole squad, Shula slowed down one play in which Orr failed to block downfield during a successful pass play.

"If you had made that block right there, we would have had a chance to go all the way," Shula explained. Shula also pointed out that Ray Renfro always made that block for Jim Brown with the Cleveland Browns. "You've got to hit somebody!" Shula exclaimed.

Orr raised his hand. "What?" asked Shula.

"You can't ask a Thoroughbred to do a mule's work," said Orr. The entire team busted up laughing, including Shula.

Alex Hawkins was another Shula favorite. One time, Hawkins badmouthed Shula to the press, complaining he didn't get enough playing time during a 38–7 blowout of the Washington Redskins in 1965. Shula called Hawkins into his office that morning when the story appeared. When Hawkins arrived, Shula held up the paper, opened to the story, and shouted, "Is this your shit?"

"Yes, he wasn't supposed to have printed it, but those are my words," admitted Hawkins.

"Well, you asshole, you've got a good thing going and you try to screw it up with shit like this?" said Shula, angrier now.

"He wasn't supposed to print that," Hawkins tried to respond.

"What you're doing is second-guessing my decision, and I won't have it," screamed Shula. "Now get your ass out of here. I don't want to see you anymore today. From now on, keep your mouth shut!"

Hawkins was once arrested at 4:45 a.m. for taking part in an illegal poker game in the back of a barber shop. Hawkins told the judge, "I just came in for a haircut." He was even less nonchalant in front of Shula. Shula dressed down the young running back, pointing out it wasn't bad enough that he had been out till all hours before an upcoming showdown with the Packers, but that one of the other players arrested had a rap sheet with thirty-three arrests. Hawkins responded, "It's hard enough finding a card game at five o'clock in the morning, without screening the applicants, too." Even Shula doubled over.

"Then there are the stories—legends, actually—that march through the file like soldiers, following him through the years: didn't allow water on the practice field when he started coaching; forbade his players to have sex after Tuesday during game week. That one was a little much. For Shula, too," wrote *Sports Illustrated's* Paul Zimmerman. That had been called, at Camp Shula, the "Tuesday rule."

"Oh, hell," Shula said. "No water during practice was one of those outdated ideas. Everyone believed it. It was supposed to give you cramps or something, just like weightlifting supposedly made you muscle-bound. So many strange things in those days. Remember that exercise everyone had to do, the duck waddle, walking around with your knees bent? Later it turned out it was absolutely the worst thing for your legs."

"The no-sex-after-Tuesday thing was just something to kid about. When I played for Cleveland, Paul Brown used to talk about it in the meetings, and everyone would laugh and tell jokes. I mean, how would they check?"

Marchetti had balked at playing one more year, but Rosenbloom, who had staked Marchetti $100,000 to open up a chain of hamburger stands called Gino's, felt obligated and agreed to one more season. By 1964, the Colts had developed four running backs: Tom Matte, Jerry Hill, Tony Lorick, and Joe Don Looney. With this quartet of backs, Unitas had more time to throw and improvise. The running game established, Unitas could now pass at will.

"We got the weapons now," Unitas told the press. "They don't tee off anymore. They've got to look for the run, and they can't put the pressure on the way they use to."

The Colts hired veteran coach Bill Arnsparger on March 6 to become their defensive line coach. He attended Paris High School and became connected with the school's then-football and basketball coach, Blanton Collier. Arnsparger served in the United States Marines during World War II. He was a line coach for four years under Woody Hayes at Ohio State University in Columbus, Ohio. Arnsparger then worked for Blanton Collier at Kentucky for eight years. It was there, in 1959, that he met Don Shula. He most recently had coached at Tulane.

"On defense, your job is to get the ball and get off the field," Arnsparger once told the *New York Times*. "Everybody depends on the people who are beside them, behind them, or in front of them."

Dropping their opening game to the Minnesota Vikings shocked the Colts, but they rebounded against their nemesis, the Green Bay Packers. Shula was constantly engaging with Lombardi's Packers, the dominant team of the 1960s.

"We spent a good deal of time working on a flood play," said Shula talking about strategy for the upcoming game. By placing three receivers on the strong side, and Berry on the weak side, it forced either man-on-man coverage for Berry, a mismatch with a linebacker, or freeing up Moore among the pack against the strong side. It worked.

"Designing a defense for the Packers was even tougher. No team is more versatile on attack then Green Bay," Shula said. "Bart Starr is a wonderful field general and a fine passer. Some people have said that he cannot throw accurately long, but that is not true. He is a complete passer who throws quickly and accurately at short, middle, and long range. He is hard to rush, because he releases the ball quickly."

On September 20, the Colts beat the Packers in a pivotal game, 21–20, at Lambeau Field. "We had proved something to ourselves. I think no one was really convinced before that we were a championship team," said Shula. "After the Packer game we knew we could do it."

By late November, *Sports Illustrated* called the Colts "The New Dynasty." After stumbling in their opener, they reeled off 11 straight wins, were beaten by the Lions, and then clubbed the Washington Redskins, 45–17, to finish the year 12–2.

"We got stung in Minnesota trying to use a safety blitz. [Fran] Tarkenton called a quick trap into it," Shula added at the end of the season. "We don't need gimmicky defenses." Shula also said the running game had improved tremendously.

"What we are doing this year is beating the clubs that beat us last year. That is our plan. Coach Shula is pointing us that way," Marchetti told the press. The Colts sewed up the Western Division title early, with three games to go. Carroll Rosenbloom asked one reporter, "What do you think? Are we as good as we looked?"

In early December, the *New York Times* trumpeted, "John Unitas, the toast of pro football in Baltimore's title days of 1958 and 1959, was voted yesterday the most valuable player of 1964 in the National Football League. Don Shula, his coach, was voted the coach of the year by an Associated Press panel. Unitas, the rags-to-riches quarterback who was rescued form the semi-pros by the Colts, won by a landslide vote of the 42-man committee, including three from each league city.

"Unitas climbed back to where he was in the golden years of Baltimore championships as he led the Colts to 11 straight victories this season after an opening day defeat by Minnesota. With Baltimore assured of a title game . . . Unitas can do no wrong."

The division title earned the Colts a championship game shot against the East Division winners, the Cleveland Browns. Shula would be coaching across the field from an old colleague. "Blanton Collier, coach of the Browns, is 58 years old and has been teaching football for 36 years. Don Shula, the Colt coach, is 34 and he is younger than two of his players, Gino Marchetti and Bill Pellington," William N. Wallace pointed out in the *New York Times*.

The Colts were installed as prohibitive favorites. As Wallace noted, "the Baltimore players are convinced they will blow the Browns right out of Cleveland Stadium. Shula has of necessity stressed Cleveland's assets to his players who are confident, if not over-confident."

"Somebody has to be the favorite," Shula said. "But we've all been around football long enough to know favoritism doesn't mean much when the bell rings." Privately, Shula was both elated and nervous. In only his second year as head coach here, he was getting ready to lead a team for the NFL championship. But he was worried, as well.

Bill Pellington, the middle linebacker who would retire after the game, said: "The Browns are a good team. We think we are better. We know we have to prove it, and the proof will be on the field Sunday, not anywhere else."

"The more we looked, the more we began to respect the Cleveland offense. You could see Paul Warfield grow from game to game as a receiver. And we never ceased to be amazed at Jim Brown," Shula said of their game planning for the contest.

One night after they had finished, Gino Marchetti said to Shula, "He's even better than I thought he was, and I thought he was the best." Shula agreed.

"After our analysis of the movies, we decided that we would have to establish a running game so that we could control the ball. That is the best defense against Jim Brown. He can't run when he is on the bench," said Shula of their plan. "Planning a defense against the Cleveland ground game is essentially trying to figure out how to stop Jim Brown. We keyed our middle linebacker, Bill Pellington, on Brown, as most clubs do. But the only effectual defense against Brown is gang-tackling, and we emphasized the need for our defensive players to keep their feet and get into the pursuit."

"Our workouts have been shorter because we had more time to get ready and because this is a heavy field we're practicing on," Shula told the press. "It tires the players. We're in real good shape. A couple guys have had colds or the flu and missed time last week, but they're all right now."

"The Colts are favored by a touchdown, but Cleveland is hoping to post an upset on the strength of its versatile offense," reported United Press International. "The Browns' running attack, led by Jim Brown and Ernie Green, is considered virtually the best in the league, and Frank Ryan at quarterback can be as good as any passer in the league when he's in form."

For many in the stands at Cleveland Municipal Stadium, this was an emotional game. The Browns faithful were out, rooting for their team. But there was a substantial number of people there who knew both Collier and Shula. Also in attendance were Shula's family and friends. A contingent of Painesville faithful were in their seats, too. His old coaches from high school and college were there. This was a personal event for Shula as much as it was a professional one.

The Colts knew they were in trouble by the end of the scoreless first half. With a tough wind, and a slightly muddy field, both teams had trouble moving the ball and holding on to it.

"The most dramatic play may have been Browns linebacker Galen Fiss blowing past three Colts' blockers to upend Colts Hall of Fame halfback Lenny Moore on his butt for an eight-yard loss in the first half—exposing the Colts' veneer of invincibility," wrote Cleveland sports historian Roger Cohen.

In the third quarter, Lou "The Toe" Groza knocked in a 43-yard field goal, Frank Ryan tossed two touchdown passes, and Collier's Browns never looked back in a 27–0 rout of the Colts. Ryan threw three touchdown passes to Gary Collins, who had five receptions on the day for 130 yards and all three touchdowns.

"It was our best defensive game of the year," said Collier. "We decided that we wanted to have everybody covered when Unitas took his first look at his primary receiver. That way, he'd have to look for a second receiver. And if he still didn't see anyone open, maybe he'd wait some more. By then our pass rush should be on him. But there's nothing so startling about that."

"We had to count on our front four and knew that had to do it," Browns linebacker Galen Fiss said.

"They used a lot of man-to-man coverage and mixed it up pretty well," Shula said. "And they used a somewhat unusual spacing in the line, but they had shown it before. We just killed our own drives by giving up the ball twice on fumbles and twice on pass interceptions. We never gave our defense a break."

"They just beat the hell out of us. That sums it up," Unitas, who was held to only 95 yards passing, said after the game.

"In the center of the dressing room, Coach Don Shula was talking to only a handful of persons. His answers indicated he was shocked as much as any of the players by the defeat," wrote sportswriter Gordon S. White Jr. "We sure found out about the Cleveland defense, didn't we. You have to, however, talk about our lack of offense with their defense. Our offense never gave our defense any break. We sure didn't execute our offense very well," said Shula.

Then Shula changed his mind a bit. "We messed up the pass defense pretty much ourselves."

Despite his complete shock over how they lost, Unitas told White, "When you go over to the Cleveland dressing room, tell Frank Ryan congratulations for me. He was great."

"I thought at the time that it was a good thing to win the Western title early," said Shula, hoping to rest his players some and give playing time to the less experienced players. "But maybe we lost our momentum. There was certainly something missing that day in Cleveland."

Son David Shula remembered it. "One of Dave's first memories is of standing on the Colts' sideline in the 1964 NFL Championship Game in Cleveland. He stayed next to the heater the entire game, and then, after Baltimore lost to the Browns, he walked into his dad's team's dressing room. For a five-year-old the sight could hardly have been more astonishing, and it is frozen in his mind," wrote sports journalist Richard Hoffer.

"Grown men crying," David says. "I don't think I'd ever seen my dad cry."

"Shocked to say the least," Shula said years later. "I was embarrassed. A fine season down the drain. Those are the things you remember." It was one of the losses that never left him his whole life.

That offseason, Don spoke at an event for more than 350 John Carroll alumni in April. He joked, "After December 27th, I thought I'd never want to return to Cleveland." The crowd laughed. "And you can be sure I won't be back in that stadium until I absolutely have to be." He could joke with this crowd, many of whom had seen the game. Many were friends, and family members.

With Marchetti's retirement in 1965, it would be the offense that would garner most of the headlines. Though they lost their second game of the season to Lombardi's Packers, they amassed a record of 9–1 before tying the Lions at Detroit on Thanksgiving Day. That game was the first color television broadcast of an NFL regular-season game. They then lost to the Bears in Baltimore. However, the news was worse than that. Unitas, after being hit high and low from both sides, needed immediate knee surgery and was lost for the rest of the season. Backup Gary Cuozzo would replace him.

Then the Colts had their home rematch with the Packers. The game was anticlimactic. Green Bay dominated them, 42–27. But, as Shula said, "Lightning struck again. Cuozzo was carried off the field, and I can remember how depressed I was." With a separated shoulder, Cuozzo needed immediate surgery, as well. He, too, was lost for the season.

Shula admitted that the pressure was on. And his coaching staff and team knew it, too. If Green Bay won their final game of the season and Baltimore lost, it would give the Western crown to the Packers. Baltimore desperately needed a win to stay alive.

Shula met with his dispirited team on a Tuesday morning. His goal was to try and convince them that they could defeat Roman Gabriel and the Rams without a bona fide quarterback. "The plan I presented to them that day was a simple one: play defense. Don't make any offensive errors. Work for field position and make the kicking game win for us," said Shula. The players looked at him with blank faces.

Pittsburgh Steelers owner Art Rooney had called Shula and offered him journeyman quarterback Ed Brown. But even if a deal was made, there would not be enough time to teach him the offense. Shula decided to go with Tom Matte. The running back had played quarterback for the legendary Woody Hayes at Ohio State. Hayes told Shula that Matte was reliable, and that he only had one drawback as a quarterback—he had trouble taking a snap from center.

Shula told the story that things got worse at practice on Wednesday. As soon as Matte started calling out the play, the defensive linemen broke up laughing at his high-pitched voice. Surely, the vaunted Los Angeles defensive line that included Rosey Grier and Merlin Olsen would be not be laughing—they'd be licking their chops. "Our practices that week resembled a high school team in its first week of fall football. Matte with his high-pitched voice, mass confusion in the huddle, uncertainty at the line of scrimmage, and finally the fumbles on the exchange from center that would stop any play before it started," said Shula.

The traditional, pocket-passer offensive plan that was used by Unitas or Cuozzo was quickly scrapped. They reduced the number of plays they would call in the game, so it would make it easier for Matte. They reduced their play calling to three different sets, which would still give the defense enough to decode. The offense consisted of a sound running game with simple handoffs, a lot of quarterback keeper plays (which turned out to be successful), and Matte, having thrown several halfback option passes, was given a number of rollouts where he could run or throw.

"Through it all, Matte kept his 'cool,'" said Shula. "Looking back, I am continually amazed as to how he reacted to this intense pressure. . . . Finally, some of the pieces began to fall into place. At times we actually resembled an offensive unit," recalled Shula.

Brown did finally clear waivers and met the team in Los Angeles. He was quickly taught even fewer plays than Matte. The offensive unit had two sets of plays: the "Matte" offense and the "Brown" offense. They put their players through their paces, trying to get as smooth a look as possible.

"I later learned the Rams had a 'spy' watching the practice," Shula said. Luckily, believing the Matte offense was there to throw them off, they only concentrated on Brown.

The night before the game, Carroll Rosenbloom took the entire team out for a special dinner to boost their morale. The only person who did not attend was Matte, who had the flu. Doom seemed imminent. "Our pregame practice that day at the Coliseum was without a doubt the flattest and most unmoving that I have ever been associate with either as a coach or as a player," said Shula. "There wasn't any chatter, and, more important, there was no execution. Matte, in warm up, didn't complete a pass, and Brown didn't, either."

On Saturday, December 18, the Colts' first four series went nowhere, and the first quarter ended in a scoreless tie. But in the second quarter, the Colts drew first blood on a 50-yard field goal by Lou Michaels. And they followed it up with a 28-yard touchdown scamper by Lenny Moore to make the score 10–0.

"Hard to believe, but there it was," said Shula. "You could feel our players gaining confidence and sensing they could win."

But a pair of touchdowns lobbed by Gabriel and a Bruce Gossett field goal put the Rams up, 17–10. Then, in the fourth quarter, Ed Brown stepped up and hit John Mackey for a 68-yard touchdown that tied the game, 17–17.

The defense played superbly, and, according to Shula, "The rest of the fourth quarter was all Matte. You would have thought he'd been our quarterback all season."

Finally, getting as close as the 23-yard line in Rams territory, Michaels booted a field goal to give the Colts a 20–17 lead. The Rams drove the length of the field with time running out, but Bobby Boyd intercepted a Gabriel pass and killed the drive. Matte ran out the clock.

"We had won our impossible game. Winning is always great, but this victory had to be the greatest," said Shula. The victory over the Rams "remains foremost in my memory because each one of us stood up to be counted . . . our team showed great character in overcoming adversity at its worst." Shula rated it as one of the best wins in his career.

The Colts still needed help. Green Bay needed to lose for the Colts to take the crown or to tie to force a playoff. Then it happened.

"The story line is so outrageously improbable that no self-respecting scriptwriter would have the temerity to use it. . . . The crippled Baltimore Colts upset the Los Angeles Rams in the last couple of minutes, solidifying their victory with a goal-line interception in the last minute," wrote Arthur Daley in the *New York Times*. "That was one stunner. The other was just as electrifying and unlikely. The Green Bay Packers, presumed to be headed inexorably for a playoff berth, were overtaken in the final 67 seconds by the San Francisco 49ers for a 24–24 tie and toppled into a deadlock with the Colts for the division lead."

Crippled or not, the Colts were headed to Green Bay for a one-game showdown with the Packers for the Western Division title and a berth in the NFL Championship Game.

"One thing we're going to have to do is throw the ball ourselves," Packers coach Lombardi told the press. "The Colts blitzed on something like 30 of 56 plays against Los Angeles."

Lombardi was in the midst of his dynasty years. Born in Brooklyn, New York, he had been one of the original Seven Blocks of Granite during Fordham University's glory years. After coaching high school and college in the metropolitan area for more than a decade (finishing with stops at Fordham and the incredible Army teams under Earl "Red" Blaik), he became the offensive coordinator of the New York Giants. In 1959, he took over the reins of the once-glorious but now faded Green Bay Packers. He would coach Green Bay from 1959 to 1967 and win five NFL championships and two Super Bowls in seven years. Lombardi was much older than Shula and was more of a father/mentor figure to the Packers players, juxtaposed to Shula's boy-genius aura. It was to Shula's frustration that his and his team's aspirations were in direct conflict with Lombardi's infamous iron will. And that his team might be overshadowed by the likes of Paul Hornung, Jerry Kramer, Jim Taylor, and Bart Starr.

What may have further vexed Shula (and Lombardi) was that Starr and Unitas were good friends. The two compared contracts and salaries on a regular basis. Starr had taken longer to rise to the top than Unitas. Still, in Starr, Unitas had found what he considered an admirable foe and an absolute equal. "We were at Pro Bowls together. We became friends," said Starr.

"The only player I ever talk money with is Bart Starr, because we're in the same business. I respect him, and I think he should know what I make," Unitas told the press.

The Packers' plan was to concede short passes to Matte and concentrate on his most lethal strength (and the Colts' strength in general)—they would try to limit his running and that of the other Colts runners.

According to Shula, "We figured we would have to play a hell of a defensive game. Our only offensive weapon was Matte's running. We couldn't throw. We had to win with defense and field position." The conditions were cold, muddy, and very windy. "When any coach goes over the Packer personnel, it gives him insomnia. I was no exception."

This would be the first playoff game televised in color. The subsequent NFL Championship Game played in January 1966 would also be the first to be broadcast in color. The most famous televised football game before this had been the 1958 Colts-Giants sudden-death football game. But even today that one is etched in the memory in garish black and white. Football was now entering a whole new world. *Bonanza, Bewitched, The Andy Griffith Show, The Beverly Hillbillies,* and a host of other popular television shows, heretofore broadcast in black and white, were now making the transition to color. And football was at the forefront of it. Starting in 1967 and 1968, Lombardi, Shula, Starr, and others were now seen in vibrant color on nationally televised games.

However, the most famous part of this playoff game was not only Matte's admirable star-turn as a playoff quarterback, but it was also the first time a quarterback played with a wristband that had all the plays written down on it. There are two versions of that wristband still in existence. One copy of it is in Don Shula's house; the other is in the Pro Football Hall of Fame.

"As sports relics go, it is nondescript: a 3-inch vinyl wristband covered with tiny writing. Visitors to the Pro Football Hall of Fame are apt to walk right past it to gawk at the more inviting lore displayed nearby," wrote Mike Klingaman in the *Baltimore Sun*. "The Colts pinned their hopes—and that wristband—on Tom Matte, 26, a reserve halfback."

"I had to learn so much offense that I didn't have time to be nervous," Matte said. "I remember that we walked through the plays in the ballroom of our hotel in Green Bay."

"We simplified everything—a few runs, a few passes, and some goal-line plays," Shula said. "Our whole objective was somehow, someway, to make a first down. And then another." However, Tom Matte's wristband wasn't the only thing that would be significant about this game.

The Packers got the ball to start off the game. On the first play, Starr completed a short pass out to the flat to Bill Anderson. Anderson turned to run up field and was hit hard, and the ball popped out. Colts linebacker Don Shinnick scooped up the ball and raced for the goal line. Starr weakly but courageously attempted a saving tackle but was viciously blocked by another Colt, injuring his ribs. The Colts had scored first, and Starr was lost for the remainder of the game.

"I didn't see what happened after I threw the ball and Anderson caught it. The next thing I knew Shinnick was coming down with a couple of blockers ahead of him." For his courage, Starr received a severe bruise to his back and ribs. "After that I couldn't raise my right arm above my shoulder." Backup Zeke Bratkowski would replace him.

Just like the Rams game before, the Colts led at halftime, 10–0. According to *Sports Illustrated*'s Tex Maule, the Packers exhibited "far more strain and tension than the Baltimore team." The Colts defense played outstanding football. The Colts made a majestic goal-line stand in the first half.

"They came out in a five-one," Packer guard Jerry Kramer said. "It fouled up our blocking, and [linebacker Dennis] Gaubatz had a clean shot at Jim Taylor. He made a good play, but we should have picked him up."

A bad snap on an attempted punt gave the Packers a short field early in the second half, placing the ball on the Colts' 35. One big pass play later from Bratkowski, and the Packers were down at the goal line once again. However, Lombardi and his staff had made the necessary adjustments, and the Packers scored this time to make it 10–7. With 1:58 remaining, Packers kicker Don Chandler lined up for a 22-yard field goal attempt to tie the game.

"All I thought about was keeping my head down and following through," said Chandler. The kick was high enough, but was the fluttering ball good?

"It went right through the middle," insisted Chandler to the press. The Colts were sure it had gone wide.

"There was no question the field goal wasn't any good. Chandler knew it when he kicked it. He knew it, and he just jerked his head in disgust. Because he knew he had missed it," Shula insisted. But the referees raised their arms, and the game was tied. As Shula himself pointed out, after that, the NFL competition committee changed the positioning of the referees and raised the height of the goal posts as a direct result of this game.

Time expired with the score 10–10, and overtime would be needed to decide the division title.

"This was one of the toughest games I ever played," said Packers offensive tackle Forrest Gregg. "They were hitting on every play. You got to give them a lot of credit for the way they played with what they had to."

"I wasn't about to let someone else play my position," said banged-up Packers guard Fuzzy Thurston. "They were going to have to carry me off the field to get me out of there."

"For a while after the sudden-death overtime period began, neither team seemed to be able to move the ball. The Colts' best opportunity in the overtime in the overtime period was a 47-yard field goal attempt by Michaels," wrote Maule.

"I was scared to death when I saw them line up. He can hit them from 50," said Starr. But a bad snap caused by the swirling wind causing a late placement by holder Bobby Boyd made Michaels stutter-step, and the kick was short. Finally, with eight minutes lapsed, Green Bay took possession on their own 20-yard line. In a series of passing plays, Bratkowski drove the team down to the Baltimore 18. Chandler then came on and kicked a less controversial game-winning field goal from 25 yards out.

"This game was very typical of the season. We did just what we had to do. I hope we can do it next week," Lombardi told the press after the game. But it didn't sit well with the Colts. "Everybody on our team was in an uproar. The game films later revealed we were right," lamented Shula.

"It became, without a doubt, the most talked-about incident in Baltimore sports history, setting off repercussions that resulted in the National Football League changing the rules, an admission of guilt, and unfortunately, depriving the Colts of at least an otherwise well-deserved championship opportunity," wrote Baltimore sports journalist John Steadman thirty years later. "It happened 31 years ago, the day after Christmas, in Green Bay, at Lambeau Field before God and 50,484 witnesses."

"When I looked up," Don Chandler admitted to Steadman in 1996, "the ball was definitely outside the post."

"The Colts were wronged, unintentionally, of course, by one of the most competent officials the league ever employed, Jim Tunney," wrote Steadman. Fate had handed the Colts a dirty deal, and no one more than their coach knew it. But he and Rosenbloom took it stoically.

"I was never more proud of a team I've had. We didn't deserve to lose. There was no justice out there today," Carroll Rosenbloom told the press after the game.

Shula said the team had nothing to be ashamed about in the loss. "You can't go into a game like this without a Johnny Unitas or a Gary Cuozzo and expect to do the same things offensively that you've been doing all season long," said Shula. "You don't belong in this league if you play a team three times and can't even beat them once."

"Think about it," said Raymond Berry. "We came within a whisker of playing for the world championship, with Tom Matte at quarterback. That's one of the darnedest things to happen in the history of football."

Little Dave Shula had been on the sidelines again for this contest, as he had been the previous year. He stood beside his father at an informal press conference, crying. "They all wrote that I cried because we lost the game," Dave said years later. "Well, I had smashed my hand in the door coming in. So, yes, I was upset."

"After the game, a disconsolate Matte tore off his wristband and threw it on the locker room floor. It was salvaged by John Steadman, the venerable Baltimore columnist who packed it off to the Pro Football Hall of Fame in Canton, Ohio. There it remains," wrote Mike Klingaman.

All Forrest Gregg could say after the longest game in the history of the NFL? "I'm glad it's over."

The Colts took a step backward in 1966. The team went 9–5 and finished in second place, three games behind Green Bay. They were 7–2 following an early November victory over the expansion Atlanta Falcons but then struggled the rest of the way, winning only two of their last five games. They lost twice to Green Bay that season.

The only notable thing about 1966 was the hiring of Chuck Noll as the defensive coach. In Noll, Shula found someone who was almost a spiritual dopplegänger. He was born and bred in Cleveland, Ohio, played football for Benedictine High School in Cleveland, and then went to University of Dayton. Playing both the line and as a linebacker earned the nickname the "Pope," for his "infallible grasp of the game." He played for Paul Brown from 1954 to 1959 and appeared in three NFL Championship Games. He was one of Brown's famous "messenger guards." He had first coached under Sid Gillman in San Diego. He would add a whole new dimension to the Colts over the next few years and then become one of the most successful coaches in the NFL for two decades. The Colts now had a defensive brain trust of Arnsparger and Noll.

"I knew the minute I sat down with him that I wanted to hire him," Shula recalled. "Chuck was that impressive. He was the complete package, total—exactly what you want in an assistant coach."

Nineteen sixty-seven was a strange year for Shula. On February 15, he was playing handball with Colts vice-president and general manager Joe Campanella. During the game, Campanella collapsed on the court and died of a massive heart attack. Campanella, a former linebacker at Ohio State and with the Colts, was only thirty-six years old with no history of heart trouble or ill health. He had complained of recent shortness of breath but had been checked by doctors. He had been in the restaurant business with Gino Marchetti and Alan Ameche.

The Colts had the No. 1 pick in the draft that year as a result of trading Cuozzo to the expansion New Orleans Saints and selected defensive lineman Bubba Smith, who had starred at Michigan State. At 6-foot-7, he was as quick as he was big.

"I was tougher on him than I ever have been with a player. The reason was simple: Bubba was a great athlete, but he was too fat. When the blubber came off, he became one of the finest players in the game—but it was hard on him, and he resented it." Shula wanted to move the big man from defensive end to the interior of the defensive line.

Eventually, Bubba asked Shula to be traded, but Shula scoffed. Smith insisted that he could not be screamed at, and Shula seemed to temporarily relent. But Smith's resentment lingered. Despite this, Smith made an impact on the Colts and became a feared defensive lineman who helped supercharge the Colts' pass rush. Smith sported a conservative, college prep style his first season, but when he reported for his second season, he'd grown an Afro and sported shades. One of the reporters asked if Shula would insist on cutting his hair, to which Bubba replied, "Is he a coach or a barber? What does my hair have to do with playing football?"

The Colts came out red-hot to start the 1967 season, crushing the Atlanta Falcons and Philadelphia Eagles in consecutive weeks, and reeled off a record of 11–0–2 going into the season's final week, with ties against the Rams and the Vikings. No victory was thought more compelling and significant than their 13–10 win over the Green Bay Packers. *Sports Illustrated* even blared the headline "An Aura of Destiny," as it seemed it would be the Colts' year.

"There comes a moment in the course of nearly every professional football season when one team rises unmistakably above the rest," wrote Tex Maule of the Colts. "An aura of destiny surrounds the club, as if its success were preordained."

For the last three years, the winner of the Green Bay-Baltimore game had gone on to take the Western Conference title, Maule pointed out. The Packers had taken the title in 1965 and 1966 and won the NFL championship. "For both teams, then, the game has come to be the most significant of the season."

With the league's new alignment, Baltimore and Green Bay were now in different divisions, and everyone's guess was that the two would now meet in the divisional playoffs. However, the last game of the season for the Colts was easily their most important. They had to play the Los Angeles Rams in California for the Coastal Division title. The Colts were favored with a record of 11–0–2 against the Rams, who were 10–1–2. The *New York Times* called it "the little Super Bowl." It was a winner-take-all scenario. If Los Angeles won, due to tiebreaker put into place, they would take the season series and thus be catapulted ahead of Baltimore, even with an identical record. If the Colts won, they would get the right to face Green Bay, the Central Division champs, in the playoffs. In Baltimore, there were dreams of an undefeated season. For the second time in his career, Shula was named Coach of the Year.

"This rematch of the two . . . contenders has captured the imagination of pro football fans," the Associated Press trumpeted. The coach across the field was the well-regarded George Allen. Allen was seen as a control freak, and one NFL owner once opined, "It was more fun to lose without him than win with him." Allen was a future Hall of Fame coach who had a lifetime .681 winning percentage and was twice named Coach of the Year. He had studied under coaching legends George Halas and Sid Gillman and was not to be trifled with. Allen, a defensive specialist, had assembled one of the greatest pass rushes in NFL history, known as the Fearsome Foursome, which featured Merlin Olsen, Deacon Jones, Lamar Lundy, and Roger Brown (acquired from Detroit after Rosey Grier went down with an injury). Allen had also assembled an offense worthy of his defense, led by Roman Gabriel, who had come into his own. After the first quarter, when Baltimore scored their only touchdown, the game was never in doubt. Gabriel tossed three touchdown passes of 80, 23, and 9 yards, while Unitas was sacked seven times for 48 yards in losses. The most humbling moment came when Unitas was sacked three out of four downs, and the Rams got the ball on the Colts' 4 yard line. The Rams also intercepted Unitas twice. Los Angeles and Allen won, 34–10. It was Baltimore's only loss of the season, but it cost them a playoff berth.

"They exerted a great amount of pressure on Unitas, and he had trouble throwing the ball," Shula said. "We were again disappointed losers."

There was a story Dorothy Shula used to like to tell. Sometime during their honeymoon, in Wildwood, New Jersey, they were walking on the boardwalk. Don asked his dark-haired, blue-eyed wife to backpedal for him.

"I thought he was kidding. But he wasn't," Dorothy recalled. She jogged backward a few steps, confused on why her new husband would make such a request.

"In football, you have to do a lot of backpedaling," Shula explained. "I just wanted to see what your moves were like so I'd have an idea of how our children will be as football players." He was only half-kidding.

Regarding his early coaching years, Shula said, "The word came across that we were a sexy couple, and I couldn't hold a job." They seemed the happy couple—the hyperfocused genius, and his chatty wife. "Don and Dorothy Shula would be at a party, and by his way of thinking, it was time to leave. Had been 15 minutes ago, in fact. There was always film to look at, plays to diagram, and [he] . . . has never been much on parties or patience. So Shula would pull his wife toward the door, parting the sea of people that wanted to talk to them. His arm would strain for the doorknob. But it never got there," wrote the *Washington Post*'s Scott Fowler in 1991.

"Dorothy smiled at everyone and she talked to everyone," Shula remembered. "I'm pulling her by the arm, and she says, 'We've got time, Don. We've got time.' Dorothy never was much on clocks."

By 1968, Don and Dorothy had a full house. Dave Shula had been born on May 28, 1959, in Lexington, Kentucky, when Don was an assistant coach there. They had two daughters when the couple lived in Detroit, Michigan, while Don was with the Lions: Donna on April 28, 1961, and Sharon on June 30, 1962. Another daughter, Anne, was born on May 7, 1964, and their youngest son, Mike Shula, came along on June 3, 1965, both born in Baltimore, Maryland, while Shula was with the Colts.

"Football has its rewards, but it also has its price," Don Shula once said. "The loss of family life was the one part of this job I always hated."

"You can't get along in my profession unless you have somebody at home," he said. "I couldn't be there as much as I wanted, but Dorothy was always great with that." There was no question that Don relied on Dorothy in some ways like he did with his mother. He had an ideal of what a woman should be. Art Donovan had once told of a stewardess whom Shula had picked up. She was beautiful, Donovan recalled, and so Shula brought her to a party. However, Don became immediately disgusted when she started smoking cigars and drinking whiskey with the boys. She was never seen again. Dorothy had indeed been the right choice.

"We went up to visit Don and Dorothy one time after he started coaching," sister Jeannette, then a high school teacher, recalled. "My mother had one of these rugs that was made out of pieces of cloth, a throw rug. She gave it to Dorothy, and Dorothy just put it on the floor.

"But my mom couldn't let that go. She got down there and made sure that it lined up perfectly. It was just a throw rug. I just looked at Dorothy and shrugged my shoulders."

"At home, she runs our family and keeps it together," son Mike once said. According to several of their children, two of her best friends were her housekeeper and her hairdresser. She volunteered in a number of community organizations and taught a little. "I love being with teachers and I love meeting kids," she had said. "I love the smell of schools."

"Dave is Don Shula's son in some ways," wrote Richard Hoffer. "[H]e seems more of an amalgam of influences. In fact, he may owe more to his mother than to his father."

"What was my mother like?" Dave says. "The best way I can put it is: within five minutes of talking to her, you'd feel entirely at ease. Not that my dad couldn't be charming. He could if he chose to."

"People tell me there's a lot of my mom in me," Mike also told the press. "She was a little more talkative, a little smoother around the edges, so to speak. One of the things I always felt was special about my mom was how within five minutes of meeting someone for the first time, she could make that person feel as though they'd known each other a long time. And when the conversation was over, that person would feel better about himself."

According to Hoffer, "Coaches did not seem supernatural to Dave. Don may have been larger than life to the players, but he seemed normal at home. Of course, there was the larger-than-life influence of Dave's mother, Dorothy, the glue in the Shula family. She kept the balance among the football pursuits of Dave and his brother, Mike, not to mention Don. And her three daughters managed to prosper, as well."

Don was not the hands-on parent that Dorothy was. He was curmudgeonly, yet "he was a doting father. Maybe he didn't make dinner every night, but while Dave was in high school, Don made 31 of his varsity games, missing only the 1974 state championship," wrote Hoffer. "It was a very fatherly thing to do, going to Dave's games, even though Don would have to sit alone in the last row of the bleachers, as far from the action as possible, and would still rouse the crowd with cries of 'Time out!' and other exhortations he just couldn't contain."

"I suppose I always sort of guided my boys to football, but it was always their choice in the end," said Shula.

"All the other kids wanted to be my best friend when the Colts won," Dave said, "or I was their worst enemy when they lost."

"[Dave] Shula can think back to that 16-year-old high school quarterback who absorbed as much punishment from fans as from opponents," wrote Bill Plaschke.

"I remember running home one day and telling my mom, 'I wish my name was Joe Shmo,'" Shula said. "But like she always did, she calmed me down and told me that I better learn to deal with it now."

"The highlight of my summer was being able to spend two or three days out at training camp with him, and it was probably the highlight of my mom's summer, getting me out of the house," said Dave. "He had a projector, and he used to let me run that. I held 'the clicker,' as it was called back in the day of the 16-mm film. It was a handheld thing with a button that you pressed to put it into reverse. That was a big thrill. I'd walk in and say, 'Can I run the clicker for you?'"

David was a ball boy when his father coached the Colts. He continued those duties in Miami. Dave did whatever was required in Miami. He painted the blocking sleds, did laundry, cleaned bathrooms, and caught passes from Bob Griese, all for $100 a month. "But then all of a sudden he decided he didn't want to pick up dirty uniforms anymore," said Don with a laugh. "He wanted to get another job."

"The thing about my dad was that when he got upset at you, it was for a good reason. It wasn't just because he was in a bad mood. It was for a good reason. And within the 30 seconds to a minute, he had forgotten about it. He had moved on. You hadn't moved on, but he had," he recalled.

"I couldn't have had a better example of great parenting than what I had from my mom and dad," Dave said. "They were both totally engaged and gave us all the support and opportunities we needed, both emotionally and they were able to provide for things financially. They were just there. They were invested in what we were doing. They cared, and they held us accountable."

"It would be poetic justice if the Colts, after their magnificent effort of last year, went all the way in 1968. If they won the National Football League title, it is likely they would be able to demolish the AFL champion even more decisively than the Packers have in the last two years," wrote Tex Maule in the pro football preview issue of *Sports Illustrated*.

In training camp of 1968, Don Shula was casting about for a new backup quarterback. Unitas's arm had been swelling up throughout training camp, and it was clear he was losing strength in that arm. He'd thrown the ball 436 times the previous season, and his arm and elbow were sore and unpredictable. Unitas kept saying he would be fine, but Shula saw in practice how Unitas was struggling, and he was worried. The Colts possessed a devastating defense and needed another quarterback in case Unitas came up lame. "Yes, I am interested in getting another quarterback into training camp," Shula told the *New York Times*.

The New York Giants were one of the targets he searched. They had four quarterbacks on their roster: Fran Tarkenton, Earl Morrall, Tom Kennedy, and Gary Wood. Morrall was thirty-four years old and a journeyman. He was from Muskegon, Michigan, and had led his local high school to a state title in 1951. He was the starting quarterback for Michigan State University and led them to a 9–1 record in 1955 and ended his career there with a Rose Bowl victory over the UCLA Bruins. He was drafted by the 49ers and then traded the following season to Pittsburgh, where he earned Pro Bowl honors in 1957. He was sent to the Detroit Lions early the following season and joined the Giants in 1965. At age thirty-four, he was seen as expendable. Though no one knew it, his greatest days lay ahead of him—he would be involved in three Super Bowls in the next 10 years.

"I had heard a lot of rumors of me being traded," Morrall recalled.

"Morrall confided to Shula that he was considering retirement, but Shula was persuasive. He convinced Morrall to join the Colts," wrote Unitas biographer Lou Sahadi.

"If you come to Baltimore, you'll join a team with a great chance to win a championship. And you may get more action than you think," Shula told Morrall.

"I didn't want to sit around for another year," Morrall said. On August 25, Morrall was traded to the Colts in exchange for Butch Wilson, a reserve tight end. "It had to be the best trade that I've ever made as a head coach," said Shula.

"Earl won a lot of games for me in Baltimore. . . . And he did it in such a humble way—he was a great team player who would do whatever was asked of him. And he was an outstanding leader who inspired confidence in his teammates," Shula once said.

Morrall had only a few weeks to learn Baltimore's offense. It was a completely new system for Morrall. "He had an enormous amount of adjusting to do, but he did it because of his great poise and intelligence. Morrall was simply fantastic."

In the final game of the preseason, Unitas opened with an 84-yard touchdown pass to Mackey, but after that it was a struggle. In the last quarter, after splitting time with Morrall, Unitas came off the field, holding his elbow, saying to Shula, "I can play, but I can't play well." He was in obvious pain.

"I'm through," Unitas told a *Baltimore Sun* reporter. "They got all they could out of me. With this arm, I couldn't knock a sick cat off a flower pot."

Morrall started the first game of the season, a 27–10 victory against San Francisco. "The first pass I threw was a touchdown," said Morrall, "for San Francisco." When Baltimore got the ball back, the offense started to click. Baltimore started moving the ball down the field with ease. On the last play of the drive, the main receiver appeared covered. Looking for another target, Morrall hit another receiver, who scampered in for the touchdown. "I'm feeling a lot better," Morrall recalled. As he approached the bench, a seething Shula shouted, "Goddamn it, what the hell are you doing out there? You're lucky that ball didn't go the other way! You've got to read the defense! That pass should have gone to the flanker! We had one-on-one coverage! Read the fucking defense! The defense will tell you where to go!"

They reeled off five straight wins to open the 1968 season, all of them with Morrall at the controls. They were averaging 33 points a game. But in Week Six, against the Cleveland Browns in Baltimore, Morrall stumbled and threw for only 63 yards in the first half. The Browns were up, 14–7. At halftime, a concerned Shula approached Unitas in the dressing room.

"Can you make it?"

"Yeah," said Unitas instantly.

"But he really couldn't," wrote biographer Lou Sahadi. Unitas's first pass fell into the arms of the Browns, setting up the Browns' third touchdown. In 10 more attempts, he threw two more interceptions. "It was the worst performance of his life," wrote Sahadi. The home crowd booed him, an ignominious send-off for such a gallant warrior, and Morrall was reinserted. The Browns won, 30–20. It was the Colts' only loss of the year. From there, they rolled right through the rest of the schedule. They scored 402 points and only surrendered 144. Morrall managed to beat all the clubs he had previously played for. That experience was a big sign for Shula. He was not sure he could trust Unitas's word again. During a November 3 meeting in New York against the Giants, Unitas had begged back in.

"I didn't want to use John in the game because I can give him another week of practice, but he's coming along," Shula told the press. Asked where that left Morrall, Shula responded, "I don't know, but it's a helluva pleasant problem to have." In truth it wasn't. Unitas was a proud man and having trouble dealing with being all but forgotten in the big run the Colts were making.

On December 7, the Colts were at Green Bay. This was a significant game for Shula and for the NFL. Lombardi was no longer the coach. The Packers had been the NFL champions five of the last seven years under Lombardi and had won two Super Bowls. "The Packers defeat by Baltimore was, in a way, a microcosm of the whole unfortunate year for Green Bay," wrote Tex Maule. "The loss snuffed out what dim hope the Packers had to win their fourth straight championship."

It was Green Bay's first losing season since 1958, and the Packers' locker room had a funereal tone to it after the loss. Green Bay had readied itself for the game. They started off with the same old Packers ferocity.

"We didn't expect them to come so much," Morrall said after the game. "Every time we went into a slot formation, they blitzed. I had to audible a lot to take care of it."

Maule stated that the Colts had the best defense and the best No. 2 quarterback in the league, and it figured in his mind, and a lot of others', that the Colts would make it to the Super Bowl as the NFL's champion.

Shula gave Unitas a chance to prove himself in the last game of the season at Los Angeles. Splitting time with Morrall, Unitas went 4-for-9, with one touchdown and one interception in a 28–24 victory over the Rams. But Shula was not impressed. Though Unitas had been efficient, and called an excellent game, it was clear to Shula what was wrong. John could still not throw deep. He was a half of a quarterback, and opposing teams would find out that weakness.

"Unitas and Morrall might have become jealous rivals, but they weren't. They quickly became chums," wrote Unitas biographer Tom Callaghan.

"The two of them fit hand in glove. We called them Hump and Rump. John had those sloping shoulders, and Earl had that big butt," said offensive tackle Fred Miller. The two, for better or worse, would play together another few years, each taking turns. The other was always there to counsel the other. "I would come to the sidelines, and he would tell me things," Morrall said. "In later years, when he got the starting job back, he would come back to the sidelines and I would tell him things. We were pros, we were pals."

"Unitas had this great belief in his own ability," Shula said. "Sooner or later, John was absolutely sure things were going to fall into place for him. And they did. . . . But he was hurt now. He had that elbow." Shula started Morrall in the playoffs.

On December 19, Morrall was named Most Valuable Player in the NFL, and two days later, Shula was named Coach of the Year for the third time. On December 22, as 11-point favorites, the Colts hosted the Minnesota Vikings in the division playoffs and won handily, 24–14. After that, the Colts were installed as two-point favorites over Blanton Collier's Cleveland Browns at Cleveland in the NFL Championship Game. Cleveland had spent a lot of energy killing off the tough Dallas Cowboys in their playoff matchup.

The game began with Morrall and the offense driving the length of the field, and then turning the ball over on an interception at the Cleveland 14-yard line. Cleveland drove downfield, but missed a field goal from 35 yards out.

"If we make the field goal, we go ahead, and it might have given us the momentum we needed," Collier told the press. "They gave us a good, sound licking." The Colts' 34–0 win was anticlimactic. "We weren't very aggressive, and Baltimore's offensive line did a great job of blocking."

"This is the last guy I'm ever going to hire as a head coach," Rosenbloom crowed about Shula, exalting in his championship glory.

"The championship victory over the Browns was especially satisfying to me. In 1964, they had embarrassed us, 27–0. We had tremendous execution this time, and we whipped Cleveland," said Shula.

Shula recounted a story that his mother was watching the game on television, screaming at the top of her lungs, "Get one more touchdown! One more touchdown! We want to beat the Browns worse than they beat us!"

"The euphoria all over the city was unbelievable. You would have thought it was Christmas," said Upton Bell, the ubiquitous Colts personnel man and executive. Shula had vanquished the Packers, the Rams, and finally the Browns and avenged all his losses up until now. He was coach of a championship team. But now, the Super Bowl against the AFL champion New York Jets loomed with their cocky star Joe Namath. Shula worried.

"The Colts have the greatest defensive team in football history," said oddsmaker Jimmy "The Greek" Snyder, installing the Colts as 17-point, and 7–1, favorites.

By now, Shula was being compared to Vince Lombardi by numerous newspapers and magazines. He and Lombardi had the best records far and away in that era. "The record that Shula has going for him in Baltimore the past six years surpasses what Vince Lombardi accomplished with the Green Bay Packers over a nine-season term. Shula hasn't won the championships Lombardi put together, but his overall percentage reads better," wrote John Steadman in the *Sporting Times*.

Shula admitted years later, after the thrashing of the Browns, a Super Bowl victory "didn't seem as if it would be difficult."

Despite all the excitement, the Jets were no easy mark. They were coached by Weeb Ewbank, Shula's old mentor, and a two-time NFL champion himself. He'd built himself a big, tough club, led by the most glamourous star in either league—Joe Namath. "Broadway Joe" had come to epitomize New York in the late 1960s. He was brash, good-looking, and talented. Signed for the then-outrageous amount of $435,000, he had been worth every penny. He was from Beaver Falls, Pennsylvania, had been recruited by four major-league baseball clubs, had won a national collegiate championship with Paul "Bear" Bryant (his record as a starter at Alabama was 29–4), and was now the most famous quarterback in pro football.

During the week leading up to the game, Namath galvanized the press like no one else. He almost started a bar fight his first night and traded barbs with the press poolside while opening fan mail and ogling the young women in bikinis. Namath had also famously attended a dinner at the Miami Touchdown Club, which had named him the outstanding football player of 1968. While at the dinner, as he accepted his award, someone in the crowd heckled him, shouting, "Namath, we're gonna kick your ass!"

Namath, now upset, looked out into the audience, and said, emphatically, "Hey, I got news for you! We're gonna win the game; I guarantee it!" The remark took on a life of its own. Soon, he had riled the old guard of the NFL. Indeed, given the times, Namath stood in stark contrast to Morrall and Unitas. He was living proof of what was then called "The Generation Gap."

"Someone asked him about the near fight early in the week between Joe Namath and Shula's kicker and former defensive end, Lou Michaels, in a Fort Lauderdale restaurant. I turned to the guy next to me and said, 'Oh, boy, now we're in for it,' fully expecting some tirade about confining our inquiries to football," recalled sports journalist Paul Zimmerman.

"Joe's the 837th guy Louis has threatened to death," Shula said, laughing, "and if he'd punched him, he'd have been the 30th guy he'd decked." Despite this, even Lombardi had confided to the famed sports columnist Jimmy Cannon, "The kid can beat them."

Indeed, defensive back Bobby Boyd was terrified of the Jets. "Bobby told me when he looked at their backfield on film . . . Matt Snell and Emerson Boozer would have beaten out our men Tom Matte and Jerry Hill," recalled Upton Bell. He also thought Jets receivers Don Maynard and George Sauer Jr. were one of the best tandem of receivers he'd ever seen. "And of course, they had Namath," said Bell.

According to Bell, defensive coordinator Chuck Noll "recognized that they had a dangerous offense." Bell added, "I began to get a sense some of our players were growing beyond overconfident."

"Johnny Unitas didn't agree with my decision to start Earl Morrall," Shula remembered. "I had no qualms about starting Morrall. Shula pointed to the incredible game Morrall had just played against the Browns in the NFL Championship Game, and his MVP award.

Their disagreements aside, Unitas behaved like a consummate professional, and good friend to Earl, telling the press, "Earl should be starting because he has been playing all year. He's an excellent quarterback, and he deserves all the honors he's getting. Why shouldn't he start Sunday after all he's done?" When asked about Namath, Unitas responded, "He's an excellent thrower. Showboat? No. Make it flamboyant. That doesn't sound as bad."

"He has done so much for us that there is hardly a way to put into words what it has meant having him," Shula said about Morrall earlier that season. "When I was in Detroit as an assistant under George Wilson, I always had a lot of respect for the way Earl could come in off the bench and win games for you."

Before the game, Shula had gone over to Ewbank, and the two chatted in a friendly tone. They were interrupted by Carroll Rosenbloom, who invited Weeb to his Super Bowl after-party. Weeb turned away in disgust. In his pregame speech, Weeb had said at one point, "Let's throw our own Super Bowl party," and at another he said to his men, "Don't carry me off the field, I have a bad hip!"

The Jets and Colts played to a 0–0 tie after the first quarter. A missed field goal by Michaels haunted the Colts. The Jets and Colts traded turnovers bordering the first and second quarters. The Colts had moved the ball with ease but faltered twice on scoring opportunities. Namath led the Jets down the field, and they scored a touchdown on a 4-yard run by Matt Snell, making the score 7–0, the first time an AFL team had led in the Super Bowl. The teams missed field goal attempts on the next two drives, then the Colts drove the length of the field, only to see an interception by former Colt Johnny Sample blunt another drive.

Later, after a New York punt, the Colts advanced the ball to Jets' 41-yard line. Baltimore then attempted a flea-flicker play. It is one of the most infamous plays of that game. Matte took the handoff, ran off tackle right, and then chucked the ball back to Morrall. The play worked perfectly, as receiver Jimmy Orr was wide open near the end zone. Morrall never saw him. Instead, Morrall threw to running back Jerry Hill, as time expired, and was intercepted by Jim Hudson. The Jets went into halftime up, 7–0. Orr said later, "Earl said he just didn't see me. I was open from here to Tampa." Ewbank and Shula had both learned the play while working for the Browns. He had told his defense they would use it sometime during the game. The Jets were unfazed by the play.

"We should have had points on the board with the way we moved the ball, and we were behind, 7–0," said a Baltimore player who preferred to remain anonymous. "We should have stuck with the game plan, but we began to panic. That's what they were supposed to do, but they played with great poise. We didn't."

During halftime, Shula decided to let Morrall have one more offensive series. If nothing happened, he would switch to Unitas. He said to John, "Be ready." Shula insisted afterward that most of the unlucky breaks in the first half were not Morrall's fault.

Tom Matte fumbled on the first play of the second half. The Jets then controlled the ball for most of the third quarter, adding two field goals to extend their lead to 13 points. Shula had seen enough and called for Unitas. But Unitas faltered, and the Colts punted.

Matt Snell said, "By this time, the Colts were pressing. You saw the frustration and worry on all their faces."

In the fourth quarter, Unitas completed a miraculous fourth-down, 17-yard pass to Orr for a first down. Aided by three Jets penalties, Unitas led the Colts on a 10-play drive, and they scored on a 1-yard run by Hill. The score was now 16–7, but there was only 3:19 left in the game. It was too little, too late.

Thirty years later, Shula mentioned in an interview, "Maybe I should have put him in the game sooner."

The Jets had shaken the football world. And Shula and the Colts were left in shock once again. "I can't begin to detail our disappointment afterward. It was like a death knell."

Shula went to midfield to shake hands with Weeb. "We got all the breaks," Ewbank said. He had preached poise and patience all week, and it had paid off.

"Your team played well," said Shula.

"Nice of you to say so," said Ewbank. The two parted. Weeb had won the two biggest games in the history of the NFL after building both teams up from nothing and had brought along two of its greatest quarterbacks—Johnny U and Broadway Joe.

Sports Illustrated's Tex Maule confidentially told a friend that the outcome of the game "made me sick." His cover story focused on Joe Namath and his heroics. He said he had to "lean over backward" to give New York credit for the victory but saw in Namath the same qualities he admired in Unitas. "What I did not point out was that the Colts, given a little more luck, might have put the ball game out of reach in the first half." Many had thought the same thing.

"We figured we were going to beat them," receiver Jimmy Orr said of the Colts, who were 15–1 entering the Super Bowl. "We went down there about 10 days before the game, and we were not taking it serious. It ended up biting us."

"It was humiliation, to be kind," said linebacker Mike Curtis forty years later. "That loss is the grave baggage."

Said center Bill Curry years later, "There is still the sense of longing, 'Gosh, if we could just do that again.'" He ended his musing by saying, "You just can't help but wish that we had done a little better. And I guess we'll go to our grave like that."

To add to Shula's disastrous day, Colts defensive back Rick Volk suffered serious convulsions after the game in his hotel room, as a result of experiencing two concussions in the game, and had been rushed by ambulance to the hospital. Shula added, "It was the darkest day of my coaching career."

According to Upton Bell, "We all knew Carroll was not happy and neither were his fellow owners. I came to realize later that an embarrassed owner is a dangerous man to work for. He's worse than an angry owner. An angry owner gets over it. An embarrassed owner never does." Bell said Rosenbloom loomed over the silent locker room, fuming. "If looks could kill, he would have been the only man standing."

"It was the biggest embarrassment of his career, to lose the Super Bowl for the first time to the AFL. I know it really hurt Carroll," said Ernie Accorsi, then-public relations director for the team who would go on to build Super Bowl teams as general manager of the New York Giants.

Just after the game, Rosenbloom stood next to Shula in the locker room and said calmly, "Now men, I am not in this business to be humiliated or embarrassed, to come in second place, ever. I've already fired one coach who won two world championships for me. I want you to understand that I am interested in one thing. I am interested in dominance, and the world championship. Are there any questions?"

"That speech was very unusual for an owner. I was thirty-one years old and I had never heard anything like it," remembered Bell. "He was demanding and brutally honest about his feelings. . . . Rosenbloom never forgot defeat. He still remembered a 27–0 loss in Cleveland in 1964, in Shula's second year as head coach. It would come up from time to time. So you can imagine what that loss in Miami was like. It was like a funeral. A funeral for all of us."

All week, Rosenbloom had been inviting people to his house for a presumed championship celebration after the game. With the team assembled at his house, it was more like a wake than a party. People spoke in hushed tones, and the atmosphere was as oppressive as the locker room had been. Rosenbloom was obviously still seething.

Unitas did not attend Rosenbloom's party. He stayed at the hotel drinking, "believing as we all did that if he'd gotten into the game sooner it would have been different," said Bell. "The Colts organization never fully recovered from Super Bowl III. Some things simply can't be erased. It was like a hangover for which there was no antidote."

Said Shula simply, "It was the lowest point in my career."

There was the famous story about NFL commissioner Pete Rozelle's aide being close to tears, expressing anguish about this historic loss, when Rozelle shrewdly pointed out, "Don't worry, this may be the biggest thing that ever happened to the game."

Indeed it was. Along with the lopsided victory of the Kansas City Chiefs over the Minnesota Vikings, 23–7, in Super Bowl IV, Super Bowl III helped to force and solidify the merger of the two leagues and catapulted the NFL into mainstream America. It was one of the two most important games ever in American football (the other being "The Greatest Game Ever Played" between the Colts and Giants in 1958). Super Bowl III would make the league rich and change the courses of lives for years to come. One of those lives would be Don Shula's.

"I felt a certain uneasiness returning to Baltimore following the Super Bowl loss. I knew that it would take [Rosenbloom] a long time to forget. The loss would gnaw at him," said Shula.

A few weeks after the Super Bowl, *Baltimore Sun* sportswriter Larry Harris wrote an article detailing an interview with Rosenbloom. In it, the Colts owner commented he was no longer "big on coaches." "The column was distinctly negative," Shula lamented.

Shula was so bothered by the article that he called Rosenbloom to discuss it. "He was quite upset that I brought up the subject of the newspaper column. He snapped at me that he had the right to say or think whatever he wanted to and that he was bitterly disappointed in our loss to the Jets."

Shula saw his two most important relationships completely crumble—the first with his previously enthusiastic owner, and the second with the aging star Unitas.

"My relationship with the owner was never quite the same after that game," Shula said of the game played eight days after his 39th birthday. "Every time he felt bad, he picked up the phone and passed that feeling onto me."

"Unitas' relationship with Shula had grown cool with every passing week of the 1969 season. The acridness had started when Unitas didn't get to play more in the Super Bowl. He had produced the Colts' only touchdown and was confident he could have gotten more if Shula had not waited until the end of the third quarter to send him on the field to relieve the struggling Morrall," wrote biographer Lou Sahadi.

The hangover was evident. Shula reinserted a healed Unitas back in as the number one quarterback, and he started 12 of the 14 games that season. The season started off with two losses, to the Rams and the Vikings (an embarrassing 52–14 blowout), then they lined up three wins against the Falcons, Eagles, and Saints. And it trudged on like that, trading wins and losses, until the team finished with a disappointing 8–5–1 record, two-and-a-half games behind first-place Los Angeles. Shula wasn't blameless. Rosenbloom was freezing him out, not taking his phone calls, meeting with him less and less. And Shula's anxiety was being translated to his players.

"Last year when we started losing, Shula went crazy," said Bubba Smith after the season was over. "He had this thing about Vince Lombardi. He wanted to be better than Lombardi. So he did a lot of screaming."

"It started in the Super Bowl. We panicked and so did Shula. We couldn't do anything right. It carried over into the next season. He became more and more of a dictator. He started sending in most of the plays to Johnny Unitas. Johnny Unitas!!!" said Hall of Fame tight end John Mackey.

"Don made a lot of enemies among the players. He was a good coach," said Unitas about that season. "But the way he handled some of the players left a lot of bad taste around here. I never let him bother me. I told him if he didn't like my job, put the other fellow in. But I guess a player who's uptight all the time, probably he couldn't get his job done."

"Maybe everybody hated Shula and maybe that's what he wanted," said linebacker Mike Curtis. "Maybe he felt it would translate into making a close team, pulling us together because we hated him. It was a bad situation."

"He' find a way to chew you out one way or another. No matter what you did, it wasn't good enough," said defensive end Roy Hilton.

Smith was incensed by Shula's screaming. "I want to talk about a trade because I cannot work with Shula," Smith told Rosenbloom. "He cannot talk to me like I am beneath him. He treats me like a child!"

Rosenbloom calmly replied, "Don't worry, Bubba, he'll be gone next year."

Rosenbloom, when questioned about the results of the 1969 season, said he would continue with Shula as coach but indicated some changes would need to be made to turn the team around. While Shula was coaching the 1970 Senior Bowl in Mobile, Alabama, Rosenbloom announced the hiring of Dan Klosterman, general manager of the Houston Oilers. Shula knew Klosterman and was aware of their talks but was worried about their implications.

It soon became clear that Klosterman would not only be included in personnel decisions, he would be approving them. And that Shula was no longer invited to attend the annual NFL winter meetings. Klosterman would be going, but not Shula. More to the point, Rosenbloom's son Steve, who had started working for the team as an equipment assistant when he was twelve, and Klosterman could not really detail Shula's new list of what he assumed were reduced responsibilities. Shula objected. He'd made trades and had huge influence on the drafting of players, and other personnel matters. Now he felt he was being marginalized as retribution for the Jets loss. With that, Shula called Carroll Rosenbloom, who was in New York preparing to take a trip to Hawaii and Asia.

"He spent the first half of the conversation telling me I was ungrateful despite everything that he had done for me and telling me that if I had some decisions to make to go ahead and make them," Shula recalled.

Rosenbloom would not back down, though. Shula would have to work with Klosterman, and he would not be invited to the league meetings. Shula saw it as a step backward. His problem was not with Klosterman, he determined, but with Rosenbloom. It would not get better.

The NFL draft was spent with Shula and Upton Bell working the war room. Klosterman would come in and out. Each time it was the team's turn to pick, Klosterman offered alternate suggestions. Bell and Klosterman didn't get along. "To me, fair or unfair, Klosterman was an interloper. Carroll put him in there hoping he could lead us into a deal where the town would accept buying exhibition games as part of their season package. It had nothing to do with football." Bell was also chafing at the restrictions caused by Klosterman's arrival.

But Klosterman was upset that all his draft-day suggestions had been ignored, and complained bitterly to Steve Rosenblom, screaming at Bell, "You kept me out of everything!" Bell told Shula, who responded to the story, jaw jutting, "I'll talk to him in the morning. I don't like this."

CHAPTER 6

Miami

Joe Robbie did not want Don Shula originally. Shula's name hadn't even crossed his mind. The Miami Dolphins' owner was hunting even bigger game to coach his team. George Wilson, Shula's old boss, had been the head coach of the Dolphins since their inaugural season of 1966. At the end of the 1969 season, his contract expired. In that time, the Dolphins had a combined record of 15–39–2. And Robbie let Wilson twist in the wind, waiting for an extension, while he raced around trying to find a big-name replacement. In fact, he'd been interviewing coaches through the latter half of the season in secret. Robbie wanted to win.

Joseph "Joe" Robbie was born on July 7, 1916, to an immigrant Lebanese father and an Irish mother (who raised him in the Catholic faith), in Sisseton, South Dakota. He had been the second of the couple's five children. His father was a restaurant manager, and his mother was a baker. Robbie worked as a lumberjack during the Great Depression and finished high school in 1936. He attended the University of South Dakota, where he met his wife, Elizabeth. They were married not long after. Robbie earned a Bronze Star during World War II while serving in the Navy, where he saw intense action. Using the GI Bill, he attended and graduated from University of South Dakota School of Law.

Robbie was a university economics professor who eventually was elected to the South Dakota House of Representatives as a Democrat in 1948. After a failed attempt at running for Governor of South Dakota, he moved to Minneapolis at the suggestion of political friend Hubert H. Humphrey. Robbie found work as a lobbyist for the tobacco industry. He appeared in front of the US Senate several times on their behalf.

While living in Minnesota, Robbie had become a season ticket holder of the

Minnesota Vikings. Robbie was friends with AFL Commissioner Joe Foss, an old school and Navy chum. Foss suggested that if Robbie could form a partnership, a new expansion opportunity was going to become available in Miami. Robbie formed a partnership with fellow Lebanese-American comedian and television star Danny Thomas. They won the bid and were the owners when the Dolphins took the field in 1966.

Robbie was no pushover. He was as hard-nosed and every bit as competitive as Carroll Rosenbloom. And was just as much a character. "Joe Robbie was used to pissing people off. He frequently berated employees—sometimes in person, sometimes in memos. People called him a tyrant. Others mocked him for having the tightest fist in the NFL," wrote sports journalist Michael Rosenberg. According to the report, Dolphins employees were not allowed a box of paper clips without Robbie's approval. He once complained about a $110 caterer's bill for food for the press box. Robbie fired the caterer and replaced the fare with hot dogs instead. "When the city of Miami refused to pay for tank repairs for the Dolphins' live mascot, Flipper, he got rid of Flipper too. Oftentimes, somebody sent Robbie a check to sign, and he returned it with notes on it, determined to negotiate better terms."

At first Robbie remained in Minnesota, and no decision on day-to-day business could be made without his approval. It made things difficult. Second, the team was cheaply run. There were no locker rooms at the practice facility. Players changed in their dormitory rooms. The practice facility wasn't bad; it was dangerous—a layer of sod stretched out over broken shells. Cuts and stitches were a common thing. The average scouting department cost about $100,000 a year to run in those days. The Dolphins had a budget of $48,000. The hotel where the players were housed served only cheap steam-table Chinese food.

The original team offices were two rooms and a dozen phones. Bud Adams, the owner of the Houston Oilers, once said of Robbie, he was "running a $2 million-a-year business like a fruit stand."

According to Robbie, "I brought football here when nobody else would get near the place. I protected football in this community. But the club and I have been under constant pressure since the day we got here. I didn't come down here to have people prove I am a cheapskate. It's been personally offensive to me. . . . We've had to live here in Miami by our wits. Once people sympathized with the guy who could climb up the ladder, the Horatio Alger thing, you know. But I think this affluent society where lots of people have lots of money, they resent a working stiff making it."

He was known to be argumentative and nasty. He was even reported to be sober occasionally. "The man could outdrink a small Irish town. Sometimes at dinner he would pass out drunk, then pop up 15 minutes later and rejoin the conversation as if nothing had ever happened," reported Rosenberg.

Reportedly, Dolphins employees were charged with bringing glasses, ice, a fifth of Wild Turkey bourbon (Joe's preferred beverage), and a fifth of vodka (his wife Elizabeth's tipple) to the couple's booth in the press box. When the referee's final whistle blew, both bottles would be empty. But the good times lingered on. On plane rides home, Robbie would slink into his seat (always 2B) and dip his hand into a secret compartment, withdrawing numerous miniature bottles of hootch to keep him inoculated. "Eventually he would pass out with his drinking glass resting on his chest, and no matter the turbulence, that glass stayed there, like it was attached to his body," wrote Rosenberg. "Tyrant, tightwad, drunkard. . . . People called Joe Robbie a lot of things. This is what he called himself: 'The idiot who hired all the geniuses.'"

By the end of the 1969 season, many of the original investors had fled. Thomas was bought out by local investors. Robbie first approached Ara Parseghian, the popular Notre Dame coach. "Always an admirer of Parseghian's cut and style," said Miami sports journalist and historian Morris McLemore. Five years earlier, Robbie had approached Parseghian before settling for Wilson. His answer still remained a solid "No."

Robbie then considered approaching Bill Petersen of Florida State University, who had built a solid program there. He had also turned down Robbie previously. He was more open than the Fighting Irish coach this time around, but Robbie hesitated.

Around Christmas of 1969, Robbie had heard that Alabama's famed coach Paul "Bear" Bryant might be open to a conversation about taking over the Miami team. The negotiations had gone very far but collapsed when Bryant could not secure a satisfactory successor for the university, and he decided to return to Tuscaloosa.

"Robbie put out feelers without results for some days and decided to wait until after the draft at the end of the month before moving forward," wrote McLemore.

Not long after the draft, Edwin Pope, the sports editor of the *Miami Herald,* approached Robbie, telling him he was aware of the Bryant negotiations and that the paper was considering doing a story. Robbie informed Pope that the negotiations had run aground and he was still looking for a successor to Wilson.

According to Robbie, Pope volunteered that Bill Braucher, the *Herald*'s Dolphins beat writer, had been a classmate of Shula's at John Carroll. The night of the draft, Robbie, Pope, and Bruacher met at the New Palm Club, and Braucher attempted to contact Shula at home. Dorothy answered the phone and told Braucher that Don had gone out to dinner that night straight from the office.

Once he was reached, Shula was in disbelief when Braucher explained the nature of his call. Shula called Robbie the next day. After a brief conversation, both men knew Shula would need permission from the Colts to talk to the Dolphins. With Carroll traveling, Shula approached Steve Rosenbloom and explained that he had an offer to own a portion of the Dolphins, and Rosenbloom, according to Shula, said that the Colts organization would not stand in his way.

Shula agreed agreed to meet Robbie at the Washington, DC, Marriott. They spoke for three hours. Shula also inquired about Wilson, whom he considered a close friend. Robbie assured Shula that he would not be retaining Wilson no matter what. Shula and Robbie met again the next day, this time with Shula bringing his lawyer, David Gordon. Salary details, tax issues, and other issues were discussed. Gordon would need to meet with some of the financial people for the Dolphins to go over other details. The next meeting would take place in Miami.

When Shula arrived in Miami not long after, he brought Dorothy and Gordon with him. Liz Robbie met them at the airport and brought the group to the Jockey Club. The three of them had dinner in the club's private dining room before retiring to their rooms that night. The Jockey Club was very posh, and generally out of view of prying eyes. These were supposedly secret negotiations. Shula was trying to keep a low profile. While dining, they were spotted. Elinor Kane, a Miami sports columnist, spotted him first. She summoned Shula to her table and introduced him to several people. Then who should spot him but Vince Lombardi, now coach of the Washington Redskins. Lombardi approached the table and asked Shula what he was doing in Miami. Shula had told both that he was just vacationing with his wife and a friend. "Imagine bumping into a writer and a rival coach at this time!" Shula marveled later.

The next day's conversations went well, and it became apparent that the time was coming to make a decision. The Shulas flew back to Baltimore. "If I went ahead, I would be uprooting my family's life once again. As she had in the past, Dorothy felt that whatever I thought was best for our family and for my work was also best for her," said Shula.

He accepted the job and called Carroll Rosenbloom himself. He was told by his son Steve that Shula would have to wait a day or so since his father was traveling from Tokyo to Hawaii. Eventually, Shula got him on the phone, and after he expained the new salary and ownership offer, Rosenbloom, reluctantly, congratulated him and told him it was an advancement he could not stand in the way of. He asked Shula if he had talked to commissioner Rozelle. When Shula said he was about to, Rosenbloom balked and said, as an owner, it was his right to call Rozelle first, but that Shula should call him. Shula told Rosenblom that Robbie would call Rosenbloom next. Both owners talked to each other and Rozelle.

When Robbie reached Rosenbloom, Carroll reportedly told him, "It's too late to talk about anything. . . . I'll say whatever I have to say to the commissioner." Then he hung up.

Rosenbloom had three stipulations according to Klosterman: Shula was not allowed to talk to any current assistant coaches until a new coach had been named to replace him; he could not take any Colts materials from his office; and any press release would have to be approved by the Colts organization. Shula told Klosterman he agreed.

Robbie now moved full speed ahead. He arranged for a press conference at the Jockey Club. He met with George Wilson beforehand to inform him of his fate. Wilson "was bitterly disappointed but took the savage blow in good grace. It probably was especially galling to him that he would be eased out for one of his former assistants," wrote McLemore.

Robbie arrived at the Jockey Club minutes before the press conference on February 18, 1970. Shula was given a five-year contract to be coach and general manager. He received a salary reported to be approximately $70,000 a year, with stock options that made the total package worth $500,000.

"I wouldn't be truthful if I didn't admit that the money was an important factor, but it certainly wasn't the decisive factor in my final decision," he said.

"I had to know without the slightest doubt that Miami's people were totally dedicated to winning football," Shula said at a news conference. But he cautioned, "I'm not a miracle man."

Wrote McLemore, "For the first day, it appeared that the coach's departure would be accepted with regret but no great passion in Baltimore. . . . But then all hell broke loose."

In the *New York Times*, William N. Wallace wrote, "It is forbidden in pro football for one owner to steal another's coach and that was what prevented Vince Lombardi's switch from Green Bay to the Giants in 1961. But there is a legal way to steal coaches—promote them to vice president or general manager and give them a piece of the franchise. Edward Bennett Williams did that last year, when Lombardi went to the Washington Redskins, and Joseph Robbie of the Miami Dolphins did it this week, when he hired Don Shula away from the Baltimore Colts. It is permissible, according to Commissioner Pete Rozelle, for a coach or another executive to move from one team to another provided he is 'bettering himself.'"

"Immediate and substantial interest in the Dolphins caused me to leave the Colts," said the forty-year-old Shula. "Being active in ownership while still coaching is something I've always wanted."

"He became most irate. That's when the fur started to fly," said Don Klosterman of Rosenbloom.

It was at the annual NFL owners meetings that March in Honolulu that Rosenbloom filed an official complaint of tampering against Robbie and the Dolphins. Rosenbloom was one of the most powerful of the NFL owners, and Robbie was a general manager of a partnership. At the same meetings, Shula approached Rosenbloom with his hand outstretched. "Rosenbloom did an about-face and presented the back of his $300 suit. Not long after, the two were accidentally juxtaposed in a men's room of a New York hotel," wrote Jack Olsen in *Sports Illustrated*.

"Hi, Carroll," said Shula, smiling.

"Rosenbloom turned coolly to a third party, issued a remark that must be rated PG (parental guidance advised), and stalked out," continued Olsen.

"It's like this. I have not talked to Robbie or Shula since this happened. I will not talk to Robbie or Shula ever again. One stole something from me. The other allowed himself to be stolen," Rosenbloom said.

The Colts' owner made bold accusations, insisting that Robbie and Shula had been in contact since before the draft, and that the Colts' poor draft was a result of this "tampering." Dumbfounded, Shula responded, "I've done nothing wrong, I informed Steve of everything I did and kept him abreast of the whole situation as it developed." Accusations continued to fly.

In the first week of April, Rosenbloom and Klosterman announced a one-year deal with Don McCafferty, Shula's old assistant, who would be taking over the helm of the Colts. During the press conference, Rosenbloom appeared "bitter" and complained to the press, "It's just not fair that coaches should be able to walk away from their obligations."

On April 14, commissioner Rozelle issued a verdict to quell the festering feud. The league found Robbie and the Dolphins guilty of tampering on three out of four counts. The penalty for the transgression would cost the Dolphins their 1971 first-round draft choice, which was awarded to the Colts.

According to Rozelle, Robbie had initiated contact with Shula through a third party outside of an employment opportunity with another team. By NFL terms, the Colts had not yet granted permission. Second, Robbie had failed to talk to Carroll or Steve Rosenbloom directly before offering anything to Shula. That also qualified as tampering. Last, Robbie had failed to inform the Colts until the day of the announcement of Shula's hiring.

"It is the conclusion of this office," said Rozelle, "that circumstances of employment constituted violation of these rules. Disciplinary action has been taken under the constitution, which provides forfeiture of draft choices." The only statute Rozelle had found on the behalf of Robbie was that the offer did stand to benefit Shula through a minority stake in ownership.

The sniping would continue for a long time, but for now, Shula was free to start working.

Shula moved quickly to assemble a staff. He instantly hired Bill Arnsparger. He had left the Colts because of personal issues but couldn't resist rejoining Shula in Miami. He would be the defensive coordinator. Next, he hired Howard Schnellenberger to be the offensive coordinator. They had coached together at Kentucky under Blanton Collier.

Also joining the staff was old friend Carl Taseff, who would be at Shula's side for decades. Taseff always had Shula's back. He had experienced a much longer playing career in the pros. He had played for Weeb Ewbank in Baltimore and was a member of his 1958 and 1959 championship teams. He was released after the seventh game of the 1961 season and then finished out the season with the Philadelphia Eagles. He joined the Buffalo Bills in 1962 and retired after the season. He had been a solid and versatile running back and a remarkable special teams player. He had started his coaching career in 1964 with the Boston Patriots and had also coached for the Detroit Lions before joining Miami. He would be with Shula to the end, working with him for the next 24 years.

"I always had great respect for Carl as a player and a coach and the special relationship with him as a friend," Shula said. "He was a very dedicated and goal-oriented person. He only knew one way to play and one way to coach. And that was to win. . . . He could have coached almost any backfield position on either side of the ball."

Susan deMuth, Taseff's daughter, said, "From a career standpoint, he was the only member of the 1958 Colts team—the one that played in the so-called greatest game in history [against the New York Giants]—and the 1972 Dolphins and their perfect season. When you look at how short some of the pro careers are, daddy played 12 seasons and then coached the Dolphins for 24 more. By today's standards, it's incredible when you consider his longevity."

New offensive line coach Monte Clark had just finished his illustrious playing career, mostly with the Cleveland Browns. The solid left tackle blocked for Jim Brown and Frank Ryan and was an important cog on their 1964 championship team.

"Monte Clark is the real secret. Monte Clark was the most important acquisition that has ever come to the Miami Dolphin franchise," said Pro Bowl guard Bob Kuechenberg. "Shula's original choice was John Sandusky. Monte Clark came down here and molded five linemen who had been discarded, five ragtag linemen . . . and Monte Clark molds them into arguably the greatest line that ever played. The offense was on the field all day long. And that was because of Monte Clark." Kuechenberg made a point of noting that four of the linemen who made up the Dolphins' offensive line had been cut by other teams and that Hall of Famer Larry Little had been acquired for next to nothing.

The only holdover from George Wilson's staff was Tom Keane. Keane had played college football at Ohio State and professionally for the Rams, Texans, Colts, and Cardinals and went to the Pro Bowl in 1953. Due to his Colts connection, he and Shula had much in common. He would stay with Shula for the next 16 years before retiring.

"It's doubtful if one of them got more than a half-sandwich for lunch in the first six months after shaking hands with the new head coach. Long, grinding days opened with eight-o'clock meetings and finished well after sundown or hours after that," wrote Morris McLemore.

"Coming up with a coaching staff that could do an objective job of teaching during the first season was foremost in my mind, and we came out quite well," Shula said. "You delegate authority and let those men pretty well run their own shows, and you, as the head coach, supervise what's happening. After seven years at Baltimore, things happened automatically on our staff. . . . That hardly was true at Miami early, for Arnsparger was the only one who had worked closely with me in recent times." His new staff had to scout each team as well as their own. The new staff spent countless hours studying films, evaluating and grading players, and creating playbooks.

"You can sit a group of people down and teach them these things by normal methods, but when the outcome of a ball game depends upon it and you haven't been able to sit them down as you would like, it compounds the problem and it takes intense concentration by everyone concerned," said Shula. "Our coaches—with the exception of a couple—had the same problem: to adapt their thinking to mine and the new system in a spread of time that didn't match the size of the problem."

America was less than a year removed from Woodstock, the immense hippy-inspired rock concert that seemed to form a generational divide. The Civil Rights movement had divided on itself, especially after the murders of Martin Luther King and Malcom X among many, and the conservative element of the society had placed its trust in Richard M. Nixon as President of the United States. Shows such as *My Three Sons* and *Bonanza* were giving way to irreverent shows like *Rowan and Martin's Laugh-In* and *The Flip Wilson Show*. The Guess Who's "American Woman" and "Let It Be" by the Beatles were among the biggest hits that year, and the best picture was the gritty *Midnight Cowboy*.

Roster construction was the next project. Norm Van Brocklin, the famous quarterback-turned-coach, used to chide Shula during his years at Baltimore. He called Shula the "push button coach." He said all Shula had to do was toss the ball to Unitas and say, "Go win the ball game." When Shula began his work in Florida, he received a note from Van Brocklin reading, "Congratulations on your first coaching job. Now you're going to know what the rest of us coaches have been going through all these years."

"Their attitude during that indoctrination session was tremendous. They did everything, without question, that I asked them to do. I think they did this because they realized that they hadn't won and they were interested in winning," said Shula.

The Miami Dolphins had gone 3–10–1 in Wilson's final season. The first order of business was to weed out those players who had performed well for Wilson during that disaster of a campaign and jettison those who did not. Twenty-two players from the 1969 roster were not on the 1970 team.

On April 25, Shula had his first contact with this team, rookies, and veterans. They met at the University of Miami. Shula explained his philosophy, outlined his objectives, and began explaining his terminology, and other instruction. Shula referred to this moment as his "indoctrination session." He told any players living in the Miami area that the team would begin working with them immediately. It was important to drill them on terminology, cadence, routes, and schemes. It was all about teaching.

Much of the team's core was already there. Bob Griese, Jim Kiick, Larry Csonka, Larry Seiple, Larry Little, Manny Frenandez, Nick Bouniconti, Bill Stanfill, Howard Twilley, Dick Anderson, and Mercury Morris all made the cut and would all still be on the team by 1972. Eleven rookies would make the squad that first year, four of whom were starters—linebackers Doug Swift and Mike Kolen, defensive back Curtis Johnson, and free safety Jake Scott. More than half the 1970 squad was homegrown, drafted talent.

Even though he was the NFL Defensive Rookie of the Year, little did the Dolphins know what they had in Dick Anderson. He was a go-getter on and off the field. He augmented his football salary by starting an insurance agency. Anderson was notorious among coaches and players alike for returning calls to clients before or after practices on his car phone.

"Shula was always telling me to get off the phone," Anderson said. "In those days, you had to have another job if you wanted to get ahead."

"Shula was like: 'Hey, guys, here's the rules. You're old enough to realize them. Don't screw up,'" said Anderson. "He was a miserable S.O.B. when we lost. . . . The best part of [the undefeated 1972 season] was by winning everything, he never got on our backs."

"Dick was very bright but careless," countered Shula. "At times he would not concentrate and made mistakes, the kind of mental errors that other guys who were not close to him in intelligence never would make. You had to get on his case to bring out the best in him."

"He was completely consistent; he screamed at everybody," said Anderson years later. "Now I have my revenge. When we play golf together or go skiing, I can yell at him, 'Come on, Shoes, get those skis together! Straighten out that swing!'"

"Our early camp training was unlike anything that's ever been experienced in football. Improvisation, the timetable has been shotgunned, we've worked with rookies harder than ever before . . . everything is different this time," Shula told the press.

Shula continued to work with the rookies and local players through the summer, but then came a strike by the players, which lasted a few days and prevented the veterans from participating. Finally, six days before their first preseason game in Jacksonville against the Steelers, Shula asked something radical—rather than the traditional two-a-day sessions or drastic three-a-day sessions, he would ask for an astounding four-a-day sessions to help indoctrinate the veterans into their system.

Shula admitted that at the time he was worried about a credibility gap between himself and the players. He'd arrived in a newsworthy maelstrom and had been accused of dirty-dealing by Carroll Rosenbloom. Accompanied by the commissioner's verdict, it had cost the team, and Shula felt that his reputation had been fairly soiled, as well. He wanted to make sure his players could trust him. Most of the press about him up to this point had been fairly negative, and so he tried to explain his story as best he could and asked that they put their trust in him. It was a humble, but necessary, gesture.

The other thing that Shula did was purposely start working on integrating the team. He and his staff tried to put players together who would pair well, and who would complement each other. Where possible, they did their best to mix roommates, black and white. The old Dolphins had tended to have a segregated locker room.

"There's a sticky situation here at Dolphin camp," running back Mercury Morris had written in his locker room diary for the *Miami News* in 1969. "I've been doing my best to get rid of it. There's de facto segregation being practiced here, and it's as much my Black brothers' fault as anyone else's."

Morris pointed out that the showers were also a place of segregation. He recalled how the water pressure was better in the area where the white athletes were showering. "So I went over there and started washing myself. These guys went, "Hey rookie, what are you doing?" I said, "I'm taking a shower, just like you." One said, 'What are you doing? You're supposed to be—' I said, "No I'm not. I'm supposed to be right here, taking a shower. Because I just came off the same practice field you did. And I got the same dirt on me that you do. And I'm washing it off the same way you are."

Morris explained years later, "These were my teammates, but they didn't know me. And I really didn't know them. So we had these expectations of having to be a certain way because I was black, or because I wasn't white."

"Shula was worried about a problem inside the team," quarterback Bob Griese said. "Shula wasn't concerned with the social evolution of blacks and whites in the broader America. His world consisted of those 100 yards. But he cared about anything that affected his team's unity and . . . performance." Griese also noted that Shula was careful to have hair care products important to black players available in an effort to make sure that all were treated fairly.

"As a football coach, I want to treat everybody the same and not worry whether a player is black or white, or whether he's Catholic, Jewish, Protestant, or whatever. The only thing I want to do is judge them objectively," said Shula.

An important addition was star receiver Paul Warfield, a future Hall of Famer, who was acquired from the Cleveland Browns in exchange for their first-round draft pick. "Hi, I'm Paul Warfield," the star receiver introduced himself to Griese, his new quarterback. Griese laughed. "I know who you are." For Shula and his staff, this was one of the best pairings they came up with. The two were intellectuals. Both from the Midwest. Smart. Dedicated athletes who kept themselves in great shape. They worked with each other on the field and talked football all night in their room. They roomed together for many years and were absolutely sure that a portion of their success came from this pairing.

Tim Foley, who was white, was paired with black secondary mate Curtis Johnson. Marv Fleming, the veteran tight end, was placed with reserve quarterback John Stofa. Another successful pairing a year later was of Maulty Moore and Vern Den Herder, a pair of long-shot defensive linemen. Den Herder, who was white, had grown up in a small town in Iowa, and Moore had grown up in the deep South. Neither had spent a lot of time with people of the opposite race. The two helped each other make the team and became lifelong friends.

"[Shula] brought in a new era, that it's about the football and what we're supposed to be out there as the team," said Morris. "Once, I said something about race, and he said, 'Hey, you know I'm not like that.' And I knew he wasn't because he only cared about one thing, and that was winning."

The biggest addition to the locker room, through a trade by Shula, was the very clear presence of Marv Fleming. Fleming already had two Super Bowl rings that he had earned with the Green Bay Packers. He had played in the famous Ice Bowl game in 1967. He was a big, smart man who had earned stockbroker and real estate agent licenses, as well as being a licensed airplane pilot. He had made serious money through investing and was already successful outside of football. He'd even taken acting lessons, preparing hopefully for some roles in Hollywood.

Players, black and white, looked up to Fleming. He was just the kind of veteran voice their locker room needed. And they all knew it. But Fleming had reservations about playing below the Mason-Dixon line, and he was not surprised when he came into the locker room and noticed that the black players had taken one side of the room, with the whites occupying the other. According to Griese, the players even showered separately.

Fleming was used to having a white roommate. He'd roomed with George

Seifert (future Super Bowl-winning coach of the 49ers) in college and roomed with white teammates on the Packers. According to Griese, Fleming was a big personality, and well liked, and broke down divides with humor and his outgoing personality, as well as with his maturity. Once, when he overheard that there had been a player party that he and other black players had not been invited to, he questioned the shocked group. Fleming had a reputation for being a hard partier. Was it a team party? Were there players there? Any black players? No arguments. Point made.

"A few days later he heard a white player's voice come across the locker room," said Griese.

"Attention, Marvin Fleming! There is a party tonight and you are invited!"

"That night, Marvin was the last to leave the party," said Griese.

Shula reassigned lockers, defense on one side of the room and offense on the other, forcing integration and diffusing the awkward scene.

With the veterans finally in camp, the team got to work.

7:00–7:40 a.m.	Kicking and special teams
8:00–9:00 a.m.	Breakfast
9:30–10:00 a.m.	Teaching/Planning
10:30–Noon	Full pads running game offense and defense
Noon–3:00 p.m.	Break
3:30–4:00 p.m.	Afternoon session briefing
4:00–6:00 p.m.	Passing game offense and defense
6:00–7:00 p.m.	Dinner
7:30–9:00 p.m.	Reviewing the day's session/scrimmage/adjustments
9:30–10:30 p.m.	Film review of the day's sessions

Shula tried to teach his players the concept of "overlearning." He wanted smart as well as physical players. "That's a term I use to emphasize how important it is to not only know what your assignment is, but the assignments of everyone around you and why you are being asked to do what you are asked to do," Shula said. "I always tried to have my practices fast-paced and everything done at full speed and as close to game conditions as I could possibly make them. That better prepared the players for the game.

"I've always felt that whatever you want to get accomplished, you've got to be willing to work hard to get it done," said Shula. "One of the things in my coaching philosophy I tried to instill in my players was the formula that hard work equals success."

"I never really felt that way in my 33 years of coaching," Shula said later in life. "I pretty much enjoyed every day. I didn't know anything about burnout or some of those things other people talk about. I had to sleep in the office and put in the 15-hour days, too. There were times when we'd do our game-plan on Tuesday night and then stay right there. I got done so late at night, and that way I wouldn't have to drive a long distance so early in the morning."

Shula also talked about the holidays. It was an odd juxtaposition for a man so strongly devoted to family to be absent during the holidays. If you were coaching on Christmas and New Year's, it meant that you were successful, a saw that without a doubt played with his head. It seemed wrong not to spend more time with his family during the holidays, but at the same time, success in his industry flourished at that time of year. That conflict within him was always grinding. He would admit, after his career was over, that he had sacrificed knowing his children as well as he would have liked and worried he might have missed out on grandchildren, too. Still, as a virile man in his prime, Shula was helplessly driven toward success like a freight train. He was in Miami to prove to the establishment that he could do it . . . again.

Shula also believed in physical conditioning. "I placed a great amount of emphasis on conditioning. As far as I am concerned, there is no end to it. It's the single most important factor that is needed to play a football game," said Shula. Shula and his coaches emphasized three different conditioning drills: The Oklahoma drill; gassers; and the twelve-minute run. The Oklahoma drill featured a running back, an offensive blocker, and a defensive man. Placed in a space approximately three yards wide, contact is initiated. The offensive man attempts to block, the runner attempts to get by, the defensive man has to make the play. This was a classic drill, aimed at improving technique and toughness.

Gassers were sprints going from one sideline to another and back. The players would run four such laps. Break. Run four more. Break. Then run four more. Ideally, the last four, which would be the most difficult, were supposed to be run at the fastest pace.

The twelve-minute run was easily the least popular. The idea was to run as many laps as possible around the field or around a rack as possible within twelve minutes. According to Shula, Dick Anderson ran two miles in twelve minutes and was easily in the best shape. Each player, by position, height, and weight, was given a target time. If you completed the time, you didn't have to run them anymore. If you failed, you needed to do it again the next day. "If I wanted to run," running back Jim Kiick told the media one year, "I would have run cross country in high school." The players tried to make light of the sessions, saying they were taking their clothes off so many times a day they felt like strippers. But Shula was proud. They had kept the schedule up for a full week.

They arrived at Gator Bowl Stadium in Jacksonville after putting in a full morning's practice before the game, which is highly unusual. But there was good news to this grind—Miami won its preseason opener, 16–10, over Chuck Noll's Pittsburgh Steelers.

In the weeks following the Super Bowl loss to the Jets, Shula had allowed the Bills and Steelers to interview Noll, who had been a hot prospect to fill a number of different head coaching vacancies. Shula had recommended Noll to Pittsburgh owner Art Rooney in January 1969, when Noll was still with Baltimore, for the head coaching spot in Pittsburgh. An avid horseplayer, Rooney said of Noll, "His pedigree is super: he was by Paul Brown, out of Sid Gillman, by Don Shula."

The Dolphins players and coaches were gratified that they had put in so much work and it had paid off so quickly. After the contest, the players gave Shula the game ball. Of all the game balls he ever received, Shula said that one was among the most special, as the group had accomplished so much in such a short amount of time, but more so because they had all been tested, and they had passed that test together.

"The Dolphins looked like they had been playing together for years—one of their more remarkable feats, actually," wrote McLemore.

Jake Scott was an instant star in that game. Scott had played for the University of Georgia, where he had snagged 16 interceptions, and a college career total of 315 interception return yards is still the most in Georgia history. Vince Dooley, the longtime, legendary coach of Georgia, said Scott was the best athlete he ever coached, bar none. He was also famous for something else at Georgia—his grades. As a student, he got only As or Fs. If he liked a subject, he dived in. If he didn't, he didn't bother.

Scott's scuffles with Joe Namath eventually became legendary. When the Jets quarterback would look at Scott's feet to read the defense, Scott would dance and move them around. Namath would curse him out from the line of scrimmage. "You're not getting me this time, motherfucker!" Namath shouted from the line one time. The two became drinking buddies.

Not only was Scott fantastic at picking off passes, he was also tough. Defensive lineman Manny Fernandez once said, "He's the one guy no one messed with." According to Fernandez, a mountain man attempted to pick a fight with Scott, in a Colorado bar. He hollered, "I'm the toughest guy in here." Scott knocked him out in seconds flat and then turned to the other patrons and asked, "No one's tougher in here than him?"

"Scott, to be sure, was respected for playing through pain: He played the final 11 games as a rookie with a separated shoulder; he played Super Bowl VI with that broken hand and wrist, even receiving punts in the game," wrote *Sun Sentinel* sports scribe Dave Hyde.

"We were playing Buffalo, and they had a big fullback named Jim Braxton, and they would do the Green Bay sweep," Scott said between swigs of Bud. "Our linebackers were waiting on O. J. [Simpson], and then they'd run this sucker play and he [Braxton] would come up the middle. I had to tackle him three times one game. We finish the game, I go off the field, I go to the wrong locker room. O. J. and I were on the same All-America team [in college]. He takes me over to the [Miami] locker room and says, 'I think he belongs to you.'"

In those days, Scott and Shula were very close. In fact, Shula's son David wore Scott's jersey number when playing football, as the young boy considered Scott to be his hero.

Karl Kremser had been the kicker for the Dolphins in 1969 and finished the season by kicking 13 field goals out of 22 attempts, was 0-for-5 from 40-yards and beyond, and had scored the fewest number of points of any active kicker in the league. He was automatic from 30 yards or less, but dreadful at the further distances. A new kicker was a definite need or Kresner needed to improve. The Dolphins brought in former Detroit Lion Garo Yepremian, who had kicked a league record six field goals in one game as a rookie in 1966. With Yepremian pressing him, Kresner responded. During the preseason, they continued to duel.

"I'd never played pro football and had only been in the country for six weeks," said Yepremian, who was a soccer player while living in Europe.

"In that first game [with the Lions]," recalls Yepremian, "we were losing by a big score, losing badly, at halftime I don't think we had crossed midfield yet. But we scored a touchdown somehow, and I kicked the extra point. I was running off the field with my arms in the air, like we had won a championship. Well, Alex Karras came over, and he put his foot on the bench, and he said to me, 'What the you-know-what are you celebrating? Why are you celebrating when we are losing so badly?' I said, 'Because I just keeked a touchdown.'" Johnny Carson, then host of *The Tonight Show,* repeated that quote for years. Meanwhile, the Lions replaced Yepremian while he served his time in the US Army Reserves in 1969. The Dolphins called in 1970.

"[Taseff] really took me under his wing and helped me out as much as he could because my English was not too good then. He gave me so much confidence and kept building it up." The running joke was that he had never seen a professional football game and had no idea how to put on an American football uniform or what to do once the ball had been kicked. Short, bald, and with a deep accent, Yepremian looked anything but like a football player. He was eventually assigned to the taxi squad at the end of the preseason. After Kremser missed a field goal in the opening game against the Boston Patriots, Shula released him and brought Garo up for the rest of the season. He made 75.9 percent (22-for-29) of his kicks. "Most important, he was to successfully kick 11 of 15 field goal tries that began between the 40- and 49-yard line, with 47 yards his longest," wrote McLemore.

"Garo was only 5'8" but stood a lot taller than that," said Bob Griese. "Mentally, he was sharp, and I think his success as a kicker was based on his intelligence and his understanding of the challenges involved with kicking a ball through the uprights. . . . Being as small as he was, I didn't know how he kicked a ball so far and so straight, but he did and made most of his field goals. He was a huge part of the success of those great teams."

"Garo went from 'I kicked a touchdown' to making some of the most pressure kicks in Dolphins history. He didn't know much about football when he started his career but certainly helped win a lot of games for us during his time in Miami," Shula said. "I enjoyed having him on the team. He was unique."

Last, and most important, Shula had played all four of his quarterbacks during the Pittsburgh game—Bob Greise, Rick Norton, John Stofa, and rookie Jesse Kay. Griese and Norton had split time the previous year. Griese had been the starter but had missed five games due to injury. At 6-foot-1 and 190 pounds, he was of slight build behind an awful offensive line. But seeing was believing, and Shula instantly knew Griese was the right choice. The idea was to build a better offensive line and protect their quarterback.

"Bob had the perfect mental approach," Shula said. "He was the master of the position of quarterback. He knew the people and how to use them. He knew defenses inside and out. Bob is probably the most unselfish guy I've ever been around. He gets as big a thrill calling the right running play for a touchdown as he does connecting on a bomb. That's just his makeup." Shula once called him the "thinking man's quarterback."

For a while, Dolphin veterans nicknamed Griese "Straight Arrow," poking fun at his professorial, clean-living style. He was no Bobby Layne. Some even called him their "milkshake quarterback." He had been labeled a running quarterback. The real reason was that the Dolphins' line was so porous, and the receivers so paltry, that he had nowhere else to go with the ball. Dolphins quarterbacks had been dropped 53 times in 14 games—an average of almost four sacks a game. In one of their first meetings, Shula said to Griese, "I want you to stay in the pocket."

Griese shot back instantly, "Make me a pocket and I'll stay in it."

"There's no great mystery to quarterbacking," Griese said. "You move personnel around in various formations, looking for the defense's patsy, and then you eat him alive."

"Bob Griese deserves to be in the Hall of Fame. Which he is. And the reason he deserves to be in the Hall of Fame is because he, better than any other quarterback in the league, knew how to utilize our offensive skills. Griese was like [racer] A. J. Foyt. He had the best car in the race, the fastest car, but more importantly he knew best how to drive it," said stalwart Dolphins guard Bob Kuechenberg.

Griese had a fondness for Shula that would last the rest of their lives. But Griese liked to repeat about Shula, "He had a high tolerance for another man's pain."

The Dolphins won their second preseason game, as well. In a 20–10 victory over the Cincinnati Bengals at Miami's Orange Bowl, Griese threw two early touchdown passes to Kiick and Warfield. In their third game, they won again, beating the San Francisco 49ers, who would go on to play in the NFC Championship Game, 17–7. The game featured a 50-yard touchdown bomb from Griese to Warfield, as well an impressive goal-line stand by the defense.

The next game of the preseason was their traditional warm-up against the Baltimore Colts. This had all the fanfare of a Super Bowl.

"It was an exhibition game, but it was played for blood by both the Dolphins and the Colts, and for good reason," wrote Tex Maule in *Sports Illustrated*. "The Colts, who are probably a better team than the Dolphins, wanted to beat their old coach, Don Shula, who deserted Baltimore for warmer weather and more money back in February. Shula, who now owns a piece of the Dolphins as part of his recompense for breaching a 5-year contract with Baltimore, naturally wanted to increase the value of his investment. He did."

"We didn't play well last year," Rosenbloom said. "We had only a couple of good games—against bad teams. We didn't even look good winning. If Robbie had come to me and asked for Shula, I wouldn't have objected strenuously."

The rhetoric before the game was tough. "I think it was a good deal for both clubs," said Colts guard Dan Sullivan. "The Dolphins needed a rah-rah guy and a strict disciplinarian, and that's what Shula is. And we're better off with Don McCafferty. He's a quiet guy, but he gets things done." While some of his old players, including Bubba Smith, said publicly that they wanted to beat their old coach, a few visited him privately at his house.

"Watching this team, it was hard to believe that Shula had had so little time to install his system. They were a well-schooled, alert club and they beat the Colts soundly with no flukes—and might even have beaten them worse," wrote Maule. The Dolphins came away with a 20–13 victory.

"We could see the difference in Miami in looking at the movies," Sullivan said before the game. "We played them a couple of years ago, and at that time, I remember, when you watched the defensive line, it looked disorganized and confused. In the movies we saw of their exhibition games this year, they knew what they were doing. It was a different club."

After the game, while being interviewed on television, Shula had been told that Rosenbloom had said to the press that Shula had won a lot of games for the Colts but "lost the big ones." Did he think of this recent Baltimore contest a big game?

"First, I'd take exception to that first statement. We won a lot of big games, too, during the years with Baltimore. We did lose the Super Bowl game to the Jets, and nobody regretted it more than I did. As for this Baltimore game last Sunday—yes, it was a big game."

The next weekend, they lost Washington Redskins, 26–21, as quarterback Sonny Jurgensen and his teammates dedicated the game to Vince Lombardi, who had passed away two days earlier of cancer. That was followed by another loss to Atlanta in their final preseason game, 20–17.

One touch the team appreciated was that during the Wilson era, the team flew in coach or tourist class. When Shula took over, the team traveled first class. The players took note. They also knew more would be expected.

As the team began to build more confidence, so did the pubic. By the end of the exhibition season, the Dolphins drew more than 246,000 spectators. They averaged 41,500 spectators per preseason game. And with one less home exhibition game than the year before, the Dolphins had drawn in more than 100,000 extra spectators than in 1969.

However, Opening Day against the Patriots in Boston went badly. The Dolphins went up, 14–3, early in the second quarter. And then the wheels fell off, and the Patriots took the game, 27–14. The Dolphins had practically given the game away. Shula was furious and berated his club in a gruesome tongue-lashing. He told them that if they were going to lose, then they had better be prepared for the criticism. And that they deserved it.

The team responded with a four-game winning streak, beating the Oakland Raiders at the Orange Bowl, and beating the Oilers, Jets, and Bills on the road. During this stretch, Griese started to find his targets in Warfield and Fleming, with Csonka and Kiick crashing and slicing through defenses.

"That Warfield is making a contender of this team," Raiders owner Al Davis said. "He gives them a threat they never had before."

Paul Dryden Warfield had already been a star in Cleveland before he came to the Dolphins. He had played at Ohio State and, as a rookie receiver in the NFL, amassed more than 900 yards and nine touchdowns. Shula once said of him, "A gifted athlete, which made coaching him so easy."

The Dolphins then lost to the Cleveland Browns, 28–0 and found themselves in Baltimore on November 1 for their first regular-season game against the Colts. The bizarre story lines continued.

"When Rosenbloom learned that a Florida sportswriter had been denied permission to travel on the Dolphins' plane after twitting Robbie publicly, he offered to fly the reporter to the Miami-Baltimore game at the Colts' expense," explained Tex Maule.

"Prodded by Rosenbloom's enemies in Baltimore and encouraged by Dolphin operatives, a Colt fan club blandly announced that it wanted to make an award to Shula before the opening kickoff Sunday.

"'How stupid can people get?' asked a Colt official. Can you imagine the scene on the field? If Shula goes out to accept the award and gets a five-minute standing ovation, we're embarrassed, and if he goes out there and gets booed for five minutes, he's embarrassed. So who can possibly benefit? We told the fan club to stuff it."

Shula was worried about what fans might do when he took the field. He needn't have. When he walked out, there was thunderous applause from a packed house. Unfortunately, Shula didn't have much to cheer about during or after the game.

Rosenbloom lashed out at Shula after the Colts beat the Dolphins, 35–0, with both Unitas and Morrall throwing touchdown passes.

"Former coach George Wilson and personnel director Joe Thomas put together a terrific team. I couldn't believe my eyes. I thought they would be better coached," said Rosenbloom after the game. "There is not a coach in the league who wouldn't like to have his material. Look at the receivers, Paul Warfield and Willie Richardson. Richardson was All-Pro last year. Look at Jim Kiick and Larry Csonka. They're both terrific running backs," Rosenbloom said before rekindling the memories of the Super Bowl loss. "The Baltimore team [that lost to the Jets] was the finest I've ever seen. Then, the next year we played one good game. We were 8–5–1. We should have lost every game we played."

To Shula's credit, he did not respond back then: "I've never answered him, and I'm not going to start now. It's too far along now."

After a 24–17 loss at Philadelphia, the Dolphins were 4–4. The team had already won more games than they had the previous year. Griese had struggled for the last three games, but Shula stayed the course. The Dolphins upped their record to 5–4 with a win over the New Orleans Saints in Miami. And that set the stage for their second meeting with the Colts.

The Colts brought with them a gaudy 7–1–1 record, while the feisty Dolphins stood at 5–4. But the team had remembered the embarrassment the Colts had handed them in Baltimore, and Shula's young team responded. The game opened with a Colts field goal before Jake Scott raced 77 yards with a punt to score the first touchdown of the game. It was an ironic moment, since Baltimore had done the same thing in their previous meeting. Griese ran the next touchdown in himself and then tossed the next one to Warfield for their third touchdown of the game. Unitas countered, throwing two touchdowns of his own, but also tossed a pair of interceptions. The Colts also lost two fumbles. By the time the day was done, the young Dolphins had returned the favor to the mighty Colts and won the game, 34–17.

Shula was elated. More important, it was the way they were doing it. A tough defense, and a solid, straight-ahead offense. Shula pointed out that the Dolphins had run a lot of gadget plays over the previous three years to try and overcome their lackluster offense. "In 1970, we needed solid play," Shula said. "We were able to develop this solidity because of the presence of Fleming and our gifted running backs behind [Larry] Little."

The Baltimore game was encouraging, because of the way in which Miami had done it. "We took the ball and rammed it down their throats, and after that game we sensed we were capable of moving the football against anybody," said Shula. "Now we were the kind of football team you like to be associated with—the kind that takes advantage of every situation presented offensively or defensively or in a special teams situation."

The Dolphins won the rest of their games on the schedule that year. They beat the Falcons in Atlanta and then won their last three games against the Patriots, the Jets, and the Bills, all at home, to finish the year 10–4.

"In our last two games," Shula told the press, "we've held two of pro football's best quarterbacks, Namath and Daryle Lamonica of the Raiders, to only one touchdown. If we can maintain that type of performance, we might surprise everybody this season."

They finished second to the Colts (11–2–1) in the AFC East. Still, with their record, they won the newly created "wild-card" playoff berth. Their opponent would be the 8–4–2 Oakland Raiders, champions of the AFC West. Don Shula had taken the laughingstock of the league and turned it around in one year, and made it a playoff team.

Robbie was ecstatic but still saw room for improvement. "Our average attendance nearly doubled from 34,000 to more than 62,000," said Robbie, grinning. "But, as great as this season has been, we've still got to 'sell' the Miami Dolphins," Robbie noted in the last game of the season with 70,000 fans in attendance but lamented the 9,010 empty seats. "After the season's over, I'll make a recruiting trip," said Robbie. "I plan to hit nearly every chamber of commerce, nearly all the newspapers in Florida. I'll also go to similar offices throughout the Caribbean."

"Joe didn't have a dime to invest," said Joe Foss, a former American Football League commissioner. "He searched for somebody else with dough, got himself a franchise, and now it's going great guns."

Shula had been Robbie's key in attracting new investors, new money, and solidifying his position.

"There'll be a price increase for tickets next season," Robbie promised his 62,000 regular fans. "We have to hike it to get close to other pro cities. We're second in the N.F.L. in attendance behind Cleveland and near the middle in gross revenue."

"People said I was cheap before I shelled out to Shula," said Robbie. Before Shula, the franchise was being run on a shoestring. Now Robbie had financing and money. The team would have to fly to Oakland during the Christmas holiday for the playoff game. According to Shula, Joe Robbie did as much as he could to help the players to enjoy the holiday season, especially those who were far from family and friends.

Before the playoff game, Shula reviewed the season with the press. He alluded to the first game against the Patriots, a loss. "After that loss, we turned our deep disappointment to absolute determination," Shula said. "When we followed by beating Houston and then Oakland, I knew this team had the kind of character and drive to be a winner." By then, Griese and Warfield were named to the Pro Bowl. Miami was truly turning around.

John Madden, the Raiders' gargantuan and effusive coach, said Warfield had been the difference for the Dophins this season, and in his club's previous loss. "He scored two of their touchdowns," Madden said. "We had double coverage on him. We even hoped Bob Griese would throw to him."

The game was tied, 7–7, at the end of the first half. In the third quarter, a Miami drive was thwarted on two key plays First Griese was sacked on a second down for a 12-yard loss. On third down and 19 yards to go, Griese attempted a pass to Warfield, but Raider defensive back Willie Brown stepped in front of Warfield and picked off the pass, racing 50 yards for a touchdown, giving the Raiders a 14–7 lead. Not long after, Oakland struck again when Daryle Lamonica threw an 82-yard touchdown pass to wide receiver Rod Sherman to make it 21–7. Miami answered when Griese passed to wide receiver Willie Richardson for a 7-yard touchdown. But Miami never really mounted another serious threat, and the Raiders' defense rose to the challenge. The final score was Raiders 21, Dolphins 14.

"All that we've accomplished all season, everything we've worked so hard for is finished. Everything we built was left out there in the mud," Griese told the press.

"Sure, I am disappointed. We came in here prepared to win, and while we didn't, I'm still pretty proud of my boys. I've been proud of them all year. They have worked hard and the results showed it. I expected them to run at us more, as they did against Kansas City. But Lamonica mixed his plays pretty effectively. His two touchdown throws were big plays, and he made them," Shula said after the game. Of Griese's interception? "Griese was trying to throw through the Oakland zone, but the ball slipped in his hand and he was short. That's all there was to it."

One of the things that developed in 1970 were the confluence of running backs Jim Kiick, Larry Csonka, and Mercury Morris and how they began to mature. Csonka and Kiick were a matched set. Mercury was originally the odd man out, an occaisonal back and kick return specialist. But that wouldn't always be true. Shula was determined to develop all three of them. It would not be easy, but it would be one of the greatest accomplishments of his early tenure with the Dolphins.

Fullback Lawrence Richard "Larry" Csonka was born in Stow, Ohio, not far from Akron. At 6-foot-3 and 237 pounds, Csonka was a straight-ahead runner. "Larry Csonka was tough to bring down. That man was like a bulldozer. You were rooting for your linebackers to stop him because if they didn't get him or slow him down, he would pick up some speed and simply run over defensive backs. It was shoulder injury time if you had to tackle Csonka on your own," said Jimmy Johnson, Hall of Fame defensive back for the San Francisco 49ers.

Another Hall of Famer, linebacker Bobby Bell of the Kansas City Chiefs, remembered: "Larry Csonka was a big back and he ran so low to the ground. I felt it every time I hit him. One time I hit Larry so hard, I ended up looking through the earhole of my helmet. I thought to myself, 'I know he's got to stay down after that hit.' But he got up and walked back to the huddle and then here he came again."

"When I think about Zonk, I think about power, strength, domination, and intelligence. He had them all and he was a very bright guy. He was a tremendous competitor and just about as big and strong as you could get at the fullback position. He was aware of everything going on and never made a mental mistake," Shula once said of Csonka. Two small stories epitomize their relationship.

Csonka was the only running back in modern football memory who received a personal foul while advancing the ball for delivering a violent forearm to the head of a defensive back who tried to tackle him. Once, during a game against Minnesota, Csonka got hit and was doubled over backward. It was a vicious hit near the sideline. Csonka slowly got up, hobbling toward the bench, when Shula screamed at him, "Get up! Get up! They're going to think you're hurt!" Csonka angrily replied, "I *am* hurt!"

The other was from Griese, who remembered watching the 1971 highlight film with the team. "Csonka lumbered into the endzone, his helmet viciously twisted, his uniform slathered with mud, his expression set in stone. He turned impassively after scoring, flipped the ball over his shoulder, and jogged to the bench." Shula called it "The image of manhood." When asked to quickly name the first thing to come to mind about Csonka, Shula said easily, "The guy you wanted on YOUR side."

No matter what, Zonk (as he was known) was the back that the famous Miami backfield revolved around. A devastating runner, a thunderous blocker, and a team player. He was also one of the few men who could tweak Shula and get away with it. There was one training camp, when Csonka walked into the room with an invisible dog leash—a leash that looked slightly slack that dangled a collar, making it look like you were walking an imaginary dog. Csonka walked the leash right up to Shula and said to the collar, "Piss on him." Few other players could get away with something like that. He was not immune to Shula's volitile temper. He was Shula's favorite lovable bad boy.

There was also the time Csonka and Kiick (it was rumored) put a four-foot alligator in Shula's shower stall. "Scared me nearly half to death," Shula said. "But I felt a little more comfortable when I saw the mouth had been taped shut." Added Shula, "The way I got the story later, the motion to tape the mouth passed a team vote by one."

Another time Shula came over to shout at Csonka during practice. The giant fullback seemed to be fooling around and looking down at the grass. Inquiring what Csonka was looking at. Csonka told him, "A snake!" and flipped a rubber strip at the coach.

"Yow!" Shula screamed and ran like one of the Keystone Cops. Shula tried to feign anger, but it was obvious to everyone that he was fighting back laughing for the next few minutes.

Shula said he would appreciate Larry Csonka even if Csonka weren't Hungarian. Csonka referred to his father and Shula as "those crazy Hungarians" (himself being inexplicably exempt). Once, Edwin Pope, a legendary Miami sportswriter, was chided by Shula for sneaking out of the head coach's press conference to talk to the star running back. Csonka commiserated with Pope, speaking loudly enough for Shula to hear, "Don't worry about it, Edwin, you heard one Honky, you heard 'em all."

In those days, it was not uncommon to see Csonka accompanied by Jim Kiick. The two had formed a lasting friendship while surviving their early years on the Dolphins. James Forrest "Jim" Kiick was born in Lincoln Park, New Jersey. His father, George, had played for the Pittsburgh Steelers in 1940 and 1945. He played running back for the University of Wyoming and led the team in rushing in 1965, 1966, and 1967. He was MVP of the 1966 Sun Bowl. Kiick was drafted in the fifth round in 1968, the same year as Csonka.

While Kiick was faster and ran to daylight, he was no less prone to violence himself. He was once seen biting the arm of a New York Jet during a game. When asked why he did it, Kiick responded, "Because he was twisting my leg." Did Kiick bite him hard? "Hard enough to make him stop twisting my leg."

"By the same token, Shula says he would appreciate Jim Kiick even if Kiick were not loath to participate in Shula's tough practices. Kiick says he hates to practice," wrote John Underwood. "He told Shula exactly that, and then ran the 12 minutes . . . bringing up the rear in lockstep with his faithful Hungarian companion Csonka. Shula said the two are so close they even get tired together."

"I've always been what you might call lackadaisical. It makes for a bad appearance. For example, I hate exercise. I hate sit-ups. Larry thrives on hard work . . . Shula yells at me for the way I do exercises. I just like to loosen up. I don't worry much about form. I don't knock myself out on the unnecessary stuff," Kiick said. "I'm not a student of anything. I stopped growing mentally at 17. I know absolutely nothing about football. I don't know how to read a defense. I'm always afraid they'll quiz me on something I'm supposed to know."

The tag line on Kiick and Csonka was that Kiick liked to run where there were holes and Csonka preferred to run into people (or through them). "Kiick and Csonka. You can't spell 'em and you can't stop 'em," said one rival coach. Shula called them "throwbacks." According to Underwood, "They are two manifestly uncomplicated football players who love the game for the simple things it can do to a man. Dirty his shirt. Bloody his chin. Satisfy his inhibitions. Relieve his tensions."

Shula told the press that he did not send Csonka and Kiick to play as much as he "cut them loose." Both craved action and hated being rested. Csonka would argue and plead with the coach. Kiick would sulk during his short breathers on the bench. "It's my way," Kiick said. "Larry is more likely to say something. 'Let me back in, coach.' I never say anything. I sulk."

"Two things can happen in a case like that," said Csonka about being roommates with Kiick. "Either you communicate and get along or you wind up hating each other. If you don't get along, it's pretty obvious. Show me the game films of a team, and I'll tell you whether the running backs get along. When Jim and I run a sweep, I can sense exactly what he's going to do, how he'll react to the defensive end or the cornerback. We don't have anything in common except friendship, but that makes it work."

"He was huge," Kiick said of Csonka. "I was embarrassed to be around him. He was taller. He was stronger. I measured my thighs and thought, boy, 28 inches. His were bigger. We kidded him every time he ran a pass pattern: 'Lineman down field!' We were nothing alike, but we hit it off. Larry likes to fish. I hate the outdoors. But I could enjoy it with him. I like to play basketball or shoot pool. He doesn't give a damn, but he'll come watch."

Csonka and Kiick were hazed their rookie season. "One time they had us drink a gallon of white lightning," Csonka says. "Kiick sat there, motionless. Sometimes he does that, just sits there, so I wasn't concerned. He looked sober. Then he said, 'We gotta go.' We made it back to the room, and he was sicker than I've ever seen a man. The next day we had to run the ropes, and we got tangled so bad you wouldn't believe it.

"No matter what your style, you have to take a beating," Csonka said. "If you're small and quick, it might catch up to you all at once, or if you're like me you might prefer to get it in regular doses, but sooner or later the bill collector comes. . . . It's all in the game. I'm no masochist, but I wouldn't want it any other way. I want to be physically involved. . . . I love the game, that's all. I bitch, but I love the whole thing, the total experience. . . . And the only thing that troubles me is that I won't be able to play forever."

The two were so inseparable and so ubiquitous, both on the field and off, that they became known as Butch Cassidy and the Sundance Kid, after the popular film starring Paul Newman and Robert Redford. Once, in a game against the Bills, Csonka's helmet cut into the bridge of his nose, and he began gushing blood. Back in the huddle, he began to drip blood on Marv Fleming's shoes. The players could hear the drops. Fleming, a Super Bowl-winning athlete, became unnerved. "So I leaned the other way to bleed on Kiick," said Csonka. "He loves it. It makes him think he's been in a game."

Both were notorious for playing through injuries. Kiick once had his arm swell to twice its normal size during a game, and told the trainer, "Hell, I'm paid to play." He also played with a broken toe, a broken finger, and a hip pointer. Csonka was once knocked out during a play and came to as the team doctor called for a stretcher. "I'm not going to be carried off in front of all those people," he said. "I'm going out the way I came in or I'm not going." He got up and walked off the field. Kiick was X-rayed once for a broken ankle. Curious, the doctor X-rayed the other ankle, as well. Both were broken. Kiick wore through the casts in less than two weeks.

It was easy to see why Shula loved the pair. During the 1970 season, Csonka carried the ball 193 times for 874 yards (averaging 4.5 yards per carry) and accumulated 94 yards receiving, as well. Kiick took 191 handoffs for 658 yards (3.4 yards per carry) but also had 42 receptions for 497 yards, giving him 1,155 total yards from scrimmage—a respectable number in any era. It was clear to see why the pair were popular on and off the field.

But there was another back on the team who was underutilized during his early years on the team—Mercury Morris. Morris had set the single-season collegiate record at West Texas State in 1968, a week before O. J. Simpson eclipsed it. He had received his nickname "Mercury" when one coach had described him as mercurial.

"The fact that I didn't get the call until Day 2 [of the draft]. That was the bad news because I thought I was going to go in the first or second round. I went in the third round because the Dolphins were drafting linemen," recalled Morris. "They drafted Bob Heinz ahead of me, and I was a third-round draft pick . . . at that time running backs were not 5–10, 185 pounds, they were 6–2, 215, like Jim Taylor and Paul Hornung, which is the same as [Larry] Csonka and [Jim] Kiick, so it was an uphill battle from the beginning."

Famed gonzo journalist Hunter S. Thompson once wrote about Morris, "Mercury Morris was a human lightning bolt when he got his hands on a football . . . 'Merc' had a wild streak in him."

Morris was a star in his own right, as a lightning-fast kick returner early on, and even had his own football diary published in a Miami newspaper. He was outspoken, whether on race, politics, or sports. And he was not afraid to clash with anybody.

Early in his career, Morris was the backup to Kiick and picked up occasional carries. He served mainly as the kickoff return man. In 1970, he was in the top ten of all categories for kick returning, and as high as No. 3 for return yardage with 812 yards. Still, spelling Kiick in 1970, Morris got the ball 60 times and raced for 409 yards (that's 6.8 yards per carry) and had 12 receptions for 149 yards. In the early years, the formula worked, but over the next three or four years, Shula fell in love with the idea of revolving the three backs. This desperately upset the equilibrium of Butch and Sundance, but Shula had a real and founded suspicion that Morris's potential was not being tapped. A series of events would crash the outspoken and mercurial Morris into the hegemony of the two starters, and the granite chin of Shula. It wouldn't always be pretty in the locker room, but it worked beautifully on the field.

Shula's concept was to create situational mismatches as often as possible, predating today's game of situational substitutions. "We started that when we had Larry Csonka, Jim Kiick, and Mercury Morris [in the backfield]," Shula said. "Kiick and Morris had very different skills, and I just tried to get them into the game when the situation dictated it.

"A lot of that was field position, down, and distance to first down. Kiick was a great goal-line runner, as was Csonka. Mercury was more of an open-field threat to break long runs. Kiick was a great receiver running routes out of the backfield; he usually got linebacker coverage and would easily get open and give the quarterback someone to throw the ball to."

The season had ended for the Dolphins, but the Baltimore Colts continued playing. On January 17, 1971, the Colts defeated Tom Landry's Dallas Cowboys, 16–13, in Super Bowl V, on a last-second kick by Jim O'Brien to win the now-named Lombardi Trophy. John Unitas had started the game but was knocked out of the game by Dallas' defense with sore ribs. Earl Morrall came in relief. The Cowboys were leading, 13–6, at that time. The Colts scored 10 points in the fourth quarter and won the game. Despite the fact that Morrall was the top passer of the game and the winning quarterback, the MVP was awarded to Dallas linebacker Chuck Howley (the only time a player from the losing team took the honor). The game was marred by so many turnovers and penalties, it was eventually nicknamed the "Blunder Bowl" and the "Stupor Bowl." But Carroll Rosenbloom had finally won it all.

The 1971 draft turned out to be a sore subject for the Dolphins and Shula. Joe Thomas was the Dolphins' immensely gifted NFL talent executive. At Miami from 1966 to 1971, he drafted Howard Twilley, Bob Griese, Larry Seiple, Larry Csonka, Jim Kiick, Dick Anderson, Mercury Morris, and Jake Scott.

The Dolphins took Joe Theismann in the fourth round. He had been a star quarterback at Notre Dame. Theismann had also been offered an opportunity in 1971 to play shortstop for the Minnesota Twins. He'd also been offered a deal by the Toronto Argonauts of the Canadian Football League. Theismann chose football. He negotiated with owner Joe Robbie himself without an agent. Theismann requested a three-year deal worth $55,000 and was amazed when Robbie agreed.

"I said, 'Oh man, it's not supposed to work this way,'" Theismann said. "There's supposed to be some give and take. But it was fine. So I go on Miami television and say, 'Come hell or high water, I'll be a Miami Dolphin.'"

Robbie added a $35,000 bonus into the deal, but Theismann balked when he realized the bonus was split over three years and was recoupable if he did not play all the years of his contract. Theismann had a very real concern that he might be drafted into the military with the Vietnam War still raging.

"I didn't know whether I was going to wind up going into the service or what," he said. "It was an issue for a very long period of time." Concerned with Robbie's tactics, Theismann began talking to Toronto. Argonauts head coach and general manager Leo Cahill offered Theismann a $200,000 package that included a $50,000 signing bonus, huge numbers in those days.

"Theismann himself wanted to break the news to now-legendary Dolphins head coach Don Shula, who was certain that the rookie would sign with Miami. But Shula found out when word of the signing leaked out through Canadian media. He was angry," wrote sports journalist Mike Richman.

"It took probably 15, 20 years for him to forgive that I had signed with Toronto, didn't go to Miami," Theismann said. Theismann went on to play in a Grey Cup in Canada and win a Super Bowl in the NFL with the Redskins.

Csonka and Kiick, who shared the same agent, Ed Keating, both reported late to camp as they held out for better contracts than they had been offered. With Joe Thomas suffering from health issues and Joe Robbie out of town, it took a few extra weeks to get them to sign their respective contracts. Shula fined each of them $2,000 for reporting late to camp. It would take three or four preseason games to round them into shape. In the offseason, Shula had insisted on better weight training and lifting routines for his linemen. He felt the Miami pass rush was weak and it needed bulking up.

The preseason performance of his team was worrisome to Shula. The record was 2–3–1, which included an embarrassing 24–0 spanking by the Minnesota Vikings in their last tune-up before the season began. And the season didn't start any better, with a lackluster 10–10 tie with the Broncos in Denver. Yepremian had missed four field goals, the running game went nowhere, and the usually sure-handed Jake Scott had fumbled on a punt return that would have put the team in good position for a possible winning field goal.

They continued to stumble. Though they beat Buffalo, they lost their home opener to the Jets, 14–10, giving up two fourth-quarter touchdowns. The team responded with an eight-game winning streak, with victories over Cincinnati, New England, the New York Jets, Los Angeles, Buffalo, Pittsburgh, Baltimore, and Chicago.

A loss to the New England Patriots broke the streak, giving them a 9–2–1 record going into a big game against their divisional nemesis, the Baltimore Colts, who entered the contest with a record of 9–3. The winner would take the lead in the AFC East. A division title was seemingly on the line with two games to play.

"For a long while on a bright, balmy afternoon in Baltimore last weekend, time stood still. Johnny Unitas, the 38-year-old quarterback who has only recently returned to the starting lineup after a crippling injury, must have thought it was 1958," wrote Tex Maule. "He was superb and preeminently clearheaded."

Unitas had said, while sitting getting his shoulder massaged before the

December 11 contest, "I feel good. I can play. It's another game. We've been in big games before. We'll be in big games again. You do what you can. You can't do any more than that." When asked what he thought he could do against the vaunted Miami lineup, he answered, "I don't know. I'll take what they give me. They got to give you something. All you got to do is find out what it is."

Unitas saw it all the way. The linebackers were dropping off fifteen yards, and the defensive backs were fifteen yards behind them. Unitas threw short passes mixed with short runs all day long, picking apart the Dolphins defense like a surgeon. Maule wrote that Unitas was giving "lessons" on "how to attack a modern zone defense."

"Unitas was fitting the ball in between the defensive backs when we were in the three-man rush," said Shula. "He did everything right. We haven't played well enough to win in two weeks." The Colts were now in the driver's seat with a game to play.

But the Dolphins took care of business, beating the mediocre Green Bay Packers, 27–6, the next weekend, taking their last regular season game. They then received help from the 6–8 New England Patriots, who played the role of spoiler against Baltimore. Patriots quarterback Jim Plunkett threw two touchdowns and Johnny Unitas threw two interceptions, including one that was returned for a touchdown, in a 21–17 New England victory. With a record of 10–3–1, the Dolphins had finished first in the AFC East, in only Shula's second year. But it was not the last time they would see the Colts.

Their first playoff game would pit them against the Chiefs at Kansas City Municipal Stadium on Christmas Day. It would be one of the most memorable games in NFL history. It was destined to be known as "The Longest Game Ever Played." Hank Stram, the legendary coach of the powerful midwestern team, thought his 1971 team was possibly the best team he had ever coached. And that was saying something, since they were only two years removed from having won the Super Bowl handily. They had an efficient offense and an immensely powerful defense. They had been among the best teams in professional football for more than half a decade. And this was their last game at the old stadium, as the next year they would begin playing at the new Arrowhead Stadium. There were more than 45,000 people in the stands, on an unseasonably warm 63-degree Christmas Day. In addition to coaches Stram and Shula, there were thirteen future Hall of Fame players competing in the game. The vaunted Chiefs were favored. They had 11 Pro Bowlers on their team versus the seven Pro Bowlers on the Dolphins. This was a real test for the scrappy Dolphins. And they knew it.

The Chiefs featured Len Dawson, the MVP of Super Bowl IV, at quarterback. His favorite target was Otis Taylor, who led the NFL that season with 1,110 receiving yards. He stood at 6-feet-3 and weighed 215 pounds. He averaged almost 20 yards per catch.

With the Chiefs leading, 10–0, in the second quarter, Jan Stenerud, arguably one of the greatest kickers of his generation, lined up for a 22-yard field goal attempt. However, Stram wanted to go for the throat early against Shula and his hard-nosed team. He called for a fake.

"I told Jan, 'You've got to be a good actor and look like you're going to kick,'" Stram recalled. "Anyway, we're on the right hash mark. Everyone on the sideline is psyched. We know we're going to score a touchdown. Bobby Bell, our center, looks through his legs and sees Jan looking down at his spot like he normally would, which is exactly what we told him to do. But it's so convincing, Bell thinks Jan missed the call. He's afraid to snap the ball to him, so he snaps it to the holder, Lenny Dawson. Lenny is surprised. Jan is surprised. Lenny puts it down and Jan takes a swipe at it and just misses to the right of the post. Meanwhile, both our guards are all alone on the right. I mean, there wasn't a soul out there with them. It would have been a certain score."

"I asked Bell why he snapped it to me, and he said, 'Because it didn't look like Jan was ready to catch it,'" Dawson said. "I said, 'Did you expect him to put out his arms?'" It was an opportunity missed.

Csonka scored the Dolphins' first touchdown, and Yepremian added a 14-yard field goal when another drive stalled, and the teams went into halftime tied, 10–10. By then, Jake Scott had been playing half that time with a broken hand and would finish the game, not missing a snap. The third quarter opened with Kansas City scoring a touchdown, and the Dolphins answered with Kiick going in from a yard out. Ed Podolak scored his second touchdown of the game in the fourth quarter and put the Chiefs ahead, 24–17. Podolak was a solid third-year back, but in this game, he was amazing. He amassed 350 total yards, still a playoff record. However, with 1:36 left in the game, Miami answered when Griese found Marv Fleming in the end zone for a touchdown. The Dolphins were still alive. The score was tied, 24–24.

"The Dolphin celebration died in their throats. Ed Podolak, incandescent that day with 350 all-purpose yards, took Yepremian's ensuing kickoff at the goal line, started up the middle and cut sharply left through a mass of bodies, and found himself in the clear, with only Yepremian standing between him and the goal line," wrote *Miami Herald* columnist Bob Rubin.

"I had a choice—run over the Kangaroo or run around him," said Podolak (he called all kickers Kangaroos). "I cut hard left to avoid him and started down the left sideline, but the time it took gave Curtis Johnson the angle to catch me. I tried to get him to commit to where I could cut back behind him, but he played it very smart and kept forcing me toward the sideline. I've looked at the film 50 times to see if there was anything I could have done different, but there wasn't."

Yepremian remembers panicking as Podolak swerved toward him at first. "I thought, 'You've got to do something or the whole season's down the drain,'" Yepremian said. Podolak went out of bounds at the Miami 22-yard line.

Three Kansas City runs went nowhere. On came Stenerud. With 35 seconds to go, he would attempt a 31-yard field goal. Stenerud had a 75 percent success rate from 30–39 yards out during his career. At 31 yards, many felt this was a gimme.

"I was planning what I was going to do with my off-season," linebacker Nick Buoniconti said. "The chances were one in a million he would miss that kick."

"I sincerely felt, as this game went on, there was no way in the world we could lose it. . . . When Miami tied it and Eddie Podolak came back with a 78-yard kickoff return—our longest of the year—we felt it was poetic justice," said Stram. "I was more concerned with the protection of Stenerud than I was the actual kicking of the field goal attempt. I still think Jan kicked the ball well but it . . . was a little bit off line. In a big game like this, you've got to take advantage of the shots you get or you're dead."

It was Stenerud's second miss of the game.

"It was like the football gods telling you, 'We're going to help you,'" Griese said. "It was like, 'Geez, another chance.'" The game went into overtime.

"The game postponed Christmas dinners around the country as fans watched on television while the Chiefs and the Dolphins battled through the afternoon and into the evening," wrote Robert Weintraub in the *New York Times*.

"Everyone I knew in Miami told me they had to shut off their ovens to avoid ruining their Christmas turkeys," said Buoniconti, who had 20 tackles that day.

The game slogged along. The field, not in good shape to begin with, turned sloppy, and finding traction was difficult. Neither team would yield. In overtime, Nick Buoniconti blocked another Stenerud attempt. The Dolphins' Yepremian missed on another.

Frustrated, Buoniconti pressed Podolak's face into the mud at one point. "The only thing he said to me was, 'Do you think this game will ever end?'" the linebacker recalled. Podolak said, "I was so tired I was operating totally on instinct."

Then the first overtime period ended. During his time sitting on the bench while the defense toiled, Griese went through the game plan and playbooks looking for a magic bullet. He found one—"a misdirection play before they were popular," said Griese.

Kansas City quarterback Len Dawson called it "a sucker play." Griese waited for the right time to spring the play. Stuck on their own 35-yard line, on a third down, with five yards to go, and the Kansas City defense tired, Griese called the play for Csonka.

"It was a roll-right trap," explained Csonka. "Kiick and Griese start toward the strong side, and I go the other way. The two guards cut with me and then it's up to me. It was a great call by Griese." Csnoka blew through the defense and went 29 yards to the Chiefs' 36-yard line. Kansas City stiffened and only yielded six more yards. Now it was time for Yepremian again.

"I couldn't help but think of what had happened to Stenerud and pray it wouldn't happen to me," Yepremian said. "As I ran out onto the field, I kept saying to myself, 'I can make it. I can make it.' The ball felt very good off my foot. I started for the sideline, then stopped. I thought, "It's so quiet. Maybe I missed.'" He didn't, and his kick gave the Dolphins an unforgettable 27–24 victory.

"The Chiefs stood disbelievingly for a moment, then slowly started trudging off the Municipal Stadium field for the last time," wrote Murray Chass in the *New York Times*.

"It was a horrifying experience," Dawson said of the sudden-death play, "because one break is going to be the game. You never heard such silence, if that's not a contradiction. Such pressure, such tension. Everyone was completely drained."

"It was such an eventful game that just when you seem to have it in proper perspective another element comes to mind and changes the picture," wrote *Kansas City Star* sports scribe Joe McGuff.

The game had lasted 82 minutes 40 seconds. Wrote Crass, "Long after this season's playoffs are forgotten, this game will remain embedded in the memories of those who saw it in person or on television as a historical event." It is still considered one of the greatest playoff games in the history of the NFL.

Yepremian was the toast of Miami after kicking the winning field goal. "The 5-foot-7-inch Yepremian was hounded by newsmen after Miami's thrilling 27–24 victory over Kansas City. He was mobbed by thousands of enthusiastic Dolphins fans who created a Kennedy Airport-sized traffic jam around Miami International early this morning as they greeted the team on its return," wrote Neil Amdur in the *New York Times*. "Karl Noonan had no such problems in the dressing room, at the airport, or at home. Yet Noonan may have been as responsible for ending the 82-minute-40-second playoff game as the left-footed Yepremian. He held the ball for Yepremian's kick."

"Nobody remembers the holder unless you muff it," Noonan said.

When he wasn't kicking for the Dolphins, Yepremian was a clotheshorse who made his own ties and sold them. "They are pretty colorful," said the 27-year-old Cypriot. "In fact, some people who see the fabric think it looks pretty ridiculous. But they wind up loving the neckties." He'd received a rush of orders after the Kansas City game and had sold up to that point around 2,000 neckties.

Shula was amazed by the 15–20,000 people who were waiting to welcome the Dolphins home. Weaving his way through the sea of humanity, Shula, with his son David in tow, finally made his way to the parking lot. The car was dead. So he and his son went back to the mobbed area and stuck out a thumb. One of the nation's premier coaches was hitching a ride on Christmas night. A fan spotted the coach, a woman with two other fans, and offered the coach a lift home. Once home, he invited the fans in for a Christmas drink, which they happily accepted, and they all talked about the game.

"I had to be the first coach in history to win a playoff game and end up hitching a ride home," said Shula.

After their win, there was good news, and bad news. The good news was that they had beaten the Chiefs and were playing for a berth in the Super Bowl. The bad news was the Colts would be waiting for them back in Miami. The defending Super Bowl champions had won on the road, clubbing the Browns, 20–3, in Cleveland, and were determined to get back to another Super Bowl.

Both teams featured brutal defenses and smart, aggressive offenses. The players' shares for the AFC Championship were $8,500 to each member of the winning team and $5,500 to each member of the losing team.

Miami was awash in football fans. The Miami faithful were joined by hordes of Baltimoreans who were in town to see their Colts hopefully defeat the surprising Dolphins. There was a drenching rain the night before the game. The heavy rain shifted to light rain and had diminished not long before the game began. Just then the sun came out.

Dave Anderson's lead sentence in the *New York Times* said it all after the game: "As if inspired by a rainbow that appeared to descend into their huddle in the first quarter, the Miami Dolphins played virtually impeccable football today in winning the American conference title with a 21–0 victory that dethroned the Baltimore Colts as world champions."

"When we saw the rainbow, we thought it was going to be our day," said Shula.

The Dolphins struck first when Griese threw a 75-yard strike to Paul Warfield that seemed to shock the Colts. But the Colts' defense stiffened. Meanwhile, Johnny Unitas went to work. The Colts drove at the Miami defense all day. Unitas carried the game on his shoulders. Baltimore's leading rusher, Norm Bulaich, was injured and unavailable, and Tom Matte was playing with an injured knee. Still, Unitas made it a game for as long as he could. The Miami defense was on the field almost twice as long as the Miami offense. At halftime, it was 7–0.

But Johnny's arm could only carry the team so far. A Unitas pass sailed deep into Miami territory. Just then Curtis Johnson deflected it, and Dick Anderson took it out of the air and, thanks to five crushing blocks by teammates, raced 62 yards the other way for a touchdown, giving Miami a 14–0 lead. Csonka scored from five yards out in the fourth quarter. The Colts were finished. It was the first time they had been shut out since 1965. The Dolphins were AFC champions.

"I can't believe it. I don't understand what happened. I still don't believe we lost that game," said Bubba Smith. "We're too good a team to lose that way. I think this is a better team than last year when we won. It's the best Baltimore team in the five years I've been on the squad. How we lost is a mystery to me. We seldom make mistakes. We capitalize on other teams' mistakes. This time we made the mistakes. I'm mad as hell. I'm not a good loser." Unitas was more insightful.

"Buoniconti is the key to the Dolphins' defense," he said after the game. "If you block him, you should be able to run on them."

"We knew what we wanted to do," said Buoniconti. According to him, Miami "worked on taking third-down situations away from them." He paused. "And we did it."

Buoniconti was among Shula's favorite sons. He had bought in from the beginning. He often told the story of Shula's arrival. Shula told the team they had a reputation for partying heavily, and that they partied even after losses. He told them that was all going to end. That they were losers in the past, but now they were going to be winners. Bouniconti believed.

After the Colts win, many stories included lines about his previous failures in "the big game." Rosenbloom's assessment had been damning, but that didn't mean there weren't others who were thinking it.

"For the Dolphin coach Shula, the victory will enable him to return to the Super Bowl, the scene of his greatest embarrassment," wrote Dave Anderson after the game.

"It's as if Gen. Robert E. Lee had another chance to win the Civil War because Shula was the coach of the Baltimore Colts when they lost to the New York Jets, 16-7, three years ago in the most historic and significant of the five previous Super Bowl games. Since that time, redemption has been an obsession with him."

In one game, he had beaten his old team and gotten to another Super Bowl. He was only the second coach to go to two Super Bowls, the other being Lombardi. Too euphoric to sleep, Shula decided to watch a rebroadcast of the game that was airing around midnight. His wife and in-laws stayed up to watch it with him. Around 1:30 a.m., he got a phone call. It was President Richard M. Nixon, calling to congratulate him and suggesting that they use the slant-in pattern to Warfield again against their next opponent.

Awaiting the Dolphins were Tom Landry's Dallas Cowboys. Landry and Shula were mirror images of each other. If ever there were a man who was as successful as Shula, and as starved for the ultimate victory, scarred and bloodied, it was Landry. Finally, in this contest, one of them would win the Super Bowl. Landry had been a good defensive back and, like Shula, slowly became a player-coach with the New York Giants, who eventually became their defensive coordinator while Lombardi had been the offensive coordinator. Landry had built the Cowboys up from nothing.

Thomas Wade "Tom" Landry had played for the University of Texas at Austin, where he studied to be an industrial engineer. He interrupted his schooling to enlist in the Army. He became a B-17 copilot and flew missions from England over Europe from November 1944 to the end of the war in Europe. He played defensive back for the New York Giants from 1950 to 1955. He then became the defensive coordinator until he took the job of building the Dallas Cowboys in 1960. In his first season, they went 0–11–1. Since then, he had suffered immense postseason defeats mostly at the hands of his old cohort Lombardi. His Cowboys had lost the brutal Ice Bowl to Vince's Packers, and just the season before, he had finally arrived at the Super Bowl, where his team played poorly and lost to the Colts. The Cowboys had topped the San Francisco 49ers to reach the Super Bowl. So close were they in kind that Landry had beaten his former assistant Dick Nolan (now head coach of the 49ers) in the NFC Championship Game the way Shula had beaten McCafferty (of the Colts) for the AFC championship.

Both had played for seven years in the pros and were kept because of their acumen. They both would win 13 division titles. Both would coach in 36 postseason games. Both would coach more than 400 games. Both coached in NFL Championship Games before they went to Super Bowls. The comparison could go on and on.

Like Shula, Landry was a defensive genius who had invented the 4–3 defense in New York. He had invented that defense specifically to thwart Lombardi's "run to daylight" philosophy, and the vaunted Packers' "power sweep." The idea was building a defense that would flow to the daylight and blot out the sun. There were two variations of this defense: 4–3 inside and 4–3 outside, changing the look to confuse or match strong-side coverages. By this time, the 4–3 flexes had morphed into something called the "Flex Defense."

"When introduced, it caused a lot of confusion, because Dallas soon came to be able to play the 43 inside/outside from the Flex set. That was the upside, as no one knew what they were actually playing," wrote author Peter Golenbock. In 1971, the Flex was brand-new, and it threw teams off immensely.

Like Shula, Landry was very religious and was a devout Christian. Where Shula was fiery and temperamental, Landry was cool and cold as ice. His demeanor rarely wavered. Like Bear Bryant, he wore a checkered fedora most of the time when coaching a game as well as a shirt, tie, and jacket.

"We haven't played them, and I've only seen them a couple of times on television. We know Warfield very well, having played against him," Landry said before the game. "I know nothing at all about their defense," he said. "Except I do know Shula, and I have to assume we'll see a lot of the same things we saw when he was coaching Baltimore."

If the writers were chiding Shula, Landry was not. He had a healthy respect for the Dolphins' coach. "I don't think we have any advantage on account of experience. Shula offsets any edge we have. He has been there before."

Asked if anything was different between his previous Super Bowl experience and now, Shula responded, "There was too much confusion three years ago," his jaw dominating his words. "Maybe I didn't shelter the players enough. But everything has changed since that game. It was considered to be a great sin that we got beat by the Jets, but everybody found out that the Jets had a pretty good football team and a pretty good quarterback. And the next year they found out that the Chiefs had a pretty good team too when they beat the Minnesota Vikings in the Super Bowl. In the last three years, everything has changed in that respect."

The Tuesday before the Super Bowl, the Dolphins' first head coach, and Shula's former mentor, George Wilson bitterly told Charlie Nobles of the *Miami News*, "I've been silent too long. . . . Joe Doakes could have taken this team to the Super Bowl. . . . As far as I am concerned he [Shula] took over a ready-made team. I was fired just when the team was ready to go. . . . You go over the roster and you'll see most of the guys who are doing the paying were committed to the Dolphins before Shula ever got here." Wilson added that he "helped to get him [Shula] the Baltimore Colts head coaching job. . . . I practically wrote his contract for him. . . . Carroll Rosenbloom wanted me to take the job and I had twelve meetings with him about it. But I got him to take Shula."

The next day, Shula stepped up to the podium at a press conference in New Orleans, where the Super Bowl was to be played, and jokingly said, "Hi there, I'm Joe Doakes." Shula made light of it and answered questions politely, still not understanding why a friend he sat next to in church (they both attended the same Roman Catholic church) each week would say such a thing publicly.

"I don't know what his reasons are, but I was unhappy to hear them," Shula told the press. "George is entitled to his own opinion. I'm very proud of what we've accomplished, and I don't think I've ever stepped forward to claim the credit for what's been accomplished." Shula pointed out that many players were already here, and that he had made wholesale changes, and brought Fleming, center Bob DeMarco, and Yepremian in himself. Privately, Shula was irate.

Griese said years later that Wilson "was a likeable guy, the kind that would go out after practice and have a beer with players." Griese also said he knew they would never win with Wilson. Even Mercury Morris pointed out that training camp under Wilson included swimming, which turned out to be far different from training camps with Shula.

Shula said years later that Wilson's real anger was that Robbie had lied to him, dangling him, intimating that Wilson would continue, all the while shopping for a new coach. Wilson, by then a contractor, was angry at Robbie and Shula both. One for firing him, and one for replacing him. But if the truth be told, the genius for supplying the original stars, as even Shula pointed out, was general manager Joe Thomas.

The Cowboys were favored. "The sentimentalists will be rooting for the Dolphins but the pragmatists will be betting on Dallas. The older and wiser Cowboys have been in this pressure-cooker before and no team in pro ball can match their record for consistent excellence over the last half-dozen years even if they did come up empty and reaching for that final big one," wrote Arthur Daley in the *New York Times*.

Most difficult for the Dolphins would be Cowboys quarterback Roger Staubach. He had played for the Naval Academy but also served out his four-year commitment, including a stretch in Vietnam. Staubach was bigger, stronger, and a better and sturdier runner than Griese. Staubach had taken over halfway through the season and had not lost a game yet. He would go on to become a Hall of Famer who would play in four Super Bowls.

In scouting the Cowboys, the Dolphins coaches watched plenty of film. "Watch this," shouted one coach, unaware of what was about to happen. "Staubach's receivers are covered and he is being forced to run with the ball. This is what we want you to do. Make him run. Don't let him throw. Make him run . . . oh!" The coach was embarrassed. He wasn't aware that he had chosen a play where Staubach scrambled 29 yards for a touchdown.

"This was the early angle on the game: Neither coach can win the big one; game might end in a tie. Don Shula of the Dolphins and Tom Landry of the Cowboys both had that rap. Now one of them had to win it, unless at midnight their teams had pounded themselves into groggy exhaustion with the score still tied—and the referee had to stop it," wrote Paul Zimmerman in *Sports Illustrated*.

As Dolphins historian Morris T. McLemore wrote of it, "When Nick Bouniconti went against form, and won the toss, the Dolphins were at their high point of the day. After that Dallas had all the options."

"I thought everything would be all right once the game started. But it wasn't. I noticed the players were tight," recalled Shula.

Containing Bouniconti was the key to the Dallas offensive game plan. What was incredibly ingenious was that they shadowed Bouniconti. The idea was always to have a body between him and the runner. They used reach blocks, double teams, anything to shield their runners or delay Bouniconti's arrival. That was their key, and added to it was that the dominant Dallas offensive line played absolutely flawlessly.

Shula was so incensed with his team's poor play by the fourth quarter, he had an argument with an official. After being penalized, Shula let out a string of high-volume obscenities. The official pointed a finger at Shula. "Shula, if you open your mouth one more time, it is going to cost you!" Shula growled but did not retort. Just then, he saw one of his players out of position on the field and screamed out, "Hey, you dummy, move over!" The official spun around, tossed a flag. When Shula insisted he was talking to one of his players, the official told him it was too late, the flag was on the ground. When the official told him it was for "coaching from the sidelines," Shula again insulted the official, who fined him five yards. Shula angrily retorted, "This proves you're stupid. It's a fifteen-yard penalty!"

"Shula," the official retorted, "for your coaching . . . five yards!"

"The Cowboys were methodical and merciless as they turned back the Miami Dolphins, 24–3, in what amounted to a rout," wrote William N. Wallace in the *New York Times.*

Zimmerman said he had two indelible memories of the game, "Dallas's Bob Lilly chasing Bob Griese practically out of the stadium for the longest sack in Super Bowl history, 29 yards," and "the magnificence of [Dallas running back Duane] Thomas, slashing and swerving for 95 yards behind a line that executed its cutoff and trap blocks with military precision."

When Lilly had tackled Griese, the Dolphins quarterback called time-out and went to the sidelines.

"Okay, you always want to call the plays," Griese told the coach, "Third and thirty, you can call this one."

"Oh no, you got us into this mess. You get us out of it!" replied Shula.

Said Landry afterward: "I can't describe how we feel. We fought so hard, came so close so many times. It's great for players like Bob Lilly and Chuck Howley, who have been with the team for so long."

Shula dejectedly said, "We played poorly. Dallas played a near-perfect game."

More important, it's what Shula said to his team after the loss that mattered most. The team had shuffled in, dazed, confused, shaken. Csonka sat down and held his head in in hands. Others sat in silence. The 1971 Dolphins were the first Super Bowl team to fail to score a touchdown. They had been humiliated. He stood there haggard but resolute.

Before the press was let into the silent locker room, he spoke. "We all hurt right now," said Shula. "It's painful. It stings. But I don't want you to forget how this feels. Take it with you everywhere. Remember it now and when you leave here. Remember it when you go home. Remember it when you start training again. Remember it next season. Remember it so when we get back to the Super Bowl next year, the highs of winning it will feel even better. I want all of you to remember how we feel right now, and I don't ever want you to feel this way again."

He then told them he was about to open the door. That they should be mindful of what they said. "We're going to be tested," Shula said. "If we turn on each other, we will become a house divided. I won't allow that. . . . What I am telling you is that we will be back. I can promise you that. We'll be back because we are champions."

Shula opened up the doors, and the writers came flooding in.

Fuming in a corner of the locker room was Mercury Morris. "The only time I got off the bench was for kickoffs and the national anthem," Morris told the press. He complained that he never got in the game. "We planned to run wide, but we weren't doing it," Morris added. At this point, an assistant had whispered into Shula's ear that Mercury was complaining to the press.

"I bit my lip to control my temper. Finally, I couldn't hold back any more," said Shula. He walked briskly to the other side of the locker room, fire in his eyes, his legendary jaw jutting out. Morris had been angry since the last few minutes of the disastrous game, and his anger was boiling over. Shula and Morris stood toe-to-toe, both seething. Neither seemingly backing down. Shula motioned for the running back to step aside where they could talk, thus temporarily ending Morris's diatribes.

"If you have anything to say about me, you should say it to me first," Shula said. Shula paused, but Morris did not respond. "Come to my hotel room tomorrow morning. Be there by ten," said the furious Shula, who then went back to the writers to answer further questions.

"I respect Merc for wanting to play, and, hopefully, we can work him into our offense a little more this next year and continue to progress and move along. We do need his outside speed," Shula told the reporters.

The simple fact was that Morris had not proven himself to Shula's liking. He was one of the best college backs of his era. He was small, but fast, and with powerful legs. But he liked fast cars, fast women, and lots of partying. He had, in Shula's eyes, done nothing to distinguish himself. Shula was always watching, and he wasn't sure he could trust Mercury to respond. Kiick would complain but play hurt, play injured, and put his whole body on the line in a game, and Shula knew that, but the outspoken, sometimes critical Morris seemed less of a team player. He wasn't sure he could count on Morris. However, Shula also knew one more thing—he needed Morris's speed desperately.

The two reached an accord—Shula promised Mercury a real chance for serious playing time, but Morris would have to work out and put himself forward in the best possible way to prove he deserved that opportunity. "This is your shot," he told Morris.

CHAPTER 7

Undefeated

As 1972 began, plenty of changes were in the works for the Dolphins. First, Joe Thomas went to Baltimore to become the general manager of the Colts. One of the first things he did was to release one of their two aging quarterbacks. Earl Morrall was the odd man out. He was ready to release him unceremoniously, when Don McCafferty insisted he give the news to Morrall himself, personally. Morrall wrote a handwritten letter to the *Baltimore News-American* thanking the fans for their years of support.

During the offseason, Shula became concerned with his backup quarterback situation, and it was around this time that the thirty-eight-year-old Morrall was placed on waivers for $100. At first, Upton Bell, now with the New England Patriots, claimed him but rescinded it at the last minute. That's when Shula acted.

He went to Robbie and made his case for bringing in the aging quarterback. By now, Robbie was a rich man. His team was making a $2 million in profits, and he had bought out many shares of the unhappy investors. Still sometimes oddly tight-fisted, he often gave Shula what he wanted, sometimes with a fight. Shula looked at Robbie, awaiting an answer. There was "just one problem," Shula pointed out.

"What's that?" asked the owner.

"He makes $75,000," said Shula, knowing it would be among the highest salaries on the team

Robbie shrugged. "Sign him."

When he arrived at the Dolphins' training camp, he noticed that there was still joking and grousing among players, but they treated it not as a game, but as a 9-to-5 job. Yes, they still went out for a beer afterward, but they were all business during the week. They treated the game as professionals, something oddly different from what he was used to. He liked the new upstart team, and was glad he had made the decision to sign up rather than retire.

The key addition Shula made was the acquisition of Marlin Briscoe from the Buffalo Bills.

Marlin Oliver Briscoe had been the first starting black quarterback in the old AFL while with the Denver Broncos. He was later converted to a receiver by the Buffalo Bills and led the league in several receiving categories in 1970. Shula had traded his top pick in the 1973 college draft to Buffalo in exchange for Briscoe, who would lead the team in touchdown receptions for the next two seasons.

The Dolphins and Bills also made a straight-up trade of Buffalo defensive lineman Jim Dunaway for reserve Miami linebacker Dale Farley. Dunaway had been a solid defensive tackle for the Bills for nine seasons, and Shula wanted to continue to bolster his defensive line.

In training camp, Mercury Morris responded to Shula's challenge. Morris worked harder and played more in the preseason games of 1972. Morris changed dramatically, becoming serious about football.

"I liked that new attitude. We all did," said Griese. Morris led the team in rushing during the preseason. It was a portent of things to come.

"He was prepared both mentally and physically. His desire was rampant," said Shula. It was obvious to everyone that Morris would make a difference. But Shula knew he had his work cut out for him. Larry Csonka and Jim Kiick were established pros and, by now, celebrities. Getting them to buy in would be difficult. He tried to explain the three-back system to Csonka and Kiick; it got an icy reception. All three backs and the press wanted to know who the starters were and who the reserve was, and Shula told them there was no such thing. The starting combination would be dictated by the defense they were playing that week.

Kiick especially didn't like it. He was the one who stood to lose the most carries. Kiick and Shula had it out during training camp. As usual, Kiick resented the running that Shula required to get in shape. One day, Kiick quit the 12-minute run after about eight minutes. Csonka knelt beside his friend. Shula approached quickly, and Kiick claimed he had the flu.

"What the hell are you doing, trying to defy me in front of everyone?" growled Shula.

"Shula was the one who stuck it to me," Kiick later said. Csonka concurred, saying, "The way I saw it, Shula handed Merc the opportunity at Jim's expense."

And that was the beginning of the end. It was a long streak of rebellious behavior for the running back from New Jersey. One day, Shula complimented Kiick on having a particularly crisp practice, and Kiick noted that the temperature had dropped from 90 to 60 degrees.

"That's what cold weather does for me," Kiick smiled.

"You like cold weather, eh? You really like to play football in cold weather?" asked Shula.

"I love cold weather. I really love it," Kiick responded.

"I know what you're hinting at, I know all about your calling [Joe] Namath and asking him to tell Weeb Ewbank that you wanted to be traded to the Jets when you were holding out. As soon as Joe talked to him, Weeb called me up. I know all about it," said a fuming Shula. Kiick just grinned at him, taunting him.

When the Dolphins played the Jets at Shea Stadium, Kiick's friends from Lincoln Park came to the game. They brought a sign that read: "Run Kiick or Trade Shula."

"The sign infuriated Shula for three days. It made Kiick happy," according to Howard Cosell.

On another occasion, Kiick had complained to the press that he hated practice. Shula confronted him, saying that he was quoted like he was talking to the whole team. The two began arguing over how many players actually liked to practice. When Kiick pointed out that Shula had played for Weeb, whose practice were known to be less strenuous, Shula was hot.

"You wouldn't win," hollered Shula.

"All right. You made my point. But that doesn't mean I have to like it," said Kiick emphatically.

So, when he told Shula he couldn't finish the run, Shula had had enough.

That was the day Kiick lost his job and Mercury Morris got his shot. From there, the three-back system was guaranteed.

"I was always—I'm not going to say rebellious—but I guess I sort of was," Kiick said. "I liked to do things my way, and I did it. I can understand Coach Shula is the head coach, because we never got along back then. I get along with him fine now."

"He said I had an attitude, and I probably did, because I wanted to play more," Kiick said. "I told Shula, 'You and Csonka have a lot in common. You're both from Ohio, you're both Hungarian, and you're both ugly.' He probably didn't like that."

"There's all kinds of things that could have happened there," Csonka said. "It could have been racial. It could have been egos over who was starting. Instead, they both came to work because the three of us got together and talked about it a little bit. Never really directly set down and addressed any of those subjects in their entirety, head-on. We just got together and decided we were willing to do whatever it took to win."

But in reality, the three-back system worked. Yes, Kiick had fewer touches in 1972, but the team prospered immensely. And it was not just Shula who liked the idea. More important, both Griese and Morrall bought into it.

"Shula began using situation substitution in its most elementary ways in 1972," said Griese. "I used hand signals to bring in the players I wanted." Griese added that if Kiick and Csonka were unhappy during the season, "I never saw it. It didn't get in the way of their work or our winning."

As the 1972 season went on, it was not unusual to see Kiick or Morris outside Shula's door if they had been lightly used the week before. Shula had a balancing act to perform and met with his stars on a weekly basis to listen to their complaints about not playing. The press constantly asked the two backs who was starting, and how the other player felt about not playing. Shula tried to make sure he balanced it out as much as possible. And the same thing was done with receivers as the team juggled Paul Warfield, Howard Twilley, and Marlin Briscoe. The idea was to take advantage of the players' skills that best fit the situation. By adding Morris and Briscoe, the Dolphins would be an offensive juggernaut. As Shula said a year later, "If switching players was new to those of us running the offense in 1972, it was entirely unrecognized by the defenses playing against us."

The other big change was the defense that became popularly known as the "No-Name Defense."

"We're the No-Name Defense, and we're proud of it," Nick Buoniconti said during the season. "Nobody has been able to give us a nickname. We love it that way. We enjoy being anonymous. We don't need a nickname. I hope we never get one."

"[Tom] Landry unintentionally nicknamed the Miami defense. When asked about the Miami defensive unit, he complimented it, and then added that it was 'a bunch of no-named guys.' The Dolphins and the sporting press had a field day, and the nickname 'No-Name Defense' was born," wrote Dave Anderson in the *New York Times*.

"We just call it our 53 defense," said Shula. "That's because 53 is Bob Matheson's number."

Defensive coach Bill Arsparger used Matheson, a linebacker, to replace Jim Dunaway, a tackle. Matheson had played the line before. He became an instant threat. He could line up as a down lineman, or stand up like a linebacker. At the same time, Lloyd Mumphord, a defensive back, replaced Mike Kolen, a linebacker, giving the defense a lot of flexibility. It confused offenses, double-teamed dangerous receivers, and allowed for a solid run defense.

Arnsparger was "a trailblazer who practically invented the dual-purpose edge-rusher that has become the backbone of every hybrid playbook in the league. It was that creation that kick-started the zone blitz as a viable tactic in NFL circles. It began with Arnsparger using linebacker Bob Matheson at end. He could drop or rush," wrote sportswriter James Duko. "When he subbed in Matheson, Arnsparger was also giving the league its first taste of the 3–4 defense."

"There's a direct line from the '53 defense,' so named for the situational use of No. 53, linebacker Bob Matheson, as a fourth linebacker in the early 1970s to the modern 3–4 defenses teams began using later that decade," David J. Neal wrote in the *Miami Herald*.

"But the impact of the 53 scheme went further than the 3–4. It was a new way to bring pressure. The foundation was a deceptive mix of rush and coverage, and defensive responsibilities were disguised until the last second," added Duko.

"He pioneered situational substitutions with the '53' defense that changed the way the game was played on that side of the ball," Shula later said.

"He never cut the picture of a commanding, jaw-jutting football coach like Shula. Balding and bespectacled, Arnsparger was a quiet football professor. Howard Schnellenberger rode to work with him in their Dolphins days," wrote *Sun Sentinel* reporter Dave Hyde.

"I'd say, 'Good morning,' and some days he'd answer," Schnellenberger said. "Other days he was already too deep into his thinking about football."

Arnsparger was not much on sartorial splendor. The running joke within the organization was his often-mismatched clothes. "Nice outfit," safety Zac Henderson once said to Arnsparger about his ensemble one day during training camp. The next day, Henderson was gone.

"He never asked you to do something you couldn't," offered cornerback Tim Foley. Foley couldn't run fast, and so Arnsparger never placed him in a situation where Foley would be exposed.

The Dolphins were now ready for the 1972 season. But there would be bumps along the way.

They opened the season at the new Arrowhead Stadium against the Kansas City Chiefs in a rematch of their epic playoff game. The Dolphins went into the fourth quarter leading, 20–3, and went on to win, 20–10. The game was never in doubt. They beat the Houston Oilers in Miami, 34–13, and then were trailing the Vikings at Metropolitan Stadium by eight points late in the fourth quarter, before scoring the game's last 10 points.

"One of my biggest memories was in the third game, we were playing the Vikings, and we were losing 14–6, and there was three and a half minutes to go. And coach Shula, with three and a half minutes to go, he sends me out for a 51-yard field goal. I lined up for it, but I had never kicked that far. But then, I started to think that if he has this much faith in me, I might as well have that much faith in myself," recalled Garo Yepremian. The Dolphins capped it off with a 3-yard touchdown pass from Griese to tight end Jim Mandich for the winning score. They then cruised to a 27–17 win over the Jets in New York.

And then they encountered what could have been a disaster but instead became one of its great surprises. In the first quarter of their game with the San Diego Chargers at the Orange Bowl, Griese went down with a broken ankle. Replacing him would be the thirty-nine-year-old backup Earl Morrall.

The young Dolphins players, and even many veterans, called Morrall "The Old Man." Even the Dolphins equipment manager, instead of placing a folding chair in front of his cubicle, placed a rocking chair there for the wizened quarterback. "And if he wasn't the first guy off the field, by the time he got to his locker, there was always someone else sitting in that chair—me, Zonk, Mercury, or one of the defensive guys. But Earl didn't care—he just laughed and pulled out a folding chair for himself. That's the kind of person he was—always a team guy," said Griese.

The other Dolphins players would routinely steal the chair. Morrall would get undressed and yell, "I'm going into the shower. That chair better be back when I return." It always was.

In a time when shaggy long hair was the norm, Morrall still wore the same identical crew cut he wore in the '50s and '60s. Bill Stanfill, the defensive end, used to tease Earl, saying, "Your hair's getting a little long, Earl. You better get it trimmed."

"If [Earl] had a tip when I was playing and he was on the sideline, he would always make it a point to come up to me and let me know what he saw. And it was the same way when I was hurt and he was playing. He would always come over to me when things weren't going well and would always ask what I saw or what he was missing. We had a great relationship, and we were a better team because of it," added Griese.

Shula stood there, looking at Griese on the ground, thinking, *Get up. Please,*

Dear God, make him get up. But it was not to be. Shula then said to Morrall, "It's all up to you now, Earl."

Morrall approached the huddle. There were a lot of bewildered eyes. Morrall looked at everyone and just said, "Let's just keep it going." He was so confident, and the team easily responded. He threw two touchdown passes that game, and the Dolphins won, 24–10. The team didn't miss a beat.

Defensive end Bill Stanfill said: "Earl was a lot more personable than Bob. No doubt about it, Bob had the best ability, but Earl might have just gone in and sparked the team."

Morrall said about Griese, "He's a great, great individual. He broke his ankle so I could play."

As Shula himself said years later, "There wouldn't have been an undefeated season and the World Championship if it wasn't for Earl." Shula once joked, "I never had to give him a pregame speech. We were always playing a team that had cut Earl. I'd say [to the team], 'We gotta get back at these guys because look what they did to poor Earl.'" He also added, "Earl was the worst practice quarterback I ever had. He couldn't hit anybody. Then you put him in the game, and all he ever does is make the plays to help you win."

They played the Bills next and won that one, trading late touchdowns, and held on to win, 24–23. They followed that by crushing the Colts (23–0), the Bills again (30–16), and the Patriots (52–0) as Shula became the first coach to win 100 games in his first 10 seasons in the NFL. They beat the Jets, 28–24, but the last Jets score came when the game was more or less decided. The Dolphins then rolled over the Cardinals, 31–10, in a Monday night game; beat the Patriots (again), 37–21, and the Giants (23–13); and blanked the Colts, 16–0, for their 14th win to complete a perfect regular season.

Csonka gained 1,117 yards that season, fourth best in the NFL. Morris gained exactly 1,000 yards and led the league with 12 touchdowns. Morrall had the best passer rating. The Dolphins scored more points, 385, than any other team in the NFL, and their defense surrendered 171 points, the fewest in the league. Miami amassed 5,036 yards, best in the league, and gave up 3,297 yards, the fewest in the league. In passing, they were only 16th out of 26 teams.

Up until 1972, there had been two undefeated, untied regular seasons in NFL history—the 1934 and 1942 Chicago Bears (they lost the NFL championship both times). The 2011 New England Patriots finished the regular season the same way but also failed to win the championship, losing the Super Bowl to the New York

Giants. The only untied, undefeated, championship team in professional football was the 1948 Cleveland Browns, then of the All-America Football Conference (AAFC), but the NFL did not recognize their records. Could the Dolphins finish this season undefeated? This one wasn't just for the trophy—they were building a legend.

The first real test of the season came from the Cleveland Browns in the AFC divisional playoffs on Christmas Eve. Cleveland took a 14–13 lead in the fourth quarter, giving the undefeated team a big scare. The Dolphins were struggling. It was eventually Warfield, who caught two passes for 50 yards and drew a pass interference call that set up Kiick for the touchdown, who put the Dolphins over the top, 20–14. In this game, each back had almost the same number of carries, with Morris (72) and Kiick (50) gaining the most yards.

"I got great blocking," Kiick said of the winning score. "Bob Kuechenberg pulled, Norm Evans turned the defensive end, and Larry Csonka got the cornerback. I had a big hole, but it was the same play that I fumbled on before, so I covered the ball with two hands. Nobody likes to fumble, especially at a crucial time," Kiick said. "But, at least, I was able to make up for it later."

The Dolphins were then three-point favorites over the young, but up-and-coming, Pittsburgh Steelers, coached by Shula's former assistant Chuck Noll, in the AFC Championship Game in the Steel City on December 31. The game was tied, 7–7, at halftime. It was there that Shula made his big switch. As he had gone to Unitas too late in 1969, he would not make that same mistake in 1972.

"You did a good job, but we're going to go with Bob," Shula told Morrall. Up to that point, Griese was resigned to be the backup, as Morrall had held the hot hand. But Shula made the switch. Morrall said, "A young guy might have created waves. Being a little older, I wasn't going to sit there and sulk. I knew from experience that we had to win that game because if we didn't, the whole season would go down the drain."

In Griese's first huddle, it was abuzz with voices and panic. "Watch the offside now," one player warned. "Ram the ball down their throats," another said. Griese snapped at all of them, commanding, "Shut up." And when they were quiet and looking at him, he said. "Let's get this drive going."

"That's the mark of a leader," Morris said. "That was his way of telling us to be cool."

"Guys were talking all at once," said Csonka. "He just said it once, that's all he had to."

By the fourth quarter, with Griese at the controls, the Dolphins were up, 21–10, and though they gave up a fourth-quarter touchdown, they held on for a hard-fought 21–17 victory. It had easily been the toughest game of the year. Later that day, George Allen's Washington Redskins, nicknamed "The Over-the-Hill Gang," defeated the defending Super Bowl champion Dallas Cowboys in the NFC Championship Game, 26–3.

Despite their undefeated season thus far, oddsmakers anointed the Redskins a three-point favorite. Several writers argued that the Miami schedule had been week, and that the Redskins had knocked off the much tougher team to get to the big game.

Super Bowl VII would be held at the Los Angeles Coliseum on January 14, 1973, and the media hype leading up to it was hot. Allen had mortgaged the team's future draft choices for a win-now mentality. His motto became "The future is now." The Redskins were the oldest team in the league.

"We've got a bunch of guys people wrote off as too old, too slow, and too heavy," Allen said. "Nobody wanted 'em."

According to Nick Buoniconti, "[Larry] Brown running out of their I-formation is a problem. He can make his cuts anywhere he wants into the seams. The game will be decided in those two yards of the scrimmage line. If we get pushed back, we're in trouble. We'll beat them some of the time and they'll beat us some of the time."

In the *New York Times*, Dave Anderson opined, "The common observation has been that Morris, running to the outside, made the Dolphins a much more formidable team than a year ago when they meekly lost the last Super Bowl to the Dallas Cowboys, 24–3. Mercury's contribution to the team's 16-game undefeated streak this season was considerable."

Redskins outside linebacker Chris Hanburger said of Morris, "We've got to get to him early before he turns upfield, before he can cut and run against the grain. You don't want a fellow like that running loose beyond the pursuit."

Many writers pointed out that the Redskins had handled power backs like Csonka before, especially John Brockington of Green Bay. As Anderson pointed out, "It is the spectre of speed, Mercury's, which frightens them. As for the Dolphins, their respect for the indefatigable Brown carrying at least 20 times is huge. No one really stops Larry Brown."

And there was a healthy respect for the formidable coach Allen. "It is not necessarily coincidental that the Watergate incident occurred in Washington after

George Allen became the Redskin coach. He has a reputation as master spy," wrote Anderson, who pointed out that the Jets didn't practice at Shea Stadium the week they played the Redskins, but at nearby Rikers Island.

"Let's see Allen sneak somebody in there," Weeb Ewbank said.

Several days before the Super Bowl, commissioner Pete Rozelle had announced two fines against Allen. He had traded away the same draft choices twice to acquire players he wanted. According to Rozelle, the move was "unprecedented." He had also traded a player without disclosing that the player was injured. There were a number of running jokes at Allen's expense that he was the favorite coach of President Richard Nixon. Shula and Joe Robbie were so sure of Allen's penchant for spying, they moved their training facility to a community college and had Dolphins employees scout the trees and shrubs for possible Allen spies.

What was scary about this Super Bowl was this: the teams were virtually the same. They both had vicious, opportunistic defenses; conservative, bone crushing offenses; and their coaches were fairly evenly matched—Shula's record against Allen was 4–3–1. They both believed in repetition and perfection. And Allen had his own quarterback situation like Shula had experienced in Baltimore, replacing popular star Sonny Jurgensen with Billy Kilmer. Allen only cared about winning, rarely smiled, and ate vanilla ice cream by the bucketful. He was uptight and prickly with the press and his staff and squad.

Allan was the ultimate control freak. He cocooned his players, distancing them from the rest of the organization, owner, and press. He was a stern taskmaster but was well known for leading his players in the three cheers for the Redskins in the locker room before each game.

"Can you imagine me leading Larry Csonka in singing 'Three Cheers for the Dolphins'?" Shula said.

In one of the press conferences in the week leading up to the game, Allen had told the sportswriters that the Miami Dolphins were the finest team of all time. It was an old coaching ploy. Shula began his conference the next day, saying, "I think they [the Redskins] are the finest team we've ever . . ." And then he and the press corps laughed.

"I don't care about winning the press conferences," said relaxed Shula, making small jokes with reporters. "I want to win the game."

And that was one of the main differences between the Dolphins of the previous year and the current undefeated team. After they had lost to the Cowboys, one of the Dallas players had stated that the Dolphins were just happy to be there, but the Cowboys, having lost the previous year, were there to win it. And so were the Miami Dolphins this year. They were loose, but serious.

The game plan was simple. Stop Larry Brown and the Redskins' running game, and force Billy Kilmer to pass. Defensive tackle Manny Fernandez was charged with clogging up the middle. On offense, they wanted to do the same things they had all year—run the ball inside and outside, and pass with precision. Washington was also dedicated to stopping Miami's run and would double-team Paul Warfield all day.

"Bill Arnsparger came into the defensive meeting room after we beat the Steelers in the 1972 AFC Championship Game," remembered Jake Scott. "I want you guys to forget everything I ever taught you," said Arnsparger. "We're not going to lose this game like we did last year [in Super Bowl VI] by sitting back. We're going to go after them."

"That certainly woke us up. He changed the whole defense for the Super Bowl and clogged up the middle of the field," said Scott. "Clogging up the middle of the field was really the key to our win because Larry Brown was a cutback runner and Billy Kilmer was a play-action passer who always threw slants to Roy Jefferson or Charley Taylor. Arnsparger didn't have us play soft that day. He played real aggressive defense, and that's why Fernandez had a great game and I had a good one."

The Apollo 17 crew, the last astronauts to land on the moon, were feted before the game, and the University of Michigan Marching Band performed. The Little Angels of Chicago's Angels Church performed the National Anthem. Neither Allen nor Shula wore a coat or tie. It was the first time in history neither coach would wear one. It was 84 degrees at the time of kickoff, the warmest Super Bowl temperature in history.

Miami won the toss and elected to receive. Nothing happened. Both defenses were stout, and the two teams traded two punts each. Then, late in the first quarter, Miami broke out. Kiick contributed 11 yards on consecutive runs, and then Griese completed a pass to Warfield that brought the Dolphins to the Redskins' 34-yard line. Two more runs, and then Griese hit Howard Twilley for his only catch of the day, a 28-yard touchdown. Twilley had faked going inside and then cut back the other way, leaving defensive back Pat Fischer behind by a few steps. It was enough separation for a score. With Garo Yepremian's extra point, the score was 7–0 going into the second quarter.

Most of the second quarter saw the two teams again trading punts. Toward the end of the quarter, Bouniconti intercepted a Kilmer pass in Miami territory and raced it back upfield the other way to the Washington 27-yard line. Consecutive runs by Csonka and Kiick were followed by a Griese-to-Mandich pass that put the Dolphins at the Redskins 2-yard line. Then Csonka and Larry Little blasted a hole that Kiick went through, and the Dolphins were up, 14–0.

The game turned deadly dull in the second half as it became a defensive struggle. Washington made a drive into Miami territory that was wasted with a failed field goal. Another Washington drive was thwarted by a Scott interception in the fourth quarter. Later in the quarter, Miami had driven far enough for Garo Yepremian to attempt a field goal and put the game completely out of reach. Garo had noticed that his first two kicks that day were of low trajectory, but both had been good. The Dolphins lined up with 2:07 on the clock. The field-goal attempt was blocked by Bill Brundige, and Yepremian, instead of falling on the ball, picked it up and started to run. He then decided to throw the ball, attempting the most awkward pass in NFL history. The ball went nowhere but up, then bobbled, and then Redskins cornerback Mike Bass plucked it from the air and raced down the sideline for a touchdown. With the kick, it made the score 14–7. It was one of the most infamous and bizarre blooper plays in Super Bowl history, and it is still known as Garo's Gaffe.

"I honestly felt as if my life was over," says Yepremian. "I never, ever had been disappointed like that in my life. Goodness, I felt as if it was the end. Norm Evans, the spiritual leader of the Dolphins, said, 'Don't worry, God is with you.' That was the best thing that ever happened to me, to have that encouragement from a friend. If the other team scored, and it would have went to overtime, that would've haunted me for the rest of my life."

"I took a negative, and I turned it into a positive," said Yepremian. "That happened in 1972, and I played ten years after that. I could have taken it as a negative, and I could have then made a failure out of myself. But I persevered, and I was voted kicker of the decade of the '70s."

When Yepremian returned to the bench, there was dead silence. A fuming Shula greeted him, "You should have fallen on the damn ball!" Many on the bench realized what it had meant. It might have been the only shutout in Super Bowl history. "I mean here we are out there, bleeding through every pore of our bodies. . . . I don't want to talk about it. I get too mad," said guard Bob Kuechenberg.

"There's not a day in my life someone doesn't mention it," said Garo years later.

Everyone thought an onside kick would ensue, but Allen ordered a deep kick.

The Redskins defense held, and Washington got the ball back with a little more with a minute left. But the Redskins offense stalled, as it had all day, and the game ended with Kilmer sacked for a nine-yard loss by Dolphins defensive lineman Vern Den Herder.

Kilmer completed six more passes than Griese (14 to 8) but also threw three picks. Said Kilmer, "I wasn't sharp at all. Good as their defense is, I still should have thrown better." Larry Csonka was the game's leading rusher, carrying 15 times for 112 yards. Kiick had gained 38 yards, caught two passes, and scored a touchdown. Morris picked up 34 yards. On the defensive side, Manny Fernandez had a monster game, amassing 11 solo tackles and six assists. Safety Jake Scott intercepted two passes and was named Super Bowl MVP. Larry Brown was held to 72 yards on 22 rushing attempts. Don Shula had finally won the big one.

"All along I've had an empty feeling," admitted Shula afterward in the winners' locker room, "of not having accomplished the ultimate. And this right here," he said, tapping the Vince Lombardi Trophy for the National Football League championship, which had been presented to him moments before by Commissioner Pete Rozelle, "is the ultimate."

"I hadn't done too well in my first two [Super Bowl games], as a lot of people kept reminding me," he said. "We weren't thinking about being 13–0, 15–0, or 16–0," Shula said. "We were only thinking about being 17–0, like right now."

It was the lowest-scoring Super Bowl of all time. As pro football historian Michael MacCambridge has pointed out, "Miami would be all too representative of its era—using a conservative offense that passed sparingly, and stifling opponents with a defense that choked the run, and a zone that thwarted long passes." He added that the Dolphins were adding to the thickening of the game, at the exact time Rozelle and the owners were highlighting the passing game and exciting moments to sell tickets and television packages. "The result made for boring football. The 1972 season saw 114 fewer touchdowns than 1966, but 141 more field goals."

Shula had been named Coach of the Year five times in his career, and had won more than 100 games in only 10 NFL seasons. No one had accomplished what he had. He had been to three Super Bowls. No one else had done that. He was finally atop the football world. He could turn his back on the sneers of those who said he couldn't win the big one. A "great weight had been lifted." He could shrug off the quips of Carroll Rosenbloom.

"At least I've proved I can win the big one to some people," he said.

In April 1973, the last critic was silenced. The spring NFL meetings were held in Scottsdale, Arizona, that year. The meetings were held at the lush Camelback Inn. It was then that Klosterman attempted a reconciliation between the two.

"Carroll was bitter about it," Klosterman said. "Don always tried to put his hand out, tried to forgive and forget. But Carroll wouldn't do it. Carroll used to always get upset when I talked about Don. We had some heated arguments. Carroll wouldn't want to admit that Don was a great coach. Then I'd say, 'Look at his record,' and Carroll couldn't argue with that."

Klosterman asked Don if he would meet with Carroll. "When does he want to get together?"

"Any time you say," said Klosterman. Shula suggested the next morning before the meetings began. Klosterman agreed. Ironically, they met in the Peace Pipe Room.

Klosterman said to the both of them, "Why don't the both of you shake hands and get all these things that have been happening between you in the past out of the way."

Shula stuck out his hand and said nothing; Carroll reached out saying, "Don, let bygones be bygones."

"That's OK with me, but an awful lot has happened in the last three years," said Shula.

They chatted some more, and Rosenbloom said, "You and I had always talked privately together on important matters."

"That's the way it had been. But our relationship had deteriorated in our last year together."

"Well, we don't have to look back at the past anymore," said Rosenbloom. Some more banter, and it ended with Shula saying, "I'm glad we had the opportunity to finally sit down and talk."

"It was strange sitting there talking to Rosenbloom again after not having done so for over three years. At least we opened up lines of communication," said Shula not long after.

Klosterman would get them together again in 1976, again effecting a more meaningful reconciliation. "I'm happy we did end up with a good relationship because he meant a lot to me and my success. He had the guts to hire me as a young assistant."

"The thrill for Dorothy Shula was to see Don settle into his chair at night and watch the peace on his face, wrote sportswriter John Underwood. 'He'd light up a big cigar, and sit there, and I'm thinking, *Happy at last.* For so long he'd been so sensitive. Small, petty things would bother him. He'd have to take out his energy on something. Lately it had been the garage. When he had nothing else to do he'd raise a storm and clean out the garage,'" said Dorothy.

Indeed, Dorothy had become local celebrity based on her charity work, and being the coach's wife. But she saw him sparingly. They were popular guests at dinners, which usually rankled Shula during the season. Once, Dorothy was asked if it wasn't unusual for the coach to be having dinner out on a week night at the Miami Club back in October of 1970 when the coach was glad-handing fans and local bankers and club partners.

"I'll say it is," she told a reporter. "This is the first time we've been out socially, at any time of week during a football season, since Don became a head coach eight years ago!"

"Don't get me wrong. He never said 'no' to anything. Our cup runneth over. I mean, this has been a woman happy. But to see him happy. At breakfast he always has coffee, black. Grapefruit, cut up. Eggs and sausage. Early. Ordinarily I get up and do it and it's just the two of us. I do it, but don't expect me to say 'good morning' when I do. Well, after the Super Bowl, I'd get up and he'd already have the coffee made. And sometimes he'd even be cutting his own grapefruit."

Shula's other passion, aside from his children and his dog, then named Colt (who was named when the family was living in Baltimore), was his unabashed affair with golf. *Sports Illustrated* reporter John Underwood wrote of Shula's passion in a 1973 profile, "As for his golf, it speaks quietly for itself. It is no small love affair he has for the game. The lawn of his five-bedroom, $150,000 home bleeds onto the 16th fairway of the Miami Lakes Country Club. Shula, in the off-season, applies to golf his customary intensity. At 43, he is still solidly built, with the blocky abdomen and thorax that serve a man well for long-ball hitting and/or dock work. But he does not get his hips into his swing and therefore hits a lot of pop flies. He is undaunted. He admits he once sliced a shot into the men's room, and if he does not scream—he has a reputation as a screamer that is deserved—over a missed putt he is likely to squirm. Jim Kiick, the halfback, took him for $10 in a friendly Nassau this summer. Kiick said Shula was too proud to take the handicap he deserved."

"As a golfer, he is much more the carpenter than the cabinet maker, doggedly chopping away at the Miami Lakes and other courses near his home," wrote Dolphins historian Morris McLemore. "To him, golf apparently serves as a quiet time for noodling problems, for picking at his own mind and deciding things. A good man at the nineteenth hole and usually a talkative one with friends." He enjoyed telling jokes, and needling friends.

According to John Steadman, quoted in Underwood's article, "We were at the par-3 12th hole at Bonnie View, in the midst of a very serious match. I think a $1 Nassau. I had a putt of about two feet for a par. Less than two feet. I lined it up, but I was really expecting him to say, 'It's good.' I stood over it a long time," recalled Steadman. "Finally I pulled up and said, 'It takes a real fucking asshole to make a guy putt one this short.' Shula came right back at me. 'It takes a real fucking asshole to ask for it.' You want to know what makes Shula tick? Try fierce competitor."

Before the start of the 1973 preseason, "Shula played a round of golf with his old coaching friend and Dolphin predecessor, George Wilson, at Wilson's golf course on North Kendall Drive. It was a hot day; they hacked around the course keeping a small gallery sweating after them," wrote Underwood. Golf had helped them to bury their issues, as well.

Then training camp began. The sign outside Shula's office read, "I'm just a guy who rolls up his sleeves and goes to work." And his message to the team was simple. Get to a third Super Bowl. Lombardi's Packers had only been their twice. They had the opportunity to go to three straight Super Bowls. No one had ever done that.

"He's even more serious than he was last year," Csonka told Edwin Pope that season. "More determined to go back. I could just see his metabolism speeding up, his eyes getting buggy and his hairline jerking the way it does once in a while. All the signs are there. It takes a Hunky to catch one .... He is no rah-rah guy. Even his pep talks make sense."

The 1973 season started with a come-from-behind win against the San Francisco 49ers at home at the Orange Bowl. The 49ers were leading, 13–6, when the Dolphins fought back during a game where the temperature was 105 degrees. There were 11,755 no-shows for their home opener due to the extreme heat.

"I expect some no-shows, but not that many. It was too hot," Robbie told the press.

The 49ers quarterback John Brodie had torched the Dolphins defense in the first half, but they bent and did not break. Griese started the fourth-quarter barrage with a 10-yard scoring pass to Paul Warfield. Yepremian added a 45-yard field goal, then Miami scored a safety for another two points. And Garo added the final nail in the coffin, a 22-yard field goal, making the final score 21–13. Their 18th consecutive victory tied a league record. "The defense and Garo kept us in the game until the offense got going," said Shula after the game.

The next game was against John Madden's Oakland Raiders. With the Oakland Coliseum unavailable due to baseball, the game was played at California Memorial Stadium on the campus of the University of California in Berkeley. The Raiders defense was stifling, and George Blanda, the wizened Raider kicker, was deadly. Blanda kicked four field goals, and the defense stopped everything the Miami offense tried to do. The Dolphins had uncharacteristically fumbled twice. And the punting of Ray Guy had pinned the Dolphins deep in their territory all day. Miami did score a touchdown in the closing minutes of the contest, but the score was merely cosmetic. The Dolphins were never in this game. The Oakland rushing game almost outgained the entire Dolphin output. The Oakland Raiders had snapped the Dolphins' winning streak, 12–7.

"I hate to talk about losing," said Shula afterward, "but give Oakland and John Madden [the Raiders' coach] all the credit in the world. Their defense controlled our offense, it didn't make any mistakes, and their offense didn't get a touchdown, but it controlled the ball. Their offensive line and running backs played well. They established their running game, and they stopped us."

The Dolphins bounced back the next week on the shoulders of Mercury Morris, who bolted out of Shula's doghouse for his two fumbles (and two dropped passes) against the 49ers in the opening game. They crushed the Patriots, 44–23, behind Morris's 197 yards on 15 carries. Morris had three big runs of 70, 35, and 24 yards.

"I had a lot of people in front of me, that's why I had such an outstanding day," explained Morris. "All three runs came on a basic play. It was nothing new. Everybody executed the way they should have."

This was the start of a ten-game run. In order, they beat the Patriots, Jets, Browns, Bills, Patriots, Jets, Colts, Bills, Cowboys, and Steelers.

The biggest game of the regular season was a rematch of Super Bowl VI, pitting the Dolphins against the Cowboys on Thanksgiving Day. Csonka rushed for 80 grueling yards, and Morris bounded for another 49 to lead the Miami attack. The Dolphins struck first, by scoring two touchdowns in the first quarter (a Csonka 1-yard plunge and a Griese-to-Warfield pass good for 45 yards) to post a 14–0 lead. Despite a fourth-quarter touchdown run by Dallas's Walt Garrison, the game was never in doubt. The Dolphins were methodical in their beating of the Cowboys. Csonka figured prominently, pounding away at the Dallas defense.

"He's so strong," Lee Roy Jordan, the Cowboys linebacker and defensive captain, said of Csonka. "You stop him for three yards and that's a feat. Then he falls down for two more."

After beating the Steelers, scoring 30 first-half points and holding on to win, 30–26, they came up against the 3–10 Baltimore Colts on a rainy December day at Memorial Stadium. The Colts had fallen on hard times and were seemingly facing the daunting task of toppling the 11–1 Dolphins. Howard Schnellenberger was now the Baltimore head coach, a reward of being a coordinator on a Super Bowl–winning team. Few thought the Colts had much to offer. With Griese sitting out with an injury, Earl Morrall went to work on a muddy and rain-soaked field. Morrall completed 11 of 22 passes and Csonka gained 70 yards, but Morris was held to only 7, and the porous Colts defense suddenly became very stout. The Colts scored in each of the first three periods, with Morrall throwing two interceptions. Baltimore defeated Miami, 16–3.

But the Detroit Lions came to Miami at just the right time, and the Dolphins fed on the carcass of yet another losing Lions team, now led by former Colts head coach Don McCafferty, who finished 6–7–1 that year. They beat the Lions, 34–7, to finish with a 12–4 record. Griese and Warfield played pitch-and-catch, hooking up for four touchdowns.

Their first-round playoff opponent was the Cincinnati Bengals, who were established in 1968 and led by Shula's old mentor, Paul Brown. With a record of 10–4, the AFC Central champions featured a stellar quarterback in Kenny Anderson and a handful of star players including wide receiver Isaac Curtis and tight end Bob Trumpy. The Dolphins boasted 11 Pro Bowlers. Both teams featured strong running games, slick passing, and stout defense. The first half was a contest, and the upstart Bengals traded body blows with the Dolphins, with the Dolphins going into halftime leading only by five points at 21–16.

"While the Hessians heaved and snorted, master and pupil prowled the sidelines each according to his style. The emotional Shula, hatless, coatless and short-sleeved, moved with the flow of action, stopped to glower down at the synthetic turf with bare arms folded, crouched with hands on knees as though to spring," wrote famed New York sports scribe Red Smith. "Outwardly impressive, Brown was a remote figure in a dark business suit, staring out from the shade of a hat brim pulled low. He might have been an inspector of homicide viewing the body." Cincinnati's defense had been the difference in the first half. The Bengals were holding their own. But the Miami defense rose up in the second half, the offense went on a small spree, and the final score was 34–16.

"In 1946 when Brown made his first mark on professional football as coach of Cleveland in the All-America Conference, Shula was a 16-year-old high school student in Painesville, Ohio, and five years later Shula was a defensive back for Brown in Cleveland. This sunny, summery afternoon, master and pupil came face-to-face on the ersatz grass of the Orange Bowl. They shook hands solemnly," wrote Smith.

"Congratulations on a fine season," Shula said to Brown. "I'm sorry this had to happen to you."

Buoniconti praised the Bengal attack, saying it was "the most explosive we saw all year. . . . They were using what we call counter influence, sending one back one direction and another the opposite way." But the Dolphins quickly made adjustments.

"This is about as thorough a throttling as our offense has had all year," said Brown. His Bengals had amassed only 194 yards against the Dolphins after averaging 322 a game during the regular season.

"Obviously, we were soundly beaten. We weren't any match for them. They defeated us in every aspect of the game," Brown told the media. And of his former pupil, Brown said, "He is a splendid man with a wonderful team. They gave us a good lesson in football. They're not the world champions for nothing. They've been to the Super Bowl twice. They've got a great football team and they showed it today."

The next step was a little harder, with the Dolphins facing the Oakland Raiders at the Orange Bowl in the AFC Championship Game on December 30. It was clear Shula's players were not happy having their streak ended by the Raiders earlier in the season. "They [the Raiders] have a real big team, but size doesn't necessarily spell a man," said Larry Little, the All-Pro guard. "They beat us up front when we played them. We barely gained 100 yards rushing and they ran over our defense. But it's not going to be that way this time. I guarantee it."

Little was serious. He was born in Groveland, Georgia. He graduated from Bethune-Cookman College in 1967 and was signed as an undrafted free agent with the San Diego Chargers. Shula had turned down Little when he asked for a tryout with the Baltimore Colts in 1967. Shula criticized Little for his excessive weight. Little was traded to the Dolphins in 1969. "I didn't particularly like the trade. The Dolphins weren't much then," Little said later.

"We were poor but we ate well. I never was hungry," Little recalled of his childhood. "I ate more than anybody in the family. If there was any food anyone didn't want, I was around to eat it. When it came to football, we'd play tackle in the street. No equipment. Four, five on a side."

When he joined the Chargers, he began to gain weight at an alarming rate, tipping the scales at nearly 300 pounds. It was during this period that he was traded to Miami. Shula insisted that Little reduce his current weight to 265 pounds, or he would be slapped with a $10 per day per-pound-over-that-weight fine.

"Larry Little had tremendous athletic ability. He needed discipline and he got it," chuckled Shula years later. Little actually collapsed during one training camp. Shula pushed him. "I see the promise of what could be the finest offensive lineman in the game," Shula remarked to an associate at the time. "I saw that Little could be an outstanding pulling guard. We had one of the NFL's best blocking tight ends in Marv Fleming. Both Jim Kiick and Csonka could block as well as run. I got the idea it would be best to go with the run and use the pass as a mixer."

"I like the running plays," Little always said. "It evens up your tools with the defensive man. You can unload on him. I remember Green Bay used to be known for those sweeps. I'd like to think the Dolphins might some day be just as famous."

He was given the nickname "Chicken Little" after he'd eaten two whole chickens during a training camp in San Diego. Csonka was amazed at Little's speed, saying, "I'll be running behind Chicken, who is blocking for me, and suddenly I realize he is pulling away from me. Sometimes I grab hold of his pants to keep up."

"Chicken's a big truck," Kiick added. "When he gets rolling on an end sweep, the traffic suddenly thins out. I feel sorry for the little backs coming up on the play. Larry wipes them out."

Little soon gained enormous respect around the league. "Trying to get around Larry Little is like trying to throw a paper airplane through a mountain," Washington Redskins defensive end Ron McDole said. Larry Little wanted another shot at the Raiders. And his teammates were also still carrying the sting of that loss. "We just didn't play good football, and they had it all together that day," said Mercury Morris. "But think about when they had it all together—they didn't score a touchdown."

The Raiders were stymied on offense, and the Dolphins ground out two touchdowns to take a 14–0 lead into the locker room at haltime. Csonka had crashed in for two rugged scores. He added a third touchdown in the second half, and the Dolphins dispatched the rough-and-tumble Raiders, 27–10. The Dolphins gained 266 yards on the ground.

"I felt the tempo of the game dictated our going with the run," said Griese. "We were prepared to pass more if need be, but you do what's working for you." Griese threw only six passes the entire game, completing three. He ran for 39 yards and only passed for 34.

"He's a quarterback who understands the running game," added Csonka, who received the game ball after rushing for 117 yards.

"This is the damndest team we've played, just the best," said Raiders linebacker Phil Villapiano. "Nobody is supposed to treat us the way they handled our club today. When we were thinking Csonka, they gave the ball to [Mercury] Morris, and vice versa. They just called a great game."

"Two fourth-down plays, with Larry Csonka smashing to a first down at the 1-yard line on one and Dick Anderson forcing Marv Hubbard to fumble near midfield an the other, symbolized the Miami Dolphins' 27–10 domination of the Oakland Raiders," wrote Dave Anderson.

"The fans always want you to go for the first down, but what they might not realize is that the players want to go for it, too. When your coach lets you go for it, it's really exciting. His confidence gives you confidence. And when you do make it, it gives you a big mental lift," said Csonka after the game. "We like that fourth-down situation. We have a lot of hard-working professionals on our line. They like to go right at the defensive linemen and establish themselves. They made it work last year, and they made it work today when we needed it. I had three alternatives, and I picked the right one."

When asked about having to prepare during the holidays for the Super Bowl, Shula responded, "I don't mind working Christmas and New Year's. Our goal is to get it all."

"The Packers are the only team that's won two Super Bowls in a row," said Shula. "The Packers, under Vince Lombardi, were talked about as *the* team in professional football and their consistency was admired by everybody. We'd like to be the team everybody talks about next."

"We've been down that road before where you get there and you don't win," said the coach. He then turned his attention to the NFC champion Minnesota Vikings. "A lot of them have been in the Super Bowl, and some of them have been great All-Pros. They're solid in every department, and they're a team that's very businesslike, very much like the Miami Dolphins. They go about getting the job done. That's why they're in the Super Bowl."

The Minnesota Vikings, led by coach Bud Grant and quarterback Fran Tarkenton, were a formidable team. They featured strong running, and a brutal defense known as the Purple People Eaters. In the NFC Championship Game, their defensive line had stopped the mighty Cowboys flat while their offense had run through the Dallas defense on their way to a 27–10 victory that was really never in doubt.

Los Angeles quarterback John Hadl said, "That front four as a unit is as good as any team that's ever been in the league." The four lineman were Jim Marshall, Alan Page, Carl Eller, and Gary Larsen. Bob Lurtsema was the alternate, usually for Larsen, but was seen as an important member of the defensive line scheme, and a solid contributor.

"Bud Grant is the master builder of the . . . purple in Minneapolis. At 46, he is an almost ascetic figure with a prematurely white flattop haircut and a wiry, svelte body that fairly exudes the proverbial pink of health," wrote Peter Ross Range in the *New York Times* magazine. "Grant thinks the Vikings' secret lies not so much in a uniqueness of system as in a perfection of known skills. His method is (1) science and (2) talent-scouting: 'Our guys are mostly college graduates, they've got more to work with—up here. We can expect them to do things exactly right.'"

Rolling Stone had sent Hunter S. Thompson to Houston to cover the Super Bowl that year. Thompson wrote, "Both Robbie and his coach, Don Shula, seem far more relaxed and given to quick flashes of humor than the kind of militaristic, puritanical jocks and PR men you normally have to deal with on the business/power levels of the NFL. This was just as obvious—especially with Shula—before the game, as well as after it. In stark contrast to Shula, Viking coach Bud Grant spent most of Super Week acting like a Marine Corps drill sergeant with a terminal case of the piles."

Thompson opined about the night before the Super Bowl, writing, "Earlier, before the bar closed, the whole ground floor had been jammed with drunken sportswriters, hard-eyed hookers, wandering geeks and hustlers (of almost every persuasion), and a legion of big and small gamblers from all over the country who roamed through the drunken, randy crowd—as casually as possible—with an eye to picking up a last-minute sucker bet from some poor bastard half-mad on booze and willing to put some money, preferably four or five big ones, on 'his boys.'"

Wrote Tex Maule in *Sports Illustrated*, "Super Bowl VIII had all the excitement and suspense of a master butcher quartering a steer. The slaughterhouse was Houston's Rice Stadium and the butcher was Miami Quarterback Bob Griese, whose deft dismemberment of the Minnesota Vikings may have had a certain esthetic appeal for serious students of the science of football, but left devotees of drama more than a little bored. The suspense in the game, which Miami won 24–7, lasted for five minutes and 27 seconds, which was the time it took Griese to march his Dolphins 62 yards in 10 plays after the opening kickoff. Most of the drive was predicated on the ability of the Miami offensive line to shunt aside the Minnesota defenders, especially Middle Linebacker Jeff Siemon, who was attacked by a bewildering variety of blockers."

On first and goal at the Vikings 5-yard line, the Dolphins guards, Bob Kuechenberg and Larry Little, pulled as if to imitate the famous Packer sweep to the right. One back went with the guards, as the Miami team looked to attempt a student body right. But the give was to Csonka, who blew through the middle. He rumbled in for the score.

"Griese asked me what I wanted," Csonka related. "I said X block to the left and the Roll Right, Trap Left. We proceeded to run that play into the ground," said Csonka. "We took advantage of their aggression. They stunted themselves out of the play several times. On my touchdown on the first drive, I started wide, then looked for a place to cut back. They went with the guards and left me a big hole to cut back through."

"I knew we were in trouble after their first drive. They didn't do anything we didn't expect. They ran the plays we saw in the movies and they blocked well. They did the things that got them here, we didn't," said Grant after the game. "They controlled the line of scrimmage both ways. There's no secrecy about this thing. They blocked well and they tackled well. If you don't do that, you're in trouble."

The rest of the game was a forgone conclusion. Csonka, voted the game's Most Valuable Player, carried 33 times for 145 yards and two touchdowns. Morris had 34 yards, and Kiick 10 yards and one touchdown. Griese only attempted seven passes, completing six for a mere 73 yards.

In the third quarter, the Dolphins were down on the Minnesota 2-yard line.

"Griese went up to the line of scrimmage with a lot on his mind," the coach said. "But he had forgotten what the snap count was." The quarterback had called the snap count "on one" and then forgot. "Bob turned around and asked Larry. Csonka never knows," said Shula with a smile. Csonka said on two. Kiick said on one. Zonk insisted. Griese called out. To his surprise, when he yelled out the ball snapped up "early." Griese almost fumbled. Csonka took the ball from him and ran it in.

At one point in the first half, linebacker Wally Hilgenberg hit Csonka in the head after the play was whistled dead. The hit had bloodied Csonka but did not deter him. "I don't know who it was, but he did it right out in the open, because he was frustrated. It was a cheap shot, but I guess you would have to say it was a clean cheap shot. He didn't try to hide it," said Csonka.

The Vikings had one interception and one fumble, and 65 yards in penalties. The Dolphins had no turnovers, and one penalty for five yards.

"The precision-jackhammer attack of the Miami Dolphins stomped the balls off the Minnesota Vikings today by stomping and hammering with one precise jack-thrust after another up the middle, mixed with pinpoint-precision passes into the flat and numerous hammer-jack stops around both ends," concluded Thompson. "Don Shula, despite his fairly obvious distaste for Nixon, has adopted the Lombardi style of football so effectively that the Dolphins are now one of the dullest teams to watch in the history of pro football."

Paul Zimmerman wrote years later, "Bob Kuechenberg, the Dolphins' left guard, once told me that the players felt the '73 team was better than the unbeaten '72 squad, mainly because the defense was better and Griese was healthy for the whole season. Kuechenberg said that in almost every game they drove and scored on their first possession."

Since taking over the Dolphins, Shula was 54–11–1. A remarkable record, which could be compared to anyone's. The comparisons to Lombardi were flying fast and furious. "Lombardi and Shula are the same type of coach," said Mary Fleming, wife of Marv Fleming, who had played in five Super Bowls by now (two with Lombardi, three with Shula). "Each is a disciplinarian. Each demands a lot. The difference is that Shula is more personable. You can walk up to him after practice and say, 'Coach, can I see you minute?' and he'll stop and talk to you. With Lombardi, you had to make an appointment."

Fleming said after the game, "Whenever anybody asks me which team would win," he said referring to the great Packers teams or these Dolphin teams, "I always tell them, 'Whichever one I'm on.'"

Shula considered this season "a greater accomplishment" than the previous, undefeated season. "This year everybody was coming after us. We were down for a couple of games [defeats by Oakland and Baltimore] and a couple where we didn't play very well but managed to win. This team rises to the occasion. . . . Anytime a team executes, you shouldn't be surprised. That's what you work for."

If Shula was proud of his team in mid-January, he didn't have long to enjoy it. The 1974 season would be one of his biggest challenges. First came the loss of Arnsparger.

On January 17, Andy Robustelli, the New York Giants' director of operations, announced the worst-kept secret of Super Bowl VIII—Dolphins defensive coordinator Bill Arnsparger had accepted a three-year contract to be the head coach of the team. Arnsparger's contract called for a salary close to $70,000 per annum.

"We felt to ask a man to leave the Super Bowl champions he needed some kind of security, so that's what we offered him," Wellington Mara, president of the Giants, said of the multiyear contract. "It's not something he demanded."

"I never really talked to anyone other than Bill," Robustelli said.

"I think it's a great opportunity that has been presented to me," Arnsparger said concerning his reasons for leaving the security of the Dolphins for his first head coaching position after twenty-three years as an assistant. "It's a successful operation and I'll have total involvement. I'm looking forward to the challenge."

"How will the loss of Bill Arnsparger affect the Dolphins?" somebody asked Csonka just after the Super Bowl.

"It's a loss," Csonka said, "but I think Coach Shula will groom a new defensive coach, and I think we can take up the slack in the meantime."

As if this weren't enough, more bad news came only eight weeks later. But its coming had been the talk of the NFL since before the Super Bowl. And of all the teams in the league, it would hit the Miami Dolphins harder than almost any other team.

"Gary Davidson, short and suntanned, invented the W.F.L. last August over lunch. His earlier inventions were the American Basketball Association and the World Hockey Association, each of which got off the ground easier than the Wright Brothers' invention did," wrote Dave Anderson in the *New York Times*.

Hunter S. Thompson had written in his Super Bowl piece, "Meanwhile, on the other side of the lobby, Doug Swift was going along with a conversation that had turned, along with Shula's, to money and next year's contracts." Swift listened to the points of the conversation. Then he looked up and responded, "You can expect to see a lot of new faces on next year's [Miami] team. A lot of important contracts are coming up for renewal, and you can bet that the guys will be asking for more than management is willing to pay."

Thompson prophetically continued, "Nobody paid much attention to the decidedly unnatural timing of Swift's matter-of-fact prediction about 'a lot of new faces next year,' but it was not the kind of talk designed to tickle either Shula's or Joe Robbie's rampant humours that morning. Jesus, here was the team's Player Representative—a star linebacker and one of the sharpest & most politically conscious people in the League—telling anyone who cared to listen, not even 12 hours after the victory party, that the embryo 'Dolphin Dynasty' was already in a very different kind of trouble than anything the Vikings or the Redskins had been able to lay on them in two straight Super Bowls."

In fact, Swift had been talking such doomsday scenarios as far back as mid-November, when he told the press that at least a dozen members of the champion Miami Dolphins would jump to the proposed World Football League that had been proposed. They were all looking for higher salaries.

"A dozen to 15 if they had the money," said Swift. "They can have Jim Mandich right now." All- Pro defensive tackle Manny Fernandez concurred. The problem was that the average salary in the NFL was approximately $30,000. Even the NHL paid $45,000 on average in the same years.

"You talk to the players, and most of them would love to see this new league get off the ground," said Fernandez. "It would finally give them a little bit of a wedge. You've got to make the money while you can. The N.F.L. has us over a barrel."

"Current sports economics makes the head turn, but the ambitions of the discontent Dolphins and the projections of the new league make one downright dizzy," concluded William N. Wallace.

In one fell swoop, the Dolphins were gutted. The Toronto Argonauts of the new World Football League had signed Larry Csonka, Jim Kiick, and Paul Warfield to big, lucrative contracts starting in 1975. "Wherever Butch and Sundance go there's bound to be trouble," said Larry Csonka. "I wonder what it'll be this time?"

They had also gotten Cadillac Sevilles as part of the deal—Csonka's was silver, Kiick brown with beige stripes, and Warfield a navy-blue model.

"Joe Robbie sells out but we won't," Toronto owner John Bassett said. "Csonka, Warfield and Kiick are worth more to us than to him. . . . Warfield wants to get into TV and radio and we own Canada's biggest TV station. There's also no racial hassle for him there. Csonka likes the outdoors. He's in Canada fishing every year. And everybody knows that Kiick isn't happy with Mercury Morris playing so much."

"When Paul Warfield, Jim Kiick and I traveled to Toronto to speak with Johnny Bassett, he seized the moment. He knew we had come to just talk but he also knew this would be his only chance to land all 3 of us with one deal. Bassett wanted to know what it would take," Csonka wrote four decades later. Csonka's agent Ed Keating, demanded three guaranteed years of salary, signing bonuses, guaranteed product endorsements, luxury apartments, automobiles, travel expenses, and so on. "But we had to make our minds up before we left Toronto. In other words, take it or leave it. But I wanted to call Coach Shula first. We spoke and I waited on a call from the Dolphins owner, Joe Robbie, which never came. So we took the deal!"

"I could understand why he doesn't want me, but he doesn't want you," Kiick said he told Csonka, referring to Robbie. "He never gave us a call."

"He was angry," Kiick said of Shula. "He blamed me for taking Csonka to the World Football League. He blamed me for leaving him high and dry. But Csonka was a big boy, and he made his own decision."

What was especially awkward about the deal was that the players would remain with Miami and play out their contracts for the 1974 season. In the meantime, the Toronto Northmen moved their franchise before the first WFL season started and eventually became the Memphis Grizzlies. Csonka knew his agent Keating and Dolphins owner Joe Robbie did not get along. Still, he insisted they gave the Dolphins every opportunity to renegotiate their contracts in good faith, before turning to the WFL: "Joe Robbie was offered the opportunity to negotiate with Paul Warfield, Jim Kiick, and I before we traveled to Toronto and, ultimately, signed with the WFL. He turned us down."

It was much the same across the NFL. Stars fled for money, but these were the three biggest names. "I do not regret my decision to jump to the WFL. It was a business decision. We all had families and the money offered would help secure our futures after football. None of us wanted to leave Miami but there was too big a gap in salary and Robbie wouldn't even consider discussing our current contracts," wrote Csonka.

Privately, many of their teammates thought well of the move. They even hoped it would lead to better pay for those who remained in the NFL. Shula said he was "disappointed, shocked, sick." Shula also said, "Losing Csonka was a bitter pill for me. It is going to take a lot of joy out of the job."

"That decimated his team, and [Shula] took it personally," Dick Anderson said. "But none of the players held any ill will [toward the three who departed]. After the WFL came in, it ended up in player salaries going up in the NFL."

Bob Kuechenberg summed it up best, saying, "The NFL couldn't stop us. It took another league to do it."

"The last six months have been the worst of our lives," Dorothy told the press. "We would sit up at night worrying who was going to go to the World Football League next. I know Don has taken it very personally. I did, too. We had pictures of Larry and Jim hanging all over the living room, but the day I heard they had signed with the WFL, I took them down."

"It was like watching a funeral," Dorothy said when they saw the announcement on television. "It felt like a death in the family."

After the Super Bowl win against Minnesota and the defection of the three to the WFL, Don and Dorothy took some time off and went to Maine for a few weeks. They went to a movie theater one evening, and when he walked in, the crowd began to cheer.

"I can't believe it," Shula said to Dorothy. "They recognize me all the way up here." When a fellow came up to shake his hand, Shula asked the man if he was a Dolphins fan.

"I don't know what you're talking about," the fellow said. "I came over to thank you for coming, because the manager said he wouldn't show the movie if we didn't get ten more people into the theater pretty soon."

That summer, the Miami Dolphins had a team awards banquet. "My wife was late coming in. And I was waiting for her to go up to the head table. And everybody had been seated at the head table. And in the audience. And so Joe wanted me to go up there and be seated so the banquet would start. He was yelling at me. And that's when I didn't want to be yelled at. So I told him how I felt," chuckled Shula years later. Don Strock, a Dolphin quarterback, was a witness.

The irate Robbie hollered at Shula in front of everyone. Shula furiously responded, "If you ever holler at me again, I'll knock you on your ass!" The priest who traveled with the team had to separate the two men. It was acknowledged that the two men rarely meddled in each other's responsibilities. Shula ran football operations. Robbie took care of administration and contracts. For many years, though, Shula, in the private company of friends and confidants, referred to Robbie as "the asshole" or "that asshole."

"After 14 days of bitter silence, it took the intervention of Archbishop Carroll before the two men would speak again. No sooner had they settled their dispute than the long and bitter player strike erupted," reported Ronald B. Scott.

Meanwhile, the NFL Players Association had called for a strike. With their collective bargaining agreement set to expire, the players made several demands, most notably the end of "The Rozelle Rule," which determined compensation for teams losing a player as a free agent. More than twenty veterans had decided to start picketing the Dolphins facilities as of July 6. Newspapers carried the stories of unhappy players and their demands. The Dolphins players agreed not to vote on how they would honor the strike (or if they would) but left that decision up to each man. Yepremian said he would follow the crowd. Tight end Jim Mandich said he would cross the picket line.

Shula was perturbed by the strike. It would obviously interfere with his coaching plans. But there was more to it than that. He had devoted his life to football and did not want to see the game's reputation squandered. Having been a player, he also understood their side. "It seems like someone's telling me how to run my football team, and I don't like that," he told the press, referring to the 90 points known as the "Freedom Issues." "Over the past four years, we're doing things the right way. The list of 90 demands makes me wonder if as a coach I've done anything right and if the National Football League's done anything right." He admitted he was a proponent of the controversial reserve clause.

Especially in those moments, Shula, a regular practicing Catholic, sought solace in the church: "Kneeling in the nearly empty chapel at Biscayne College in Miami, his face still smarting from a quick shave, the coach of the Miami Dolphins, Donald Francis Shula, recites the prayers of the rosary while waiting for 7 a.m. mass. He has begun nearly every day of his adult life in church, and Shula at 44 likes to think it has helped," Ronald B. Scott wrote in *People*. "To withstand the formidable pressure of championship coaching, Shula turns unselfconsciously to church and family."

Despite these incidents, Shula still found time to watch his sons, David, then fifteen, and Michael, nine, play football. "He shouts encouragement like any parent but rarely criticizes the coaches' decisions. He doesn't hesitate to fault the refereeing," added Scott.

"Sometimes they call holding too quickly," he complained. "Hell, they've got to let the kids play the game." Daughters Donna, thirteen, and Annie, ten, rode in equestrian events. Daughter Sharon, twelve, was a cheerleader. "I try to get to know my family," Shula says. "They're so caught up in my life, I feel it's important to get involved in theirs, too."

Every Sunday afternoon when the Dolphins played at home, the three younger children sat in the stands with Lucy Howard, the family maid. Meanwhile, Dorothy enjoyed the air-conditioned luxury box high in the Orange Bowl reserved for the coaches' wives and VIPs.

As the season began, despite the rebellious actions of Csonka, Kiick, and Warfield, there was no question that the Dolphins would continue on in the same fashion, relying on a stalwart defense and a solid running game built around its star running backs and its well-regarded offensive line.

To offset the loss of Bill Arnsparger, Shula hired Vince Costello. Costello was a 12-year veteran linebacker who'd played for the Cleveland Browns (1957–66) and New York Giants (1967–68). After retiring as a player, he became the linebackers coach for Paul Brown with the Cincinnati Bengals (1969–73). His pedigree was solid. He was old school NFL, right up Shula's alley, and right out of Paul Brown school of coaching.

It would have been hard for anyone to follow Bill Arnsparger. He was easily one of the best defensive coordinators in the history of the game. Unfortunately, Costello was overmatched as a coordinator from the beginning.

"There are easier jobs to go to," said Costello. "But I knew what I was getting into. I knew what they had done in the past, and I knew I would be living in the shadow of a coach who was considered a genius."

The players had been used to better, more forward-thinking game plans, and the players who had been playing together now for four seasons seemed to know more than their coach.

The always outspoken Jake Scott stopped a practice once, screaming at Costello, "I don't like you and I don't like your damn defense!" Scott told the coach he didn't know what he was talking about. When Shula hustled across the field to ask what happened, Scott said, "I wasn't fucking talking to you!" He wasn't alone.

It was like "going from nirvana to hell," said Buoniconti, who disliked Costello more than Scott did. The entire season, Shula put up with griping about Costello from various team members, the most notable being defensive leader Buoniconti, with whom he was also close.

"The change had to affect us," Bob Matheson explained. "Arns is a great defensive genius; he's a super coach. He's the guy who refined the zones to what they are. When you have a new coach come in, he knows his zones and his Xs and 0s, but when you get to the fine details of the game, well, we knew more about our defense than he did. There was a little communication problem at first, not where we weren't talking to each other, but we had to get used to the way he does things and he had to get used to doing things the way we were used to."

Just before the season, the *New York Times* started off its NFL kickoff preview: "Can a team win the American Football Conference championship for the fourth straight year despite the departure of its defensive genius, the impending defection of three star players to another league and a feud between the coach and the owner?" That pretty much summed it all up. If not, the newspaper summarized, the rising Pittsburgh Steelers would be more than happy to take advantage of the situation.

The deck was stacked against Shula, and the first game of the season at New England was an eye-opener. The Patriots jumped out to a 24–10 halftime lead and never looked back, spanking Shula's Dolphins, 34–24. Shula, angry and depressed, told the press, "We stink. They played a hell of game. . . . I felt going into the season that New England and Buffalo would be two of the most improved teams. Now, after losing to New England, we're going to have to get it done against Buffalo to get back to.500. Last year after two games, we were 1–1. After losing to New England, this is what we are shooting for. O. J. Simpson has a lot more help for this season, and this is going to mold them into a better team."

There was good news and bad news the second week. The good news was that the Dolphins beat the Bills in Buffalo, 24–16. The bad news was that the WFL Birmingham Americans announced that they had signed both Tim Foley and Bob Kuechenberg for the 1975 season. Shula told the press he was not surprised, as he had heard rumblings early in the month, and that the two players had failed to sign new contracts.

"I'm disappointed, obviously, but you can't second-guess what they're doing," said Shula. Regarding the loss of Kuechenberg, Shula said, "This is obviously going to create a rebuilding process in our offensive line."

The Dolphins rebounded, beating the Chargers and Jets in consecutive weeks, but then faced the daunting task of playing the Washington Redskins, whom they had beaten the Super Bowl two years earlier. It didn't go well. In the fourth quarter, Sonny Jurgensen drove his team 60 yards in 90 seconds and threw the winning touchdown in the waning moments of the game to give the Redskins a 20–17 victory at RFK Stadium.

"That's one of the toughest losses we've ever suffered. To lose it in the end like that," said Shula. "We didn't stop Sonny. He just kept coming up with plays. He was magnificent."

They bounced back again, beating the Chiefs, Colts, and Falcons, bringing their record to 6–2 by early November. Right after that, Shula suspended Mercury Morris. Morris, injured for most of the season, had missed treatments on the Monday and Tuesday after the Falcons game. He had snapped at Shula, "Go ahead and suspend me."

"It really was the only thing he could do," said Morris. "It's unfortunate that right at the time when I felt ready to play, this had to happen. But I've been out for so long now, that it really can't make that much difference. I just have to stay in shape both physically and mentally for whenever I do get a chance to play."

They beat New Orleans and Buffalo with Morris back on the team, but playing behind Kiick, to run their winning streak to six games. Then they lost to the Jets, 17–14, in New York. The score was tied, 7–7, going into the fourth quarter. Pat Leahy put the Jets ahead with a 34-yard field goal, but the Dolphins answered with a touchdown when Kiick got in from eight yards out, making the score 14–10 in favor of Miami. Then, with five minutes left, Joe Namath threw a 45-yard touchdown pass to Rich Caster, and the Jets walked away upset winners, 17–14.

They rounded out the season with wins over the Bengals, Colts, and avenging their opening day loss to the Patriots, repaying them in kind, 34–27, to finish the season at 11–3, and winning yet another AFC East division crown.

Their first test in the playoffs would be the 12–2 Oakland Raiders led by quarterback Ken Stabler. This would be one of the biggest playoff games of the year. And going into it, Shula had enough on his plate. "You have to understand the background here. Back in 1974 Morris was so upset with Shula that he put a voodoo curse on him. He had been unhappy about splitting time with Jim Kiick at halfback," wrote *Sports Illustrated*'s Paul Zimmerman. "He had ripped Shula in the papers. The Dolphins would end the '74 regular season against the Patriots and then face the Oakland Raiders in the first round of the playoffs. Morris had been out with a bad knee. Shula and the team doctor said he was ready to play. Morris said he wasn't. There was a bitter exchange, and after the Patriot game Morris, who didn't play, put the voodoo on the coach."

"I went to see this Haitian root man, King Solomon, on 54th and 12th," Morris says. "I told him, 'Shula's trying to kill me. I don't want him hurt, but I want him off me.' I see that you're laughing, but believe me, you'd go down to his place, and you'd see lawyers there and people like that waiting for him to put some roots on somebody."

"The night before we left for Oakland, I was out in the backyard at 2 a.m., saying chants. I made a Shula doll and put it in a box and buried it. Before the game I was chewing roots on the field. In my shoe I had a piece of paper with a spider web on it, and written underneath was the word *confused*."

The Miami-Oakland rivaly was becoming legendary, and anticipation for this rematch was high. "Many of the players on both teams are veterans of those games, and the mutual respect is enormous. So is the emotional buildup. Each group is approaching this as the title game—a feeling that will change instantly for the winners as they start to look ahead, but is real enough today," wrote Leonard Koppett. The Raiders were favored over the Dolphins by three points.

"I have never heard any louder cheering in the Coliseum than when we came out to be introduced," said longtime Raiders executive Al LoCasale. "The stadium left the ground."

The game couldn't have started better for the Dolphins. Nat Moore took the opening kickoff 89 yards for a touchdown to quiet the crowd and give Miami an instant 7–0 lead. The Raiders evened the score in the second quarter with a Stabler-to-Charlie Smith 31-yard touchdown pass. With a Yepremian field goal, the Dolphins went into the half leading 10–7, but with a real street fight on their hands.

The teams traded touchdowns in the third quarter, but Miami failed on their point-after attempt, leaving the score 16–14 going into the fourth quarter. The Dolphins added another Yepremian field goal to make it 19–14. Then the Raiders countered with another Stabler touchdown pass, a 72-yard bomb to Cliff Branch to go ahead, 21–19. Then the Dolphins struck back with another touchdown, when Benny Malone swept 23 yards to the end zone, giving them a 26–24 lead for their defense to protect with 2:08 to go.

Starting at their own 32-yard line, Stabler drove the Raiders deep into Dolphins territory with the clock running down. The Miami defense was handicapped, as two of their best defensive backs were not on the field during the final drive. Jake Scott had left the game with a sprained knee. He was replaced by Charlie Babb. "That hurt because Miami's deep middle zone is always covered when Jake is playing. And that was the zone where [Clarence] Davis roamed on the big play at the end," wrote William N. Wallace.

Curtis Johnson was also lost to a sprained knee. Scott and Johnson brandished temporary casts around their knees on the sidelines. But those were not the only injuries. "During the game our starting cornerback, Tim Foley, got hurt, and they put in Henry Stuckey, the third-stringer, instead of Lloyd Mumphord, the regular backup. Cliff Branch ran by Stuckey for a 72-yard touchdown. On the bench everyone's asking our defensive coordinator, Vince Costello, 'Why is Stuckey in there?' Then someone said, 'He must be confused,'" said Mercury Morris. Stabler and the Raiders picked on the depleted secondary all day, feasting to the tune of 293 yards passing.

With 26 seconds left, the Raiders were eight yards away from the end zone. "On the winning play, Vern Den Herder, the Miami defensive end, had his arms around Stabler's ankles as the pass went off and the Oakland quarterback then fell to the grass. 'I felt him,' said Stabler. All Den Herder needed was another split second to dump Stabler and save a game that Miami had controlled during most of the afternoon. Yes, football is indeed a game of inches and tenths- of-seconds. Vern

Den Herder, the Miami defensive end, had his arms around Stabler's ankles as the pass went off and the Oakland quarterback then fell to the grass," wrote Wallace.

According to Stabler, "I saw Clarence. He had come back. But there were an awful lot of people around him, and it didn't look like he was going to be able to catch the ball." In between three Dolphins defenders, the ball floated, wobbly, and settled into Clarence Davis's hands in the end zone. "It was a dumb play. I never should have thrown the ball to Clarence. Or maybe I should have thrown it out of the end zone. Sometimes you get away with a dumb play and sometimes you don't," said Stabler. It became known as the "Sea of Hands" play.

Esteemed NBC football announcer Curt Gowdy called it "the greatest game I have ever seen."

After the game, Shula openly cried. A man who had stood proudly, his famous jaw out, who publicly tried to show as little emotion as possible, was devastated. He knew as well as everyone else. This was the end. The end of one of the greatest runs in professional football history. The end of a dynasty. And more important, the end of his team.

It was also the end of his kind of football. Teams like the Raiders, and especially the Steelers, favored the passing game, and it was clear that the times were changing. The league wanted the more wide-open passing game to eclipse the ball control running game. Shula's style of ground game was the last great gasp of the old era. It would take a long time for him to get back to this place.

"That loss denied us a third straight Super Bowl win," said Kuechenberg years later. "Of all the years I've known Coach Shula, I would say that loss bothered him the most."

Costello resigned on the plane ride home from Oakland.

CHAPTER 8

Woodstrock and the Killer Bees

In his drive for perfection and accomplishment, Shula had spent a lot of time away from home. Coaching, planning, traveling with the team, and the football operations ate up most of his time. In order to accomplish his goal, he had sacrificed. He had brought his sons with him when he could. But the fact remained it took a toll on his life—his marriage and his children. Still, he did the best he could.

"The Shulas were close, and at home, Don was a progressive husband and father who listened intently to what Dorothy had to say even when it was difficult to hear," wrote journalist and author Mike Freeman.

"The first five years, I was almost envious of my husband," Dorothy once said. "I was tied down with babies. He did try to include me, but he was trying to prove himself as a head football coach. I felt football was getting more attention than I was. And when he came home, instead of letting him relax, I unloaded all of my problems. I had three in diapers at a time, and he had all the glory, it seemed."

"I used to hate it," she said. "I was all alone. It's a very lonesome job, being a coach's wife."

At one point, Shula told Dorothy, "You know, I think you're jealous."

"Maybe I am," she responded.

Through it all, Dorothy remained a stalwart companion to the driven coach. She had been there for his defeats and cheered his victories. She had delved into charity work in Baltimore and did so in Miami, as well. But by 1975, the stress began to show on Dorothy. There was a price to be paid for the successes they had achieved together. And she was a big factor in his success, which he was quick to admit.

"He won't smile," Dorothy once told an interviewer. "He's afraid that iron jaw will break. He thinks laughing will hurt his image. It's the same thing with dancing. He's a good dancer. But someone might see him do it."

In May of that same year, there had been speculation that after having been to three Super Bowls, Shula might in fact bolt to another team, again. Robbie and Shula renegotiated his deal. Shula sold a portion of his stock in the football team but remained with the team after securing another new three-year commitment.

He was not the only Dolphins employee to receive a renegotiated contract. Tim Foley and Bob Kuechenberg had both agreed to play for the Birmingham Americans in 1975, when their Dolphins contracts expired. But by mid-May, both were back in the fold. "Both have signed contracts for more than one year," said a Dolphins spokesman. In truth, both had extricated themselves from their WFL commitments after contending the Alabama club did not live up to the agreements, as well as signing more lucrative contracts with the Miami club than in previous years. When Csonka, Kiick, and Warfield and other stars had signed on to the WFL, it forced NFL owners to start paying better salaries to their star players.

That summer, before training camp, Shula took his parents back to Hungary. "My dad came over when he was 11 years old. And we had a chance to go back on his 75th birthday. And we went back and he found some of the relatives that he had over there, and found a little village and house. It was pretty interesting. Budapest is a beautiful city, beautiful." Shula said at another time. Don himself still had a decent vocabulary of Hungarian. Once asked well after retirement what his favorite Hungarian word was, he answered, laughing, "Chicken Paprikash."

By July, the Dolphins, in need of new running back, acquired Norm Bulaich from the Philadelphia Eagles in exchange for a fourth-round draft choice in 1976. "I'm hoping Bulaich will team up with Don Nottingham and give us the player we need at the fullback position," said Shula. Bulaich had been the Colts' first-round draft choice in 1970 when Shula was still with the team. He never had the chance to coach the big back there, as he left for Miami shortly afterward. The Colts had traded Bulaich to the Eagles in 1973. He had become expendable after being troubled by injuries the previous season.

George Young had come to work for the Dolphins in 1974, and he evolved into a much bigger influence on the organization over the years. By 1975, he was making a big difference. A Baltimore native, Young had played the defensive line at Bucknell. He later became the head coach of the Baltimore City College prep school football team. In 15 years, he established himself as a successful coach, winning six champoionships. When Young wasn't coaching or teaching history and political science, he would sit and watch Baltimore Colts practices. Shula hired Young as an assistant in the personnel department when he was still with the Baltimore Colts in 1968.

"In 1968, Shula's coaching staff was working at the Pro Bowl that year, so he asked Young to grade college prospects. Young's reports were so detailed and accurate that Shula hired him to evaluate personnel for the Colts," wrote Bob Glauber in *Newsday*. Young went on to hold positions of scout, offensive line coach, director of player personnel, and offensive coordinator.

"If Don Shula didn't come along, I'd still be a teacher and still be with people who discuss books and ideas all the time," recalled Young. "He's the one who believed in me."

"Shula brought Young to the Dolphins in 1974, replacing Pat Peppler, the former director of player personnel who went to the Houston Oilers. Shula first assigned Young as the director of pro scouting, then put him back on the sidelines as an assistant coach in 1975. Young's responsibilities grew, however, with an emphasis placed on college and pro scouting, and on the negotiating of salaries," wrote sportswriter Eric Lincoln.

"Don just didn't want to be in an adversary position with the players, and he knew George could do the right kind of job. It sounds funny, but the players loved him. He was completely fair with them. He is a gentle, kind man who is sympathetic, yet completely fairly had the respect of the players," said a Dolphin executive. "After Larry Csonka, Jim Kiick, and Paul Warfield left the team, there was a lot of grumbling about fairness and salaries. But when George stepped in, that stopped. He handles people well, and cares about them."

One of Young's responsibilities was preparing analysis for Miami's upcoming games. Young reviewed the films of their opponent's previous games. "He was so thorough," Shula says. Young meticulously reported each offensive and defensive strategy. "We went into games well prepared basically because of George. He was my right-hand man," said Shula.

"At 11 o'clock one night, we were sitting in a meeting, and Don took out the report from the doctors and started asking each of us what our potassium level was, our uric acid level," recalled Young many years later.

"Don, people think we're in here making great decisions, and you're talking about our urinalysis?" responded Young.

"I'm going to subpoena your medical report!'" answered Shula.

Young eventually went on to be the general manager of the New York Giants was named NFL Executive of the Year five times, and built two Super Bowl winners. He and Shula would serve many years together on the competition committee.

"George Young went from a high school history teacher and football coach to one of the most powerful men in the NFL," Shula said. "His counsel was sought by everyone in the league, and he was respected by players, coaches, administrators, and owners alike."

Expectations for the 1975 season were much lower than usual. Suddenly, the Miami Dolphins were just another pro football team again. "Two years after they swept to a second successive Super Bowl crown, the Dolphins are trying to retain respectability in the face of defections, injuries and a drop of almost 30,000 season-ticket sales," wrote Neil Amdur in the *New York Times*. The large Burdine's department stores according to one buyer had "narrowed the breadth" of their assortment of Dolphins football merchandise. The number one selling jersey of the three previous years, 39 (Csonka's number), was not available at all.

Csonka, Warfield, and Kiick were gone, and Nick Buoniconti and Dick Anderson both had injuries that kept them on the sidelines. Bob Griese struggled during the preseason, and when asked why, he responded, "There's no question we've had different receivers and they react differently."

The running backs were now Don Nottingham and Norm Bulaich, both retreads from other teams, as well as Benny Malone, a second-round pick the previous season who had scored what looked to be the game-winning touchdown in Oakland until Stabler brought the Raiders back. Second-year prodigy Nat Moore was one of the primary wide receivers along with rookie Freddie Solomon and veteran Howard Twilley. The defense featured five new starters, due to injuries, the most notable of the missing starters being Nick Bouniconti.

Bobby Beathard was now in charge of player personnel and began making moves that would start to restock the Dolphins' roster, but it would take time.

In 1972, Beathard was still working for the Falcons when he read that personnel director Joe Thomas was leaving the Dolphins. After returning home to Atlanta from a scouting trip, Falcons coach Norm Van Brocklin told him that Shula had called. Beathard remained with the Falcons through the draft and then flew to Miami. He stayed at Shula's house, and the two of them talked football nonstop. Shula offered him the job as the Dolphins' personnel director.

"Bobby did a real fine job for us," Shula said. "He's a guy with a great eye for talent—there's no question about that. Sometimes he would draft a guy we all agreed on, but it just didn't work out. That happens with every team in the league. Nobody has a perfect record, and you're going to make mistakes. But Bobby made fewer mistakes than most. And he found some kids for us nobody else would take a chance on. He wasn't ever afraid to take a risk."

Beathard was not afraid to argue with Shula. "We went back and forth on a lot of guys," Shula said. "That's the way it should be. He won some, and he lost some, like anybody else. But he was never afraid to speak his convictions on a player. It was his job to find the players, but he knew that I made the ultimate decision. He didn't always agree, but we had a fine working relationship." While Beathard and Shula found an equilibrium, Bobby never got on with owner Joe Robbie. It seemed clear to Beathard that Robbie couldn't care less about the Dolphins' scouts. It seemed to Beathard a constant battle to get his men raises and comparable professional working conditions enjoyed by other scouts around the league. "Beathard finally asked Robbie if he could tell the rest of the NFL his scouts were available. Robbie agreed, Beathard sent out the word and, within a day, one scout had a new job and a $9,000 raise, another had a new job and a $6,000 raise. Robbie was furious, but the scouts had already joined their new teams," wrote Paul Attner and Leonard Shapiro in the *Washington Post*.

"Generally, you learn so much just being around Don Shula," Beathard told the *Miami Herald* in 1983. "That was great experience for me."

"The years at the Miami Dolphins including the '72 season of undefeated teams and being with [Don] Shula, I learned a lot more than I ever had up until that time about football," Beathard said.

The first game of the 1975 season pitted the Dolphins against their playoff nemesis, the Oakland Raiders, this time at the Orange Bowl on *Monday Night Football*. The Raiders were the odds-on favorites to reach the Super Bowl that year, and they proved it here.

The Raiders jumped to a 17–0 lead and never looked back. They unleashed six running backs who accumulated 159 yards on the ground, while eight Raiders caught a pass. Harold Hart returned a kickoff 102 yards as the Raiders routed the Dolphins, 31–21. It was the Dolphins' first loss at home in 31 games.

"A fumble by Don Nottingham in the game's second minute at his 38-yard line launched the Oakland assault. The Raiders were in the Miami end zone 10 plays later as Pete Banaszak scored the first of his two touchdowns by leaping over the goal from 2 yards away," wrote William N. Wallace in the *New York Times*. Griese threw four interceptions in that game, two in the end zone in the last three minutes. At the end came a scattering of boos from the crowd of 78,744 (1,250 short of capacity).

Shula was not happy with his team's performance. "Every time we got something going, we'd make a mistake," he said. Hart's kickoff return, in which no Dolphin came close, galled him. "I thought," he said, "we would have excellent special teams because of the youth and enthusiasm."

"Well, we're not about to panic," said Griese afterward. But the Dolphins had only rushed for 118 yards.

The Dolphins righted their ship the next week against the New England Patriots, 22–14, in New England. That began a seven-game winning streak, including two games in which they scored more than 40 points that season.

The Dolphins stubbed their toe in Houston on November 16. After Nottingham had scored a touchdown in the fourth quarter to put the Dolphins ahead, 19–13, Yepremian's point-after attempt failed. The Oilers responded with a Ronnie Coleman 7-yard burst and a successful PAT to win the game by one. Miami dominated the stats but had lost on the scoreboard.

The next weekend brought on a showdown against the resurgent Baltimore Colts. The Dolphins went into halftime leading, 14–9, having given up a touchdown and a safety. But when they took the field of the Orange Bowl for the second half, the Colts made a spectacle of the place and beat the Dolphins, 33–17. By the end of the game, Colt running back Don McCauley had rushed for three touchdowns and Lydell Mitchell for one. The result left the 7–3 Dolphins with a one-game lead over the 6–4 Colts in the AFC East.

The Dolphins went about their business dismantling the Patriots and Bills in strong showings, but more bad news hit. Bob Griese had suffered torn tendons in the late November loss to Baltimore. Morrall was lost in the win over New England after suffering a partial ligament tear in his left knee.

"We're going to keep Earl quiet and see if there's any swelling in the next two to three weeks," Shula said. "Only with a knee brace will he be able to play." Third-stringer Don Strock beat the Bills and was slated to be the starter against the Colts for their showdown in the bedlam of Baltimore. A win would virtually guarantee a Dolphins division crown. The Colts needed the win to stay alive.

The two teams met on December 14 at Memorial Stadium. Shula had his hands full, as the Colts were now a mirror image of the Dolphins. Nick Buoniconti, Manny Fernandez, and Dick Anderson joined Griese and Morrall on the injured list. The first half finished scoreless. This was the hard-fought game everyone was expecting.

"The Miami line conducted a clinic out there," said Baltimore defensive end John Dutton. "I never knew where their blockers were coming from next—or how many of them there would be. It was a learning experience."

Miami broke through on a Mercury Morris 3-yard touchdown plunge in the third quarter. But Lydell Mitchell returned the favor in the fourth quarter, making it 7–7.

"Linhart kicked the game-tying extra point through the fog, and suddenly 59,398 Baltimore fanatics were blowing their kazoos and chanting 'dee-fense, dee-fense.' Both defenses responded, as time ran out," wrote Mark Mulvoy in *Sports Illustrated.*

Miami won the toss at the start of overtime but went three and out. A Larry Seiple punt, which he angled out of bounds at the Baltimore 4, was a clear setback for the Colts.

"After Larry's kick, I thought we were all set," said Shula. "We couldn't have asked for anything better."

But Colts upstart quarterback Bert Jones stepped in. After a few runs had established breathing room, Jones was sacked for a 10-yard loss. But Jones came right back and lobbed a deep sideline pass that tight end Raymond Chester hauled in as he stepped out of bounds at the 36.

"Two years ago, I wouldn't have completed that pass because I wouldn't have thrown it," said Jones, who completed 23 of 39 for 232 yards. "The coverage dictated the pass. Lydell was covered over the middle, so I went wide and Raymond was there." Jones directed a 82-yard drive, setting up the winning 31-yard field goal by Linhart for a 10–7 Colt win.

"We'll have to back into the playoffs now," said the shocked Shula.

"Miami was on top for a long time," Mitchell said in the Baltimore dressing room. "Really, there's no love lost between these teams. Don't get me wrong. We're not a great team yet. We're not there. We've got to keep our heads screwed on and keep together."

There were no excuses from the Dolphins, who had struggled through an injury-riddled season, losing such key players such as Bob Griese, "They beat us," said offensive lineman Jim Langer. "The Colts right now are like the young Dolphins of about 1970. They're nothing to laugh at." Both teams walked away 10–4.

"If we beat Denver next week and either Baltimore loses to New England or Cincinnati loses to San Diego, we get into the playoffs," Miami Coach Don Shula said, trying to sound hopeful. Then he admitted, "I've never been much of a back-door guy, though. I like to do things myself. We had the chance to control our own destiny. All we had to do was beat the Colts. We didn't. And now I don't see Baltimore or Cincinnati losing next week."

The next week, the Dolphins inched past the Denver Broncos 14–13, while the Colts dismantled the Patriots, 34–21. The Colts and Dolphins both finished with 10–4 records, but the Colts won the tiebreaker by virtue of their two victories over Miami. Meanwhile the 11–3 Cincinnati Bengals claimed the AFC wild-card spot. Miami was out of the playoffs.

Follwing the season, Shula announced in a team meeting that players' attendance was mandatory at a banquet. "I won't be there," Jake Scott said.

"Everyone will be there or they'll be fined $5,000," Shula said.

Scott never showed, and true to his word, Shula fined him. That offseason, Scott asked to be traded. "Shula said I'd never have to wear a Dolphins uniform again," Scott admitted years later. Scott was on the team in the 1976 preseason but said he couldn't practice because of a bum shoulder. Shula claimed team doctors told him Scott was healthy. Shula remembered, "He told me he'd say when he was ready to practice and play. I said, 'We can't operate like that. I can't have one set of rules for you.'"

Shula and Scott got into a screaming match before a 1976 preseason game. Scott refused to shoot up with painkillers for the game. The next day, Scott was gone—traded to Redskins for another safety, Bryant Salter, whom the Dolphins would release late in the season. Six years later, in 1982, at the 10-year celebration of ther undefeated team, Scott and Shula shared an Orange Bowl elevator together.

"I said to him, 'We've got to meet next week and iron out this thing between us,'" Scott explained.

"Fuck you," Shula said. The door to the elevator opened, and Scott walked out of it, and out of the stadium, and didn't return for decades. It was the most painful feud either man experienced in his life.

Shula said later, "I don't remember that. Why would I say that?" There were many reunions where Shula missed Scott. He told a reporter one year, "I loved Jake on that team, and I know the kind of player he was. I don't think there has been a better safety combination than him and Anderson."

Their estrangement would last almost three decades and would pain both men.

The next year was a whirlwind. Offensive coordinator Monte Clark, with Shula for five years, was named as the new head coach of the San Francisco 49ers in January. There were more coaching changes, as Howard Schellenberger and Bill Arnsparger returned to Miami. This was a pivotal moment. Arnsparger had failed spectaculalrly with the Giants and was released in mid-October. Shula picked him up immediately. Schnellenberger had rejoined the team in 1975. With Beathard drafting, and with Arnsparger and Schnellenberger back on staff, there was a sense in the room that this group of men, now reunited, might create another run toward a championship. NFL observers agreed with this assessment. They were correct, but it would take time.

In March, Shula was appointed by Pete Rozelle to the competition committee. He would go on to serve on the committee for the next twenty years. He would serve with the likes of committee chairman Tex Schramm of the Dallas Cowboys, who lauded Shula for his ability to remain objective in the pursuit of bettering the game. Shula and the committee significantly changed the rules to help the passing game, which was diametrically opposed to the Dolphins' run-oriented style.

"He was a unique individual who could look at what was best for the game and the league rather than what was necessarily best for his team," Schramm said. "That's not easy for the people in this league to do."

Though he admitted himself that he could sometimes be an official's worst nightmare, Shula would say often that he was immensely proud of his work on the committee, in helping to shape the modern game. Years later, he and George Young, his former assistant and NFL legend, would change the game in a way no one could have imagined and bring in the modern game.

Also in March, Pete Rozelle reinstated Csonka, Kiick, and Warfield. They were free to talk to any club in the league. The WFL had collapsed on October 22, 1975. In that short period, Csonka attempted to rejoin Miami, where Shula surely could have used him. "I had my agent contact Joe Robbie in Miami ASAP. In hindsight, I should've called Coach Shula. Keating and Robbie never got along and, unfortunately, picked up right where they left off and the time to negotiate ran out. The NFL deadline for major player movement was approaching on October 28th, so the possibility of returning to Miami for the remaining '75 season quickly disappeared," said Csonka years later.

Other NFL teams started talks with Keating. Csonka urged Keating to negotiate with Miami. Keating sent Robbie an unsigned copy of the contract Bassett had personally guaranteed to pay Csonka. "Needless to say, Robbie exploded and immediately had my 'demands' published in the *Miami Herald*—calling it ridiculous and absurd to expect such a deal," said Csonka many years later. Three days later, the New York Giants extended a full contract if Csonka would sign with them. Csonka would be a New York Giant. Warfield and Kiick ended up with the Cleveland Browns.

"I was made out to be a fool," Csonka said. "What he [Robbie] did hurt me deep down."

That August, the Dolphins cut Mercury Morris and brought Nick Buoniconti back for one more year. It was a forgettable year for the Miami Dolphins. They were stockpiling new players through the draft and slowly revamping the team. It would take a little while. But 1976 was a horrific season. They beat the Bills on opening day but could not get untracked. After the sixth game of the season, they were 2–4. They won their next three games and then turned around and lost three in a row. They repaid the Bills with a big win, in the second to last game of the season, but then got walloped by the Vikings, 29–7, to end the campaign at 6–8. Shula had never suffered a losing a season up to that point.

The following year saw a number of changes. The biggest news of 1977 was that of Bob Griese, who now sported eyeglasses and threw for 2,252 yards, with 22 touchdowns and only 13 interceptions. He threw for six touchdowns against the St. Louis Cardinals in a 55–14 Thanksgiving Day win. He was named the Player of the Year. Linebacker A. J. Duhe, their first-round pick, was named Defensive Rookie of the Year.

"I played for Coach Shula in the Senior Bowl. So he and his staff had a sneak peek at me for a week. I worked my butt off. I did everything that was asked of me. I remember like it was yesterday that one time after we scored a touchdown and needed somebody to cover the kickoff, Coach Shula started to look around," recalled Duhe. "I said I would cover it and ran onto the field. I think I impressed him and his staff with how hard I wanted to work and how much the game meant to me. My interview was basically what I did for six days with them."

"A. J.'s our fire-up guy," said Dolphins nose guard Bob Baumhower. "It's the fourth quarter, everybody's draggin' but there's ol' A. J. just ready to go. It makes everybody play better."

"When you're tired and you see him still jumping around, it lifts you," said defensive end Kim Bokamper. "He's definitely a leader, and definitely not a silent leader."

"We drafted A. J. No. 1 a while back, and we had to find a spot for his leadership," Shula said. "He's an emotional guy who can turn a game around with those big plays. The thing we noticed immediately was Duhe's ability to run. He runs so smoothly.

"There were times in the past when he was learning the position that we had some problems. It's been painful at times for us and for him. He's a guy who had so much natural ability, but he was an undersize defensive end. Then we made the switch with Bokamper from the line to linebacker. Those two moves have really helped this defense."

Duhe was sure the staff was prepared to tell him to hand in his playbook and pack his bags. But then Shula took Duhe aside and told him that the staff was doing it because they thought that he, Duhe, could make a bigger impact. Shula told him, "We're not just going to let you play linebacker. If you can't make the adjustment, you won't play." As Duhe explains, "So there was really a lot of pressure put on me to make the adjustment. I took pride in it."

The team won their first three games convincingly, but the Baltimore Colts clubbed them at Memorial Stadium, 45–28, to hand them their first loss. They would avenge the loss late in the season but ended up at 10–4. While they showed marked improvement, the team missed the playoffs. They finished behind the Colts on tiebreakers, and the Oakland Raiders, who finished 11–3, took the wild-card berth. It was the third year in a row that Miami failed to qualify for the playoffs. In the meantime, the increase in wins showed at the box office, as attendance rose from the previous year.

In 1977, Beathard had a falling out with Joe Robbie and quit after the draft. He eventually ended up with the Washington Redskins, where he helped to build several Super Bowl champions.

Shula had spoken to Washington owner Edward Bennett Williams several times about Beathard, saying, "I gave him my strongest recommendation. Bobby's an excellent man. He knows what's going on around the league, and he'll be a great asset to the Redskins."

Joe Robbie made his son Mike the team's general manager. Chuck Connor was named head of player personnel.

"I get excited the closer the draft gets, but it's not a thing where I can't sleep, or where you're constantly on edge or anything," Connor said. "It's just a matter of working at it and evaluating as thoroughly as you can, then lining them up and hoping they're there when it comes time to pick. Someone asked the other day what's tougher, college recruiting or drafting. The advantage we have in the pros is we don't have to babysit the kids and sell the school to them. But the disadvantage we have—and it's a big one—is you have to hope the guy you want is there."

"The only thing we can do is voice our opinion, but Don is going to make the final choice," Connor said. "If it's our turn and we look up at our [draft] board and see two people awfully close at two positions, he calls the final shots. If those two players have got a wide variance in abilities, we just go with the best player."

"The draft is Chuck's Super Bowl," Shula said. Connor had a staff of three people. The 1978 draft featured wide receiver Jimmy Cefalo, tackle Eric Laakso, center Mark Dennard, defensive end Doug Betters, and defensive back Gerald Small. The Dolphins also acquired dynamic running back Delvin Williams from the San Francisco 49ers in exchange for their first-round pick.

The 1978 season started off with a loss to the Jets in New York, but then they won five of their next seven games to reach the midpoint of the season with a 5–3 record. They rebounded from a loss to New England by beating the Colts, Cowboys, and Bills in succession and then ran into the rising Oilers and their phenomenal rookie running back Earl Campbell in Houston on a Monday night. Miami had the No. 1 offense in the NFL going into the game. A fine effort from Bob Griese, who completed 23 of 33 pass attempts for 349 yards and two touchdowns, was a gutsy response. Without question, it was one of the most memorable games of the 1978 season.

The game featured two of the most successful backs of the season in Williams and Campbell. The Dolphins led off the scoring with an impressive drive, capped by a Griese-to-Nat Moore touchdown. But Houston answered with a drive of its own, with Earl Campbell brutalizing the Dolphins, scoring from the 1-yard line. Houston continued to roll in the second quarter, powering through the Dolphins, with Dan Pastorini capping the drive with a touchdown pass to Mike Barber. Before the half ended, it was the Dolphins who responded with a Delvin Williams 1-yard plunge to make it 14–14. It was the heavyweight match many had been anticipating. In the third quarter, the teams traded rushing touchdowns, Campbell with his second of the night and Leroy Harris countering for the Dolphins. The game remained deadlocked going into the fourth quarter, 21–21.

Then what looked like the turning point of the game came, when A. J. Duhe tackled Pastorini in the end zone for a safety, giving the Dolphins a 23–21 lead. However, the momentum in the stadium was about to change. The stadium now erupted. Houston was just coming into its own as a team, and the Oilers, who had beaten the Steelers earlier in the season, pushed back. Campbell scored yet another rushing touchdown to put Houston on top, 28–23. Griese drove the Dolphins into Oilers territory, but his pass intended for tight end Andre Tillman was deflected by safety Mike Reinfeldt and intercepted by linebacker Steve Kiner with 3:05 left in the game. Houston just needed to kill the clock. Shula used a timeout and the two-minute warning to slow down the game. But then on a second-and-eight, Campbell ripped off an 81-yard run against the shocked Miami defense, and the game was over. It put the score at 35–23 with 1:11 remaining. An 11-yard touchdown catch by Jimmy Cefalo made the final score 35–30.

It was a showcase performance by the powerful but swift and mobile runner, and the stadium full of delirious Oilers fans waving blue pom-poms is an indelible memory. The Dolphins did not go down easily. Shula had never seen Campbell in person. Shula was shocked how the rugged back tore through his defense. "Campbell," he said, "is everything they said and more."

"Earl won't listen to instructions," said a delighted Phillips. "I told him just to get the first down and run out the clock."

When asked about his performance, Campbell, worn out, responded, "I don't know how many touchdowns I scored. I'm not aware of that at all." He had rushed for 199 yards and four touchdowns. A fine effort from Bob Griese, who completed 23 of 33 pass attempts for 349 yards and two touchdowns, was a gutsy response in defeat.

The Dolphins, stung by the loss, stumbled home to lose to the Jets but then rebounded with a three-game homestand that saw them defeat the Redskins, Raiders, and Patriots to close out the regular season. The game against the Raiders had been pivotal in establishing the playoff picture. The victory helped eliminate the Raiders from the playoffs for the first time since 1971. The Raiders had 21 first downs to the Dolphins' 13. Shula said, "Our defense and Garo (who kicked three field goals) kept us in the game." After the season, Raiders coach John Madden retired, claiming one Super Bowl ring, one ulcer, and 103 wins. He was one of the few in the business who had accomplished that feat, and he said the grind had worn him out.

The Dolphins finished at an impressive 11–5 and were in the playoffs for the first time since 1974. However, the New England Patriots took the AFC East crown due to tiebreakers, so they settled for a wild-card berth. Miami had the second-best offense that year, only behind the Dallas Cowboys (whom they had beaten), and were ranked sixth on defense. Griese had the fourth-best passer rating, and Delvin Williams was number four in rushing yards with 1,258. It was the first season in which there were two wild-card teams, and they drew a rematch with the 10–6 Houston Oilers, who had finished second in the AFC Central behind the Pittsburgh Steelers, in the wild-card round game on December 24.

Oilers quarterback Dan Pastorini had spent days prior to the game in the hospital with fractured ribs, a wobbly knee, a banged-up elbow, and a tender hamstring. This became a historic game because of Pastorini's ribs more than anything else. Because of his delicate health in the waning weeks of that season, Pastorini might have had to sit out the playoff game if it were not for a man named Byron Donzis.

"In the late 1970s . . . Mr. Donzis roamed the country, visiting colleges and high schools to demonstrate what became known in football as the flak jacket—a device that has saved quarterbacks, running backs and wide receivers from many a rebruised or broken rib," wrote Dennis Hevesi in the *New York Times*. "Initially, there was that day in the fall of 1978 when Mr. Donzis and a colleague talked their way into a hospital room in Houston where Dan Pastorini, the Houston Oilers quarterback at the time, was recovering from three broken ribs."

"I thought he was some kind of nut," Pastorini said. To demonstrate its toughness, Mr. Donzis opened his trenchcoat, revealing the jacket, and "without flinching, took several whacks from the bat swung, full-out, by his associate," wrote Hevesi. Three weeks later, Pastorini donned the jacket for the Miami game. It was the first time any quarterback wore one in an NFL game. "That type of jacket is still worn today by every quarterback in our league," said Joe Browne, an NFL executive, in 2012.

Houston was ranked fourteenth on offense, and sixteenth on defense. But this time they would have to beat Miami at the Orange Bowl. The opening salvos of this game were a repeat of the previous game. Griese started off the scoring with a 13-yard strike to Andre Tillman in the first quarter. The Oilers responded with a 13-yard touchdown pass from Pastorini to Tim Wilson, and the game was tied, 7–7. And there it remained, neither team scoring again until the fourth quarter. Finally, the Miami defense cracked, giving up a 35-yard field goal by Tony Fritsch and later an Earl Campbell 1-yard plunge. The Dolphins earned a late safety, but it was too little, too late, as the Dolphins went down to a 17–9 defeat.

Griese was suffering from bruised ribs that day but without a flak jacket played through the pain. Houston had bottled up Delvin Williams, holding him to 41 yards, while Griese completed only 11 of his 28 passes for 114 yards. Meanwhile, Houston's offense gained 455 yards and slowly wore down the Miami defense with 77 offensive plays.

"That's their game," said linebacker Kim Bokamper. "The threat of Earl Campbell's running moved the linebackers up, and then came the pass." Pastorini completed 20 of 29 attempts for 306 yards and one touchdown. Pastorini froze the Dolphins defense with play action to Campbell all afternoon. Campbell gained 84 yards on 26 carries.

"Bob can't even take a deep breath," said Bob Matheson, the Miami linebacker, of Griese, who was as injured as Pastorini. "People have no idea what it's like to try to play football when you're in that kind of shape."

"I'm sorry I couldn't do better for you," Griese told Mike Current, a teammate, in the locker room.

"Griese never complained. We had so many opportunities but we didn't make the big plays that win games. They did. Pastorini was terrific," Shula told the press.

In January 1979, Pete Rozelle suggested that George Young take over as the general manager of the New York Giants. Shula was intimately involved in the appointment. When Rozelle approached him about the position, asking for recommendations, Shula recommended Young instantly for Rozelle's shortlist of potential executives. It was a precarious spot. The warring Mara family, Wellington and Tim, who fought over who could order light bulbs and boxes of pencils, had turned what was once one of the league's flagship organizations into a laughingstock. Shula was immensely proud of Young, the one-time history teacher. Shula called him "a walking encyclopedia of information."

"Back in Baltimore, I once gave him the key to my office and asked him to evaluate players from game films," Shula said. "After the season, he had evaluated each and every player we considered and told us why we should accept or reject them. He was seldom wrong."

"He was very much influenced by his tenure under Don Shula," said Jim Mandich, former Dolphins tight end.

In February of 1979, Larry Csonka called Don Shula. "I negotiated with Coach Shula, not Joe Robbie. That deal was agreed to in just 3 days, and in 1979 we made the playoffs."

Csonka flew to Miami to finish the negotiations. "Once Zonk and Robbie got in the same room together, things went pretty smooth," said Shula. "It's hard to be mad at a guy that's meant so much, that's been such a part of the success."

"I signed the first time we met," he said. "Robbie wasn't harsh in any way in the negotiations. Neither was I. That was a little surprising because of everything we had been through, but our past problems were based on business, not personalities. There was no hassle over money." The one-year contract was for $125,000.

There was no doubt in that there was plenty of football left in Csonka, but it was clear he was not happy in New York. Yet his Giants teammates liked him a lot. Doug Kotar, a fellow running back, recalled that Csonka had run over Gary Fencik of the Chicago Bears—on purpose. Fencik had sent a Giants player to the sidelines with what Csonka had considered a cheap shot. He requested the ball on the next play. He burst through the line with his old ferocity and then purposely ran right at Fencik. At the last minute, he hit Fencik with his massive forearm and drove into the Bears safety with all his weight and force, driving Fencik to the ground.

"I'm convinced in my mind that Larry still has a lot of football left in him," Shula told the press. "There hasn't been much of it used up in the last four years."

"Our past relationship was something good and special," Shula said, "and I have a good memory for guys that really put it on the line for me, but if I ever let emotion enter into it, I wouldn't be doing my job as a football coach. It wouldn't be fair to my staff, to my players, or to myself. If he gets down and proves he can do anything near what he did in his old days, he'll be useful to our team. But there are no guarantees. He still has to win a job on the football team."

Csonka knew what to expect, even if he wasn't prepared. Csonka signed up with a bad knee and came in at a whopping 265 pounds. Shula immediately set his new weight goal at 237, his old playing weight. Csonka immediately worked out at the training facility, even working out with the now-retired Jim Kiick.

His work on his knee was difficult and required special equipment. Csonka knew his knee was not ready for an NFL season. He, however, was committed. It was not uncommon to hear him scream and holler during those exercises. "What's all this moanin'?" asked Kiick. "Go to hell," Csonka mumbled. "Zonk, this is only the beginning," laughed Kiick.

Shula also attended a good number of Csonka's workouts. "I don't think he ever worked half as hard as he did this off-season," Shula said. "He had to, because of the situation he's in. He had to get that weight off, and it was a struggle. He can't make it if he plays at 250 pounds. Age is creeping up on him."

To show his commitment, he also showed up a week early to training camp and practiced with the rookies and second-year players. And he was not spared the infamous 12-minute run. He completed it without complaint. "That's the furthest he's ever been," chuckled Shula. "Before, it was a big deal to get him headed in one direction and keep his momentum going without having him stop to walk."

Csonka told the press he still hated training camp with every ounce of passion that he had when he was young and full of fire. He insisted he was no "yes-man." But for the first time in his life, he was willing to commit and keep his mouth shut.

"I'm ready to make any sacrifice he demands. I just want to be on the field as much as I can," said Csonka. "Because of my age, my knee, and the fact I might be a step slower, I've got to make up for it in enthusiasm and by making a good impression. I just want to be on a winning team. That might sound humble for a guy that's in his 12th year, but that's exactly where I'm at. There's no future for me. My future is behind me. I've got one year, and I'm going for broke. Each game is my career, and that's the way I'm going at it. I don't believe I'll ever be in another training camp."

"I think he wants it in the worst of ways," said the coach. "He wants to end on a positive note. The guy has immense pride."

"The starting fullback job is between Csonka and [Leroy] Harris," said Shula. "Listen, I didn't bring Csonka down here just to use him on third-and-one." It was clear Csonka's comeback was a just a one-year commitment. But he was earnest. Shula knew what Csonka was capable of. He knew he could carry a capable team on his back. And it was good to have the prodigal son home at last.

The 1979 draft was a solid one for the Dolphins, as they acquired running back Tony Nathan, offensive tackle Jon Geisler, kicker Uwe von Shamann, and defensive back Glenn Blackwood. A notable thing about this draft was that 10 of their 16 selections appeared on the franchise's active roster at some point in their careers.

Shula was busy at the winter meetings. Owners spent much time discussing Super Bowl sites for 1981 and 1982. The big focus that year was on the competition committee. The powerful group of five (Tex Schramm, Dallas; Don Shula, Miami; Paul Brown, Cincinnati; Peter Hadhazy, Cleveland; and Bart Starr, Green Bay) were set to address four areas of concern. "One is rules, notably the difficult one concerning defensive pass interference. A second is improvement of equipment using new technology. Another is the player limit and continuing violations of the injured-reserve provisions. A fourth is the practicality of instant television replay to collaborate officials' decisions," reported the *New York Times* in mid-March.

There was a lot of pressure from fans and media alike to bring in some system of instant replay. Rozelle and other NFL executives were skeptical it would make a difference other than slowing the game down. But player safety was uppermost in minds of the owners and the Players Union.

"With the paralysis last summer of Darryl Stingley, the New England wide receiver, still fresh in mind, the concern over better equipment remains real. Schramm and Shula have been looking into new kinds of equipment which would absorb body blows. Of particular interest was the flak vest that protected the broken ribs of the Houston quarterback, Dan Pastorini, in last year's playoff games," continued the *Times*.

The rules committee did in fact offer many new safety rules, including no spearing with the helmet, no blocking below the waist during special teams play, all players had to wear their helmets with chins straps on, unsportsmanlike penalties were expanded to include punching, no striking with arms or elbows or kicking opponents, and others. Since Shula had joined, the committee had issued almost twenty new rules changes aimed at increasing player safety.

"These things were allowed to creep into the game without any intent of rules makers. If the offensive lineman tried to do anything he was flagged for holding. Now you can protect the quarterback and he can throw the ball. That's the basis of everything.

"Tex Schramm, president of the Dallas Cowboys, and Don Shula, coach of the Miami Dolphins, are the catalysts of the Competitions Committee, which was following a mandate. In the 1970s, pro football had stereotyped itself with run-oriented offenses slamming and efficient zone defenses," wrote William N. Wallace.

"The rules changes seemed to be what everyone wanted, the fans, the owners," said Shula. "So far I haven't heard any complaints. The committee is flexible enough that if we determine it's gone too far, we can adjust."

"The defense had too much of an edge," said Steelers head coach Chuck Noll. "The linesmen had fun. There were no restrictions as to what they could do, slap helmets, grab jerseys."

On April 2, the news came that Carroll Rosenbloom had died swimming in the waters of Golden Beach, Florida, just north of Miami. There was conjecture that his death may have been the result of foul play, but Florida officials ruled that out. Instead, they posited, he was one of the first recipients of a heart bypass operation. He had probably suffered a heart attack and then drowned. More than 900 people attended Rosenbloom's memorial service, including fifteen NFL owners, the sportscaster Howard Cosell, the entire Rams organization, and celebrities such as Warren Beatty, Kirk Douglas, Cary Grant, Jimmy Stewart, Rod Steiger, and Henry Mancini.

The 1979 season started off with a tough 9–7 win over the Bills at Rich Stadium. Buffalo had made a second-quarter touchdown until Uwe von Schamann's

34-yard field goal got the Dolphins on the board in the third quarter. But it wasn't until Csonka burst through for a 1-yard touchdown in the fourth quarter that the Dolphins finally led for the first time. After that, they beat the Seahawks, Vikings, and Bears to improve to 4–0, lost the next two games to the Jets and the Raiders, then set themselves right again at 5–2 against the Buffalo Bills. It was Shula's record 20th consecutive win against the Bills. Shula had never lost a game to Buffalo in his first ten seasons with the Dolphins.

The Dolphins seesawed between victories and losses all the way to Week 14, a showdown with their division rival New England Patriots. Both teams were 8–5. Their second meeting of the year took place at the Orange Bowl. They went into halftime with the Patriots in the lead, 17–13. The second-half scoring started with a Griese-to-Nat Moore 38-yard touchdown, followed by a safety when the Patriots snapped the ball out of the end zone. From there, it was a rout, which the Dolphins won, 39–24. Then they split their last two games and finished the season 10–6.

Though they finished a game worse than the year before, they finished first in the AFC East. The team ranked fourth on defense, and 11th on offense. Csonka had rushed for 827 yards, and Delvin Williams for 703. Griese had a subpar season for him, throwing 14 touchdowns and 16 interceptions.

One of their most surprising defeats that year had come only after a day of one of Shula's sweetest joys. The Dolphins were in Cleveland to play the Browns on November 18. The day before, the entire Shula clan had made plans for a family reunion dinner, and then for attending the game the next day at Cleveland Municipal Stadium to root on the Dolphins. This crowd required thirty tickets alltogether (including one each for Father Robert Hanzo, who was the pastor at St. Mary's, and Sister Denise, Don's second grade teacher, also from St. Mary's). But on Saturday night, Dan and Mary's five children, eighteen grandchildren, and one great-grandchild, and other family members, converged to celebrate Don as the guest of honor. The family crowd was so extensive that they took up an entire banquet room at the Bond Court Hotel in downtown Cleveland.

"I always root for the Dolphins to win, and I'm a bad loser just like Don," his mother once told the press.

After a night of seeing familiar faces he saw only too seldom, the Dolphins lost to the Browns in overtime, 30–24.

"They didn't know a lot about football. Dad was born in the old country, and mom didn't know about sports, either," said Shula. "Now they live and die with our team. They've been to Super Bowls and know the pressures of the game. My parents are great people. Both worked hard all their lives to raise a family," said Shula warmly. "I don't see my parents as much as I like because I am always in and out. Dad is not moving around too good lately, either."

"Don had always been a good boy, very thoughtful," his mother proudly stated. "He sometimes has so much on his mind, but he never forgets to call up and see how we are." Still, Don was missed by his family. As his mother said, it would have been better if he had coached the Browns. "It would be so nice to have him nearby and we'd see more of him and especially his family of five children. But we've never talked about moving. All our children are here except Don and his brother Jim in Chicago. We're too old to make a change."

In the fall of 1975, Don twice came home to visit his father in the hospital, once in Painesville, once in Cleveland. His father had a severe stomach ailment incorrectly diagnosed at the beginning. "He almost died," Mary Shula said. The illness sapped his strength and required him to now walk with a cane. By 1979, Shula's parents had been married fifty-eight years. However, when the couple had celebrated their 50th wedding anniversary, the party had to be relocated to Cincinnati, because the Dolphins were playing there.

On December 30, at Three Rivers Stadium, the Pittsburgh Steelers annihilated the Miami Dolphins in a divisional playoff game. Shula was frustrated. Noll and the Steelers had experienced a Dolphins-like run of their own, and their dominance since Miami's fall irked Shula. The Steelers had the best postseason record in the 1970s and would win four Super Bowls, and this made for a more emotional Shula.

"I feel it's time for Miami," said Shula. "That's what I hope. Pittsburgh has been there long enough."

The Steelers scored 20 unanswered points in the first quarter, and the Dolphins were never in the game, a bitter 34–14 defeat. Miami rushed for just 25 yards in 22 attempts. "It's hard to find anything positive. It was so disappointing. We just never challenged them," said Shula.

In September 1980, there was conjecture that Shula was a candidate for the head coaching job at the University of Notre Dame. Shula was now considered the greatest living coach. He had more than 180 wins, with only George Halas and Curly Lambeau ahead of him on the NFL's all-time list, Halas with 324 victories in 40 years and Lambeau with 229 in 33.

"I really don't spend much time thinking about my place in history." he said. "That's for other people to do. Now, during the season, your whole thrust is winning this year, winning on Sunday and the week after that and after that."

Said safety Tim Foley, "He does a better job than anyone in football at filling a variety of roles. Some head coaches are great administrators, some have great football minds, and some are great at public relations. Shula does everything well. I think he's the best for one very important reason. When we won those (two) Super Bowls, we won with less material than anyone else ever did. We didn't have the great talent a lot of championship teams had. But he got more out of us than anybody ever could.

"No. I don't think he's changed much. His hair is a little grayer, but he still has as much intensity as he ever did. I find that I've changed more than he has. As I grow older, I understand more and more what he's trying to do. I'm not as intimidated as much as I used to be, and my respect grows for him the longer I'm around him."

"I don't try and jam a system down a player's throat or a team's throat. I guess you would say I'm adaptable," said Shula. "I also believe in the draft . . . I love to bring in six, seven, eight young people every year. It keeps your special teams enthusiastic and aggressive, and eventually you hope they'll compete for starting jobs. And if there's a trade I think will help us, like the Delvin Williams deal, I make it."

"Our relationship hasn't gotten any better," Shula said, referring to owner Joe Robbie, "but it hasn't gotten any worse. He runs the business, I run the team, and I've never had a problem trying to get someone I wanted."

Shula's relationship with Robbie never warmed. They maintained separate offices thirteen miles away from each other. Other than salaries, Robbie was good for his word and did not interfere with player personnel moves or changes in staff. They were never close to being friends.

"There has always been speculation that they would eventually split, but each time his contract came due Shula wound up signing on for another tour," reported *Sports Illustrated*.

Shula told the story about being recruited by Notre Dame. "I played golf with Moose Krause [then the Notre Dame athletic director]. Moose said there was no hurry. He'd accept my decision after we finished the front nine."

In the end, Shula signed a new three-year deal with the Dolphins. His salary had been rumored at $450,000 per year, and though Robbie would not announce the exact figure, he said the new deal made Shula the highest-paid coach in the game. And he was. For as diabolical as Robbie could be, he made good on Shula.

The 1980 squad would finish a disappointing 8–8. It was time for Shula to make a break with his own past and build anew. Suddenly he became renewed with energy to build back up again. His optimism began to return. He began to see things no one else saw.

The one bright spot for the Dolphins in 1980 was the drafting of future Hall of Famer Dwight Stephenson, who was an All-American under Bear Bryant at Alabama. Bryant said he was the best center he ever coached and called him "a man among children."

"Years ago they felt the centers lacked the ability," said John Sandusky, the offensive-line coach. "Now, it's a passé notion. The center's the anchor of the line. Dwight's quickness allows us to do a lot of other things. Because of the three-man line, the center now has to be like a regular offensive lineman, block and be quick enough and protect against the pass."

"The reason he's so important to us is he comes off the ball on our running game," says Shula, "and on the pass he sets up so well. He does a great job of backing up in the pocket."

In practice, Stephenson and Baumhower (on defense) were both so intense that flare-ups between the two led to full-scale fisticuffs. The Dolphins line regularly gave up the fewest sacks in the league. He made five straight Pro Bowl appearances in the 1980s.

The Dolphins played in two milestone games on television that December. The first one was a Monday night overtime game against the New England Patriots. The game was tied, 6–6, coming out of the half. Then the Patriots went up, 13–6, early in the the fourth quarter. The Dolphins responded with a touchdown, tying the game. In the waning seconds, the Patriots attempted a field goal. But then ABC broadcaster Howard Cosell made an announcement.

"This is just a football game, no matter who wins or loses," said Cosell as Patriots kicker John Smith prepared to kick a field goal with three seconds remaining in the game. "An unspeakable tragedy recently confirmed to us by ABC News, in New York City. John Lennon, outside of his apartment building, on the West Side of New York City, the most famous perhaps of all the Beatles, shot twice in the back, rushed to Roosevelt Hospital, dead on arrival. Hard to go back to the game after that news flash."

The Dolphins blocked Smith's field goal attempt and forced overtime. In the extra period, rookie quarterback David Woodley heaved a 54-yard bomb down the right sideline, where Duriel Harris pulled it in. That set up the winning Uwe von Schamann field goal, with Miami winning, 16–13. The surreal experience is still considered one of the most memorable *Monday Night Football* games of all time.

The other notable game was the December 20 contest against the New York Jets at the Orange Bowl. The Jets were 3–12, and the Dolphins were 8–7. NBC television decided to do something different. "Here we had this dog of a game," NBC Executive Producer Don Ohlmeyer said. "Part of my thinking was what could we possibly do to get fans to watch this? People could follow a game with pictures, graphics, and hearing the PA announcer in the background." Ohlmeyer proposed a game with no announcers. The idea was to make it a you-are-there experience. Dick Enberg, then NBC's lead football announcer, was not impressed. "My first reaction was of incredible nerve, nervousness," he said. "We're paid to talk, so all of us want to fill the air with lots of exciting words. We all gathered together, hoping that Ohlmeyer was dead wrong. I mean, he was flirting with the rest of our lives. What if this crazy idea really worked?"

Bryant Gumbel did an off-the-cuff pregame summation and then walked off the screen. Highly sensitive microphones were placed throughout the stadium. Lots of graphics were flashed. But on the television screen? Just the game. No announcers.

Said Enberg: "The final outcome, with much relief, was the fact after watching for a quarter or two that, you know, something was missing. It was us. While we are not the most important ingredients in the pie, we certainly are a slice of that pie that gives the whole experience full flavor."

Gumbel said later, "I can't believe it's anything more than a footnote."

Said Ohlmeyer, "It certainly did a much better [ratings] number for us than that dog deserved." It was the only time an NFL game was ever televised without announcers. The Jets won, 24–17.

On June 25, 1981, Bob Griese officially retired, saying, "I've had 14 years, and they've been 14 good years . . . I've been in a lot of big games, and I've won the big one," he said, a reference to the Super Bowl victories he directed in 1973 and 1974. "I can't help but feel some sorrow for some players around the league who never get a chance to experience anything like that."

There was a rare kind of Shula family reunion on September 27, 1981, at Memorial Stadium in Baltimore. That day, the Dolphins were playing the Colts. On one side of the field was Don Shula, scowling, jaw out, and on the other side, stretching and focusing, was David Shula. Miami coach against Colts special-teams player. It was a very proud moment for Don and Dorothy.

Dorothy felt squarely in the middle. "I'm for my kid and my family," she said. "That's simple. I want David to do great and score touchdowns if he can on every punt return. And, of course, I want Don to be successful."

"I'm sure I'll be more nervous for this game than others," David Shula said. "But I can't get that nervous about it or I'll screw up."

"I want him to do well. But at the same time I make a living coaching this football team," said Shula. But he was also concerned. "This is a tough, competitive game, but I certainly wouldn't want one of my players to cheapshot David. I might get upset. I might go running on the field saying, 'Hey, don't cheapshot my kid.'"

David Shula, a two-time All-Ivy selection, had been a star receiver at Dartmouth College from 1978 to 1980. In his three years at Dartmouth, he caught 133 passes for 1,822 yards and 9 touchdowns. Joe Yukica was the head coach at Dartmouth in 1980, the team's centennial season. Jeff Dufresne was the top running back, Jeff Kemp was the quarterback, and David Shula was the receiver who held most of Dartmouth's receiving records. Kemp's father, Jack, who played from 1960 to 1969 for the Chargers and Bills, was at the time a leading Republican congressman.

Kemp said of David, "His moves and body control were head and shoulders above everybody else's. He always knew the defense, always realized that football was also an intellectual pursuit. He was open every time."

"He makes All-Ivy his sophomore season and could have rested on his laurels," said Dartmouth coach Yukica. "Instead, looking for a little extra speed, maybe one more step at the start, he joined the track team. Not good enough for the varsity, you understand. The jayvee track team. I'd look out my window, and there was my All-Ivy receiver finishing dead last in the 100. The jayvee 100. He didn't care. And who knows, maybe it did help him, although I don't think we ever timed him better than 4.95, no matter what he did."

"A lot of kids came from more interesting backgrounds than Dave's," Yukica said of the youngster's desire to blend in. "Who knows how many Colt camps he'd been in? But you'd never know he was Don Shula's son. On the field it was always, 'How do you want it done, Coach?' That's what I remember the most about him."

"I don't mean to say he was a boring guy," Kemp said. "But he was more levelheaded, protective, and cautious than the rest of us. He was very deliberate and superprepared, whether it was studying or in football."

Jeff caught on with the Los Angeles Rams, while Dave was a free agent with Baltimore. "I knew the team and the town from when my dad coached there. It sounded great, and I have no regrets."

His father had called and made him a free-agent offer, but David refused. "No matter what happened or how well I did, it would be a difficult situation with the

Dolphins. My father and I would both be on the spot." The Colts called not long after. David had made the Colts, despite his disadvantages, like his lack of height (5-foot-10) and his lack of speed (a relatively slow 4.85 speed in the 40-yard dash).

"Perhaps there was some sentiment behind the signing of young Shula by the Colts. The general manager, Dick Szymanski, was a player for Shula when Don coached the Colts in the 1960's. And Fred Schubach, the player personnel director, was equipment manager during the same era, the best years in the club's history," wrote Gerald Eskenazi in the *New York Times*.

"We're both conscious of not revealing too much to each other," David says of his weekly Monday telephone conversations with his father and mother. "He'll ask how I did and we'll go over that. He'll ask about the big plays in the game. . . . Sometimes, my mom gets on the other line and says to both of us, 'Now you don't tell him anything that might eventually hurt you.'"

"I think it's such a lot of pressure, unnecessary pressure on him," said concerned mom Dorothy. "But I'm sure it was inevitable being in the same division. I think he'll handle it, like he has everything else in his life. We're very proud of him."

The night before the game, David had dinner with his father, mother, his fiancée, and several other family members in the hotel restaurant where the Dolphins were staying. "It was hectic all week, though. And it was the same way for my father. And then just before the game, we saw each other on the field and shook hands," recalled David. "The media swarmed around us like bees around honey. It was as though they were covering a summit conference."

In the stands with Dorothy was David's brother Michael, then a sixteen-year-old high school quarterback. Michael had taken up David's old Dolphins duties back home, running projectors, carrying clipboards, and other duties. Daughter Sharon, who was a sophomore at the University of Miami, roamed the Dolphins sidelines with a camera to take pictures of both Don and David during the course of the game. The Dolphins won, 31–28, giving the 1981 squad a 4–0 start. When the Colts played the Cleveland Browns a month later, a large contingent of family and friends came to visit him, and to cheer him on unabashedly. And of course, it was a return home when he played in Miami the next week, a 27–10 Dolphins victory.

"Just how does Shula get these performances, year in and year out? How does he get youngsters to play error-free football? Is there a Don Shula secret in striving for perfection?" wrote Eskenazi.

"It's the way I grew up," said Shula. "I've always been neat and clean."

"He isn't kidding. You make a mistake on the Dolphins and you won't repeat it," wrote Eskenazi.

"It isn't unusual for him to put the club through a walk-through at 7:30 at night in the summer if he didn't like the way the two-a-days went," said a staffer.

"We don't think it's a joke," said Shula about holding calls in practice. "We stop practice." Shula did not want his players committing penalties, even in practice. "There are times teams gamble because there are no calls," said Shula. But, he added, "You make a decision on what football should be." Shula's teams were always among the league's least penalized. "When I played, I couldn't stand for teammates to make mistakes. I'd get after them if they made errors. They called me Captain Redneck. I believe that as long as you're doing something, you do it right."

Don Shula fined David Woodley before one game that season because the quarterback wasn't at a meeting—even though the meeting started ahead of schedule. "To be in there every game," said Shula, "you have to master coverages. Griese very rarely threw to the wrong receiver, and neither did Strock. But Woodley came from a college system of rollouts [at LSU]. What had to be done was learn."

"Other teams sink or swim on their quarterback," said Woodley. "But the success or failure of this team is tied to Don Shula."

"He seems to get the most out of his players," cornerback Ed Taylor said of Shula. "He puts them in situations in which they excel. When I came here, they said they knew I could play good man-to-man coverage. So they used me as a nickel back. Part of the tradition here is that they're used to winning and expect it of you. In all my years in pro football, I had never been in a winning situation."

"He's all over us like a cheap suit if we make a mistake in practice," Cefalo said of Shula. "In a game he's such an intense man. But he is in practice, too. It's the mental mistakes he can't stand. Physical errors are something different to him."

At New England on November 8, the Dolphins were tied with the Patriots after John Smith kicked a 34-yard field goal with 11 seconds remaining in the fourth quarter. Then in overtime, Dolphins linebacker Bob Brudzinski intercepted a pass by Steve Grogan that led to Uwe von Schamann's 30-yard field goal to win it for Miami, 30–27. It also happened to be Coach Shula's 200th NFL win.

They dropped their next two games to the Raiders and Jets but finished with four consecutive victories, defeating the Eagles, Patriots, Chiefs, and Bills, to end the season at 11–5–1. The defense was beginning to coalesce in a very special way.

Arnsparger was still fiddling, but the first inklings of what would become a sensation in 1982 was taking shape as the unit was ranked fifth in the NFL.

The Dolphins had won the AFC East and were the No. 2 seed in the AFC playoffs. They would face the No. 3-seeded San Diego Chargers, who had won the AFC West with a record of 10–6. The divisional playoff game was played on Saturday, January 2, 1982, at the Orange Bowl.

The Chargers were an offensive juggernaut and had amassed a then-unheard-of 6,744 yards with a unit that had been dubbed "Air Coryell" that would lead the NFL in passing each season from 1978 to 1983. Don Coryell, San Diego's head coach, developed what they called the "vertical passing" game, which was possible now with a lot of the new rules the competition committee had enacted to make the game more exciting. This offense was explicitly made possible by what became known as the "Mel Blount rule," named after the hard-hitting Pittsburgh Steelers defensive back known for his physical style of play, stipulating that defenders could not bump receivers beyond five yards of the line of scrimmage.

Taking advantage of the new rules, Coryell set out to exploit them for his own purposes. The offense required the defense to defend the entire field. Many of the pass plays were based on timing and rhythm.

But Coryell also had the people to exploit this offense, as well. The unit featured one of the most prolific passers of all time, Dan Fouts, who was the first quarterback to throw for more than 4,000 yards in a season four seasons in a row. Fouts had two dangerous wide receivers in Charlie Joiner and Wes Chandler, a rugged running back in Chuck Muncie, and Kellen Winslow, a big, rangy tight end.

"This is a game where we can't afford to make a mistake," said Coryell before the game. "That's what they're looking for us to do. They're a very well-coached team. If we turn over the ball and don't take advantage of our opportunities, it could be a very long afternoon. Defensively, we've had a tough time against the pass. We fear Miami's passing attack. They have two different-style quarterbacks you have to prepare for, and it's a different kind of rush for each one of them. But I think our defense has come together the last four or five games. It's better than it was early in the year."

"We need a big game from our defense, but we also need for our offense to play well. We can't count on holding an offense like San Diego to just one touchdown. We're going to have to score some points," said Shula. "The thing you have to do with the Chargers is realize just how explosive they are and not lose your poise defensively. You have to stay in the game and try to make your plays defensively and have your offense get something going. Fouts is probably the best in the league at reading defenses. We have to counteract them."

The writers were jokingly referring to the Miami quarterback as Woodstrock, for the seamless way Shula interchanged his quarterbacks. Don Strock had thought he was the quarterback of the future when he was drafted 1974. He sat behind Griese and Morrall. In 1980, he thought he might finally inherit the mantle, but the Dolphins drafted David Woodley from LSU, and Strock found himself passed over for Woodley, who started all but one of Miami's games in 1981.

Yet Shula had turned Strock into the football version of a relief pitcher. "I can't think of anyone else in football," said Strock, "who does the same thing I do." At that time, Strock had worked in 89 games as a Dolphin, 86 in the regular season and three in the playoffs. He also acted as the holder for the placekicker for many seasons.

"It takes a guy with a certain temperament to do what he does," said Shula. "I don't think everybody could handle it. Certainly, not every pitcher in baseball can handle being a reliever. You have to be cut out of a certain mold."

"The key thing for me," said Strock, "is to stay prepared. . . . I have been put in games after eight minutes of the first quarter, after the half, and, like last week, with four minutes to go. What I do along the sidelines is stay ready on every play, know what to call, know what I would like to do on the next play. Because a lot of times, I don't know when I'm going to go in."

Strock and Woodley were never mistaken for the other. Strock was a 6-foot-5 classic pocket passer who liked to loft long throws. The 6-foot-2 Woodley was a scrambler who threw darts. The fascinating thing was that Strock was allowed to call his own plays, while Shula called Woodley's.

"It's hard to explain what happens when he comes in," said receiver Duriel Harris. "You feel like, 'O.K., this is it. It's time to do it.' He brings in an intensity that there's no way to explain."

"When he's in there," Shula said of Strock, "he's usually throwing every down."

"I don't know," Shula said. "Different things happened to him. He just hasn't been able to get it all going when he's had the chance."

"Because of the atmosphere in there when I go in, I have no time to get tense," Strock said. "Especially if we're in the two-minute drill."

The temperature at kickoff was 76 degrees with intense humidity. Fouts remembered fans "blowing their nose on you as you walked out of the tunnel." Kellen Winslow said, before the game, "They call me the sissy, the San Diego chicken. I'm the tight end who won't block. They say I need a heart transplant . . . that our whole team has no heart. But I know what I can do."

The game did not start well for Shula and the Dolphins. The high-powered Chargers offense shredded one of the stingiest defenses in the league for 24 points in the first quarter. It was a stunning display of offensive power and finesse. Rolf Benirschke started it all with a 32-yard field goal, Wes Chandler returned a punt 58 yards for a touchdown, Chuck Muncie crashed in for a 1-yard touchdown, and Fouts hit James Brooks with an 8-yard touchdown pass. Woodley, who started the game, was a paltry 2-for-5 passing, for 20 yards. The Dolphins were being booed by 73,735 fans in the Orange Bowl.

Veteran Chargers receiver Charlie Joiner had his head in his hands on the sideline. "What's wrong?" asked teammate Winslow.

"Man, you just don't do this to a Don Shula team," Joiner moaned. "He's gonna pull Woodley, put in Strock, start throwing the ball, and we're gonna be here all damn day." Joiner was right. By 12:05 of the second quarter, Shula had seen enough, and Strock was called in.

If the first quarter had been all Chargers, the Dolphins under Strock answered the bell. As if waking from a slumber, the Dolphins started their scoring with a 34-yard Uwe von Schamann field goal, followed by a 1-yard Strock touchdown pass to tight end Joe Rose. Then came one of the most famous playoff plays in the history of the NFL.

Miami held the ball with six seconds left and the ball at the San Diego 40. Miami called a time-out. Strock went to the sidelines.

"What about the hook-and-ladder?" said Shula. Why not? Don Strock faded back to pass and found Duriel Harris in between the two zones. Harris then immediately, in danger of being tackled, lateraled the ball to the trailing running back, Tony Nathan, who ran the remaining 25 yards for a touchdown as time expired in the half, making the score 24–17. The stadium exploded, and the Dolphins had suddenly taken back the momentum.

"It's pretty hard to believe that a guy would bite on that with six seconds to go," Strock later said of 87 Circle Curl Lateral, "but when it worked, it made every high school coach in the world happy because every high school has that play."

"It was a beautiful, beautiful play," remembered Coryell. "Perfectly executed."

Fouts shouted out, "Aw, fuck! Here we go again."

The stadium roared to life, and the din just kept on going. "I've never heard anything like it,"said Strock. "It was like we were still on the field. It was that loud. We were in the locker room, what—10, 15 minutes?—and it never stopped!"

"You could just sense the difference," said Chargers linebacker Linden King. "Strock had a real presence out there." The momentum shift continued into the third quarter when Strock directed a 74-yard drive capped by a 15-yard pass to Joe Rose, making the score 24–24. The Chargers responded, with Fouts hitting Winslow for a 25-yard touchdown. And then Strock and the Dolphins struck back with a 50-yard pass play to backup tight end Bruce Hardy to tie the score at 31-all. Following an interception of a Dan Fouts pass by Lyle Blackwood, Miami scored another touchdown with Tony Nathan rushing from 12 yards out, to make the score 38–31, Dolphins. The Dolphins were finally in the lead.

With 4:39 left in the fourth quarter, Dolphins running back Andra Franklin fumbled deep in San Diego territory, and the Chargers averted another Miami score when safety Pete Shaw recovered it. Fouts led the Chargers to the Dolphin 9-yard line, with only 58 seconds left in regulation. The Dolphins sent a heavy pass rush. Fouts threw up a prayer intended for Winslow in the end zone. The pass missed Winslow but sailed right into the arms of James Brooks for a touchdown to tie the game, 38–38. Not only had Fouts thrown the pass blindly, but Brooks wasn't even supposed to be there on that play. He had run out for a pass when he was supposed to have stayed in and blocked.

"That was one of the all-time brilliant heads-up plays I've ever seen," Fouts said. "In all the hundreds of times we'd run that play, I'd never thrown to anybody back there."

After the ensuing squib kick, Strock moved the Dolphins to the San Diego 26-yard line for a possible game-winning field goal. But the 6-foot-5 Winslow ever so slightly tipped the ball as it sailed from Uwe von Shamann's foot just enough to deflect it.

"It was the biggest thrill of my life," Winslow said. "I felt like I scored three touchdowns." Winslow caught 13 passes, a playoff record, for 166 yards. The game headed to overtime.

In the overtime, the Chargers drove to the Dolphins' 10-yard line, and Benirschke missed a 27-yard field-goal attempt after a bad snap and a bad hold. The Dolphins marched the ball deep into Chargers territory, where von Shamann's attempt was again blocked, this time by Leroy Jones. "He kicked it kind of low," Jones said, "and I stuck my arm up and got it." Taking the ball from deep into their own territory, Fouts drove the Chargers back to the Dolphins' 10-yard line.

"Shula was hot that his players were helping Winslow up after a play only to see him beat them with another great catch," wrote Rick Reilly in *Sports Illustrated* years later. "Let him get up by himself!" Shula kept yelling.

Then Benirschke finally made the game-winning 29-yard field goal. The Chargers had won one of the great playoff games in history, 41–38. At the time, it was the highest-scoring playoff game in NFL history and had lasted four hours and five minutes.

"I have coached for 31 or 32 years, and this is tremendous, . . . There has never been a game like this. It was probably the most exciting game in pro football history," said Coryell.

Shula concurred, "A great game. . . . Maybe the greatest ever." The game has since become known as the "Epic in Miami," and *Sports Illustrated* called it "A Game No One Should Have Lost."

"Doubly ironic for the Dolphins was that, almost 10 years ago to the day, they had won such a game: the longest game in playoff history, a double-overtimer in which Kansas City's Jan Stenerud missed, and then Miami's Garo Yepremian made, the winning field goal," pointed out John Underwood in *Sports Illustrated*.

"The game had everything—seven turnovers, 100 yards in penalties, 79 points, 96 pass attempts, seven TD passes and a Wes Chandler punt return for a touchdown—and didn't finish until there was barely a minute left in overtime," wrote Barry Werner for FOX Sports thirty-five years later. The Dolphins had gained 472 net yards and San Diego 564, for a total of 1,036 total yards of offense.

"The locker-room celebration was more low-key than other locker rooms I'd been in," Chargers running back Hank Bauer told reporters. "It was more of 'Thank God that's over. Thank God we got out alive.'"

Shula did not deal with losses well. And whether he liked to admit it or not, he brought them home with him. Sometimes Dorothy could talk him out of his despair. Sometimes not.

"I can remember him sitting alone on the patio one time, staring out over the pool," his daughter Annie said. "I watched him from the bathroom window, and I felt so sorry for him, I started to cry. I wished I could have jumped on his lap and put my arms around him."

"He'd scare the crap out of you," recalled daughter Sharon. "He's built like a wall, and there's such a powerful force inside him. We did not talk about losses. Period. I kept myself hidden in my bedroom. As I've gotten older, I've just stayed away. I can't even bring myself to go to his box at Joe Robbie Stadium after a loss."

As consolation, Shula coached the AFC in the Pro Bowl in Honolulu. Shula faced the NFC's John McKay of the Tampa Bay Buccaneers. "This is my third time coaching the Pro Bowl, and it's a joy to work with these talented players," said Shula. He had coached the winning teams in the 1965 and 1968 Pro Bowls.

In June 1982, *Sports Illustrated* published an exposé on drugs in the NFL. This also mirrored what was going on in Major League Baseball in that same period. Don Reese, a thirty-year-old retired defensive end, who had played for the Dolphins (1974–76), Saints (1978–80), and Chargers (1981), told the magazine that there were major drug problems on all three teams. Reese was sentenced to prison in 1977 for selling cocaine and declared that cocaine "now controls and corrupts the game because so many players are on it."

On May 4, 1977, Reese and another Dolphins player, Randy Crowder, had been arrested in Miami for selling a pound of cocaine to an undercover policeman. Both were sentenced to one year in jail.

"Cocaine can be found in quantity throughout the N.F.L. It's pushed on players, often from the edge of the practice field. Sometimes it's pushed by players. Prominent players," said Reese. "A cocaine cloud covers the entire league. I think most coaches know this or have a good idea. Except the dumb ones. Dick Nolan must have suspected that we were on the stuff in New Orleans because he asked me about it a couple of times. Don Shula was too sharp to let it go by unnoticed in Miami, and we had to be extra careful around him." In the Miami area, it would be a continuing story line for another decade.

"I first became aware of the cocaine thing when Reese and Randy Crowder were arrested delivering it in 1977," said Shula in response to the story. "But I never thought it was prevalent, and I don't know. I don't think you can indict a football team on what Don Reese has said."

"Players and management have to attack this problem jointly," said Gene Upshaw, the Oakland Raiders' offensive guard and president of the Players Association. "Drug testing won't solve the problem. It will only detect users. What the clubs propose is a witch hunt, an invasion of privacy."

"We have tested for drugs," said Shula of the new controversial policy of drug testing at the time. "As far back as I can remember, I can't remember any positive results. But we will continue to test."

"There are occasional rumors," Shula continued. "There are poor performances. But in all the years I've been coaching, no player has ever admitted a drug problem to me. I think they fear they would lose their job. Now, with the emphasis on employee assistance, I think a player who needs help is more likely to step forward."

In November of that year, former Dolphin Mercury Morris was convicted of cocaine trafficking and would spend three and half years in jail.

"Merc got a tough verdict. I hate to see a life ruined like that. But he's like anybody else—if you know the rules, then you've got to live by 'em. If you're an N.F.L. player, you're looked on as a role model, whether you like it or not. Especially if you're a star, like Merc was. Anything that deviates from the norm is immediately noticed and talked about," said Shula. "We used to get a rumor a year on Merc with drugs. One time I asked him about it directly. I told him that this was what I'd heard and I wanted him to be honest with me. He told me there was nothing to it. In any confrontation like that, I didn't expect a confession, but I wanted him to know that I'd heard the rumors.

"Reese wasn't here as long as Merc was. Reese was apt to do or say anything without thinking. Crowder was more of a quiet guy. He wasn't outgoing at all. It was tough to get a line on him. At the meetings and practices, he did what he was supposed to do. But with Reese, it was a matter of the coaches having to continually prod him. You knew the ability was there."

As for the team having these problems, Shula was honest, saying, "The only explanation I have is that Miami players might be more susceptible by the nature of southern Florida, being an area where drugs apparently come into the country. Another factor could be that when we had the Super Bowl champions in the 1972 and 1973 seasons, their accomplishments and recognition created more temptation for them.

"We've had some real problems here off the field. They have been real disappointments. They can be real downers if you let them drag you down. But life goes on. You just try to prepare the next guy so he doesn't make the same mistake.

"You try to do the best job you can with your players, on and off the field. But you have very little control once a player leaves practice, or during the offseason. And you never assume guilt from a rumor. You never think any of your players will wind up the way Merc and Reese did. That's the tragic part. But, as a result of Reese's article in *Sports Illustrated* about drugs in the N.F.L., there should be more awareness on everyone's part now."

Just before the season opener against the Jets at Shea Stadium, a dustup occurred between Shula and New York coach Walt Michaels. As required by NFL rules, each team sent three of their most recent game films to their opponent.

Michaels contended that the film quality of their most recent contest, the preseason finale against the Giants, was of such poor quality, they couldn't even see the numbers on the jerseys. "You need to find where certain people are, and it's hard to see the numbers," Michaels said but was quick to add, "It's got no bearing on the game." Still, Jets Film Director Jim Pons filed a formal complaint with the NFL.

"There's definitely no hanky-panky. I've been doing this for 12 years," said Al King, the Dolphins film director. When asked what happened, he responded, "I can't tell until I look at the films."

"Whatever was done wasn't done intentionally," said Shula. "I don't spend a lot of time trying to play those games."

Both teams were well positioned to finish atop the AFC East, and the opening game was as highly charged as a playoff game. The Jets held a 7–0–1 edge over the Dolphins in the last four seasons, even while Shula was 40–16 against the rest of the league. The Jets, conversely, had been 23–33. As Gerald Eskenazi wrote in the New York Times, "It would not be such a renowned streak—everyone in pro football is aware of it—if the Jets had dominated other teams over that span and the Dolphins were soft touches for everyone else."

"When he loses to the Jets so many times, it's got to drive him bananas, I'm sure. But he won't say it," said Frank Buetel, a Dolphins executive.

What were Shula's thoughts on the odd run? "If I was an authority on that, I wouldn't have the trouble."

As it turned out, there was little reason for the Dolphins to worry, as they annihilated the Jets on opening day in New York, taking a 24–14 lead into the third quarter before scoring 21 unanswered points and cruisng to a 45–28 blowout.

The Dolphins bested the Colts the next week, but then the NFL went on strike, with the Players Association calling for a work stoppage until the owners came to the table on a number of issues. Play would not resume until late November. In the meantime, Shula stewed.

Shula grew increasingly frustrated. He admitted that he was drinking gallons of coffee in the meantime instead of coaching; his wastepaper basket resembled a volcano of white used Styrofoam. "That's been the toughest part for me, not doing anything. I'm so geared to be doing something. I've felt all along that if you got the players back on a Tuesday, maybe even a Wednesday, you could play on Sunday," Shula said in mid-November

While he was a coach, he was also a former player and addressed the strife between striking players, and those who were against the work stoppage. "I've stressed all along that the players have to respect each other, that a strike affects different people in different ways, that the players should be able to express themselves."

He reflected back on his career and coaching style. "One of the things I've second-guessed myself on is not praising the good guys more, the ones who never give you any trouble, the ones you take for granted. Jim Langer, Bob Griese, Wayne Moore, Paul Warfield, players like that. Every day they help you to be successful, but you don't acknowledge it like you should. All it takes is a word or a look or a pat. Not to take the time to do it is really being shortsighted," said a thoughtful Shula.

One of the things Shula had read and heard was that he had been coaching for 20 years and that he had changed. "I keep hearing I've mellowed," Shula chuckled. "I've mellowed."

"I don't know if *mellowed* is the right word. It's more a maturity, which comes with age and reasoning," said Dorothy Shula. "As Don has grown, he has grown wiser. He has become a more mature man. He's still hyper after a game, still very hyper. But I think the degree of hyperactivity is less than it once was."

Longtime ESPN announcer Beano Cook, once a Dolphins publicist in the early years, remembered Shula screaming at an official in front of the bench, livid, fists clenched, "You're ruining my life! You're ruining my life!" It was during an exhibition game. "I don't think I ever started a fight," Shula says. "But I had a short fuse."

"He's a screamer," said wide receiver Jimmy Cefalo. "He screams over mental mistakes. He tells us you'll get beat physically once in a while, but don't make mental mistakes. You stay here longer if you don't make mental mistakes."

Gerald Eskanazi once wrote, "It was a Monday night game and there was a call against his team that angered him. He held his fingers to his throat in the 'choke' sign—in front of the national television audience. The criticism eventually resulted in a $1,000 fine. That didn't distress him so much as a call he got the next day from a nun in Baltimore who had known him since his days with the Colts."

"I realized how bad I looked when I got that call from her," Shula said. The next season, he flew her to Dolphins games against the Jets, Bills, and Patriots.

"As a younger coach, I was very intense," Shula said. "Sometimes I was less than understanding. I hope I have been able to balance it out a little, but I also hope that I never give up being intense.

"I'd like to think I've learned things over the years," he said. "This is the 20th year I've been a head coach—seven years in Baltimore, 13 years here. I have also raised a family of five children. You go through that at home, then you come out here and go through coaching young players, turning them into veteran players. You do all that work, you tie it together and it helps you become more mature, more intelligent about your responsibilities."

"Being flexible was never a problem for me. I have always tried to adapt, to get the most out of the people I have, to utilize their strengths, rather than stick a system down their throats," Shula said.

"Mellow? Mellow?" said Stu Weinstein, the Dolphins' director of security. "I've been here nine years, and I've yet to see the mellow. Consistent, yes, but mellow is not the adjective I'd use."

"I don't mind personalities or individuals. In fact, I encourage it. I don't want everyone to be in the same mold, and it has never been that way," Shula said, perturbed by the notion. "They all have to operate under the same basic rules and regulations because I can't control the team if I'm treating one guy one way and the other 48 another way. From there, they can extend into their own personalities. It's refreshing, more than anything else. You look for things that give your team an identity."

During the strike, Daniel Shula, Don's father, passed away in early October 1982. He had been in declining health. Still a resident of Painesville, he left behind his wife, Mary; his sons Joseph of Painesville, Donald in Miami, and James in Chicago; and three daughters Irene, Jeanette, and Jane. He was grandfather of 20 children, and great-grandfather to eight.

The strike was settled on November 16 after 57 days. The season was shortened to nine games, with the top eight teams from each conference qualifying for the playoffs regardless of division. The Dolphins resumed the season and won five of their seven remaining games after the work stoppage, losing only to their cross-state rival Tampa Bay Buccaneers and to the New England Patriots in controversial fashion in what became infamously known as "The Snowplow Game."

On December 12, the Dolphins and Patriots played to a scoreless tie going into the fourth quarter on a frozen field at Shaefer Stadium in New England. There had been ice and snow, and only the yard lines had been plowed the snow was so thick. Both teams slipped and slid throughout the game, finding no traction on the covered field.

"I woke up that morning and looked out the window and just saw snow everywhere. I could see it was going to be that kind of day. It was always tough for us to play up in New England, but during the game the snow was on the field nonstop," recalled Kim Bokamper.

Bokamper remembered that during any break in the action the field crew would plow the yard lines "just so you could see where you were out on the field." The crew worked feverishly throughout the game. "There were two field goal attempts in the game and neither was made. The kickers couldn't get any footing because under the snow there was ice."

The Patriots had struggled into Dolphins territory with 4:45 left in the game. Patriots head coach Ron Meyer signaled for his kicker, John Smith, to attempt a 33-yard field goal. But before he did, Meyer suddenly turned to a man sitting on a John Deere tractor and motioned to him.

"Get out there and do something," yelled Meyer.

"I knew exactly what he meant," said operator Mark Henderson. Henderson was a convicted burglar on work-release who volunteered to operate the field equipment. He had come directly from the MCI-Norfolk prison.

"I remember standing on the field and they were going to attempt another field goal and I see the snowplow going on the field," said Bokamper. "I didn't think anything of it because he had been clearing the yard lines and it was a stop in play. He got about 10 or 15 feet away from me, then he veered back on to the field and went right to where the kicker was and he cleared out a path for him."

Holder Matt Cavanaugh now had a place to kneel, and Smith had a clear place where he could plant his foot. Smith kicked the ball through the goalposts for a 3–0 Patriots lead. The crowd went crazy. His picture was put on the scoreboard with his name underneath. Patriots fans chanted Henderson's name and "MVP! MVP! MVP!"

"Matt Cavanaugh was already getting down on one knee to hold for John Smith's field-goal attempt. This part of the story is very misconstrued," recalled Hall of Fame Patriots offensive tackle John Hannah. "In reality, the tractor had not swept the exact spot where the ball was going to be placed. Instead the driver had actually thrown a whole bunch more loose snow over the spot Cav had cleared. So Cav and Smith had to quickly get down and sweep the spot clear with their hands again just in the nick of time."

"John and Matt will tell you to this day that what Henderson did didn't help the cause, it hurt it, because where he brushed was the spot where the ball gets placed," said Patriots PR man Tom Hoffman. "John's position was that the snow got brushed off on to the spot where he put his plant foot and that made it less stable than it already was. It made it more difficult to kick."

"Coach Shula started yelling from the sideline. He was just livid. The one thing about Coach Shula is that we were always the least-penalized team in the league. He believed in the letter of the law. If it wasn't legal, he wasn't going to do it. Even if he could gain an advantage, he wasn't going to do it. So anytime anyone circumvented the rules, he just went livid. He was beside himself on the sideline throughout the whole thing," remembered Bokamper.

"I could see the Dolphins sideline explode on the opposite side of the field, and instantly Shula was leading a charge of assistant coaches and players toward the middle of the field. They were all yelling and screaming, throwing playbooks, headsets, and helmets," remembered Hannah. "After what seemed like an eternity of argument, protests, screaming, and hollering, the game resumed, and the play stood."

"I think it's the most unfair thing that I've ever been associated within coaching. It's the most unsportsmanlike act that I've ever been around," said Shula. "I was bewildered. I really was bewildered about what was happening out there on the field in front of my eyes. The magnitude of it never really set in until after he had lined up to kick the field goal."

"We got a chance to tie the game at the other end. No snowplow. Our kicker slips and falls on his butt," chuckled Shula years later. The Patriots won, 3–0.

"It's the first time since I've been in professional football we've ever taken such serious exception to something which happened on the field," said an incensed Joe Robbie. "That kind of thing should not occur as a result of somebody putting a snowplow run by a convict with a day off from prison, out on to the field to give special advantage to the home team."

"I'm sure if you were the other coach on the other sideline, you would say it would be a black mark." said Patriots Coach Ron Meyer "But I know one thing: I can live with myself on it, and it wasn't an attempt to deceive or it wasn't an attempt to cheat anybody."

"I get up at 5 o'clock Monday morning, go into work, and what's on the front page of the *Globe* and the *Herald* but the picture of Mark with the sweeper," recalled Hoffman. "I have a 4 o'clock flight out of Logan and have to change planes at O'Hare [Airport]. I grab a copy of the *Chicago Tribune* and the *Sun-Times,* and right above the fold on both of them there's a giant picture of Mark Henderson. Then I land in Seattle, and in the *Post-Intelligencer* and the *Seattle Times,* above the top of the fold in both of those papers, is a picture of Mark Henderson with [holder] Matt Cavanaugh and Smitty bent over him. So here's these six major newspapers, and they all had the same picture and the same story plastered on the front page."

Shula continued to protest to NFL commissioner Pete Rozelle. Rozelle agreed but could do nothing about it after the fact. Not surprisingly, the NFL Competition Committee banned the use of snowplows on the field during a game.

Several weeks after the incident, the Minnesota Vikings coach commented that he thought it was "terrific" what Meyer and Henderson had done.

"It's hard for me to imagine that he said what happened to us was terrific," Shula said. "Sooner or later, that could happen to them, and it clearly was an unfair advantage. Both kickers already had missed off the snow. Why should one kicker be allowed to have a path cleared for him to kick?"

Privately, Shula was both angry and wounded that Grant should speak so publicly. Grant's comments had come after a four-page set of rules to prevent similar incidents was issued so soon after the freak occurrence.

"Get a guy from Miami who is on the competition committee and get his nose tweaked. Now he's got four pages of rules in case it snows again," said Grant.

"Miami made a huge deal about the fact that the Patriots had sent in a criminal to execute another criminal act. Whenever we played Miami in Florida during the years after that game, they sold a bunch of fake plastic snowballs to the fans. The fans would pelt us with thousands of those things as we ran into the stadium," recalled Hannah later.

Said Bokamper years later, "It's funny, the Dolphins played up there many years later when they were closing the stadium before they moved into Gillette Stadium. They had a ceremony where they brought back some of the legends who had played there like Russ Francis and Steve Grogan. I'll never forget who got the loudest ovation. It was Mark Henderson." The John Deere Model 314 tractor, complete with sweeper attached, was commemorated at the Hall at Patriot Place at the new Gillette Stadium, where it hung from the ceiling.

The most important thing that season was the maturing of the Miami defense. It had now become known as the Killer Bees. And they were peaking just at the right moment. The Killer Bees got their name from so many defensive players whose last names began with the letter *B*. The units featured players Bob Baumhower, Doug Betters, Kim Bokamper, Charles Bowser, Bob Brudzinski, and Glenn and Lyle Blackwood. In just nine games, they recorded a league-leading 19 interceptions to go along with 29 sacks. They allowed the second-fewest points and led the league in fewest yards yielded. They were the number-one rated passing defense, but they had an Achilles heel—they were 24th against the run.

Of course, the architect of this defense had been Bill Arnsparger again. They used the versatility of their players to confuse defenses. A. J. Duhe played in multiple positions throughout the season, sometimes lining up as a linebacker, sometimes as an end. Sometimes he would rush the passer, sometimes he would drop off in coverage. Bokamper did the same.

"They move Duhe around," New York Jets offensive coordinator Joe Walton said. "One play he's in the line, the next he's backing up into coverage, the next he's blitzing, the next he's on the right side, the next he's back on the left side. When you look at their defense, one of the first things you have to do is see where Duhe is. Larry Gordon, their right outside linebacker, is another excellent player. But they're all good players. Some people might think of them as no-names, but they're almost all high draft choices."

"Basically, I feel I'm a teacher," Arnsparger said. "You have to have a teaching atmosphere. If you don't, you have to get their attention some other way, and it may involve a louder approach. It's hard to prepare yourselves to get better without having total concentration. Oh, I can get loud."

"In meetings, especially in meetings after we lose," said Bob Baumhower, "He's not that mild-mannered then. Everybody gets beat on a play. When that happens, you pull yourself up and beat the guy on the next play. All the coaches understand that. But if you blow an assignment or haven't done your job mentally, Bill lets you know it. He lets everybody in the room know it. And that's the way it should be."

On January 8, 1983, the Dolphins played the New England Patriots in a first-round playoff game at the Orange Bowl. The pressure on the team was immense. The Dolphins had not won a playoff game since they defeated the Minnesota Vikings in January 1974. It was the longest the team had gone without winning a playoff game—almost nine years. And it was weighing on the coach as well as the players. When asked about it, Shula replied, "Once we have played a game, it's history."

The Dolphins took a 14–3 lead into half time. "Once we shut them down pretty well in the first half, we knew what they were going to do," said defensive end Doug Betters. The Dolphins never looked back on their way to a 28–13 victory. The Dolphins dominated the entire game. And Shula and his team had avenged a serious injustice.

"It's nice to get that nine-year monkey off our backs," said Dolphins lineman Bob Kuechenberg. "But the most important thing about today's victory is the kind of football we played to win. If we continue to play this way, it should take us all the way to the championship game."

The defense was outstanding, but the biggest surprise of the game was David Woodley, who completed 16 of 19 passes for 246 yards and a pair of touchdown passes. And Tony Nathan, who had battled injuries throughout 1982, ran brilliantly for 71 yards. Shula had worried publicly if the offense had been "too one-dimensional," relying on a heavy dose of fullback Andra Franklin, and who gained 112 against the Patriots. "But David, having that kind of game, should give him more confidence as we continue in the playoffs," Shula said.

"We have played great defense all year," said Shula. "And today, we played great when we had to, early in the game when we forced the Patriots to settle for field goals instead of touchdowns."

The next game was against the San Diego Chargers in a rematch of the Epic in Miami. It was one of the most anticipated playoff games of the weekend. The Chargers were again the league's most prolific offense. The game was once again in Miami. Duhe had told the press that the defense would "find a way to stay in Fouts's face."

This was not a replay of the game a season earlier. This was revenge pure and sweet. This time, Miami posted 24 unanswered points in the first 23 minutes and took a 27–13 lead into halftime.

"When it got to 24–0, I thought about last year," said Woodley, who astonished all with another fine performance (17 completions, 22 attempts, 195 yards, 2 touchdowns). "But I don't think anybody said anything. Nobody wanted to bring it up." And while Kellen Winslow had had the game of his life against the Dolphins the previous year, he was a nonfactor on this particular day, mostly due to injuries.

"We told them to go out there with the idea that the score was 0–0, win the second half, and don't think about the 14 points we had in the bank," Shula said. "Over all, it was a great team effort."

In the first quarter, Fouts was only on the field five minutes. Bokamper sacked Fouts on San Diego's first pass play. Bokamper screamed a string of explatives standing over Fouts and gave him an obscene gesture just to boot. Explained Bokamper later, "Just to let him know that I intended to be back there all day."

The Chargers fumbled two kickoffs in the first half, and the game was over. "They did a tremendous job of disguising what they were going to do. Once we receivers got through their jams at the line of scrimmage, the safeties took away our bread and butter. I know that today, for the first time I can remember, I was having thoughts about whether to release inside or outside. I started trying to do some things differently, give them a different look," said Chargers receiver Wes Chandler.

The defense shut out the Chargers in the second half, taking the game, 34–13. Said the exhausted Fouts after the game, "Miami didn't give us anything. Its defense is the best we've seen." *Sports Illustrated* called it "The Revenge of the Killer Bees."

"I can't tell you how much he enjoyed last Sunday," Dorothy told the press after the win over the Chargers. "He came home and spent a few hours with the family and some friends from California. It was a real joy for him."

Next up was the New York Jets. A division rival with real desire to beat them, the Jets were no joke that year. The Jets had scored the third-most points in the league and had their own branded defense nicknamed The New York Sack Exchange. The offense featured gunslinger quarterback Richard Todd, and the defensive line had brutish talent in Marty Lyons, Mark Gastineau, Joe Klecko, and Abdul Salaam. This would be no easy contest.

"How can you compete against Don Shula?" Jets coach Walt Michaels asked a reporter. "The only thing I can say about where we play is that I don't have to make a time change on this watch," said Michaels pointing to his digital watch. "There's a lot of buttons to push."

The daunting task in front of Shula was this—only one team in NFL history had defeated another three times in one season: The Green Bay Packers had defeated Shula's Colts three times in 1965. When asked how he would approach the game, Shula said, "I don't feel they have any bearing on us playing the Jets this Sunday. I look at it as trying to beat them for the first time, in 1983 . . . When you develop a rivalry, you get to know the coaches, the players, the team's tendencies. You know a lot more about them. But it also works the other way around.

"Fouts will take three, five, or seven steps straight back, he's a pure pocket passer," Shula said. "Todd will do more things. He'll throw some drop back, but he'll also give you a lot of movement one way or the other with a bootleg. And he mixes in the run well."

On January 23, the Dolphins and Jets faced off in the AFC Championship Game on a windy, soggy Orange Bowl field with a Super Bowl berth on the line.

"The idea was to stop their running game and force them to make mistakes with their passing game," said Baumhower. Todd threw for just 103 yards on 15-of-37 passing. "In the beginning, we didn't know what they were going to try to do. We figured we would let them run their pattern, we would do our own scheme of things, and if they were doing things that were hurting us, then we would adjust. We never had to adjust."

And A. J. Duhe had the game of his life, with three interceptions, including one in the fourth quarter that he returned 35 yards for a score that sealed Miami's 14–0 victory. "This was the most exciting game of my career," he said. "I know I missed a couple of assignments, and I'll hear about it tomorrow. But I know I made a couple of big plays, too."

"We were slipping, sliding, twisting, and turning out there today and we didn't get the breaks," said a disappointed Walt Michaels. "I think we were prepared. We just didn't execute. . . . I could make a lot of excuses about the loss, but when it's done it's done. Sometimes you just shouldn't get up in the morning."

After the game, Baumhower went to dinner with Todd and his wife. They had been college teammates at Alabama. "Richard was down," remembered Baumhower. "He was saying that the Jets came down here real confident, figuring that they were going to the Super Bowl, but we had shut them down. He said our defensive backs were jamming their receivers so well at the line of scrimmage that they couldn't run any of their patterns and were never where they were supposed to be. And that confused him. He said for me to tell our secondary that they are the best he's ever played against."

"Basically, we're a three-man-line team. We have our stunts. For example, Baumhower does not always go straight into the center. He'll go one way or the other, our defensive ends will step in or out, and our linebackers will compensate with their 'games.' Those are all parts of the sophistication of the three-man line you have in your game plan," said Shula. "That caused some indecision on the part of the offense. When they're looking at a three-man line, and at the snap we're doing different things, like three, four, even five guys rushing, we can get some pretty good things going for us.

"We were zoning him some. Other times we used six defensive backs to make sure we had some double-coverage on him, either short and deep or in and out," explained Shula. "Defensively, we wanted to continue to improve. We have played pretty well all year. But in the last two weeks, in particular, we have been outstanding."

Don Shula and the Dolphins were back, and going to the Super Bowl the following Sunday at the Rose Bowl in Pasadena, California. And this time, maybe, Don Shula was a little mellower. He told the players to enjoy the experience. One of the few people who could truly appreciate what it felt like to not go back for nine years was Bob Kuechenberg. Kooch had been the last holdover of the Undefeated team. Then a young man, he was now a grizzled veteran at thirty-five years old.

"Don has changed a little," Kuechenberg said that week. "Our society has changed. I think of Vince Lombardi, one of the greatest all-time coaches, very rigid, very demanding. There are times when I would go through a brick wall, but Don Shula has transcended that era of asking a player to go through a brick wall without asking questions. Coach Shula is more relaxed now. He's enjoying the hunt. He still wants to win, but he's able to smile and crack a joke."

"When it's quiet, I reflect on how there are anniversaries in life. This is the 10th anniversary of that 17–0 team. It's really kind of eerie to think we're back playing Washington again," said Kuechenberg. "You sometimes wonder, with all the pain and disappointments, if it will ever come around again. In pro football, there's no guarantee. This will make it a little sweeter this time. This reminds me of what I already knew. The Super Bowl is singularly what makes pro football worthwhile. You guys in the press laugh when I say you don't play for the money. Look how short the average career is: four-point-two years. You couldn't sacrifice to play unless you loved it. This week and this game make it all worthwhile."

The Redskins were a mirror image of the Dolphins. Coached by Joe Gibbs, they featured the league's top-ranked defense and depended on power running back John Riggins and scrambling quarterback Joe Theismann, to move the chains offensively. The Redskins featured a huge offensive line that was nicknamed The Hogs. Despite that, their offense sputtered that year, ranking only 12th. Like the Dolphins, head coach Joe Gibbs's Redskins were built to wear you down. But the reputation of the Killer Bees was such, by virtue of their 12 playoff interceptions, that Miami was favored by anywhere from one-and-a-half to three points.

The first big play of the game came when Cefalo hauled in a David Woodley pass and raced 76 yards for a touchdown to give the Dolphins a 7–0 lead. Then the two clubs traded field goals before the Redskins tied the game with a short pass from Theismann to Alvin Garrett, making it a 10–10 game. But Dolphins return man Fulton Walker took the ensuing kickoff and returned it all the way for a 98-yard touchdown. It was the longest kick return in NFL postseason history and the first kickoff returned for a touchdown in a Super Bowl. The Dolphins headed into the locker room at halftime up, 17–10.

The teams exchanged body blows in the third quarter, and the Redskins managed a field goal. But going into the fourth quarter, the Dolphins held onto a thin 17–13 lead. And while they were a superior defense, their offense was not going anywhere. The offense struggled all through the second half, and the defense started to slow down. The mammoth offensive line of the Redskins wore down the lighter, quicker Dolphins. And Riggins, a power back in the mold of Csonka, crashed through the Dolphins. The indelible image of that game is Riggins pounding into the Dolphins defense, breaking tackles and carrying players with him. The Redskins finally took the lead when Riggins broke free and rumbled for a 43-yard touchdown on a 4th-and-1 play, giving the Redskins the lead with ten minutes remaining in the game. They would not relinquish it.

"I should have made the play," said Dolphin cornerback Don McNeal. McNeal was a special player who had overcome huge odds and was someone of special character. He carried the weight of that play on his shoulders for years. It was a heavy load. "I slipped, but that's no excuse. I've seen the picture a million times, and I've even got the picture on my wall at home. Why? I don't dwell on it, but it's part of my career."

Washington scored another touchdown with less than two minutes remaining and took Super Bowl XVII, 27–17.

The Redskins had 24 first downs to the Dolphins' 9. Riggins carried for 166 yards and was named the game's Most Valuable Player. In contrast, the Dolphins had run for only 97 yards as a team and passed for 80 yards. After three great games, Woodley was suddenly human again, completing only four of 14 attempts. Strock was 0-for-3. During the playoffs, the Dolphins had averaged 242 yards per game, versus the 176 that day. The Redskins rolled up 400 yards that day.

"If they didn't change anything during the game, we felt we could really manhandle them" Redskins safety Tony Peters said. "They just weren't that complicated on offense. If we could force Woodley to pass, it was all over."

Said Woodley, "When nothing works, it's completely frustrating. When it would look like we would complete a pass, one of their guys would come in and knock it down. They were able to shut down our backs (Woodley's favorite targets in most games) because they blitzed and we had to keep the back in to block."

Shula told his team after the game, "It could have been a great story. But now it will only be on the Redskins. I realize better than anyone else that after a Super Bowl they're only going to be talking about one team, and it won't be the Dolphins. We had a fine season, and we have to turn this loss into a learning experience, which is the only positive thing I can possibly say about it.

"They deserve to be champions. They had the best record of anybody in the regular season and now they come out of the Super Bowl with the best record, and when you do that, you're the best, and they are the best.

"This team has accomplished a lot of things, and it took a successful season to reach Super Bowl XVII. But we just couldn't get it done in the second half. Washington beat us every way you can beat a team in the third and fourth quarters," said Shula. "We try to get our running attack going and can't do it, and they're making the big plays against our pass attack, too. We went deep a lot because I thought we could throw long with them crowding us the way they were. It just didn't click. We just go three and out, three and out, three and out.

"I considered making a quarterbacking change, from Woodley to Don Strock, late in the third quarter and early in the fourth," he said. "We had it ready to go, but they used up a lot of clock on us. Strock never was able to get untracked the little time he was in there." He later said, "I couldn't do a goddam thing."

"When Riggins went 43 for the touch in the fourth quarter," Shula recalled, "we were in a short-yardage defense, and he went off the left corner, and we had a man slip and a man miss an arm-tackle on him, and it didn't work. He was a tremendously dominating force, and their offensive line also had some of the surges we've seen in the films that they've done against other teams.

"Their scheme, and it's something I'm sure Gibbs brought from San Diego and Don Coryell, has been constant movement," Shula said. "I thought we were prepared for it. The bottom line is that, despite the fancy things they tried, it was the pounding, the old-fashioned stuff, that did us in."

"That was probably the pinnacle of our defensive core," said Doug Betters later. "The Killer Bs. We were playing at the top of our game, but our offense was lagging behind. If we had Dan [Marino] in that Super Bowl, we could have beaten the Redskins."

"All season, Betters says, the Dolphins' defensive coaches told them not to worry about the offense, to shut down teams and seize games on their own. But this was before defenses regularly substituted. The cumulative impact was a defense worn down by the time it reached the Super Bowl," wrote Greg Bishop in *Sports Illustrated* several years later.

"We felt like we had been a quarterback or a player away from winning it all," said Nat Moore.

The team was a success because Shula had willed it. With exceptional assistant coaching and great coordinators, he'd taken a team that shouldn't have been there and put them in a place where they were in over their heads. His defense was tired. They had been shutting down teams all year, playing long, hard minutes in the face of an offense that was middle-of-the-road at best. And history showed the NFL that as much as Shula had put his faith in Woodley, he was nowhere near being a Super Bowl-caliber quarterback required in the modern era. While detractors over the years have pointed to such shortfalls (the 1964 and Super Bowl III Colts—neither of whom should have lost), the 1982 team was evidence of what a superior coach could do with a squad of good players. While the Dolphins believed they could win, in truth, the defense was tired, undersized, and got exposed. The Redskins were a better team. It was a bitter loss, but Shula had gotten more out of that team, and beat many other better teams, than many other coaches would have with the same group of talent. This was the curse of being able to do more with less.

CHAPTER 9

Marino

Football was always at odds with Don's love of family. The game required more and more hours in the modern era. But for someone for whom family was so important, he did his best to try and reconcile the two. It was not always successful, as success in the NFL required more and more time away from those he loved. In December 1982, David signed on as a full-time assistant coach on the Dolphins' staff in charge of receivers, replacing Wally English, who had left to become coach of Tulane.

"I decided to go to law school," David said. "I enrolled and was in my first year in 1982. I remember I was home for the holidays, and I was about to go out to play some golf, and my father got a call that Wally English just left to go to Tulane. My father asked if I could come over and help with the game films—you know, just break them down, fill in some things. There were only two games left, and that's how it started." He was then attending the University of Baltimore Law School.

"I was going to return the second week in January," he recalled. "But then we got into the playoffs, and we won the first game, and we won the second game, and then we went to the Super Bowl, so I got a deferment. Then my father asked me to stay on for the next season, with the idea that I'd go back to school. But everything fell into place. I was working as a coach, and it just evolved that I signed a two-year contract."

This was both good and bad, as either man would tell you. David had to negotiate his first contract with his own dad. And Don remained ever the perfectionist, and David was not spared his wrath. But it was a chance to spend more time with his son.

"It's the little things that happen that don't let you forget you're at the bottom of the totem pole," David said. "In the morning, I'm the last guy to get the paper to read. Whenever something has to be done, it's 'Send the kid to do it.'"

There was one time in a film session that David suggested that if Jimmy Cefalo, who had dived for and missed a pass, had extended a bit more, he might have made the reception. David immediately knew he had said the wrong thing. Don spoke to David privately. "I didn't try to force anything with him," said Don. "I'd say, 'Dave, you shouldn't have said that,' or 'Why not keep that opinion to yourself.' I never hesitated to step in. I'm not a very tactful person when it comes to that. Nobody has ever accused me of too much finesse.

"Some players respond to yelling. Some respond to a quiet word. Some respond to a pat on the back," Shula said. "They're all different, and you have to treat them as individuals and yet continue to get the most out of their abilities so they can help the team and grow as individual players. That's another thing I've come to understand over the years."

On the other hand, Mike Shula was now a 6-foot-3 senior at Christopher Columbus High School in Miami. He was the starting quarterback and had been voted to Florida's all-state team. He was one of the most heavily recruited high school seniors in the country, and by some of the biggest programs.

"Me and Mike Shula arrived there at the same time," said Alonzo Highsmith, about the time they played together at the same high school. "He didn't have a whole lot of friends. I didn't know anybody. So he befriended me. We'd talk. We'd have lunch together every day. He started bringing me home with him, and because I knew him, I had the chance to go with him to visit the Dolphins training camp."

While visiting the Dolphins training camp, Highsmith was asked to help arrange uniforms. He was wearing headphones.

"Don Shula came over and said to me, 'We concentrate on football around here, not rock music,'" Highsmith said. He was one of the great defensive players in Florida high school football. He went on to a career as a running back at the University of Miami and six years in the NFL. By 2018, he was the vice president of player personnel for the Cleveland Browns after spending six years in the front office of the Green Bay Packers. "Meeting and talking football with the Dolphins players, having Don Shula tell me to watch this or that. That's all because of me knowing Mike Shula. I've never told Mike this, but meeting him helped shape my life and helped determine who I am and where I am today. . . . If I become a GM one day," Highsmith said, "he'd be one of the first people I'd call to be my head coach."

In his senior year in high school, Mike completed 146 passes, 20 for touchdowns, and ran for four more touchdowns. He started his junior and senior seasons, and the team was 21–3 under his command. In 1982, though, his school fell short, losing the state championship game to Pensacola Woodham, 23–14.

His father was able to attend every game except the state championship game. "He never intruded on the team, but he made it known he was available if we needed any sort of help," said Coach Dennis Lavelle. "Once, when he heard that we had lost our three top tailbacks to injuries, he sent over some material for a one-back offense with four receivers that we used until our runners were healthy."

Since it was a strike season, Don had extra time to spend with Mike, attending games and reviewing films. "He was a big factor in helping me to prepare, and that meant a lot to me," Mike recalled. "I don't look at him as a football coach. But he does expect discipline from others. That doesn't take away from his caring or love for us. It's just part of his character."

Key among Mike's suitors had been the University of Alabama. But the death of Bear Bryant on January 26, 1983, had thrown that school into a whirlwind. In a shocking move, the lords of Tuscaloosa called on alumnus Ray Perkins, then the head coach of the New York Giants, to come rescue the school in their hour of need and pick up Bryant's mantle (heavy as it was). Perkins heeded the call and returned to the Crimson Tide nest immediately. Don Shula had coached Ray Perkins with the Baltimore Colts for three years in the 1960s. On February 16, Michael Shula signed a letter of intent to attend Alabama. His father was ecstatic.

"Alabama has a great football tradition, and we've got a lot of players from Alabama with the Dolphins," Don told the media.

Back at his office at Biscayne College (now known as St. Thomas University), Don Shula had to consider new contract negotiations and somehow, almost more important, what he was going to do with his football team. He knew he had another good nucleus, but not enough parts. He needed more to get the team over the hump.

Shula sat at his brown wooden executive desk. It was nothing particularly outlandish, more the same kind of desk you might see at a middle manager's desk in a bank or in an executive suite. Nice, but not eye-catching. On the front was a wooden hand-carved sign that read, COACH DON SHULA, as if anyone needed to be reminded.

There were "other tools of his trade, including blank play sheets, along with his personal copies of the highlight reels of Super Bowls VII and VIII produced by NFL Films. Unseen in the top right hand drawer is a piece of NFL history—the famous wristband Shula assembled with a miniature version of the game plan that Colts' halfback Tom Matte used when he was forced to play quarterback in a 1965 playoff game," wrote Dolphins historian Harvey Greene. "Behind the desk in a bookcase is a variety of memorabilia. Most prominent are media guides from all the NFL teams in organized binders, as well as NFL fact books dating back to 1956. There are family photos, as well as shots of Shula with dignitaries in and outside of football (ranging from presidents to golfers). The shelves are lined with an assortment of inspirational and motivational books, along with biographies of sports greats, including a few about Shula himself and his great Dolphin teams. There are also practice schedules, team and league statistical sheets, and scouting reports scattered around the bookcase."

Shula could often be found reading the local and national newspapers, rifling the sports pages for stories about his teams and other tidbits he could store away for future games. By now, Ronald Reagan was president of the United States, the the hottest shows on television were *Dallas, Dynasty, Falcon Crest,* and *Magnum P.I.* Popular music tastes had also shifted. The country's favorite music artists now included The Police, Michael Jackson, Eurythmics, Culture Club, and many others. *Ghandi* had won best picture in 1983.

But as Shula scanned the papers, he especially read the local writers avidly, to know who was friend or foe. What concerned him most was the upcoming draft. The 1983 NFL Draft was arguably the richest singular draft in the history of the NFL. Everyone knew it was special, but it would take the league a generation to see how much so. Six quarterbacks would be taken in the first round. Four of them would play in at least one Super Bowl. In 11 of the next 16 years, the AFC representative in the Super Bowl would be quarterbacked by one of them. Overall, six players from the first round (and seven overall) were eventually inducted into the Hall of Fame. Thirty-four additional Pro Bowlers also came out of this draft. It was a feeding bonanza.

Quarterback John Elway of Stanford was the big prize. Other candidates were fellow signal-callers Jim Kelly, Tony Eason, Todd Blackledge, and Dan Marino. Marino had been the absolute undoubtable star of the 1981 season, his junior year at Pitt, but his senior year was a flop in 1982, and his stock had fallen.

The problem was simple for the Dolphins. Who would be available with the 27th pick? They had gone to the Super Bowl and lost, and now they would get to pick second-to-last in the draft. Shula felt for sure no quality quarterback would be left at the end of the first round. As the draft drew near, he focused on Mike Charles, a defensive lineman from Syracuse.

The story how Marino fell so badly is still legendary. In 1982 and 1983, there had been rumors that he was using drugs. Were they true?

"It was certainly out there that there were 'issues' with Marino," said Ray Didinger of the *Philadelphia Daily News*. Chuck Noll, a decade after the draft, admitted the Steelers had passed on Marino because of those rumors. "It started off with just the idea that he was partying. Then it grew more sinister from that," Didinger recalled.

"I never took any tests," Marino said later. "One time somebody wrote that, but that's something I can't control. If I worried about everything that was written about me, I wouldn't have a good time."

Foge Fazio, Marino's head coach his senior season, later admitted to the press that he felt vindictive gamblers started the rumors. "A lot of it was disappointment we didn't beat the point spread," Fazio said. "That's where the viciousness came out."

As expected, Elway went No. 1, and his selection by Ernie Accorsi, then of the Colts, was the most controversial of all the picks, since Elway had told the organization he would never play a down for them, mostly due to his father's antipathy for Colts coach Frank Kush, an unpopular disciplinarian in both college and pro circles. Accorsi drafted Elway anyway, hoping to use him as a bartering chip to get extra draft picks. He was eventually traded to the Denver Broncos.

Todd Blackledge of Penn State was the next quarterback picked at the No. 6 spot by the Kansas City Chiefs. Jim Kelly of Miami went to the Buffalo Bills at No. 14, and Tony Eason of Illinois went next at No. 15 to the New England Patriots.

"It's a weird day, really," Marino remembered. "You're sitting there . . . I know it's football, you're going to play in the NFL, but every other kid that graduates college and has a chance to get a job, they kind of know where they're going or what their profession is going to be or what they're going to do, and you can sit there and not know if you're going to be in Seattle or Miami or Arizona. That part is tough, I think." Added Marino later, "I just remember it being a long day."

"People started finding reasons to not like Marino, and I think that the drug rumors were just another thing that they threw on the pile," agent Marvin Demoff said.

To be fair, the entire media had started to play Marino down. Gordon Forbes of *USA Today* wrote of Marino, "Stands tall in the pocket and has a good view of the field. Sets up quickly and gets good, deep pass drops but lacks a classic delivery. Scouts say he often forces the ball into a crowd and is frequently intercepted." In the *Miami Herald*, Larry Dorman wrote, "After Marino's inexplicably poor senior season, he's lucky to still be considered a first-rounder. Still, as a prospect, he's worth taking a chance on."

Also in the *Miami Herald*, Edwin Pope wrote, "The word from Marino's hometown is that the Panthers' all-time passing leader declined last year as a twin result of a) inflated ego, and b) pressing to impress the pros after he finished fourth in Heisman Trophy voting as a junior. He developed the idea that he was God's gift to football. Dan was a down-home Pittsburgher who started thinking he was Joe Namath. It hurt the team, along with some other things, like losing some top receivers and also that head-coaching switch-over from Jackie Sherrill to Foge Fazio."

"This happens in a lot of drafts," Didinger said. "Once a guy starts falling, everybody runs the other way. Everyone assumes everyone else knows something, and they back away."

"People were scared that they couldn't handle him," said one NFL scout later. "Why waste a No. 1 on a problem?"

At No. 24 in the first round, the Jets were on the clock. Days before, Fazio, a good friend of Jets head coach Joe Walton, who had just replaced Walt Michaels, called to vouch for Marino. As the tension mounted, Jets fans in the balcony of the New York Sheraton hotel, where the draft was conducted, could be heard chanting loudly, "Dan Marino! Dan Marino!" Commissioner Pete Rozelle announced, "With the twenty-fourth pick, the New York Jets select quarterback . . ."

There was a pause. "I don't think Rozelle did it on purpose. But for dramatic effect, he couldn't have done it better," remembered Didinger.

"Ken O'Brien, University of California-Davis," Rozelle finished.

"The cheers turned to screams of anguish—and then boos, in just a second," Didinger said.

The Bengals and Raiders also passed on Marino, and then came the Dolphins at 27. Bill Arnsparger pushed Shula hard to take Charles. "The pressure was on me to take the defensive lineman," Shula recalled. Future Hall of Fame defensive back Darrell Green was also on their list of available players.

"Everybody's trying to figure out now why he was drafted so late," said Shula. The Dolphins head coach was thrilled to find Marino available. "We had a strong commitment on Marino that others did not. We heard rumors, different kinds of rumors. We checked them out and did not hear anything that changed our minds.

I called Foge Fazio, and he gave me his strongest recommendation. We knew all we needed to know."

Fazio said Marino was a "Pittsburgh Guy." Said Fazio: "A Pittsburgh Guy carries himself with an air that he knows what's going on. He smiles and has something nice to say about everybody. He can relax on either side of the tracks but basically is a shot-and-beer guy."

With our situation and our evaluation of Dan Marino, we felt he was a good pick," said Shula. "Certainly good credentials. Didn't have the best senior year, but when you look at him and evaluate him throughout his career, you have to be pretty impressed."

"What Shula saw was a franchise player who could carry a team for a decade or more. He saw an already polished drop-back passer who had spent four college seasons in a pass-oriented offense. He saw the MVP of both the Senior Bowl and Hula Bowl who had thrown for 8,416 yards and 79 touchdowns at Pitt," wrote Paul Attner in the *Washington Post.*

"I was happy the Dolphins got me, said Marino. "This is all I've wanted to do, to get a chance to play in the pros, and Miami is giving me this chance. Everything else is behind me, and I let it go at that."

"You probably got the best guy in the draft," said Chuck Noll to Shula by phone after the Dolphins picked Marino.

There was a story that was oft repeated in Miami sports circles in the subsequent years. Shula was quiet as he watched Marino work out for the first time that spring of 1983. Shula was sure he'd gotten a "steal" in the draft, though how much of a steal he wasn't sure.

"Shula stood behind Marino, watching him effortlessly flick pass after pass, using not much more than his wrist. He looked like a man fly-casting with a fishing rod, but the ball would zing downfield 40 to 50 yards. Then Shula did something he almost never does. He walked to the sideline to chat with a friend, Edwin Pope, sports editor of the *Miami News,*" remembered sportswriter Larry Felser.

"Have you ever seen anything like that in your life?" Shula asked Pope quietly.

"Right from the time he stepped out on the practice field, it's been nothing but upbeat excitement. It was evident from the beginning we were dealing with a real talent. When he makes up his mind to throw the ball, he really uncorks it. It's boom! . . . the release and the throw," recalled Shula.

The rest of that draft went very well for the Dolphins. In the second round, they ended up getting Mike Charles anyway, and they also selected defensive end

Charles Benson from Baylor, punter Reggie Roby from Iowa, wide receiver Mark Clayton from Louisville, and linebacker Mark Brown from Purdue. They would make the roster, and several of them would play for the team for years to come.

That May, Shula, as he had done many years, was in Painesville visiting his parents and relatives and raising money for John Carroll University. He was appearing at the Pepper Pike Country Club when he was asked about any signs of burn-out and how he felt about the impending birth of his first grandchild.

"I am not anticipating any burnout. I don't feel old. I'm going to jog when I get out of here. I also play a lot of golf and tennis in the off-season," he chuckled. "But I am looking forward to becoming a grandfather." David and his wife were due to have a child.

David, at twenty-five, was the league's youngest assistant coach. "It's very simple," he said of his father's style. "If you make an error as a coach, he won't let it go. Say you're presenting a game plan. I'm responsible for showing the defense against us. If something's wrong with it, he'll say, 'Why didn't we have this figured?'

"But he's changed. The family is grown up now, three sisters and another brother. He now sees that the problems we had are similar to the problems ballplayers have. He's a grandfather now and his job is to spoil. He sees things differently than he did. People who have known him through the years say he's more understanding and open-minded." David and his wife, Leslie Ann, would have three boys, Dan, Chris, and Matt.

On May 21, it was reported that the South Dade Expressway, a seven-mile stretch of road, would be renamed the Don Shula Expressway. State Road 874 was renamed by an act of the Florida Legislature in his honor and was dedicated on August 4.

It was a tumultuous summer. On June 25, starting outside linebacker Larry Gordon collapsed while running in the desert outside Phoenix, Arizona, and died about an hour later at an area hospital. The twenty-eight-year-old had been the Dolphins' first round pick in 1976 from Arizona State. He hadn't missed a game during his seven-year career, starting in all but two of them. He had one sack against the Redskins in Super Bowl XVII.

A month later, Larry Csonka walked into Shula's office and informed his old coach that he was now a scout for the Jacksonville franchise of the United States Football League, a new rival league. He explained he was charged with converting as many players to the USFL as he possibly could. A report surfaced that Shula and the players were being wooed by the new league.

"He came in and told me that he would be getting in touch with players entering their options. I understand that's part of his responsibilities now. I understand it's his job. The entire league is going to have to face more of this," Shula told the press. "I am sure Csonka will have to talk with other players from other teams also. But because he played with these guys, because he knows them, it's only natural that he'd contact players from this team."

Players coming up on contract options included Duhe, Baumhower, Woodley, Betters, Lyle Blackwood, and others. Like the players, Shula would use this to his own advantage.

Despite Marino's presence, Shula decided to let Woodley start the season. They started off with wins over the Bills and the Patriots. Then they lost to the Raiders and rebounded against the Chiefs. Then they lost an ugly game to the New Orleans Saints, 17–7, and that was enough for Shula. Marino had seen some action against the Raiders and Saints, but in the sixth game of the season, Shula started him for the first time. Marino responded brilliantly, passing for 370 yards, three touchdowns, and two interceptions, and the team amassed 488 yards of offense and accumulated 31 first downs. They still lost the game to Buffalo, 38–35, due to several defensive breakdowns, but Shula was impressed.

"They were nobody's idea of an exciting team," said *Miami Herald* writer Greg Cote of the staid Dolphins. "Marino was the opposite. He was a sexy, curly-headed kid with a lot of bravado about him."

Greg Bishop wrote in *Sports Illustrated*, "In his first practices, Marino impressed Shula. He was better than expected: stronger arm, quicker release, faster at making decisions. He also had an innate sense of when the pass rush was closing in and a nifty slide step to avoid pressure. That bought him extra time to throw farther down the field."

"He had a reputation from college as being very confident," said broadcaster Jim Lampley. "But it was what he did on the field that was amazing. He's the first guy I remember who could make the back-shoulder throw. He had a unique arm. Unbelievable velocity."

Marino had wowed the league. Paired with receivers Mark Duper and Mark Clayton, Marino went 7–2 as a starter that season. He threw 20 touchdown passes, and only six interceptions. In a full season, the most scoring passes David Woodley had thrown was 14, with 17 interceptions as a rookie in 1980. The Dolphins had found their new quarterback.

"Not even Nostradamus, the great 15th century seer who could see into the future, could have shown so much foresight because Marino has made the transformation from college to pro quarterback splendidly and in doing so has transformed Miami's offense into the feared unit it once was," said sportscaster Hank Goldberg at the time.

"What you saw is what he can give us—big play potential," Shula said after Marino posted his first win as a starting quarterback in New York on October 16. "He's got the quick arm that you need, especially against a team with a pass rush like the Jets. John Unitas had a pretty good gun. Marino has that gun; he also has quickness, and he sees downfield well." When asked for a comparison with Elway, Shula responded, "Elway is a better athlete, but Marino was the best at throwing the drop-back pass. We didn't think he'd still be there when we drafted, but when he was, nobody argued with me about taking him."

Paul Zimmerman wrote, "Have I ever felt Shula's wrath? Oh, brother, let me count the ways. When Miami drafted Marino, I was one of the TV analysts for ESPN. I issued one of those mindless pronouncements some scout had told me, that Marino's mechanics were wrong, that he pushed the ball. The next time I saw Shula, he stuck his finger in my chest."

"Pusher, huh? Pusher? What do you think of my pusher now?" said Shula.

"He stayed on me for two years, while Marino was putting up all those outasight numbers," recalled Zimmerman.

"Here's the guy who said I've got a pusher for a quarterback," Shula would repeat.

Contract talks between Shula and Robbie became heated again during that season. Shula found a new suitor in Donald Trump. The future president of the United States was then a New York real estate mogul who had recently purchased the United States Football League's New Jersey Generals. Trump was looking to pay big money to lure a big coach. The Generals had already signed college star Herschel Walker to a $4.2 million contract.

"Shula also confirmed today that he'd been holding weekly telephone conversations with USFL New Jersey Generals owner Donald Trump," announced Goldberg (a longtime Shula friend) on television in mid-October during the season. "Shula has also begun contract talks with Dolphins owner Joe Robbie, and while they haven't made any progress yet, they're moving along."

"I've talked to Mr. Trump on the telephone on several occasions," Shula told the New York press in mid-October while in town to play the Jets, "but I don't let it interfere with my preparations as a coach. He always calls me at home just before the Monday night game. I didn't see him this weekend. I told him there was no way I'd consider meeting him here when I'm here with my team for a game."

Both Shula and Trump intimated that the contract offer for Shula was in the range of $1 million per year, for five years.

However, Trump completely overplayed his hand when he went to the media to discuss his dealings with the normally private Shula. Trump went on the *NFL Today* pregame show on CBS and declared, "Don Shula would like to come to New York. He'd like to be in New York, New Jersey, the metropolitan area. It's really a question of economics for Don, and I believe if we want I believe Don will be in New York. It's really a question of whether I want to pay a certain price." Trump also told program host Brent Musburger that Shula had demanded as part of his compensation package an apartment in Trump Tower on Manhattan's Fifth Avenue. Shula was furious. He was in Baltimore when reporters reached him with the news of Trump's television gambit.

"All I've done is listen to what he's had to say," Shula told the Associated Press. "They approached me. I didn't approach them."

Then Shula fired back at a press conference, saying to television reporters, "I've decided I'm not interested in the United States Football League and the New Jersey Generals in particular. Contrary to reports that I was on the verge of signing, that was not true. He mentioned I was on the verge of agreeing to an offer. All he had to do was agree to the things that I wanted. A condominium on Fifth Avenue?" Shula chuckled, "I guarantee you it wasn't down to that."

Trump claimed in a statement later that he had "terminated" the negotiations with Shula because "the arrangements to obtain a coach like Don Shula were just too complex and time-consuming at this point." Shula told the press the talks had become a "huge distraction" and added it was "time to draw the line."

Still, rumors persisted that Shula would go to the Generals. This wedge was driven into the press by Shula's camp to spur negotiations with Robbie. Trump used the negotiations to promote his league, and Shula used it to get a better deal from Robbie. Regardless, any time Shula's contract was up, there always seemed to be interested owners and colleges who would be happy to talk to him. Shula had a record at that time of 210–80–6 in 21 seasons. His winning percentage made him the most successful coach in professional football. At Miami alone, he had 138 victories already in 197 games. In the meantime, Robbie also worked the rumor mill, telling local reporters that he would pay Shula in the neighborhood of $1 million per year. By late November, the drama had played itself out, and Shula accepted a new contract somewhere in that neighborhood.

"We were never far apart," Robbie said, adding that he thought the Generals' offer was "orchestrated" by the USFL to attract headlines and attention to the new league. Nobody in the NFL or media thought Shula would leave Miami at that time. But Shula needed to make the point to Robbie that his asking price was easily obtainable. Someone would pay him his price. And Robbie got the point.

"The key to this was a one-bedroom efficiency on Biscayne Boulevard," Shula quipped, referring to Miami's main thoroughfare.

As the season progressed, the usually stern-looking Shula was sometimes even referred to as bubbly and went so far as to say at one point, "the thrill is back."

"Shula," wrote Paul Attner in *The Sporting News*, "had enjoyed this year as much as any other in his storied career. Marino's boyish enthusiasm rubbed off on his coach."

For his part, Marino was saying all the right things. "I've got a lot to learn, but I am getting more confident every week," Marino said. "I'm just trying to play the way they want me to, and do the best I can. I didn't know what was in store for me this season, so I decided to come in and learn the offense and then just see what happens."

Shula said that Marino was "a player with a quick release and a gun for an arm, stronger than Griese's. He has decent mobility and a way to get the ball where he wants it. He sees well downfield. No matter what anyone throws at him, he doesn't get rattled. He's just a natural leader."

Marino was named the first rookie quarterback ever to start in a Pro Bowl game. "If I said I expected him to be the first rookie quarterback to start in the Pro Bowl game, I'd be lying," Shula said. "Frankly, though, I would have been disappointed if he hadn't done the job when he was given the opportunity. And he certainly has so far."

The Dolphins had clinched the AFC East by December 5, so Shula rested Marino and had Woodley start the final two games of the season. With a 12–4 record, they hosted the Seattle Seahawks in a divisional playoff game at the Orange Bowl on December 31. This would be no easy task. The Seahawks were a good team powered by rookie sensation running back Curt Warner, who led the AFC with 1,449 rushing yards during the regular season. It was the first playoff appearance for the Seahawks since joining the NFL seven years earlier. Seattle had a solid quarterback in Dave Krieg, and an efficient receiver in Steve Largent to compliment Warner and stretch the field. Led by coach Chuck Knox, a playoff veteran with both the Rams and Bills, the Seahawks had beaten the Denver Broncos, 31–7, in the AFC wild-card game.

"Their basic offense is a handoff to Warner in deep position behind the line," Shula said. "What makes him so dangerous is that when he cuts back, he does it with a lot of quickness and power, which makes it hard to bring him down. We stress with our defense to keep in their proper lanes of pursuit. But if one of our guys gets cut off, he can break it."

The first quarter was scoreless, but Marino took care of that quickly in the second quarter, tossing two touchdown passes. Seattle stood firm, and Krieg threw one of his own, as Miami led, 13–7, at halftime. In the second half, Warner started to wear down the Dolphins defense and scored a touchdown in the third quarter as the Seahawks took the lead, 14–13, and extended it to 17–13 at the top of the fourth quarter with a field goal. The Dolphins responded with Woody Bennett's 3-yard TD plunge and took a 20–17 lead midway through the fourth quarter. Many in the building thought the game would have been put away by the heavily favored Dolphins by now.

But Miami played an uncharacteristically sloppy game, turning the ball over five times. Marino, who completed 15 of 25 passes for 193 yards, threw two picks, and there were also three fumbles. In the second half alone, running back David Overstreet fumbled, Marino threw an interception, and Fulton Walker fumbled two kickoff returns. Thirteen of the Seahawks' 20 second-half points were attributable to these miscues. Curt Warner's 2-yard touchdown plunge took the air out of the stadium when he put the Seahawks up, 24–20, later in the fourth quarter. Norm Johnson's 37-yard field goal sealed the deal, and the Miami faithful filed out of the stadium stunned. The Dolphins, favored to go to the AFC Championship Game, and likely the Super Bowl, had been upset. Warner rushed 29 times for 113 yards and two touchdowns.

"When we came down here, nobody gave us a chance," said Knox. "They thought we were going to be blown out. Even after the Dolphins went ahead late in the fourth quarter, I thought we could come back. Our whole bench thought we could come back."

"They had been running the ball so well, really grinding it out, making first downs. Then we got it in after we hadn't done anything in the second half. I thought that would get us going," said Shula. "Defensively, they have a lot of good athletes, and they were all over the joint."

Miamians were not starved for a win for long. On the night of January 2, 1984, the University of Miami, under Shula's old friend Howard Schnellenberger, entered its first major bowl game in thirty-three years to play the Nebraska Cornhuskers for the National Championship. Though they were ranked below Auburn, Schnellenberger campaigned hard for a title, claiming his team deserved it if they beat the unbeaten Nebraska squad, which they did, 31–30.

In late January, an acquaintance saw Don standing in line to register for his hotel room in New Orleans. Had he gone to the Super Bowl? "Yeah, I was there. I did the color commentary for the radio broadcast of the game to Great Britain," said Shula grinning. "Now I'm big in England. I can't go anywhere over there now without people recognizing me." As they spoke, Shula approached the check-in desk.

"Shula," he said.

"Is that S. . .c. . .h?" the clerk asked.

There were some changes in the offseason. Duriel Harris was traded to Cleveland, and running back David Overstreet tragically died in a car crash. And the stalwart Bob Kuechenberg retired, about which Shula said, "It's a pretty important loss to our team, not only for his playing ability, but for the great leadership he has given us for the last few years." Kuechenberg had played in every playoff game in the franchise's history up to that point and was the last player active from the undefeated 1972 squad.

The Dolphins lost Andra Franklin early in the season and scouted around for another running back. In mid-September, they picked up Pete Johnson from the San Diego Chargers. San Diego had earlier traded the troubled Chuck Muncie to Miami in exchange for a second-round pick. However, the deal fell through after Muncie failed his urine test. The Dolphins had then attempted to sign Rickey Young, who had been released by the Minnesota Vikings during the offseason, but he also failed the drug test. Johnson was a big back, 6-foot, 265-pounds. The irony was that Johnson at one time in his career had been suspended after being caught purchasing cocaine. But he was clean by this time, and the Dolphins were happy to have him. It was another sign that the times were changing.

"Pete has been an excellent short-yardage, goal-line player for us," said Don Coryell, the Chargers coach. "This is a great opportunity for him to play in Miami's two-back offense. We will miss him on the goal line." Shula told the press that Johnson "picks things up in a hurry and can catch the ball."

"If you need a player, it's better to get a guy who's on a team, rather than a guy who's unemployed," said Charley Winner, the Dolphins director of pro personnel. "What makes us think we're the only ones who can build talent?"

"I've been a guy who's gone both ways. I believe in making trades for key players. I wouldn't have made the deal if we wouldn't have lost Andra. But that was a key player. I could never operate the way George Allen did, trading away all your draft choices. But I couldn't operate the way some clubs do by never making a trade," Shula told the press. The Johnson trade paid off handsomely. He scored nine touchdowns that year for the Dolphins.

When Johnson made the club, Shula held an extra Sunday morning practice, just for Johnson. The team had a walk-through Sunday morning in Baltimore, just before a meeting with the Colts.

"We gave him a crash course on short-yardage and goal-line situations by holding a walk-through in the cafeteria this morning," Shula told the press.

Despite all this wrangling, the Dolphins were no longer a running team in 1984. They were a pass-first ballclub, with two 1,300-yard receivers, Clayton and Duper. Running back Tony Nathan was Marino's third favorite option, with wide receiver Nat Moore being the fourth-most targeted. Even the third-string quarterback, Jim Jensen, was being used as a receiver, and to good effect.

Marino completed 362 of 564 passes for 5,084 yards, becoming the first player in NFL history to throw for more than 5,000 yards. The team led the league with 5,936 yards of total offense.

The Dolphins raced off to an 11–0 start. The first weekend in October was a homecoming of sorts for Marino when the team played the Steelers in Pittsburgh. "He has a twinkle in his eye this week," said Shula of Marino. The opposing quarterback was David Woodley. The Dolphins annihilated the Steelers, 31–7, and Woodley left the game early after suffering a concussion and was replaced by Mark Malone.

At the halfway point of the schedule, they had beaten New England, 44–24. Marino set three club records in that one game alone. "He did today what he has been doing all year long in making the big plays," said Shula. "He doesn't seem to be awed or intimidated by anybody."

"We had an extremely difficult time containing Miami's offense," said Patriots coach Ron Meyer. "They have an outstanding football team, an outstanding quarterback, and outstanding players around him. The Dolphins are the most explosive outfit in the NFL today."

"You go out there with one thing in mind, to score every time you have the ball," Marino said. "If you're not thinking that, what's the point of being out there?"

"There's a balance of things," said guard Ed Newman. "Opponents have become wary of our deep threat, so they have been playing us a little softer on the run. Their linebackers were playing us a little deeper, which made their pocket a little softer."

"In the dazzling development of Dan Marino as the Miami Dolphins' quarterback, it's natural to talk about how Coach Don Shula has been lucky to have this husky youngster, who throws a football as easily as if it were a dart," wrote sports columnist Dave Anderson. "But instead, Dan Marino might be even more lucky to have Don Shula coaching him. Under another coach on another team, it's conceivable that, for all his now-apparent ability, Dan Marino might still be wearing a telephone headset on the sideline, or he might have been rushed into playing before he was ready."

Anderson reasoned that the club's success was not just about Marino. "The Shula System is to understand the coach's search for perfection in practice," wrote Anderson.

"We never let an error go unchallenged," Don Shula says. "Uncorrected errors will multiply."

Once, a reporter asked Shula if it was OK to sometimes overlook a small flaw.

Shula smiled. "What is a small flaw?"

"Never mind who's lucky to have who," Shula told the press. "Marino should be recognized for what he's done. I'm not out there when the ball is snapped. No young quarterback has ever done what he's done, being picked to start the Pro Bowl as a rookie before his knee injury kept him out, and now having a year like he's having. We spend a lot of time giving Dan the picture he should have of the opposing defenses, our philosophy of what to do with the ball."

There was no question that Shula and Marino had transcended the regular coach-player relationship. Shula had real admiration and affection for his second-year phenom. "Dan's got an outgoing, attack-type personality. He's a winner because he's not afraid to do the things you have to do to win. He's like Joe Namath was in that respect, and he's like Dan Fouts is with his quick arm, his knowing what to do, his accuracy," lauded the veteran coach. "From the moment he walked in, everything you saw about him, you liked. He's just a down-to-earth guy from Pittsburgh, blue-collar people, warm people. I've compared this guy to Larry Csonka in personality. He's always around the locker room like Zonk was in our Super Bowl years, he just enjoys being around the other players."

"When Dan arrived, he was surrounded by excellent personnel—a good line,

Memorial Stadium, Baltimore, Maryland, home of the Baltimore Colts 1947–1983. (Photo courtesy of Wikimedia Commons)

Three Hall of Famers: Bob Griese, Don Shula, and Dan Marino. November 2015. (Reprinted with permission from the *Palm Beach Post*)

Blanton Collier was a major influence on Shula. (Photo courtesy of Special Collections, Cleveland State University Library)

George Wilson was the head coach of the Detroit Lions and later the Miami Dolphins. He won the NFL Championship in 1957 and was later fired by Joe Robbie to be replaced by his former assistant. (Reprinted with permission from the *Palm Beach Post*)

Herb Eisele was the head coach of John Carroll University from 1947 to 1958. A legend in Ohio athletics, Eisele remained the school's athletic director until 1970. Eisele had a big influence on Shula, and they remained close the rest of their lives. (Photo reprinted with permission of John Carroll University)

Don Shula during his college playing days for the John Carroll University Blue Streaks, circa 1947. (Photo reprinted with permission of John Carroll University)

The former Miami Orange Bowl from the west end zone, as it appeared in the 1960s through the 1980s. The Dolphins played their last game there in 1986. It was demolished in 2008. (Haaron755; Photo courtesy of Wikimedia Commons)

Something rare . . .

A rarity on the University campus are the Shula triplets, from left, Jeannette, Jane, and James. Nineteen years old, the triplets live in Painesville.

Jeannette, Jane, and James Shula attending Bowling Green University in Ohio together in 1956. (Photo reprinted with permission, Bowling Green State University, "The B-G News April 24, 1956" (1956), BGSU Student Newspaper, Book 1302)

Dan Marino, Hall of Fame quarterback of the Miami Dolphins. (Reprinted with permission from Shutterstock)

Wilbur Charles "Weeb" Ewbank drafted Shula while an assistant coach with the Browns. He won two of the most important games in the history of the NFL and beat the Colts and Shula, who took his job in Baltimore, in Super Bowl III. (Associated Press)

Don Shula Stadium at Wasmer Field at John Carroll University was opened on September 27, 2003, and has a capacity of 5,416 people. (Photo reprinted with permission of John Carroll University)

Baltimore Colts running back Tom Matte (41), who played quarterback on this occasion, confers with Hall of Fame head coach Don Shula on the sideline during the 1965 NFL Divisional Playoff game against the Green Bay Packers in Green Bay, Wisconsin, December 26, 1965. The Packers defeated the Colts, 13–10, in overtime. The wristband is in the NFL Hall of Fame. (AP Photo/Vernon Biever)

Coach Shula of the Detroit Lions reads the riot act to back Jim Steffen for missing a block in the game in the Coliseum in Los Angeles on October 29, 1961, against the Los Angeles Rams. (Associated Press)

Photo of Shula (standing) and John Unitas (kneeling) in training camp, July 24, 1964. Both were signed to extensions before the photo was taken. Shula would be Coach of the Year in 1964, and Unitas Player of the Year. The two often butted heads during Shula's tenure but were successful together. (Associated Press)

Coach Shula takes time out from spring practice to show his two young daughters the basics of the game on July 21, 1966, in Westminster, Maryland. At left is Donna, 5, while Sharon, 4, is on the right. (Associated Press)

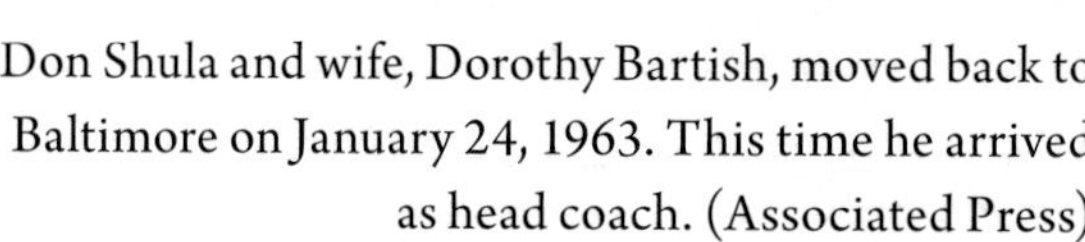

Don Shula and wife, Dorothy Bartish, moved back to Baltimore on January 24, 1963. This time he arrived as head coach. (Associated Press)

Two of the most successful coaches of the 1960s, Don Shula of the Baltimore Colts, left, and Vince Lombardi of the Green Bay Packers, separate after the traditional handshake at the end of the game at County Stadium in Milwaukee on September 27. 1965. Their expressions tell the outcome of the game: Lombardi's Packers won, 20–17. (Associated Press)

Shula and wife, Dorothy, pose with their five children for this picture in their Miami Lakes home on January 3, 1973, in Miami, Florida. Anne is foreground, left; Michael leans on his dad's leg; Donna, left, and Sharon are behind Michael; and David stands behind Shula. The photo was taken just before the Super Bowl against the Washington Redskins during their undefeated season. (AP Photo/MTF)

Marino, left, and Coach Shula get together for photographers during media day at Oakland Stadium Tuesday, January 15, 1985, Oakland, California. The Dolphins played the San Francisco 49ers Sunday in Super Bowl XIX. (Associated Press)

Former Miami Dolphins head coach Don Shula, right, and his wife, Mary Ann, arrive at Shula's 80th birthday party being held at Land Shark Stadium in Miami, Saturday, January 2, 2010. (AP Photo/Jeffrey M. Boan)

Don Shula, center, stands with his sons, David, left, and Mike, after being enshrined into the Pro Football Hall of Fame Saturday, July 26, 1997, in Canton, Ohio. Son David was the head coach of the Cincinnati Bengals, and Mike was a coach in the Super Bowl with the Carolina Panthers. (AP Photo/Mark Duncan)

Shula, left, with Earl Morrall, center, and Bob Griese, right, January 3, 1973. Shula said Morrall was the best trade he ever made (twice) and Griese was a thinking man's quarterback. (AP Photo/Mark Foley)

good running backs, good receivers, a good defense," said veteran backup quarterback Don Strock. "He also had played with a pro-set offense in Pitt, so his only big adjustment was to reading defenses. In college, they show you the defense. In the pros, they disguise it."

"Shula is really the Dolphins' offensive coordinator; he gives a quarterback confidence. He doesn't jerk a quarterback around. If a quarterback has a suggestion that makes sense, he listens. Shula's the captain of the ship, but he's not above listening to somebody else," said Bob Griese. "If the quarterback doesn't like a play, Shula won't make you run it. Dan already is getting to the point where he talks to Shula about plays and personnel. Shula has given Dan more leeway. He lets Dan call the third-down plays, but Shula still calls all the first-down and second-down plays." By contrast, Woodley had never called a play during his time with the Dolphins.

The first loss of the season came on November 18, at San Diego's Jack Murphy Stadium. The Chargers were still potent, and the Marino-Fouts matchup was one of the most highly anticipated of the year. And it did not disappoint. The Chargers scored first, the clubs traded touchdowns throughout the first half, and Miami led at the break, 21–14. The Dolphins came out in the third quarter and put up another touchdown, making the score 28–14. But Fouts threw two touchdown strikes in the fourth quarter to tie the game and send it into overtime, where the Chargers' Buford McGee rushed 25 yards for the winning score. Marino had passed for 338 yards, two touchdowns, and one interception, while Fouts had answered with 380 yards, 4 touchdowns, and one interception.

The Dolphins then beat the Jets, lost to Oakland, and beat the Colts and Cowboys to end the season 14–2. Their first playoff opponent was the 12–4 Seattle Seahawks at the Orange Bowl in a rematch of last year's divisional playoff. A reporter asked Knox if he and Shula had a rivalry going. "Last year is history," said the Seattle coach. "What do we know about each other? Don Shula-coached teams are well prepared. Everyone gets a feeling of how it's going to be, but there's not a lot of mystique about it. It comes down to players—the chance to make an interception; if you're blitzing, making the big play. This is what the game will come down to. Their players versus our players."

But if Knox didn't hold a grudge, the Dolphins players remembered that playoff loss bitterly. Miami came out and put two touchdowns on the board in the first half, and Seattle answered with a touchdown and field goal, as the Dolphins took a 14–10 lead into halftime. Marino threw two touchdown passes in the third quarter, and the defense held the Seahawks scoreless in the second half as Miami came away with 31–10 win.

"I feel very good about our team right now," said Shula. "The defense was a real concern. But when you think we gave the Seahawks only 58 yards rushing. They would have liked to do the same stuff job against us as they did against the Raiders. I think the defense feels good about what it's doing now. We're doing things aggressively on the other side of the line of scrimmage."

The Dolphins had the league's seventh-ranked defense that year in points allowed and were 14th against the pass, and 22nd against the run. While they had carried the team for the past four seasons, they were not the leading edge of this team. The offense had scored 513 points that year, even outscoring the vaunted 49ers, who had scored 475. What Shula already knew was that the offense was scoring too fast and leaving his defense on the field exposed time and again. This was the Achilles heel of the team, though it was hard to see at the time. At the beginning of the season, the Dolphin defense had given up 17 points or less in eight of their first 10 games. But with injuries and time, the numbers in the second half of the season were alarming, as they allowed 35 to the Chargers and 45 to the Raiders. Were these flukes, or a sign of something coming down the road?

"We weren't ready for the success the offense was going to have. Fifty-four seconds on the field and the offense scores in four plays, and we have to go back. It's a high-powered offense, so we started playing a laid-back game. I'm glad we finally pulled out of it," said Dolphins defensive end Doug Betters, attempting to explain the Dolphins' late-season defensive slump. "Because we play in this heat, we were always conscious of our weight, keeping it down so that in the fourth quarter we wouldn't come apart."

Chuck Studley, the new defensive coordinator, who had replaced Arnsparger (who had become head coach at Louisiana State), wanted the defense to attack more. The idea was to force mistakes.

"Arns was always coming up with new schemes," Betters said of Arnsparger, "and he'd show something each week and then double-cross the scouts from the other team when we did something different in a game. He wanted the smart players. Now we want to get some movement on our line, be more aggressive."

"This is our best defense and the best football team I've played on," said Betters, who was in his seventh campaign. "When things were going bad for us, we went back to defensive basics. We realized we had an opportunity like this once in a lifetime with Marino and Clayton and Duper."

The Dolphins next faced the 9–7 Steelers in the AFC Championship Game at the Orange Bowl on January 6, 1985. Pittsburgh was now led by Mark Malone, who had gone 7–2 as the starting quarterback since he had relieved Woodley. The Steelers were still a formidable team. "The first thing I have to think of is stopping the run," Baumhower explained. "They're a play-action team. Malone's not a drop-back passer. But if we don't stop the run, it makes the play-action more effective."

At that time, the Dolphins were thought to have the best offensive line in the NFL. Two were named to the Pro Bowl, Ed Newman and Dwight Stephenson. Without question, Stephenson was the anchor of that line. The Dolphins gave up the fewest amount of sacks that season, 14, while the Steelers defense allowed 47 sacks that year. The Dolphins felt the game would be won in the trenches.

"The Steelers off-set their nose tackle instead of playing him straight up," line coach John Sandusky said of the Steelers defense. "[Nose tackle Gary] Dunn has excellent strength and quickness. That creates a problem. He may take an angle on your center, and that could force your guard to do something else. You don't know where you have to help out."

"I expect them to start blitzing when they get off the bus," Shula told the press.

The Steelers and Dolphins traded touchdowns in the opening quarter. Then the Dolphins responded with an Uwe von Schamann field goal, and Pittsburgh countered with a touchdown, giving them a 14–10 lead. The Dolphins would score two touchdowns before the half, with Marino combining with Duper on a 41-yard touchdown pass and Nathan scoring on a 2-yard run, giving the Dolphins a 24–14 lead at halftime. It never got any closer than that, with the Dolphins cruising through a physical but easy victory, 45–28. While Malone had thrown for 318 yards and three touchdowns in a losing cause, Marino had thrown for 435 yards, four touchdowns, and an interception as the Dolphins amassed 569 yards of offense. Tony Nathan had been a dynamo, with 178 yards of combined rushing and receiving, and also completed a pass for 14 more yards. Mark Duper had 148 yards receiving, and Clayton 95.

"We like blitzing teams," Marino said after the game. "It gives the offense a chance to make the big plays."

"We did an outstanding job against the blitz," said Shula. "There were a couple of times our line didn't pick it up, but with Dan's quick gun, he was able to get the ball off. That combination worked for us the whole game."

"Marino is the best quarterback we've seen—no question," said Noll.

"Marino is something, I'd say he's sensational," said Mike Webster, the Steelers' center. "Twice we had him on his back, and he threw it on a string."

"You can't ever predict that a guy is going to be better than anybody else has ever been, but this guy rises to every occasion," said Shula. "We've never had to tell him he's too young to do this, or that he's not ready to do that."

"You've got to pat Shula on the back," said CBS announcer and Terry Bradshaw, a Hall of Fame quarterback. "He didn't change Marino, *he* changed. Shula used to run the ball a lot more, but as soon as he got Marino, he started throwing the ball a lot more. This kid is the greatest I've ever seen, but whether he'll be the best ever still has to be proven. But give Shula credit for knowing what to do with this kid."

"It's just so enjoyable," Shula said in the locker room. "Usually you can scratch your head and come up with a negative about any player. But not with this kid, not yet anyway."

The Dolphins were an offensive juggernaut. They scored an average of every 16 plays. The NFL average that year was 30. More frighteningly, Marino scored a touchdown on every eighth pass he threw. The Dolphins were No. 1 in twenty-four different offensive statistics measured by the NFL. It was unheard of. What was even more amazing, where the Dolphins were No. 1, their Super Bowl opponents, the San Francisco 49ers, were most often No. 2. It took more than 32 points to beat the Dolphins (their average of scoring). Mark Clayton and Mark Duper had combined for a total of 144 receptions, 18 by Clayton for 2,695 yards and 26 touchdowns, 18 by Duper.

"They were both dynamic," Shula said. "Both could leap. They'd go up and get the ball."

"Each week when we put together our package, we try to get them both in the game," said David Shula. "But Dupe knows that a lot of times he'll be setting up a route for Clayton, and Clayton knows that he might be setting up something for Dupe. There's never been a point where they resented that."

In a sense, the old rubric was to run to set up the pass; the Dolphins inverted that, throwing almost 70 percent of the time, but they used the pass to set up the run.

They had the No. 16 rushing attack. Miami's leading rusher was fullback Woody Bennett, with 606 yards. Tony Nathan averaged 4.7 yards per carry, and 1,137 yards of combined offense. And rookie running back Joe Carter averaged five yards per carry and chipped in 548 combined yards.

It was the first time Bennett, a perennial journeyman who blocked well and ran occasionally, had led a team in rushing. "We take pride in sustaining our blocks and picking up blitzes, because we know if we give Dan time, he'll score," Bennett said. "I'll have to help the offensive linemen because we're going to see a big rush from Fred Dean and those guys," he said. "I'm going to play a big role of blocking this weekend."

Dave Anderson summed it up best in the *New York Times,* writing, "The Super Bowl XIX scenario is as obvious as it is theatrical—the Dolphins against the 49ers, Dan Marino against Joe Montana, Don Shula against Bill Walsh, southeast Florida against northern California on Jan. 20 out there in Palo Alto in northern California itself." Both Shula and Bill Walsh, head coach of the 49ers, had worked for Paul Brown. These were arguably two of Brown's greatest disciples and were evidence of his far-reaching influence into the modern game.

"It only seems right that the two best teams are going to play to see who is the best team," said Shula. "It's ironic that the 49ers already have won 17 games, which ties our 17–0 season in 1972. And a Super Bowl win for us would be our 17th this season. What I'd love to do is go out there and beat 'em in their own backyard. It'd cap off a great year."

For 18 of the previous 21 seasons, Bill Arnsparger had been Shula's defensive coordinator. This season it was Chuck Studley. Shula called Studley his secret weapon. Bill Walsh and Chuck Studley had been assistant coaches under Brown on the Bengals. The two coaches commuted to work together each day, wherein Walsh would call out an offensive play and Woodley would call his corresponding defense. Sometimes, it worked the other way, and Studley mentioned a defensive play first.

"Bill would bounce a lot of his offensive thoughts off me," Studley recalled. "And he's got a million of 'em. Bill Walsh was the first guy to move the tight end back and put him in motion, he's very ingenious about offensive innovations. . . . But the thing is, you can't get obsessed with all the different plays Bill might use. If you get consumed by them, he'll beat you with solid stuff. Another thing about Bill is that he never runs the same passing attack. . . . I imagine Bill will try to have a different passing attack against us."

Sports Illustrated's Paul Zimmerman opined that Miami's numbers were "mesmerizing, seductive," noting that the tough running of Csonka, Kiick, and Morris (and more recently by Andra Franklin), and the bruising defenses like the No-Name Defense and the Killer Bees, seemed lost to time. "Flash had replaced substance, but what the heck difference did that make? Miami still was taking a

14–2 record into the Super Bowl against San Francisco. The next season I was talking to Shula before a game, and I asked him if he was really comfortable with this kind of club. I said he seemed like a coachman riding behind a team of wild horses; all he could do was hold on tight. He got annoyed."

"We reached the Super Bowl with this kind of team," Shula replied. "What do you want us to do, throw 15 passes a game?"

"We started something that people couldn't stop. I'll never forget when we arrived there at the Super Bowl. I was like, 'We better get used to this. We'll be here the next three, four, five years,'" said Mark Clayton.

It was important to note that only 12 of the 20 offensive and defensive players who had started the Super Bowl against the Redskins two years earlier were still on the squad. On the offensive side of the ball, only Nathan, left tackle Jon Giesler, and center Dwight Stephenson remained.

"We had something special going," Nathan said. "We could be as good as we wanted to be, if we put points on the board and kept our defense off the field. Our only problem was scoring too quick."

Shula was such a perfectionist that during Super Bowl week he even mapped out how the players should come in for their player-media breakfast, so they would not get jostled by the more than 500 media members. "Don doesn't want the players coming through here," said a club executive. "He wants them coming through another entrance so they don't get shoved around."

"One of the biggest enjoyments I get out of accomplishments is that I do it within the rules," Shula said.

"The rules. They are made to be followed, and no one in pro football is obsessed with them as is Shula. For nine straight seasons, his team has been the least penalized in the National Football League," wrote Gerald Eskanazi.

"I guess people know from that jaw who I am," Shula once said in a Ford television commercial. But he said that week, "I try to be myself. I've got a long memory and a lot of people who have helped me along the way."

"This has been one of the most enjoyable years of coaching I've had," Shula told the Associated Press. "To see how these young guys have developed, come along, is very satisfying."

However, the 49ers weren't half as impressed as the media world. "After looking at the films, we said, 'This is a Super Bowl defense?'" said 49ers line coach Bobb McKittrick. "It's unusual for a one-dimensional team to make it to the Super Bowl, but Miami was unusual. . . . We could see in the films we could run against them."

Doug Betters remembered waiting in the tunnel before the game, "We were all pretty loose, pretty cocky and confident," he says. A crowd of 84,000 people was in the stands, 120 million people were watching on television, and 30 additional countries were broadcasting the game. The game was played at Stanford Stadium, making it for all intents and purposes a 49ers home game.

"We sensed it the minute we got off the plane," said William Judson, the Dolphin cornerback. "The crowd tonight was 75 percent for the 49ers."

The Dolphins scored first on Uwe von Schamann's 37-yard field goal, and Joe Montana responded with a 33-yard touchdown pass to Carl Monroe, making it 7–3, San Francisco. Marino retaliated with a 2-yard TD pass of his own to tight end Dan Johnson, and the Dolphins were up, 10–7. "That first quarter was a hell of a football game; it was exciting and we did well," Shula recalled. Then the second quarter happened.

First, Reggie Roby, considered one of the best punters in the game, uncharacteristically shanked three punts. "The three punts just messed things up," Roby said. "It was a combination of things—too fast, too hard, too anxious." The 49ers scored three straight touchdowns, two rushing and one passing. Miami responded with two field goals. And the two teams went into halftime with the 49ers leading, 28–16. Whether the Dolphins sensed it or not, the game was over.

"Both teams are so emotionally up," said Mike Kozlowski, a Dolphin defensive back. "It's hard to get back on the springboard once you're trailing. At the half, we said, let's start out and come back, but then we had three plays and a punt, and then we were just hanging on. When you're down and a team is emotionally up, it's hard to come back."

"I know it's tough to come back," said Shula. "But I had that feeling at halftime, especially after we got that last field goal. We usually can move the ball in the third quarter. We're never stopped. That's what I'd hoped would happen.

"In the second quarter, we just quit playing, and the 49ers couldn't do anything wrong. That second quarter was a nightmare. We had worked so hard to get there, and we let it slip away," Shula added.

"Early in the game, we didn't use a huddle and we scored a touchdown," said Shula. "That made the 49ers decide to go to a four-man line and six defensive backs. We got a lot of that at the end of the season and felt we would get it today. We didn't go to the hurry-up offense when they switched to a four-man front. We tried to get some runs against it, but the runs we used didn't work. They also had the lead, and we were fighting that. Our offense has been slowed down this season.

But it was stopped for the first time today. Offensively, it was our poorest game of the year. We didn't make things happen."

"Montana was outstanding in every way," said Shula. "Every time we tried to put some pressure on him, he scrambled for a big play on his own or he bought time to hit one of his receivers. He hurt us in every way. He broke the record and did the job."

The 49ers defense harassed Marino all the through the second half, disrupting their plays by only rushing four men and dropping seven back. He threw two interceptions and was sacked four times after halftime.

"They were able to get some pressure on us and cover our receivers well," Marino said. "The chances we did have, when guys were open, sometimes I didn't hit 'em."

"It all started from up front, with the line," said 49ers linebacker Keena Turner. "Once they got pressure on Marino, he couldn't wait as long to throw, and we could do a better job of coverage."

George Seifert, the 49ers defensive coordinator, put in new stunts up the middle for the game. They saw Stephensen as the anchor of the line. He had to be neutralized or overwhelmed. "We had to tie him up on every play so we could go right up the middle on Marino," 49ers defensive lineman Gary "Big Hands" Johnson said. "You could see [Marino] getting rattled out there. Marino would throw away passes or he would talk more than usual to his linemen. We could see we were getting to him, but you'd be upset, too, if you were getting hit a lot."

Marino stood tall after the game, as well. "Their defense played me better than anybody all year. They got the job done. I probably could have played a better game. We knew what we had to do, but they took us right out of our game," said Marino, who attempted 50 passes, completing 29 for 318 yards. The 49ers tacked on another 10 points in the third quarter. The rest was academic, as San Francisco won, 38–16.

"Defensively," Shula added, "we never stopped them." The Dolphins defense yielded 537 yards, in the most in Super Bowl history up to that point.

Betters later recalled that the weather changed as the game did. "Fog rolled around, in his recollection, and blocked out the sun. Meanwhile, the cracks that had shown in the Dolphins defense only widened. Roger Craig scored three times. Not only could Miami not tackle him, they couldn't cover him," wrote *Sports Illustrated*'s Greg Bishop. "In each of their Super Bowl losses, the Dolphins had one thing and needed something else. In '82, their defense needed a better quarterback. In '84, their quarterback needed a better defense."

"You don't mind being overlooked that much, but sometimes it seemed they [reporters] forgot there were two teams in the game," Montana said later, regarding the pregame hype about Marino. "It got to all of us after a while. But you couldn't argue with Dan's statistics. He had a great season."

"Joe will never say it, but it's understandable that with all the talk about Marino, he would like to do well," said 49ers wide receiver Dwight Clark. "The talk pushed him. I know I am prejudiced, but he is the best quarterback around today, no question."

"Our defense let us down," Duper said.

"We knew they were coming. We saw them coming, but we missed the tackles," said Judson.

"I'll admit it. After a while, we were in a state of shock," said Baumhower. "They left no doubt about who was the better team out there."

"The 49ers drilled us. Nobody else ever did what they did to us," said Betters.

"After the game, I was already into my depression of losing a second Super Bowl," Moore later said. "When we lost in '82, it was gut-wrenching. To come back two years later and not just lose, but we weren't that competitive. . . . I still believe if we played them 10 times we would win six. It wasn't that we were outclassed."

"We said to ourselves all week we'd be able to stop him. We should have executed better, but there were breakdowns. We weren't always where we were supposed to be, and that puts a lot of pressure on the three-man rush. If there's the correct coverage, he can't get away," said Betters after the game. Years later, he added, "Our defense didn't peak at the time Dan started peaking."

"We have got to improve our football team," said Shula. "This game exposed some weaknesses."

"If you're going to get here," Marino said, "you want to win. It's a disappointing feeling. You worked hard to get here. It's a tough feeling. It's something you'd like to have over again."

"I always thought I would be back a number of times, and win a Super Bowl," said Marino after his playing career. "My advice to people is always take advantage of that. Don't take things for granted. We were young guys. We were a pretty young team. As far as Clayton and myself and some of the other guys on the team . . . we all thought we'd be back several times. And we never did get there."

Nathan said later that Shula "took it harder than the majority of us did."

"Yeah, I was there. I remember that game. The last one I went to with my dad, I was in college [at Alabama]. Sure, it spoils you a little going to so many as a kid.

But from a personal level, you actually find out who your true friends really are, because everybody's your friend when your dad's going to the Super Bowl and winning Super Bowls," Mike Shula said. "Then all of a sudden you realize it's not like that for everyone, and you realize how hard it is to get there. You realize how high the highs are and how low the lows are. You realize how important the game is to your father, and how he always preached doing things the right way, and that hard work equals success."

"When you get beat the way we got beat, you have to take your hat off to them, and that's what I'll do," said Shula. "Their defense stopped our team. Dan Marino certainly didn't play the way he had done all year. The disappointment of not getting it done today will live with all of us."

Don Shula had no idea how prophetic his statement would be. Neither he nor Marino would ever walk the sidelines as a Super Bowl competitor again. And the pain of going 2–4 in the Super Bowl would nag him the rest of his life, as well as the loss to the Browns in 1964. While he had proved he could win the big one, another ring might have secured him as the greatest coach of all time. Even without another Lombardi Trophy, he could certainly stake his claim. But these last two losses, especially the one against the 49ers, hurt. It hurt bad. It hurt almost as bad as the Super Bowl III loss to the Jets.

CHAPTER 10

Pursuing Halas

Shula had only one other goal to chase now, whether he knew it or not. While he would ache to get back to another Super Bowl, the last, unassailable record beckoned to be broken. And with Marino at the helm, it suddenly seemed within reach. He would attempt to break George Halas's record of 318 regular-season wins. It was the Moby Dick of NFL coaching records. Shula would chase it.

"Even with his closest friends, Shula doesn't say much about his pursuit of Halas's mark. Instead, he claims he's really aiming at the Super Bowl, so that he can become the only coach to have made it to Super Bowls in four decades," wrote Jill Lieber in *Sports Illustrated*.

However, when he was nearing victory number 300, he said to his daughter Sharon, who wanted to commemorate the event with a special momento, which occurred on September 22, 1991 (a 16–13 win at Green Bay), "I don't want to do anything too fancy, because I want to wait until I break the record. That's the time when you can do something really special.'"

In 1985, the Dolphins drafted running back Lorenzo Hampton, offensive lineman Jeff Dellenbach, and kicker Fuad Reveiz, who would become key contributors. However, there was real trouble brewing. Dan Marino was in the middle of a contract holdout. The *New York Times* blared the headline, "Dolphins' New Play: Waiting For Marino." Outside Shula's office, there had been a poster of Marino from the previous season. Handsome, with his curly hair, blue eyes, and toothy white smile, the poster hung over the copier in the hall. But since late July, through the course of Marino's holdout, players and staffers had come to make subtle changes to the poster's appearance. Several of Marino's teeth had been blacked out. Someone had drawn red zigzaggy lines in the whites of his eyes. Marino had come into camp but was upset with Joe Robbie, who had promised the quarterback a new contract during Super Bowl week, but it never came.

Marino had shown good faith and come to the spring workouts. "He had a great minicamp," Shula said. "It was exciting to watch him practice. He looked sharp. He ran well. The knee looked good. The day he left, he was under 218 [pounds] and looked in great shape."

In April, Marvin Demoff had offered a proposal that asked for more money than Joe Montana was making, figuring the price would come down but would still be in the ballpark. Robbie's response was relative silence. He talked with the agent, but he would not discuss numbers. When Robbie hesitated, Marino left training camp in late July. When Marino walked, Robbie balked. And the whole thing mushroomed. By August, the rhetoric worsened.

"We have been trying to talk about a new contract for four months and haven't gotten anything done," Demoff said. "Now, Robbie is saying that if Dan comes in, he'll talk. That's like saying, 'Trust me,' which is what the three bears said to Goldilocks."

"I think they're all behind Danny," said Baumhower, referring to the other Dolphins. "We all want him in here. Everybody knows what the guy means to the team. At the same time, this is his future, his career. He has to do what's right for him."

And, as the September 8 season opener at Houston approached, others were also out, including fullback Andra Franklin, tackle Eric Laakso, guard Ed Newman, nose tackle Bob Baumhower, and linebacker A. J. Duhe, who were battling injuries. Shula was despondent. Far more than the strike, Shula found this difficult to deal with.

"This has been the most disheartening, confusing, and disruptive time I've ever had in coaching," he said about the lack of star talent. Then he added, "You hate to see Marino out of camp."

"I wasn't that interested in playing him a lot in the preseason," Shula said. "But he's still in a learning process. He needs to study films, become more and more of an expert, be sure of our offensive philosophy and terminology, to get to where he has the kind of knowledge Bob Griese once had. He has a long way to go before he understands things the way Griese did."

By this time, as Dolphins head coach, Shula had won the division title in nine of his fifteen years. In that time, Shula lost only one home game in the month of September. Many wondered what kept driving him. "He's already more of a myth than a man in the minds of many fans, and he has to compete with his own legend every Sunday," said George Young, then-general manager of the New York Giants and one of Shula's closest friends. "To coach in the NFL is to be wounded . . . often. And Shula has a lot of wounds. He moans and groans like everyone else, but he's adjusted to adversity better than the others. That's why he's survived so long."

"If anyone believes Don Shula can rest easy with a 2–4 Super Bowl record, he doesn't know the man. Shula is embarrassed by it and means to change it. His record doesn't leave the same acrid taste in his mouth as did the sense of humiliation that pursued him after the Super Bowl III defeat. But he won't be content with a mere 4–4 standoff. What he wants, what he hungers for, is three more Super Bowl wins before calling it quits," wrote journalist Jon Nordheimer.

"Competitive?" asked his former assistant coach Monte Clark. "Don Shula is competitive in everything. He's competitive eating breakfast. . . . People don't realize how tough-minded he is. He's a tough, tough competitor and very demanding. There were lots of times when I walked off the practice field into the parking lot thinking about punching out a windshield or something." The fans who saw Shula coaching that training camp in 1985 saw a man still full of passion and energy.

"No, no, no," Shula barked at a cowed linebacker who made an excuse for missing an assignment. "None of that 'I thought he said' bull! You've got to know your assignment!" When a young receiver dropped an easy pass, Shula clapped his hands and sighed. The player, seeing Shula's disappointment, hung his head in shame. "Relax," Shula told the young receiver off to the side in a calm, fatherly voice. "Think about looking the pass in, like this," mimicking the moves of cradling the reception. "You'll make the next play."

"Dolphin meetings can turn into players' worst classroom nightmares. Taking copious notes is encouraged, and concentration is a must because Shula can be counted on to pop a quiz. In front of the whole team he'll jump on a player who screwed up on the field, and he will run game tape again and again to emphasize somebody's ineptitude," reported *Sports Illustrated* on Shula, then in his fourth decade of coaching.

"I'll embarrass a player publicly, if that's what it takes," said Shula. "You've got to shape up, or I'm looking for somebody else," said Shula. "If I see somebody doing something casually that I don't think should be handled casually, I don't hesitate to correct. On the spot. I can't let that creep into my football."

Shula still jogged almost thirty minutes a day in an effort to keep his weight down. He was constantly monitoring his times against previous performances. By

1992, his doctor would request he knock off at least a minute or two sooner than previous years. Shula was unhappy. "I could have gutted it out," he said.

"I've never seen a guy with more energy," said Clark. "I think the church he goes to is called Our Lady of Perpetual Motion."

"To me, coaching is finding out what makes an individual play to the best of his ability. I have to understand how best to motivate each and every one, and of the 45 players I'm going to be responsible for this year, there are no two alike," said Shula. "Some are not naturally aggressive, and I have to do something to make them aggressive. It could be yelling and screaming. It could be a kick in the pants. But that's the wrong approach on those who can't handle that treatment."

"This is my secret: I let all of my emotions out. I've screamed so hard on the sideline, at players, coaches, and officials, that I don't even recognize myself when I see pictures of my face in that state. I've punched walls. I've stomped off from press conferences. My adrenaline flows, and everything just comes right out of me," said Shula. "I've always believed that you have to feel the disappointments, heartaches, and losses to be able to move on. You put so much time into it, you can't ever feel it too deeply. You've got to feel it down to your bones. You just can't allow yourself to get consumed."

"Shula's home is in Miami Lakes, a suburb a few miles west of the St. Thomas campus. But, beginning in July, he lives in the dormitory with the players and stays there for the rest of the regular and postseason play, having dinner with his wife, Dorothy, on Thursday evenings and after home games," reported Nordheimer. "He puts in 17-hour days, starting with mass in the college chapel and ending with evening meetings that include players and coaches and run past 10 p.m. Shula's ability to drive himself hard for long hours, seven days a week, cuts off any complaints about the regimen he demands of his players and assistants."

"Once the season starts, you have to be totally dedicated to the job, there is no other way," Shula said, reflecting on all the lost family time. "I'm fortunate that Dorothy understands it. She's been there when I haven't, and she's been just outstanding in raising the kids and substituting for some of the things I should've been doing. There are many benefits to a head coach's job, but the loss of family life is one of the negatives."

The Dolphins received some good news on September 1, when Marino announced that he would return to the Dolphins, even without having reached an agreement. "I am returning to the team as of today," Marino said at a news conference. "I can no longer let these circumstances with Mr. Robbie affect my personal life. I want to return because I feel a strong obligation to my teammates, my family, and the fans of the Miami Dolphins. I want to help my teammates work to have another great season. At this time, I'm not being forced to return. This is totally my own decision. I expect a new offer from Mr. Robbie shortly, now that I have returned to the team."

"I'm obviously happy," Shula said. "It's too bad that it's gone on for so long. He looks in excellent shape, and now we're just going to work him over time to get him caught up with all the things he's missed."

The Dolphins lost the 1985 season opener to the Oilers at the Astrodome, 26–23. Marino started the game but was replaced in the fourth quarter by Strock, whose 67-yard TD pass to Duper gave them a 23–19 lead before Mike Rozier scored the winning touchdown with 24 seconds remaining on a 1-yard plunge. Miami then won their next four games, beating the Indianapolis Colts, Chiefs, Broncos, and Steelers. A Monday night loss to the Jets in New York began a stretch in which they lost three of four games to put them at 5–4, stacked up behind the Patriots and Jets in the AFC East. They then went on a seven-game run, finished the season with a 12–4 record, and took another AFC East divisional crown.

One of the most memorable games in Dolphins history was the Monday Night Football contest against the undefeated Chicago Bears at the Orange Bowl on December 2. It featured the NFL's No. 1 offense against the No. 1 defense. The 12–0 Bears featured one of the greatest defenses in NFL history. The talk in Chicago was that Marino had wilted before the 49ers in the Super Bowl, and he would do so again. While the Dolphins were 8–4, the Bears were undefeated, and many thought that they would match the '72 Dolphins' perfect season.

Bears Head Coach Mike Ditka said before the game, "To say you might end up undefeated, even if you thought it, you wouldn't say it. You're almost afraid to think it because it's almost like treading on sacred ground. It's like nobody is even supposed to think that good. But I'm kind of foolish about things. I do think optimistically."

"I know just what Ditka is going through. [A perfect season] is such an elusive dream, and you don't dare dream it too often. Maybe the Bears have the kind of football team that can go all the way," Shula said. Gentlemanly in front of the press, Shula wanted this game in the worst possible way.

As Bob Kuechenberg told the press, "Nobody likes to share immortality."

Even the boisterous Bears' defensive coordinator, Buddy Ryan, said before the game, "I'm scared of this game. Their strength [Marino] is our weakness [cornerbacks]."

The home field was an advantage. Plus, the Dolphins brought back the undefeated 1972 team for a ceremony before the game started. It was enough to whip the crowd into a frenzy. It was easily the most hyped-up regular season game of the 1985 season.

"Here's the dynamic: Put yourself in charge of a bunch of 25-year-old guys going to Miami and they all think they are Mick Jagger, they are all rock stars. It had the earmarkings of trouble, and years have gone by and I have heard of certain guys maybe sneaking out and doing this and that. Now remember, we had been practicing on a rock-hard field of ice for weeks. We go out for pregame, and after that I came in, went into the shower, took my shoulder pads off, and laid on the cold tile floor trying to get my body temperature down. It was like a shock," remembered Bears defensive lineman Dan Hampton.

"They did everything to beat us. They brought back their 17–0 team, and they made us stand around and watch all that (ceremony) as it was going on," remembered linebacker Ron Rivera. "The game didn't start until well after 9 and it was really hot and the humidity kicked our ass."

"It was just a pretty magical night because the Bears were very good and we wanted to keep our streak alive. It was amazing the way the fans got there early and the '72 players showed up on the sideline and really got into it. It was a game that I will always remember," said Shula years later.

"As we watched film that week, we felt like we could have success throwing the ball against them provided Dan had enough time. And we also added a wrinkle to the offense that week. We went three wide and took out the tight end [for] Nat Moore, which made [linebacker] Wilber Marshall have to cover Nat," remembered Mark Clayton.

"What Coach Shula said was, 'We're just going to have a positive play. We're going to throw around the blitzer in the flat, and there's not going to be anybody there to cover you.' My job was to read the blitz. We felt if we could get them to play our game with our matchups, we could put some points on the board," recalled Nat Moore. Most experts only gave the Dolphins a puncher's chance.

"We were the best offense in football," Moore said. "It was the best offense going up against the best defense, and we're playing at home on a Monday night. So to think that you could come into Miami and play us and we don't have a chance was somewhat far-fetched. To be looked upon as a team that had no chance just didn't fly well with us."

"In the locker room before the game," Shula said, "I told our players, 'The important thing is what happens here and now, but there's a lot of Dolphin history on the line, things that are important to the coaching staff and to the organization.' I would never ask them to win one for the Gipper, but I wanted them to know what was at stake."

In the first series, to buy time, they had Marino roll away from wherever All-Pro defensive end Richard Dent was, in order to buy more time. Anything to either beat the line or the blitz they did. Against a more ferocious defense than the 49ers, Marino carved up the Bears. By halftime, the score was 31–10.

At halftime, the Bears had a full-blown meltdown in their locker room. "Down the tunnel, you could see the entrance to their locker room, and I could see Buddy Ryan and Mike Ditka about to throw down with one another because Ditka was telling Buddy to take Wilber [Marshall] off of Nat Moore. I said, 'We got 'em,'" said Clayton. "Ditka is saying, 'Wilber is a good player, but he can't cover Moore.' Duh. He was right. Sooner or later, you have to face reality, and Nat Moore is a great player. It was a reality check, and I think it really affected Buddy.... Nat Moore was wearing Wilber out. There were a lot of reasons it was like a meltdown situation."

Said Rivera, "We were sitting there waiting for [Ryan] to come in, and all of a sudden we hear in one of the back shower areas they're just screaming at each other. So we go running around the corner and see them toe-to-toe just yelling at each other, a little belly bumping. It was the first time I ever thought, 'Wow, these guys aren't really happy with each other.'"

The Bears came out and put up a touchdown in the third quarter. Then the final nail in the coffin came from a crazy carom. Marino's pass hit Hampton in the helmet and popped into the air. Mark Clayton saw the ball flutter into the air, grabbed it, and raced for a 42-yard touchdown that made the score 38–17. The Bears scored another touchdown, but the damage was already done. The Dolphins won the game, 38–24. It was the only time the Bears allowed 30 or more points all year, in a season where they allowed 10 points or less 11 times.

"I don't know when we've had a bigger regular-season game," said Shula, "as far as people being excited."

"He needed to win a big one. Not to prove that he could, but to remind everybody that he did," wrote columnist Dave Anderson. "Don Shula's stature as the National Football League's most respected current coach is secure."

"We probably played one of the best games that I've ever been around. We just set up situations where we felt we would have the advantage and made it happen," recalled Shula. "When you beat a team that was as good as the Bears were and beat them the way that we beat them, it gave us unlimited confidence in what we were capable of doing." In 2015, it was selected as the greatest game in Miami Dolphins history by a fan vote.

In the first round of the playoffs, they faced the 8–8 Cleveland Browns, coached by Marty Schottenheimer. Brash young quarterback Bernie Kosar, who had starred at the University of Miami and led them to the national championship in 1982, had ignited the Browns franchise. With his shock of wavy hair, and his ability to make plays, Kosar seemed to be almost the second coming of Marino. Along with running backs Earnest Byner and Kevin Mack, both of whom gained 1,000 yards, the Browns were a formidable opponent. The two teams faced off on January 4, 1986, in Miami. The Dolphins scored first on a 51-yard field goal by Fuad Reveiz. But then the Browns came to life. With a brutal ground attack somewhat reminiscent of the old Dolphins, Byner and Mack crashed their way through the Miami defense. All-Pro tight end Ozzie Newsome took in a 16-yard Kosar pass for Cleveland's first score, and early in the third quarter, Byner cashed in his second touchdown of the game, giving the Browns a 21–3 lead.

"We felt at halftime that we were going to find out a lot about our football team," said Shula after the game. "That was as tough a situation as we've been in."

"If you want to go home, let's go ahead and lay down," Nathan remembered thinking. "If you want to go to next week, let's get up and be counted."

Then, in a span of three and a half minutes, Miami put up two scores—a 6-yard Marino touchdown pass to Nat Moore and a 31-yard touchdown burst by Ron Davenport—and suddenly the Dolphins cut their deficit to four points. Schottenheimer continued to call a conservative game, hoping to grind out a win. Kosar, who had experienced some of his biggest games in the Orange Bowl while playing for Miami, was kept in check by his own coach. After a huge defensive stop, Marino led a 73-yard, nine-play drive that was capped off by Davenport's 1-yard touchdown run, and the Dolphins took the lead with 1:57 remaining and held on to win, 24–21.

If there were heroics the week before, there were none to be found when the Dolphins hosted Raymond Berry's New England Patriots in the AFC Championship Game at the Orange Bowl. Berry had been a star receiver for Shula's Baltimore Colts and was now a successful coach. Miami had split with their division rival and had taken the AFC East crown, with the Patriots settling for a wild-card berth. New England proceeded to win playoff games against the Jets and Raiders, both on the road. The day promised to be a good one. The Dolphins, 5–0 in AFC Championship games at that point, were favored, and the media were salivating for a Dolphins-Bears rematch.

The contest started badly for the Dolphins, as Tony Nathan's fumble on the first play of the game led to a 27-yard field goal by Tony Franklin. Marino stormed back and tossed a 7-yard touchdown pass to Dan Johnson to make the score 7–3. That was the high point of the game for the Dolphins. The Dolphins turned the ball over six times (compared to the Patriots' two), and Tony Eason, a class of 1983 quarterback, threw for three touchdowns as New England snapped an 18-game losing streak in Miami, as a shell-shocked Dolphins crowd walked away silently with the Dolphins losing, 31–14. The Patriots, not the Dolphins, would face the Bears in Super Bowl XX, which was won by Chicago, 46–10. Miami was the only team to knock off the Bears, who finished 15–1.

"Don Shula was alone in his office, his renowned jutting chin below lips that were turned down. It wasn't only the obvious distress that his Dolphins had lost the American Conference championship on Sunday to the Patriots. His team had made mistakes. Because they created six turnovers . . . Shula was seething. He was also thinking about next season," according to the *New York Times*.

"It's so damn disappointing, after fighting and scratching," he said, "to leave the ball on the ground like that." Shula shook his head in disgust.

"The disappointment was losing the game the way that we lost. Our team worked hard to come back from 5–4," Shula said of the season a day later. "I didn't sleep much last night. I kept thinking about all those turnovers."

"My overriding philosophy," said Shula, "is I don't dwell on things I can't control. Too many good things have happened to me. We spend a lot of time giving young people or backups an opportunity to beat out the guy, and if something happens—well, the backups have the confidence that our work has given them and they know they'll do well."

In February 1986, Shula appointed his son Dave, then twenty-six, as his chief assistant. Dave had been the Dolphins' receivers and quarterbacks coach for the past four seasons. He had been a candidate for the Philadelphia Eagles' head coaching vacancy. However, Buddy Ryan, who had been the Bears' defensive coordinator, got the job instead.

Shula suffered a huge loss when his mother, Mary, passed away on April 1 at the age of eighty-three at the Greenlawn Nursing Home in her native Lake County after a long illness. She had been battling several ailments, including rheumatoid arthritis. In addition to her six children, she had twenty-two grandchildren and fourteen great-grandchildren.

The 1986 season would be a difficult one for Shula. Veteran guard Ed Newman, who suffered a knee injury in training camp the previous season, never recovered and retired in July. Even with the addition of draft picks John Offerdahl, T. J. Turner, James Pruitt, and defensive back Reyna Thompson, the team struggled. The season started with a loss, and ended with a loss. By the time they reached the halfway point of the season, they were 3–5. Shula was in a foul mood.

"Do not—repeat, do not—challenge Shula on a football matter unless you're on very firm ground," wrote Paul Zimmerman. "Dr. Z" (as Zimmerman became known) admittedly repeated his own mistakes. In 1986, after a press conference in Foxboro, Massachusetts, where the struggling Dolphins were scheduled to play the New England Patriots, Zimmerman was oblivious to Shula's sensitivity. Zimmerman walked with the coach outside the hotel. He described the conversation: "I said that I had the feeling he wasn't comfortable with the kind of team he was coaching, all that passing, not much running, that things were much better in the '70s, when he had those machines that would crank out 250 yards on the ground and throw the ball 15 times a game. I was too caught up in my own thought to notice the rage that was building. Finally it exploded."

"What would you do if you had a quarterback like Marino?" Shula snapped. "Have him hand the ball off 50 times a game? Geez, these experts."

By late September, the defense had suffered significant losses, including Mike Charles, John Offerdahl, and Hugh Green. The defense was a mess. And the Orange Bowl crowds were calling for defensive coordinator Studley's head. Catcalls of "Go back to San Francisco, Studley," "You need to fire McNeal, Studley," and "Studley's a wimp" grew louder and louder. In the stands, during a 31–16 drubbing by the 49ers, at Miami, a banner read simply, FIRE STUDLEY.

"I don't know what the problem is," said Lyle Blackwood, the strong safety. "Whether it's one man breaking down, or two men, or whatever, it's not good. I wouldn't want to be in Chuck's shoes, having to put up with the ridicule. The responsibility is not all his. Some of it is the coach, but a lot of it is the players."

"He's more disappointed than anybody else when it doesn't happen," said Shula, defending his coach. "He knows what he's doing. He says things that make sense."

Truth was, the defense was getting old, and the new players brought in to bolster it up had been hurt. Their draft picks hadn't worked out. The players they traded for either didn't pan out or were injured.

Hugh Green, whom they had acquired from the Tampa Bay Buccaneers the previous season for two first-round draft picks, suffered a fractured kneecap against the Jets in Week Three.

"I went out on a limb, making a big investment for a guy who could play with intensity and make big plays for us, and he did," he said. "Everybody thought it was a great deal. Now, we don't have Hugh Green or the draft choices we gave up."

And the breakdown of communication on the field between players, and sloppy play, were the result of a ragtag series of substitutions that also hurt the defense. On the offensive side of the ball, the front line had suffered losses, and the play of the backs had not been consistent.

By the middle of November, Shula's contract had not yet been renewed, and another round of rumors was now circulating around the NFL. The speculation this time was that Shula would leave at the end of the contract and go upstate to Tampa Bay and become the head coach of the Buccaneers.

"I have no comment on it," Shula said. "I'm not confirming or denying anything. A few years ago, when my contract was going to be up, everybody got carried away. That became the news, and football wasn't." Shula was then making approximately $700,000 a year. Hugh Culverhouse, the owner of the Buccaneers, dismissed it as "conjecture and speculation"; at the same time, he neither confirmed nor denied it. By end of the month, Robbie announced Shula had re-signed with the Dolphins.

"I'm happy to put all the rumors to rest," said Shula. "I could have waited to see what was out there if I had coached until the contract was up. But I made the decision that as long as I had the good relationship with Joe and he continued to support me in every way, I'm going to be loyal to him in every way."

The decline of the team was a popular story. Two years removed from a Super Bowl loss, and one year from an AFC Championship Game failure, the slide of the Dolphins was exhaustively documented.

"No one is more disappointed than Shula, who has watched his world crumble under a barrage of injuries, penalties, bad plays and bad luck. That said, life goes on: Shula isn't one to cry over spilled milk or fractured kneecaps," Michael Janofsky wrote.

"The real problem is that we haven't had the same people on the field we feel good about so the defense can get better," said Shula. "We're fighting now to be good enough just to get by."

"He hasn't been too bad with us, considering the rocky start and that some people didn't work out as expected," said Doug Betters. "I've seen other times where he's been worse. He realizes the players are just as upset, confused, and downhearted as the coaching staff. If he ran us down more, that would only break our spirits altogether. He pushes us harder when we win and get cocky and think all we have to do to win is show up."

"I've had to handle some things with kid gloves," Shula said. "You can't always scream and jump down somebody's throat. Some individuals need a pat on the back more than just screaming."

The final jab of fate in 1986 came in the final game of the season at the Orange Bowl, on Monday night, December 22. More important, it was the last game to be played by the Dolphins in that stadium, as they were moving the next year to the new, luxurious Joe Robbie Stadium.

"It's going to be a night of nostalgia," admitted Shula, the coach for 17 of the Dolphins' 21 seasons. "The Orange Bowl has been very good to us. I've enjoyed all the years being the head coach of the home team in the Orange Bowl. I'm sure that after the game, a lot of memories will come back about the great games here."

After the Dolphins lost to the Patriots, 34–27, to finish the season at 8–8, Shula left from the stadium to catch a flight to El Paso, Texas, where he would be spending Christmas that year. He was going to see his son Mike lead the Alabama Crimson Tide against the Washington Huskies in the Sun Bowl.

Mike Shula was a quarterback with the Crimson Tide from 1983 to 1986. He played in one game as a freshman and appeared in eight games as a backup in 1984. What he lacked in height, speed, and arm strength, he more than made up in character and understanding of the game. In 1983, the program went 8–4, and in 1984, the program had its first losing season since 1957, going 5–6 overall under coach Ray Perkins, which ended Alabama's streak of 25 straight bowl appearances.

The 1985 season opened on a Monday night, with Alabama facing the University of Georgia Bulldogs.

"On an oppressively hot and humid Labor Day night in Athens, Ga., her son Mike, a lefthanded quarterback at the University of Alabama, began his season with a game against Georgia," wrote Malcom Moran about Dorothy Shula, who had gone to see her son play. "Her husband was back home, preparing for his team's opening game, reduced to being simply a father in front of a television. There were more than 81,000 people surrounding the hedges at Sanford Stadium that night, and few of them were rooting for her team. In the first 59 minutes 10 seconds, her son had thrown for just 64 yards."

Toward the end of the game, Georgia blocked a punt and scored a touchdown, giving the Bulldogs a 16–13 lead with only 50 seconds left. Don Shula, watched from his home in Miami, watching on television, like everyone else. But he was not thinking like a coach.

"I was devastated," Don said. "All you could think of was how could they lose the game. I was more of a parent than a coach. You get involved with the emotions of being a father. Rather than thinking about strategy, you're thinking about your son out there, and what he's going through."

"I got so sick to my stomach, I had to find a bathroom," Dorothy recalled. "I wound up actually down by the hedge. I couldn't see a thing except the balls Mike was throwing as they went through the air."

The Tide had 71 yards to go to win the game. Shula moved the team down the field in five plays and connected on a 17-yard TD pass with 15 seconds to go to give Alabama its first win of the season. It was a huge rite of passage for him. "The only way I knew Mike's team won," Dorothy remembered, "was by the way the Bama fans went crazy."

"I hope he stayed up for the end of the game," Mike Shula told the press about his dad.

Dorothy and Don laughed. They stayed up way after the game was over. "She couldn't sleep, and I couldn't sleep," Shula said. "That was really a pro two-minute drill," Shula said proudly.

"I know it's going to be a good feeling calling home," Mike said.

Shula led the Crimson Tide to 4–0 start before a pair of two-point losess to Penn State and Tennessee. However, they rebounded, going 9–2–1 overall. Mike threw for 2,009 yards and 16 touchdowns. They ended the year with a win over USC in the Aloha Bowl, 24–3, where Mike threw a touchdown pass to help the cause.

At the beginning of the 1986 collegiate season, Gordon S. White Jr. wrote, "Mike Shula, the southpaw son of the Miami Dolphins' coach, Don Shula, is not as spectacular a passer as [Vinny] Testaverde, but he is a sure winner with a strong team. Coach Ray Perkins can now point the team toward the mythical national title for the first time since he replaced the late Paul (Bear) Bryant in 1983." Mike was being mentioned alongside Michigan's Jim Harbaugh, Penn State's Testaverde, and Jamelle Holieway of Oklahoma.

Alabama started the 1986 season with a 7–0 run, including a 21–7 road win over the Florida Gators.

"I think we played well together as a team," said Mike in classic coachspeak. He had completed 11 of 16 passes for 118 yards, with one touchdown pass and two interceptions. "Our running kept the defense off balance. I was looking to throw more, but in the second half we knew what we had to do."

"It was hairy enough there for a while," said Dorothy, who watched the game from the press box.

That night, Don would come home, and turn on the VCR. "It's the first thing he watches when he gets home," Dorothy said.

"I really didn't think I knew that many people in Gainesville," Shula said of his sort-of homecoming in his home state of Florida. "Then, when I got here, I realized I knew more than I thought."

"I don't know that Mike Shula made a bad decision playing quarterback for us at Alabama," said head coach Ray Perkins. "I can't remember a time when I thought he made a bad decision."

Now the father had come to watch the son. It was the first time he'd seen him play in person as a college player. The Crimson Tide had a 9–3 record as they faced the 8–2–1 Washington Huskies in the Sun Bowl in El Paso, Texas. Mike tossed a 32-yard touchdown pass to Greg Richardson in the third quarter and threw another 18-yard strike to Bobby Humphrey to give the Crimson Tide a 21–6 lead. The Tide defeated the Huskies, 28–6. Father Don was beaming.

It was announced by Senior Bowl officials on January 10, 1987, that since John Mackovic had been fired by the Chiefs, he would not coach the North team in the annual college all-star game as previously planned. It was agreed by all who participated that John Robinson of the Los Angeles Rams, instead of coaching the South, would instead coach the North, so that Don Shula could coach the South, and of course, his own son Mike. The 1987 North-South game then became a family affair. Shula's assistant head coach would be Dave, and the starting quarterback would be Mike.

"I played for both of them for one game. Dad's staff was coaching the Senior Bowl, and I was a senior coming out of Alabama and Dave was the offensive coordinator. He called all the plays in the game. And I was happy about that. And Dad gave me the starting nod for the game," laughed Mike during a television interview along with his father years later.

"And we won, too!" Don interjected. They both laughed. But it was a telling moment. Even in a game that was meaningless to his career, it was important to him that he won. The South won, 42–38. In the NFL draft that year, Mike was taken in the 12th round, by the Tampa Bay Buccaneers. He was the 313th player picked overall. He was on the team's roster for part of the season but did not appear in a game and took a coaching position with the team the following year.

The 1987 (8–7), 1988 (6–10), and 1989 (8–8) Dolphins seasons were marked by more mediocrity. It was the nadir of Shula's coaching career. He'd never really run into a swell of lackluster performances in his career. The 1988 season was only the second losing campaign in his entire career.

"The priorities for Miami this season included an improved defense, improved rushing attack, a better record against the AFC East, and a winning record," wrote Bob Keim of UPI in 1988. "But the Dolphins again finished with the league's 26th-ranked defense, had the worst rushing attack in the NFL, compiled an 0–8 mark against AFC East opponents, and finished with a 6–10 overall record that is the worst of Don Shula's career. Miami's dismal year was capped by a 40–24 loss at Pittsburgh Sunday in which the Steelers gained 305 yards rushing."

"It's just a disappointing end to a disappointing year," Shula said. "We went into the season with a lot of goals. We just weren't able to accomplish any of them. There doesn't seem to be a lot of difference between winning and losing in the league. We lost five games by 15 points. We need the players that can get us over that hurdle there. Someone that can pick you up, make you a winner in that kind of ball game. I don't know how you make major changes. I'm happy with the coaching staff. We have a nucleus of good football players. What we have to do is find more of them."

Miami had always relied on the draft. Shula believed in new blood and youth. But while the draft had supplied a few solid role players, they had not acquired any of Pro Bowl caliber the way they had in earlier years with Thomas, Beathard, or Young. The Dolphins weren't one player away, they were a dozen players away. They still had a terrific quarterback and receivers. But they lacked a pass rush, their offensive line was weak, they needed a decent fullback, their secondary was suspect, and they lacked a solid outside linebacker.

"In addition to the problems on the field, the Dolphins have been plagued this year with off-field troubles as well. Early in the season there were reports of friction between David Shula and Dan Marino following the departure of Don Strock. Later in the season, there was the suspension of receiver Mark Duper that led to reports that some players had been seen with convicted drug traffickers. Finally, Marino hinted before the Pittsburgh game that he might like to leave Miami after his current contract expires in three years," concluded Keim.

"We need to get some sort of balance on offense and be much more consistent on defense," said Shula.

Most worrisome were the allegations against Duper. In 1986, Shula and Robbie had been informed that Duper was hanging around with suspected cocaine drug lord Nelson Aguilar and other dealers. In December 1988, *Sports Illustrated* ran a story basically accusing Shula of doing nothing to stop it. Shula was incensed and went on record immediately. "I was very disturbed by the implication that I was aware of the alleged drug use or consorting with drug dealers and didn't do anything about it," said Shula. "As soon as I was aware of the photographs that were taken of two of our ballplayers with two convicted drug dealers, I immediately made the league security department aware of this and called the ballplayers in. I talked to them about having their pictures taken with these convicted drug dealers."

The fact was the Dolphins were aware of Duper's constant cocaine use, and the article detailed two deliveries of briefcases filled with cocaine to Duper's condo delivered by a driver in January 1986 in exchange for $18,000 in cash. Kim Knight, the estranged wife of one of Aguilar's former partners, admitted to snorting cocaine with the star athlete in a limousine in 1986. As late as 1988, John Rafael Gomez, a suspect in a $3 million drug case, had regularly attended Dolphins practices as a known friend of Duper's. The team and league officials were aware of Duper's use, but he received star treatment due to his performance on the field. However, Shula was incensed and termed the *Sports Illustrated* article "an insult to my integrity and to the discipline that I demand from myself and my players." Shula insisted that the team and the league were aware of Duper's associations, and that he himself had warned Duper in person.

The fact was Duper was not a dealer or pusher of any kind. He was a self-professed cocaine eating machine, whose addiction grew worse and worse. He loved partying with underworld figures, and the pretty fans who were constantly drawn to him. The drug would eventually rob him of all his hard-earned money and self-respect, in a downward spiral that would take him through the 1990s and early 2000s.

In simpler football terms, the league was catching up to the Dolphins. Shula's teams were running into the increasingly better-prepared, more talented clubs like the Patriots and the emerging Buffalo Bills.

"We were playing against Buffalo in the 1980s when they dominated us. On one play Dan [Marino] got up to the ball and got under the center. He looked over at Bruce Smith, who was killing him all day. Smith was over Delly [Jeff Dellenbach]," recalled Mark Duper. Duper said that Marino was so vexed, that while calling out the cadence, he then suddenly interrupted his own signals.

Duper said that Marino was so vexed, that while calling out the cadence, he then suddenly interrupted his own signals. "Delly, you gotta block him—you gotta block Bruce—nobody but him," yelled Marino.

"I died laughing, but I didn't want to be in Delly's shoes. But he did a good job against Smith on that play and the rest of the game. But there's no way anyone can stop him all the time; Blocking Bruce Smith all game, he's going to get loose sometime no matter who is blocking him."

Nineteen eighty-nine started off with some news that made Shula beam, even in the face of utter chaos. In February, his son Dave had been named assistant head coach of the Dallas Cowboys, and Dave Wannstedt had been named defensive coordinator under new coach Jimmy Johnson. Wannstedt had been the Dolphins' defensive coordinator for a month but resigned to join his mentor and friend in Dallas. Shula could not have been prouder of his son.

"David took a lot of heat," Shula said, for being made Miami's assistant head coach at such a young age. "But all he's ever done is help me and help us be a better team."

On November 19, the 6–4 Dolphins faced the rebuilding Cowboys, who were 1–10, at Texas Stadium. This was the first Shula-Shula matchup, Head Coach Don Shula of the Dolphins against son Dave, the offensive coordinator of the Cowboys. The elder Shula's team came away with a 17–14 victory.

"Dorothy Shula's handling of the family tradition has rarely involved the act of staying away. She did one weekend in the 1989 season, when the Dolphins were playing the Dallas Cowboys. Facing the prospect of watching her husband on one sideline and her oldest son, David, an assistant coach with the Cowboys, on the other—and having to choose whom to sit with and whom to root for—she decided to stay home," wrote Malcom Moran in the *New York Times*.

According to local Dallas sportswriters, Dave was a regular target for fan discontent on Dallas's three morning talk shows. "The poor guy got crucified. Every week it was Dave Shula this, and Dave Shula that," recalled Mickey Spagnola of the *Dallas Times-Herald*. "Players didn't come right out and say it, but they felt his offense was too complicated for a young team."

"We laid a foundation down there for a winning football franchise. That's what happened," said Dave calmly. "It was as close to being an expansion franchise as you can get. We got to within one game of the playoffs in 1990. That's what happened. Now all the other things, when you get right down to it, they're not important.

"When I went to Dallas, it was the first time I had authority over other coaches. At times, I think it was more difficult for them than it was for me. But it was not a problem by any stretch," said Dave. Eventually Dave's contract would be renewed by Johnson, and Dave appreciated the act of faith exhibited by the coach, but he was reassigned to the position of quarterbacks coach. Dave remembered it as being "hurtful." Don had a falling out with Johnson around this time, as Don was fiercely proud and protective of his son.

"I could have done without a 1–15 season the next year, but despite everything it was definitely a worthwhile experience. It's something every coach should go through. I did take a lot of criticism," Dave said. "We were 27th in offense in 1989 and 28th in 1990 and sure weren't bowling anyone over. When it happened [the demotion], one of the reporters asked me if I thought I'd been the scapegoat. I said, 'I guess I am.' It was the sound bite they all wanted to hear. I bit on the bite. But I wasn't coerced into it or anything like that. It was a knee-jerk reaction on my part, and I truly regretted it."

That spring and summer, with one eye toward retirement, Shula got into the restaurant business. "The last thing on my mind when I was coaching football was going into the restaurant business," said Shula. "I resisted for a long period of time and finally thought, 'Let's give it a try.'"

Shula had been courted by the Graham family for more than two years before Shula considered it seriously. The Grahams were a famous family. There was Phil Graham, who had been the publisher of the *Washington Post,* and there was former Florida governor and former US senator Bob Graham. Since the 1970s, when Shula and his family first moved to Florida, the Shulas and Grahams had been friends. The Shulas had moved to the exclusive neighborhood of the Loch Lomond section of Miami Lakes. The Grahams had owned a restaurant called Legends, and in 1989, they proposed keeping the restaurant, refurbishing it, giving it a complete makeover, and opening it as Shula's Steak House. The new exclusive restaurant would be a high-end steak house. Service would be of the highest quality, the wine and whiskey selection representing only the best.

"Shula, football, steak. It all went together," said Dave Shula years later. According to Dave, it was his mother, Dorothy, who helped seal the deal. "Eventually, you're going to hang up your whistle," she said, urging him to consider the Grahams' offer. "The Grahams also pitched that the steak house would be themed after the accomplishments of the '72 Dolphins team that went undefeated," Dave says. "That legacy would be carried on throughout the restaurant. He finally agreed to do that in 1989."

"I just didn't have a feeling that I had any aptitude for the restaurant business, other than eating a lot of food," said Don.

"Probably the biggest hitch, the part that slowed you down, is you realized that you can only lose your reputation once," Dave said to his father in a joint interview. "He wasn't going to be running it and had put a lot of faith in the Grahams and their ability to be able to run this facility in a way that would represent his name and the reputation that went along with it in a positive way."

William A. "Bill" Graham, Bob's half-brother, and David Younts opened the first Shula's Steak House location with Coach Shula. The Graham family owned a high-grade Angus farm, Buckhead Beef, located just outside of Albany, Georgia. The family has owned it since the 1930s. With Graham and Yount's expertise, Shula agreed to serve only their Premium Black Angus Beef in their first restaurant, from steaks to burgers.

They also came up with a new cut of beef, which they called The Shula Cut®. Rather than referring to butchery, the cut refers to the quality of meat served at the restaurant. The beef had to exhibit eight specifications including medium-to-fine marbling, abundant marbling, "A" maturity, superior muscling, no dark cutters, leaness, no ruptured capillaries, and no Brahmin-influenced cattle. Each steak was aged no less than twenty-eight days and was cut two inches thick.

Because Graham and Yount insisted on high-quality beef less than 1 percent of all beef sold in America qualifies for The Shula Cut®. With Shula's name blazing atop the doorway, sales increased fourfold in the first year. Shula beamed with pride.

The restaurant would not only go on to become a success, but it would spawn a chain of resaurants, including five other Shula "themed" restaurants. All included, the list of restaurants was Shula's American Steak House, Shula's Grill 347 (six locations), Shula's two Steak & Sports (Cleveland and Miami Lakes), 347 Steak Bar by Shula's, Shula's Bar and Grill (three locations), and Shula Burger (with six locations), all coming under the parent licensing company of Don Shula Family Restaurants.

The licensing did not stop there. Shula was an avid golfer. He played regularly at the Graham's local Bill Watts-designed golf course and hotel. Shula often had the Dolphin team stay at the hotel on the eve of home games. Shula licensed his name to that, too. The Graham property brandished the name of Shula's Hotel & Golf Club.

The 1989 season was when Don Shula began to right the Dolphins' ship, but not without a lot of self-doubt and second guesses. Marino had a down year for him, with 24 touchdown passes but 22 interceptions, while Mark Clayton enjoyed a 1,000-yard season, but Duper was way down in production. The offense sank to 15th in the NFL. And the defense was worse, despite the brilliant play of John Offerdahl.

The Dolphins went 1–3 in the first four games. By midseason, the team was 4–4 and looking decidedly better, reaching a record of 7–4 after beating Dallas in the father-son matchup and in the hunt for a playoff spot. However, they then ended the season losing four out of their last five, finishing 8–8. They were out of the playoffs for the fourth straight year, unheard of in Shula's reign. However, there were signs that the team was improving. They'd beaten several playoff teams and played well against others. On the other hand, they gave up 69 points in their last two games, which pained Shula.

If Shula could point to a game in the 1989 season that was a signpost for him, it was a 31–17 thrashing by the Bills in Rich Stadium. "We were 4–3, and I felt we were on the way to turning things around on the defense. Going up there and getting hammered like that with them just running over us and holding onto the ball for something like 43 minutes and then us winding up losing four of our last five games as everything fell apart—that was it. I knew we had to become more physical."

An 8–8 record. Four years without a playoff game. The nadir had arrived. The team needed a revamp, and Shula knew it. On December 26, Shula held his end-of-year press conference, just after their Christmas Eve loss to the Chiefs.

"Back then, missing the playoffs was a sin for Shula's team, so there was obvious concern that Miami needed to do something dynamic to change direction. Shula wanted back in the playoffs, and the idea of trading Dan Marino was starting to gain traction among fans," wrote Armando Salguero in the *Miami Herald*.

At the press conference, a reporter asked Shula if he had ever considered trading away Marino. "I don't . . . my actions aren't governed by . . .," Shula, surprised, mumbled. Then recovering, he said with authority, "Furtherest thing from my mind."

But Hank Goldberg, then of WQAM, was a friend of Shula and Raiders owner Al Davis. He later confirmed the story. In the offseason, Shula was filled with doubt. He and Davis discussed the possibilities of trading Marino to the West Coast.

Finally, after many discussions, Davis and Shula agreed in principle to a trade. But Shula got cold feet and raised the price. Davis said yes. Then Shula asked for more, and Davis had enough, balking at the lopsided deal Shula now insisted on.

These kinds of conversations take place all the time in professional sports, but trading away Marino was like trading away a son. He had a bond with Marino that was on the same level as Csonka and Griese. Maybe it was sentiment. Maybe not. But it was a sign that the coach was grasping at almost anything.

On January 7, 1990, Joe Robbie died at seventy-three. In his legacy, he left three things: the Miami Dolphins franchise, one of the most successful in the country; Joe Robbie Stadium, one of the most highly prized stadiums in North America; and a family feud to make the Hatfields and McCoys look like a daytime television game show. His death began a family feud that would spill out into the national newspapers and take its toll on the organization and the city.

"When the Robbie family in Miami celebrates Thanksgiving next week, it won't be a Norman Rockwell setting. Instead of carving up the turkey, they could be carving up each other," wrote Vito Stellino in the *Baltimore Sun* in November of 1991. "A bitter family feud among the nine children of Joe and Elizabeth Robbie has threatened the family's control of the Miami Dolphins and could lead to the club's being sold. It started when Joe Robbie died Jan. 7, 1990. His will left control of the team to three trustees—his sons, Tim and Dan, and daughter, Janet."

Shortly after Joe's death, Tim, Dan and Janet sold Blockbuster Video chairman H. Wayne Huizenga Jr. 15 percent of the team and 50 percent of the stadium. They also fired their brother Mike from the front office. After these actions, Elizabeth Robbie, Joe Robbie's widow and mother of these children, and six others, insisted on obtaining her "widow's share" of 30 percent of the existing estate. She filed papers insisting on it in Probate Court in September 1991. The estate was valued at $73 million. Her three children responded in court that her payment would cause the trust immensely expensive legal fees and taxes, amounting to approximately $25 million. She was unrelenting. In fact, the final taxes would be a sum of more than $73 million.

"Mrs. Robbie has been in ill health ever since this dispute started, but her death came suddenly," her attorney, Dan Paul, told the Associated Press. "Since the dispute with her children, Mrs. Robbie's health has deteriorated over the last couple of months." Elizabeth Robbie died on November 5, 1991. But her will left her 30 percent to other members of the family, other than the three children running the trust.

Joe Robbie Stadium was paid for by Joe Robbie himself, who built it at a cost of $115 million. "When Mr. Robbie first announced plans to build the stadium in 1984, he was greeted with skepticism. But he put up all his possessions—including the Dolphins' franchise—as collateral to assure completion of construction," reported the *New York Times*.

"This is just my perverse nature," Robbie said at the time. "I'll have everything paid for by 2016." Using the new stadium as lure, Robbie had brought spring training baseball and international soccer to Miami. Robbie was also the owner of the American Soccer League's Fort Lauderdale Strikers. This drama would continue to fester until 1994.

Amid the chaos, in an effort to show continuity, on January 18, 1990, team President Tim Robbie announced that the Dolphins had extended Shula's contract yet again. He agreed to a three-year contract worth $1.2 million a year. The deal was announced while Shula was in Mobile scouting the North-South game. "Coach Shula wants to come back. We want him back," said Tim Robbie.

But there was wariness. The Robbies needed to show consistency in their organization. They also needed to sell out their new stadium. The recent dreadful seasons had softened ticket sales. "Too often in the last four football seasons, the ear-splitting devotion of South Florida for its Miami Dolphins has seemed to vanish into the suburban sprawl, forfeited when the team headed north from the Orange Bowl in search of the comfortable seat and the convenient parking spot," wrote Malcom Moran.

That February, Dolphins ownership wanted Shula to unload some of his responsibilities. Shula had seen old friend Monte Clark while vacationing in South Florida. Shula added Clark to the staff as the pro personnel director.

"It was all I heard when I got here, that we have to have more muscle in our linemen and linebackers," Clark said. "We had to have some strength and power and size to match up with people. The players have risen to the occasion. Take [linebacker David] Griggs. The coaches didn't even know this guy in training camp. Now, Griggs is about 6–3 and up to about 250 and hitting and playing."

"It was very frustrating," Shula recalled. "But we realized the areas that had to be improved. We needed a better running game for more balance, to give Marino more weapons. We needed a better run defense so that other teams couldn't control the ball on us."

The NFL had implemented what was known as "Plan B" free agency in 1989. Under the plan, teams could retain limited rights to 37 players on their roster. A protected player could not sign with a new team without giving his old team the chance to sign him. The remainder of the players were free to sign with any team. This method of free agency lasted until 1992, when it was found that it violated antitrust laws.

When the Plan B free agent signing period began, the Dolphins were ready. Miami signed Tony Paige, a powerful blocker and runner, unprotected by Detroit. They moved David Griggs from practice squad onto the defense. Shawn Lee was acquired from Tampa Bay in a trade for a conditional draft pick. Outside linebacker Cliff Odom was another Plan B signing. And J. B. Brown, a 12th-round pick a year earlier, became a starter at cornerback. Offensive tackle Richmond Webb, their first-round pick in 1990 from Texas A&M, became a perennial Pro Bowl player beginning with his rookie season.

No one knew quite what to expect from the 1990 Dolphins. Least of all *Sports Illustrated*, whose Paul Zimmerman wrote, "O.K., here it is, and you've heard it before. Over the past five years, ever since the MIAMI DOLPHINS last appeared in the Super Bowl, no team has given up more yards. Cumulatively, Miami has had the worst defense in the league. Yet the Dolphins have had only one losing record in that stretch. That speaks highly of Dan Marino and Miami's big-pass offense."

As Dr. Z pointed out, Miami had drafted 33 defensive players of whom only four made significant contributions, including John Offerdahl, safety Jarvis Williams, end Jeff Cross, and safety Louis Oliver. Miami was taking in older free agents, such as Mike Reichenbach and Cliff Odom, to pair with also slighty older yet effective linebackers they had acquired the previous year, E .J. Junior and Barry Krauss. Zimmerman also mentioned acquiring better running backs, and better lineman.

"Run the ball, block better for Marino, hide your defense. That should keep Miami right around .500," said Zimmerman in his preseason preview.

The Dolphins started off the season by winning two of their first three games, and nobody noticed. But by Week 10 in the NFL, along with a bye, the Dolphins were 8–1, a run that included a 30–7 shellacking of the Buffalo Bills.

"We're a phoenix. Best defense in the league. Boom! . . . Risen from the dead. Everybody in the league's wondering, What's happening down there in Miami? What's McKyer hollering about now?" boasted cornerback Tim McKyer, a former San Francisco 49er. The Miami defense had ranked 26th, 26th, and 24th the past three seasons. Now it was the top-rated defense in the NFL.

"I don't like all this attention we're getting," said Tom Olivadotti, the Dolphins' defensive coordinator. "It's no good for the players."

The Dolphins weren't just wining with defense. They were running the ball more often, and having Marino throw shorter passes, and holding onto the ball longer than other teams. The run-pass mix was now almost 50/50. Still, Shula was a stickler for preparation, even with a seasoned quarterback like Marino.

"We'll start off the week by outlining the 25 most important plays in the game plan with a yellow highlighter," Marino said in 1993. "We'll meet and meet and meet, and he'll go over and over the game plan, and by the end of the week, I've marked up about 150 plays in our playbook. Everything is yellow. He never stops expecting the best of people. We'll be ahead in games by three touchdowns, with only two minutes left, and he'll still be going 150 miles an hour. You want to say, It's O.K., Coach, we won the game. Relax a little."

"He's not having to carry the load by himself by trying to throw the ball upfield," said Jets linebacker Kyle Clifton about Marino. "It makes him tougher, because he can pick and choose and put them in the best situation to win."

"It just goes to show how quickly teams sometimes can turn around in this league. Marino's status has been reduced almost to that of a role player. The Dolphins who participated in an informal poll by the *Miami Herald* voted fullback Tony Paige, a Plan B pickup last winter, as the team's midseason MVP," wrote Zimmerman. "Miami has given up 13 fewer points and 140 fewer yards than the New York Giants—who have the second-ranked defense in the NFL—and hasn't allowed an opposing offense to score a touchdown since Oct. 18. The Los Angeles Raiders, who have the third-rated defense in the league, have yielded 343 more yards than the Dolphins and 41 more points.

"One more thing: All of these castoffs," continued Zimmerman, "know what it's like to have nothing, so now they want everything. Don't underestimate that attitude, or the motivational skills of coach Don Shula, in this turnaround."

But it was also some of the players they had brought in. Some brought an attitude the Dolphins had long been lacking. "I just didn't see the things I was used to seeing with a world championship team," continued McKyer. "I saw disarray. So I told them, 'If you're satisfied with just being in the NFL and not being a world champion, then you're just another player, no matter how good you are.'" Not everyone was happy with McKyer's admonishment. "I think at times here they had an every-man-for-himself attitude. It became a 'we' attitude."

"I think we were lacking in confidence, and Tim gave the whole team some of that, on both sides of the ball," said Louis Oliver. "It began building each practice, each game. We already had some quiet leaders, but Tim was a new breeze around here."

"When we broke down their film for the last three games," said New York Jets coach Bruce Coslet, "there wasn't one snap against their goal-line defense. And those teams had been in the red zone [inside the Miami 20-yard line] on six plays. Six plays in three games. That's unbelievable. They're not doing a damn thing different than they were last year. They're just doing it better, with better players."

The accolades began rolling in. After several years of languishing, the Dolphins were back. And everyone saw it. The *New York Times* ran a headline, "Don Shula: Still the Best Coach."

New York Times columnist Dave Anderson wrote that great competitors eventually only compete against themselves. Their current successes are only ever measured against their past accomplishments. Anderson wrote, "It's this way with Don Shula now. As his 7–1 Miami Dolphins share first place in the American Conference East with the Buffalo Bills, he is trying to do what he has done more than any other coach: lift his team to the Super Bowl game.... Unlike those coaches who resent change, Shula has adjusted to different players and a different game."

"I never felt I knew it all. I always felt there's something new to learn, something new to do," said the 60-year-old Shula. "Coaching football is still the same. You try to get the most out of the talent. Make 'em work and let 'em play."

"That's what makes Don the best coach," former 49er coach Bill Walsh told the *Times*. "His ability to win with different teams in different eras. He's done it with passers like Unitas and Marino. He's done it with runners like Csonka, Jim Kiick, and Mercury Morris. He's even done it with a rollout quarterback like Woodley who really wasn't much of a passer. Don Shula is the best."

"They lumped the three of us, Tom [Landry], Chuck [Noll], and myself," Shula said. "Tom doesn't have to apologize for his record. Chuck has shown he's still a great coach. I'm not going to worry about the critics until some of my peers start saying I'm a softie."

"He'll be 61 on Jan. 4, the day before the Super Bowl playoffs begin. Over his 27 seasons, several other coaches have burned out, some ascending to the front office or the television booth. He has remained on the sideline where he belongs," continued Anderson.

"To keep this team winning," Shula said, "is my responsibility."

"Miami was on its way to a 12–4 season, Shula fielded a question during a media session and then looked at the reporter," recalled Paul Zimmerman.

"Eleven times you've picked us to lose. Do you really think we're that bad?" said a clearly perturbed Shula.

"The guy tried to explain that he was doing a handicapping column and that he'd been picking the Dolphins to fail to cover the spread," remembered Zimmerman.

"Eleven times," Shula said, shaking his head. "Eleven."

The team stumbled some from there and was in a battle for the AFC East right up to the end, including a heartbreaking loss in Buffalo in late December that essentially decided the division. The halftime score was 7–0 in favor of the Bills, but the game had been a struggle for both teams. On the opening kickoff of the second half, the usually reliable Dolphins return man Marc Logan fumbled the ball, and it skipped forward into a crowd of Bills. Carlton Bailey recovered for Buffalo at the Miami 32. Buffalo scored on a Jim Kelly-to-Andre Reed 11-yard touchdown pass. That play broke the Dolphins' backs. The Bills never looked back. After the game, more than 70,000 fans stormed the field and tore down the goalposts. The Bills went 13–3 and won the division under Marv Levy, and the Dolphins finished 12–4 and were a wild-card team.

The other story that began to emerge that season concerned Dorothy's plight. Her fight against cancer was becoming more difficult, and Shula had to admit it publicly. Dorothy had been battling lung and breast cancer for almost six years.

"In the spring of 1989, Miami Dolphins Coach Don Shula and his wife, Dorothy, made a 6,000-mile pilgrimage to Medjugorje, in Croatia, hoping to find a cure for the cancer that was ravaging Dorothy's body. Medjugorje, a primitive village located 100 miles northwest of Dubrovnik, is a symbol of hope to Christians. The Virgin Mary is said to make daily appearances there, and many sick persons are reported to have been healed during visits to the village," wrote Jill Lieber. "For four days the Shulas, who had joined 10 fellow parishioners from Our Lady of the Lakes Catholic Church in Miami Lakes, attended hours of religious services in Medjugorje. Every morning, as they walked through a meadow en route to church, Don would look up at the sky for signs of the Virgin."

"I was always hoping for something positive to happen," Shula said. "I loved Dorothy. I wanted to do everything in my power to save her life. I would have gone anywhere for her."

While in Medjugorje, Don helped the immensely weakened Dorothy trek two hours up a narrow, rocky path to the well-known crucifix at the top of a mountain. As a bonfire reached into the sky, Don searched the billowing smoke and flame for images of the Virgin Mary. Don bowed underneath it all, leaning heavily on his faith, hoping for a miracle.

"Mom was so full of happiness and excitement when she got home," said Annie Shula, then 29, Don and Dorothy's youngest daughter. "It was a religious rebirth. She brought back crosses, plastic bottles filled with holy water, and videotapes of people being interviewed in Medjugorje, which she watched over and over. The trip gave her the strength to go on. It changed her. It changed both of them. It gave them hope and a sense of ease."

From the time of their trip to Medjugorje on, Don and Dorothy's relationship intensified. They had become closer than ever, and for the last two years of her life, Don was more in love with her than ever.

"He held her when she trembled. He awakened early in the morning and lay beside her in bed and told her there was nothing to be afraid of. In the evening he watched *Wheel of Fortune* and *Jeopardy!* with her. They competed to see who could come up with answers the quickest," wrote Lieber.

"She'd wink at me, showing that she knew the answer," recalls Lucy Howard, the Shulas' longtime housekeeper. "Usually she let him win. He didn't like losing at anything."

Now it was getting worse. Don was missing practices. Meetings. People were beginning to notice. People, friends knew. Some people say it softened him. Others didn't see it. But it was clearly a struggle for the coach and his family. He had missed three days of training camp in 1989 to attend to his wife's surgery. "It pinpoints the parts of your life that are most important," Shula said.

"When I left the house to go to work each day, I was just as afraid as Dorothy," said Shula. "It was hard. I was so distracted. Football seemed unimportant. Death is something you read about happening over there, but now it's right here, on your doorstep.

"In all that time, I can't remember missing a practice because of illness. The only times I've missed were since Dorothy's been ill," said a despondent Shula. "It's put everything into perspective; I know that," he admitted. "But as for translating into my coaching, I don't know that it's done that." It would continue to be a day-to-day issue for the coach and his family.

"It was a tough, tough year. You could just see how she was slipping," Shula said. "We had gone through six years of battling."

After the 1990 playoffs, Dorothy began to close her eyes to anything to do with the future, a futre she was not going to be a part of. At one point, Dorothy even stopped seeing her grandchildren.

"Even some days when I didn't want to go to work," Shula said sadly. "I was afraid all the time. I cried lots of nights."

"Her cancer was a continual hurt, and it wore me out," said Shula later.

The Dolphins hosted the resurgent Kansas City Chiefs at Joe Robbie Stadium on January 5, 1991, in the wild-card round. The first half had been a 3–3 struggle until Steve DeBerg threw a 26-yard touchdown pass to Stephone Paige to give Kansas City a 10–3 lead at halftime. It gave the visiting Chiefs a lift at the end of the half that carried over into the third quarter. The Chiefs added two Nick Lowery field goals to extend the visitors' lead to 16–3.

It was then that the Dolphins finally started to put things together. Marino threw a pair of touchdowns, the last one a 12-yard pass to Mark Clayton, just behind a diving Albert Lewis with 3:28 remaining in the game, and Miami had escaped with a 17–16 win and another playoff date.

"I told him I was going to throw it to him if they were off, and if they weren't I was going to change the play," said Marino about the play.

"I knew they didn't have a great deal of room to work with," Lewis said. "If they ran an out, I could make a big play and put the game out of reach. I never considered what would happen if I missed it."

"On those kind of plays, when you're throwing against a guy like him," Marino said of Lewis, "you've got to make sure you throw it outside, that if you don't complete it, it's an incomplete pass and no one can get it. That's what I tried to do, just throw it low and away. It was first down, and I figured if I hit it, fine. If I don't, we've got two more downs."

"Unfortunately," Lewis said, "the ball tailed off on me. It went a lot lower than I anticipated. I was close enough to touch it. I just missed it."

No one was happier than Shula, who beamed with pride after having been out of the playoffs for so long. "Is everybody going to Buffalo?" Shula asked the press corps. "We're going there or someplace, but we're going to play again. What a great feeling."

"There are other things in this stadium that are going on that are critical," said a befuddled Marty Schottenheimer after the Kansas City game. "It's a personal thing," he said, almost apologetically. "I really can't." Reporters realized later, after the excitement of the game, that the Chiefs head coach had been referring to

Dorothy Shula. Shula later admitted that the Kansas City victory was one of the most emotional moments of his life. A celebration of victory, but a massive hurt for one who was not there to share it with him.

"Much of that concern is a result of the fact that such a vital part of football's first family—the wife of pro football's top-winning active coach, the mother of two assistant coaches among their five children, and the grandmother of five other children, whose birthdays are each celebrated by a mounted football in Don Shula's office—is conspicuous by her absence," wrote Malcolm Moran.

"That's what made yesterday so special," Shula said the day after the Chiefs game. "An emotionally packed game. We've had maybe four or five games at the new stadium when the fans seemed to be involved emotionally, but never anything like yesterday. The combination of the fans' support, the players being totally immersed in what they were doing, the excitement of the ballgame, that brought back a lot of great memories."

As Shula was preparing for his trip north to face the Buffalo Bills, he was asked about Dorothy's health. "She's trying to do the best that she can," he said, "and we're trying to do the best that we can."

The divisional playoff game between the Bills and the Dolphins took place at Rich Stadium on January 12.The Bills were an amazing team, filled with stars and personalities, including quarterback Jim Kelly, running back Thurman Thomas, receiver Andre Rison, and a hard-hitting defense led by All -Pro defensive end Bruce Smith. The Bills jumped out to a 13–3 lead in the first quarter. Early in the second quarter, Thomas's 5-yard touchdown run extended their lead to 17 points. Things looked bleak for Miami. Marino threw one touchdown, and ran in another himself, as the Dolphins battled back, making the halftime score 27–17, Bills. The teams traded field goals early in the third quarter before Marino drew the Dolphins closer with a 2-yard trick pass play to eligible offensive tackle Roy Foster, making it 30–27 by the beginning of the fourth quarter. It looked like this game would go down to the last minute. However, that was as close as it got.

"We tried to put pressure on Kelly. We blitzed him, he killed us blitzing. When we stayed back off, he had all day to throw the football," Shula said.

The Bills put up two touchdowns and closed out the game, winning it, 44–34. Marino had thrown three touchdowns but also two costly interceptions. But in fairness, the running game had stalled, and he had been playing from behind all game. The Bills simply had too many weapons. It was a disappointing ending for Shula and his revamped team. After the game, this time, the 77,087 fans were more restrained, and no goal posts were torn down. They were enthusiastic but kept at bay by a cavalry of mounted police officers, a phalanx of officers on foot, and three kinds of attack dogs.

"It's tough to feel good after a heartbreak, but there are a lot of things that happened," said Shula. "I just hate to see it end here in Buffalo."

In truth, this was a tough season for Shula. A season of immense mood swings. He was happily spurred on by his team's success, like a gift from heaven, but at the same he was despondent, struggling with his wife's life-and-death struggle as it was progressing toward its ultimate end. It was an emotional season for all the Shulas.

On February 12, Shula appeared at a dinner in his honor, at "Don Shula Night" at the LaMalfa Party Center in Mentor, Ohio. The reception and dinner were sponsored by a local radio station, and all proceeds would be donated to the Don Shula Foundation to fight breast cancer. Dorothy had established the foundation to help fund research to fight breast cancer. This was a cause near and dear to her heart in her last years, and she spoke emotionally about it. The foundation would go on for more than two decades. Shula himself would speak on the subject as an avid and passionate voice for this cause. Carl Taseff was among the invited guests.

Dorothy Shula died at her home in Miami Lakes on February 25, 1991, at the age of fifty-seven after an eight-year battle with breast cancer. She once summed up her outlook on life as "love, listening, counseling."

"She went peacefully, thank God," Shula said. "It was about as peaceful as it could be. She went into a coma and just drifted away. Thank God everybody was here, all the five children. That's what she wanted."

"I just thank God now that she's at peace and doesn't have to suffer anymore. And I know that's how she would want us to feel," said Mike afterward.

"Any time you anticipate death, when the final moment comes, it's always a very sad moment," said Shula's longtime assistant coach and friend John Sandusky. "She fought it for a long time. They were a rough couple of years, but she held up well. She was tough."

"Dorothy was good for Shula. His wife got him to think about things other than the Dolphins and who they were playing that week. She caught him up on the kids' school plays and Little League games, sat with him when he ate his late dinners, played gin rummy with him, teased him," wrote Scott Fowler in the *Washington Post.*

"You know, we had five kids in our first six years of married life, changed jobs four times. . . . We never thought anything about having kids or picking up and moving. It just went like that," Shula said snapping his fingers. "I couldn't have accomplished or stayed in the coaching profession as long as I have if I didn't have the strength that Dorothy gave me.

"When I got home, no matter how bad it was, there would be somebody there to help me through it. We never got into technical stuff, but I used to kid her about being my Sunday-night quarterback. I'd say, 'I don't have to wait until Monday morning. I've got you Sunday night,'" Shula recalled. "No matter how bad the football was going—and there were some bad days—you could always count on Dorothy being there when you got home. She would be there to pick you up and get you through it, give you the confidence for tomorrow and next week," he said.

Dorothy Shula was a ubiquitous presence as Dolphins games. She rarely missed them. But in the last six years she lacked the strength and stamina to attend as many as she once had. In her last year, she didn't come at all. "I just tried to support her as best as I could," said a depressed Shula.

"Sometimes she'd get down." Dorothy was always known for her chatty and optimistic viewpoints. As her battle stretched over the years, the disease sapped her usually chipper attitude. "It's such a brutal disease. Occasionally a doctor would give us some reason for optimism, and then a test would come back, and that optimism would be squashed. That was the worst."

"We haven't had to fight the battle she has had to fight," Dave recalled telling a respectful crowd in 1987 at the Broward Booster Club's tribute to his mother. He turned to her, trying not to cry, with tears in his eyes, saying, "When I feel down and sorry for myself, I think of your fight with cancer. I don't think I could have matched it."

Shula recalled Dorothy attended a $100-a-plate dinner benefiting the American Cancer Society in August 1989. It was one of her last public appearances. She spoke passionately about the need for cancer research. "Talk about courage," an emotional Shula said later. "This is what it's all about."

"I couldn't be there as much as I wanted, but Dorothy was always great with that," the unusally emotional Shula said. "That's the big concept I can't understand. I feel so sorry for her being cheated out of the grandmother role."

"There was relief at the end, but a deep, deep emptiness," said Shula.

"Of course you always ask the 'Why?' question. 'Why?' But what she looked forward to more than anything was the grandkids, enjoying being a grandmother. She was like the mother hen. She was so great with our kids. And then the grandkids were going to be what she would really enjoy. She didn't really have the opportunity to do that. That's what I think I regret more than anything else," Shula added.

"What I learned from Dorothy more than anything is always take the necessary time. Don't ever be in too big a hurry. To do the right thing, no matter the inconvenience or whatever. She always had time for people, to say or do things to help make their lives more pleasant, to feel better about themselves. At this stage in my life, that's something I want to do. I don't need to rush anymore."

Shula was wounded as he dragged himself into the 1991 season. The one good thing about work was that he avoided thinking about his wife. "This is actually going to be my first year in coaching that Dorothy hasn't been around," he said.

Shula sought counsel from Father Edmond Whyte, the pastor at Our Lady of the Lakes, Shula's church. "Dorothy was such a good wife and mother," Father Whyte told Shula. "She helped you through difficult times, and now she's gone. You have to learn to live without her. You have to go on."

"I've tried to keep extra busy. I've been conscious of that, of keeping busy," he said. He golfed—a lot. He vacationed with the Shula clan in North Carolina. And he still went to mass every morning. "I enjoy starting the day that way."

"And the kids have been great. Like Michael made the decision to—he could have gone with the [Cleveland] Browns. They offered him a job. He thought about it, but he also had a chance to stay here with me. And he just felt at this stage in his life that it was better for him to stay at home," said Shula. "I have Michael to spend time with and talk to. Otherwise, I'd walk in here and there'd be nobody. At least now, after a game and during the week when we've got time, we can discuss things and communicate. He knows what I'm going through."

Mike, then twenty-six, was the youngest of the five Shula children. By then, he was a Dolphins assistant coach like his brother before. He moved into the house with his father that February. He was the only other person living in the house. Mike had been the receivers coach for the Tampa Bay Buccaneers for two years, from 1988 to 1990. He would be a coaches' assistant for 1991 and 1992. Meanwhile, Dave would move from Dallas to Cincinnati to be the receivers coach for the Bengals.

"People ask me, 'How's he been?' I say, 'He's been fine,'" Mike said. "He's never been one to show his emotions a whole lot anyway, except to referees on the football field. But on our vacation, we talked a lot about our mom, certain little things. They're mostly all good things."

Mike made the effort of attending mass with his father every morning for a while. They would have dinner together and relax in the den of Shula's house. "He'd always be the one to bring her up," said Mike. "He wanted us to talk about how we were feeling."

In July, Mike went away with friends for the weekend to the Keys. Lucy Howard, the Shulas' trusted housekeeper of twenty-three years, was in and out. She, too, had been devastated by the loss.

"I think yesterday was probably one of the few days I've had with nobody around . . . I didn't make any plans to play golf or anything. I just sat around. I took a walk in the morning and sat around watching tennis. Didn't do anything at all. That was a lonely day."

Shula admitted that he eventually found himself sitting at Dorothy's desk, in her office. That's where she dealt with Shula family correspondence, fan mail, and paying bills. She also organized her volunteer work there. The room was as she had left it, complete with a Dolphins helmet lamp and black-and-white wedding photos on the wall. He pined for her.

"He was difficult to reach," said longtime friend Rep. Bill Stanton.

"It was terrible grief, beyond words. He was lost without my mother," said daughter Donna Shula Jannach. "He's really made an effort to take over a lot of the things my mother used to do. My mother was like all things to all people, especially to her children. My dad has made more of an effort to reach out to each of the children. Things that we never used to talk to him about, we talk to him about now. I see him as more vulnerable. I used to see him as this almighty person. I don't think he used to like to let anyone see that he was vulnerable or hurt or scared," she said. "He comes to me a lot of times with things to talk about. It feels good."

"I've always been a more private than open sort of a person. It's not natural for me," Shula said. "It was natural for Dorothy. She just could talk with anybody about anything and make them feel good. I don't have that gift. I have to work at it more."

"Coach Shula's changed in very subtle ways," said Bob Kuechenberg, one of Shula's favorite players, years later. "Maybe the death of his wife, Dorothy, a couple of years ago had something to do with it, the slow and tragic way it happened. I saw him at a dinner after that. He hugged me. He said, 'I love you, Bob.' When he walked away, I said to my wife, 'Did you just hear what I think I heard?' It's something he never would have said in the old days. The Lombardi in him wouldn't have let him. Now he can say something like that. He isn't afraid to show that kind of emotion."

"Everybody sees him on the sideline with that stern jaw sticking out. Everybody thinks he's so much in control, and he is. But we all have to go home in the evening," said Bob Griese, still a close friend of Shula's. "Dorothy was a big support for him."

"It has long been suspected that the day would come when a coach would not require his players to be tucked in every night at training camp, but no one knew who the pioneer would be. Guess what? It was Miami Dolphins coach Don Shula, the darling of the establishment. That's right, his lads spent every night of the preseason at home with the wife and kiddies. What does this tell you?" wrote Paul Zimmerman in the 1991 *Sports Illustrated* NFL preview issue. Zimmerman felt the Dolphins were "a solid playoff team, but the first part of the schedule will be troublesome, with five of the first seven games on the road."

The high point of the season came early when Shula got his 300th win in the fourth game of the season against the Green Bay Packers at Joe Robbie Stadium on September 22. The Dolphins missed the first opportunity for the milestone a week earlier, losing at Detroit, 17–13, dropping their record to 1–2. The Packers, coached by Lindy Infante, had a charismatic quarterback in Don Majkowski. Pete Stoyanovich booted a pair of field goals in the first quarter, and Green Bay matched them in the second quarter. The Dolphins offense struggled mightily, and the unhappy fans let the team and the coach know their displeasure, booing the Miami offense lustily throughout the game. Then Majkowksi threw a 14-yard touchdown pass to Ed West, and the Packers held on to their 13–6 lead into the fourth quarter.

Miami tied the game when nose tackle Chuck Klingbeil recovered a fumble by Majkowski in the end zone. "I sort of spun to the inside," Klingbeil said. "I saw him pump the ball, and it slipped right out and there it was, just about on my lap, and I jumped on it. You don't get too many chances like that as a defensive lineman, especially that easy."

"My hands were really just perspiring. They were very wet, and the ball just slipped out of my hands. I wish I didn't do it, but I can't take that back now," Majkowski said.

Pete Stoyanovich notched a 31-yard field goal to with 8:25 left on the clock, and Miami preserved the lead for a 16–13 win. Shula's record at the time was 300–139–6. Coincidentally, it was exactly twenty-eight years to the day that Shula had gained his first NFL victory as a coach, when his Baltimore Colts beat the San Francisco 49ers, 20–14.

"Everybody was sort of tense this week," said Klingbeil. "But we had to have this one. It was necessary. He wanted to put it behind him so he could concentrate on other things." At the conclusion of the game, Shula got a Gatorade bath.

"I think that's the first time. I've never been a Gatorade kind of guy," Shula said. "It was cold, but I'll tell you I enjoyed every minute of it."

"I've always wanted to do that to Coach Shula," receiver Jim Jensen said, "one way or another."

"Shula was mobbed at midfield by television cameras as he shook the hand of Green Bay Coach Lindy Infante. Shula jogged off, smiling, pausing near the tunnel that leads to the bowels of the stadium to give fans a two-handed wave," wrote sportswriter Mike Freeman. "Shula was presented a game ball and a trophy from the players." The plaque on the trophy read "Congratulations on 300 career victories. From the 1991 Dolphins."

"The team was great about it after the game," Shula said. "I've been fortunate to work for two such class organizations as the Colts and the Dolphins. Organizations that allowed me the freedom to do things my way. Plus I've had the opportunities to coach with such outstanding assistants as John Sandusky, who have been with me such a long time. Thinking back through the years—the great wins, the great players and assistant coaches. . . . When you think about numbers, you can't help but think about those things. I'm glad [No. 300] is in the can, but it won't be one that I will pull out and look at a lot."

"The only time I heard him say anything about it was when reporters asked him. That's the way he is—not caught up in the records. But I can tell you he's proud of it underneath, but he won't brag about it. He's always looking forward to the future," said son Mike.

Even with the win, Shula had reason for concern. The game was their season in microcosm. By midseason, the Dolphins were 3–5. Five of those games had been on the road. Shula steered the team back on course by Week 14. They were still in the playoff race with an 8–6 record with two games to go after defeating Dave's Cincinnati Bengals, 37–13, in a Monday night game in Miami on December 9. As per usual, the father and sons had dinner before the game. But the Dolphins lost their last two games, including a crushing 23–20 overtime loss to the Jets in Miami that cost them a playoff spot.

Mark Clayton had talked big all week, and the Jets admitted to a man that his brash talk (and a chance at the playoffs) had fueled the Jets' desire to beat the Dolphins.

"You don't say things like that," Jets running back Johnny Hector said. "It sparks teams. It definitely did us."

"It's one that's going to last a long time with me and with us, I'm sure," Shula said. "You hate to go out. All of a sudden there's nowhere to go and nothing to do."

It was a bitter bookend to the previous year's success.

That December, Dave was promoted to head coach of the Cincinnati Bengals. At thirty-two, he was one of the youngest head coaches in the history of the NFL, a year younger than his father was when he took over the Colts, and three months younger than John Madden when he had been named the coach of the Raiders in 1969. Dave was younger than three of his own players: kicker Jim Breech (thirty-five), offensive tackle Anthony Muñoz (thirty-three), and running back James Brooks (thirty-three). Sam Wyche had been the previous Bengals head coach and had taken the team to the Super Bowl three seasons earlier. The team had gone 3–13 in 1991. Owner Mike Brown, who inherited the team from his father, Paul, fired Wyche and hired Dave. The circle was now complete. Another Shula was working for another Brown.

"Shula might have gotten a hint of his standing with the Bengals when he and his family were invited to a Memorial Day gathering at Paul Brown's Indian Hill estate a year ago. Although the Bengals' 82-year-old patriarch was in failing health, he sat outside for a spell, talking with his guests and watching the kids frolic in the pool," wrote Michael Graham in *Cincinnati* magazine.

"That was the kind of thing he would do for a friend's son," said Mike Brown.

"Poor Dave Shula. Named to replace Sam Wyche last winter in the Bengals' Desperately Seeking Sanity campaign, he is twice blessed by the god of novelty: He's young (33), but more important, he's the son of a Super Bowl coach," wrote Richard Hoffer in *Sports Illustrated*.

"I didn't come to Bengals with the idea that I'd be the head coach, said Dave. "I was looking forward to working under Sam Wyche and his offensive wizardry, and he had had a lot of success in the 80s and I was hoping to be a part of that for a long time, but it didn't turn out that way.

"Sam was definitely different. But I learned from him, just like I learned from Jimmy, just like I learned from my father. My experience in Dallas hardened my shell. I also saw the way Jimmy dealt with his players. He'd play mind games with them. Oh, the stories he would tell. Sam was very close to the players, he wanted to involve them in the process. My dad's approach was more businesslike. His style has always been 'Buffalo is 5–1, we're 4–2, here's what we have to do to win.'"

When Wyche was let go, Shula asked the other coaches if they had put in their names for the top spot. None had. Dave made up his mind and talked to Mike Brown.

"I don't know if it was more than one discussion that I remember," Shula recalled of his talk with Brown. "It didn't seem like it took very long that he gave me the opportunity and we came to an agreement on a three-year deal. So that's how it came together."

"He was an outstanding coach," Wyche said. "Then Mike hired him, which was a surprise to me, that he would hire a young coach that really wasn't quite ready to be a head coach. I don't know. I don't know why Mike did that. That was his choice. I was gone."

"Some people are going to think that David is a little young to be an NFL head coach," Mike Brown said at the news conference. "But you should bear in mind that he has been an NFL assistant for 10 years. Not only that, my first recollection of him is as a young boy on the sideline down at Miami next to his dad, taking down the plays during the game, keeping notes that way."

"I think we were in a transition not only just the coaching but players, too," said veteran Bengals safety David Fulcher. "That free agent money, Plan B free agency, and guys were taking this money to go other places. They got him here as a young coach, and everybody's like wow, he's going to be our coach. I hope he's as good as his dad."

"Was I ready?" Dave asked. "At the time, I thought so. As I look back on it now, I appreciate the enormousness of the job and all the experiences I've had in the six years since then to learn."

"We talked about it, certainly," Don Shula said. "I felt it was a great opportunity. The thing a lot of people don't realize is that they had a year to look at David. He was an assistant there, and he had a year to find out about the team. It's not like they hired him off the street."

"A lot of people, especially assistant coaches, were upset about it," one league personnel man said. "You heard it everywhere: 'How many years has he been there? What's he done? He's only getting it because of his name.' There was a lot of resentment. You also heard that Cincinnati makes decisions based on money and getting a guy they can control. That's one of the reasons Sam left. Their scouting is a joke. But everybody was talking about him [Shula]. Some people will always resent him just because of who he is."

Resigned to his notoriety, Dave said to *Sports Illustrated*, "They want to know what it's like to be Don Shula's son. There are eight other head coaches making their debuts in the NFL. I doubt your magazine covered all their openers."

"That name was an anchor," said former Dolphins tight end Jim Mandich. "If you observed this kid in a laboratory setting, no name to him, you'd have made him a head coach in a very short time."

Dave had liked working for Wyche. "Wyche was an eye-opener for Shula. Wyche would sit in his office on Mondays and fill legal pads with new plays. Game-plan day was a frenzy of innovation," wrote Hoffer.

"Thursday, 7:30," said Dave, gently poking fun at his father's famous rigid schedule. "I can tell you for a fact he's meeting with his special-teams coach."

"Don's idea of change is moving 15 paces to the north," said George Young.

"At Miami, you could take film from a game 10 years ago and recognize plays you used last week. With Sam, you might not recognize plays from week to week. The fun was, 'How were we going to get our players to execute those plays?' I always looked forward to seeing what was on those yellow pads," recalled Dave. "Sam was much more concerned with how a player felt about a matter than any coach I had been associated with before. He'd talk to them, call them. Maybe because he'd been a player for so long himself."

Theories in the press abounded. Had Mike Brown hired Shula because he was someone he could control (unlike Wyche) and who would not cost a lot of money? The Bengals were rumored to be among the most penurious teams in the NFL. The local press and disapproving fans jokingly called Dave "Doogie Shula" after the television show *Doogie Howser* about a teenage doctor.

The Bengals' first game under Shula was an upset victory over the Seattle Seahawks. Boomer Esiason, the Bengals quarterback and spiritual leader, gave Dave his first Gatorade bath. There would be few in the future. "He's businesslike," said Boomer. "Hey, I love him. Besides, he's kinda soft and cuddly."

Had his father called to congratulate him? Dave said he would never forget it: "He said, 'Congratulations, I've got to go to a meeting.'"

Dolphins training camp had its moments of seriousness and levity but gained the most notice because of the team's late-night carousing. The first incident was with nose tackle Alfred Oglesby, who failed to show up at practice. He had spent a night drinking at a nude bar. When confronted, he made up a story about being kidnapped by car thieves. Shula fined Oglesby $4,000. Upset, he insisted that veteran players no longer be allowed to live at home during training camp, but live in dorms with the rookies for the rest of the preseason.

Then on August 3, Opalocka police announced tight end Ferrell Edmunds and rookie defensive end Larry Webster were arrested just before curfew in an undercover prostitution sting. Both faced $500 fines and possible jail time.

"You'd like to think the players learn their lesson and understand and try to use some discretion on what they do and where they go," said Shula, who was livid about the later incident.

"We know we have to get stronger overall on defense and especially up front," Shula said before the season. "The road to the A.F.C. East championship and to the Super Bowl in the A.F.C. now goes through Buffalo."

The Dolphins roared out of the gate and started off 6–0, highlighted by a thrashing of the Bills on October 4 at Rich Stadium, 37–10. It was meant to be a statement game. And it was. The Dolphins marched to a record of 11–5, ending with a thrilling overtime victory against the Patriots in Miami on December 27. The Dolphins, down 13–3, came back in the second half, scoring 10 unanswered points to tie the hard-fought game and send it to overtime, where Pete Stoyanovich's 35-yard field goal finished the Pats. The win clinched the AFC East and secured a first-round bye and home-field advantage throughout the playoffs.

Marino had a good statistical year, throwing for 4,116 yards with 24 touchdowns and 16 interceptions. The team was eighth in offense, with the second-ranked passing attack and the 24th-rated rushing attack. The defense was ranked 11th, 14th against the pass, and sixth against the run. They were a formidable playoff team, in a season of good teams. The road to the Super Bowl would be a difficult one.

On January 10, 1993, the San Diego Chargers came to town for the division playoffs. The Chargers had beat the Chiefs in the wild-card round to earn a ticket to Miami. It was all Dolphins. In the second quarter, the Dolphins broke open a soggy, rainy scoreless game, with three unanswered Dan Marino touchdown passes to take a 21–0 lead. The defense completed the shut out of the Chargers in the second half, and the Dolphins won easily, 31–0.

"We just took an old-fashioned licking—on both sides of the ball," said San Diego Coach Bobby Ross. "They're an underrated defensive team. Some people say they're small, but I don't see that. They've got great quickness, and they defended us with great intensity and skill. Their whole team was focused and coming off a week of rest."

"I slept for two hours, as I usually do," Shula said the next day, "and then I got up and started thinking about the game and then I'd think about Buffalo." There was no hiding it. Shula was obsessed with beating Buffalo, who were seeking their third consecutive Super Bowl appearance.

"We've been the only team to get to the Super Bowl three straight years," said Shula. "It never happened before, and it hasn't happened since."

But Shula was thinking about more than that. He was thinking of coaching mortality. After the 1992 season, Mike Ditka of the Chicago Bears and Dan Reeves of the Denver Broncos had both been fired. Like him, they were throwbacks, old-fashioned taskmasters who had experienced and accomplished tremendous success. There was no question that the NFL establishment considered them to symbolize a different era. Yet Shula remained. He still thirsted for success.

"That's just tough for me to understand," he said of the dismissals. "I felt that way with Landry; I felt that way with Chuck Noll. I appreciated them as men." Reeves would ultimately find redemption in New York and Atlanta. Ditka would get another chance in New Orleans, but it was clear the establishment and the industry were tougher than ever. It was only about wins and losses.

The AFC Championship game was played at Joe Robbie Stadium on January 17. Both teams had powerful offensive attacks, and stout defenders. But it was not the Dolphins' day. The game saw the teams trade fields goals in the first quarter, and then Jim Kelly threw a 17-yard TD pass to Thurman Thomas to give Buffalo the lead. A 33-yard field goal by Steve Christie increased the margin to 13–3 at the half. The Dolphins never really challenged in the second half. The Bills added another touchdown and field goal in the third quarter and took the AFC crown, 29–10. In truth, it wasn't even that close. Marino, who was sacked four times and hurried all day, threw two interceptions and fumbled once, and the Dolphins lost two other fumbles.

"The big difference is we weren't able to run with it," said Shula. "We struggled to run every time. They played an outstanding game. That's the kind of team we need to be able to beat to get to our final goal, and we weren't able to handle it."

"I don't think they'll win," controversial Miami linebacker Bryan Cox said on the field moments after the game ended. "I don't like them. But they're going and we're not. I'll root against them."

"It was a real disappointment that we didn't play better in a game that meant so much to us today," said Shula. "This was the big test that we had to overcome in order to get into the final ball game, but we weren't ready for it." Don Shula was sixty-three years old, and he was now 5–2 in AFC Championship games. It would be the last time he would coach in one. The glory days were behind him.

Don Shula attended a New Year's Day party in 1992 hosted by golfer Ray Floyd and his wife, Maria, at their Indian Creek Island home, north of Miami Beach. While at the party, he met Mary Anne Stephens. She was a forty-eight-year-old, incredibly wealthy divorcée, and the two began to spend a lot of time with each other in the spring of that year.

"He has a tremendous sense of morals and ethics," said Maria Floyd. "I think those kinds of people gravitate toward each other. That, in one sentence, says everything that I can say about Mary Anne."

"The fifth of six children, Stephens is from the small town of Coal Hill, Ark., between the Ozarks and the Arkansas River valley. Her father was a soybean and cotton farmer and cattle rancher, her mother, a nurse and Bible teacher," wrote Jill Young Miller in the *Sun Sentinel*. "When she was 15, Mary Anne went to live with her older sister Colleen, whose husband was in the military. Years later, she would return to Coal Hill and donate $30,000 to build a child-care center."

"They were a mighty poor family," says Ben Yates, a neighbor and former mayor of Coal Hill. "You could look through the cracks on the floor and see the chickens underneath. We're proud of her here in Coal Hill. She has helped us in several ways."

Mary Anne Hurst had been married when she was eighteen and then remarried when she was twenty-four. She had a daughter and two sons from her first two marriages and then married Jackson T. "Jack" Stephens, a wealthy financier, after meeting him at a political rally in Hot Springs, Arkansas. She was used to power, wealth, and influence right up to the steps of the Capitol building in Washington, DC. And she knew how to wield it, as well. In the early 1980s, Jack and Mary Anne were known as "Mr. and Mrs. Republican of Arkansas." Mary Anne was cochairwoman of George Bush's successful 1988 presidential campaign in the state.

By the time she'd met Shula, Mary Anne was a grandmother.

"Wilton Robert ["Witt"] Stephens founded Stephens, Inc., which once was the largest brokerage firm off Wall Street . . . and exerted great influence on the political and economic fortunes of Arkansas during the second half of the twentieth century," wrote local historian Ernest Dumas. "In 1956, Stephens became president and chairman of the board of Arkla, leaving the investment company in the hands of his brother, Jackson T. Stephens, who had joined the company in 1946."

In the late 1980s, the Stephens brothers were very active in politics. Republican strategist Lee Atwater wanted to run a preemptive campaign against Bill Clinton and his potential presidential run. Atwater was hoping to co-opt Democratic

Representative Tommy Robinson to the Republican party in an effort to defeat Clinton in Arkansas.

"Running Robinson against Clinton was an idea that appealed greatly to the Republican Party's most important patrons in Little Rock, eighty-year-old billionaire Jack Stephens and his second wife, Mary Anne Stephens. . . . He had long served as chairman of the nation's ultimate country club, the Augusta National Golf Club in Georgia, annual home of the Masters tournament," wrote Joe Conason and Gene Lyons in their book *The Hunting of the President.* Ultimately, the scheme failed. Mary Anne was instrumental in getting Robinson to defect to the Republican party, but he lost in the Republican primaries, and Clinton won the 1990 Arkansas gubernatorial election.

In his lifetime, Jackson had made hundreds of millions of dollars. In 1970, he had underwritten the first public offering of Walmart Stores.

"A person married to a Stephens in Arkansas is pretty much like somebody who might be married to a Rockefeller in New York," said Betsy Blass, a friend in Little Rock. As a present, Jack had bought Mary Anne a Rolls Royce, but she refused to drive it around Little Rock. "She felt it was OK in Palm Beach, but not in Little Rock," Blass says. "She is definitely not pretentious," wrote Miller.

Stephens had a strong philanthropic side, as well. In 1990, the March of Dimes named her Arkansas Citizen of the Year. She was cited especially for her work on behalf of students with learning disabilities. Mary Anne also organized a $28 million fund-raising campaign for a national learning center at the University of the Ozarks in Clarksville, Arkansas. She also donated time and money to such causes as cancer research and alcohol and drug abuse. "Mrs. Stephens, who states her occupation as philanthropist/interior decorator, has given ample sums to an untold number of needy causes," reported the *Arkansas Democrat-Gazette* in 1991.

"She was such a bundle of energy. When she put her heart and mind and time behind a project for Arkansas, then it was successful because she would see that it was," said friend Sue Cato.

Social columnist Phyllis Brandon of the *Arkansas Democrat-Gazette* remembered Mary Anne as "very, very attractive and very, very personable and extremely popular in Little Rock." She was known for throwing lavish dinner parties as well as bigger soirees. When her daughter became a debutante, she held a New Orleans-themed Mardi Gras party on the family estate, with her daughter riding on a float. "They recreated Bourbon Street, fabulously so, on the drive to the estate," said Brandon.

"It was the most spectacular party ever given in Little Rock," agreed Blass.

In 1991, she divorced Stephens, who was then worth $380 million. As part of their divorce settlement, she received their luxurious 12,674-square-foot home (worth $3.9 million) in the exclusive Indian Creek Island area in Florida and $1 million a year for the rest of her life.

Immediately, Mary Anne began working her fund-raising magic in South Florida. In 1993, she was chairwoman of Miami Heart Institute gala at the Fontainebleau Hilton in Miami Beach, which raised more than $400,000.

"Mary Anne has the ability to get people on the bandwagon and participate, if she believes in a cause," said Ray Floyd's wife, Maria. It was Maria who introduced her close friend Mary Anne to Shula. "I think that everyone east of the Mississippi—and probably west of the Mississippi—was trying to fix up Don Shula."

In a bizarre moment, on July 7, 1993, it was reported that vandals had broken into the gravesite of Dorothy Shula during the Fourth of July holiday weekend. "They were in the process of breaking into her coffin," Mary Ross Agosta, spokeswoman for the Archdiocese of Miami, which ran the cemetery, told the *Sun Sentinel*. "This is a shocking, horrible crime. When someone passes away you pray they will rest in peace." The intruders had either left or been scared away; thus her coffin had been left marked, but unopened.

Shula himself was on vacation and told the press, "I was stunned when I was told about what happened, shortly after the vandalism occurred." And so was the rest of the family. Eventually, her remains were moved to an undisclosed location.

By August, there were rumors that the two had married in secret, but that was not true. "I think they're good for each other, after they both made transitions in their lives. His wife dying. And Mary Anne's divorce," said Rep. John Paul Hammerschmidt, a U.S. congressman from Arkansas who was friends with Stephens and Shula. "They probably are a comfort to each other."

It was alleged that it took Don two months to ask Mary Anne out on a date. "He kept asking me questions about her for weeks and weeks," says Shula's friend Dick Elias. "He said, 'Tell me about her. What do you think about her?' I said she was very attractive and very easy to talk to. The first time he went to her house, for lunch, I had to take him, literally lead him, by the arm. He was petrified."

"Don and Mary Anne are blissfully happy together," said her sister Colleen Williams. "They have fun, hold hands. They're very romantic and have a lot of respect for each other."

"It's great to see a guy his age in love and able to express it," said Elias. "Mary

Anne has a way of tearing down the guard he has always had with his players and everyone else. For the first time in the 20 years that I've known him, this defense mechanism is broken." Shula took to updating his wardrobe, buying $1,500 suits, and going snorkeling. They had their lighter moments, as well. Mary Anne spoke of little notes he would leave her. Once comfortable, he let loose a little. "That is the ugliest picture I've ever seen," said Shula to Stephens, pointing to a painting she had in her home.

"Really, Don?" replied Stephens. "Well, if you don't like it, I'll sell it."

"Who would want to buy that?" said Shula.

"Well, Don," said Stephens gently, "it is a Picasso."

"We both had a lot of grief to work through—him, a death; me, a divorce," said Stephens. "We could share those things, and we became very good friends. Probably the most beautiful thing about Don is that he loved his wife and he loves his children."

Shula found immense relief in reaching out to his children. In February 1993, the two-year anniversary of Dorothy's death, the Shula clan descended on Miami for a family weekend of golf, tennis, and fishing. They also hosted and attended a black-tie dinner that raised $600,000 for breast cancer research.

"This is a relationship we've needed for a long time," said daughter Annie. "There were times I wished that the closeness and togetherness could be there a little more. We've needed to be able to go cry on his shoulder if we had to, or to just talk to him and express our opinions and concerns without being judged. Our loss drew us all together."

"Since Mom died, he has made an effort to be closer to us. She flatout begged him to be there for us. I talk to him about things that I used to go to Mom with. He was never the kind of father who could tell you he loved you, who would hold you or kiss you. It was real awkward for him. But these days, he's very connected. He tells us he loves us a lot more," said Donna.

In 1993, Shula began to embrace grandfatherhood. He bought a vacation home in Linville, North Carolina. From the deck of this large sprawling country retreat, you can see Grandfather Mountain, one of the most famous peaks in the Blue Ridge Mountains. During the summers, all the grandchildren would arrive. He would read them *Green Eggs and Ham* and other Dr. Seuss stories. He allowed them to climb all over him in a way he never had before.

There, he organizes tennis tournaments on his courts that are part of his grounds, a game of basketball or shootaround, or drills them in the fundamentals of the game. The children sooner or later tire and go inside. They call him Grandfather Mountain. "They're just like you, Don," Stephens kidded Shula. "Little Sherman tanks."

"One time Matt stormed in the front door after three minutes, saying it was 'stupid, stupid, stupid,'" daughter Sharon said of one of Shula's grandchildren. "And my father kept saying, 'Where does he get that word from?' Come on, Dad."

The difference in Shula was remarkable. One time, the family sat glumly around the house after yet another Dolphin loss. Things were quiet. Then the highlights of the game appeared on television. "Boy, Grandpa," granddaughter Lindsey blurted out, "the Dolphins sure stunk." Shula laughed out loud. But when training camp started, Grandpa Mountain had all but disappeared.

The 1993 season would be an immensely memorable and satisfying season for Don Shula on a personal level, yet the playoffs would elude the Dolphins that year. Shula entered the season needing only seven more wins to surpass George Halas's record of 324 victories. It was a forgone conclusion that Shula would break the record. But the question was when?

There was concern that his chase of the record would overshadow Miami's season. "The Dolphins are, and always will be, the big story," Shula had said during training camp at the team's new $8.5 million practice facility at Nova University. "Getting back to the Super Bowl, and hopefully winning it . . . that's the story I want to be associated with. [Halas's record] is one I'd someday like to have, but I can't let it get me off my focus. The only reason I have this opportunity is because I've stayed focused and didn't worry about individual or personal goals. My numbers are a by-product of the team's success." His modesty notwithstanding, Shula was still obsessed with winning.

"Now I have a chance to win the most games and have a team in the Super Bowl in the '60s, '70s, '80s, and '90s. Those are the things I'd like to accomplish before I hang it up. I still look forward to training camp. I enjoy the month of June because I know that's vacation time, a chance for the family to get together. But when it's over, I know that training camp is right around the corner. And once it starts, I get totally immersed in everything I do," said Shula. "[Training camp] is the best way to get back into it, get totally involved morning, noon, and night. We start with coaches' meetings as early as 7 or 7:15 in the morning and sometimes, with player meetings and two-a-day practices, don't finish until 11:30 at night. I enjoy what I do. I don't know what the word 'burnout' means. I realize the demands of my job, and I'm willing to pay the price."

"Don's the type of coach who won't leave any stone unturned. He wants to know everything about our opponents; he's very meticulous. He doesn't like surprises," said Carl Taseff. "He's going to get Halas's record, but it's not something he's planning for. He doesn't plan beyond one game at a time, and when you do what you have to do, things fall in place." Taseff was still with Shula all these years later. Taseff coached running backs from 1970 to 1992 and was a staff assistant in 1993. He'd been with Shula 24 seasons as a reliable and trustworthy friend and assistant. Taseff had coached such players as Larry Csonka, Jim Kiick, and Mercury Morris, as well as Tony Nathan, Delvin Williams, and others. "From a career standpoint, he was the only member of the 1958 Colts team—the one that played in the so-called greatest game in history [against the New York Giants]—and the 1972 Dolphins and their perfect season," Taseff's daughter, Susan deMuth, said. "When you look at how short some of the pro careers are, daddy played 12 seasons and then coached the Dolphins for 24 more. By today's standards, it's incredible when you consider his longevity."

Even with so many changes going on in his life, Shula was still very much aware that the one person he had shared so much of this journey with would not be there to see his ultimate accomplishment. "Dorothy was such an important part of any success I've had as a coach," he said with a catch in his voice. "It gave me tremendous confidence to know she was always there for our kids and for me."

For whatever reason that went beyond division rivals, the Dolphins' matchups with the Jets seemed to find even extra fire in 1993. The Dolphins started off with a win over the Colts in Indianapolis and then flew home to Miami to play the Jets.

"Like a rock striking flint, there is a spark whenever the Jets and the Dolphins meet. As [Jets cornerback James] Hasty said earlier in the week, the two teams could play in Guadalajara and the electricity would still be there," wrote Timothy W. Smith in the *New York Times*. Under Bruce Coslet, the Jets continued to have a better record against the Dolphins, than other, lesser teams in their division.

"We're trying not to put a label on that," said Pete Carroll, then the Jets' defensive coordinator. "We're going to try to get away from that when we play those other guys this season. Sometimes people talk like in our division the big games are Buffalo and Miami. But there are none that are bigger than the other, and we need to approach them that way and get that displayed. So far it hasn't happened. New England has been up and down with us and Indianapolis has just been down."

The Dolphins had a solid corps of veteran receivers, including Irving Fryar, running back/tight end Keith Byars, tight end Keith Jackson, and Mark Ingram. "Jackson is really the focus of the throwing-game intermediate areas," Carroll said. "He's the No. 1 target it looks like they're trying to get the ball to. They're real good at it."

The Jets won, 24–14, at Joe Robbie Stadium. New York quarterback Boomer Esiason threw for 323 yards and two touchdowns. Keith Jackson caught a 57-yard touchdown in the first quarter but missed the rest of the game with a pulled hamstring. "He's a big part of our offense, but someone has to step up and make the plays," said Shula.

The next game was at Buffalo. Linebacker Bryan Cox had been talking all during the Dolphins' bye week about how much he hated Buffalo and stated in an interview that he would "retire from football if I am ever traded up there."

His antics started before the game. The Buffalo fans were ruthless that day. Cox was catcalled with all manner of obscenities, and there were numerous signs in the stands, including CRYIN' BRYAN, KNOCK THE SOX OFF OF COX, and a number of banners whose foul messages were not repeated in reports of the day. Sportswriter Bill Plaschke called the game "a considerable step toward making their rivalry the ugliest in the league."

"[Cox] was greeted by agitated fans when he walked onto the field. Cox responded by waving the middle finger of both hands at the crowd, and his gestures were shown on national television. He said he was sorry the obscene gestures were seen beyond his intended audience," reported the Associated Press. Cox could be seen coming out of the tunnel with his double-barreled response. The league fined Cox $10,000 the next day. It was nothing less than a gladiatorial welcome worthy of *Wrestlemania*. Cox sacked Bills quarterback Jim Kelly on the very first Buffalo offensive series. The other Dolphins players later admitted that Cox had inspired them that day. The defense was monstrous. The Dolphins had a 19–0 lead before the Bills had a first down. The final score was 22–13.

Miami beat the Redskins the following week and were playing the Cleveland Browns at Municipal Stadium when Marino ruptured his Achilles tendon. "I thought I got kicked, but I was told I wasn't," Marino said later. "I was trying to move up in the pocket, and, when I threw the ball, I just landed on the foot the wrong way. I haven't been hurt much, so I haven't had this experience. It's kind of a shock. Just not being able to play the next game is going to be the hardest part—let alone the ones after that." The Browns, coached by Bill Belichick, took a 14–10 lead into halftime. But backup quarterback Scott Mitchell came in, threw two touchdown passes in the second half, and the offense didn't miss a beat. The Dolphins defense rose to the occasion, and Shula left with a 24–14 win.

There were two bye weeks that season. So Don Shula did something he rarely did on the Friday of the Dolphins' second bye week, October 15, 1993—he took the day off. That Friday night, in a small, private ceremony at St. Joseph's Catholic Church in Miami Beach, Don married Mary Anne. It was mostly immediate family. Mike, who was now an assistant coach for the Bears, flew in for the ceremony, in all about twenty guests, including Raymond and Maria Floyd. Mike Shula was the best man, and Carrie Stephens, Mary Anne's daughter, was the maid of honor. Dave could not attend, as he was preparing his Bengals for a game against the Browns that weekend.

"Good for him," said Carl Taseff. "I figured he'd get married sooner, but I'm happy for him."

When Shula showed up for work Monday, a gallery of reporters and photographers were there. He said to them, tongue planted firmly in cheek, "What's up?" with a big smile on his face. Shula shared few facts about the wedding. "I'd like it to be private. It was a very beautiful evening with family and just a few friends," Shula said.

On October 31, Shula and the 5–1 Dolphins played host to Joe Montana and the Kansas City Chiefs, with Shula one victory away from tying Halas. But was Shula's quest suddenly to be undone by Marino's injury? Who was Scott Mitchell? A relative unknown as far as the NFL was concerned. He was a 6-foot-6-inch, 230-pound left-hander from Utah drafted in the fourth round back in 1990. He was in his fourth year as a backup. However, that day, he connected on 22 of 33 passes for 344 yards and three touchdowns. And Montana? He injured his hamstring during the first half. Montana and Marino stared at each other in crutches from across the field.

"What can you say about Scott Mitchell? He made every play," Shula said.

"It's been a lot of years," Shula said. "What makes tying the record that much more important to me was it came in such a good football game." Not only that, the Dolphins had won six of their first seven games and were sitting atop their division.

"People have been giving Joe Montana all the accolades this week," Cox said after the game. It was Cox who had given Shula his Gatorade bath after the record-tying victory. "We have our own legend in Coach Shula. Sometimes he's underappreciated." Shula gave Cox a meaningful hug afterward.

When asked, Shula said he would not fine Cox for the dousing. When asked what he said, Shula said, "I told him I loved him." The game had been so lopsided that many of 67,765 who had come to anoint Shula had left before the game's end. However, a hardy, stalwart group was left to chant, "Shula! Shula! Shula!"

There were numerous comparisons of the two coaches. Halas and Shula had both played and coached. They had both gone from leather helmet days to the days of long hair and big mustaches. Both were hard-working, no-nonsense guys. Both never lost their zeal for winning. Halas had been one of the founders of the NFL and was thought of as the Father of Football. Halas had coached in four decades, the 1930s, 1940s, 1950s, and 1960s. Shula had had also coached in four decades, including the 1960s, 1970s, 1980s, and 1990s. At the time, the top three winning coaches of all time had been George Halas, Tom Landry, and Curly Lambeau. Shula was about to top all of them.

The stage was set. Shula was remarried and tied the record in grand manner. The Dolphins arrived in New York at the top of the division, and the host Jets were 3–4, coming off of a win against their crosstown rival Giants. The media and the NFL were prepared to crown Shula that day. NFL commissioner Paul Tagliabue was there. Most of Shula's family was on hand. A telephone company planning to film a live commercial was there. There was only one problem. The Jets were there, too. The New York Jets had been the football team that had beaten Shula more than any other.

"Dad won't say it, but it would be especially sweet to get the record in this game," Shula's daughter Donna said beforehand. "He has been through a lot with the Jets. A lot of bad memories. A lot of bad times." His sting still stretched all the way back to 1969. But the Jets had other plans for the NFL's coronation.

"Bottom line, we weren't going to let Don Shula film his AT&T commercial here," quarterback Boomer Esiason told the press after the game. "It all made us want to defend ourselves. We were like bulldogs backed into a corner."

"You've got these presidents waiting on the line, you've got all this stuff . . . it was like they were almost predicting a win for the Dolphins," said the Jets' Dave Cadigan. "In this league, you just can't do that."

New York jumped out to a 10–0 lead and built on it the rest of the day. Scott Mitchell looked suddenly human, and the Dolphins didn't score a touchdown until the third quarter, when they were down, 20–3. The final score was a disappointing 27–10. "I cannot figure it out," Shula said. "The Jets are a good team when they play us. . . . I don't know what happens any other time." The Jets had done it to him once more. As Shula stepped up to the podium for his postgame press conference, he said to the media with a wry smile, "No Gatorade." The Dolphins were now 6–2, with both losses to the Jets. That same week, the Dolphins, desperate for quarterback help, signed thirty-nine-year-old Steve DeBerg, the oldest player in the NFL, who had recently been released by Tampa Bay.

"There were subplots aplenty when the Miami Dolphins met the Philadelphia Eagles here this afternoon on a warm, sunny day ideal for something special to unfold. It was William (Refrigerator) Perry's first game in an Eagles uniform. It was the return of three former Eagles—Keith Jackson, Mike Golic and Keith Byars—to Veterans Stadium. It was Miami Coach Don Shula's attempt to surpass George Halas as the National Football League coach with the most victories," wrote Thomas George in the *New York Times* of the Dolphins' next game in the City of Brotherly Love on November 14. By this time, Mitchell was leading the league in passer rating, and the Dolphins were riding high.

The Dolphins scored first as Mitchell threw an 8-yard touchdown pass to running back Terry Kirby, but the extra point attempt was missed. The Eagles responded in the second quarter with a touchdown, which made it 7–6. They traded touchdowns once again, and the teams went into halftime with Philadelphia in the lead, 14–13. The Eagles defense was stout all afternoon, especially with the addition of William "The Refrigerator" Perry. "It really shored up their run defense when they got the 'Fridge' in there," said Shula.

The game would be decided by an unlikely hero. Early in the third quarter, Mitchell was scrambling and went down hard, suffering a separated shoulder. Enter third-string back-up Doug Pederson from Northeast Louisiana, who had never thrown a pass in the NFL. "Shula might have preferred Tom Matte, the halfback who once had to start at quarterback for Shula's Baltimore Colts. At least Shula knew Matte's name. A month ago, Shula couldn't remember Pederson's name when the kid was called from the practice squad after Marino got hurt," wrote Don Pierson in the *Chicago Tribune*.

"I was nervous the first two plays, and Coach Shula just kind of settled me down and told me to do the things that I knew how to do. I just didn't want to make the big mistake that cost us the game," said Pederson. "He [Shula] just told me to keep my head up. He told me to just do the things I knew how to do. Kept giving me support and encouragement."

"He was an outstanding student of the game, prepared diligently even though he wasn't the starter, and was ready to play when he was given the opportunity," Shula said of Pederson. "He was a real professional."

"He's so resourceful," said Pederson. "We came in wanting to throw, and immediately he was making moves after Scott got hurt to rely on the running game and defense. This kind of game fits into his legacy."

Meanwhile, the Miami defense played brilliantly in the second half, forcing three Eagles turnovers. Pederson threw six short passes underneath the zone, connecting on three of them for modest gains. The running game pressed hard, and the Dolphins put up two Pete Stoyanovich field goals to take the lead, 19–14, in the fourth quarter.

However, the Eagles were set to spoil Shula's quest. The Eagles were at the Miami 22-yard line with less than three minutes left in the game. On a 2nd-and-2, Ken O'Brien, the former Jet, lofted a pass over the middle. Veteran All-Pro receiver James Lofton was wide open at the five-yard line. Normally sure-handed, he dropped the pass.

"I'm going to wake up in the middle of the night when I'm 65 and drawing Social Security and remember that one," Lofton said. "That's a pass everyone in the stadium could have caught."

"There are reasons sometimes when guys drop balls. I mean, it was a slugfest out there, and there were people around him ready to make a big hit. This is special the way our defense played because we talked about shutting them out at halftime, and when Scott Mitchell got hurt, we knew that was the only way we would win. And that's just what we did," said Miami defensive end Jeff Cross, who made three sacks that day. The game ended essentially when O'Brien fumbled the ball on a fourth-down play and Cross fell on it. Game over.

"I give coach Shula credit. He keeps things simple, he strives for perfection, and he asks his players to do the same thing. His real key is leading by example. He is not just lip service. He pays attention to detail, and he works as hard as anyone. That is how he has our respect. He gets ready to play, you get ready to play. Really, what more could you ask? It's really not much. It's his secret to success," said Cross.

"Over the years, there have been a lot of great victories and memories," said Shula. "This one is pretty special to me, mainly because of the way that we won, the adversity we overcame. When Mitchell went down with the injury, Doug Pederson, who hasn't played any kind of real football to speak of, handled himself with a lot of poise and got the job done. It reminded me of the Matte days," said Shula after the game.

"A classy man," said guard Keith Sims. "We looked at the Gatorade and said, 'You know, we need to do a classy thing.'" So they carried him off instead. Even his players knew that Don Shula was head and shoulders above everyone else.

"The last time I was up there was '72 in the 17–0 season," Shula said. "It's been a long time since I've been up on anybody's shoulders. It is something down the road I'm going to have the luxury to sit back and enjoy. I have said that I hoped it would come in a year of accomplishment for the team. We are 7–2, we've got a chance for the playoffs and maybe the Super Bowl. That would mean so much. I thanked my football team for their effort in a game that meant so much to me.

"I just thanked the football team for hanging in there and doing the things necessary to win," Shula said. "Hopefully, there won't be any more talk about individual records, and we'll get back to the things that brought us here. We're going to try and get it together, and we have Steve DeBerg, who we'll have to give a lot of work," said Shula. "I would love to see this football team continue to win and go all the way to the Super Bowl. We have to continue to believe in ourselves."

Not long after, *Sports Illustrated* named Shula Sportsman of the Year. "For nearly 31 years, first as coach of the Baltimore Colts and for the last 24 years at the helm of the Miami Dolphins, Shula has thrived in a world of pressure so intense that it has burned out even those who have succeeded at the highest level, or close to it. Joe Gibbs, 12 years and out. Health reasons, family reasons. Bill Walsh, 10 years. Trapped at the top, crushed by the pressure to stay there. Dick Vermeil, haunted by the vision of what he had become, a robot consumed and almost destroyed by the game. John Robinson, Don Coryell, John Madden—the list is long," wrote Paul Zimmerman. "Through it all, year after year, watching them burn out and drop out all around him, Shula marches on." Zimmerman said Shula was to be saluted for his "unparalleled success and pursuit of excellence. . . . Even now, Shula's Dolphins are Super Bowl contenders despite being on their fourth quarterback of the season."

Sure enough, Steve DeBerg started the next week and guided the Dolphins to a win over the New England Patriots, and then the Dolphins were set to play the Dallas Cowboys in Dallas on Thanksgiving Day. This was billed as a titanic meeting between two clubs headed for the playoffs. This was Jimmy Johnson's defending Super Bowl champion Dallas Cowboys led by quarterback Troy Aikman, running back Emmitt Smith, and wide receiver Michael Irvin.

It was thirty-two degrees in Dallas that Thanksgiving Day, with rain, sleet, and snow showering in through the roof of Texas Stadium. The hash marks could barely be seen. The weather was unrelenting, and it would be an ugly game forever known as "The Snow Bowl."

"I hate cold weather, absolutely hate it," said Johnson.

"We've got to play no matter what happens. We've got to handle it," said Shula.

"We did not expect snow when we left for Dallas. Officials have different kinds of shoes. We have a longer cleat for games with snow for better traction. And we wear a longer cleat for grass. But for artificial turf, some officials just wear a flat shoe, like a basketball sneaker for turf. We didn't bring our longer cleats that day, and we were slipping and sliding. We couldn't stop. You basically had to slide on the ice to eventually come to a stop," remembered official Ed Hochuli. "That is absolutely the worst traction I've ever had as an official in 25 years. We've been in worse snow, but with the shoes we had, and the old surface at Texas Stadium, it was basically a carpet. There was a lot of sliding around that day."

"It was so bad that we might as well have worn ice skates," said Emmitt Smith later.

"You had to run control routes because it was so sloppy that you couldn't get any kind of traction. You couldn't come out of cuts and couldn't break hard," recalled Irvin.

The game started off well for the Dolphins. Keith Byars ripped off a 77-yard touchdown run, and the Dolphins had a 7–0 lead. But the Cowboys responded strongly in the second quarter. Aikman threw a short touchdown pass to Kevin Williams to tie it, and then Williams returned a punt 64 yards to the end zone to make it 14–7 in favor of Dallas at the half.

As the game progressed, the field got worse. Finding any traction in the ice and snow seemed nearly impossible. In the second half, the defense again rose to the challenge. Cox and company blanked the powerful Dallas offense for the entire second half. However, the Dolphins would have to earn every yard. In this horrid weather with bad footing, Dolphins kicker Pete Stoyanovich kicked a 20-yard field goal in the third and a 31-yard field goal in the fourth to bring Miami back to within a point.

"Twice in the final five minutes, ahead by 14–13, the Cowboys made two huge defensive plays that appeared to seal the victory. The first was safety James Washington's crunching hit that forced a fumble by the Dolphins rookie Terry Kirby at the Miami 30 with 4 minutes 19 seconds left. After that, Dallas missed a field goal," wrote Thomas George.

Then there was the final drive. With Steve DeBerg at the helm, the Dolphins rammed forward. DeBerg, despite the snow, had thrown 24 completions in 41 attempts for 287 yards. "This really became a man's game, a big man's game because all we could do was go straight ahead," said DeBerg after the game.

"Sunshine is nice, but when the elements come into play, that's when we find out which players can step up and play. The Dallas defense's strength is their speed, so we tried to come out and play physical, and just ram it down their throats. That way we're playing to our strength and their weakness," said Dolphins running back Keith Byars.

The Dolphins pushed forward, but with only seconds remaining, their final drive stalled. That's when Dallas made its second attempt to end the game. Stoyanovich attempted a 41-yard field goal, but Jimmie Jones blocked the kick.

"We had 'block right' on, and I was lined up one-on-one with their center. I just did a quick swim with him, and I was able to get penetration and get my hands up [for the block]. I thought the game was over with. Everybody was celebrating," said Jones.

The ball skittered around in the snow. The Dolphins were lost, Dallas had prevailed. Except a gaggle of Dolphins followed the ball, but it was not theirs to touch. The ball would not be live unless touched by Dallas player first. Enter Leon Lett, a Pro Bowl defensive tackle who came diving through the slippery ice and snow and kicked the ball forward. A mad scrum followed.

"I knew the rule," Lett recalled years later. "I had blocked field goals in the past. It's not like it was my first time on the field-goal block team. Maybe it was that season, but not in my career. I have been trying to think back for, what, 20 years now, and I don't know what happened. It was a brain freeze."

Dolphins lineman Jeff Dellenbach came up with the ball as the pile of twisted bodies and white snow slid from the field of play into the end zone. But this was a difficult moment. In 1992, the owners had decided to discontinue instant replay, and so there were no camera angles to judge or spot the ball in 1993. The crowd roared with astonishment and disapproval.

"I didn't see anything after the block," Hochuli recalled years later. "That's common in terms of what our specific areas of responsibility are. My eyes are trained to be on the kicker, the holder, the snap, not where the ball landed downfield. So the crew came together, and there was a little input from everyone, and we put the pieces together. I have so much confidence in my crew. We have complete trust and confidence in each other. And we got the call right."

There was mass confusion. After the ball was blocked, many people, including players and coaches, had looked away, figuring the game was over.

"I always go down to the field right before the game ends. I was down there with Jimmie when the blocked field goal happened, and he turned to me," remembered Dallas public relations director Rich Dalrymple.

"I didn't see what happened. What the hell happened?" asked Jimmy Johnson.

"I don't know," responded Dalrymple. Dalrymple recalled later, "There was all this mass confusion and running around. For those of us on the field, we really didn't know what happened. We all thought the game was over. And the next thing you know, Miami is lining up to kick another field goal. It was total exhilaration to total frustration in about 30 seconds."

"As I reached the sideline, I heard something in the crowd, like a gasp, and my teammates all looked scared. I turned around and had no idea what happened. They told us to go back out, and I'm like, 'Are you serious?'" recalled Dallas safety Darren Woodson.

There were still three seconds left in the game. The officials claimed that the ball was downed when the kicking team recovered the ball. The Dolphins were awarded a first down at the Dallas 8-yard line. With three seconds left, Stoyanovich lined up for what was a second chance, with a 19-yard attempt. This time the kick was good, and with time expiring, the Dolphins won the game, 16–14.

"This was a crazy, crazy game with a fitting finish," wrote George.

"We've lost two in a row to start the season, and we've lost two in a row now," said Dallas Coach Jimmy Johnson. "There is no reason we can't put another streak together. This was a very disappointing loss. In fact, I don't know whether I've ever had a loss that hurts like this one right now. The play by Lett, it was a mistake and we all make 'em and it's part of the game. There were hundreds of mistakes made in the ball game before that. It just so happens that that came at the end, and it will be remembered as the one that cost us the ball game."

"This is as big as any win I've ever played in, and it looks like the games are going to get bigger and bigger," DeBerg said after the game.

"I vividly remember the moments after that game. Leon was so emotional, and I wanted to reach out to him. No one felt worse than Leon. That team was so special. I think everyone understood that and supported him. I made sure he knew how Jimmy and I felt about him. Also, we both stressed to him that there's never one play that totally makes a difference in a football game. Never," said owner Jerry Jones.

"All I remember about after the game was Leon in the training room, and he was despondent. Jimmy went in there and put his arm around him and talked. I didn't even ask him about talking to the press. I just told everyone that, 'Look, he's painfully shy, and he's not talking.' And to their credit, the media was pretty understanding that this was an unusual circumstance, and they gave him a pass for not talking about it," said Jones.

"I've been around a lot of football games, but I never saw a game end like that before. There have been a lot of [wins], but that one is special," said Shula.

Right after this game, the Dolphins were 9–2, considered the team to beat in the AFC, and appeared a lock, not only for the playoffs, but a good chance at the Super Bowl. There were a lot of questions about what would happen to the Cowboys.

However, this was a seminal game for both teams. The Cowboys would not lose another game the entire season, up to and including the Super Bowl. And for the Dolphins, it began one of the worst slides in franchise history. They would not win another game the rest of the season.

"There is plenty of blame to go around for Miami's collapse: injuries, inconsistency at quarterback, no running game, butterfingered receivers, turnovers, weak tackling, a defense that has become an almost-overnight sieve," wrote Charlie Nobles in the *New York Times*.

"I don't ever remember losing four in a row," Jeff Dellenbach said. "It's hard to put up with. There's no way after being 9–2 that we should be sitting where we are. We just have to deal with it. I think people are sensing that if we're going to do something, we've got to get it done right now."

"You can't talk yourself through this situation," Cox said. "You just have to get the job done."

Then the Dolphins went to New England for their last regular game of the season, January 2, 1994. If Miami won, they would be in the playoffs. Former Giants Head Coach Bill Parcells was now on the Patriots' sideline in the middle of a rebuilding year, with a team that was 4–11. The game was a tough one in the cold weather elements, and the teams went into halftime with the Patriots up, 10–7.

Pete Stoyanovich kicked a 29-yard field goal to tie the game in the third quarter, but the Patriots answered as Drew Bledsoe threw an 11-yard touchdown pass to Vincent Brisby. Then came the crazy fourth quarter. Scott Mitchell, who had returned with four games remaining, threw a 9-yard touchdown to Mark Ingram to tie the game, 17–17. The Patriots responded with a field goal by Matt Bahr to regain the lead. Terry Kirby ran one in from 11 yards out to give the Dolphins the lead for the first time, 24–20, with 3:40 remaining, but the Patriots responded with a Drew Bledsoe-to-Ben Coates touchdown pass good for 11 yards, making it 27–24, Patriots. With six seconds remaining, Pete Stoyanovich kicked a 24-yard field goal to tie the game with six seconds remaining after after a leaping Mark Ingram was ruled to have one foot out of bounds after grabbing a Mitchell pass in the end zone. The game went into overtime, where Drew Bledsoe threw a 36-yard pass to Michael Timpson to win the game, 33–27, and knock the 9–7 Dolphins out of the playoffs.

The 1993 team went from the supreme highs to the supreme lows.

"I feel kind of numb now," said wide receiver Irving Fryar. "At the same time, I'm angry and frustrated because of the mudslide we've been in." The offense had not helped, but the defense had been awful, surrendering an average of 42 points in their last three games.

"Knowing our whole season was on the line the last two weeks and not winning, this hurt," said the devastated Shula, who at 9–2 truly thought his team had a chance of going all the way. "This is something that will be hard to live with."

"How could you believe when we were 9–2, with the best record in the NFL, that this could happen?" said Shula. In retrospect, it was a testament to his and his staff's coaching that they had done as well as they did. They were playing with second-, third-, and fourth-string quarterbacks, and a defense patched together with free agents that had suffered injuries and tired at the end of the year. How does any coach get to 9–2 in the National Football League winning with a fourth-string quarterback? In any decade? Still, from the extreme highs of the season's peak, this was a bitter, bitter pill to swallow. His chances for one more Lombardi Trophy were shrinking.

That February, the movie *Ace Ventura: Pet Detective* starring comedian Jim Carrey was released. "Make no mistake: 'Ace Ventura: Pet Detective,' . . . is a mindless stretch of nonsense. The plot, as such, involves Miami-based animal-tracer Carrey's search for a missing dolphin—the mascot to the Miami Dolphins football team," read the review in the *Washington Post*. "It includes lamely scripted appearances from Sean Young, as Carrey's tight-lipped lieutenant; Courteney Cox, as his gratuitous love interest; Tone Loc, as his gratuitous friend; and quarterback Dan Marino, coach Don Shula and a huddle of other Miami Dolphins as gratuitous cameos."

Shula's scene is a quick cameo. The football team hires Carrey as Ace Ventura to track down their missing mascot, a live dolphin. Ace needs, he believes, to find someone with a 1984 AFC Championship ring with its stones missing to find the kidnapper. In the scene, Shula approaches a mailbox and unthinkingly inserts his mail into it. Carrey, hiding in there, tugs the coach's arm hard, until he can see whether the ring is complete. Shula's reaction is hilarious. It is actually one of the funnier moments in a silly movie.

In March, the league's competiton committee announced the most drastic set of rules changes in the league's history. "From 1983 through 1993, the number of touchdowns scored in NFL games decreased by 22 percent, while the number of field goals attempted rose 14 percent. During the 1993 season, half of the league's teams averaged less than two touchdowns per game. Average yardage was also on the decline—pro football had become a game of inches. Critics derisively referred to it as the National Field Goal League. Longtime NFL writer Len Pasquarelli, then with the *Atlanta Journal-Constitution,* said pro football had become 'moribund' and 'stale and predictable,'" wrote Kevin Craft for Slate.com.

Craft wrote that the committee, chaired by Shula and George Young, had attempted to make life easier for the offensive teams, to introduce rules that deterred the kicking game, and to point the league into a new, more spectacular dimension. The changes included prohibiting "downfield chucking," making it more difficult for defensive backs to jam receivers more than five yards beyond the line of scrimmage; allowing offensive lineman the option of lining up with one foot behind them at the line of scrimmage; instituting two-point conversions; putting more emphasis on the roughing the passer rule; stiffer rules intended to deter defenders from hitting the quarterback after the ball was released; moving the spot of the ball after missed field goal attempts; and inserting radio transmitters to quarterbacks' helmets, allowing coaches to talk directly to them. These changes would usher in the newest and most prolifc offensive era in football history and help revitalize the game for another generation.

On June 28, 1994, H. Wayne Huizenga completed his purchase of the Miami Dolphins and Joe Robbie Stadium. He met with Shula to discuss his future with the franchise. Shula was sixty-four years old and said publicly that he wasn't sure whether he wanted to coach beyond the upcoming season, when his current contract expired.

"If he says he wants one more year or two more years or four more years, that's the coach's decision," said Huizenga. "I think he's entitled to that." However, there were rumors in the media that Jimmy Johnson, who had resigned in March of that year from the Super Bowl champion Dallas Cowboys and had also coached the Miami Hurricanes to an NCAA championship, would replace Shula after the coming season. However, two weeks later, Shula and Huizenga announced a new two-year extension on his contract.

"I'm healthy and looking forward to this next year of coaching and also coaching in the remaining years of my contract," said Shula. "Some of the things about the retirement or going up to the front office have been blown out of proportion or exaggerated. Leaving the sideline is the furthest thing from my mind right now."

"He would only be a thought in my mind if Don came in this morning and said he didn't want to coach anymore," Huizenga said of Johnson. "But Don wants to coach, and he has an option to coach for as long as he wants."

All eyes were on Marino that season. Would the soon-to-be thirty-three-year-old quarterback be able to come back? "It's a whole different deal. I'm gonna turn it loose, because it's the real deal on Sunday," he said. "I'm making progress; it's like a weekly thing. I've just got to continue to work hard. Frankly, I think everybody is making too much out of this. What it really comes down to is me being in the game and doing the job. My leg is going to be the way my leg is going to be. It's going to get healthy gradually, and I've got to deal with it on a daily basis."

"I'm not going to get into that speculation," Shula answered, regarding questions of substituting for Marino. "I'm going to think positive about the ball game and about Dan. He's played some great ball games for us, and nobody wants it worse than he does. He's worked hard to get to this point. He'll be ready to go."

"No game was bigger for me personally than the 1994 opener against New England," Marino later recalled.

In that September 4 game, Marino left no doubt about his comeback. The visiting Patriots got a front-row seat. It was a Wild West shootout. Drew Bledsoe (32 of 51, 421 yards), back from his own injury, threw four touchdowns on the day. Marino (23 of 42, 473 yards) threw five. There were 997 yards of total offense between the two teams. After the Patriots went up, 35–32, on Bledsoe's 23-yard strike to Ray Crittenden in the fourth quarter, Marino threw a 35-yard scoring pass to Irving Fryar on 4th-and-5 with 3:19 left in the game for a 39–35 Dolphins victory.

Following the game, Patriots coach Bill Parcells said to Marino, "Not bad for a guy on one ankle."

From there, the Dolphins beat the Packers and the Jets, before losing in a shootout with the Minnesota Vikings, 38–35, at the Hubert H. Humphrey Metrodome. The Vikings had jumped out to a 28–0 lead before the Dolphins offense woke up in the second half, but it was not enough. Miami would arrive in Cincinnati with a 3–1 record to face the 0–4 Bengals. This was one of the most anticipated games of the 1994 NFL season for its historical significance.

Dave had been given a contract extension December. He had finished his first season 5–11 and went 3–12 in his second season," Mike Brown, Cincinnati's vice president and general manager, said. "He has done a good job under trying circumstances, and I'm confident he can shape the Bengals into a winner in the near future."

But things hadn't been that easy. There had been a lot of losing, as was expected for any rebuilding team. After winning their first two games in 1992, the Bengals hit the skids. They were up, 17–3, against Green Bay and had knocked Packers starting quarterback Don Majkowski out of the game. Backup Brett Favre came in and threw three fourth-quarter touchdowns to hand Cincinnati a shocking 24–23 loss.

"It's not the coach's fault we're not getting it done," despondent and battered Bengals quarterback Boomer Esiason said during the 1992 season. "He's doing everything he can think of. He's been through tough times in Dallas, and Miami, too. And I believe he can turn this team around." But Esiason soon lost faith.

"The first four games of that season I'll never forget, man. I mean, I was calling all the plays, all the formations, all the personnel groups. I was doing it all from the field. I was literally calling the entire offense. I remember we lost a home game to Minnesota (42–7), and I was mentally shot four games into the season." Esiason asked to be traded at the end of the season. He got his wish. He went to the Jets in 1993.

In 1994, the Shulas were the first father-son coaching matchup in the history of any of the major American professional sports. "I'm looking forward to it," Dave said. "It'll be a great challenge. They're a fine team and certainly well coached."

Dave admitted to the press that he'd been talking more with his father in recent days leading up to the game. "It seems we're talking less and less about the specifics of team strategies and personnel and more about how we're going to handle all the friends and family coming to the game," he said.

The game was not only nationally televised by TNT, but the Shulas had between 60 and 70 family members and friends at Riverfront Stadium for the October 2 game.

"I'm very much looking forward to it," said Dave. "It'd sure as hell be easier going into the game 4–0 or 3–1 or 2–2, but this is where we are, and we have to grin and bear it. They all said they were pulling for the Bengals this week," David said. "But they're sitting in seats I've given to them, so they better be."

"This is all team. You can't ever think about anything individually," said Don. "My responsibility is this football team, and Dave's responsibility is his football team. He does the best job he can, and I try to do the best job I can."

Dave said, "I'd rather the attention be focused on the players. The most tangible good thing to come from all this is that we know it's going to make some money for a very good cause." For the game, the Don Shula Foundation for breast cancer research sold more than 100 commemorative "Shula vs. Shula" autographed footballs that were sold for $500 each.

About an hour-and-a-half before the 8 p.m. kickoff, father and son shared a warm embrace that was recorded before a bank of television cameras and a mob of photographers. They then parted and went their separate ways. This was a difficult situation for both men. Don Shula admitted that when the national anthem ended, he looked across at the other sideline toward his son, and his thoughts turned to winning.

The Bengals drew first blood with a 51-yard touchdown pass from David Klingler to Darnay Scott for a 7–0 lead. It was the only thing Dave would be able to smile about the rest of the game. The Dolphins came back with 23 unanswered points. Marino threw for 204 yards and two touchdowns with no interceptions. Klingler was intercepted three times, fumbled once, and the Bengals totaled five drive-killing turnovers in the second half.

"You can't spot the Miami Dolphins five turnovers and expect to win the game," David Shula said. "That was the difference."

"We were trying to get ourselves turned around, get a win," said Bengals cornerback Mike Brim. "But in the back of your mind you know it's important for Dave. We needed the victory as much for him as for ourselves."

"I'm glad our football team won," Don Shula said. "I'm sorry for Dave and the fact that they didn't do as well as they're capable of doing. Those five takeaways really hurt their team. But I didn't feel sorry for Dave when they went up, 7–0."

"Once the game began, there was no thought that Dad was the opposing coach," said Dave. "There were too many other things to think about."

"I told [David] how much I thought of him after the game," said Don. "I know how hard he has worked. This is tough when you are on the losing end. I've been there. But anytime you're involved in something significant like this and you look across the field and it's your son coaching against you in the NFL, you have to be proud."

The Dolphins were 7–4 and were coming off consecutive losses to the Bears and Steelers when they faced the 6–5 Jets for a second time that season on November 27 at the Meadowlands . "It's the Jets, you know," said Dolphins defensive end Jeff Cross before the game. "The hype and hoopla is one thing, but it's a division game—that's what makes it special to me. And they're a hot team right now."

By the middle of the third quarter, the Jets had built up a 24–6 lead and seemingly were in control of the game. "I remember being so up for that Miami game because it was so important to us. I can remember practice that week; it was unbelievable. The meetings were great. We put a lot of effort into that game. It was a huge game. It was for first place in the division," recalled Jets quarterback Boomer Esiason.

But then Marino and the Dolphins stormed back.

"All of a sudden, Dan got hot. Things started clicking," remembered Miami cornerback Troy Vincent. "As Coach Shula used to say, 'Hey, don't get in the man's way, let him throw the ball.' I remember [linebacker] Bryan Cox going up and down the sideline, going nuts, saying, 'Hey, Danny's hot, we gotta get him the ball back.' Before you knew it, we were back in the game."

Marino threw two touchdown passes to bring Miami to within 24–21. Then, with time running out in the game, Marino drove his team down the field again. As they neared the line of scrimmage on the Jets 8-yard line, Marino pumped his arm up and down, signaling to his team he would spike the ball to stop the clock.

"We always referred to that as Bernie's play. He came up with it," said Mike Westhoff, Dolphins special teams coach, referring to Dolphins backup quarterback Bernie Kosar.

"Bernie's play? Who told you that, Bernie?" chuckled Shula. "It was a play we practiced during the week."

"If you watch the Jets-Browns [playoff] game in 1986, you'll see the first two times the clock play was run. With about a minute to go [in regulation], on the 2- or 3-yard line, I used the clock play. Webster Slaughter was open, and I underthrew him," recalled Kosar. "Everywhere I went, we practiced that play, whether it was the Browns, the Cowboys, or the Dolphins. It took eight years for the stars to be aligned for that situation to come up again."

"We worked on it on a weekly basis. Watching film, we saw some of their guys weren't really doing a whole lot when they knew the ball was going to be spiked, so we talked about this could be the week we do this," said center Jeff Dellenbach.

"I was on the headphones to Dan," said Kosar. "We had it called even before he got inside the 20-yard line. Don Shula, [offensive coordinator] Gary Stevens, Dan Marino . . . we were in it together. Whether I called it or not, it didn't matter. We were so ingrained that we knew what we were going to do. Aaron Glenn was a phenomenal rookie cornerback, and he went on to have an excellent career, but we had Mark Ingram and Dan Marino. We decided to pick on the rookie."

"Bernie tried that bullshit against us when he was with the Cleveland Browns and I was in Cincinnati," Esiason recalled. Marino screamed for everyone to get set, flailing his arm up and down. Then he looked over the field quickly and put his hands under center.

"It seems like that play was in slow motion, in my view, from beginning to end. The receiver was lining up, and I'm looking at Marino's face," said Glenn. "When I finally caught on, the ball already was snapped. It was one of those plays where . . . you know sometimes in your life when you have a feeling that something is about to happen and you just react? I had that feeling, but my reaction wasn't quick enough."

"That play was ahead of its time. To run that shit at that time, no one did that," said Jets linebacker Marvin Jones. "I was thinking it was some type of illegal play. We were out of sync. After he threw it and Ingram caught it, I was like, 'What the hell just happened?' I guess he had some secret signal with the receiver."

"You know what the Jets are thinking?" said Paul Maguire on the NBC telecast. "He's gonna take the ball and throw it into the ground. . . . They all stopped. If you take a look at it, the offensive linemen, all they did was stand up. And Marino says to Ingram, that's a communication thing they have. I mean, this is a beautiful play. They catch the Jets napping." The easy 8-yard touchdown pass floated into the arms of Mark Ingram. The stadium had gone quiet for a few seconds, the fans not sure of what they had just witnessed. Then the Dolphins sideline and the fans erupted. The Dolphins had won, 28–24, and strengthened their hold on first place in the AFC East.

In the second week of December, the sixty-four-year-old Shula ruptured his Achilles tendon, and he had to miss practice for an outpatient surgery to repair it. But he was on the sidelines for the next game against the Kansas City Chiefs, a 45–28 victory. Pictures showed up across the nation with Shula on a golf cart with his leg up. The Dolphins finished with a 10–6 record, wrapping up the AFC East crown with a 27–20 victory over the Detroit Lions in their final game of the season on Christmas night. It was the 11th and final AFC East title the team would win under Shula.

The Dolphins opened the playoffs at Joe Robbie Stadium on New Year's Eve against the Kansas City Chiefs, whom they had beaten in Miami three weeks earlier. Kansas City featured veterans Marcus Allen and Joe Montana on offense and a strong, big-play defense. The two teams traded body blows all through the first half, which ended 17–17. Marino gave Miami the lead for good when he connected with Irving Fryar on a 7-yard TD pass in the third quarter, and Pete Stoyanovich added a 40-yard field goal as Miami advanced with a 27–17 victory. Kansas City had outgained Miami 414 yards to 381, but two Chiefs turnovers proved to be the difference.

The Dolphins' divisional round opponent was the San Diego Chargers at Jack Murphy Stadium in San Diego on January 8, 1995. Miami jumped out to a 21–6 lead in the first half as Marino threw three touchdown passes, the first two to Keith Jackson and the third to Mike Williams. However, the second half was all San Diego. The Chargers picked up a safety by tackling Dolphins running back Bennie Parmalee in the end zone, then Natrone Means ran 24 yards for a touchdown to make it 21–15.

It was a game full of strange plays and controversial calls. Replays showed Means had stepped out of bounds before scoring a touchdown. The referees upheld the play. The Chargers were denied a touchdown when a 37-yard pass from Stan Humphries to Shawn Jefferson was ruled out of bounds. Replays showed it was a touchdown.

Marino completed a 20-yard pass to Jackson in the fourth quarter. Inexplicably, Jackson lateraled the ball as he fell down. However, no Dolphin player was anywhere near him. San Diego defensive back Darren Carrington recovered what appeared to be a fumble. Wrote Steve Springer in the *Los Angeles Times,* "After consultation, officials ruled that it was an illegal forward pass, drawing a five-yard penalty and loss of down, but not loss of possession. Referee Johnny Grier said he had never seen a call like that made on anyone other than a quarterback."

With 35 seconds left, Mark Seay caught an 8-yard TD pass from Humphries to give San Diego a 22–21 lead. Marino then drove the Dolphins into Charger territory, and with six seconds left, Pete Stoyanovich attempted a 48-yard field goal. That year, he had made 9 of 12 tries from 40 or more yards that season.

"I stretched my arms out to get [the snap], and I got the ball down as fast as I could," said holder John Kidd of the high snap. "We saw it going to the right and looked at each other and there wasn't anything to say. The season was over." And with it, any chance of playing in the Super Bowl, which would be played at Joe Robbie Stadium that year.

"I looked to the crowd, not even at the kick," said Chargers coach Bobby Ross. "They always tell you in that situation what you need to know. The photographers near our sideline were saying, 'Oh, he's got plenty of leg. That's easy for him. He's going to make it.' I said, 'You guys just don't believe. We do.' God was looking out for us. You know that that kicker could line up nine more times and make that kick nine times in a row."

"I saw the kick go wide," said Chargers safety Stanley Richard. "Then I sprinted to the far end zone and saluted the fans. Then I ran behind our bench and jumped up and down with the guys. Then I sprinted to the other end zone. Then I ran back onto the field. I couldn't stop."

"That's about as tough a loss as I've ever been around. It's a bitter disappointment. The bottom line is we couldn't stop their running and we couldn't run. It looked like the snap was high. When Stoyanovich hit it, it didn't have anything behind it," said Shula.

"It was a long third quarter," said Dolphins cornerback Troy Vincent. "They came out in the second half and played like champions. They kept the ball away from our offense. I was very surprised they ran so well because we basically had an eight-man line out there. They played a better game in the second half."

A day later, Shula spoke out regarding instant replay. "There were some missed calls out there that really affected the outcome of the ball game," said Shula. Ross echoed those sentiments. By then, Shula was cochairman of the National Football League's competition committee. He was always in favor of instant replay and never wavered in the need for it. "My opinion hasn't changed, and I know the negatives. It's not a perfect system. You're still dealing with the human element."

"It was a big, big disappointment, to be up, 21–6, at halftime and not score another point in the second half," Huizenga said. "We didn't deserve to win. Now, we just have to put on our happy face. In a split second, it was gone." Huizenga was now the American sports world's only three-team owner. Besides the Dolphins, he also owned the Florida Marlins baseball team and the Florida Panthers of the NHL.

"We have an opportunity the next couple of years, and we have to build on what we have now. I'll be 34 in September and I feel pretty good about my throwing ability. My arm last year felt better as the year went on," said Marino. "As far as my arm is concerned, I feel like I can throw the ball for a long time. It's the rest of my body I have to keep in shape. I'd love to play as long as I possibly can, as long as I can be effective and help the team win and be consistent on a weekly basis."

CHAPTER 11

Retirement

In the offseason, Wayne Huizenga shelled out more than $18 million in signing bonuses. The idea was to load up the team and make a big run at the Super Bowl. The team had 19 first-round draft picks on their roster. Expectations were high. A Super Bowl appearance was expected by Huizenga, league insiders, and NFL experts. Shula had two seasons left on his contract. Shula told the press in preseason, "I like this team. I like it a lot," adding, "I like our chances."

"Shula took an already good Dolphin team and made it better during an offseason of wheeling and dealing. He lavished a six-year, $12 million contract on free-agent tight end Eric Green, traded for Chicago Bear defensive end Trace Armstrong and Green Bay Packer cornerback Terrell Buckley, and signed free-agent wideouts Gary Clark and Randal Hill," wrote Johnette Howard in *Sports Illustrated* that July.

Nationally syndicated sports columnist Mike Lupica sat in Shula's office before that season began. "Shula joked about his golf game. He did not look like his 65 years or sound that way or even move that way in a golf shirt and shorts. He looked as if he had plenty of years left, plenty of time. Not just one year, one season. There was no way to know that this was the beginning of a season gone wrong. . . . In his office that day, I asked Shula what I thought was an innocent question, 'Even after everything you've done and everything you've won, do you ever feel insecure about your own coaching?'"

"I'm not sure I understand your meaning," Shula said sharply. "Do you feel anxiety?"

"Golfers talk about how they feel as if they can hit the ball as well as they ever did, but their nerves aren't the same," Lupica tried to explain.

"I never feel those insecurities," said Shula.

"And that was that. It was as if the morning left the room," recalled Lupica.

In August, Dolphins running back Irving Spikes had been arrested for assault and battery charges for allegedly beating his wife, Stacy, and was released on $5,000 bail.

Shula immediately placed the reserve running back on season-long probation. "While I realize that Irving is entitled to his day in court to determine the validity of these charges, right now there is no question that it's been an embarrassment to our football team, and as a result I am placing him on probation for conduct detrimental to the football team," said an angry Shula. "Hopefully it will send a message and hopefully he will get his act straightened out."

The year started off with a bang. The Dolphins thrashed the upstart, tough-talking Jets, 52–14. They won their next two against New England and Pittsburgh, before having a bye week. Then came another matchup with the Bengals in Cincinnati on October 1. This time, the Bengals took the fight to the Dolphins.

"Any son that has played some one-on-one in the driveway with his father knows the feeling. Just when you think you've got the old man beat, he pulls one more trick out of the bag," reported UPI. The Bengals had just gone up, 23–19, when Jeff Blake threw a 10-yard touchdown to Carl Pickens with 3:39 remaining in the game.

Marino then drove the Dolphins 91 yards, tossing a 16-yard touchdown pass to O. J. McDuffie with 1:03 remaining in the game, giving them a 26–23 win over the Bengals. Marino completed 33 of 48 passes for 450 yards and two touchdowns. "It was a tough loss for Dave," Shula said. "About as tough as you can get . . . when you seemingly have a game won and then lose it at the end."

The Dolphins were now 4–0 and looked like world beaters. But by the middle of October, Marino was sidelined with a knee injury, and Bernie Kosar took over. By Week 14, the Dolphins were 6–6.

Discontent began to fester. Bryan Cox, the vocal and sometimes outrageous leader of the defense, pointed to an overtime loss at Indianapolis in which Marino was injured as the turning point in the season. In that game, Marino broke Fran Tarkenton's NFL record for career completions, and the Dolphins were up by 21 points at the half. The Colts tied the game and then won it in overtime. Cox was upset by his teammates' lack of passion, and the club seemingly drifting.

"I'm one that believes it had a devastating effect on us. I think after we lost that game, we walked around in a daze for a couple of weeks and we lost two more games. It was the start of our debacle, but none of that is really important anymore. We need to start playing football the way we're capable of playing," said Cox. Cox's outburst was seen as traitorous, but the Miami fans were getting restless too, especially after an embarrassing 44–20 loss to the San Francisco 49ers on *Monday Night Football*. There were no recent championship banners. There were too many losses. The fans were siding with Cox. Amid a 2–5 slump, Shula was feeling the pressure.

"Everybody is dejected, no question, but we have to get that out of our mind and get on with the preparation for the Colts," said Shula about the upcoming November 26 rematch with the Colts, a 36–28 loss. "We just have to realize that if we don't hang together, there's nothing to keep us together. That's pretty much the things I stressed in a meeting with the team. We have to understand that the criticism is going to be there." In that loss, Marino threw four touchdown passes, giving him 346 for his career, breaking Tarkenton's league record.

In the Monday night game when they were trounced by the 49ers, Cox was seen storming the sidelines. Cox claimed he was "frustrated." "We just haven't played. With all the expectations that we put on this team and then you don't play, you're in for a butt kicking every week," said Cox. "There has been too much talk. It's time for some doing. Each guy has to look at the situation hard and decide whether they want to come out fighting or give up."

In reference to Cox's outburst, Shula responded, "He was upset about the way everybody was playing in general. Everybody who knows Bryan knows he has a short fuse." While Cox was controversial, the one thing everyone could agree on was that he was passionate about winning, and backing up with good play. It was around this time that local columnists started asking if now wasn't the right time for Shula to retire. And in all fairness to Cox, while he caused controversy, he never blamed Shula, only those of his fellow players who were not putting their hearts into it. But his passion was feeding the discontented fans.

In one of the most hurtful and wincing moments of his career, as Shula walked off the field after the San Francisco debacle, the fans were chanting lustily, "Jimmy! Jimmy! Jimmy!"

The local columnists agreed. "Assuming Jimmy Johnson was watching San Francisco stir-fry the Miami Dolphins on Monday night, I envision him hoisting a rum runner or two down in the Florida Keys, saying goodbye to his envious life of leisure. Jimmy Johnson should return to coaching in the NFL next season. Miami appears the perfect fit," wrote George Diaz in the *Sun Sentinel*. "Perhaps this is heresy in a city whose coach is so beloved that an expressway is named in his honor. Don Shula deservedly has established himself as an icon in South Florida and throughout the NFL. Shula stands alone as the greatest football coach in NFL history, but his footing is treacherous, marked by the failures of an underachieving team that plays without a pulse."

"Shula is not dead yet. He has survived longer than any NFL coach. But there is blood in the water now, for the first time, and Jimmy Johnson circles, just off-shore, at his home in the Florida Keys," wrote Larry Dorman in the *New York Times*. What had made this whole scenario even worse was that Johnson had been part of the group that ignominiously had jettisoned fellow NFL icon Tom Landry a decade before in Dallas.

Like Shula, Landry had won two Super Bowls and lost three. Both had assistant coaches who won college championships (Howard Schnellenberger at Miami; Gene Stallings at Alabama). Each had been fired by a flamboyant owner—Shula by Rosenbloom (who, if he did not fire him, surely pushed him out) and Landry by Jerry Jones. Both would see their former team win a Super Bowl—the Colts in 1970 and the Cowboys in 1992 and 1993. The end for both would be disrespectful, hard to swallow, and grotesquely public. Both would be replaced by the same man—Jimmy Johnson.

Shula had always been horrified by how Landry was summarily dismissed by the organization he had helped create, and the new owner, Jerry Jones, who had taken it over. Now, here was the same man, cheerily denouncing the Dolphins on television broadcasts while stating publicly that he was only an observer. Johnson had written in his weekly local Florida newspaper column during that season about the Dolphins, "The 6–5 Miami Dolphins are a mystery to everyone. They have 19 first-round draft picks and, it is widely acknowledged, as much individual talent as any team. Perhaps that is the key. They have a group of individuals. They don't have a team."

In the old days, a banner used to hang, almost every home game on a Sunday, that read, SHULA IS GOD. That had been long gone. During a home game against the Atlanta Falcons, a plane had circled overhead, with a banner trailing, reading, MOVE OVER ROVER, AND LET JIMMY TAKE OVER.

There was also another alarming statistic. Despite having won 11 AFC East titles in 25 years, what was more glaring was the failure of his teams in the late part of the season. Since 1988, his teams had a record of 33–36 in games played in November and December up to that point.

According to reader polls in the *Miami Herald*, *Sun Sentinel*, and *Palm Beach Post*, Shula's popularity was nonexistent. In the meanwhile, fans fully endorsed for Jimmy Johnson to succeed Shula. The *Sun Sentinel* had even run the headline "Don Voyage," stating that 69 percent of their respondents thought Shula should be fired immediately. The *Miami Herald* stated their polls revealed an 80 percent response who agreed.

Diaz also wrote, "You feel for Marino. You feel for Cox, who plays with the same intensity regardless of the score or circumstances. His gutless teammates should take notice."

By mid-December, Michael Silver wrote in *Sports Illustrated*, "Shula bemoaned his team's performance in recent weeks even as he tried to soften the impact of the public outbursts by some of his players, most notably that of linebacker Bryan Cox, the defensive captain. Shula did his best to laugh off the barrage of criticism he has been facing, including three highly unscientific newspaper polls in which roughly 80% of the respondents urged his firing."

"I can't let anything that Jimmy does or doesn't do influence any decisions that I make regarding my career. I've worked long and hard to get to where I am, and I'm going to continue to do the things that have got me here and to make decisions based on how I feel. Right now I feel about as low as you can feel. But my responsibility is leadership, and the minute I get negative, that's going to have an influence on the team. So I have to make sure that I don't let all of the turmoil drag me down," responded Shula to the criticism. "It does hurt, especially the viciousness and the cruelty that enter into any criticism. These are unpleasant times."

"Shula's popularity suffers as Johnson's legend continues to grow. It was Johnson who guided the University of Miami to the second of its four national championships before departing to rebuild the Cowboys. As Shula walks the Dolphin sidelines, absorbing the boos, Johnson operates from the comfort of the Fox-TV studio, where he is free to launch broadsides at Shula and any other coach whose team is stumbling," wrote Silver.

"The fans would like to see somebody who brings a little more fire," said former Dolphins utility man Jim Jensen. "People are saying that Shula is not motivating his players, that it's time to get someone who can do that."

"There are too many 'me' guys on that team," said former Dolphins guard Harry Galbreath.

"People want to point fingers, especially when expectations are so high," said Troy Vincent. "When you lose, the top just flies off the jar." Vincent went so far as to insinuate that there was an anti-Shula faction in the locker room. There was also a feeling that the coaches played favorites with the players. "The whole atmosphere is negative," said a recent unnamed free agent. "The coaches are always on your ass, unless you're one of the chosen ones."

"He used to get right in your face if you screwed up," recalled former Dolphin Kim Bokamper. "And now players get in his face? And he's patting guys on the butt when they mess up?"

"This year I kind of felt that he didn't have the control he once had," Duhe said. "Maybe today's player doesn't respect him. When he would correct me, I would say, 'Yessir.' Today's guys just snap right back at him."

Other former coaches also wondered out loud. Ron Meyer, of the infamous "Snowplow Game" in New England, opined that "Shula has lost control of his team." Even old friend Mike Ditka said the Dolphins were "a team without heart" and added, "ultimately, the head coach has to take the responsibility."

Shula had grown so frustrated, Keith Sims said, that the coach told his charges toward the end of the year, "I'm just tired of kissing your butts."

"If the Dolphins aren't Don Shula's fault," wrote Mike Lupica, "I sure would like to know who does get the blame in Miami."

What made things worse for Shula was that Pat Riley, late of the Los Angeles Lakers and the New York Knicks, was now coaching and running the National Basketball Association's Miami Heat. The Heat was a hot team. Riley's pizzazz and charisma made it even more difficult on Shula. The Heat featured a new advertising campaign that read, "New Coach, New Team, New Attitude." The unofficial team song was from the classic television show *The Jeffersons* with the players singing, "Well, we're movin' on up . . ." This contrast made the locals even more hungry for change in the Dolphins organization.

"Right about now, though, the folks in Miami want to send Shula to his hotel/golf course/mini-mall/steak house complex north of the city in permanent retirement as punishment for the Dolphins' disappointing season. And they want to kiss Riley's ring finger, in hopes that his championship history will somehow rub off," reported Jennifer Frey in the *Washington Post*.

They beat the Atlanta Falcons on December 3, which provided some relief to Shula, who said that "without a doubt the toughest week I've spent in my coaching career. . . . The people who say this team is out of control, they're not around here, they don't know. We had a meeting Monday that was very positive, that couldn't have been more positive. I can't control the criticism. It's something you certainly don't appreciate, but by the same token, everybody is entitled to their opinion. I just signed a two-year extension, so I've got this year and next year. What I've done all through my career at the end of that time I take a look at where I am and what I want to do and make decisions that are thought out, not emotional.

"You try to shut the criticism out," Shula said, "but it's pretty hard to do. You see people on the street, friends, people that you know are in your corner, and they come and tell you how bad they feel, and that's not the kind of conversation you want. I don't want anyone to feel bad for me."

They triumphed over the Kansas City Chiefs the next week and things seemed headed in the right direction, but then Miami then lost a close game in Buffalo. In the season's final week, they beat the Rams in St. Louis, 41–22, to qualify for the playoffs with a 9–7 record (with the help of the Denver Broncos, who defeated the Oakland Raiders).

On December 30, the Buffalo Bills hosted the Miami Dolphins in the wild-card round.

"We've struggled all year, but this gives us a chance to make up for it and maybe do something special," Marino said. "We felt pretty good about the way we played. And just the experience of being up there in a hostile atmosphere is something we can take away from that game."

"It's kind of chilling to be a player in that stadium," said Dolphins cornerback J. B. Brown "Some of the stuff that they say to us, they really mean it. It's not just competitive fire, they really mean it. They want to bury us every time we're up there."

"I think it's going to be real difficult to take this crowd out of the game early or late. They're a smart crowd, too. They yell when we have the ball and they're quiet when Buffalo has it, so Jim Kelly can make all of his checks at the line of scrimmage," added Marino. "I'm more concerned with this team and how we've been doing, the game at hand," Marino said. When asked about Shula's situation, Marino said, shrugging, "I don't know about the past or the future—I'm not worried about that. I'm worried about what I can do, what the team can do."

"You people fail to realize Marv's done that against everyone else, and its not only against my team. When you look at his record—four Super Bowls in a row—the thing that's kept him from getting the recognition is that he hasn't won Super Bowls. But he's got more wins over that period of time than anyone else," Shula said about Bills coach Marv Levy. "They know us; we know them. They pretty much dominated us in recent years. We know it will be tough—the home crowd, the weather. But the things that happened in the past don't affect this game."

Bryan Cox would require extra security at and during the game. More than two dozen Erie County police in riot gear patrolled the areas behind the Dolphins bench and around the stadium. "Cox had another incident late in a 23–20 Dolphins loss, on Dec. 17, 1995, a game that was Shula's final regular-season defeat. Cox and Bills fullback Carwell Gardner were ejected for fighting and nearly came to blows again in the tunnel between the locker rooms. Cox, booed lustily by fans, responded by spitting on the field in the direction of the fans five times. The league hit Cox with a $17,500 fine—the NFL's largest that season," wrote Barry Jackson in the *Miami Herald*.

The playoff game was not much of a contest. The Bills put up 24 unanswered points in the first half and another 13 in the second half and then withstood a Marino barrage. Marino was 33-for-64, for 422 yards, two touchdowns, and three interceptions. The Bills rushed for a playoff-record 341 yards, including 158 by Thurman Thomas. The final score of 37–22 is as close as the Dolphins ever got.

"They were never in their opening playoff game against the Bills," wrote Lupica. "There were times when Shula's Dolphins looked as overmatched trying to stop the Bills. . . . It was a collapse to go with the collapse that had begun after 4–0. And if you didn't blame Shula for this, then who did you blame? He picked these players, he coached them. It is Shula who has not built a Super Bowl defense in too many years, or a Super Bowl running game. Or a Super Bowl champion. There have been very few coaching or managing immortals who have ever gone the two decades Shula has now gone without a title. It is on his record along with the most pro football wins of anybody in history."

"As long as [defensive coordinator Tom] Olivadotti has been there," Thomas said, "when you do things to hurt him, he really doesn't make a lot of changes. When we saw what defense he was in, we thought this could be a good day for rushing the football."

"The disappointment was in Don Shula's jaw. Instead of being thrust up and out as if it were on Mount Rushmore, his jaw just hung there, above his white turtleneck with the Dolphins logo and below his silver hair," wrote Dave Anderson in the *New York Times*.

"[He] looked 65 now, sounded 65. Every day of it. The other day in Buffalo, he finally looked like an old man. Now comes the news that Shula himself has decided it is time to go. It is time," wrote Lupica. "He deserved better than he got this season, from the newspapers and their polls and all the shrieking people on talk radio calling for his head. If there is no grace for Shula as he moves off the stage, you wonder who will ever earn that kind of grace in sports. . . . The Dolphins had a bad few months, and all of a sudden fans who had known two losing seasons in 26 under Shula considered themselves long-suffering. They came across as the worst and whiniest front-runners anywhere."

"I know coach Shula was frustrated," said former defensive back Dick Anderson. "Frustrated by the performance of the players and harassed by the talk shows and the media. It was really sad."

"This is the one we're going to have to remember and think about. In a game that meant so much, not challenging, not competing, that's what's so disappointing," said Shula. "We worked hard to get here. We'd beaten four or five teams that were in the playoffs." During the course of the season, Miami had beaten the Bills, the Chiefs, the Steelers, the Chargers, and the Falcons, all of whom were in the playoffs.

There were few true believers in Shula left by this point, but the most vocal was Dave Anderson, who opined, "It's as if Shula's career 347–172–6 record doesn't count anymore. As if somebody else won all those games. As if somebody else won those back-to-back Super Bowls nearly a quarter of a century ago." Anderson recited Shula's many amazing moments, such as getting to a Super Bowl with quarterback David Woodley, or who else would have brought Marino along so brilliantly? "For all of yesterday's disappointment, Don Shula deserves to coach as long as he wants to. Years ago the snipers thought pro football had passed George Halas by, but he was 68 when he coached the Bears to the 1963 N.F.L. title. The snipers thought pro football had passed Paul Brown by, but he was the 70-year-old brain behind the 1988 Bengals that went to Super Bowl XXIII," wrote Anderson.

Shula was halfway out the door at this point. Huizenga publicly said he would not fire Shula despite the current public outcry. For his own part, Shula said he would take time, as he always did, at the end of each season, to decide on his path. Early comments to the media showed his stubbornness: "Things haven't worked out the way I thought they would when I signed that contract, but that doesn't change my responsibilities. My responsibilities are to honor this contract and hopefully get this team back on top.

"The important thing to me is how you're judged by your peers, and how you're judged by people who know what it takes to coach the football team. If I felt I wasn't respected in those areas, then I really would look hard at what I'm doing," said Shula. "The thing that's happened is the agents have gotten in many cases in between the player and coach relationship," he said. "It used to be a player-coach relationship. Now it's a player-agent-coach relationship. That tends to keep you from having the close relationships that you had in the early years."

"When you play a game like that, you can't feel too good about anything," Shula said. "It makes us realize we've made a lot of mistakes in our assessment of certain personnel. Now we have to try to rectify those errors. In the past we've always tried to keep the guys here who've been productive players for us. Now we've got to go back and review all those decisions that we made."

After the playoff loss, Huizenga had had enough. Wholesale changes needed to be made. Shula refused to "surrender power after a season that scuffed his image," wrote Bill Plaschke in the *Los Angeles Times*. "According to Dolphin sources, Shula was ordered by owner Wayne Huizenga in a meeting Wednesday to make widespread changes in his coaching and personnel staffs. In response, Shula told Huizenga he would not make others scapegoats for a season during which their collection of stars finished 9–7, leading to a first-round playoff humiliation in Buffalo. When Huizenga would not back down on his demands, Shula decided to retire."

"What happened just goes to show you, it was always Don's team," said former defensive end Vern Den Herder. "It doesn't surprise me that he wouldn't fire his staff if he was ordered to do it. This was his team, and no one else's."

"I don't think Don was ready for another change," said another former Dolphin, Fulton Walker. "I watched him, and I just don't think he could take it anymore."

"I think he had a staff that probably wasn't doing the job for him, but he has a lot of loyalty for people," said Jim Shula, Don's brother, a Chicago-area businessman. "He expects the same thing in return."

Shula realized it would be difficult to make the necessary coaching changes with only a one-year deal. Even if he were to replace Olividatti, what coach would leave a good job to join a staff for only one year? And what players would join a team with a legendary coach who had only one year to go? If he stayed, he was a lame duck. And there was no question he had used up a fair amount of Huizenga's goodwill with their $18 million gamble.

On January 4, 1996, Shula's sixty-sixth birthday, rumors began to fly. By now, Bill Clinton was president of the United States. Artists like Coolio, TLC, and Boyz II Men were topping the charts; *ER*, *Seinfeld*, and *Friends* were TV's hottest shows; Barings Bank, one of the largest in the world, had collapsed; and the *New York Times* and the *Washington Post* both published the Unibomber's manifesto, an essay opposing industrialization by the domestic terrorist who had mailed or planted sixteen packages of bombs that had killed three people and injured 23 over an 18-year period . He would be arrested in April and identified as Ted Kaczynski, a former mathematician who had become a recluse living in a Montana cabin. The world had changed significantly since Shula had begun his pro career. This was not lost on his critics. He told a local television station late in the evening that "It was a tough decision, one I haven't had to make in 33 years."

"This is one of the saddest days this area has had in its history," said Jimmy Cefalo, former wide receiver and cohost of Shula's weekly television show. "In his 26 years here, you never had a question where his heart and head were. You might disagree with his philosophy, but you would never, ever disagree with the character of the man."

Bryan Cox was among the first to speak out, saying, "South Florida doesn't know what they're going to miss yet. Next year at this time they'll be talking about 'We want Shula back.'"

"Passion was not Shula's problem. Loyalty was. Shula refused to replace Tom Olivadotti as defensive coordinator long after it became apparent that the Dolphins defense could not stop opposing offenses in crucial games. This was not just a problem this season but one that has festered for several seasons," wrote Anderson." There were many pundits who agreed.

Shula spoke at his press conference:

> *In talking to Wayne about this, he said, "Well, if that's the case, why don't we extend your contract?" And when he mentioned this, he took me back some. Because that was the furthest thing from my mind. And at that time I wasn't prepared to make any further commitment. That was the last thing I wanted to do to make a further commitment. In being at this stage of my life.*
>
> *I'd being lying to you if I didn't say it's going to be gut-wrenching when that ball is kicked off in September because this is going to be the first time in 43 years that I haven't been on the sideline in the National Football League. I can tell you I'm at peace with myself. And I am looking forward to spending time with my lovely wife, Mary Anne, and getting to know my kids, and my grandkids.*

A number of Shula's former players attended the press conference. Manny Fernandez, Bob Griese, Earl Morrall, Dick Anderson, Jim Kiick, Jim Mandich, Joe Rose,

John Offerdahl, Kim Bokamper, Dan Marino, Irving Fryar, Keith Byars, and Bernie Kosar were all there.

"You can see the decline," Bokamper said. "It's time for the guy to go. There's no disrespect in that for Don Shula. He's been a great coach over a long period."

"I'm putting up a noble front," Shula said. "This week has been the most difficult—soul-searching, gut-wrenching, all those things." He then turned to wife Mary Anne, adding, "When the ball is kicked off, I don't know where I'll be next September, but you better be careful."

"I'm a little sad, a little happy right now," said Fernandez. "I'm sad that he was driven out by all the criticism, a lot of it totally uncalled for. I'm saying a lot of the criticism he took on the radio was solicited, which is a shoddy way to operate. But I'm happy for him that it's over. He doesn't have to put up with all this anymore."

"It's an end of an era," said son Dave, whose Bengals lost their two head-to-head games against Dad's Dolphins. "I suppose if I had one regret, it's that I'm not going to get an opportunity to finally notch a win against him. Now I'll have to take our battles onto the golf course and to the tennis courts and try to get my game in shape so that he doesn't dominate me there."

"This week's proof of our cannibal nature is Don Shula," wrote Dave Kindred in *The Sporting News*. "He moved from single-bar face mask to Darth Vader visors on players who evolved from crew cuts to curls to shaved heads. He won with Hall of Famers, and he won with a quarterback who taped the plays to his wrist. He won smashing mouths and won airing it out. Always, he won by being a man on fire."

Huizenga was asked if Jimmy Johnson was being considered as the next coach. He answered, "I have no thoughts on Jimmy that are any different than anyone else out there. The next three, four, five weeks will be a busy time. I've never heard from Jimmy that he was interested in coming here. I've heard it from everyone else. I haven't talked to Jimmy. I've never talked to Jimmy about coming here. He obviously has to be one of the names on the list. When the time is right, we'll call him or he'll call us."

"His sly and unconscionable two-year campaign to unseat Don Shula has succeeded, and now the Miami Dolphins belong to Jimmy Johnson. . . . He is a calculating opportunist unburdened by guilt," wrote Philadelphia sports columnist Bill Lyon. "The coy Johnson has made himself so popular in South Florida and has so shrewdly ingratiated himself that Dolphins fans probably would have boycotted their team had Huizenga hired anyone else."

"It happened to Tom Landry at the end. They make mistakes they never made when they were on top, when they were real coaching giants instead of just legends hanging on," wrote Lupica. "Marino was supposed to go to more than one Super Bowl. Shula was supposed to take him there. He was one of the greats, and he knew how. He just forgot. It happens to the best of them. Sometimes the end of the line comes before the end of the contract. Only the lucky exit as heroes."

CHAPTER 12

Life After Football

"A day after he turned 66, Don Shula said he was starting the first day of the rest of his life. He said he would now have more time to get to know his children and grandchildren. It was a sad commentary on what it takes to be a successful coach," wrote Paul Attner in *The Sporting News.* The rumor mill started a few days after the victory laps ended. After a one-hour special on local television with Dolphin-turned-sportscaster Jimmy Cefalo, and a one-on-one interview with Larry King, Shula's name was attached to several possible opportunities.

First, he was mentioned in passing as a possible coach for a new Cleveland Browns team (Art Modell's team was moving to Baltimore, but the name Browns was staying in Cleveland). Then he was mentioned as a coach or front office man for the Baltimore Ravens. "Baltimore needs Don Shula almost as bad as Don Shula needs Baltimore," crowed Bill Plaschke in *The Sporting News.*

"I've liked Don Shula for 33 years; I'm enamored with the man," Modell said. "He came up here yesterday to have a drink with me and my wife. . . . We had an exchange of views on what he wants to do with his life. . . . I think he'd like to be involved with an NFL team in a major capacity. I'm going to follow it up. I don't know if he wants to coach again in the NFL. Yesterday he didn't seem to be going in that direction, but that could change tomorrow. That's all I can tell you."

"When Shula turned him down, Modell then asked him to be an integral part of the front office. Shula-to-Baltimore would have been an interesting fit: He played in Baltimore four years and coached there seven," wrote Gary Myers in the *New York Daily News.*

"I told [Modell] that after I made the decision to step aside, I wasn't interested in going back on the field," said Shula, who seriously considered the front office job offer. "That would have taken a morning, noon, and night commitment on my part. At this stage of my life, I didn't feel I wanted to do that."

Shula's name would continue to be bandied about over the next few years, each time an NFL coaching vacancy came up. Columnists in New York begged the Jets and Giants to at least reach out to the grand old coach. This happened in other NFL cities, as well. Shula had conversations with several of the networks, but no television job came about. At commissioner Paul Tagliabue's request, Shula remained involved with the NFL as chairman of a committee on officiating. He would not rule out a return to coaching, but for the interim, he dedicated himself to following the coaching careers of his sons Dave and Mike.

"No practice field . . . No locker room. Shula's office, in a quiet business area, is 20 minutes from the Dolphins' facility. And on a day he'd be running his team through practice, the NFL's winningest coach is talking with associates about: meat for his chain of steakhouses, a recent three-day trip to the Olympics, the 800-person invitation-only guest list for a $500,000 party Dolphins owner Wayne Huizenga is throwing in his honor Sept. 12," wrote Myers on the eve of the 1996 season. "Before long, Shula will be going through coaching withdrawal."

"To this point, I really haven't missed anything. I've been busy doing a lot of things," Shula said. "The one time that it felt like I should be doing something is when the draft rolled around and I wasn't, for the first time, involved in the decision making."

"When I feel it's really going to hit home will be the first Sunday in September," he said. "That will be the first time in 43 years that I haven't been involved: seven years as a player, three as an assistant, and 33 as a head coach. I think that's when the reality of it is going to sink in."

As the 1996 football season approached, good things were expected from Jimmy Johnson and his staff. Johnson's braggadocio was unmistakable. He jettisoned Bryan Cox, unwilling to tolerate anything that would sideline the team's focus. He gave the impression that things had been lax the previous year and made tough statements like "I only know our guys are on time for meetings and working hard now." He insisted his team would make the playoffs and win a playoff game.

Shula remained bitter, but classy in the face of such withering chiding. "I respect Wayne for making the best judgment that he can make for his investment," Shula said. "Obviously, when he made the decision to bring Jimmy in, and he certainly was the best available coach out there, I understood that Jimmy was going to want to do his own thing. He's won Super Bowls. He knows how he wants to get things done. In a similar situation, I would have wanted to do it my way. If they would have brought in a young coach, I would have certainly been more available."

Johnson's first Dolphins team started 3–0 but finished 8–8, fourth in the AFC East. In 1997, they finished 9–7 and lost a wild-card round game to the Patriots. In 1998, they went 10–6, finished second in the AFC East, and lost to the Broncos, 38–3, in the divisional round of the playoffs. In 1999, the Dolphins went 9–7, finished third in their division, but made the playoffs. They beat the Seahawks in the wild-card round and then lost to the Jacksonville Jaguars, 62–7. For all his huge talk, Johnson, while coach of the Dolphins, never won a division title, let alone an AFC Championship Game or a Super Bowl. In their last two postseason losses under Johnson, the team had been outscored, 100–10. He was 38–31 as Dolphins head coach. He resigned after that season. Shula admitted years later that it didn't bother him much that the Dolphins had not accomplished much during Johnson's reign.

Dave had struggled with the Bengals. The 1992 Bengals were a work in progress, finishing 5–11. Boomer Esiason became unhappy and asked to be traded and was sent to the Jets. The team regressed to 3–13 records each of the next two seasons. But, in 1995, Cincinnati improved to 7–9. With Larry Peccatiello as defensive coordinator and Bruce Coslet as offensive coordinator, the Bengals were picking up steam. And new quarterback Jeff Blake and wide receiver Carl Pickens went to the Pro Bowl. Things were finally looking up.

"I could have done a better job of holding people more accountable to earn more respect," Dave said years later. "I sit back and remember having a team leader meeting, I don't know if it was during the season or if it was in the offseason and I'm not going to get into the names of the people, but looking at those players that were in that meeting—and they were undisputedly the leaders of the team—this was after Boomer was gone and Anthony [Muñoz], and you look back at who was in that room, not one of them turned out to be leaders. And they've had some issues off the field since then. Once again, I was bringing those people in. There were some players, and again I won't get into names, but there were some players that we knew we had issues with and we held on to longer than we should've. I could have been, I should have been more forceful in saying look, in order to move the team forward we need to build with character and we didn't do that in certain decisions."

"I cannot blame David Shula for us going 3–13," defensive back Fulcher said. "I blame the players because we have to do a job. Coaches can only do so much." Still, he was not without his own moments. In 1994, his 0–7 Bengals were scheduled to host the surging Dallas Cowboys (6–1). It was Barry Switzer's first season coaching in Dallas after replacing Jimmy Johnson.

"The reference point I always used is Iowa State. I was always wary of these games when I was at Oklahoma," Switzer said at his weekly press conference five days before the game. "If we play our game, it should be no problem."

"It turned out to be a big problem. Despite facing a quarterback who was making his first NFL start (Jeff Blake), the Cowboys trailed 14–0. Dallas eventually escaped with a 23–20 win when rookie Chris Boniol booted a 38-yard field goal with 5:00 to play," wrote sportswriter Mike Baldwin in *The Oklahoman.*

"Take Iowa State and stick it up your ass!" Dave barked at Switzer after the game.

"We made some decisions on players that didn't quite work out," Shula said. "And then we didn't get, as a coaching staff, we didn't get the guys that we had to perform as well as they could've. And that adds up to losing games and losing close games and unfortunate things."

"They were still trying to recover from the David Klinger fiasco," Coslet said years later, referring to a series of bad first-round picks made by the Bengals organization. "I wasn't here for that, thank God. But we went through a lineup of quarterbacks that were less than NFL quality, let's put it that way. Until I recommended that I had this kid in New York as a backup, Jeff Blake. So we got him and he was our quarterback for two, three, or four years. He was serviceable. But I mean he wasn't going to take you to the promised land. He was a good player but not a Super Bowl-caliber player, let's put it that way."

On October 20, 1996, the 1–5 Bengals traveled to San Francisco. They took a 21–0 lead in the second quarter against a hobbled Steve Young and the 49ers, a perennial NFL power that had won the Super Bowl two years earlier. But they went scoreless the rest of the game and lost in the waning minutes, 28–21. Mike Brown had seen enough and replaced Shula with Coslet. Dave had established a 19–52 record with a winning percentage of .278 during his tenure with the Bengals. His father had been the coach who had won 50 games faster than any other coach in NFL history, Dave had lost 50 games faster than any coach in NFL history. At the time it was not the worst winning percentage in NFL history. That dubious honor belonged to Bert Bell, who later became NFL commissioner.

"He was a wonderful person," Brown said. "Honest to God, he had the youth and experience enough and energy. Yet it never happened. And it just was one thing after another. Some of it really wasn't his fault. Some of it probably was.

We couldn't solve the quarterback problem. We didn't have the quarterback we needed, and whatever we kept trying to do didn't make it better. Nobody deserved a better result. It just wasn't the way it ended up."

"You make a decision like this, it just evolves in your mind. I did think it had to be done for the benefit of our future here. Again, this is not a reflection on Dave, and the job he's done," Mike Brown told the press the day after the loss to San Francisco.

"I wish Bruce Coslet and the Bengals all the luck in the world," said Dave in front of the mikes. "I thank Mike for the patience he's shown through the years as we've struggled to put a winner on the field. The record is what I'm judged by. That obviously was not adequate."

Privately, he was devastated. "It was a real blow to my ego, and a tough time for my family," he said. "Getting fired is never easy."

"There was enough talent on this team to make a playoff run. Now it's up to Bengals President Mike Brown to make a run at a new head coach," wrote New York *Newsday* football columnist Bob Glauber.

The Bengals rallied under Coslet, finishing with a 7–2 run, to make the team's final record 8–8. "You think, 'What changed?' Well, you did," Dave laughed years later. "So it's hard not to think that you were a major cause of the problem, right?" The Bengals never won more than eight games over the next eight seasons, including coaching stints by Bruce Coslet, Dick LeBeau, and Marvin Lewis, who finally led them back to respectability.

"So it kind of evened out over a period of time where I didn't feel quite as bad. So, yeah, now, with 20 years perspective looking back on it, you realize that maybe it wasn't all me," said Dave.

In 1997, Dave and his wife and their three sons pulled up stakes in Cincinnati and moved south to Florida, settling in Cooper City. David Younts, one of the partners in the Shula Steak House restaurant, approached Dave.

"When I came down to talk to David about working here, I had just finished a book called *Raving Fans* by Ken Blanchard," Don said. Shula and Blanchard co-wrote Don Shula's book, *Everyone's a Coach,* which was published in 1996. "Well, David had that book displayed on his desk, and it turns out that everybody here is told to read Blanchard's books. We try to empower our employees and make sure they have a stake in this place; we want every customer to have a perfect dining experience and to leave a raving fan."

"I don't pretend to have any expertise with the food and beverage industry except as a consumer, but we have other people in the office who do," said the 38-year-old Shula. "What I think I bring to the table is my expertise in managing people for the last 15 years, and the ability to impart a culture for our company—the passion behind the numbers."

"At the time, it was the furthest thing from my mind," said Don, who still coaching the Dolphins at the time. "So the agreement we had going into this was that David wasn't going to tell me how to coach, and I wasn't going to tell him how to run a restaurant.

"David Younts has always run the restaurant business like a football coach running a football business, which is why he was so enthused about bringing in my son," said proud father Don. "Dave's joining the company was a natural fit. His presence is going to take a lot of pressure off David Younts, who really needed a right-hand man."

Don Shula had spent much more time working on the restaurants once he retired. He spent most of his time creating promotional concepts, or promoting the restaurants in person. Shula created special menus that were printed on footballs and created the famous "48-Ounce Club," a 5,000-member club for special customers. He also spent more time making personal appearances at each of the restaurants as well as promoting the restaurants with the media and press.

"One of the differences between the business I was in and this business is that it takes a lot longer to make things happen," Shula said. "There are a lot of layers you have to go through to get something done."

Many of Shula's restaurants are housed inside a hotel, an arrangement that helps the chain hit its target market of business travelers on expense accounts. Each location hires and pays their own help. Many of the high-end restaurants are licensed. Each location pays the corporation an up-front franchise fee, and a percentage of the gross revenue. In return, Shula's licenses the Shula name, all logos, associated memorabilia, operating procedures, recipes, food contracts (especially the beef), and a guaranteed number of appearances by the coach himself each year.

In 1997, the Shula's in Miami Lakes grossed revenue of $5 million. The restaurants grossed $4 million in Troy and Tampa, and the Cleveland location added another $3.5 million. In just seven months, Shula's On the Beach grossed another $5 million. The Tampa restaurant had been previously named J. Fitzgerald's. But after the makeover, revenues jumped tenfold in the same location. The Shula name now had the Midas touch. The company was having great success convincing partnerships with hotels.

"Traditionally, the hotel people don't want to be in the restaurant business," Dave said. "So for them to turn their food and beverage operations into a moneymaker is a real plus." With the coach retired from the NFL, and his son ensconced in the operation, Shula's Restaurants had become energized and pointed toward aggressive growth.

In October 1996, Shula was listed among the nominees for the Pro Football Hall of Fame. On January 27, 1997, he had just come from having breakfast at Brennan's when he got the phone call he had long been expecting. He had been elected to the Hall of Fame. "That 17–0 tells you how tough the competition is, that it's never been done," Shula said. "I remember when the Bears had the chance in 1985, and we beat them." Among the other enshrinees were defensive back Mike Haynes, Giants owner Wellington Mara, and center Mike Webster.

This would not be Shula's first visit to the Canton main stage. He had been there before. In August 1987, Shula had introduced both Larry Csonka and Jim Langer when they were inducted.

"Our offense had the keen ability to keep the ball away from opponents with long, time-consuming drives," Shula had said. "[Csonka] was simply the best fullback of his time. He was blood and guts and dirt all over him. In his career, high school, college, and the pros, he had 12 broken noses."

Shula also presented Bob Griese for induction in 1990. He had missed the cut the previous year. "What does a guy have to do to get into the Hall of Fame?" Shula griped to the press at the time. He was thrilled to introduce Griese in 1990. "Bob had the perfect mental approach," Shula said. "He was the master of the position of quarterback. He knew the people and how to use them. He knew defenses inside and out."

Larry Little had requested Shula to introduce him for his 1993 induction. "There was no one more misnamed," Shula said, "than Larry Little, who was a giant in his profession."

Dwight Stephenson also requested Shula to present him in 1998 at Canton. The *New York Times* reported of the event, "His presenter, Don Shula, his former coach, said that because Stephenson was always in great shape, Stephenson would still be playing pro football had it not been for a knee injury. As is, Shula said, Canton today added a touch of class."

Marino would be inducted in 2005. Shula attended that as well, though Marino was presented by his son Daniel. In his acceptance speech, Dan stated, "Today, I want to thank those 26 teams for passing on me. You gave me an opportunity to play for one of the greatest franchises in the NFL—the Miami Dolphins. And to be coached by the greatest coach ever—Don Shula. Coach, other than my father, you're the most significant influence on my football career. You pushed me and demanded my best. Coach, you were always a true professional, and I want to thank you for the example that you set for me on the field, but also in the community. We didn't win a Super Bowl together, and that's something I will always regret not knowing what that feels like. But you and I have won more games together than any quarterback and coach in the history—the culmination—the history of the NFL. That's something I'm very proud of."

Shula had always been miffed by the fact that more defensive players from the undefeated 1972 team had not been inducted, especially Manny Fernandez, Dick Anderson, and Jake Scott. He felt that the "No-Name Defense" spoke well of the unit's unselfishness but had actually hurt them when it came time to make the Hall. Bouniconti's induction in 2001 helped mollify that.

"It's something I've been waiting for—somebody to be recognized from those great defensive football teams, and Nick is the logical one. He was the captain of our defense, had great instinct, never made mental errors, and was one of the great competitors I've ever been around on the football field," said Shula. "If a teammate made a mistake, he was on the teammate before the coach. He wanted to be perfect. He wouldn't tolerate anybody not being totally prepared the way he was totally prepared. That's the kind of guy you want leading your defense."

Buoniconti's was possibly the most emotional of all the inductions. He was introduced by his son, Marc. Marc had followed in his father's footsteps, playing middle linebacker. He had been seriously injured in a game while playing for the Citadel against East Tennessee State in 1985. Marc became a quadriplegic, suffering almost total body paralysis that would plague him the rest of his life. Nick, who became CEO of US Tobacco (maker of Skoal tobacco products as well as Chateau Ste. Michelle and other wine brands), dedicated the rest of his life to his son's recovery. Nick founded The Miami Project to Cure Paralysis with the University of Miami, where he helped to raise more than $450 million for a cure for paralysis. The research has changed the way these kinds of injuries are treated today. Marc was confined to a wheelchair the rest of his life. But he was able to present his father at Canton, where Marc received a standing ovation. Shula sat behind the two of them, beaming.

For Shula, Canton, Ohio, was only fifty miles from Grand River, Ohio. It takes about an hour to travel between the two small towns. Canton is the home of the

Pro Football Hall of Fame. But, on induction day, it might as well have been called Painesville or Miami, because Shula drew one of the largest contingents ever in the history of the Hall's induction ceremonies. He had to find tickets for family members and longtime friends who came from Painesville, Chicago, Baltimore, and Miami. At the very least, it was a Shula family reunion. It seemed at least like half of Painesville was in Canton that day. In addition to all those attendees, massive crowds cheered outside the Hall, surely bolstered by the induction of a son of their home state.

Shula's bust had been sculpted by Blair Buswell of Provo, Utah. Shula could not have been more pleased with it. "The jaw is prominently featured in the bust," Shula said, "and that's the way it should be. When you get away from all the numbers, the jaw is the one thing people associate with me. I really like the bust."

"He has been described, in part, because of his jutting jaw as the NFL's national monument," Mike Shula said.

Craig Barnes, from the *Sun Sentinel,* quipped, "The jaw has been bronzed forever."

Asked if he thought it would be difficult to break his record in the current NFL, Shula answered, "The climate would be tough. There were 11 coaching changes this year. If that continues to happen, there's nobody who is going to hang around as long as I did. You have to win early and often to establish enough of a reputation to stick around until you have one losing season."

"I've never seen him happier or more relaxed," said his brother Jim, in from Chicago. "He's known where he wanted to go for a long time, and now he's there."

"Nobody would like to have won more Super Bowls," said owner H. Wayne Huizenga, "but the other numbers that he compiled far outshadow that one. His record speaks for itself."

"He was competing against himself," friend and former defensive coordinator Bill Arnsparger said. "It doesn't happen often. Unless you win the Super Bowl every season, you don't meet the demands of the organization or the fans."

On July 26, 1997, Don Shula was presented by both David and Mike Shula. This had never happened before. All inductees had been asked to select only one person, but Shula petitioned that both his sons be given a short time to present him, and his wish was granted.

Dave Shula spoke first. He recapped his father's life from Painesville to the back-to-back Super Bowl wins. "He would not ask his players to do something he would not do himself, so he ran gassers after practice with his team. If he had something on his mind, you were soon to hear about it, good or bad. Honesty is his credo. No team went into a game better prepared. Being better than everyone else is all he ever thought about. Excellence was expected."

Then Mike spoke. He recounted his father's personal life as a husband and father. "Don Shula has a tender side, as well, you just have to dig a little to find it. . . . He became a horseman because his daughters loved to ride and travel to horse shows. Now he loves to spoil his six grandchildren. He even spent over a $100 in a candy store to make them happy. . . . Devotion to his religion, his family, and the NFL have brought dad here today. He has been described in part because of his jutting jaw as the NFL's National Monument. His devotion to his real and his football family inspire tremendous loyalty for all of us."

Then it was Don's turn to give his acceptance speech. "I can't tell you how much of a proud father I am to have those two up here to present me. I coached against Dave the last couple of years, and I was very proud to be the first time a father ever coached against his son. He beat me for thirty minutes the first time and fifty-nine-and-a-half minutes the second time. And I coached against Mike when he was an assistant with the Bears, and they won that football game. But both of them clean my clock now on the tennis court and also on the golf course." Said Shula, "You know it's only fifty miles from Grand River to Canton, but it took me sixty-seven years to travel that distance."

Shula then recounted his journey from Painesville to John Carroll, to the Browns and onward. He thanked many people along the way. He recounted, "Back-to-back Super Bowls, the 17–0 perfect season. The next year, 15–2, 32–2 in two years, what a football team. I think what coaching is all about is taking players and analyzing there ability, put them in a position where they can excel within the framework of the team winning. And I hope that I've done that in my 33 years as a head coach."

He credited many of his players and coaches. "The one thing that I know is that you win with good people. The Hall of Famers that I've coached, you got Bob Griese, Jim Langer, Larry Little, Larry Csonka sitting over there, Paul Warfield, some other guys offensively that I hope are soon going to be considered for the Hall of Fame, Bob Kuechenberg, Dwight Stephenson. We got Nat Moore sitting out here who has done so many things. And a defense, what a defense, a 'No-Name Defense' in those years led by Bill Arnsparger, who's here today and what a defensive coach. Nick Buoniconti, Dick Anderson, Jake Scott, Manny Fernandez, Bill Stanfill. Two Super Bowls, 32–2 in two years, we've got to get a defensive player from those teams into the Hall of Fame, and I hope someday we're going to be able to recognize one of those players. And I also want to talk about other players that gave me everything that they had to give on special teams, practice squads, whatever. Their dedication and effort was the main reason that I was able to win so many games.

"Earl Morrall, I got to say a word about Earl Morrall. When Unitas went down, it was Earl Morrall. I was smart enough to bring him to Miami, and when Bob Griese went down, it was Earl Morrall. The toughest decision that I've ever had to make as a coach was after Bob was hurt, Earl led us to the unbeaten season. We get into the Super Bowl, after Bob's healthy, he comes back and helps us beat Pittsburgh, in Pittsburgh. And then I had to make a decision, and I made the decision to start Bob Greise. I made the decision to start Bob Griese, and Earl took it like the man that he is. And Earl, thank you for all of your contributions.

Then Shula addressed the present day. He mentioned how he had worked with Marino for thirteen years. Shula noted that it had taken Marino thirteen years to break all the records that it had taken Fran Tarketon eighteen years to establish a generation before. "I've had opportunity to coach Dan Marino. Dan Marino makes practice exciting," said the misty-eyed old coach. "And I hope and pray that Dan gets the opportunity to wear this ring before he retires."

Shula then recounted highlights of his career. "I'm proud of being able to break the record of a man that has meant so much to the National Football League, a record that nobody ever thought would be broken, George Halas's record of 324. And then to end up with a total of 347 wins . . . 17–0, the only team in history, and a special bond has developed with that group of players. They wear this ring with pride. And this year is going to be the 25th anniversary of the 17–0 team, the only undefeated season. The lowlight in my career, the loss to the Jets in Super Bowl III. Weeb Ewbank is the coach here, and what a coach Weeb is. And then they had a quarterback by the name of, I keep forgetting, Joe, Joe Namath was the quarterback. And what a game that he had against us. But I did learn from that negative experience, I hope the hell I learned something from that negative experience. And I'm also a little bit upset because my career didn't end in a blaze of glory, I would have liked to have rode off into the sunset. But instead, we got beat in the first round of the playoffs in the last game that I coached. And I felt at that time the team underachieved. I would have loved to have bowed out with a Super Bowl win, but it didn't happen." He then went on to thank the various members of the competition committee.

"I've only been carried off the field two times, one was after the 17–0 and the other was after 325, and I'll always remember those rides. . . . A lot of special people, family that is here today and all of the sacrifices and the loyalty and the support. Friends that have been loyal in good and bad times.

"What's life been after the National Football League? I miss the action, there's no question, on Sunday afternoon, nothing could replace that. But my wife, Mary Anne . . . she's helped keep me busy by making life interesting and enjoyable." He ended by saying, "You know it's only fifty miles, but I've relished every moment of the longer route to get here. Thanks for letting me reflect on those great moments. Thank you."

In June of 1998, Shula signed a five-year contract with the Dolan Family Ownership Group, who were one of at least six investment groups seeking to purchase the expansion rights to the new Cleveland Browns franchise vacated by Art Modell after he moved his team to Baltimore and renamed them the Ravens. Shula would be the team's executive vice president of football operations and would hire their coach and general manager.

"We needed a football person," said Larry Dolan, the group's general partner along with Charles Dolan of Cablevision. Shula would resign his position as vice chairman of the board of the Dolphins if the Dolan family won the bid. The Browns would begin play in 1999. Shula, who negotiated a 5 percent stake in the Dolan bid, would help be responsible for developing the club's football operations. Actor Bill Cosby was also a part of the bid with a 5 percent stake. The group was prepared to pay from $350 million to $500 million for the franchise fee at that time.

"Once talk fades about which bidder has the most famous or local investors, which group can best uphold the Browns' legacy, or which ownership has the best community relations plan, money will surely shout the loudest," wrote Richard Sandomir in the *New York Times*.

By September 9, it had been decided. "Al Lerner, who helped Art Modell move the former Cleveland Browns to Baltimore in 1996, was chosen unanimously today by National Football League owners to buy the new Browns for $530 million, outdistancing his closest pursuer by $30 million," wrote Sandomir.

On December 13, many of the 1972 Dolphins team gathered at the renamed Pro Player Stadium for an 8:20 p.m. kickoff against the New York Jets. "Nick Buoniconti called me and told me he was going to the Dolphins game tonight," former defensive back Dick Anderson said. "So I told him I was going to bring a bottle of champagne to our alumni suite and share it with him and all other members of the 1972 team."

At the time, the Denver Broncos were 13–0 and bidding for a perfect record. However, in an afternoon game at Giants Stadium, the Giants had defeated the Broncos, breaking up their undefeated season. Many members of the 1972 team had their eyes glued to the Giants-Broncos game. Phones rang, call were answered, relief shared. Anderson, Buoniconti, and Shula gathered in a suite at the Miami stadium for the Jets-Dolphins game. But they also celebrated the Broncos' demise. Shula said the Broncos loss "underscores what a great accomplishment going undefeated really was."

"I hoped that if a team was going to go undefeated and tied our record, it would be the Broncos because of Brian being on the team," said Bob Griese, whose son was drafted by Denver that year. "I feel close to the players on that team and feel a special kinship with the team, and their accomplishment this season is really something special. But on the other hand, I have to admit that I feel happy that the record remains intact, not for myself, but for the entire 1972 team."

It was a small impromptu moment that eventually turned into an urban myth. There eventually developed a story about how the players each bought champagne every year and toasted the defeat of that season's last undefeated team. While they were all very proud of their accomplishment, and few wanted to see their record equaled, this kind of organized celebration was a myth. Yes, they did breathe a sigh of relief. Their accomplishment was theirs alone. Who wants to see their record beaten? Especially something so unique?

"That's probably the most talked-about thing that just doesn't happen. We've got players scattered all across the country. Nick Buoniconti, Bob Griese, and Dick Anderson all live in Coral Gables, and they'll go to a parking lot and open a bottle of champagne, but those three are too cheap to invite the rest of us down there," Shula once quipped.

In 2005, the Dolphins were accused of celebrating again when the Indianapolis Colts lost after winning their first 13 games. Shula again told the media, "We've been accused of being angry old men and just hoping and praying that the last team would lose, and that's not true. If the Colts do it, I'd be the first guy to call [Colts head Coach Tony] Dungy and congratulate him, and I'm sure our players would congratulate their players."

Again, in 2011, Green Bay went 13–0 before losing their fourteenth game. "Records are made to be broken," former Dolphins tight end Marv Fleming said. "I told my players, we celebrate our victory, not the person's defeat when someone gets beat. It's not a matter of them getting beat. We have kept it so long. We've kept it long enough, probably."

"If you're going to drink it, drink it in the closet," Fleming said of the alleged infamous toast. "It was a great feat that we did. For it to last so long is cause for celebration. You celebrate in the closet. And we only did that one time. C'mon, we don't do that anymore. Did it once and it took off. Everybody thinks we do it now. We're not a bunch of old men thinking the record should not be broken. It can't be broken. Whoever gets there will be a tie. They'll be the second team that's become undefeated."

In February of 2000, Mike Shula was fired as the offensive coordinator of the Tampa Bay Buccaneers, a job he had held for four years. He had been hired by Tony Dungy to help rebuild the Bucs' program. Dungy had created one of the best defenses in the NFL, but they never seemed to have the offensive weapons to put them over the top in Dungy's time there.

Mike had been hired in 1996, stating, "I'll be the first to admit that my dad, who he is, has opened doors. I'd be lying if I said it didn't. But I've always tried to be extremely appreciative and take nothing for granted." It was his second tour of duty with the Bucs, as he had been an assistant with them from 1988 to 1990.

The defense was stocked with stars, but not so the offense. The primary weapons on the Bucs had been Mike Alstott, a bruising fullback who was more like Csonka, hitting people rather than running to daylight; Warrick Dunn, a dynamic and powerful as well as shifty runner; Trent Dilfer, a solid if unspectacular quarterback, who was an excellent game manager; and, in his final season there, wide receiver Jacquez Green.

"Mike [Shula] was always good at designing the offense to the strength of his players," Dungy said. "He did the same thing with Warrick Dunn and Mike Alstott. It was different having a fullback like Mike who was really a big running back."

In January of 2000, The Buccaneers visited the St. Louis Rams, nicknamed "The Greatest Show on Turf" for its dynamic passing offense led by Kurt Warner. The defense performed brilliantly, holding the league's leading offense to only 11 points. But the Tampa Bay offense never really got on track, either. They gave up a safety and scored only two field goals all day. Tampa lost, 11–6. Dungy, his coaches, and players had turned around a moribund team and come within a game of the Super Bowl. Rookie Shaun King, their third-string quarterback, started that day, and the offensive line had backup players starting at tackle. Despite their 11–5 record, the Bucs' offense had failed to score a touchdown in five games that season.

"In those days, the staff of the losing teams in the conference title games coached the NFC and AFC teams in the Pro Bowl. Shula was running practice for the NFC offense when Dungy was informed the Glazer family, which owns the Bucs, and then-general manager Rich McKay did not want to offer Shula a new contract," wrote Rick Stroud of the *Tampa Bay Times*. "Dungy's contract gave him control of the coaching staff, and he wanted to retain all his assistants. After practice, Dungy was asked about his staff and whether he had a responsibility to hold the offensive staff accountable."

"Of course I do," Dungy said at the time. "I also know this. We've been through one round of the playoffs (in '97). We've been to the NFC championship. And we're trying to get to the Super Bowl. I know people have their opinions on how to get there, and I may have my opinions on how to get there, too. And I may be wrong, but I have my opinion."

"Unfortunately for him, the Glazers [the Bucs owners] didn't share that opinion. Dungy informed Shula of his dismissal during a private meeting at the Ihilani Resort in Honolulu. He told other members of the Bucs' coaching staff of Shula's firing during a meeting described as somber at 10:30 p.m. Eastern, just before a scheduled luau. Shula left the next morning," continued Stroud.

"That's one of my few regrets," Dungy said later. "I don't have many of them. From Day 1 when it happened, I knew it probably wasn't the right thing to do and very soon after I felt bad about it."

A week later, Mike was picked up by Dave Wannstedt, then the head coach of the Dolphins, who had succeeded Jimmy Johnson. Mike's job was to help new Offensive Coordinator Chan Gailey revamp the offense. He was the last person Wannstedt hired to complete his staff.

"His dad gave me my first NFL coaching job," Wannstedt said, referring to his seven-week stint as Miami's linebackers coach in 1989 before joining Jimmy Johnson in Dallas. "Obviously that's there, but understand that Mike's here because he's a heck of a coach and he's going to make this organization better."

Meanwhile, David was serving as president of Shula's Steak House. By 2002, he had overseen the growth of their company to become the fourth-largest chain of upscale steak houses in the nation.

"That's a huge hook we have to get people's attention, to get their foot in the door because of their interest in football and in my father's career," David told the media. The restaurant's famed 48-ounce porterhouse had been a showcase plate as the chain's sales soared to $60 million in 2002. With Shula on board, they had added seven restaurants and had as many as 23 locations.

"David has been a tremendous asset for us," said the chain's founder and chairman, David Younts. "It has worked out very, very well. I thought the experience an NFL head coach has could be transferred very easily into our business. There are only 30 of those guys each year. I don't care if you have a winning record or not, what you learn in that process correlates very well to running a business."

"I've been very happy," said Dave, then forty-three. "I learned the Xs and Os of the restaurant business as I went along, and I still learn something new every day. That was a life-changing decision. I was 37 years old and had been doing one thing for 16 years. It was a big leap."

In mid-2002, the chain opened up a restaurant in midtown New York City, in the theater district, in the Westin New York hotel near Times Square.

"The dim, masculine dining room is filled with framed photographs of Mr. Shula in his moments of glory—no shots of the 1969 Super Bowl, when his Baltimore Colts lost to the New York Jets. The menu arrives, printed on a football, which is set before you on a tee," wrote Eric Asimov in the *New York Times*. "Shula's specializes in lineman-size portions."

That same year marked the thirtieth anniversary of their undefeated season. An official Dolphins team commemorative event was set for December 9 at Pro Player Stadium. That summer, nine of them sat at a banquet table at Shula's Steak House in Miami Lakes.

"Hey, give this to Rick Reilly for me," said former tight end Jim Mandich to *Sports Illustrated* reporter Michael Silver, offering a middle finger. His fellow diners broke out laughing. "He called us bitter old men, but this is the kind of record you want to hold on to."

"Every family has its strife, and the Dolphins are no exception. Teammates say that Scott, the MVP of Super Bowl VII, remains bitter toward Shula for the '76 trade that sent him to the Redskins. Other than the two deceased team members, linebacker Bob Matheson and offensive tackle Wayne Moore, Scott is the only one not expected to participate in reunion events," wrote Silver. "Mostly, though, the Dolphins' bonds have remained strong. Several extended financial assistance to wideout Marlin Briscoe, who after leaving football in the late '70s became addicted to crack cocaine—L.A. dealers nicknamed him 17 and 0—and once was kidnapped by Crips because of a drug debt. He now works for the Watts/Willowbrook Boys and Girls Club."

"Shula got up and talked about how much that season meant to him and how every player contributed," wide receiver Howard Twilley said. "He basically gave a five-minute exposé, without notes, on every player on offense and defense. That's what meant the most to me. Shula always brought out the best in people."

"We really don't talk much about that season," said defensive end Jim Riley. "We talk very little football. We ask about the kids, what's going on with life. Of course, we reflect back on some of the times we had, but it's not necessarily our playing days or certain games."

"How many times across the decades, during a lull at another Perfect Season reunion, had Scott's teammates gotten the conversation rolling again just by mentioning his missing name? Someone would provide an update on him. Everyone would remember a story involving him—a real story, too, not just a heroic football story like they all had, the kind a 17–0 season and two Super Bowl rings breeds," wrote longtime *Sun Sentinel* columnist Dave Hyde on the occasion of the reunion of the 1972 team in December. "Riding a motorcycle over a basketball arena. Renting out a bar for every Sunday's postgame party. Ribbing a tense Don Shula on the bus headed to Super Bowl VII, 'What's the matter, you thinking about going down as the losingest coach in Super Bowl history?'" Jake had been unique.

"Jake, why don't you come to the reunion this time?" asked Jim Langer.

"Ain't no way," Scott said.

"Jake is Jake" was a popular refrain at the numerous reunions over the years.

"He's the one guy no one messed with," remembered Manny Fernandez, who had last seen Scott in 1979.

"He just doesn't like to go to events where they're just, well, he says, 'kissing ass,'" said his mother, Mary Scott, eight-one years old at the time.

Scott and Anderson had bought a ranch in Colorado with their first Super Bowl earnings. Jake remained a Dolphins fan, watching all the games. He fished and golfed in Hawaii and skied in Colorado. Later, Scott built a house higher up the mountain. "I visited him there once in the winter, and we needed a [snow caterpillar] to get to the house," Shula later recalled.

"Scott was traded to Washington, along with a third-round draft pick, for safety Bryant Salter in arguably the worst trade in Dolphins history. Salter lasted a season. Scott retired after three seasons with the Redskins, but his anger isn't the retiring kind. It's not just reunions. It's everything Shula," wrote Hyde. They even told the story how he had a date with a model. He was all set, day, time, until he asked her where she wanted to eat. Shula's Steak House. The date was off. "All these years later, he hasn't let go of the hurt in a way other teammates have," continued Hyde.

Mary Scott relayed the story again how Jake had approached Shula in 1982 and "asked to talk with him. Shula just turned around and walked away. So he won't show up wherever Shula is."

Shula, for his part, said, "I wish Jake was at this reunion. He was a big part of everything we accomplished." The night of the reunion at Pro Player Stadium (now known as Hard Rock Stadium), 47 players and coaches as well as family members of the three deceased players from the 1972 team were introduced at halftime of the Dolphins' 27–9 victory over the Chicago Bears.

A few weeks earlier, the very first Shula Bowl was played at Pro Player Stadium. The annual college football game features two rival schools, the Florida Atlantic University Owls and the Florida International University Panthers, with the winner receiving the traveling trophy named the "Don Shula Award." The have stewardship over the trophy until the rematch the following year, when it is up for grabs once again.

The contest got its name because in 2002, the game pitted Florida Atlantic's first head coach, Howard Schnellenberger (Shula's former coordinator and friend), against FIU's first head coach, Don Strock (Shula's former backup quarterback and friend). The game alternates between the two schools' home fields, and both programs have sent players to the NFL.

In early May 2003, the University of Alabama announced that Mike Shula would be the new head coach of the Crimson Tide. Their former quarterback was replacing the controversial and hard-partying interim Tide coach Mike Price, who had been spotted in a Florida strip club in Pensacola and who mysteriously had more than $1,000 charged to his university credit card by an unknown woman for undisclosed services.

Shula had already been at the top of the university's accelerated search list, having been an assistant coach for 15 seasons in the NFL. He signed a six-year deal worth $5.4 million. At the time, Mike was a 37-year-old guy, who with his wife, Shari, had a daughter, Samantha, and was expecting their second child that fall. He was the youngest head coach in the modern era of the Crimson Tide program.

"I am obviously excited about this job," Shula said. "There is a bright future ahead for Alabama, especially with the new construction plans for the addition to the Football Building, the new weight room, and the renovation of Bryant Hall. These new facilities will all be great recruiting tools for this staff. I am thrilled to once again be a part of Alabama football."

"Likely to hinder any immediate attempts to return Alabama to national prominence are the N.C.A.A. sanctions, which limit the number of scholarships Alabama may offer and which bar the Crimson Tide from playing in a bowl game this season," wrote sports scribe Judy Battista. In fact, the program had been placed on a five-year probation period in 2002.

"Alabama reached out to someone who could bring calm to the turmoil," Mark Rodgers, Mike Shula's attorney, said. "Mike Shula was that guy. Mike knew what he was inheriting . . . he definitely inherited very difficult circumstances."

"When I was here, it went by too fast," Mike said of his Crimson Tide playing days. "I tried to slow it down, and I couldn't. I loved this place when I was here. And to be able to be head coach at a place where you played, a place that's got the tradition that this place has, is a dream that a lot of guys it won't ever happen to. Now, all of the sudden I've got the opportunity."

"There's no long haul at Alabama," said famed coach and ESPN college football analyst Lee Corso. "You win quick or you're gone."

On September 27, 2003, the new Don Shula Stadium was dedicated at John Carroll University in Cleveland before the homecoming weekend football game between the John Carroll Blue Streaks and the Polar Bears of Ohio Northern University. The multipurpose stadium was and continues to be home to the Division III Blue Streaks. It has an official capacity of 5,416 spectators. It remains a multiuse stadium and serves as home for many of the school's varsity, club, and intramural athletic programs.

The day of the dedication, the stands of Shula Stadium at Wasmer Field were packed, as Don and Mary Anne waved to a capacity crowd at the newly christened stadium and watched the Blue Streaks win, 28–23. The 2003 squad went 7–3 overall, and 6–3 in the Ohio Athletic Conference, finishing fourth in the conference that year. In 2014, they went 11–2 with an 8–1 conference record, finishing second, and took second the following year, as well. In 2016, they went 12–2 with a perfect 9–0 conference record to finish on top of the OAC.

Don Shula Stadium was built around the preexisting Wasmer Field. Wasmer Field has been the "home turf" for the JCU Blue Streaks since 1968. The completion of the stadium facilities "added new locker rooms and coaches' offices to the complex. It also replaced the old weight room with a new, state-of-the-art version and added an updated training room. A new press box and coaches booths were also added," stated the university. The new facility also added new equipment and storage areas as well as a new main concourse that houses the Shula Memorabilia Room as well as a fully functioning concession stand.

Shula had continued all his life to be involved with John Carroll University. He spoke at fund-raising dinners and sports dinners throughout the years. He and Carl Taseff went back almost every year. But Shula continued to work with the various administrations through the years to make sure the sports programs, especially football, would continue to be a vibrant part of the school. He visited with players and coaches over the years. The stadium would not be the end of his involvement with the school or the football program. Shula later endowed the Don Shula Chair in Philosophy, which supports the philosophy department by presenting programs of interest to philosophers and the general public.

As part of a government public awareness campaign, Shula was the first American to sign up for the Medicare Part D prescription drug plan benefit. He enrolled just after midnight on November 15, 2005, at a Walmart. A year later, in 2006 Shula, along with wife, Mary Anne, became Nutrisystem spokespersons.

"I saw how well my quarterback Dan Marino did on Nutrisystem, so I tried it. Thanks to Nutrisystem, I lost 32 pounds. And do I feel great," said Shula in his endorsement. "When I retired from coaching, things changed for me. I no longer was burning calories like I used to. Also, my eating habits changed for the worse. It didn't take long for me to feel my pants getting tighter. The bottom line was I didn't like the way I looked, and I didn't like the way I felt."

"Once he saw the note, Mike Shula knew that his coaching career at the University of Alabama was over. It was handed to him Sunday night by Director of Football Operations Randy Ross, moments after Shula met with Crimson Tide players to make sure they all had made it safely back to the Capstone following Thanksgiving break. It said only three words: 'Call Mal Moore,'" said local sportswriter Christopher Walsh in the *Tuscaloosa News*.

On November 28, 2006, Mike was fired from Alabama. He had gone 4–9 in 2003, which was difficult for the faithful, but not far from what had been expected. After starting 3–0, the Crimson Tide struggled to a 6–6 finish in 2004, and their first bowl appearance since 2001. Then in 2005, the program turned, and the team finished 10–2 and finished with a victory in the Cotton Bowl over the Texas Tech Red Raiders. Mike had been rewarded for such success with a contract extension for six years at $1.8 million per year. However, the team faltered in 2006, and Shula was let go with a 6–6 record. The university was forced to pay him the $4 million remaining on his contract.

"Alabama thought for a time it had the right fit with Shula. While he had no previous head coaching experience, he was a former Crimson Tide quarterback and heir to a famous pro football name," reported ESPN. "But a 6–6 season, ending in three straight losses—to SEC weakling Mississippi State along with LSU and Auburn, two Western Division rivals Shula never could beat—signaled the end. Shula was a combined 0-for-8 against LSU and Auburn and is the only Tide coach to lose four straight to Auburn. Moore and university president Robert Witt decided late Sunday afternoon to fire Shula and start over again."

"His leadership has provided our program with much-needed stability during the past four years, and we appreciate that, as our coach, he has demonstrated impeccable character and class in every way," Witt said in a written statement.

"I just feel like coach Shula had everything in place," said Tide center Antoine Caldwell. "I feel like he had complete, 100 percent control of this football team. I feel like he had our program on track. It's almost like we didn't go 10–2, we didn't finish ranked No. 8 in the country—like that didn't even happen."

Speculation began immediately that Nick Saban was among the most favored of coaching choices for the Crimson Tide. Saban had been a lifelong college coach with a tremendous track record, including his last two stops at Michigan State and LSU, before joining the Miami Dolphins in 2005. But Saban's stop in Miami had been a difficult one. The invincible college coach was seemingly human in the pro game, going a mediocre 15–17 in the NFL in two seasons.

"Mike Shula is a good guy," Saban told reporters in Florida "He's a friend. I hate to see anybody not being able to maintain. I think he's done a good job there and should have been given an opportunity to stay there."

Saban intended outwardly to end the unending speculation of his possible departure to Alabama, telling the press emphatically, on December 6, "I guess I have to say it. I'm not going to be the Alabama coach." Saban told the *Miami Herald*, "I don't care to be. I don't want to be. . . . This is the challenge that I wanted. I had a good college job, so why would I have left that if I would be interested in another college job?"

But it was all a ruse. While remodeling his lake home in Georgia years ago, Saban hired home builder Chuck Moore. Chuck had a famous uncle—Mal Moore, the Crimson Tide athletic director. The connection wasn't lost on either man, and Moore's "dogged pursuit eventually succeeded—with an assist from Saban's wife, Terry," wrote Hal Habib in the *Palm Beach Post*.

"She made it clear to Moore that Saban was miserable in the NFL and dearly missed coaching in college," Burke wrote. "She also made it clear that she wanted out."

On January 5, 2007, Nick Saban was named the new head coach of the Alabama Crimson Tide, receiving a $32 million, eight-year deal, making him the highest-paid college coach in North America.

Dan Le Batard blasted Saban in the *Miami Herald*, writing, "The punctuation on the Nick Saban Error is greasy, dishonorable, and cowardly. You know what he was as Dolphins coach? A failure. A loser. A gasbag. And one of the worst investments Dolphins owner Wayne Huizenga has ever made. There has been nothing in franchise history that came with more expectations and fewer results than this hypocrite who fled at the end to avoid the hard questions one last time. The tombstone on his Dolphins career reads, 'Talked like a warrior, acted like a weasel.'"

Don Shula was furious. "The Alabama firing vexed Don Shula, who to this day dislikes former Dolphins coach Nick Saban for saying he would not take the Alabama coaching job while he was still coaching the Dolphins while apparently allowing his agent to flirt with Alabama officials about his future availability," wrote *Miami Herald* reporter Armonado Salguero. "The Shula family is fiercely loyal to one another and guard each other's back and reputation with a passion. Not that Mike Shula needs people to guard his reputation because stories about who he is do that on his behalf."

"He lied," Shula told the *Miami Herald*, referring to Saban. "There's no other way to put it. There were four or five direct statements that were blatant lies." Shula added, "That tells you a bit about the guy. The guy likes to hear himself talk and then doesn't follow up on what he says."

Before the end of January, Mike was named quarterbacks coach of the Jacksonville Jaguars. He would remain there for four years and helped David Garrard achieve the third-highest passer rating that year in the NFL, with a 102.2 rating—a 23-point improvement. Garrard would make the Pro Bowl two years later.

"Usually we just go out and do something quiet," Shula said about his impending 80th birthday in January 2010. "This one, I guess, it's a little special. Eight-Oh! I used to think 80 was old. But I've changed my whole thinking," he said with a smile.

In 2010, the National Football League Foundation first awarded the Don Shula NFL Coach of the Year Award. Coaches from the high school, college, and professional levels were nominated and eligible to receive it. However, in 2011, it became an exclusively high school award and was part of the first annual NFL Honors.

According to the NFL, "The coaches were nominated by NFL teams and by USA Football, the sport's national governing body on youth and amateur levels.

Nominees are active football coaches at NFL, college, high school, and youth levels. They were chosen for their character and integrity, inspirational leadership, commitment to the community, and on-field success."

On January 31, 2010, the Dolphins unveiled the "Perfect Moment in Time" statue. It was a bronze statue of Don Shula that stood at the entrance of the new Dolphins corporate headquarters at Sun Life Stadium, as it was then known. The statute and the new offices marked the return of the Dolphins front office to Miami-Dade County after sixteen years. Additionally, the stadium address was announced as 347 Don Shula Drive in honor of Shula's career victory total.

Most profound, however, on a personal level was another event altogether. And it was monumental to a whole group of concerned gentlemen. "There was no plan. No script. Nothing but the sight of Don Shula across the room that made Jake Scott walk over," wrote Dave Hyde.

Scott smiled at his old coach and said, "I've missed you so much." Then he hugged Shula, who reciprocated the gesture.

"And in the moment of that embrace, as friends watched in silence, a wall that stood for decades tumbled down. Hearts opened. Eyes misted," continued Hyde. "Scott asked about Shula's sons, Mike and Dave. Shula asked about Scott's life in Hawaii. It was a brief conversation. Five minutes. Maybe 10. But that small talk represented a big step to the onlooking Boys of '72, those Perfect Season Dolphins who wondered if this day would ever come."

"You're taller than I remember," Shula said, smiling at Scott.

"I've got to see this," Manny Fernandez said, walking closer.

"Get a picture," someone else said. Dick Anderson snapped a shot quickly.

"We felt like a piece of the jigsaw was missing," Dick Anderson said.

"The hell with it, it'd been too many years," Scott was saying, then back home in Hawaii. "No sense in holding a grudge with Shula for 112 years."

"I knew he was going to be there," Shula was saying, then home in Miami. "I was hoping we'd say hello and get the other thing out of the way."

"The other thing. To understand what this embrace meant, you have to understand this other thing. Not to relive it. Not to pick at it like a sore. Just to see why it's hung over this team's golden memories in a way that made all warmed by this embrace," continued Hyde.

"There's no sense to have a grudge with Shula," Scott says.

"It's silly we haven't seen each other all this time," Shula says. "The big thing was I got to say how I felt about him, how much he's always meant to me."

"You and Dick [Anderson] were the best safety combination ever in football," Shula told Scott.

"I wish you'd said that when I was negotiating my contract," Scott said. They both laughed. A giant hole had been filled in not only for each man on the other end of that feud, but for an entire group of men who felt that one of their most beloved brothers-in-arms was missing and that their reunions and convocations were somehow less due to his absence. Part of that broken circle was now complete. Especially for Shula, whose love of Scott had been an ache in the elderly coach's heart.

In 2012, there was yet another reunion. More parties. More stories. More memories. It was the 40th reunion, which was highlighted by a documentary entitled *More Than Perfect,* billed as the untold story of the '72 Dolphins, which came out from NFL Films.

"Forty is a big number," Kuechenberg said. "It's not 50. But I don't know how many will be here at 50."

Added Manny Fernandez, "They're becoming more special because of our age. It didn't initially start that way, but it does seem that every reunion we lose another player, another member of the family. I'm not keeping score. It's something we do think about."

"Don Shula weaved his electric scooter Tuesday morning through a hotel lobby full of aging men who had arrived early, 'just as Coach Shula taught us,' Hall of Fame fullback Larry Csonka said. Csonka was in from Alaska. Larry Little carried a Dolphins hat, signed by the team's seven Hall of Famers, as a gift. Otto Stowe wore an 'I Have A Dream' button to honor the coming 50th anniversary of Martin Luther King Jr.'s speech and Obama," wrote Dave Hyde.

Shula stopped his cart in front of the ever-loquacious Mercury Morris, saying to him, "You're not going to speak today, are you Merc?"

"I'm only going to politely ask the president to correct calling the '85 Bears the greatest team ever," Morris said.

"Oh, boy, politely, Merc," Marv Fleming said.

"OK, let's get going," Shula said, rolling to the doors. "And I don't want to have to fine anyone for being late."

The 1972 Dolphins had been cheated out of their White House visit in 1973 due to the Watergate scandal. Here they were now, 40 years later, finally getting their opportunity to visit the president of the United States, and the people's home. Time had changed. Richard Nixon had been president, there was still a war going on in Vietnam, and the administration was at war with the press and the Congress over a break-in at a real estate complex known as Watergate. On August 20, 2013, President Barack Obama, the first African-American president, was straddling several wars, including one against a terrorist organization, and battling a mostly opposing political party Congress hell-bent on subverting his agenda. The politics was just as rough. *All in the Family* was the number rated television show in the country back in 1972. In 2013, *The Big Bang Theory* was number one.

The team, a large gaggle of older men mostly in their sixties and older, waddled through security around 11 a.m, making jokes about their hips and knees and the metal detectors, and continuing their conversations. They went through four security checkpoints and would enjoy the confines of the East Wing for at least two hours.

Bob Kuechenberg, Manny Fernandez, and Hall of Fame center Jim Langer did not partake of the festivities, due to their political affiliations. They were not the first Super Bowl winners, conservative or liberal, who had resisted the charms of visiting the White House. As several writers pointed out, the teams did not normally visit in those days, and this was a public relations contrivance. But tell that to the men who did attend. Dick Anderson organized numerous team pictures. Then President Obama entered the room about 1:30.

"Was this guy a great receiver or what?" President Obama said upon meeting Paul Warfield.

"You look like you can still play," he said to Csonka.

"I've only got one play left and I'm saving that one," Csonka said.

"How's your passing, Garo?" asked the president.

"Well, I'm one-for-one, the highest-rated quarterback in the Super Bowl," Yepremian said.

"Can you still pass?" the president said.

"Sure," Yepremian said.

"When the players left for the official ceremony, it was just Obama and Shula and the coach's wife, Mary Anne. And they talked football. They talked football strategy, talked of the upcoming season, then got off on a tangent about Carolina quarterback Cam Newton, who is coached by Shula's son, Mike," wrote Dave Hyde. "For five minutes, the old coach talked with the President again. He'd done back in that 1972 season, Richard Nixon even calling his home one day to suggest running a slant pass to Warfield. The coach said it was a good idea, acted is if he didn't have that play in the book. Now, at 83, with his scooter a reminder of time's cost, Shula received a private gift from Obama, a signed football that read, 'Coach Shula, congratulations on a memorable season.'"

In July of 2014, Don and Mary Anne Shula announced that The Don Shula Foundation had donated $1.5 million to help fund breast cancer research projects at Moffitt Cancer Center in Tampa, the only facility in Florida designated by the National Cancer Institute as a comprehensive cancer center. Moffitt used the monies to establish The Don Shula Breast Cancer Research Fund. The Shula fund supported projects that focused on generating new treatment and prevention strategies for breast cancer patients in Florida and elsewhere.

"Cancer has touched our family personally, and I know that the more we give to cancer research, the closer we are to finding a cure," said Coach Shula, who had been a member of Moffitt's national Board of Advisors since 2008 (at that time, Sam Donaldson, veteran ABC journalist, had chaired the board).

"We are proud of our new partnership with Moffitt Cancer Center and look forward to the participation of Shula's Restaurants during the month of October!" said Dave when the two organizations joined forces in 2014. By 2016, there were 29 Shula restaurant locations overall, down from 32 in 2010. With David's help, the chain regularly sponsored events and fund-raisers for the Don Shula Foundation and the Moffitt Center. For example, in February of 2016, the Foundation co-hosted a fundraising event with Shula Restaurants at the new "No Name Lounge" at the Shula's Steak House at the Intercontinental Hotel in Tampa.

Shula was also quick to praise Mary Anne's major influence and efforts to continue to grow the fund-raising effort. "My wife is the business mind in the family," Shula said. "She knows the bottom line and what it takes to win. We've been good partners, and we've enjoyed it together." She was president of Shula Enterprises and was a former director of the Miami Heart Institute.

That same year, Coach Shula and Mary Anne established a $10,000 annual scholarship endowment fund at St. Joseph Parish in Miami Beach that would assist one local family with a child in public schools in making the transition to a Catholic high school in the Miami Archdiocese. The endowment was in the Shulas' names and supervised by a parish committee.

Shula was a longtime parishioner at Our Lady of the Lakes Parish in Miami Lakes, where he attended mass almost daily, travel schedule permitting. But Don and Mary Anne had enabled the Catholic elementary school there to finish a three-story state-of-the-art educational facility with a music room, computer lab, and spacious offices. St. Joseph School then became a charter school. Shula also had a lifetime of Catholic education. He'd gone to a small Catholic grade school and college, and his children and grandchildren attended Catholic schools in South Florida, including St. Thomas Aquinas High School and Chaminade-Madonna College Preparatory.

Shula had many lifelong associations with several parishes in the region and many close relationships with Miami archdiocesan clergy and bishops alike, who jokingly called him "*Don* Shula," as a term of respect, emphasizing it as a title, instead of his name.

"Archbishop Wenski presented Shula with a lifetime achievement and appreciation award at a recent parish gala for 150 guests at the Miami Beach Resort, and thanked Shula for his support of Catholic education and in particular for creating the new scholarship fund at St. Joseph Parish," reported the Catholic News Service. "Also on hand were Sean Clancy, a former Miami Dolphin player, who was master of ceremonies for the event, and Msgr. Frank Casale, president of St. Thomas University in Miami."

"Every other organization, the sports world, the business world, the social world of South Florida, and even the US president recognized the [Dolphins] team from his era, and many documentaries have been made about him, but I don't think the church was recognizing him," said Father Juan Sosa, pastor of St. Joseph Parish.

"It's nice to be remembered," said Shula said, smiling.

Chris Shula was the son of David and Leslie Shula and became the third generation of Shula coaches in the NFL. Chris had gone to Thomas Aquinas High School, where he played linebacker. He had lettered all four years as an outside linebacker, totaling 68.5 tackles and five interceptions his senior season, helping the Raiders to a combined three-year record of 34–6. He was first-team all-county his last two seasons.

He played in every game of his junior year at Miami (Ohio) University in 2006, his highlight game coming against Syracuse University, where he made a season-high six tackles and forced a fumble. In his senior year, he appeared in all but one game and was the team's seventh-leading tackler. He had two quarterback sacks that year and recovered a fumble. According to the university, "coaches say he is the most intelligent linebacker on the field . . . one of the RedHawks' most valuable players, he can play all three linebacker positions."

"I could tell [he'd get into coaching] when he was growing up," Dave said. "He always asked a lot of questions. He wanted to understand the whys and the how comes. He loved going to practice. He loved preparing on his own. When there weren't organized activities, he would always grab me and want to either work out or work on techniques and things. So, it didn't surprise me at all when he showed an interest in coaching."

"Yeah, I was the same way," Dave said. "Just loved being around, loved when I was a little guy and he'd bring me over to the Dolphins training camp. Or the Colts training camp before that. I did the same thing. [My wife, Leslie, and I] have three sons, Chris and his brothers [Dan, a college assistant coach most recently at Florida Atlantic; and Matt, who works in the Dolphins' video department], and we'd bring them up to Cincinnati and they'd spend a couple weekends with me at training camp and they just loved it."

He became linebackers coach at Ball State in 2010, and from 2011 to 2013, he was the defensive backs coach at Indiana University. In 2014, he got the opportunity to be the defensive coordinator for John Carroll University. That made headlines.

"The Shula coaching tree has grown another branch, this time close to its roots. Chris Shula has been hired as defensive coordinator at John Carroll University, head coach Tom Arth said. Shula is the son of former Cincinnati Bengals coach Dave Shula and the grandson of football Hall of Fame coach Don Shula, who grew up in Grand River and graduated from John Carroll. The Blue Streaks' home field is Don Shula Stadium," wrote the *Cleveland Plain Dealer*'s Tim Warsinskey.

Arth said that proud grandpa Don did not lobby on behalf of his grandson. "We did not hire him because his last name is Shula," John Carroll coach Tom Arth said. "After getting to know him and what his philosophies are on defense, it fit very well with what we are doing. And he is someone who this job is going to mean something to. It wasn't going to just be a stepping-stone situation for him. He has ties to John Carroll. Chris was a perfect fit. Chris has done an absolutely phenomenal job. He's an incredibly smart football coach, and he's done a great job building those relationships and trust with players, who know this guy is going to put us in the right position to be successful."

Wrote Warsinskey, "Chris Shula was running behind. He was in a meeting, upstairs in the Shula Room at Don Shula Stadium. When he hurried back down to John Carroll's locker room area, he strolled by a display of the many alums who have worked in the NFL, beginning with Hall of Fame Coach Don Shula."

"It's been a blast," said Chris. By the end of the season, John Carroll's defense was ranked No. 2 in the NCAA Division III.

"Chris keeps in close contact with his grandfather and father. At the end of the week, he shares the game plan with David, then talks to him again after the game about what worked and what didn't," said Chris.

"He gives me a lot of advice, about motivation, thought process, and dealing with adversity," Chris said of his dad, David.

Don had visited with the team and his grandson before the season began.

"I'm very happy and proud of him," Don Shula said. "I think he's really enjoying it."

"It's taking it full circle," Dave Shula told the *Plain Dealer* in May. "John Carroll has always been a very special place to him."

"I'm better-looking," Don quipped regarding his grandson.

John Carroll advanced to the quarterfinals of the NCAA Division III playoffs. The Blue Streaks lost the last game, but Shula's defense had been an eye-opener. Chris, then 29, was honored as College Assistant Coach of the Year by the Northeastern Ohio Chapter of the National Football Foundation and Cleveland Touchdown Club Charities.

"I'm really proud of Chris. He was in a tough situation coming in this year having to kind of follow up to what we did in 2013 with how good our defense was. He exceeded every expectation that I had, that our players had and our coaches had," said coach Arth.

However, Chris had caught the eye of the NFL. In February 2015, the San Diego Chargers announced that they had hired Chris to be their defensive quality control coach. He worked for the Chargers for two years and was then hired as the linebackers coach for the Los Angeles Rams. Chris was hired by first-year Los Angeles Rams Head Coach and college teammate Sean McVay as assistant linebackers coach.

"It really is awesome to have a resource like that," said Chris, referring to his father, David. "Even when times are rough, to be able to call and get advice from someone who has been through a lot of the same things. And whether he would deal with it differently or not, to be able to just to use him as a sounding board has been unbelievable. [My Grandpa is] very excited for me. My dad kind of learned everything from my grandpa, so it's kind of funny hearing them both give me advice."

Also on the team was longtime Head Coach and Defensive Coordinator Wade Phillips. The Phillipses were the other three-generation coaching family in NFL history. Bum Phillips had been the head coach of the Houston Oilers and New Orleans Saints, and now Wade's son, Wes, was the tight ends coach for the Washington Redskins.

"I was really superexcited to hear that Sean was able to bring Wade on for a lot of reasons," Dave said. "Especially, selfishly speaking, that Chris will be able to be mentored by a guy like Wade. I've known him for many years and have tremendous respect for him and what he's done in his career and the kind of person he is. The teacher that he is and the way he goes about coaching the game. I'm thrilled that Chris is going to have the opportunity to be with him."

"My dad never coached with him," Chris said, "but they had obviously gone against him and just everything you hear from my dad and my grandfather about the type of person he is. . . . My dad said, 'I've never heard one bad thing about Wade Phillips.' And he had a chance to know Bum too, who I've heard a bunch of stories about him being a great guy and a great coach. It's really just an honor to coach with a guy like Wade Phillips. I almost have to pinch myself sometimes when I'm sitting right next to him in staff meetings."

Don Shula was understandably excited. He turned to *Miami Herald* columnist Greg Cote during an interview, and said, "By the way, did you know my grandson Chris works for the Rams? I'm very proud of him."

February 2016 brought another laurel to the Shula coaching tree, when Mike Shula, who was now the offensive coordinator for the Carolina Panthers under Head Coach Ron Rivera, had helped point them to the Super Bowl. Mike had left the Jacksonville Jaguars in 2010 and headed to Carolina, where he was the quarterbacks coach between 2011 and 2012, working with the talented Cam Newton.

In 2013, the team's offensive coordinator, Rob Chudzinski, had left to accept the head coach position of the Cleveland Browns. Shula was asked to step in and was named Offensive Coordinator of the Year by *Pro Football Focus* during the 2015 NFL season.

Cecil Hurt wrote in the *Tuscaloosa News* that Shula was then "in a position where his strengths could shine. He is an excellent offensive coordinator, studious and patient. Perhaps it was good luck to be paired with the uber-talented Newton but Shula has handled his star pupil perfectly. His play calling in the NFC Championship game was impeccable."

"The 6–5, 245-pound Newton is built like Superman, and this season he has played like him, too. During the regular season, he threw for 3,837 yards, 35 TDs, and 10 INTs. He also ran for 636 yards and 10 more scores. He's the first NFL player to throw for at least 30 TDs and run for at least 10 in a season," wrote SEC football writer Stan Chrapowicki. "On top of that, Newton's 21,740 total yards over his first five seasons are the most by any NFL player over that span, so he's been super for quite some time now, and he has Shula, among others, to thank for it."

On January 4, Ian Rapoport, National Insider for NFL Network, stated, "Teams will be interested in Panthers OC Mike Shula, but I'm told he won't interview while his team is still playing. He wants to focus." But the rumor in the industry was that Shula did not want to interview at all. There had been seven head coaching vacancies. All were filled. Shula, with the NFL's top offense, was never called.

"All I said was I'm focused on the playoffs," Shula told FOX Sports. "The other quote was if it did happen, if I was approached, I'd have to consider that at the time. Those were my only quotes."

According to Mike Florio of NBC Sports, "In hindsight, Shula should have said something at the time Rapoport reported that Shula wasn't interested in interviewing. Or Shula's agent should have said something. But there's one small problem with that...

"Somebody said I had an agent out there talking, too," Shula said. "I don't have an agent. I have a friend that helps me, but he definitely wasn't that person.... I don't know where that [report] came from."

"It apparently came from an agent who represents one or more coaches other than Shula," reported Florio. "Perhaps the message to Shula is this: Hire an agent. If agents representing other coaches are going to say things aimed at helping those coaches and hurting Shula, Shula needs an agent who can push back. Otherwise, Shula will continue to be the offensive coordinator of the Panthers until he retires or is fired. At some point before then, the window of opportunity for Shula to become an NFL head coach will slam shut."

In 2015, Shula's offense led the NFL in scoring, was second in passing, and 11th in total yards. And quarterback Cam Newton was named the NFL's Most Valuable Player.

"I think a secret weapon that I've had since Day One for me has been Mike Shula. I won't let him hear me say that. He's been a father figure for so many of us on the field, in meeting rooms," said Newton. "For him to be a part of my career, him being my quarterback coach my rookie year, and him moving and staying on the same coaching staff as being the offensive coordinator, him knowing me throughout this whole process has been very important for my growth."

The Panthers became known for players handing footballs to young children after scoring touchdowns. Mike Shula sparked the idea back in 2011. Newton had scored against Washington during a home game. Newton was naturally celebrating, with the ball still in his hand. According to the *Charlotte Observer*, Shula spoke into Newton's ear through his helmet headset.

"[Shula] says when you celebrate, it's not a celebration unless you give back," Newton told the newspaper. "He says, 'You do all that riffraff, whatever you do, but at the end you give that football to a little kid. You find a little kid.'

"So after I did whatever I did, I heard [Shula] in my headset saying, 'Give it to a little kid! Give it to a little kid!' I looked and there was this kid just gleaming from ear to ear, so I gave it to him."

A Panthers tradition was born. But ask Shula about giving Newton the idea, and this is his answer: "Ah, I don't know what you're talking about." Mike smiled.

"Getting to the Super Bowl and winning the Super Bowl is what you get into coaching for," Don Shula said. "Mike's been around the game all his life. He got a taste of what it was like early in his life, and I'm glad he pursued coaching because now he's at the pinnacle of what it's all about as a coach. I can't be more proud of him."

"It's nearly unfathomable to think it has been 31 long years since a Shula last coached in a Super Bowl setting," wrote Don Banks in *Sports Illustrated*. Both Mike Shula and the Super Bowl were 50 years old.

"I'm the same age as the Super Bowl," Shula said, smiling at the thought. "But the Super Bowl has aged better than I have. I will say I was trying to not let so much time pass since the last time a Shula was in the Super Bowl. But time was trotting along."

"If you like symmetry and the linkage of generations connected by the game, Mike Shula making Super Bowl 50 offers even more: Don Shula's final Super Bowl appearance came in Palo Alto, Calif., when his 1984 Miami Dolphins lost to San Francisco in Stanford Stadium, not far from where Mike Shula's first Super Bowl coaching experience will unfold in Santa Clara, in the 49ers' home stadium. You can't make this stuff up," wrote Banks.

Mike talked with his father just after the NFC Championship game. The Panthers had decimated the Arizona Cardinals, 49–15. "He was up at quarter till 12 when I called him, so that was big. He grabbed the phone right away from whoever answered it, and he was just really excited and very proud. He said your hard work's been paying off and you've got one more to go, just keep doing the things you've been doing."

"That's what just makes you that much more proud of the accomplishment, the way it ties in with family history," Don Shula said. "He's been around the game all his life, and now he's at the pinnacle of what it's all about. It's just as good as it can get in coaching, to get to that level. I want him to enjoy it, and I want everyone else to be proud of him. Everybody's going to want to go, now we've got to try and figure out how to do it. I think it's just going to be so meaningful when all of us get out there and are at the stadium and at the game and are cheering him on."

Mike Shula continued to think about the gathering to come, in San Francisco, his family converging. Mike's voice was "caught with the emotion of the opportunity that lies ahead, and the history and meaning of this game in his famous family," wrote Banks.

"It kind of got me a little bit last night [Sunday] when I walked down on the field and saw the big stage up there," Mike Shula said. "What I think of is my family, just that I know how much they mean to me and just to have them be a part of this, to be able to go back to the Super Bowl. That's kind of how I view this. But, oh yeah, my dad will be there. He's coming. They told us that last week. So it was a little more motivation [for the NFC title game]."

"He's excited," Mike said about the Super Bowl and his dad. "He's a dad first. He and [his wife], Mary Anne, are very happy for us. It has been fun this year. Each and every year, as you guys know, when there is a team that is heading down the road and they haven't lost, they start getting him more interviews and more quotes, and we always kind of chuckle because they are in the paper more. Well, this year it was fun because we were the team doing it. We were the team keeping those guys in the paper. He has always been extremely supportive and one of our biggest fans."

"I talk to him all the time. I'm so proud of the things he is accomplishing. He has an excellent football mind," Don told the media at that time. "I guess you could say I'm a big fan of two teams: Carolina and the Dolphins. But it's not 50–50, it's 100 percent for both teams."

"I can't wait to head out that way and be there to root him on and support him, and just be around. It's just so exciting," Shula said regarding Mike being in the Super Bowl. Asked what Mike was like, father Don responded, saying, "He was a stickler for detail, even at a young age. He just wanted to make sure he did it right. He wasn't always the most gifted athlete around, but he was around a lot of gifted athletes, and he wasn't bashful to learn from them.

"I watch him, they show him a lot during the game, up [in the coach's box], he's got his glasses on, he got his charts. I know exactly what he's thinking, what he's going through," Shula said of watching his son. "I'm just proud that my son's going be the one that's going to carry the torch."

Super Bowl 50 (the only Super Bowl not to bear the classic Roman Numerals) was played on February 7, 2016, at Levi's Stadium, Santa Clara, California. The Panthers would be opposing the Denver Broncos. Mike Shula's adversary was going to be defensive guru Wade Phillips. It was the third most-watched Super Bowl in history. The Broncos closed out the first half with a 13–7 lead.

The Panthers came out and drove down to the Denver 26-yard line on their first drive of the second half, but the drive stalled when the Denver defense stiffened, and a missed field goal left the Panthers rattled. The teams then traded field goals, making the score 16–10 early in the fourth quarter. The game's decisive play happened with less than five minutes remaining in a one-possession game. Following a Denver punt, Carolina took possession on their own 24-yard line. On a 3rd-and-9, Newton faded back to pass, and Broncos linebacker strip-sacked Newton. Numerous players went for the ball. Standing still was Newton. Dumbfounded, Newton failed to fall on the ball and recover it for his team. By the time he decided to act, the ball popped out of the scrum of players and skittered back toward the Panthers' end zone. Denver recovered, and a few plays later, C. J. Anderson's 2-yard touchdown run sealed the game, making the final score 24–10.

The Broncos' front seven played great. The linemen were stout, the linebackers disciplined, the defense tough as nails. The Panthers linemen were simply overpowered and never forced Denver to abandon the base seven throughout the game. Additionally, the Panthers had gained two-thirds of their rushing yards that year out of three-receiver sets. The Broncos shut that down too, which is why Mike abandoned the run. "For a coach, no pill is more bitter than being beat tactically. But that's what happens when you face a wily old defensive coach like Wade Phillips and that wily old coach has an extra week to prepare."

It was indeed a bitter pill to swallow. As other teams in the league copied Wade's approach, Newton struggled through the following season. After having gone 15–1 in 2015, the Panthers fell to 6–10 in 2016.

"We've shown around here that we've been a very good offense. So a lot of that is typical overreaction to bad games," said Greg Olsen, Carolina's Pro Bowl tight end. "That's the easy way out. That's the easy critique for people who, watching from a distance, don't really have an idea what's going on. So that's the easy solution to everybody who doesn't have much knowledge of what we're actually doing."

"While Rivera defended Shula, he did say the Panthers could stand to simplify things to help all the newcomers on offense. Besides drafting running back Christian McCaffrey and wideout Curtis Samuel in the first two rounds, the Panthers also added a new slot receiver in Russell Shepard and $55.5 million left tackle Matt Kalil," wrote Joseph Person in the *Charlotte Observer.*

"We're in a situation now where you've got so many new guys as you're going through this communication, it takes a little bit to register," Rivera said.

"We need to look at that," Mike said. "And that's a fine line. You don't want to cut it down too much. We've had some moving parts. Not to make an excuse, but it's something we've got to look at. The No. 1 thing, you can have all you want and feel like it'll be good stuff, but if they're not playing fast or not making adjustments we need to make, maybe if it's not the look we think we're going to get, yeah, we've got to make sure we do whatever it takes to make them feel good about it."

"I've been so lucky to have been around coaches who have great perspective, starting in my family," Shula said. "You've got to go win. We know we've got to go win, and even sometimes then you're going to get criticism. I mean, I'll go with the win every week. You know if you don't, there's going to be criticism."

The Panthers bounced back and finished 11–5 in 2017. With their record, the Panthers won a wild-card berth and would face the New Orleans Saints in the playoffs.

Mike remained a lightning rod. Every time the offense struggled, he seemed to be burned in effigy by the Panthers faithful. But Panthers columnist DBelt of SBNation wrote, "While following Shula's scripted plays, the Panthers are easily one of the better offenses in the league. Ron Rivera and Mike Shula like to have long, drawn out scoring drives that eat up the clock and Shula is literally the best in the league this year at doing just that in the first two offensive drives. The league average for scoring percentage is 35%, while the Panthers put points on the board 50% of the time. Scoring on half their possessions in these scenarios puts them behind offensive geniuses Sean McVay and Andy Reid. That's it. Mike Shula is able to script plays on par with the best offensive minds in the game. We cut Cam a lot of slack for his lack of weapons, but if we take that into account for Shula as well, it's clear he is fantastic at designing an offense."

However, DBelt also wrote, "It is very clear that Mike Shula is an offensive genius that struggles with situational play calling and making adjustments. Much akin to Andy Reid in Kansas City, the offense would perform better if Shula focused on being the head coach while the offensive coordinator focused on coordinating the offense on Sundays. Shula would be a fantastic offensive assistant and, even though he's an average at best offensive coordinator, he could also be a successful head coach in the NFL."

On January 7, 2018, the New Orleans Saints rolled to a 21–9 lead over the Panthers at the Superdome in New Orleans. Despite some late heroics from Newton and the Panthers' offense, Carolina lost, 31–26.

After the loss, Ron Rivera received a two-year contract extension. A few days later, Mike Shula was fired as the offensive coordinator. Many columnists were quick to point out the numerous challenges of the 2017 season. Newton had limited practice in the preseason due to shoulder surgery. They had many new players. They also had their share of injuries. The glaring failure in many eyes, however, was that Shula had failed to turn Newton into a pocket passer.

Louis Riddick of ESPN said of Newton and the Shula firing, "As much high hopes as we have for someone with [Newton's] physical ability, he just not consistently mastered the fundamentals and the technical things needs to play the quarterback position from the pocket in such a way that an offensive coordinator or quarterback coach's point would be called into question. He is a very streaky type of passer. He's a generational athlete. He's a generational runner from the quarterback positon. But his passing has never really taken off to the point where he's taken the next step. I will say this in defense of him also, their passing game, structurally this year, was very, very basic. They need to improve the weapons, as well. That falls upon the general manager. Whenever coaches like this start getting fired, there's always more to it. There's always a whole bunch of people who are involved. And it's unfortunate to see people lose their jobs over it."

Many columnists pointed out that Shula was not very good at playing the media. He tended to deflect successes to others and spent only limited time with media, of which he seemed very wary.

Four days later, Mike was hired by the New York Giants as offensive coordinator and quarterbacks coach by new head coach Pat Shurmur, who said, "He's done an outstanding job developing and working with quarterbacks. He was the offensive coordinator of a team that was recently playing in the Super Bowl."

In May 2016, Don Shula was hospitalized as a result of fluid retention and sleep apnea, his wife, Mary Anne, told the press. "The family is looking for a speedy recovery," Mary Anne stated. Shula had been in South Florida when he became ill on a Monday evening. Shula, by then eighty-six, had been in and out of the hospital for the last several weeks. He'd been keeping his health a secret.

Just weeks earlier, in April, he had presented Heat President Pat Riley with the Don Shula Legend Award at the annual Reid & Fiorentino Call of the Game Dinner, which was a fundraiser for the Lauren's Kids and Dade Schools Athletic

Foundation. And the previous December, he was seen cruising around on his motorized wheelchair, in good spirits, at the Dolphins' 50th anniversary gala in December at the Hollywood Westin.

Shula remained fully aware of what was going on, his family stressed, and was fully involved in his own health decisions. "Coach has been entertaining staff with jokes, and we expect him to be home very soon," said family spokesman Carrie LaNoce. There had been other health concerns the family did not release to the public. That May, Shula received a pacemaker.

"He's doing fine. He had the pacemaker put in back in May, and since then, he's recovered nicely and he has good quality of life and he's able to enjoy things," said Dave Shula later that year at an unveiling of a Don Shula mural at Hard Rock Stadium in Miami. "Things were slowing down overall. And his doctors thought it was the best course of action for him to have overall bodily functions." Dave explained that Don and Mary Anne had been spending summers in their home in the San Francisco Bay area "to get through hurricane season." In 2018, Dave returned to coaching after 22 years away from the game when he was hired as wide receivers coach at Dartmouth, his alma mater, as well as that of his son, Dan.

In May 2017, *Sports Illustrated* peeled back the dark curtain on CTE by writing about two of the Dolphins' greatest icons—Nick Buoniconti and Jim Kiick. As the men of the undefeated team aged, the dark side of the NFL was suddenly exposed.

"Buoniconti doesn't explain that he can't figure out how to knot a tie or towel his back. He doesn't speak of his increasingly useless left hand, the increasingly frequent trips to the emergency room or how, just a few days earlier at his home on Long Island, he hurtled backward down a staircase and sprayed blood all over the hardwood," wrote S. L. Price.

"I should just kill myself! It doesn't matter!" Buoniconti yelled at wife, Lynn, after.

"Some of Buoniconti's Dolphins teammates, meanwhile, are crumbling. Quarterback Earl Morrall, the supersub so key to the Perfect Season, died at 79, in 2014, with Stage 4 CTE. Running back Jim Kiick, 70, lived in squalor until he was placed in an assisted living facility last summer with dementia/early onset Alzheimer's. Bill Stanfill, a defensive end who long suffered from dementia, died in November at 69. His brain and spine were sent to the CTE center at Boston University, where the disease has been found in 96% of players' brains studied," continued Price.

Mike Kadish, Miami's No. 1 pick in 1972, had recognized his own deterioration around 2000. A successful business owner, he had sold his company and put his affairs in order. He'd told the press, "I'm a little scared to be honest. . . . Without all the pills I take, I couldn't even be speaking with you right now. In fact, talking is one of the most difficult things about my condition. There's so many muscles involved in making the mouth form sounds and words that it's really noticeable when I don't have medication." By 2015, he'd stop taking phone calls at all due to his advanced illness.

"I feel lost," Buoniconti said. "I feel like a child."

Price's subsequent piece on Jim Kiick was just as devastating. Price painted a sad picture of Kiick. His children "had to withstand the mental demise of . . . former Miami Dolphins halfback Jim Kiick, 70, who after years of erratic behavior and squalid living was placed in a South Florida assisted living facility in July 2016. And that experience hardly lends itself to tidy closure," wrote Price.

When daughter Allie Kiick calls to "check up on him, he calls me—I kid you not—probably 30, 40 times after if I don't pick up the phone. He just keeps calling and calling and calling, to the point where, at night, I actually have to block him from my phone because he'll call at 3 in the morning. He just doesn't know any better."

As Price pointed out, Kiick hadn't been half as successful as Buoniconti (few people had been), and so Kiick was reduced to living on much, much less. "Divorced from [daughter] Allie and [son] Austin's mother, Mary, since 2000, Jim lived alone in Davie, Fla.—i.e., with no on-site partner to gauge his symptoms, track medical appointments or monitor his use of pain-killers and prescription medications. And solitude was never his strong suit," reported Price.

Csonka, living far away and having read the *Sports Illustrated* article, was in "an almost unbelievable shock." He called Morris right away. "The three of us know each other pretty well, and what Mercury says is what I tend to put the most stock in," said Csonka.

Mercury Morris had visited Kiick several times. According to reports, Morris told Csonka that Kiick was placed in an assisted-living facility because he needed assistance, nothing more. He needed someone to tell him when to take his medications, to remind him to clean his apartment, to pick up after him or to pick up after himself.

Csonka added, "When you say assisted living, you picture somebody as a complete invalid. I don't think that's the case at all. I think he needs someone in his life that can make sure that the details that are giving him trouble are kept straight, and

I think that's what's happening." As Morris and Csonka conferred, the idea was, someone would come in and say, 'Take your 3 p.m. pill,' and they would remain until the pill was taken. "That's what he needs, and that's the assistance that he's getting," said Csonka.

Csonka said at the reunions of the undefeated squad and such gatherings that comparative health has become "more and more the issue.... It's an update on how everybody's doing and who's still here."

The reunions were fast becoming a chance of not only saying hello, again, but of saying good-bye.

"I sleep late and get up to take a nap," Shula joked about his retirement. He'd filmed commercials with Dan Marino, appeared at all the celebration events of the Miami Dolphins' 50th season, and had even appeared on the HBO hit series *Ballers*.

Ballers starred many real gridiron legends, as well as megastar Dwayne "The Rock" Johnson. But the pilot featured a cameo of coach Shula and Larry Csonka. They appeared on the back of a luxury boat, when Shula yelled at one of the series' protagonists, "You are an asshole!" The cameo was quick, but audiences loved it.

"I go to all the games," said Shula, referring to the Dolphins. "My wife and I go down on the field before the game and say hello to the coaches and the players that are out early and then we watch them from up above."

Shula was often seen sitting at his desk in his opulent home office, being visited by numerous celebrities, including Dan Marino, Bob Griese, and Larry Csonka, among others. Surrounded by trophies and various game balls, there was always the nameplate. Readying himself for a photo op, he famously reached for the thick mahogany block, with his named etched in gold, joking, "Let's pull this closer, so they'll know who I am."

Life in his eighties was good for Don Shula. He reveled in the success of his career, in the success of his children and their families, and enjoyed the relationships he still maintained with players all these years later.

"Coach," Bob Griese says, "how you doing?" Shula was seated with Dave Hyde from the *Sun Sentinel*. Hyde had been allowed to take a peek into one of the regular lunch dates of two old friends.

"Robert," Shula says, his wheelchair off to the side, his shock of white hair perfectly combed, "I'm like the bottom of a stove . . ."

"Oh, no," Griese says.

"Smoking hot," Shula says.

"Griese rolls his eyes and reminds the coach he was given a new joke book a while back to update his material. Shula looks at Griese, deadpan, and raises his three middle fingers," detailed Hyde.

"Read between the lines," Shula says.

"The interplay between them comes so easy, so natural, and why not? They've known each other long enough to win Super Bowls together, raise children simultaneously, retire from careers, get inducted into the Pro Football Hall of Fame and share the grief of burying their first wives and the joy of finding their second wives," wrote Hyde. "They bought summer homes on the same mountain in North Carolina. They had a regular golf game for years and often ate dinners with their wives at each other's homes."

The lunches vary. Usually Hank Goldberg, the sports radio host and ESPN announcer, attended. Over the years others came and went. But Griese and Shula remained constant. Sometimes the meeting was at a Shula Steak House, other times they might meet at the track.

As Hyde noticed, they are not stuck in a time warp. "They talk of family, of football, of summer plans. So it's not like they're locked in the 1970s, though the conversation drops in there at times." Then when some verbal sparing breaks out, Shula casually says, "Minus-26." It's an obvious reference to Griese's Super Bowl record 26-yard loss for a sack against the Cowboys.

"It's minus-29 yards, jackass," Griese said to Shula. "That's the only Super Bowl record I still have. And I'm glad you brought that up, the way you always bring it up." And with that, Griese theatrically produces a letter from August 17, 2004, out of his pocket.

"I went and found this," Griese said.

Griese waves the letter from former NFL referee Jim Tunney, who was a member of the crew that officiated that Super Bowl. Tunney is also a good friend of Shula's. In the letter, Tunney confirmed for Griese that he was hunted down by no fewer than three Cowboys for that historic moment.

"You always say it was one Cowboy," Griese says.

"It was one," Shula responds.

"I have confirmation, right here, from the official, it was three," Griese says.

"You know Tunney was voted the second-best of 200-and-something officials, right?"

"Coach, can I pose for a picture with you?" a woman asks, stopping by the table.

Shula looks up. "It'll cost you $35." The woman paused, then Shula started laughing, and soon everyone, even the woman, is laughing.

"Griese plays the role of his straight man. He'll set Shula up for some one-liners. The coach and the quarterback. Still close friends. Still needling one another," wrote dolphins.com columnist Andy Cohen.

"Love to be with all of them," the coach said. "I'm really enjoying my retirement. I've got a lovely wife. Great home life. Great grandkids that I see as often as I can. I spend most of the year in South Florida now, though we do also spend some time in California. As I think about my life, it really can't get any better than this.

"I miss game day. I miss the excitement of getting a football team ready to go. I miss the anticipation of the opening kickoff, the adjustments you make at halftime, how everything can ride on one or two plays. Those are the things you can't fabricate in life. You have to go through it to appreciate it. Of course, I also miss the relationships. You meet so many wonderful people and form so many great bonds. But nothing compares to game day. There are no do-overs. You can't change the grade once the game is over. I really enjoyed that excitement," said Shula.

And looking forward? Shula told Cohen, "I want to continue to live the good life and appreciate all the wonderful things and people around me. To be able to sit back and enjoy some great memories. There were so many, and so many unforgettable experiences. I'm a very fortunate man. I was able to enjoy a lot of success. Now I can sit back and reminisce with my wonderful wife, Mary Anne, and my children and grandchildren. It's been a great ride."

Endnotes

Chapter 1: The Fisherman's Son

"Painesville and the surrounding . . . Cole, Jason, "Painesville, Est. 1832, A Hometown That Values Substance Over Style," *Sun Sentinel*, Deerfield Beach, January 7, 1996.

"We never knew them . . . Cole, January 7, 1996.

"Dan met Mary Miller . . . Cole, January 7, 1996.

"He just scrawled out his name . . . Moffet, Dan, "Coming Full Circle" *Palm Beach Post*, Palm Beach, FL, July 6, 1997.

"Each morning, Dan Shula woke . . . Hyde, Dave, "Super bowl a Family Affair for Shulas," *Sun Sentinel*, Deerfield Beach, January 30, 2016.

"[Don] didn't like the fishing life . . . Hyde, January 30, 2016.

"A work ethic," Shula said . . . Hyde, January 30,2016.

"You're going back to . . . Eskanazi, Gerald, "Super Bowl XIX; Don Shula Leaves Nothing To Chance," *New York Times*, New York, January 20, 1985.

"I never got used to the rough . . . Schudel, Jeff, "Don Shula at 80: From Harvey to Hall," *The News-Herald*, Willoughby, OH, July 18, 2010.

"Dad said, 'You'll get over it.' . . . Underwood, John, "Sitting on Top of the World," *Sports Illustrated*, New York, September 17, 1973.

"My father was one of those guys . . . Dexter, Pete, "The Things He Found In People," *Esquire* magazine, New York, NY, September 1983.

"My dad was never an athlete . . . Dexter, September 1983.

"He has always maintained that . . . Eskanazi, January 20, 1985.

"This is a town built on rock . . . Moffett, November 15, 1993.

"I still have relatives in . . . Schudel, July 18, 2010.

"The Mar-Val Bowling Alley . . . Moffett, July 26, 1997.

"Our father may not have been . . . Cole, January 7, 1996.

"She was a strict Hungarian mom . . . Moffett, November 15, 1993.

"Every morning she would . . . Moffett November 15, 1993.

"He hated to lose even when . . . Shula, Don (with Lou Sahadi), *The Winning Edge*. New York, NY: EP Dutton, 1973, p. 31.

"It was strictly taboo . . . *The Winning Edge*, p. 31.

"When I grew up my parents lived next . . . *Sports Illustrated* video interview, The Vault, February 13, 2012.

"That's the first beating I ever took . . . *The Winning Edge,* p. 37.

"As a kid, I was the one . . . Katz, Michael, "The Coach Who Has the Last Laugh," *New York Times,* New York, NY January 15, 1973.

"He hates to lose . . . Katz, January 15, 1973.

"Things were really tough . . . Plaschke, Bill, "For Miami's Don Shula, Who Needs Only Seven Victories to Break George Halas' Record, Family Now Ranks Far Above Football," *Los Angeles Times,* Los Angeles, CA, September 02, 1993.

"I forged my mother's signature . . . Scott, Ronald B., "Coach Don Shula, the Would-Be Priest Who Makes Miami Mean," *People* magazine, New York, NY, December 02, 1974.

"Don was also the one who . . . Plaschke, *Los Angeles Times,* September 02, 1993.

"That's been a part of my makeup . . . Horrigan, Joe, "Don Shula: All Time Winner," Professional Football Researchers Association, Coffin Corner, Vol. 19, N.2 (1997).

"It was a habit he would . . . Underwood, John, "Sitting on Top of the World," *Sports Illustrated,* New York, NY September 17, 1973.

"The coaches didn't always . . . Underwood, *Sports Illustrated* September 17, 1983.

Once, when Shula got out of hand . . . Martin, Donald E., "Memories of Don Shula at Painesville," *Cleveland Plain Dealer,* Cleveland, OH December 16,1964.

"There were other guys who were . . . Moffett November 15, 1993.

"Don performed capably as . . . Moffett November 15, 1993.

"Our last two meets, we . . . Shula's Roots, November 15, 1993.

"I don't remember him saying it . . . Shula's Roots, November 15, 1993.

"Charlie Schupska was the quarterback . . . Shula's Roots, November 15, 1993.

"[Guarnieri] said it was the . . . . . . Shula's Roots, November 15, 1993.

"And he was the one who . . . Plaschke, *Los Angeles Times,* September 02, 1993.

"When I got out of high school . . . Schudel, July 18, 2010.

"He set up the interview . . . Schudel, July 18, 2010.

"I think about needing gas . . . Schudel, July 18, 2010.

"Eisele was an exceptional coach . . . *The Winning Edge,* p. 41.

"At Carroll, Don played both . . . Zunt, Dick, "Don Shula: Those who knew him the best," *Cleveland Plain Dealer, Sports Weekender,* Cleveland, OH, January 24, 1976.

"He wanted to know where . . . Zunt, Dick, *Cleveland Plain Dealer,* January 24, 1976.

"I remember one day . . . Zunt, Dick, *Cleveland Plain Dealer,* January 24, 1976.

"On the practice field he always . . . Zunt, Dick, *Cleveland Plain Dealer,* January 24, 1976.

"Don came from a small town . . . Zunt, Dick, *Cleveland Plain Dealer,* January 24, 1976.

"At Carroll we had a play called . . . Zunt, Dick, *Cleveland Plain Dealer,* January 24, 1976.

"Another promising halfback . . . N/A, "Carroll Is Tuning Up New Battery", *Cleveland Plain Dealer,* Cleveland, OH, November 21, 1947.

"Jim Moran, veteran . . . Heaton, Charles, "Shula, Carroll's Sophomore Backfield Find, Starts Against B.W. Saturday," *Cleveland Plain Dealer,* Cleveland, OH, October 14, 1948.

"I think he's going to rate . . . Heaton, Charles, *Cleveland Plain Dealer,* October 14, 1948.

"filled in so capably in the two . . . Heaton, Charles, *Reserve, Carroll Grid Hosts Today, Cleveland Plain Dealer,* Cleveland, OH, October 24, 1948.

"The most important backfield addition . . . Heaton, Charles, "Carroll In Tip Top Shape for Bowl Game," *Cleveland Plain Dealer,* Cleveland, OH, November 29, 1948.

"Shula, who also ran in... Heaton, Charles, "Taseff, Schaffer, Pace 4th In A Row," *Cleveland Plain Dealer,* Cleveland, OH, November 14, 1949.
"I was interviewed with him for... *The Winning Edge,* p.30.
"A great many of the ideas and... *The Winning Edge,* p. 30.
"I once seriously considered...... Scott, Ronald B. *People* magazine, December 02, 1974.
"When the football game between... Hudak, Timothy L., "'Who is John Carroll?' Syracuse Finds Out in 1950," LA84 Foundation, Los Angeles, CA, August 25, 2014.
"Not only was he a four-year... Hudak, August 25, 1994.
"Time had expired during... Hudak, August 25, 1994.
"Don Shula, who turned in another... Heaton, Charles, "Carroll Upsets Syracuse, 21–16," *Cleveland Plain Dealer,* Cleveland, OH, November 11, 1950.
"So I called the Browns... Underwood, *Sports Illustrated,* September 17, 1973.
"I never had one either... Shula, *The Winning Edge,* p. 47.
"We toasted each other... Shula, *The Winning Edge,* p. 47.

Chapter 2: Playing Days

"Most other members of... Cobbledick, Bill, "37th Makes Mock Warfare in Serious and Alert Stride," *Cleveland Plain Dealer,* Cleveland, OH, July 19, 1951.
"This is a good deal... Cobbledick, Bill, *Cleveland Plain Dealer,* July 19, 1951.
"As the safety man... Sauerbrei, Harold, "Brown Eyes Stan Heath for Defensive Spot," *Cleveland Plain Dealer,* Cleveland, OH, July 24, 1951.
"Shula and Taseff may be making their... Sauerbrei, Harold, "40,000 To Watch Browns Battle Rams Here Today," *Cleveland Plain Dealer,* Cleveland, OH, September 14, 1951.
"I've always been a big...... Underwood, *Sports Illustrated,* September 17, 1973.
"The first time I met... Shula, *The Winning Edge,* p. 45.
"It's interesting, in a way... Rhoden, Bill, "When Paul Brown Smashed the Color Barrier," *New York Times,* New York, NY, September 25, 1997.
"When he coached at Massillon... Rhoden, Bill, September 25, 1997.
"Paul was a top business... Rhoden, Bill, September 25, 1997.
"Check the record... Scalzo, Joe, "Stark Icons: Paul Brown's influence still extends far beyond Massillon," *Columbus Monthly,* March 27, 2016.
"He wanted to control... Cosenza, Anthony, "Paul Brown: The Man, The Myth, The Legend," CinciJungle.com, November 15, 2015.
"The biggest influence on my... Berger, Phil, "Football Innovator Paul Brown Dead at 82," Orlando Sentinel, Orlando, FL, August 6, 1991.
"As I looked around the room... Shula, *The Winning Edge,* p. 81–82.
"We were as close as... Shula, *The Winning Edge,* p. 48.
"Nice tackle Taseff!"... Anderson, Dave, "The Moon Shot," *New York Times,* New York, December 16, 1972.
"I saw a lot of men wounded... Keim, John, *Legends by the Lake: The Cleveland Browns at Municipal Stadium.* Akron, Ohio: University of Akron Press, 1999.
"Lou never got all the credit... Keim.
"Later we found out why... *The Winning Edge,* p. 48.
"I remember the thrill... *The Winning Edge,* p. 49.

"Otto Graham was my idol . . . Saccomano, Jim, "Sacco Sez: Automatic Otto," *DenverBroncos.com*, Denver, CO, April 7, 2018.

"You instilled more attitude . . . N/A "Closer to My Heart: Blanton Collier: That's Blanton Collier, Induction of Blanton Collier into the Kentucky Pro Football Hall of Fame," The Blanton Collier Sportsmanship Group, June 24, 2016.

"I later found out that one . . . *The Winning Edge*, p. 51.

"Fears caught his first pass . . . *The Winning Edge*, p. 51.

"the John Carroll boy . . . Sauerbrei, Harold, "Shula Stands Out," *Cleveland Plain Dealer*, Cleveland, OH, September 20, 1950.

"Each time I failed to cover . . . *The Winning Edge*, p. 52.

"As a player, he was interested . . . Heaton, Chuck, "Collier Gives View on Shula," *Cleveland Plain Dealer*, January 2, 1979.

"Don Shula, John Carroll alumnus . . . Jones, Harry, "Eagles Toss Everything at Browns—Even Water Bucket," *Cleveland Plain Dealer*, November 12, 1951.

"The absence of James is not . . . Sauerbrei, Harold, "Giants ready for First Place Battle," *Cleveland Plain Dealer*, Cleveland, OH, November 13, 1951.

"Don Shula intercepted a Chicago . . . Jones, Harry, "Bears and Browns Assessed 374 Yards in Penalties for New NL Record," *Cleveland Plain Dealer*, November 26,1951.

"This was the first league game . . . Grosshandler, Stan, "The Day Dub Jones Ran Wild," *Football Digest*, Nov. 1972.

"It seemed the harder we . . . Grosshandler, Stan, "The Day Dub Jones Ran Wild," *Football Digest*, Nov. 1972.

"I was back on the bench . . . *The Winning Edge*, p. 55.

"I could be back in Cleveland . . . *The Winning Edge*, p. 57.

"You should have seen . . . Moffett *Sun Sentinel* November 15, 1993.

"Head Coach Paul Brown . . . Yowell, Keith, "1953: Browns and Colts Conclude 15-Player Trade, Today in Pro Football History," March 26, 2012.

"That's the first time . . . *The Winning Edge*, p. 58.

Mike Devitt, "Baltimore mayor Thomas D'Alesandro Jr . . . Devitt, Mike, "Descendants of the Mayflower: A History of the Indianapolis Colts," Indianapolis Colts Infopedia, 2000.

"We got all the breaks . . . N/A, "The Last Team to Go Belly Up, The Dallas Texans," NFL Pro Football Hall of Fame, 2018.

"As Commissioner Bell was trying . . . Shuck, Barry, "Original Texans: 1952 Dallas Texans," SB Nation, October 13, 2017.

"Carroll Rosenbloom is a . . . Boyle, Robert H., The Pleasure of Dying on Sundays, *Sports Illustrated*, December 31, 1965.

"I was associated with . . . Brady, Dave, "Carrol Rosenbloom Drowns in Surf," *Washington Post*, April3, 1979.

"There was never a dull . . . Eisenberg, John, "Carroll Rosenbloom: Man of Mystery," Press Box Online, December 18, 2017.

"You knew he was robbing . . . Bell, Upton, and Borges, Ron, *Present at the Creation*. Lincoln, NB: University of Nebraska Press, 2017, p. 51.

"There's Carroll, rolling dice . . . Bell, p. 51.

"The coach, Russ Murphy . . . *The Winning Edge*, p. 59.

"I came to my first Colts . . . Donovan, Arthur J., Jr., (with Bob Drury), *Fatso*. New York, NY: William Morrow & Co. (1987), p. 15.

"I played with Don Shula . . . Donovan, p. 15.

"We know one of you Colts . . . Donovan, p. 15.

"We really didn't steal it . . . Callahan, Tom, *Johnny U.* New York, NY: Three Rivers Press, 2007, p. 68.

"When her daughter died . . . *The Winning Edge*, p. 61.

"tremendous coaching talent . . . Michael, MacCambridge, *America's Game.* New York, NY: Anchor, 2005, p. 81.

"Ewbank began by doing things . . . MacCambridge, p. 81.

"Many changes and adjustments . . . Fleischer, Jack, *My Sunday Best.* New York, NY: Grosset & Dunlap, 1972, p. 27.

"Some rough guys there . . . Zimmerman, Paul, Don Shula, *Sports Illustrated,* December 20, 1993.

"Ewbank is a very meticulous person . . . *The Winning Edge*, p. 62.

"When Ewbank came over as . . . Snyder, Brad, "Ex-Colts fondly salute 'the general' Donovan, Matte laud his '50s-'60s leadership," *Baltimore Sun*, January 6, 1996.

"Ewbank had entrusted me . . . *The Winning Edge*, p. 63.

"Captain Red Neck" . . . John Steadman, "Win or Else Berth for Shula, Colts" *The Sporting News*, January 19, 1963, p. 27.

"I'd heard that was the . . . Underwood, John, "Sitting on Top of the World," *Sports Illustrated,* September 17, 1973.

"On the first play of the game . . . Donovan, p. 156.

"He blended in with them real good . . . *The Winning Edge*, p. 63.

"Donovan would get into . . . Callahan, p. 68.

"I'm so sorry, coach! . . . Nash, Bruce, and Zullo, Alan, *Football Hall of Fame 2*. New York, NY: Simon & Schuster, 1991, p. 8.

"Shula was one of the first . . . Callahan, p. 69.

"It all started when . . . Fleischer, p. 26.

"It's an exaggeration to . . . Callahan, p. 68.

"John was just starting to . . . Callahan, p. 69.

"mean sonofabitch, and . . . Donovan, p. 167.

"So the choosy prick . . . Donovan, p. 167.

"My future wasn't good . . . *The Winning Edge*, p. 64.

"He wasn't quite fast enough . . . Snyder, *Baltimore Sun*, January 6, 1996.

"All of a sudden I had the . . . *The Winning Edge*, p. 64.

Chapter 3: College Days Redux

"It was just a stepping stone . . . Martin, Donald E., "A Coach's Memory of Don Shula at Painesville," *Cleveland Plain Dealer*, Cleveland, OH, December 16, 1964.

Richard J. "Dick" Voris was . . . N/A, "Dick Voris," Madera Tribune, Number 261, 15 February 1955 *and* N/A, "James Voris," Obituaries, *Santa Cruz Sentinel*, CA, December 26, 2008.

"It was an odd beginning . . . *The Winning Edge*, p. 71.

"Then I began to think of Dorothy . . . Miller, Jill Young, "Death of Dorothy: Shula Misses Staunchest Fan," *Fort Lauderdale Sun Sentinel*, FL, July 7, 1991.
"I was playing it cool . . . Underwood, *Sports Illustrated,* September 17, 1973.
"I got three letters . . . Underwood, *Sports Illustrated,* September 17, 1973.
"Blanton is probably the best . . . *The Winning Edge*, p. 75.
"Years later, when my . . . Martin, *Cleveland Plain Dealer,* December 16, 1964.
"From the standpoint of . . . *The Winning Edge*, p. 77.
"I've got a situation here . . . Maule, Tex, "Lambs Into Lions," *Sports Illustrated,* New York, December 2, 1957.
"Actually, Bobby doesn't live . . . Maule, *Sports Illustrated,* December 2, 1957.
"I joke around a lot . . . Maule, *Sports Illustrated,* December 2, 1957.
"I talked over the opportunities . . . *The Winning Edge,* p. 77.
"Technique-wise, Blanton Collier . . . Nordheimer, John, "The Enduring Obsession: Don Shula's Need to Win," *New York Times,* NY, September 1, 1985.

Chapter 4: Detroit

"Welcome to the Lions . . . Plimpton, George, *Paper Lion*. New York, NY: Little Brown & Co., 2016, p. 21.
"He and the other coaches . . . Plimpton, p. 32.
"Wilson felt that if a player . . . Karras, Alex, *Even Big Guys Cry*. New York, NY: Signet, 1978, p. 124.
"I guess you fellows know . . . Karras, p. 124.
"It was easy to spot George . . . Plimpton, p. 66.
"He had been with most . . . Plimpton, p. 97.
"He was a tough, hard-nosed . . . *The Winning Edge,* p. 80.
"No fooling around . . . Plimpton, p. 97.
"At Detroit the bed checks . . . Plimpton, p. 114.
"George Wilson knew he . . . Karras, p. 140.
"[Tom] Fears liked to play . . . Goldstein, Richard, "Night Train Lane, 73, N.F.L. Defensive Star," *New York Times,* NY, February 1, 2002.
"But the same competitiveness . . . Plimpton, p. 74.
"a 'must-win' game for us . . . Fleischer, p. 48.
"On any given Sunday during . . . Karras, p. 141.
"We spent much of that . . . Fleischer, p. 51.
"It was the type of tension that . . . Fleischer, p. 51.
"I thought he had a heart attack . . . Karras, p. 142.
"I took my helmet off and . . . Karras, p. 142.
"I don't know how we got . . . Karras, p. 142.
"Pass, Milt, three times, then punt . . . Plimpton, p. 74.
"Much of the credit for the . . . Gordon Cobbledick, "Lions Defensive Unit Offsets Lack of Outstanding Quarterback," *Cleveland Plain Dealer,* OH, September 7, 1961.
"the most famous football game . . . Bak, Richard, "Remembering the greatest game in Lions history," *Detroit Athletic Club,* MI, December 9, 2012.
"C'mon, C'mon . . . . I'm gonna . . . Karras, p. 150.

"It still ticks me off . . . Bak, December 9, 2012.
"On the Packers' first play from . . . Bak, December 9, 2012.
"Everything we did that day . . . Bak, December 9, 2012.
"We knocked the bejabbers . . . Karras, p. 152.
"We demolished them . . . *The Winning Edge*, p. 80.
"Bill Glass says the Detroit . . . Gordon Cobbledick, "Browns First Half-Million Home Season Within Reach Tomorrow," *Cleveland Plain Dealer,* OH, November 24, 1962.
"The defensive book was . . . Plimpton, p. 35.
"Gino was the one who . . . Callahan, p. 198.
"We got hammered by the Chicago . . . Steadman, John, "Marchetti reflects on earlier era," *Baltimore Sun,* MD, October 24, 1994.
"Don't worry; now I got my . . . Steadman, October 24, 1994.
"He asked me to recommend . . . Steadman, October 24, 1994.
"Don Shula should have been . . . Seidel, Jeff, "A revealing look at the 1957 Detroit Lions in Joe Schmidt's basement," *Detroit Free Press,* MI, September 9, 2017.
"Letting Ewbank go was . . . N/A, "Lions' Don Shula Replaces Ewbank As Colts Coach," *Traverse City Record Eagle,* MI, January 9, 1963.

Chapter 5: Baltimore

"On a day when the Baltimore . . . Boyle, Robert H., "The Pleasure of Dying On Sunday," *Sports Illustrated,* New York, NY, December 13, 1965.
"I don't want any yachts . . . Boyle, December 13, 1965.
"He always gave you the feeling . . . Bell, p. 204.
"The Colts had gotten old . . . *The Winning Edge*, p. 87.
"I think the players were . . . Callahan, p. 200.
"The first guy I had to tell . . . *The Winning Edge,* p. 87.
I had been an . . . Bagli, Vince, and Macht, Norman L., *Sundays at 2:00 With The Baltimore Colts.* Centreville, MD: Tidewater Publishing, 1995, p. 107.
"We were at about 19,000 feet . . . Cote, Greg, "From war hero to Don Shula's right-hand man: The life of Charley Winner," *Miami Herald,* FL, May 27, 2016.
"Weeb taking his socks off . . . Cote, May 27, 2016.
"Much of Unitas' success was . . . Sahadi, Lou. *Johnny Unitas: America's Quarterback.* Chicago, IL: Triumph Books, 2004, p. 84.
"As a quarterback, I have to . . . Sahadi, *Johnny Unitas,* p. 84.
"Look, you're the boss . . . Sahadi, *Johnny Unitas,* p. 85.
"If you're going to show me up . . . Callahan, p. 202.
"It was John's personality . . . Callahan, p. 202.
"Don't let me down . . . Callahan, p. 202.
"After the play John glared . . . *The Winning Edge,* p. 101.
"He came in as a young head . . . Amore, Dom, "Passing Through the Shula Era," *Hartford Courant,* CT, November 7, 1993.
"John had a real toughness . . . Nordheimer, September 1, 1985.
"Don't ask me, ask Shula . . . Callahan, p. 201.
"If that son of a bitch . . . Callahan, p. 201.

"We always left for West Coast . . . Pierson, Don, "Sports can seem inconsequential in moments of crisis, but they reflect our humanity," *Chicago Tribune,* IL, September 16, 2001.

"He asked me what I thought . . . Pierce, Charles, "Black Sunday: The NFL plays on after JFK's Assassination," *Sports Illustrated,* New York, November 24, 2003.

"Jack would have said . . . Pierce, November 24, 2003.

"I remember sitting in the . . . Pierson, September 16, 2011.

"That was the only game . . . Pierce, November 24, 2003.

"Absolutely, it was the right . . . Layden, Tim, "JFK 50 Years Later: The NFL's Darkest Weekend," *Sports Illustrated,* New York, November 20, 2013.

"He came into our locker . . . Layden, November 20, 2013.

"What stands out in my mind . . . N/A, "Former Aggie, NFL player, TV mogul Danny Villanueva dies at age 77," *Albuquerque Journal,* NM, June 19, 1963.

"Like a lot of disciplinarians . . . Callahan, p. 198.

"Orr was not a very physical . . . Callahan, p. 199.

"If you had made that block . . . Callahan, p. 199.

"I don't want to hear any . . . Callahan, p. 199.

"Is this your shit?" . . . Freeman, Mike, *Undefeated.* New York, NY: It Books, 2012, p. 8.

"What you're doing is . . . Freeman, p. 8.

"I just came in for a haircut . . . Callahan, p. 200.

"Then there are the stories . . . Zimmerman, *Sports Illustrated,* December 20, 1993.

"Oh, hell," Shula said . . . Zimmerman, *Sports Illustrated,* December 20, 1993.

"We got the weapons now . . . Maule, Tex, "The Makings of a New Dynasty," *Sports Illustrated,* NY, October 12, 1964.

"On defense, your job . . . Goldstein, Richard, "Bill Arnsparger, Architect of Feared Dolphins Defenses, Dies at 88," *New York Times,* NY, July 18, 2015.

"We spent a good deal of time . . . Shula, Don (with Tex Maule), "The road to the title in the West," *Sports Illustrated,* NY, January 18, 1965.

"Designing a defense for . . . Shula with Maule, January 18, 1965.

"We had proved something . . . Shula with Maule, January 18, 1965.

"We got stung in Minnesota . . . Maule, Dynasty, October 12, 1964.

"What we are doing this year . . . Maule, Dynasty, October 12, 1964.

"John Unitas, the toast of profootball . . . N/A "Unitas and Coach Shula Receive Honors in Poll," *New York Times,* NY, December 11, 1964.

"Blanton Collier, coach of the . . . Wallace, William N., "Browns and Colts Resume Drills for N.F.L. Title Game After Weekend Off," *New York Times,* NY, December 23, 1964.

"the Baltimore players are . . . Wallace, *Browns and Colts,* December 23, 2964.

"Somebody has to be the favorite . . . N/A, "Football Fans Get QB duel For Christmas," *Detroit Free Press,* MI, December 25, 1964.

"The Browns are a good team . . . Shula, Don (with Tex Maule), "How The Colts Met Triumph—and Disaster," *Sports Illustrated,* New York, January 11, 1965.

"The more we looked . . . Shula and Maule, Disaster, January 11, 1965.

"He's even better . . . Shula and Maule, Disaster, January 11, 1965.

"After our analysis of the movies . . . Shula and Maule, Disaster, January 11, 1965.

"The team was spirited in . . . Shula and Maule, Disaster, January 11, 1965.

"Our workouts have been shorter . . . N/A, "Avoid Complacency for Title Game With Browns on Sunday," *United Press International,* December 25, 1964.

"The Colts are favored by . . ."Avoid Complacency," December 25, 1964.

"The most dramatic play . . . Cohen, Roger, "Cleveland Browns: Memories of 1964 Title Game," *Dog Pound Daily.com,* Cleveland, OH, November 24, 2015.

"It was our best defensive game . . . N/A, "Cleveland Blitz Leaves Colts in Ruins," *Associated Press,* December 28, 1964.

"They used a lot of . . . Cleveland Blitz, December 28, 1964.

"They just beat the hell . . . White, Gordon S., "Colts' Post-Mortem: Offense Disappoints Shula," *New York Times,* NY, December 28, 1964.

"In the center of the dressing . . . White, Post-Mortem, December 28, 1964.

"When you go over to the . . . White, Post-Mortem, December 28, 1964.

"I thought at the time . . . Shula, Don (with Tex Maule), "The road to the title in the West," *Sports Illustrated,* NY, January 18, 1965.

"One of Dave's first memories . . . Hoffer, Richard, "Here Comes the Son," *Sports Illustrated,* NY, October 12, 1992.

"Shocked to say the least . . . *The Winning Edge,* p. 87.

"After December 17th, I . . . Heaton, Charles, Shula "One Step Ahead of Posse," *Cleveland Plain Dealer,* OH, April 12, 1965.

"I couldn't have hand-picked . . . Heaton, Posse, April 12, 1965.

"There was still hope . . . *The Winning Edge* p. 114.

"Our practices that week . . . Fleischer, p. 120.

"I later learned the Rams . . . Fleischer, p. 122.

"Our pregame practice . . . Fleischer, p. 123.

"We showed no signs of . . . Fleischer, p. 128.

"The story line is so outrageously . . . Daley, Arthur, "Storybook finishes," *New York Times,* NY, December 21, 1965.

"One thing we're going . . . N/A, "Lombardi Fears Matte May Throw Book at Green Bay In Western Playoff," *Anderson Herald,* IN, December 24, 1965.

"We were at Pro Bowls . . . Callahan, p. 197.

"The only player I ever talk . . . Callahan, p. 197.

"We figured we would have . . . Shula and Maule, Disaster, January 11, 1965.

"As sports relics go . . . Klingaman, Mike, "Matte's band still binds, 40 years later," *Baltimore Sun,* MD, December 25, 2005.

"I had to learn so much offense . . . Klingaman, December 25, 2005.

"We simplified everything . . . Klingaman, December 25, 2005.

"I didn't see what happened . . . Maule, Tex, "The Point of Some Return," *Sports Illustrated,* NY, January 3, 1966.

"far more strain and tension . . . Maule, Return, January 3, 1965.

"They came out in a five-one . . . Maule, Return, January 3, 1965.

"This was one of the toughest . . . Maule, Return, January 3, 1965.

"I was scared to death . . . Maule, Return, January 3, 1965.

"All I thought about was . . . John Steadman, "Chandler's admission helps take sting out of 31-year-old bad call," *Baltimore Sun,* MD, November 3, 1996.

"There was no question the . . . Steadman, *Chandler's Admission,* November 3, 1996.

"It went right through the middle . . . Steadman, *Chandler's Admission,* November 3, 1996.

"It became, without a doubt . . . Steadman, *Chandler's Admission,* November 3, 1996.
"When I looked up . . . Steadman, *Chandler's Admission,* November 3, 1996.
"The Colts were wronged . . . Steadman, *Chandler's Admission,* November 3, 1996.
"I was never more proud . . . Maule, Return, January 3, 1965.
"You can't go into a game . . . Maule, Return, January 3, 1965.
"Think about it . . . Maule, Return, January 3, 1965.
"They all wrote that I cried . . . Hoffer, Son, October 12, 1992.
"After the game, a disconsolate . . . . . . Klingaman, December 25, 2005.
"I'm glad it's over . . . Maule, Return, January 3, 1965.
"I knew the minute I . . . MacCambridge, Michael, *Chuck Noll: A Life's Work*. Pittsburgh, PA: University of Pittsburgh Press, 2016.
"I was tougher on him . . . McLemore, Morris T., *The Miami Dolphins.* New York, NY: Doubleday, 1972, p. 138.
"Is he a coach or a barber? . . . Garrison, Rita, *Big Bubba*. XLibris US, Bloomington, IN: XLibris US, 2013, p. 94.
"There comes a moment . . . Maule, Tex, "An Aura of Destiny," *Sports Illustrated,* NY, November 13, 1967.
"For both teams, then . . . Maule, Destiny, November 13, 1967.
"This rematch of the two . . . Becker, Bill, "Rams Trounce Colts, 34–10," *New York Times,* NY, December 18, 1967.
"They exerted a great amount . . . *The Winning Edge,* p. 97.
"I thought he was kidding . . . Fowler, Scott, "Shula's Biggest Test Is Handling Wife's Death," *Washington Post,* DC, September 2, 1991.
"In football, you have to . . . Scott, September 2, 1991.
"Dorothy smiled at everyone . . . Scott, September 2, 1991.
"Football has its rewards . . . Davidson, Tom, and Lynch, Dorothy Shula, Wife Of Dolphins` Coach, *Sun Sentinel,* Deerfield Beach, Florida, February 26, 1991.
"You can`t get along in . . . Davidson and Lynch, February 26, 1991.
"We went up to visit Don . . . Davidson and Lynch, February 26, 1991.
"But my mom couldn't let . . . Davidson and Lynch, February 26, 1991.
"At home, she runs our . . . Cote, Greg and Long, Gary, "Dorothy Shula was the true coach in a family of them," *Sun Sentinel,* Deerfield, FL, February 26, 1991.
"Dave is Don Shula's son . . . Hoffer, Son, October 1991.
"What was my mother like? . . . Hoffer, Son, October 1991.
"People tell me there's a lot . . . Graham, Michael, "The Son Also Rises," *Cincinnati* magazine, OH, May 1992.
"Coaches did not seem . . . Hoffer, Son, October 1992.
"he was a doting father . . . Hoffer, Son, October 1992.
"I suppose I always sort of . . . Hoffer, Son, October 1992.
"All the other kids wanted . . . McCarthy, Charlie, "Don Shula's parenting as impressive as his coaching," *FOX Sports,* NY, June 15, 2013.
"[Dave] Shula can think back . . . Plaschke, Bill, "Will the Son Come Up? Dave Shula Deals With Last Name and Last Place," *Los Angeles Times,* CA, November 24, 1993.
"I remember running home . . . Plaschke, Son Come Up, November 24, 1993.
"The highlights of my summer . . . Plaschke, Son Come Up, November 24, 1993.

"But then all of a sudden he . . . Janofsky, Michael, "David Shula: Hard Worker With The Correct Lineage," *New York Times*, NY, December 18, 1985.
"The thing about my dad . . . McCarthy, June 15, 2013.
"I couldn't have had a . . . McCarthy, June 15, 2013.
"It would be poetic justice if . . . Maule, Tex, "Pre-Season Guide," *Sports Illustrated*, NY, September 16, 1968.
"Yes, I am interested in getting . . . Sahadi, *Johnny Unitas*, p. 90.
"Morrall confided to Shula . . . Sahadi, *Johnny Unitas*, p. 90.
"If you come to Baltimore . . . Sahadi, *Johnny Unitas*, p. 90.
"I didn't want to sit around . . . George Vecsey, "Morrall: Colts Fill-In Quarterback Who Fills The Bill," *New York Times*, NY, November 4, 1968.
"It had to be the best . . . *The Winning Edge*, p. 97.
"Earl won a lot of games . . . *The Winning Edge*, p. 97.
"I'm through," Unitas . . . Sahadi, *Johnny Unitas*, p. 93.
"The first pass I threw . . . Callahan, p. 213.
"Shula used to piss me off . . . Callahan, p. 214.
"But he really couldn't . . . Sahadi, *Johnny Unitas*, p. 94.
"I didn't want to use John . . . Callahan, p. 215.
"The Packers defeat by . . . Maule, Tex, "Au Revoir," *Sports Illustrated*, NY, December 16, 1967.
"We didn't expect them . . . Maule, Au Revoir, December 16, 1968.
"Unitas and Morral might . . . Callahan, p. 214.
"The two of them fit hand . . . Callahan, p. 214.
"So this is the great Barrier Reef . . . Callahan, p. 214.
"Unitas had this great belief . . . *The Winning Edge*, p. 100.
"If we make the field goal . . . Bagli and Macht, p. 108.
"This is the last guy I'm ever . . . Bagli and Macht, p. 108.
"The championship victory over . . . *The Winning Edge*, p. 97.
"The euphoria all over the . . . Bell, p. 182.
"The Colts have the greatest . . . Stedman, John, "Coach of the Year? Iron-Willed Don Shula," *The Sporting News*, KY, January 4, 1969.
"The record that Shula . . . Steadman, Iron-Willed, January 4, 1969.
"Someone asked him about . . . Zimmerman, Paul, "Don Shula: SI Salutes the Most Successful NFL Coach In History, A Man Whose Mastery of The Game Spans Four Decades," *Sports Illustrated*, New York, NY, December 20, 1993.
"Joe's the 837th guy Louis . . . Zimmerman, *Don Shula*, December 20, 1993.
"recognized that they had a dangerous . . . Bell, p. 183.
"Johnny Unitas didn't agree . . . *The Winning Edge*, p. 99.
"Earl should be starting . . . Sahadi, *Johnny Unitas*, p. 102.
"He has done so much . . . N/A, "Lions Sent Earl to New York," *The Sporting News*, KY, November 30, 1968.
"Let's throw our own Super Bowl . . . Gruver, Ed, *From Baltimore to Broadway*, Chicago, IL: Triumph Books, 2009, p. 177.
"I know I can stop . . . Garrison, p. 110.
"Just play you're fucking . . . Garrison, p. 110.
"Earl said he just didn't see me . . . Gruver, p. 261.
"We should have had points . . . Gruver, p. 261.

"Be ready." Shula insisted . . . Gruver, p. 261.

"By this time, the Colts . . . Perry, Danny, editor, Matt Snell, "Super Bowl III," *Super Bowl: The Game of Their Lives.* NY: Macmillan, 1997.

"Maybe I should have put him . . . Sahadi, *Johnny Unitas,* p. 122.

"I can't begin to detail . . . *The Winning Edge,* p. 107.

"We got all the breaks . . . Gruver, p. 257.

"made me sick . . . Gruver, p. 260.

"We figured we were going . . . D'Angelo, Tom, "Jets' win in Super Bowl III changed NFL history and Shula's career," *Palm Beach Post,* FL, February 1, 2010.

"It was humiliation, to be kind . . . Mike Curtis, Interview, *America's Game, 1970,* NFL Films, January 1994.

"Super Bowl III? I still haven't . . . Bubba Smith, Interview, *America's Game, 1970,* NFL Films, January 1994.

"We all knew Carroll was . . . Bell, p. 193.

"It was the biggest embarrassment . . . Bell, p. 194.

"Now men, I am not in this . . . Bell, p. 194.

"That speech was very usual . . . Bell, p. 194.

"Rosenbloom never forgot defeat . . . Bell, p. 193.

"believing as we all did . . . Bell, pp. 196–198.

"Don't worry, this may be . . . MacCambridge, *America's Game,* p. 255.

"I felt a certain uneasiness . . . *The Winning Edge,* 109.

"He was quite upset that I brought . . . *The Winning Edge,* p. 1090.

"My relationship with the owner . . . D'Angelo, *Super Bowl III,* February 1, 2010.

"Unitas' relationship with Shula . . . Sahadi, *Johnny Unitas,* p. 122.

"Last year when we started . . . Olsen, Jack, "The Rosenbloom-Robbie Bowl," *Sports Illustrated,* NY, November 9, 1970.

"Don made a lot of enemies . . . Olsen, November 9, 1970.

"Maybe everybody hated Shula . . . Olsen, November 9, 1970.

"He' find a way to chew . . . Olsen, November 9, 1970.

"I want to talk about a trade . . . Garrison, p. 98.

"Don't worry, Bubba . . . Garrison, p. 98.

"He spent the first half of the . . . *The Winning Edge,* pp. 109–110.

"To me, fair or unfair, Klosterman . . . Bell, p. 206.

Chapter 6: Miami

"Joe Robbie was used to . . . Rosenberg, Michael, "The Super Bowl that tore a family apart, forever changed stadium deals," *Sports Illustrated,* NY, November 23, 2015.

"I brought football here . . . Kram, Mark, "This Man Fired Flipper," *Sports Illustrated,* NY, December 15, 1969.

"We've had to live here . . . Kram, December 15, 1969.

"The man could outdrink . . . Rosenberg, November 23, 2015.

"Tyrant, tightwad, drunkard . . . Rosenberg, November 23, 2015.

"Robbie put out feelers . . . McLemore, p. 99.

"Imagine bumping into . . . *The Winning Edge,* p. 123.

"If I went ahead I would be . . . *The Winning Edge,* p. 124.

"It's too late to talk about...... Olsen, *Bowl,* November 9, 1970.

"I wouldn't be truthful... N/A, "Dolphins Land Shula as Coach With a 5-Year, $500,000 Pact," *New York Times,* NY, February 19, 1970.

"I had to know without... "Dolphins Land Shula," February 19, 1970.

"For the first day, it appeared... McLemore, p. 104.

"It is forbidden in pro football... Wallace, William N., "Rozelle Upholds Baltimore Claim," *New York Times,* NY, April 14, 1970.

"Immediate and substantial... Wallace, April 14, 1970.

"He became most irate... Cole, Jason, "The Colts Loss Was Dolphins' Gain," *Sun Sentinel,* FL, November 7, 1993.

"Rosenbloom turned coolly... Olsen, November 9, 1970.

"It's like this.... Olsen, November 9, 1970.

"I've done nothing wrong... McLemore, p. 104.

"It's just not fair that coaches... N/A, "Colts Promote McCafferty to Head Football Coach as the Successor to Shula," *United Press International,* April 6, 1970.

"It is the conclusion... Wallace, April 14, 1970.

"I always had great respect... Schad, Joe, and Carl Taseff, "Former Dolphins assistant dies of pneumonia," *Palm Beach Post,* Palm Beach, FL, February 28, 2005.

"From a career standpoint... Marvez, Alex, and Hyde, Dave, Carl Taseff, "Former Dolphins assistant coach, ex-NFL player," *Sun Sentinel,* Deerfield Beach, FL, February 28, 2005.

"Monte Clark is the real... Kuechenberg, Bob, Interview, "The Story of the 1972 Dolphins," *Miami Dolphins.com,* November 23, 2012.

"It's doubtful if one of them... McLemore, p. 128.

"Coming up with a coaching... McLemore, p. 131.

"You can sit a group... McLemore, p. 133.

"Congratulations on your first... *The Winning Edge,* p. 140.

"Their attitude during that... McLemore p. 133.

"Shula was always telling... Nobles, Charles, "1972 Dolphins: Undefeated on Field, Undeterred Off It," *New York Times,* NY, February 3, 2008.

"Shula was like... Habib, Hal, "Playoff-bound Miami Dolphins are kicking backsides, gleeful alums say," *Palm Beach Post,* FL, December 27, 2016.

"He was a miserable S.O.B... Nordheimer, September 1, 1985.

"Dick was very bright... Nordheimer, September 1, 1985.

"He was completely consistent... Nordheimer, September 1, 1985.

"Our early camp training... McLemore, p. 134.

"There's a sticky situation here... Griese, Bob (with Dave Hyde). *Perfection: The Inside Story of the 1972 Miami Dolphins' Perfect Season.* New York, NY: Wiley Publishing, 2012, p. 53.

"So I went over there... Morris, Eugene ("Mercury"), "Former Dolphin 'Mercury' Morris recalls good and bad in late-'60s Miami," *Miami Herald,* FL, September 15, 2016.

"Shula was worried about... Griese, p. 52.

"As a football coach I want... *The Winning Edge,* p. 159.

"Hi, I'm Paul Warfield... Griese, p. 52.

"[Shula] brought in a new era... Morris, September 15, 2016.

"A few days later... Griese, p. 56.

"That's a term I use . . . Schleier, Curt, "Don Shula Dived into Details and Made a Miami Splash," *Investor's Business Daily,* Los Angeles, CA, October 8, 2012.

"I've always felt that . . . Schleier, October 8, 2012.

"I never really felt that . . . Lee, Andy, "Shula 'Enjoyed Every Day' Coaching," *Sun Sentinel,* FL, January 15, 1995.

"I placed a great amount . . . Griese, p. 24.

"His pedigree is super . . . MacCambridge, *Chuck Noll: His Life's Work,* p. 146.

"The Dolphins looked like they . . . McLemore, p. 135.

"You're not getting me . . . Freeman, p. 52.

"Scott, to be sure, was . . . Hyde, Dave, "Where's Jake Scott? Dave Hyde found him," *Sun Sentinel,* FL, November 19, 2006.

"We were playing Buffalo . . . Kantowski, Ron, "Jake Scott, Super Bowl forgotten hero, resurfaces at Las Vegas drag race," *Review Journal,* Las Vegas, NV, May 2, 2016.

"I'd never played pro football . . . D'Ambrosio, Brian, "Garo Yepremian on Super Bowl Gaffe: 'I turned it into a positive,'" *Huffington Post,* NY, December 6, 2017.

"In that first game . . . D'Ambrosio, December 6, 2017.

"[Taseff] really took me under . . . D'Ambrosio, December 6, 2017.

"Most important, he was . . . McLemore, p. 135.

"Garo was only 5'8" . . . Nogle, Kevin, "Don Shula, Bob Griese statements on passing of Garo Yepremian," *The Phinster, SBNation,* NY, May 16, 2015.

"Garo went from . . . Nogle, May 16, 2015.

"Bob had the perfect mental . . . Rollow, Cooper, "Griese Enters Hall Despite Injuries, Critics," *Chicago Tribune,* IL, July 27, 1990.

"I want you to stay in . . . Griese, p. 28.

"Bob Griese deserves to be . . . Kuechenberg Interview.

"It was an exhibition game . . . Maule, Tex, "Miami Gets A Miracle Worker," *Sports Illustrated,* NY, September 7, 1970.

"We didn't play well last . . . Maule, September 7, 1970.

"I think it was a good . . . Maule, September 7, 1970.

"Watching this team, it . . . Maule, September 7, 1970.

"We could see the difference . . . Maule, September 7, 1970.

"First, I'd take exception . . . McLemore, p. 138.

"That Warfield is making . . . McLemore, p. 141.

"When Rosenbloom learned . . . Olsen, November 9, 1970.

"Prodded by Rosenbloom's enemies . . . Olsen, November 9, 1970.

"How stupid can people . . . Olsen, November 9, 1970.

"Former coach George Wilson . . . Olsen, November 9, 1970.

"I've never answered . . . Cole, November 7, 1993.

"In 1970, we needed . . . McLemore, p. 147.

"We took the ball and . . . McLemore, p. 147.

"In our last two games . . . Anderson, Dave, "Jets' Title Hopes Seem Doomed," *New York Times,* NY, October 12, 1970.

"Our average attendance . . . N/A, "Miami Flips for Dolphins but Owner's Not Joyful," *Associated Press,* December 25, 1970.

"Joe didn't have a dime . . . "Miami Flips," December 25, 1970.

"There'll be a price increase . . . "Miami Flips," December 25, 1970.

"People said I was cheap . . . "Miami Flips," December 25, 1970.

"After that loss, we turned . . . N/A, "Dolphins Ready to Test Raiders," *Associated Press*, December 25, 1970.

"He scored two of their . . . N/A, "Disappointed Shula of Dolphins Calls Lamonica the Difference," *United Press International*, NY, December 27, 1970.

"All that we've accomplished . . . "Lamonica the Difference," December 27, 1970.

"Sure, I am disappointed . . . "Lamonica the Difference," December 27, 1970.

"Larry Csonka was tough . . . Reyonolds, Neil, *Pain Gang: Pro Football's 50 Toughest Players.* Dulles, VA: Potomac Books Inc., 2006, p. 86.

Larry Csonka was a big back . . . Reynolds, p. 86.

"When I think about Zonk . . . Reynold, p. 86.

"Get up! Get up! . . . Griese, p. 19.

"Csonka lumbered into . . . Griese, p. 19.

"Scared me nearly half . . . Melody, Tom, "Shula learned humility in a Maine movie theater," *Bangor News*, January 24, 1985.

"Yow!" Shula screamed . . . Underwood, John, "The Blood and Thunder Boys," *Sports Illustrated*, NY, August 6, 1972.

"Don't worry about it . . . Underwood, August 6, 1972.

"By the same token . . . Underwood, August 6, 1972.

"I've always been what you . . . Underwood, August 6, 1972.

"Kiick and Csonka . . . Underwood, August 6, 1972.

"Two things can happen . . . Underwood, August 6, 1972.

"He was huge . . . Underwood, August 6, 1972.

"No matter what your style . . . Underwood, August 6, 1972.

"So I leaned the other way . . . Underwood, August 6, 1972.

"The fact that I didn't . . . Morris, Eugene ("Mercury"), "Interview, Draft Memories: Wooden and Morris," *Finsiders, Miami Dolphins.com*, April 18, 2015.

"Mercury Morris was a human . . . Thompson Hunter S., "Jack Kerouac and the Football Hall of Fame," *ESPN.com*, NY, October 10, 2001.

"We started that when we . . . Schleiler, October 8, 2012.

"I said, 'Oh man, it's . . . Richman, Mike, "Flashback: Theismann Has a History with the Dolphins," *The Redskins Historian*, April 16, 2012.

"I didn't know whether . . . Richman, April 16, 2012.

"It took probably 15 . . . Richman, April 16, 2012.

"For a long while on a bright . . . Maule, Tex, "Keeping it short and sweet," *Sports Illustrated*, NY, December 20, 1971.

"I feel good. I can play . . . Maule, December 20, 1971.

"Unitas was fitting the ball . . . Maule, December 20, 1971.

"They try to keep their . . . Crass, Murray, "Chiefs Are Picked Against Dolphins," *New York Times*, NY, December 25, 1971.

"If they get 6 or 7 yards . . . Crass, December 25, 1971.

"I told Jan, 'You've . . . Rubin, Bob, "When Christmas dinner was delayed as the Miami Dolphins played on and on," *Miami Herald*, FL, December 19, 2016.

"I asked Bell why he . . . Rubin, December 19, 2016.

"The Dolphins celebration died . . . Rubin, December 19, 2016.

"I had a choice—run . . . Rubin, December 19, 2016.

"I thought, 'You've . . . Rubin, December 19, 2016.
"I was planning what . . . McLemore, p. 245.
"I sincerely felt, as this . . . McLemore, p. 245.
"It was like the football . . . Weintraub, Robert, "Endless Emotions Over NFL's Longest Game," *New York Times*, NY December 24, 2012.
"The game postponed Christmas . . . Weintraub, December 24, 2012.
"Everyone I knew in Miami . . . Weintraub, December 24, 2012.
"The only thing he said to . . . Weintraub, December 24, 2012.
"a misdirection play before . . . Rubin, December 19, 2016.
"It was a roll-right trap . . . Crass, Murray, "Kick Beats Chiefs," *New York Times*, NY, December 26, 1971.
"I couldn't help but think . . . Crass, December 26, 1971.
"The Chiefs stood disbelievingly . . . Crass, December 26, 1971.
"It was a horrifying experience . . . Crass, December 26, 1971.
"It was such an eventful . . . McLemore, p. 249.
"Long after this season's . . . Crass, December 26, 1971.
"The 5-foot-7-inch Yepremian . . . Amdur, Neil, "Miami Hails Hero Kicker as Holder Basks in the Shadows," *New York Times*, NY, December 27, 1971.
"Nobody remembers the . . . Amdur, December 27, 1971.
"They are pretty colorful . . . Klemesrud, Judy, "Football Player With a Business to Fall Back On," *New York Times*, NY, January 20, 1972.
"I had to be the first coach . . . *The Winning Edge*, p. 180.
"As if inspired by a rainbow . . . Anderson, Dave, "Colts Dethroned by Dolphins, 21–0," *New York Times*, NY January 2, 1972.
"When we saw the rainbow . . . Anderson, January 2, 1972.
"I can't believe it . . . N/A, "Loss Taken Hard by Bubba Smith," *Associated Press*, January 2, 1972.
"I don't understand what . . . "Loss Taken Hard," January 2, 1972.
"Buoniconti is the key . . . Amdur, Neil, "Buoniconti Is Singled Out by Unitas as Key Man in Dolphins" *New York Times*, NY January 3, 1972.
"We knew what we wanted . . . Amdur, January 3, 1972.
"Even at his warmest he . . . Price, S.L., "'I Feel Lost. I Feel Like a Child': The Complicated Decline of Nick Buoniconti," *Sports Illustrated*, NY, May 9, 2017.
"When Butkus hits you . . . Price, May 9, 2017.
"For the Dolphins coach Shula . . . Anderson, Dave, "Onto the Super Bowl," *New York Times*, NY, January 2, 1972.
"His jaw is Don Shula's . . . Anderson, Dave, "Don Shula's Super Obsession," *New York Times*, NY, January 9, 1972.
"Don's put on weight . . . Anderson, January 9, 1972.
"If so, it's 50 pounds . . . Anderson, January 9, 1972.
"We haven't played them . . . Wallace, William N, "Cowboys Fear Warfield—And With Good Reason," *New York Times*, NY, January 4, 1972.
"There was too much . . . Anderson, January 9, 1972.
"I've been silent too long . . . McLemore, p. 260.
"I don't know what his reasons . . . N/A, "Dolphins Fear Cowboy's Bob Lilly," *Indiana Gazette*, Indiana, PA, January 12, 1972.

"was a likeable guy, the kind . . . Williams, Pat, and Denney, Jim, *Extreme Focus*. Deerfield Beach, FL: HCI Publishing, p. 70.
"The sentimentalists will be rooting . . . Daley, Arthur, "In the Swim With Dolphins," *New York Times*, NY, January 16, 1972.
"Watch this," shouted a Miami . . . Daley, January 16, 1972.
"Let's say that I'm a . . . Daley, January 16, 1972.
"This was the early angle . . . Zimmerman, Paul, "Super Bowl VI Mute But Mighty," *Sports Illustrated*, NY, January 2, 1989.
"When Nick Bouniconti went . . . McLemore, p. 263.
"I thought everything would . . . *The Winning Edge*, pp. 197–198.
"Shula, if you open your mouth . . . *The Winning Edge*, pp. 197–198.
"I still slip occasionally . . . Underwood, "Top of the World," *Sports Illustrated*, New York NY, September 17, 1973.
"Didn't you see it?" . . . Underwood, September 17, 1973.
"The Cowboys were methodical . . . Wallace, William N., "Dallas Routs Miami in Super Bowl, 24–3," *New York Times*, NY January 17, 1972.
"Dallas's Bob Lilly chasing . . . Zimmerman, January 2, 1989.
"Okay, you always want . . . Griese, pp. 10–11.
"Oh no, you got us . . . Griese, pp. 10–11.
"I can't describe how we feel . . . Wallace, January 17, 1972.
"We played poorly . . . Wallace, January 17, 1972.
"We all hurt right now . . . Freeman, pp. 3–4.
"We're going to be tested . . . Freeman, pp. 3–4.
"The only time I got . . . Freeman, pp. 3–4.
"I bit my lip to control my . . . Freeman, pp. 3–4.
"I respect Merc for wanting . . . Griese, pp. 23.

Chapter 7: Undefeated

"I liked that new attitude . . . Griese, pp. 24–25.
"He was prepared both . . . Griese, pp. 24–25.
"What the hell are you doing . . . Csonka, Larry and Kiick, Jim (with Dave Anderson). *Always On the Run*, New York, NY: Random House, 1973, p. 32.
"Shula was the one who stuck . . . Csonka and Kiick, p. 32.
"You like cold weather, eh? . . . Csonka and Kiick, p. 32.
"I know what you're hinting at . . . Csonka and Kiick, p. 32.
"You wouldn't win," hollered Shula. . . . Csonka and Kiick, p. 32.
"I was always . . . Tomasson, Chris, "Jim Kiick now a Giants fan, but Shula feud over," *Foxsports*, December 11, 2012.
"He said I had an attitude . . . Tomasson, December 11, 2012.
"There's all kinds of things . . . Habib, Hal, "Ex-Dolphins Larry Csonka, Mercury Morris, Jim Kiick subject of special," *Palm Beach Post*, FL, November 11, 2014.
"Shula began using situation . . . Griese, p. 25.
"If switching players was . . . Griese, p. 25.
"We're the no-name defense . . . Anderson, Dave, "Namath and Jets Introduced to Dolphins' No-Name Defense," *New York Times*, NY, October 9, 1972.

"We just call it our 53 . . . Anderson, October 9, 1972.

"Landry unintentionally nicknamed . . . Anderson, October 9, 1972.

"a trailblazer who practically . . . Dudko, James, "Bill Arnsparger: Remembering the Godfather of the Zone Blitz and Hybrid Defense," *bleacherreport.com,* July 19, 2015.

"There's a direct line from . . . Dudko, July 19, 2015.

"But the impact of the . . . Dudko, July 19, 2015.

"He pioneered situational . . . N/A, "Bill Arnsparger, Miami's 'No-Name Defense' coach, dies at 88," *USA Today,* July 17, 2015.

"He never cut the picture . . . Hyde, Dave, "Bill Arnsparger was the perfect match for Don Shula," *Sun Sentinel,* FL, July 18, 2015.

"I'd say, 'Good morning . . . Hyde, July 18, 2015.

"He never asked you to do . . . Hyde, July 18, 2015.

"One of my biggest memories . . . Dambrosio, January 27, 2014.

"And if he wasn't the first . . . De Los Santos, Brian, "Bob Griese on the death of former Dolphins teammate Earl Morrall," *FOXSports,* NY, April 25, 2015.

"Your hair's getting a . . . Csonka and Kiick, p. 170.

"If [Earl] had a tip when . . . De Los Santos, April 25, 2015.

"It's all up to you now, Earl . . . Crouse, Karen, "An Understudy Helped Make the Dolphins 17–0," *New York Times,* NY, December 16, 2007.

"Let's just keep it going . . . Crouse, December 16, 2007.

"Earl was a lot more personable . . . Crouse, December 16, 2007.

"He's a great, great individual . . . Crouse, December 16, 2007.

"There wouldn't have been an . . . Crouse, December 16, 2007.

"After the Dolphins defeated the . . . Crouse, December 16, 2007.

"I got great blocking . . . Anderson, Dave, "Warfield Stars In Late Drive for Score," *New York Times,* NY, December 25, 1972.

"You did a good job . . . Crouse, December 16, 2007.

"As a starter, Morrall . . . Anderson, Dave, "The Star and the Stand-In," *New York Times,* NY, January 7, 1973.

"Let's get this drive going . . . Anderson, January 7, 1973.

"That's the mark of a leader . . . Anderson, January 7, 1973.

"We've got a bunch of . . . Anderson, Dave, "Fans Are Emotional," *New York Times,* NY, January 1, 1973.

"[Larry] Brown running out . . . N/A, "Ground attack seen as the key," *Associated Press,* January 14, 1973.

"The common observation . . . "Ground attack," January 14, 1973.

"We've got to get to him . . . "Ground attack," January 14, 1973.

"Let's see Allen sneak . . . Anderson, Dave, "George Allen," *New York Times,* NY, November 6, 1972.

"Can you imagine me leading . . . N/A, "Shula: Tough, Practical And a Low-Key Coach," *New York Times,* NY, January 14, 1973.

"I don't care about winning . . . "Shula: Tough," January 14, 1973.

"I want you guys to forget . . . Greene, Harvey, "Fins Flashback: Dolphins Complete The Perfect Season," *Miami Dolphins.com,* FL, September 11, 2015.

"I honestly felt as if my life . . . Wilner, Barry and Rappaport, Ken, *Super Bowl Heroes.* Gilford, CT: Lyons Press, 2016, p. 29.

"I took a negative and I . . . Wilner, Rappaport, p. 29.
"I mean here we are . . . Wilner, Rappaport, p. 30.
"There's not a day in . . . Silver, July 15, 2002.
"I wasn't sharp at all . . . Underwood, September 17, 1973.
"All along I've had an empty . . . Katz, Michael, "The Coach Who Has the Last Laugh," *New York Times*, NY, January 15, 1973.
"I hadn't done too well in . . . Katz, January 15, 1973.
"Miami would be all too . . . MacCambridge, *America's Game*, p. 310.
"Carroll was bitter about it . . . Cole, November 7, 1993.
"Any time you say . . . Cole, November 7, 1993.
"Why don't the both of you . . . Cole, November 7, 1993.
"Well, we don't have to look . . . Cole, November 7, 1993.
"It was strange sitting . . . *The Winning Edge*, p. 242.
"I'm happy we did end up . . . *The Winning Edge*, p. 242.
"The thrill for Dorothy Shula . . . Underwood, September 17, 1973.
"I'll say it is," she told . . . McLemore, p. 108.
"Don't get me wrong . . . Underwood, September 17, 1973.
"As for his golf . . . Underwood, September 17, 1973.
"As a golfer, he is much . . . McLemore, p. 108.
"We were at the par-3 12th hole . . . Underwood, September 17, 1973.
"Shula played a round of golf . . . Underwood, September 17, 1973.
"He's even more serious . . . Underwood, September 17, 1973.
"I hate to talk about losing . . . Koppett, Leonard, "Blanda Kicks End Dolphin String," *New York Times*, NY, September 24, 1973.
"I had a lot of people in front . . . Wallace, William N., "Dolphins Subdue Cowboys, 14–7, for 9th in Row," *New York Times*, NY, November 23, 1973.
"He's so strong," Lee Roy Jordan . . . Wallace, November 23, 1973.
"While the Hessians heaved . . . Smith, Red, "Pupil Shows Teacher How It's Done," *New York Times*, NY, December 24, 1973.
"In 1946 when Brown made . . . Smith, December 24, 1973.
"Congratulations on a fine season . . . Smith, December 24, 1973.
"This is about as thorough . . . Crass, Murray, "Near-Perfect Miami Gains A.F.C. Final—Defense Excels," *New York Times*, NY, December 24, 1973.
"Obviously, we were soundly . . . N/A, "Bengals Tip Helmets to Conquerors," *United Press International*, December 24, 1973.
"They [the Raiders] have a real . . . Crass, Murray, "But Miami Recalls Early Defeat by Raiders," *New York Times*, NY, December 25, 1973.
"We were poor but we ate . . . Don Smith, *Coffin Corner, Larry Little*, Vol 15. No. 4., 1993.
"Larry Little had tremendous . . . Smith, Vol 15. No. 4., 1993.
"I like the running plays . . . Smith, Vol 15. No. 4., 1993.
"I'll be running behind Chicken . . . Smith, Vol 15. No. 4., 1993.
"Chicken's a big truck . . . Smith, Vol 15. No. 4., 1993.
"Trying to get around Larry Little . . . Smith, Vol 15. No. 4., 1993.
"We just didn't play good football . . . Crass, December 25, 1973.
"I felt the tempo . . . Crass, Murray, "Csonka Scores 3 as Miami Rushes for 266 Yards," *New York Times*, NY, December 31, 1973.

"He's a quarterback . . . Crass, December 31, 1973.

"This is the damndest team . . . Crass, December 31, 1973.

"Two fourth-down plays . . . Anderson, Dave, "Shula Clicks on 2 Fourth-Down Decisions," *New York Times*, NY, December 31, 1973.

"The fans always want you . . . Anderson, December 31, 1973.

"I don't mind working . . . Anderson, December 31, 1973.

"That front four as a unit . . . Range, Peter Ross, "A Team Within a Team: The Purple People Eaters," *New York Times* magazine, NY, December 23, 1973.

"Bud Grant is the master builder . . . Range, December 23, 1973.

"In stark contrast to Shula . . . Thompson, Hunter S., "Fear and Loathing at the Super Bowl," *Rolling Stone* magazine, NY, February 28, 1974.

"Super Bowl VIII had all . . . Thompson, February 28, 1974.

"Griese asked me what I . . . Maule, Tex, "It Was The Day Of The Dolphins," *Sports Illustrated*, NY, January 21, 1974.

"I knew we were in trouble . . . Maule, January 21, 1974.

"Griese went up to the . . . Maule, January 21, 1974.

"The precision-jackhammer . . . Thompson, February 28, 1974.

"Bob Kuechenberg, the Dolphins . . . Zimmerman, Paul, "Miami Dolphins Vs. Minnesota Vikings Super Bowl VIII Another Crown To Miami," *Sports Illustrated*, NY, January 2, 1989.

"Lombardi and Shula are . . . Anderson, Dave, "Dolphins Better Than The Packers," *New York Times*, NY, January 8, 1974.

"Whenever anybody asks . . . Anderson, January 8, 1974.

"This year everybody . . . Wallace, William N., "Dolphins So Much in Charge Even Blunders Didn't Matter," *New York Times*, NY, January 15, 1974.

"We felt to ask a man . . . Smith, Red, "Zonk, A Point on the Richter Scale," *New York Times*, NY, January 23, 1974.

"I think it's a great . . . Smith, January 23, 1974.

"It's a loss . . . Smith, January 23, 1974.

"Gary Davidson, short . . . Anderson, Dave, "'The Whiffle' Comes Into Focus," *New York Times*, NY, March 19, 1974.

"Meanwhile, on the other . . . Thompson, February 28, 1974.

"Nobody paid much . . . Thompson, February 28, 1974.

"A dozen to 15 . . . Wallace, William N., "Many Dolphins Unhappy On Pay, Eye New League," *New York Times*, NY November 28, 1973.

"You talk to the players . . . Wallace, November 28, 1973.

"Wherever Butch and Sundance . . . Jones, Robert F., "They're Grinning and Bearing," *Sports Illustrated*, NY July 27, 1975.

"Joe Robbie sells out . . . Anderson, March 19, 1974.

"When Paul Warfield, Jim Kiick . . . Habib, Hal, "Miami Dolphins' Larry Csonka: Owner's cold shoulder forced jump to WFL," *Palm Beach Post*, FL, July 29, 2017.

"I could understand . . . Habib, Cold Shoulder, July 29, 2017.

"He was angry," Kiick said . . . Tomasson, December 11, 2012.

"Joe Robbie was offered . . . Csonka, Larry, "FAQs on WFL," *Larry Csonka.com*, July 29, 2017.

"I do not regret my decision . . . Csonka, July 29, 2017.

"disappointed, shocked, sick . . . Tomasson, December 11, 2012.
"That decimated his team . . . Tomasson, December 11, 2012.
"The NFL couldn't stop us . . . Scott, December 2, 1974.
"The last six months have . . . Scott, December 2, 1974.
"It was like watching . . . N/A, "Signings bring out Dolfans' Hankies," *Associated Press*, April 2, 1974.
"I can't believe it . . . Melody, January 24, 1985.
"I don't know what you're . . . Melody, January 24, 1985.
"My wife was late coming in . . . Shula, Don, taped interview, "Don Shula on almost fighting owner Joe Robbie," *Sports Illustrated*, NY, August 7, 2015.
"If you ever holler at me . . . Shula, August 7, 2015.
"After 14 days of bitter silence . . . Scott, December 2, 1974.
More than twenty veterans . . . N/A, "20 Dolphins to picket camp," *Associated Press*, NY, July 6, 1974.
"It seems like someone's telling . . . N/A, "Strike Angers Shula," *Associated Press*, NY, July 6, 1974 .
"Kneeling in the nearly . . . Scott, December 2, 1974.
"Sometimes they call holding . . . Scott, December 2, 1974.
"There, are easier jobs . . . Crass, Murray, "Dolphins 53 Defense Is Changed, but Jets Will Find It Is Sturdy," *New York Times*, NY, November 24, 1974.
"I don't like you . . . Hyde, Dave, "Where's Jake Scott? Dave Hyde found him," *Sun Sentinel*, FL, November 19, 2006.
It was like "going from . . . Crass, November 24, 1974.
"The change had to affect us . . . Crass, November 24, 1974.
"Can a team win the American . . . N/A, "American Conference: Steelers Waiting in the Wings if Dolphins Cannot Go," *New York Times*, NY, September 8, 1974.
"We stink. They played . . . N/A, "Dolphins in Danger of Losing Lease At Top of the A.F.C. East This Year," *New York Times*, NY, September 22, 1974.
"I'm disappointed, obviously . . . N/A, "2 More Dolphins Sign With W.F.L.," *Associated Press*, September 24, 1974.
"That's one of the toughest . . . Rogers, Thomas, "Dolphins Lose in Final Minute," *New York Times*, NY, October 14, 1974.
"It really was the only thing . . . N/A, "Morris Suspended by Dolphin Coach," *New York Times*, NY, November 8, 1974.
"You have to understand . . . Zimmerman, December 20, 1993.
"I went to see this . . . Zimmerman, December 20, 1993.
"The night before we . . . Zimmerman, December 20, 1993.
"Many of the players on . . . Koppett, Leonard, "Pro Football Playoffs to Begin Today," *New York Times*, NY, December 21, 1974.
"That hurt because Miami's . . . Wallace, William N., "Dolphins' Reign Ends on Late Catch, 28–26," *New York Times*, NY, December 22, 1974.
"During the game our . . . Zimmerman, December 20, 1993.
"It was the first down . . . Wallace, December 22, 1974.
"I felt him," said Stabler . . . Wallace, December 22, 1974.
"I saw Clarence . . . Wallace, December 22, 1974.
"Afterward our left tackle . . . Zimmerman, December 20, 1993.

"I have never heard any . . . N/A, "The Sea of Hands Game," *Raiders.com,* Los Angeles, CA, December 21, 2013.

"That loss denied us . . . Janofsky, Michael, "Shula's Style: A Mellow Intensity," *New York Times,* NY, October 1, 1983.

Chapter 8: Woodstrock and the Killer Bees

"The Shulas were close . . . Freeman, p. 14.

"The first five years . . . N/A, "Wife of Dolphin's Coach Mum on Football," *Akron Beacon Journal,* Akron, OH, January 12, 1972.

"I used to hate it . . . "Wife of Dolphins' Coach," January 12, 1972.

"The women were dubbed . . . Klemesrud, Judy, "The Woman Who Isn't Slim Desires High Fashion, Too," *New York Times,* NY, April 10, 1975.

"My husband's always . . . Klemesrud, April 10, 1975.

"Stressing that she was . . . Klemesrud, April 10, 1975.

"He won't smile . . . Freeman, p. 14.

In May of that same year . . . N/A, "Shula Sells Stock," *Associated Press,* May 15, 1975.

"Both have signed contracts . . . Strauss, Michael, "Foley, Kuechenberg 'Return' to Dolphins," *New York Times,* NY, May 31, 1975.

"My dad came over when . . . Szeleky, Tomas, "Hungarian Roots: Don Shula, Legendary American Football Coach," *Hungary Today,* Budapest, Hungary, March 30, 2016.

"I'm hoping Bulaich . . . Harvin, Al, "Bulaich and Lane In Football Trades," *New York Times,* NY, July 10, 1975.

"In 1968, Shula's coaching . . . Litzky, Frank, "George Young, 71, Former Giants General Manager, Dies, "*New York Times,* NY, December 9, 2001.

"If Don Shula didn't . . . Litzky, December 9, 2001.

"Shula brought Young to . . . Leiber, Jill, "Grandfather Mountain," *Sports Illustrated,* NY, July 26, 1993.

"Don just didn't want to . . . Leiber, July 26, 1993.

"He was so thorough . . . Leiber, July 26, 1993.

"Don, people think we're . . . Leiber, Grandfather Mountain, July 26, 1993.

"George Young went . . . N/A, "Praise for the late George Young," *United Press International,* December 9, 2001.

"Two years after they swept . . . Amdur, Neil, "Dolphins Develop Fan Lag," *New York Times,* NY, September 13, 1975.

"There's no question we've . . . Amdur, September 13, 1975.

In 1972, Beathard was . . . Zimmerman, Paul, "Smartest Man in the NFL," *Sports Illustrated,* NY, August 29, 1989.

"Bobby did a real fine . . . Attner, Paul, and Shapiro, Leonard, "Bobby Beathard," *Washington Post,* Washington, DC, April 12, 1981.

"We went back and forth . . . Attner, April 12, 1981.

"The same could not be . . . Attner, April 12, 1981.

"Generally, you learn so . . . Habib, Hal, "Ex-Miami Dolphins personnel man Bobby Beathard a Hall of Fame finalist," *Palm Beach Post,* FL, August 25, 2017.

"The years at the Miami . . . N/A, "Bobby Beathard's Favorite Memories From Career Came With Redskins," *Redskins.com,* Washington, DC.

"A fumble by Don Nottingham . . . Wallace, William N., "Raiders Conquer Dolphins," *New York Times,* NY, September 23, 1975.

"Every time we got something . . . Wallace, William N., "Dolphins Learn Defense Needs Patching," *New York Times,* NY, September 24, 1975.

"Well, we're not about . . . Wallace, September 24, 1975.

"We're going to keep . . . N/A, "Dolphins Lose Morrall in Victory over Patriots," *United Press International,* December 3, 1975.

"The Miami line conducted . . . Mulvoy, Mark, "The Colts Don't Horse Around," *Sports Illustrated,* NY, December 22, 1975.

"We screwed up their game . . . Mulvoy, December 22, 1975.

"We take what the other . . . Mulvoy, December 22, 1975.

"Linhart kicked the game-tying . . . Wallace, William N., "Colts Subdue Dolphins on Overtime Kick 10–7; Colts Beat Dolphins," *New York Times,* NY, December 15, 1975.

"After Larry's kick . . . Wallace, December 15, 1975.

"Two years ago I wouldn't . . . Mulvoy, December 22, 1975.

"Miami was on top for . . . Mulvoy, December 22, 1975.

"They beat us . . . Mulvoy, December 22, 1975.

"If we beat Denver next . . . Mulvoy, December 22, 1975.

"I won't be there . . . Hyde, November 19, 2006.

"I said to him . . . Hyde, November 19, 2006.

"I don't remember that . . . Hyde, November 19, 2006.

"He was a unique individual . . . Cole, Jason, "Shula Ends 20 Years On NFL Committee," *Sun Sentinel,* FL, March 2, 1996.

"I had my agent contact . . . Csonka, July 29, 2017.

"Robbie and Keating continued . . . Csonka, July 29, 2017.

"I was made out to . . . Archdeacon, Tom, "Last Call for Number 39," *Sports Illustrated,* NY, July 30, 1979.

"I played for Coach Shula . . . Greene, Harvey, "My Draft Memories: A.J. Duhe," *MiamiDolphins.com,* Miami, Florida, April 6, 2017.

"After the Dolphins drafted . . . Greene, April 6, 2017.

"A.J.'s our fire-up guy . . . Shapiro, Leonard, "When A.J. Duhe Talks, The Dolphins Listen," *Washington Post,* Washington, DC, January 31, 1983.

"When you're tired . . . Shapiro, January 31, 1983.

"We drafted A.J. No. 1 . . . Shapiro, January 31, 1983.

"There were times in the . . . Shapiro, January 31, 1983.

"I just thought they . . . Shapiro, January 31, 1983.

"I gave him my strongest . . . Shapiro, Leonard, "Beathard Redskin GM," *Washington Post,* Washington, DC, February 25, 1978.

"I get excited the closer . . . Hill, Bob, "Connor Cramming For 2-day Final Exam," *Sun Sentinel,* FL, April 24, 1988.

"The only thing we . . . Hill, April 24, 1988.

"Not everybody on this . . . Hill, April 24, 1988.

"I don't know how many . . . Wallace, William N., "Campbell Shy About His Feats," *New York Times,* NY, November 22, 1978.

"In the late 1970s . . . Hevesi, Dennis, "Byron Donzis, Inventor of Football Flak Jacket, Dies at 79," *New York Times*, NY, January 19, 2012.

"I thought he was some . . . Hevesi, January 19, 2012.

"That's their game . . . Wallace, William N., "Pastorini Passes for 306 Yards in 17–9 Triumph," *New York Times*, NY, December 25, 1978.

"Bob can't even take . . . Wallace, December 25, 1978.

"Griese never complained . . . Wallace, December 25, 1978.

"Back in Baltimore . . . Lincoln, Eric, "Young Rated Highly As Talent Evaluator," *New York Times*, NY, February 15, 1979.

"He was very much influenced . . . Lincoln, February 15, 1979.

"I negotiated with Coach . . . Csonka, July 29, 2017.

"Once Zonk and Robbie got . . . Archdeacon, July 30, 1979.

"I signed the first time we . . . Archdeacon, July 30, 1979.

"He hits as hard as he . . . Katz, February 4, 1979.

"I'm convinced in my . . . Archdeacon, July 30, 1979.

"Our past relationship was . . . Archdeacon, July 30, 1979.

"What's all this moanin'?" . . . Archdeacon, July 30, 1979.

"I'm ready to make any . . . Archdeacon, July 30, 1979.

"The starting fullback . . . Archdeacon, July 30, 1979.

"Apart from choosing sites . . . Wallace, William N. "NFL Is Basking In Its Income," *New York Times*, NY, March 11, 1979.

"With the paralysis last . . . Wallace, March 11, 1979.

"These things were allowed . . . Wallace, William N., "Coaches See Leveling Off Of Splurge by Offenses," *New York Times*, NY, August 31, 1981.

"Tex Schramm, president . . . Wallace, August 31, 1981.

"The rules changes seemed . . . Wallace, August 31, 1981.

"The defense had too . . . Wallace, August 31, 1981.

"I always root for . . . Lustig, Dennis, "Shula's Back In Town," *Cleveland Plain Dealer*, OH, November 18, 1979.

"They didn't know a . . . Lustig, November 18, 1979.

"Don had always been . . . Lustig, November 18, 1979.

"I feel it's time for Miami . . . Lustig, November 18, 1979.

"I really don't spend . . . Underwood, John, "His Eyes Have Seen the Glory," *Sports Illustrated*, NY July 27, 1981.

"He does a better job . . . Underwood, July 27, 1981.

"No. I don't think he's . . . Underwood, July 27, 1981.

"Shula's a very emotional . . . Underwood, July 27, 1981.

"Our relationship hasn't . . . Underwood, July 27, 1981.

"There has always been . . . Underwood, July 27, 1981.

In the end, Shula . . . Shapiro, Leonard, "Shula Secret: Adaptability," *Washington Post*, Washington, DC, September 30, 1978.

"Years ago they felt . . . Eskenazi, Gerald, "Stephenson: A Modern Center with Strength and Versatility," *New York Times*, NY, January 6, 1985.

"The reason he's so . . . Eskenazi, January 6, 1985.

"This is just a football game . . . Cosell, Howard, *Monday Night Football*, ABC Television, December 8, 1980.

"Here we had this . . . Garber, Greg, "In this NFL game, silence was golden," *ESPN.com,* NY, December 12, 2010.
"The final outcome . . . Garber, December 12, 2010.
"It certainly did a . . . Garber, December 12, 2010.
"I'm for my kid and . . . N/A, "The Miami Dolphins'-Baltimore Colts' game in Baltimore Sunday will . . ." *United Press International,* September 23, 1981.
"I want him to do well . . . "The Miami Dolphins'-Baltimore Colts'," September 23, 1981.
"His moves and body control . . . Hoffer, Richard, "Here Comes the Son," *Sports Illustrated,* NY, October 12, 1992.
"He makes All-Ivy his . . . Hoffer, October 12, 1992.
"A lot of kids came from . . . Hoffer, October 12, 1992.
"No matter what happened . . . Heaton, Chuck, "We'll both be on the spot," *Cleveland Plain Dealer,* OH, October 23, 1981.
"Perhaps there was . . . Eskanazi, Gerald, "Sons of Shula, Kemp Try Training Camp," *New York Times,* NY, June 6, 1981.
"We're both conscious . . . "The Miami Dolphins'-Baltimore Colts'," September 23, 1981.
"I think it's such a . . . Heaton, October 23, 1981.
"It was hectic all week though . . . "The Miami Dolphins'-Baltimore Colts'," September 23, 1981.
"Just how does Shula . . . Eskanazi, Gerald, "Don Shula And The Dolphins Are Sizzling Once More," *New York Times,* NY, October 4, 1981.
"We don't think it's . . . Eskanazi, October 4, 1981.
"To be in there every game . . . Eskanazi, October 4, 1981.
"He seems to get the . . . Eskanazi, October 4, 1981.
"This is a game where . . . N/A, "Chargers' Offense Threat to Dolphins," *United Press International,* January 2, 1982.
"We need a big game from . . . "Chargers' Offense Threat," January 2, 1982.
"I can't think of anyone . . . Janofsky, Michael, "Strock Carves Role As Miami Reliever," *New York Times,* NY, December 27, 1982.
"It takes a guy with a certain . . . Janofsky, December 27, 1982.
"The key thing for me . . . Janofsky, December 27, 1982.
"It's hard to explain . . . Janofsky, December 27, 1982.
"Because of the atmosphere . . . Janofsky, December 27, 1982.
"blowing their nose . . . Werner, Barry, "35 years ago, Chargers-Dolphins was one of the best games in NFL history," *FOXSports.com,* NY, November 15, 2016.
"Man, you just don't . . . Werner, November 15, 2016.
"What about the hook . . . Werner, November 15, 2016.
"It's pretty hard to believe . . . Werner, November 15, 2016.
"It was a beautiful . . . Reilly, Rick, "A Matter of Life and Sudden Death," *Sports Illustrated,* NY, October 24, 1999.
"Aw, fuck! Here we . . . Reilly, October 24, 1999.
"I've never heard . . . Reilly, October 24, 1999.
"You could just sense . . . Reilly, October 24, 1999.
"That was one of the . . . Reilly, October 24, 1999.
"It was the biggest . . . Reilly, October 24, 1999.
"Shula was hot that . . . Reilly, October 24, 1999.

"A great game . . . Reilly, October 24, 1999.
"Doubly ironic for the . . . Underwood, John, "A Game No One Should Have Lost," *Sports Illustrated*, NY, January 11, 1982.
"The game had everything . . . Werner, November 15, 2016.
"The locker room . . . Werner, November 15, 2016.
"I can remember him . . . Leiber, July 26, 1993.
"He'd scare the crap . . . Leiber, July 26, 1993.
"Cocaine can be found . . . Litsky, Frank, "Player Tells Of Wide Drug Use In N.F.L.," *New York Times*, NY, June 10, 1982.
"I first became aware . . . Durso, Joseph, "Reese May Face Return to Prison," *New York Times*, NY, June 11, 1982.
"Players and management . . . Litsky, Frank, "N.F.L. Teams Split On Tests for Drugs," *New York Times*, NY, July 18, 1982.
"There are occasional . . . Litsky, July 18, 1982.
"Merc got a tough verdict . . . Anderson, Dave, "The Empty Coffee Cups of Don Shula," *New York Times*, NY, November 16, 1982.
"Reese wasn't here . . . Anderson, November 16, 1982.
"The only explanation . . . Anderson, November 16, 1982.
"We've had some real . . . Janofsky, October 1, 1983.
"You try to do the best . . . Anderson, November 16, 1982.
"You need to find where . . . Mifflin, Lawrie, and Eskanazi, Gerald, "Dolphins Offer Jets a Dim View," *New York Times*, NY, September 9, 1982.
"Whatever was done . . . Mifflin and Eskanazi, September 9, 1982.
"When he loses to the . . . Eskanazi, Gerald, "Strong Feelings Surround Jets-Dolphins," *New York Times*, NY, September 12, 1982.
"If I was an authority . . . Eskanazi, September 12, 1982.
"That's been the . . . Anderson, November 16, 1982.
"With a 10-game schedule . . . Anderson, November 16, 1982.
"I've stressed all along . . . Anderson, November 16, 1982.
"I keep hearing I've . . . Zimmerman, December 20, 1993.
"You're ruining my . . . Zimmerman, December 20, 1993.
"He's a screamer . . . Eskanazi, Gerald, "Super Bowl XIX; Don Shula Leaves Nothing to Chance," *New York Times*, NY, January 20, 1985.
"It was a Monday night game . . . Eskanazi, January 20, 1985.
"I realized how bad . . . Eskanazi, January 20, 1985.
"As a younger coach . . . Anderson, November 16, 1982.
"I'd like to think I've . . . Anderson, November 16, 1982.
"Mellow? Mellow?" . . . Zimmerman, December 20, 1993.
"I don't mind personalities . . . Rubin, Bob, "Tiny Clayton has made big mark," *The Sporting News*, Kansas City, Missouri, January 21, 1985.
"I remember it was . . . Bokamper, Kim, "Bo Knows: The Snowplow Game," *MiamiDolphins.com*, December 12, 2017.
"Get out there . . . Marquad, Bryan, "Ron Meyer, 76; was Patriots coach for 'snowplow game' in 1982," Boston Globe, MA, December 7, 2017.
"I knew exactly what . . . Marquad, December 7, 2017.
"I remember standing . . . Bokamper, December 12, 2017.

"MVP! MVP! MVP!" . . . Marquad, December 7, 2017.

"Matt Cavanaugh had . . . Hannah, John, with Hale, Tom, "Patriots Hall Of Famer John Hannah: Why the 'Snowplow Game' Is Misunderstood," *The Post Game.com*, December 9, 2013.

"John and Matt will tell . . . Farley, Glenn, "Hingham's Tom Hoffman has vivid memories of Patriots' 'Snowplow Game,'" *Patriot Ledger*, Boston, MA, December 12, 2012.

"Coach [Don] Shula started . . . Bokamper, December 12, 2017.

"I could see the . . . Hannah, with Hale, December 9, 2013.

"I think it's the most . . . Rivaldo, Joey, "Anniversary of 'The Snowplow' Game," *ProPlayerInsider.com*, December 11, 2012.

"It's the first time since . . . Rivaldo, December 11, 2012.

"I get up at 5 o'clock . . . Farley, December 12, 2012.

"It's hard for me to . . . N/A, "Icy Aftermath," *New York Times*, NY, December 26, 1982.

"Get a guy from Miami . . . "Icy Aftermath," December 26, 1982.

"Miami made a huge . . . Hannah, with Hale, December 9, 2013.

"It's funny, the Dolphins . . . Bokamper, December 12, 2017.

"They move Duhe around . . . Anderson, Dave, "Subplot On the Sidelines," *New York Times*, NY, January 23, 1983.

"Basically, I feel I'm a . . . Janofsky, Michael, "Dolphins Adapt To Arnsparger Method," *New York Times*, NY, January 19, 1983.

"Once we shut them . . . Janofsky, Michael, "Surprises Are the Routine in Playoffs," *New York Times*, NY, January 11, 1983.

"It's nice to get that nine-year . . . Janofsky, January 11, 1983.

"We have played great . . . Janofsky, Michael, "Dolphins and Packers Gain in Playoffs," *New York Times*, NY, January 9, 1983.

"When it got to 24–0 . . . Janofsky, Michael, Dolphins Top Chargers, *New York Times*, NY, January 17, 1983.

"Just to let him know . . . Papanek, John, "The Revenge of the Killer Bees," *Sports Illustrated*, NY, January 24, 1983.

"They did a tremendous . . . Papanek, January 24, 1983.

"How can you compete . . . Janofsky, Michael, "Shula Is Wary of Jet Rivalry," *New York Times*, NY, January 18, 1983.

"Fouts will take three . . . Janofsky, January 18, 1983.

"In the beginning . . . Janofsky, Michael, "Key Role For Duhe In Dolphin Shutout," *New York Times*, NY, January 24, 1983.

"I thought today was . . . Janofsky, January 24, 1983.

"We were slipping . . . Yowell, Keith, "1983: Dolphins Defense Shuts Down Jets to Win AFC," *Today In Pro Football History*, January 23, 2011.

"He was saying that . . . Janofsky, Michael, "Jets Give Credit to Dolphins Defense," *New York Times*, NY, January 25, 1983.

"Basically, we're a . . . Janofsky, January 25, 1983.

"Don has changed a little . . . Vecsey, George, "Returning to the Scene," *New York Times*, NY, January 30, 1983.

"When it's quiet . . . Vecsey, January 30, 1983.

"I should have made . . . Vecsey, George, "The Dolphin Who Can Cope," *New York Times*, NY, January 18, 1983.

"If they didn't change . . . Attner, Paul, "Riggins, Redskins Run to Super Bowl Title, 27–17," *Washington Post,* Washington, DC, January 31, 1982.

"When nothing works . . . Attner, January 31, 1982.

"It could have been . . . Pope, Edwin, "Don Shula knows Dolphins were manhandled as Redskins run away with Super Bowl XVII," Miami Herald, FL, February 3, 2017.

"This team has accomplished . . . Pope, February 3, 2017.

"I thought Woodley played . . . Pope, February 3, 2017.

"I considered making . . . Pope, February 3, 2017.

"When Riggins went 43 . . . Pope, February 3, 2017.

"Their scheme, and . . . Zimmerman, Paul, "Hail to the Redskins," *Sports Illustrated,* NY, February 7, 1983.

"That was probably the . . . Bishop, Greg (with Rohan Nadkarni), "The One and Only," *Sports Illustrated,* NY, January 20, 1985.

"All season, Betters says . . . Bishop, "The One and Only," January 20, 1985.

Chapter 9: Marino

"I decided to go to . . . Eskanazi, Gerald, "Shula Son Works His Own Way," *New York Times,* NY, January 14, 1985.

"I was going to return . . . Eskanazi, January 14, 1985.

"It's the little things . . . Dorman, Larry, "Above All, Shula Has Learned to Adjust," *New York Times,* NY, January 21, 1985.

"Some players respond . . . Dorman, January 21, 1985.

"Me and Mike Shula . . . Salguero, Armando, "Miami's legendary family returns to the Super Bowl with the Carolina Panthers' Mike Shula," *Miami Herald,* FL, February 06, 2016.

"Don Shula came over . . . Salguero, February 06, 2016.

"Mike is truly outstanding . . . Rogers, Thomas, "All in the Family," *New York Times,* NY, January 31, 1983.

"He never intruded . . . Rogers, All in the Family, January 31, 1983.

"He was a big factor . . . Wallace, William N., "Alabama's Shula Prepared For Challenge," *New York Times,* NY, August 25, 1986.

"other tools of his . . . Greene, Harvey, "Rummaging Through The Attic: Don Shula's Desk," *MiamiDolphin.com,* September 11, 2014.

"It was certainly . . . Tanier, Mike, "NFL Urban Legends: Dan Marino, Drug Rumors and the Draft-Day Slide," *Bleacher Report.com,* August 11, 2015.

"I never took any tests . . . Raffo, Dave, "When Dan Marino was coming out of college, his . . .," *United Press International,* January 18, 1985.

"A lot of it was . . . Tanier, August 11, 2015.

"It's a weird day . . . Poupart, Alain, "Marino's Memories Of The 1983 Draft," *MiamiDolphins.com,* FL, April 29, 2015.

"People started finding . . . Tanier, August 11, 2015.

"This happens in a . . . Tanier, August 11, 2015.

"The cheers turned to . . . Tanier, August 11, 2015.

"Everybody's trying to . . . Raffo, January 18, 1985.

"Pittsburgh Guy . . . Attner, Paul, "Marino: The Great Quarterback Heist," *Washington Post,* Washington, DC, November 3, 1983.
"With our situation . . . Attner, November 3, 1983.
"What Shula saw was . . . Attner, November 3, 1983.
"You probably got the . . . MacCambridge, *Chuck Noll: His Life's Work,* p. 321.
"Shula stood behind . . . Felser, Larry, "The greatest passer? Marino, naturally," *The Sporting News,* Kansas City, Missouri, January 21, 1985.
"Right from the time . . . Nordheimer, Jon, "The enduring obsession," *New York Times* magazine, NY September 1 1985.
"I am not anticipating . . . Eskanazi, January 20, 1985.
"It's very simple . . . Eskanazi, January 20, 1985.
"But he's changed . . . Eskanazi, January 20, 1985.
"He came in and . . . Ed Chay, "USFL is Wooing Shula, Dolphins," *Cleveland Plain Dealer,* OH, July 14, 1983.
"They were nobody's . . . Bishop, January 20, 1985.
"In his first practices . . . Bishop, January 20, 1985.
"Not even Nostrodamus . . . Goldberg, Hank, commentary, "Hank Goldberg Talks Dan Marino, Don Shula, Week 7, 1983," WFOR-TV, CBS, 1983.
"What you saw is . . . Anderson, Dave, "Shula Solid In Miami," *New York Times,* NY, October 17, 1983.
"Have I ever felt . . . Zimmerman, December 20, 1993.
"Here's the guy . . . Zimmerman, December 20, 1993.
"Shula also confirmed . . . Anderson, October 17, 1983.
"I've talked to Mr. Trump . . . Anderson, October 17, 1983.
"All I've done is listen . . . N/A, "Trump Site's Shula's Price," *New York Times,* NY, October 23, 1983.
"I've decided I'm not . . . N/A, "Shula Talks Break Off," *New York Times,* NY, October 25, 1983.
"We were never far . . . N/A, "Shula Signs New Miami Pact," *Associated Press,* November 29, 1983.
"Shula," wrote Paul Attner . . . Attner, Paul, "Two for the Show," *The Sporting News,* Kansas City, MO, January 21, 1985.
"Their basic offense is . . . Janofsky, Michael, "Dolphins Main Job is Halting Warner," *New York Times,* NY, December 31, 1983.
"If I said I expected . . . Janofsky, December 31, 1983.
"When we came down . . . N/A, "Seahawks Beat Dolphins," *New York Times,* NY, January 1, 1984.
"They had been running . . . "Seahawks Beat Dolphins," January 1, 1984.
"Yeah, I was there . . . Rogers, Thomas, "Fleeting Fame," *New York Times,* NY, January 27, 1984.
"It's a pretty important . . . N/A, "Dolphins Lost Season," *New York Times,* NY, August 11, 1984.
"Pete has been . . . N/A, "Dolphins Get Johnson," *New York Times,* NY, September 23, 1984.
"We gave him a crash . . . N/A, "Unbeaten Dolphins trounce Colts, 44–7," Palm Beach Post, FL, September 24, 1984.

"If you need a player . . . Eskanazi, Gerald, "Pete Johnson, A Castoff, Finds The Goal Line With Dolphins," *New York Times*, NY, November 26, 1984.

"I've been a guy who's gone . . . Eskanazi, November 26, 1984.

"He has a twinkle . . . Janofsky, Michael, "Dolphins Roll to a Perfect Half Way Mark," *New York Times*, NY, October 22, 1984.

"We had an extremely . . . Janofsky, October 22, 1984.

"There's a balance . . . Janofsky, October 22, 1984.

"In the dazzling . . . Anderson, Dave, "Marino and Shula's System," *New York Times*, NY, November 4, 1984.

"Never mind who's . . . Anderson, November 4, 1984.

"When Dan arrived . . . Anderson, November 4, 1984.

"Shula is really the . . . Anderson, November 4, 1984.

"Last year is history . . . N/A, Knox, "Shula Dismiss History," *New York Times*, NY, December 29, 1984.

"I feel very good about . . . Eskanazi, Gerald, "Dolphins Performance Cheers Shula," *New York Times*, NY, December 31, 1984.

"We weren't ready . . . Eskanazi, Gerald, "Dolphins Defenders No Time to Relax," *New York Times*, NY, January 4, 1985.

"Arns was always . . . Eskanazi, January 4, 1985.

"The first thing I . . . Eskanazi, Gerald, "Dolphins Disregard Early-Season Rout of Steelers," *New York Times*, NY, January 6, 1985.

"The Steelers off-set . . . Eskenazi, January 6, 1985.

"We like blitzing teams . . . Anderson, Dave, "A Mouthful of Marino," *New York Times*, NY, January 7, 1985.

"We did an outstanding . . . Eskanazi, Gerald, "Dolphins Exploited The Blitz," *New York Times*, NY, January 8, 1985.

"You can't ever predict . . . Anderson, January 7, 1985.

"You've got to pat . . . Anderson, January 7, 1985.

"Each week when . . . Eskanazi, January 14, 1985.

"We take pride . . . Eskanazi, Gerald, "Top Miami Rusher Almost Forgotten," *New York Times*, NY, January 19, 1985.

"It only seems right . . . Anderson, Dave, "Dolphins' Secret Weapon," *New York Times*, NY, January 8, 1985.

"Bill would bounce . . . Anderson, January 8, 1985.

"Both have tremendous . . . Anderson, January 8, 1985.

"Marino's like William . . . Anderson, Dave, "Evolution of The Pass: Luckman to Marino," *New York Times*, NY, January 14, 1985.

"Flash had replaced substance . . . Zimmerman, Paul, "Miami Bites the Dust," *Sports Illustrated*, NY, January 2, 1989.

"We started something . . . Bishop, January 20, 1985.

"We had something . . . Bishop, January 20, 1985.

"I guess people . . . Eskanazi, January 20, 1985.

"This has been one . . . Bishop, January 20, 1985.

"After looking at the . . . N/A, "Super Bowl XIX," *The Sporting News*, Kansas City, MO, January 28, 1985.

"The three punts . . . Eskanazi, Gerald, "Super Bowl XIX; Dolphin Problems Grew and Grew," *New York Times*, NY, January 21, 1985.

"Both teams are so . . . Eskanazi, Gerald, "Montana's Wizardry, Defensive Pressure Proved Keys," *New York Times*, NY, January 22, 1985.

"In the second quarter . . . Nordheimer, September 1, 1985.

"Early in the game we . . . Janofsky, Michael, "Super Bowl XIX; 49ers Overwhelm Dolphins For 38–16 Victory," *New York Times*, NY, January 21, 1985.

"It all started from . . . "Super Bowl XIX," January 28, 1985.

"Their defense played . . . "Super Bowl XIX," January 28, 1985.

"Fog rolled around . . . "Super Bowl XIX," January 28, 1985.

"Joe will never say it . . . "Super Bowl XIX," January 28, 1985.

"We knew they were . . . Barnidge, Tom, "Niners Drill Some Myths Over Miami," *The Sporting News*, Kansas City, MO, January 28, 1985.

"The 49ers drilled us . . . Barnidge, January 28, 1985.

"After the game I . . . Vecsey, George, "Super Bowl XIX; Marino Laments An Unproductive Effort," *New York Times*, NY, January 21, 1985.

"We have got to . . . Vecsey, January 21, 1985.

"I always thought I . . . Bishop, January 20, 1985.

"Yeah, I was there . . . Banks, Don, "At long last, a Shula returns to Super Bowl: Panthers OC on his NFL journey," *Sports Illustrated*, NY, January 26, 2016.

"When you get beat, . . . Eskanazi, Gerald, "Super Bowl XIX; 49ers Overwhelm Dolphins For 38–16 Victory," *New York Times*, NY, January 21, 1985.

Chapter 10: Pursuing Halas

"Even with his closest . . . Leiber, July 26, 1993.

"He had a great minicamp . . . Janofsky, Michael, "Dolphins' New Play: Waiting For Marino," *New York Times*, NY, August 18, 1985.

"I think they're all . . . Janofsky, August 18, 1985.

"I wasn't that interested . . . Janofsky, August 18, 1985.

"If anyone believes . . . Nordheimer, September 1, 1985.

"Competitive? . . . Nordheimer, September 1, 1985.

"Dolphin meetings can . . . Leiber, July 26, 1993.

"I'll embarrass a . . . Leiber, July 26, 1993.

"To me, coaching is . . . Nordheimer, September 1, 1985.

"This is my secret . . . Leiber, July 26, 1993.

"Shula's home is . . . Nordheimer, September 1, 1985.

"To say you might . . . Biggs, Brad, "1985 Bears-Dolphins on Monday Night Football: A perfect season evaporated," *Chicago Tribune*, November 29, 2015.

"I know just what . . . Biggs, November 29, 2015.

"I'm scared of this game . . . Biggs, November 29, 2015.

"They did everything . . . Biggs, November 29, 2015.

"As we watched film . . . Biggs, November 29, 2015.

"We were the best . . . Biggs, November 29, 2015.

"In the locker room . . . Anderson, Dave, "Winning one for the flipper," *New York Times*, NY, December 4, 1985.

"Down the tunnel . . . Biggs, November 29, 2015.

"I don't know when . . . Anderson, December 4, 1985.

"We probably played . . . Gardner, Sam, "One & Done: Thirty years ago, Dolphins ruined Bears' perfect season," *FOX Sports,* December 8, 2015.

"We felt at halftime . . . Moran, Malcolm, "Rams Top Cowboys; Dolphins Win, 24–21," *New York Times,* NY, January 5, 1985.

"Don Shula was alone . . . N/A, "Turnovers Cost Shula Sleep As Well As Game," *New York Times,* NY, January 14, 1986.

"The disappointment was . . . "Turnovers Cost Shula Sleep," January 14, 1986.

Then in April, Shula suffered . . . N/A, "Mary Shula, 83, Was Mother Of Coach For Miami Dolphins," *Sun Sentinel,* FL, April 3, 1986.

"Do not—repeat, do not . . . Zimmerman, December 20, 1993.

"I don't know what . . . Moran, Malcolm, "Players; Dolphins' Defense Stung By Criticism," *New York Times,* NY, September 30, 1986.

"I went out on a limb . . . Janofsky, Michael, "Precipitous Decline Disappoints Shula," *New York Times,* NY, November 24, 1986.

"I have no comment . . . N/A, "Fish Story," *New York Times,* New York NY, November 6, 1986.

"I'm happy to put . . . Janofsky, November 24, 1986.

"No one is more . . . Janofsky, November 24, 1986.

"I've had to handle . . . Janofsky, November 24, 1986.

"On an oppressively . . . Moran, Malcolm, "Alabama's Shula Passes Test," *New York Times,* NY, September 4, 1985.

"I was devastated . . . Moran, September 4, 1985.

"I got so sick to my . . . Moran, Malcom, "A Time for Cheers and Fears," *New York Times,* NY, January 12, 1991.

"I hope he stayed . . . Moran, September 4, 1985.

"Mike Shula, the southpaw . . . White, Gordron S., Jr., "Quarterbacks Tip Balance Of Power," *College Football '86 magazine,* 1986.

"I think we played well . . . Winderman, Ira, "Just Another Victory for Shula," *Sun Sentinel,* FL, September 21, 1986.

"It was hairy enough . . . Winderman, September 21, 1986.

"I don't know that . . . Scarbinsky, Kevin, "You surprised Mike Shula's become a Super Bowl coach?" *Advance Local,* Tuscaloosa, Alabama, February 2, 2016.

"I played for both of . . . Mike Shula, interview, "Don Shula Retires," narrated by Jimmy Cefalo, Ann Bishop, *WPLG-TV,* Miami, Florida, January 5, 1996.

"And we won, too!" . . . Don Shula, interview, "Don Shula Retires," narrated by Jimmy Cefalo, Ann Bishop, *WPLG-TV,* Miami, Florida, January 5, 1996.

"The priorities for Miami . . . Keim, Bob, "The Miami Dolphins went into the 1988 season with . . ." *United Press International,* December 20, 1988.

"It's just a disappointing . . . Keim, December 20, 1988.

"In addition to the . . . Keim, December 20, 1988.

"I was very disturbed . . . N/A, "Shula says he warned Duper," *Associated Press,* December 8, 1988.

"We were playing against . . . Greene, Harvey, "Alumni 5: Five Questions With Mark Duper," Miami Dolphins.com July 6, 2017.

"I died laughing . . . Greene, July 6, 2017.

"David took a lot . . . Jenkins, Sally, "David Shula to Head Johnson's Dallas Staff," *Washington Post*, , February 28, 1989.

"Dorothy Shula's . . . Moran, January 2, 1991.

"We laid a foundation . . . Graham, Michael, "The Son Also Rises," *Cincinnati* magazine, Cincinnati, Ohio, May 1992.

"When I went to Dallas . . . Graham, May 1992.

"I could have done . . . Shapiro, Leonard, "For David Shula, A Legacy Of Victory," *Washington Post*, Washington, DC, October 27, 1992.

"Shula, football, steak . . . Morrissey, Siobahn, "The winning touch: Shula's Steak House marks 25 years in business," *Miami Herald*, FL, January 4, 2015.

"Probably the biggest . . . Morrissey, January 4, 2015.

"We were 4–3 and . . . George, Thomas," Dolphins Complete Defensive Renewal," *New York Times*, NY, November 19, 1990.

"I don't . . . My actions . . . Salguero, Armando, "The day Marino almost joined the Raiders," *Miami Herald*, FL, March 31, 2010.

"When the Robbie . . . N/A, "Joe Robbie, 73, N.F.L. Owner Who Founded Miami Dolphins," *Associated Press*, January 9, 1990.

"Mrs. Robbie has . . . "Joe Robbie, 73, N.F.L. Owner Who Founded," January 9, 1990.

"This is just my perverse . . . "Joe Robbie, 73, N.F.L. Owner Who Founded," January 9, 1990.

"Coach Shula wants . . . Moran, Malcolm, "Revised Dolphins Make Shula Beam," *New York Times*, NY, January 7, 1991.

"It was all I heard . . . George, November 19, 1990.

"It was very . . . Anderson, Dave, "Don Shula, Still the Best Coach," *New York Times*, NY, November 11, 1990.

"O.K., here it is . . . Zimmerman, Paul, "AFC East Division, NFL Preview," *Sport Illustrated*, NY, September 10, 1990.

"Run the ball . . . Zimmerman, September 10, 1990.

"During those four . . . Anderson, November 11, 1990.

"We're a phoenix . . . Leiber, July 26, 1993.

"We'll start off the . . . Leiber, July 26, 1993.

"He's not having to . . . Leiber, July 26, 1993.

"It just goes to show . . . Zimmerman, Paul, "Miami Heat," *Sports Illustrated*, NY, November 19, 1990.

"I just didn't see . . . George, November 19, 1990.

"When we broke . . . Zimmerman, November 19, 1990.

"In sports, the living . . . Anderson, November 11, 1990.

"That's what makes Don . . . Anderson, November 11, 1990.

"Miami was on its way . . . Zimmerman, November 19, 1990.

"Eleven times you've picked . . . Zimmerman, December 20, 1993.

"In the spring of 1989 . . . Leiber, July 26, 1993.

"I was always hoping . . . Leiber, July 26, 1993.

"Mom was so full . . . Leiber, July 26, 1993.

"He held her when . . . Leiber, July 26, 1993.

"It pinpoints the parts . . . Anderson, November 11, 1990.

"When I left the . . . Leiber, Mountain, July 26, 1993.
"In all that time . . . Anderson, November 11, 1990.
"It was a tough . . . Miller, Jill Young, "Shula Misses Staunchest Fan," *Seattle Times,* WA, July 21, 1991.
"Even some days when . . . Hyde, Dave, "Shula Will Be Rooting For Mickelson And a Cure," *Sun Sentinel,* FL, June 18, 2009.
"Her cancer was a . . . Leiber, July 26, 1993.
"I told him I was . . . Moran, Malcolm, "Costly Chiefs Error Spurs Dolphins," *New York Times,* NY, January 6, 1991.
"On those kind of . . . Moran, January 6, 1991.
"That's what made . . . Moran, January 12, 1991.
"There are other . . . Moran, January 12, 1991.
"Much of that concern . . . Moran, January 12, 1991.
"Don Shula Night" . . . N/A. "Honoring Don," *Cleveland Plain Dealer,* OH, January 2, 1991.
"She went peacefully . . . Fowler, Scott, "Shula's Biggest Test is handling wife's death," *Washington Post,* September 2, 1991.
"I just thank God . . . Miller, July 21, 1991.
"Any time you . . . Fowler, September 2, 1991.
"When I got home . . . Miller, July 21, 1991.
"Sometimes she'd . . . Fowler, September 2, 1991.
"Talk about courage . . . Cote, Greg and Long, Gary, "Dorothy Shula was the true coach of the family," *Baltimore Sun,* MD, February 26, 1991.
"I couldn't be there . . . Fowler, September 2, 1991.
"There was relief . . . Leiber, July 26, 1993.
"Of course you . . . Miller, July 21, 1991.
"Dorothy was such . . . Leiber, July 26, 1993.
"I've tried to keep . . . Miller, July 21, 1991.
"People ask me . . . Miller, July 21, 1991.
"He'd always be the . . . Leiber, July 26, 1993.
"I think yesterday . . . Miller, July 21, 1991.
"He was difficult . . . Leiber, July 26, 1993.
"He's really made an . . . Miller, July 21, 1991.
"Coach Shula's changed . . . Zimmerman, December 20, 1993.
"Everybody sees him . . . Miller, July 21, 1991.
"It has long been . . . Zimmerman, September 2, 1991.
"I sort of spun . . . Kjos, Les, "Dolphins 16, Packers 13," *United Press International,* September 22, 1991.
"Everybody was sort . . . Freeman, Mike, "Shula Gets 300 The Hard Way," *Washington Post,* Washington, DC, September 23, 1991.
"I've always wanted . . . Freeman, September 23, 1991.
"The only time I heard . . . Freeman, September 23, 1991.
"Late in the season . . . Shapiro, October 27, 1992.
"You don't say things . . . Nobles, Charles, "End of Concert for Clayton, the One-Man Brash Band," *New York Times,* NY, December 23, 1991.
"Shula might have gotten . . . Owczarski, Jim, "Dave Shula: 'You can't blame everything on me'," *Cincinnati Enquirer,* OH, July 7, 2017.

"Poor Dave Shula . . . Owczarski, July 7, 2017.
"Sam was definitely . . . Shapiro, October 27, 1992.
"I don't know if it . . . Owczarski, July 7, 2017.
"He was an outstanding . . . Owczarski, July 7, 2017.
"I think we were in a . . . Owczarski, July 7, 2017.
"Was I ready?" David . . . Shapiro, October 27, 1992.
"A lot of people, especially . . . Shapiro, October 27, 1992.
"They want to know . . . Hoffer, October 12, 1992.
"Thursday, 7:30 . . . Hoffer, October 12, 1992.
"Don's idea of change . . . Leiber, July 26, 1993.
"At Miami you could . . . Hoffer, October 12, 1992.
"He's businesslike . . . Hoffer, October 12, 1992.
"You'd like to think . . . Wallace, William N., "NFL Training Camp Report," *New York Times,* NY, August 4, 1992.
"We just took an . . . Nobles, Charlie, "An Old-Style Licking," *New York Times,* NY, January 11, 1993.
"I slept for two . . . Eskenazi, Gerald, "Just Point Shula In the Bills Direction," *New York Times,* NY, January 12, 1993.
"We've been the only . . . Eskenazi, Gerald, "Conference Championships," *New York Times,* NY, January 16, 1993.
"That's just tough . . . Eskenazi, Gerald, January 12, 1993.
"The big difference . . . Maiorana, Sal, "Remember: Jan 17, 1993 Bills vs. Dolphins," *Democrat & Chronicle,* NY, January 17, 2015.
"I don't think they'll . . . Smith, Timothy W., "Conference Championships," *New York Times,* NY, January 18, 1993.
"It was a real disappointment . . . Smith, January 18, 1993.
"He has a tremendous . . . Miller, Jill Young, "Shula-Stephens Affair Ignites Rumors," *Tulsa World,* OK, August 15, 1993 .
"The fifth of six children . . . Miller, August 15, 1993 .
"They were a mighty . . . Miller, August 15, 1993 .
"Wilton Robert ["Witt"] . . . Dumas, Ernest, "Witt Stephens (1907–1991) aka: Wilton Robert Stephens," *The Encyclopedia of Arkansas History & Culture,* AK, August 26, 2016.
"Running Robinson against . . . N/A, "Profile: Jackson T. Stephens (with Mary Anne)," *Mother Jones,* CA, April 5, 2004.
"[Jack] Stephens attended . . ."Profile: Jackson T. Stephens (with Mary Anne)," April 5, 2004.
"A person married . . . Miller, Jill Young, "Who Is The Woman On Don Shula`s Arm?," *Sun Sentinel,* FL, August 8, 1993.
"For decades a . . . Miller, August 8, 1993.
"Mary Anne's plan . . . Miller, August 8, 1993.
"In certain respects . . . Miller, August 8, 1993.
"very, very attractive . . . Miller, August 8, 1993.
"Mary Anne has the . . . Miller, August 8, 1993.
It was alleged that . . . Leiber, July 26, 1993.
"It's great to see a guy . . . Leiber, July 26, 1993.

"This is a relationship . . . Leiber, July 26, 1993.
"Since Mom died . . . Leiber, July 26, 1993.
"One time Matt stormed . . . Leiber, July 26, 1993.
"The Dolphins are . . . Olson, Gary, "Dolphins' Shula Close On The Heels Of Halas," *Knight-Ridder Newspapers,* September 5, 1993.
"Now I have a chance . . . Olson, September 5, 1993.
"Don's the type of coach . . . Olson, September 5, 1993.
"Like a rock striking flint . . . Smith, Timothy W., "Expect Sparks to Fly," *New York Times,* NY, September 12, 1993.
"We're trying not to . . . Smith, September 12, 1993.
"a considerable step . . . Plaschke, Bill, "The Dolphins Take Out Their Trash on Bills, 22–13," *Los Angeles Times,* CA, September 27, 1993.
"I thought I got kicked . . . George, Thomas, "Dolphins Lose Marino but Not the Victory," *New York Times,* NY, October 11, 1993.
"Good for him . . . Cole, Jason, "Shula Won't Say Much about Surprise Wedding," *Sun Sentinel,* FL, October 19, 1993.
"What can you say . . . Pierson, Don, "Mitchell Lifts Shula, Dolphins to The Top," *Chicago Tribune,* IL, November 1, 1993.
"People have been giving . . . Pierson, November 1, 1993.
"Dad won't say it . . . Plaschke, Bill, "Jets Rain on Shula's Victory Parade," *Los Angeles Times,* CA, November 8, 1993.
"You've got these presidents . . . Plaschke, November 8, 1993.
"There were subplots . . . George, Thomas, "No. 325: Shula Rides the Shoulders," *New York Times,* NY, November 15, 1993.
"Shula might have preferred . . . Pierson, Don, "Down To 3rd QB, Shula Still Wins," *Chicago Tribune,* IL, November 15, 1993.
"I was nervous the . . . Greene, Harvey, "Fins Flashback: Coach Shula Wins 325," *MiamiDolphins.com,* FL, November 13, 2015.
"He was an outstanding . . . N/A, "Shula Recalls Pederson's Role In Milestone Dolphins Win," *CBS Local,* Miami, FL, January 19, 2016.
"He's so resourceful . . . Greene, November 13, 2015.
"I'm going to wake up . . . Pierson, November 15, 1993.
"There are reasons . . . Pierson, November 15, 1993.
"I give coach Shula . . . Pierson, November 15, 1993.
"A classy man . . . Greene, November 13, 2015.
"The last time I was . . . Pierson, November 15, 1993.
"I just thanked the . . . Pierson, November 15, 1993.
"For nearly 31 years . . . Zimmerman, December 20, 1993.
"I hate cold weather . . . Sullivan, Jeff, "Frozen in Time—Thanksgiving 1993 Memories," *DallasCowboys.com,* TX, November 27, 2013.
"We've got to play no . . . Sullivan, November 27, 2013.
"We did not expect . . . Sullivan, November 27, 2013.
"It was so bad that . . . Sullivan, November 27, 2013.
"You had to run control routes . . . Sullivan, November 27, 2013.
"Twice in the final five . . . George, Thomas, "Slipshod Play: Cowboys Give Game," *New York Times,* NY, November 26, 1993.

"This really became . . . George, November 26, 1993.
"Sunshine is nice but . . . George, November 26, 1993.
"We had 'block right' . . . Malinowski, Erik, "5 things you forgot about Dallas and Miami's epic 1993 'Snow Bowl'," *FOXSports,* NY, November 25, 2014.
"I knew the rule . . . Malinowski, November 25, 2014.
"I didn't see anything . . . Malinowski, November 25, 2014.
"I always go down . . . Sullivan, November 27, 2013.
"As I reached the . . . Sullivan, November 27, 2013.
"This was a crazy . . . George, November 26, 1993.
"We've lost two in a . . . George, November 26, 1993.
"I vividly remember the . . . Sullivan, November 27, 2013.
"All I remember about . . . Sullivan, November 27, 2013.
"I've been around . . . Sullivan, November 27, 2013.
"There is plenty of blame . . . Nobles, Charlie, "A Once-Banner Season for Dolphins Sinks to One Desperate Game," *New York Times,* NY, January 2, 1994.
"The blame can be sliced . . . Friend, Tom, "The UnShula Dolphins: A 4th Straight Defeat," *New York Times,* NY, December 28. 1993.
"I don't ever remember . . . Nobles, January 2, 1994.
"You can't talk yourself . . . Nobles, January 2, 1994.
"I feel kind of numb now . . . Eskanazi, Gerald, "Dolphin Disappearance Leaves Shula Hurting," *New York Times,* NY, January 3, 1994.
"How could you believe . . . Eskanazi, January 3, 1994.
"Make no mistake . . . Howe, Desson, "Ace Ventura: Pet Detective," *Washington Post,* Washington, DC, February 4, 1994.
"From 1983 through 1993 . . . Craft, Kevin, "Hail Mary," *Slate.com,* September 3, 2014.
"If he says he wants . . . N/A, "Dolphins Owner Wants to Keep Shula," *Associated Press,* June 29, 1994.
"I'm healthy and . . . Nobles, Charlie, "Shula at Dolphins' Helm For Three More Seasons," *New York Times,* NY, July 22, 1994.
"It's a whole different deal . . . Nobles, Charlie, "Marino Back on Track from Injury, According to Him," *New York Times,* NY, September 1, 1994.
"He has done a good . . . N/A, "Bengals Give Shula A 2-Year Contract," *New York Times,* NY, December 30, 1994.
"We were running . . . Shapiro, October 27, 1992.
"The first four games . . . Owczarski, July 7, 2017.
"I'm looking forward . . . N/A, "Shulas to Face Off," *Associated Press,* January 4, 1994.
"It seems we're talking . . . Joseph, Dave, "Shula Family Getting Ready For Matchup," *Sun Sentinel,* FL, September 27, 1994.
"I'm very much looking . . . Joseph, September 27, 1994.
"This is all team . . . Greene, Harvey, "All In The Family: Shula Vs. Shula," *MiamiDolphins.com,* October 2, 2014.
"I'd rather the attention . . . Joseph, September 27, 1994.
"You can't spot the . . . Smith, Timothy, "A First for Father vs. Son Coaching But Not a First Victory for Bengals," *New York Times,* NY, October 3, 1994.
"I'm glad our football . . . Smith, October 3, 1994.
"Once the game began . . . Greene, October 2, 2014.

"I told (David) how much . . . Greene, October 2, 2014.
"It's the Jets, you know . . . Nobles, Charlie, "Dolphins After One Thing: Momentum," *New York Times,* NY, November 27, 1994.
"I remember being . . . Cimini, Rich, "The Fake Spike, 20 years later," *ESPN.com,* NY, November 26, 2014.
"All of a sudden, Dan . . . Cimini, November 26, 2014.
"We always referred to . . . Cimini, November 26, 2014.
"If you watch the . . . Cimini, November 26, 2014.
"I was on the headphones . . . Cimini, November 26, 2014.
"It seems like that play . . . Cimini, November 26, 2014.
"You know what the Jets . . . Cimini, November 26, 2014.
"I worked for the NBC . . . Sanders, Kerry, "Dropping the Pounds with Don Shula," *PMallDAY Today* NBC, Miami, FL, June 23, 2007.
"I arrived at the airport . . . Sanders, June 23, 2007.
"At this exact moment . . . Sanders, June 23, 2007.
"What do you think? . . . Sanders, June 23, 2007.
"In the fourth quarter . . . Springer, Steve, "Lightning Strikes for Chargers," *Los Angeles Times,* CA, January 9, 1995.
"It was a long third . . . Springer, January 9, 1995.
"I stretched my arms . . . Springer, January 9, 1995.
"I looked to the crowd . . . George, Thomas, "Wide Right, and the Chargers Are Left Standing," *New York Times,* NY, January 9, 1995.
"I saw the kick go wide . . . George, January 9, 1995.
"That's about as tough . . . George, January 9, 1995.
"There were some missed . . . Thomas, Robert McG. Jr., "Championships: Notebook; After Missed Calls, Shula Misses Instant Replay," *New York Times,* NY, January 10, 1995.
"It was a big, big . . . Sandomir, Richard, "Super Bowl XXIX; Huizenga's Field, but Minus Dolphins," *New York Times,* NY, January 29, 1995.

Chapter 11: Retirement

"Even after everything . . . Lupica, Mike, "Started Strong, Stayed Too Long," *New York Daily News,* NY, January 5, 1996.
"I never feel those . . . Lupica, January 5, 1996.
"And that was that . . . Lupica, January 5, 1996.
"Any son that has . . . N/A, "Dolphins 26, Bengals 23," *United Press International,* October 1, 1995.
"It was a tough loss . . ."Dolphins 26, Bengals 23," October 1, 1995.
"I'm one that believes . . . Reitman, Tom, "Dolphins Search for Answers to Losing Spell," *Indianapolis Star,* IN, November 24, 1995.
"Everybody is dejected . . . Reitman, November 24, 1995.
"We just haven't played . . . Diaz, George, "Shula Deserves Better Send-off, but Expect Dolphins to Flounder," *Sun Sentinel,* FL, November 24, 1995.
"He was upset about . . . Diaz, November 24, 1995.
"Assuming Jimmy Johnson . . . Diaz, November 24, 1995.

"Shula is not dead yet... N/A, "Don Shula and Tom Landry: The 13 Amazing Coincidences," *Past Imperfect*, June 23, 2007.

"The 6–5 Miami Dolphins ... Dorman, Larry, "Suddenly a Minor Deity," *New York Times*, NY, December 5, 1995.

"I can't let anything ... Silver, Michael, "The Waning of a Legend," *Sports Illustrated*, NY, December 11, 1995.

"Shula's popularity suffers ... Silver, December 11, 1995.

"He used to get right ... Dorman, December 5, 1995.

"This year I kind of ... Plaschke, Bill, "NFL Legend Shula Quits Dolphins," *Palm Beach Post*, FL, January 5, 1996.

"Shula has lost control ... Dorman, December 5, 1995.

"I'm just tired of kissing ... Attner, Paul, "The task ahead: A Mess Made for Jimmy," *The Sporting News*, MO, January 15, 1996.

"If the Dolphins ... Lupica, Mike, "Put Anderson in the Garden and Watch Him Grow," *Asbury Park Press*, NJ, December 3, 1995.

"Right about now, though ... Frey, Jennifer, "In Miami, Pat Riley Cranks Up The Heat," *Washington Post*, Washington, DC, November 24, 1995.

"without a doubt the ... Rhoden, William C., "Tradition and Teflon in Miami," *New York Times*, NY, November 25, 1995.

"You try to shut the ... Dorman, December 5, 1995.

"We've struggled all year ... Nobles, Charlie, "Dubious Playoff Privilege," *New York Times*, NY, December 28, 1995.

"It's kind of chilling to ... Nobles, December 28, 1995.

"I think it's going to be ... Nobles, December 28, 1995.

"You people fail to ... Eskanazi, Gerald, "Levy and Shula insist it's not 'Me vs. Him'," *New York Times*, NY, December 30, 1995.

"Cox had another incident ... Jackson, Barry, "Six Moments of Dolphins Pain and Suffering in Buffalo," *Miami Herald*, FL, December 21, 2016.

"They were never in ... Eskanazi, Gerald, "Bills Win The Old-Fashioned Way," *New York Times*, NY, December 31, 1995.

"As long as Olivadotti ... Eskanazi, December 31, 1995.

"The disappointment was ... Anderson, Dave, "The Measures of Miami," *New York Times*, NY, December 31, 1995.

"[He] looked 65 now ... Lupica, January 5, 1996.

"I know coach Shula ... Kindred, Dave, "The Last of the Football Legends," *The Sporting News*, MO, January 15,1996.

"This is the one we're ... Anderson, Dave, December 31, 1995.

"It's as if Shula's career ... Anderson, December 31, 1995.

"Things haven't worked ... Nobles, Charlie, "Shula Reflects on Finishing His Contract," *New York Times*, NY, January 1, 1996.

"The important thing ... Nobles, January 1, 1996.

"When you play a game ... Nobles, January 1, 1996.

"What happened just goes ... Plaschke, Bill, "NFL Legend Shula Quits Dolphins Job," *Palm Beach Post*, FL, January 5, 1996.

"I think he had a staff ... Plaschke, January 5, 1996.

"it was a tough decision ... Plaschke, January 5, 1996.

"This is one of the saddest . . . Nobles, Charlie, "Shula Packing Up Trophies and Wins," *New York Times*, NY, January 5, 1996.
"South Florida doesn't . . . N/A, "Shula to Resign after 33 years," *Standard-Speaker*, PA, January 5, 1996.
"Passion was not . . . Rhoden, William C., "Standoffs And Fond Farewells," *New York Times*, NY, January 6, 1996.
"You can see the decline . . . Shapiro, Leonard, "Dolphins' Shula Calls It A Career," *Washington Post*, Washington, DC, January 6, 1996.
"I'm putting up a noble . . . Shapiro, January 6, 1996.
"I'm a little sad . . . Nobles, Charlie, "Sadness, Praise, Relief, From Dolphin Faithful," *New York Times*, NY, January 6, 1996.
"It's an end of an era . . . Nobles, January 6, 1996.
"This week's proof of . . . Kindred, January 15, 1996.
"I have no thoughts . . . Shapiro, January 6, 1996.
"His sly and unconscionable . . . Lyon, Bill, "City of Miami, Jimmy Johnson deserve each other," *The Oklahoman*, OK, January 12, 1996.
"It happened to Tom . . . Lupica, January 5, 1996.

Chapter 12: Life After Football

"A day after he turned . . . Attner, Paul, "Dave Shula, Mike Shula, Maty Anne Shula . . . .," *The Sporting News*, MO, January 15, 1996.
"Baltimore needs Don . . . Plaschke, Bill, "Here's Your Chance, Don," *The Sporting News*, MO, February 19, 1996.
"I've liked Don Shula . . . Shapiro, Leonard, "Shula May Be Courted To Coach Baltimore Team," *Washington Post*, Washington, DC, February 8, 1996.
"I spoke to him yesterday . . . Shapiro, February 8, 1996.
"When Shula turned . . . Shapiro, February 8, 1996.
"I told [Modell] that . . . Shapiro, February 8, 1996.
"It's a weekday . . . Myers, Gary, "This Is My-Ami Shula's One Regret: No Ring for Marino," *New York Daily News*, NY, August 12, 1996.
"To this point . . . Myers, August 12, 1996.
"When I feel it's . . . Myers, August 12, 1996.
"I only know our guys . . . Myers, August 12, 1996.
"I respect Wayne for . . . Myers, August 12, 1996.
"I could have done . . . Owczarski, July 7, 2017.
"I cannot blame David . . . Owczarski, July 7, 2017.
"The reference point . . . Pierson, Don, "After Great Start, Blake Just Grateful," *Chicago Tribune*, IL, November 1, 1994.
"I always used is Iowa . . . Pierson, November 1, 1994.
"It turned out to be . . . Baldwin, Mike, "Iowa State Reference Haunts Switzer," *The Oklahoman*, OK, October 16, 1996.
"We made some . . . Owczarski, July 7, 2017.
"They were still trying . . . Owczarski, July 7, 2017.
"What running game?" . . . Smith, Timothy W. "After 2 Games, Bengals Are Running on Empty," *New York Times*, NY, September 15, 1996.

"He's earned the right... N/A, "Shula Rewards Hearst's Performance," *Cincinnati Enquirer,* OH, October 3, 1996.

"This guy breaks down... N/A, "AFC review," *The Sporting News,* MO, October 7,1996.

"He was a wonderful... Owczarski, July 7, 2017.

"Privately, he was... Wine, Stephen, "Shula finds peace—in steak house," *Associated Press,* July 28, 2002.

"There was enough... Glauber, Bob, "Mid-season grades are in," *The Sporting News,* MO, October 28,1996.

"So it kind of evened... Owczarski, July 7, 2017.

"When I came down... Wine, July 28, 2002.

"I don't pretend to... Wine, July 28, 2002.

"David Younts has... Wine, July 28, 2002.

"Traditionally, the hotel... Heimlich, Cheryl Kane, "With coaching dynasty dead, Shulas trying to tackle steaks," *Cincinnati Business Courier,* July 14, 1997.

"Our offense had the... N/A, "Football Hall Of Fame Inducts Seven," *Washington Post,* Washington, DC, August 9, 1987.

"My family is here... "Football Hall Of Fame Inducts Seven," August 9, 1987.

"It's something I've... Long, Mark, "Buoniconti Set To Enter Pro Football Hall Of Fame," *Associated Press,* August 3, 2001 .

"The jaw is prominently... Barnes, Craig, "Don Shula: Dolphins coach, his jaw make their mark on Hall," *Sun Sentinel,* FL, July 27, 1997.

"I can't tell you how... Shula, Don, Induction speech, National Football League Hall of Fame, Canton, OH, July 26, 1997.

"We needed a football... N/A, "Group Bidding for Browns Hires Shula," *Bloomberg News,* NY, June 17, 1998.

"Once talk fades about... Sandomir, Richard, "The Chase for the Browns: Big Names, Big Money," *New York Times,* NY, July 21, 1998.

"Al Lerner, who helped... Sandomir, Richard, "Lerner Wins Browns for $530 Million," *New York Times,* NY, September 9, 1998.

"That's probably the... N/A, "1972 Miami Dolphins Toast First Losses by Undefeated Teams," *snopes.com,* 2005; Banks, Don, "Burning Questions," *Sports Illustrated,* October 21, 2003; Bell, Jarrett, "Colts Pursue Perfection of 1972 Dolphins," *USA Today,* December 16, 2005 (p. A1); Bell, Jarrett, "Chargers Leave Colts at a Loss," *USA Today,* December 19, 2005 (p. C1); Culpepper, Chuck, "Unblemished '72 Dolphins Faced Rivals with Lots of Warts," *Newsday,* November 27, 2005 (p. B27); Diaz, George, "Shula: Champagne Story About '72 Dolphins Is a Myth, *Orlando Sentinel,* November 22, 2005; Rhoden, William C., "'72 Dolphins Unbeaten, Unbowed, But Sweating," *New York Times,* NY, December 10, 2007; Rountree, Mark, "Riley Says Myth Surrounds '72 Team," *Enid News & Eagle,* December 18, 2007; "1972 Dolphins Watch Packers' March to Perfection with Mix of Emotions," *Green Bay Press-Gazette,* December 17, 2011.

"I'll be the first to admit... Stroud, Rick, "'Football genius' Mike Shula had rocky end with Bucs," *Tampa Bay Times,* March 19, 2018.

"Mike [Shula] was always... Stroud, March 19, 2018.

"In those days, the... Stroud, March 19, 2018.

"Unfortunately for him... Stroud, March 19, 2018.

"His dad gave me my . . . N/A, "Mike Shula Added to Dolphins Staff," *Associated Press*, February 8. 2000.

"That's a huge hook . . . Wine, July 28, 2002.

"I've been very happy . . . Wine, July 28, 2002.

"Dad will remind me . . . Wine, July 28, 2002.

"The dim, masculine . . . Asimov, Eric, "Diner's Journal," *New York Times*, November 29, 2002.

"Hey, give this to . . . Silver, July 15, 2002.

"Every family has its . . . Silver, July 15, 2002.

"That's why Shula hates . . . Silver, July 15, 2002.

"We never ever . . . Baldwin, Mike, "Perfect inspiration Twilley, Riley recall event that led to only unbeaten NFL season," *The Oklahoman*, OK, November 3, 2002.

"Shula got up and . . . Baldwin, November 3, 2002.

"During the season . . . Baldwin, November 3, 2002.

"I'm the first to say . . . Baldwin, November 3, 2002.

"How many times . . . Hyde, Dave, "Looking Back In Anger," *Sun Sentinel*, FL, December 9, 2002.

"Jake, why don't you . . . Hyde, December 9, 2002.

"He just doesn't like to . . . Hyde, December 9, 2002.

"Scott was traded . . . Hyde, December 9, 2002.

"I wish Jake was at . . . Hyde, December 9, 2002.

"It is with a great . . . Press Release, "Mike Shula Named 26th Alabama Head Football Coach," *University of Alabama*, May 9, 2003.

"I am obviously . . . Press Release, May 9, 2003.

"Likely to hinder . . . Battista, Judy, "Alabama Decides to Hire Mike Shula as Its Coach," *New York Times*, NY, May 9, 2003.

"Alabama reached out . . . Salguero, Armando, "Miami's legendary family returns to the Super Bowl with the Carolina Panthers' Mike Shula," *Miami Herald*, FL, February 6 2016.

"When I was here . . . Bernstein, Viv, "Shula Era Begins Amid Hope and Doubt," *New York Times*, NY, July 20, 2003.

The original NutriSystem . . . Bittar, Christine, "Don Shula Set To Pitch NutriSystem Diet Line," *Marketing Daily*, November 20, 2006.

"I kind of had a beer . . . Zezima, Katie, "It Takes a Big Man to Seek Help on Weight Loss," *New York Times*, NY, November 8, 2007.

"I saw how well my . . . Sanders, June 23, 2007.

"At 77 years old, now . . . Sanders, June 23, 2007.

"Once he saw the . . . Walsh, Christopher, "Shula fired by Alabama after 6–6 season," *Tuscaloosa News*, AL, November 28, 2006.

"Alabama thought for . . . Zenor, Rob, "Crimson Tide Rolling onto New Coach," *Associated Press*, November 28, 2006.

"His leadership has . . . Zenor, November 28, 2006.

"I just feel like coach . . . Zenor, November 28, 2006.

"Mike Shula is a good . . . Walsh, November 28, 2006.

"I guess I have to say . . . Sabin, Rainer, "Looking back at when Nick Saban said he wasn't 'going to be the Alabama coach'," *Advance Local*, AL, February 21, 2017.

"During the last few . . . Habib, Hal, "New book: Nick Saban's wife wanted out of Miami, pushed him to Alabama," *Palm Beach Post,* FL, July 19, 2015.

"She made it clear to . . . Habib, July 19, 2015.

"The punctuation on the . . . Le Batard, Dan, "The anti-Shula bails out as a greasy, dishonorable coward," *Miami Herald,* FL, January 4, 2007.

"There were four or . . . N/A, "As Saban Starts New Era, Don Shula Talks of 'Lies'," *New York Times,* NY, January 5, 2007.

"The Alabama firing . . . Salguero, February 6, 2016.

"Usually we just go out . . . Fadely, Chuck, "Don Shula on Turning 80," *Miami Herald,* FL, December 31, 2009.

"My husband is 80 years . . . Garcia-Roberts, Gus, "Mary Anne Shula Sues for Her Dead Ex-Husband's Alimony Millions," *Miami New Times,* FL, May 12, 2010.

"There was no plan . . . Hyde, Dave, "Jake Scott and Don Shula start again with a hug," *Sun Sentinel,* FL, May 8, 2010.

"And Shula hugged him . . . Hyde, May 8, 2010.

"Get a picture . . . Hyde, May 8, 2010.

"We felt like a piece . . . Hyde, Dave, "The feel-good story of Jake Scott and Don Shula," *Sun Sentinel,* FL, May 9, 2010.

"The hell with it . . . Hyde, May 8, 2010.

"The other thing . . . Hyde, May 8, 2010.

"Forty is a big number . . . Beasley, Adam H., "Miami Dolphins' perfect 1972 season a source of pride for former players, even 40 years later," *Miami Herald,* FL, December 16, 2012.

"Don Shula weaved his . . . Hyde, Dave, "1972 Dolphins toasted at White House," *Sun Sentinel,* FL, August 20, 2013.

"I'm only going to . . . Hyde, August 20, 2013.

"Was this guy a great . . . Hyde, August 20, 2013.

"When the players left . . . Hyde, August 20, 2013.

"Cancer has touched . . . N/A, "Don Shula Foundation Donates $1.5 Million to Moffitt Cancer Center," *The American Society of Clinical Oncology,* August 15, 2014.

The fund created . . . Manning, Margie, "Don Shula Foundation gives Moffitt $1.5M to tackle breast cancer," *Tampa Bay Business Journal,* FL, July 14, 2014.

"We are proud of our . . . Manning, July 14, 2014.

"My wife is the business . . . Warech, Jon, "How Ex-Miami Dolphins Coach Don Shula Remains A Success After Football," *Ocean Drive* magazine, FL, October 1, 2015.

"Archbishop Wenski . . . Tracy, Tom, "Shula's lifetime commitment to Catholic education, other causes honored," *Catholic News Service,* November 26, 2014.

"Every other organization . . . Tracy, November 26, 2014.

"coaches say he is the . . . N/A, "Shula, Chris, Profile," *MiamiRedhawks,com,* Miami University, January 1, 2018.

"I think I always knew . . . Warsinkey, Tim, "Chris Shula named defensive coordinator at John Carroll," *Cleveland Plain Dealer,* OH, February 26, 2014.

"I could tell . . . Warsinkey, February 26, 2014.

"Yeah, I was the . . . Warsinkey, February 26, 2014.

"The Shula coaching . . . Warsinkey, February 26, 2014.

"We're excited to work . . . Warsinkey, February 26, 2014.

"We did not hire him . . . Warsinskey, Tim, "Chris Shula extends Don Shula's legacy at John Carroll with No. 2-ranked defense," *Cleveland Plain Dealer,* OH, November 13, 2014.

"Chris Shula was running . . . Warsinskey, November 13, 2014.

"Chris keeps in close . . . Warsinskey, November 13, 2014.

"I'm very happy . . . Warsinskey, November 13, 2014.

"It means a lot to me . . . Warsinskey, November 13, 2014.

"I'm really proud . . . Warsinskey, Tim, "San Diego Chargers hire Chris Shula away from John Carroll University," *Cleveland Plain Dealer,* OH, February 13, 2015.

"It really is awesome . . . Gehman, Jim, "Rams Assistant Chris Shula Is Third Generation of Shula Coaches," *Inside The Rams.com,* CA, March 22, 2017.

"I was really super . . . Gehman, March 22, 2017.

"My dad never coached . . . Gehman, March 22, 2017.

"By the way, did . . . Cote, Greg, "Don Shula's health scare makes us reflect on an irreplaceable time," *Miami Herald,* FL, May 4, 2016.

"This Super Bowl, the . . . Hurt, Cecil, "Super Bowl title for Mike Shula would be nice," *Tuscaloosa News,* AL, February 6, 2016.

"in a position where his . . . Hurt, February 6, 2016.

"The 6–5, 245-pound Newton . . . Chrapowicki, Stan, "The odd couple: Auburn's Cam Newton and Bama's Mike Shula make super team," *Saturday Down South.com,* January 2016.

"Teams will be interested . . . Florio, Mike, "Mike Shula says he would have interviewed for coaching jobs," *NBC Sports.com,* January 20, 2016.

"All I said was I'm . . . Florio, January 20, 2016.

"Somebody said I had . . . Florio, January 20, 2016.

"It apparently came from . . . Florio, January 20, 2016.

"I think a secret weapon . . . Salguero, February 6, 2016.

"[Shula] says when you . . . Salguero, February 6, 2016.

"Getting to the Super . . . Salguero, February 6, 2016.

"It's nearly unfathomable . . . Banks, Don, "At long last, a Shula returns to Super Bowl: Panthers OC on his NFL journey," *Sports Illustrated,* NY, January 26, 2016.

"If you like symmetry . . . Banks, January 26, 2016.

"That's what just makes . . . Banks, January 26, 2016.

"It kind of got me a . . . Banks, January 26, 2016.

"He's excited," Mike . . . Poupart, Alain, "Super Bowl Trips Were Once Routine For Mike Shula," *Miami Dolphin.com,* FL, February 3, 2016.

"I talk to him all the . . . Cote, Greg, "Kid Shula vs. Son of a Bum," *Miami Herald,* FL, February 5, 2016.

"I can't wait to head . . . Berry, Jim, "Don Shula Ready To Watch Son In Super Bowl 50," *CBS Miami,* January 29, 2016.

"I think his attention . . . Berry, January 29, 2016.

"It's an honor to be . . . Berry, January 29, 2016.

"[Cam] actually had a . . . Banks, January 26, 2016.

"Mike is a master at . . . Scarbinsky, February 2, 2016.

"We've shown around . . . Person, Joseph, "Concerns for Panthers OC Mike Shula? He has some, but not about his job," *Charlotte Observer,* NC, October 23, 2017.

"While Rivera defended . . . Person, October 23, 2017.

"We need to look at . . . Newton, David, "Mike Shula's answer to critics: Have perspective, simplify, throw spirals," *ESPN.com,* October 24, 2017.

"I've been so lucky to . . . Newton, October 24, 2017.

"It is very clear that . . . DBelt, "The curious case for Mike Shula as an NFL head coach," *CatScratchReader.com,* December 28, 2017.

"As much high hopes . . . Riddick, Louis, "Panthers Fire OC Mike Shula," *NFL Live, ESPN,* January 9, 2018.

"Shula was not very good at playing . . . Inabinnett, Mark, "Carolina Panthers fire offensive coordinator Mike Shula," *Advance Local,* AL, January 9, 2018.

"I've known Mike a . . . Eisen, Michael, "Giants coaching staff announced; Mike Shula named offensive coordinator," *Giants.com,* NJ, February 15, 2018.

"The family is looking . . . Habib, Hal, "Don Shula, 86, hospitalized; family hopes for 'speedy recovery'," *Palm Beach Post,* FL, May 3, 2016.

"According to the Mayo . . . N/A, "Sleep apnea," *MayoClinic.org,* 1998–2018.

"Coach has been . . . Habib, May 3, 2016.

"He's doing fine . . . Habib, Hal," Don Shula, honored with mural, 'doing well' health-wise with pacemaker," *Palm Beach Post,* FL, September 22, 2016.

"It really captured . . . Habib, September 22, 2016.

"It's one of those . . . Habib, September 22, 2016.

"Buoniconti doesn't explain . . . Price, May 9, 2017.

"Some of Buoniconti's . . . Price, May 9, 2017.

"I feel lost . . . Price, May 9, 2017.

"check up on him . . . Price, S.L. "How Jim Kiick Fell Through The Cracks," *Sports Illustrated,* NY, May 9, 2017.

"As Price pointed . . . Price, May 9, 2017.

"an almost unbelievable . . . Habib, Hal, "Miami Dolphins' Larry Csonka: For most part, Jim Kiick 'still at 100 percent'," *Palm Beach Post,* FL, May 12, 2017.

"When you say assisted . . . Habib, May 12, 2017.

"more and more the issue . . . Habib, May 12, 2017.

"I sleep late and . . . Warech, October 1, 2015.

"I go to all the games . . . Warech, October 1, 2015.

"Coach," Bob Griese says . . . Hyde, Dave, "Decades later, Don Shula and Bob Griese have a friendship that transcends coach and quarterback," *Sun Sentinel,* FL, March 21, 2018.

"The interplay between . . . Hyde, March 21, 2018.

"They talk of family . . . Hyde, March 21, 2018.

"You know Tunney . . . Hyde, March 21, 2018.

"Coach, can I pose . . . Cohen, Andy, "AC in the AM: Don Shula Still Going Strong," *MiamiDolphins.com,* FL, December 21, 2017.

"Tell the story about . . . Cohen, December 21, 2017.

"Love to be with all . . . Cohen, December 21, 2017.

"I miss game day . . . Cohen, December 21, 2017.

"I want to continue . . . Cohen, December 21, 2017.

Select Bibliography

BOOKS

Bagil, Vince, and Macht, Norman L., *Sundays at 2:00 with the Baltimore Colts*. Tidewater Publishers, Centreville, Maryland: Tidewater Publishers, 1995.

Bell, Upton, and Borges, Ron, *Present at the Creation*. University of Nebraska Press, Lincoln, NB: University of Nebraska Press, 2017.

Callahan, Tom, *Johnny U*, Three Rivers Press, New York, NY, 2007.

Csonka, Larry and Kiick, Jim (with Dave Anderson), *Always On The Run*, Random House, New York, NY, 1973.

Donovan, Arthur J., Jr. (with Bob Drury) *Fatso*, William Morrow & Co., New York, NY, 1987.

Fleischer, Jack, *My Sunday Best*, Grosset & Dunlap, New York, NY, 1972.

Freeman, Mike, *Undefeated*, It Books, New York, NY, 2012.

Garrison, Rita, *Big Bubba*, XLibris US, Bloomington, Indiana, 2013.

Gildea, William, *When the Colts Belonged to Baltimore*, Tickner & Fields, New York, NY, 1994.

Griese, Bob, with Hyde, Dave, *Perfection*, John Wiley & Sons, Hoboken, NJ, 2012.

Gruver, Ed, *From Baltimore to Broadway*, Triumph Books, Chicago, IL, 2009.

Gutman, Bill, *Csonka*, Grosset & Dunlap, New York, NY, 1974.

Karras, Alex, *Even Big Guys Cry*, Signet, New York, NY, 1978.

Karras, *My Life in Football, Television & Movies*, Doubleday & Co., Garden City, NY, 1979.

Kriegel, Mark, *Namath: A Biography*, Viking, New York, NY, 2004.

MacCambridge, Michael, *America's Game*, Anchor, New York, NY 2005.

MacCambridge, Michael, *Chuck Noll: A Life's Work*, University of Pittsburgh Press, Pittsburgh, Pennsylvania, 2016.

Marino, Dan, *Dan Marino: My Life In Football*, Triumph Publishing, Chicago, IL, 2005.

McCullough, Bob, *My Greatest Day in Football*, St. Martins Press, New York, NY, 2001.

McLemore, Morris T., *The Miami Dolphins*, Doubleday, Garden City, NY, 1973.

Mendell, Ronald L. and Phares, Timothy B., *Who's Who in Football*, Arlington, New Rochelle, NY, 1974.

Miller, Jeff, *Going Long*, McGraw-Hill, New York, NY, 2003.

Mudd, Howard, and Lister, Richard, *The View From the O-Line*, Sports Publishing, New York, NY, 2016.

Nash, Bruce, and Zullo, Alan, *Football Hall of Shame 2*, New York, NY: Simon & Schuster, 1991.

Plimpton, George, *Paper Lion*, Little Brown & Co., New York, NY 2016.

Sahadi, Lou, *Johnny Unitas: America's Quarterback*, Triumph Books, Chicago, IL, 2004.

Shula, Don, with Sahadi, Lou, *The Winning Edge*, E.P. Dutton, 1973.

Smith, Red, *Strawberries in the Wintertime*, New York Times Books, New York, NY, 1974.

Williams, Pat, and Denney, Jim, *Extreme Focus*, HCI Publishing, Deerfield Beach, Florida, 2011.

ARTICLES AND INTERVIEWS

Amore, Dom, "Passing Through the Shula Era," *Hartford Courant*, Hartford, CT, November 7, 1993.

Anderson, Dave, "Don Shula's Super Obsession," New York, NY, January 9, 1972.

Anderson, Dave, "The Empty Coffee Cups of Don Shula," *New York Times*, New York, NY, November 16, 1982.

Anderson, Dave, "Don Shula, Still the Best Coach," *New York Times*, New York, NY, November 11, 1990.

Attner, Paul, "Marino: The Great Quarterback Heist," *Washington Post*, Washington, DC, November 3, 1983.

Baldwin, Mike, "Perfect inspiration Twilley, Riley recall event that led to only unbeaten NFL season," *The Oklahoman*, OK, November 3, 2002.

Banks, Don, "Burning Questions," *Sports Illustrated*, October 21, 2003.

Banks, Don, "At long last, a Shula returns to Super Bowl: Panthers OC on his NFL journey," *Sports Illustrated*, New York, NY, January 26, 2016.

Barnes, Craig, "Don Shula: Dolphins coach, his jaw make their mark on Hall," *Sun Sentinel*, July 27, 1997.

Bell, Jarrett, "Colts Pursue Perfection of 1972 Dolphins," *USA Today*, December 16, 2005.

Berry, Jim, "Don Shula Ready To Watch Son In Super Bowl 50," CBS Miami, January 29, 2016.

Bokamper, Kim, "Bo Knows: The Snowplow Game," *MiamiDolphins.com*, December 12, 2017.

Boyle, Robert H., "The Pleasure of Dying on Sundays," *Sports Illustrated*, December 31, 1965.

Cefalo, Jimmy, "Cefalo: Drafted Into a Dream," *New York Times*, New York, NY, July 13, 1978.

Cefalo, Jimmy, interview with, "Don Shula Retires," narrated by Jimmy Cefalo, Ann Bishop, WPLG-TV, Miami, Florida, January 5, 1996.

Cimini, Rich, "The Fake Spike, 20 years later," ESPN.com, New York, NY November 26, 2014.

Cohen, Andy, "AC in the AM: Don Shula Still Going Strong," *MiamiDolphins.com*, December 21, 2017.

Cole, Jason, "Shula Ends 20 Years On NFL Committee," *Sun Sentinel*, Deerfield Beach, Florida, March 2, 1996.

Cote, Greg, and Long, Gary, "Dorothy Shula was the true coach of the family," *Baltimore Sun*, Baltimore, MD, February 26, 1991.

Cote, Greg, "Kid Shula vs. Son of a Bum," *Miami Herald*, Doral, FL, February 5, 2016.

Csonka, Larry, "FAQs on the WFL," *LarryCsonka.com*, July 29, 2017.

Culpepper, Chuck, "Unblemished '72 Dolphins Faced Rivals with Lots of Warts," *Newsday*, November 27, 2005.

Curtis, Mike, interview, "America's Game," 1970, NFL Films, January 1994.

D'Ambrosio, Brian, "Garo Yepremian on Super Bowl Gaffe: 'I turned it into a positive', *Huffington Post*, New York, NY, December 6, 2017.

D'Angelo, Tom, "Jets' win in Super Bowl III changed NFL history and Shula's career," *Palm Beach Post*, Palm Beach, FL, February 1, 2010.

Dennis Lustig "Shula's Back In Town," *Cleveland Plain Dealer*, Cleveland, OH, November 18, 1979.

Devitt, Mike, "Descendants of the Mayflower: A History of the Indianapolis Colts," *Indianapolis Colts Infopedia*, 2000.

Dexter, Pete, "The Things He Found In People," *Esquire* magazine, New York, NY, September 1983.

Diaz, George, "Shula: Champagne Story About '72 Dolphins Is a Myth, *Orlando Sentinel*, Orlando, FL, November 22, 2005.

Dudko, James, "Bill Arnsparger: Remembering the Godfather of the Zone Blitz and Hybrid Defense," *bleacherreport.com*, July 19, 2015.

Eskanazi, Gerald, "Super Bowl XIX; Don Shula Leaves Nothing To Chance," *New York Times*, New York, NY, January 20, 1985.

Frey, Jennifer, "In Miami, Pat Riley Cranks Up The Heat," *Washington Post*, Washington, DC, November 24, 1995.

Gehman, Jim, "Rams Assistant Chris Shula Is Third Generation of Shula Coaches," *Inside The Rams.com*, Los Angeles, CA, March 22, 2017.

Graham, Michael, "The Son Also Rises," *Cincinnati* magazine, Cincinnati, Ohio, May, 1992.

Greene, Harvey, "All In The Family: Shula Vs. Shula," *MiamiDolphins.com*, October 2, 2014.

Habib, Hal, "New book: Nick Saban's wife wanted out of Miami, pushed him to Alabama," *Palm Beach Post*, Palm Beach, FL, July 19, 2015.

Hoffer, Richard, "Here Comes the Son," *Sports Illustrated*, New York, NY, October 12, 1992.

Hyde, Dave, "Looking Back In Anger," *Sun Sentinel*, Deerfield Beach, FL, December 9, 2002.

Hyde, Dave, "Where's Jake Scott? Dave Hyde found him," *Sun Sentinel*, Deerfield Beach, FL, November 19, 2006.

Hyde, Dave, "Bill Arnsparger was the perfect match for Don Shula," *Sun Sentinel*, Deerfield Beach, FL, July 18, 2015.

Janofsky, Michael, "David Shula: Hard Worker With The Correct Lineage," *New York Times*, New York, NY, December 18, 1985.

Janofsky, Michael, "Shula's Style: A Mellow Intensity," *New York Times*, New York, NY, October 1, 1983.

Joseph, Dave, "Shula Family Getting Ready For Matchup," *Sun Sentinel*, Deerfield Beach, FL, September 27, 1994.

Kantowski, Ron, "Jake Scott, Super Bowl forgotten hero, resurfaces at Las Vegas drag race," *Review Journal*, Las Vegas, NV, May 2, 2016.

Kindred, Dave, "The Last of the Football Legends," *The Sporting News*, Kansas City, MO, January 15, 1996.

Kram Mark, "This Man Fired Flipper," *Sports Illustrated*, New York, NY, December 15, 1969.

Kuechenberg, Bob, interview, "The Story of the 1972 Dolphins," *Miami Dolphins.com*, November 23, 2012.

Litzky, Frank, "George Young, 71, Former Giants General Manager, Dies," *New York Times*, New York, NY, December 9, 2001.

Lupica, Mike, "Started Strong, Stayed Too Long," *New York Daily News*, New York, NY, January 5, 1996.

Martin, Donald E., "A Coach's Memory of Don Shula at Painesville," *Cleveland Plain Dealer*, Cleveland, OH, December 16, 1964.

Maule, Tex, "The Makings of a New Dynasty," *Sports Illustrated*, New York, NY, October 12, 1964.

Maule, Tex, "An Aura of Destiny," *Sports Illustrated*, New York, NY, November 13, 1967.

Maule, Tex, "Au Revoir," *Sports Illustrated*, New York, NY, December 16, 1967.

Maule, Tex, "Miami Gets A Miracle Worker," *Sports Illustrated*, New York, NY, September 7, 1970.

Maule, Tex, "Keeping it short and sweet," *Sports Illustrated*, New York, NY , December 20, 1971.

Maule, Tex, "It Was The Day Of The Dolphins," *Sports Illustrated*, New York, NY, January 21, 1974.

Miller, Jill Young, "Shula-Stephens Affair Ignites Rumors," *Tulsa World*, Tulsa, OK, August 15, 1993.

Miller, Jill Young, "Who Is The Woman On Don Shula`s Arm?," *Sun Sentinel*, Deerfield Beach, FL, August 8, 1993.

Morris, Eugene ("Mercury"), "Draft Memories: Wooden and Morris," Finsiders, *Miami Dolphins.com*, April 18, 2015.

Nathan, Tony, interview, The DA Show, Damon Amendolara, CBS Sports Radio, September 26, 2015.

Nordheimer, Jon, "The enduring obsession," *New York Times* magazine, New York, NY, September 1 1985.

Olsen, Jack, "The Rosenbloom-Robbie Bowl," *Sports Illustrated*, New York, NY, November 9, 1970.

Olson, Gary, "Dolphins' Shula Close On The Heels Of Halas", Knight-Ridder Newspapers, September 5, 1993.

Owczarski, Jim, "Dave Shula: 'You can't blame everything on me'," *Cincinnati Enquirer*, Cincinnati, OH, July 7, 2017.

Plaschke, Bill, "Will the Son Come Up?: Dave Shula Deals With Last Name and Last Place," *Los Angeles Times*, Los Angeles, CA, November 24, 1993.

Plaschke, Bill, "NFL Legend Shula Quits Dolphins," *Palm Beach Post*, Palm Beach, FL, January 5, 1996.

Pope, Edwin, "Don Shula knows Dolphins were manhandled as Redskins run away with Super Bowl XVII," *Miami Herald*, Miami, FL, February 3, 2017.

Price, S.L., "'I Feel Lost. I Feel Like a Child': The Complicated Decline of Nick Buoniconti," *Sports Illustrated*, May 9, 2017.

Price, S.L., "How Jim Kiick Fell Throught The Cracks," *Sports Illustrated*, New York, NY, May 9, 2017.

Reilly, Rick, "A Matter of Life and Sudden Death," *Sports Illustrated*, New York, NY, October 24, 1999.

Rhoden, William C., "Tradition and Teflon in Miami," *New York Times*, New York, NY, November 25, 1995.

Sabin, Rainer, "Looking back at when Nick Saban said he wasn't 'going to be the Alabama coach'," *Advance Local*, Tuscaloosa, AL, February 21, 2017.

Scalzo, Joe, "Stark Icons: Paul Brown's influence still extends far beyond Massillon," *Columbus Monthly*, Columbus, OH, March 27, 2016.

Scott, Ronald B., "Coach Don Shula, the Would-Be Priest Who Makes Miami Mean," *People* magazine, December 02, 1974.

Shapiro, Leonard, "For David Shula, a Legacy of Victory," *Washington Post*, Washington, DC, October 27, 1992.

Shapiro, Leonard, "Dolphins' Shula Calls It A Career," *Washington Post*, Washington, DC, January 6, 1996.

Shapiro, Leonard, "Shula Secret: Adaptability," *Washington Post*, Washington, DC, September 30, 1978.

Shula, Don (with Tex Maule), "How The Colts Met Triumph—and Disaster," *Sports Illustrated*, New York, NY, January 11, 1965.

Shula, Don (with Tex Maule), "The road to the title in the West," *Sports Illustrated*, New York, NY, January 18, 1965.

Shula, Don, Induction speech, NFL Hall of Fame, National Football League Hall of Fame, Canton, OH, 1997.

Shula, Don, interview, Sport Illustrated video interview, The Vault, February 13, 2012.

Shula, Don, interview, "Don Shula on almost fighting owner Joe Robbie," *Sports Illustrated*, taped video interview, Sports Illustrated, New York, NY, August 7, 2015.

Silver, Michael, "Nobody's Perfect (Except Us)," *Sports Illustrated*, New York, NY, July 15, 2002.

Smith, Bubba, interview, "America's Game, 1970," NFL Films, January 1994.

Stedman, John, "Coach of the Year? Iron-Willed Don Shula," *Sporting Times*, Bowling Green, KY, January 4, 1969.

Thompson, Hunter S., "Jack Kerouac and the Football Hall of Fame," ESPN.com, New York, NY, October 10, 2001.

Tracy, Tom, "Shula's lifetime commitment to Catholic education, other causes honored," Catholic News Service, November 26, 2014.

Underwood, John, "A Game No One Should Have Lost," *Sports Illustrated*, New York, NY, January 11, 1982.

Underwood, John, "His Eyes Have Seen the Glory," *Sports Illustrated*, New York, NY, July 27, 1981.

Underwood, John, "Sitting on Top of the World," *Sports Illustrated*, New York, NY, September 17, 1973.

Underwood, John, "The Blood and Thunder Boys," *Sports Illustrated,* New York, NY, August 6, 1972.

Warsinkey, Tim, "Chris Shula named defensive coordinator at John Carroll," *Cleveland Plain Dealer,* Cleveland, OH, February 26, 2014.

Zimmerman, Paul, "Don Shula, Sports of the Year," *Sports Illustrated,* December 20, 1993.

Zimmerman, Paul, "Miami Dolphins Vs. Minnesota Vikings Super Bowl VIII Another Crown To Miami," *Sports Illustrated,* New York, NY, January 2, 1989.

Zunt, Dick, "Don Shula: Those who knew him the best," *Cleveland Plain Dealer, Sports Weekender,* Cleveland, OH, January 24, 1976.

Acknowledgments

Any author of such an effort owes a great debt of gratitude to those who went before him. In researching this project, I read more than 3,000 articles, interviews, profiles, books, and correspondence, as well as old programs, college newspapers, and memoirs of both public and private citizens.

Several writers' works have proved invaluable, including those of Michael MacCambridge, Mike Freeman, Leonard T. McElmore, Ed Gruver, Lou Sahadi, Tom Callahan, William Gildea, Mark Kreigel, Pete Dexter, Hunter S. Thompson, and many others. Of course, there are a multitude of memoirs as well, most important of which were written by George Plimpton, Alex Karras, Art Donovan, Upton Bell, Bill Curry, Mike Curtis, Bob Griese, Larry Csonka and Jim Kiick, John Hannah, Dan Marino, and several others.

Also, sportswriters including Paul Zimmerman, Tex Maule, Edwin Pope, Dave Hyde, Dan Le Batard, Armando Salguero, Greg Cote, Bill Plaschke, and many more. Countless archives pages were scoured from the *Cleveland Plain Dealer, Baltimore Sun, New York Times, Miami Herald, Palm Beach Post, Detroit Free Press, Sun Sentinel, Tampa Bay Tribune, The Sporting News,* and *Sports Illustrated.*

I also wish to thank Ken Samelson of Sports Publishing, who helped make this book a reality. Were it not for his excitement, enthusiasm, and faith in me, I would not have had this opportunity. Special thanks to Julie Ganz for all her help and patience.

I would like to thank my sons, Dylan and Dawson, whom I have taken too much time away from to pursue not only this work, but also my other professional aspirations. I have tried to attend as many of their basketball, baseball, and track meets as possible, but there is no replacement for a chat or a dinner out, many of which were robbed by my other pursuits. I vow to them to spend more time hanging out and less time working.